STREET ATLAS

Berkshire

First published in 1990 by

Philip's, a division of
Octopus Publishing Group Ltd
2–4 Heron Quays, London E14 4JP

Second colour edition 2000
Fifth impression 2004

ISBN 0-540-07676-7 (hardback)
ISBN 0-540-07677-5 (spiral)

© Philip's 2003

Ordnance Survey®

This product includes mapping data licensed
from Ordnance Survey® with the permission of
the Controller of Her Majesty's Stationery Office.
© Crown copyright 2003. All rights reserved.
Licence number 100011710.

Printed and bound in Spain
by Cayfosa-Quebecor

Contents

III	**Key to map symbols**
IV	**Key to map pages**
VI	**Route planning**
VIII	**Administrative and Postcode boundaries**
1	**Street maps** at 3½ inches to 1 mile
154	**Index** of towns and villages
155	**Index** of streets, hospitals, industrial estates, railway stations, schools, shopping centres and universities

Digital Data

The exceptionally high-quality mapping found in this atlas is available as digital data in TIFF format, which is easily convertible to other bitmapped (raster) image formats.

The index is also available in digital form as a standard database table. It contains all the details found in the printed index together with the National Grid reference for the map square in which each entry is named.

For further information and to discuss your requirements, please contact Philip's on 020 7644 6932 or james.mann@philips-maps.co.uk

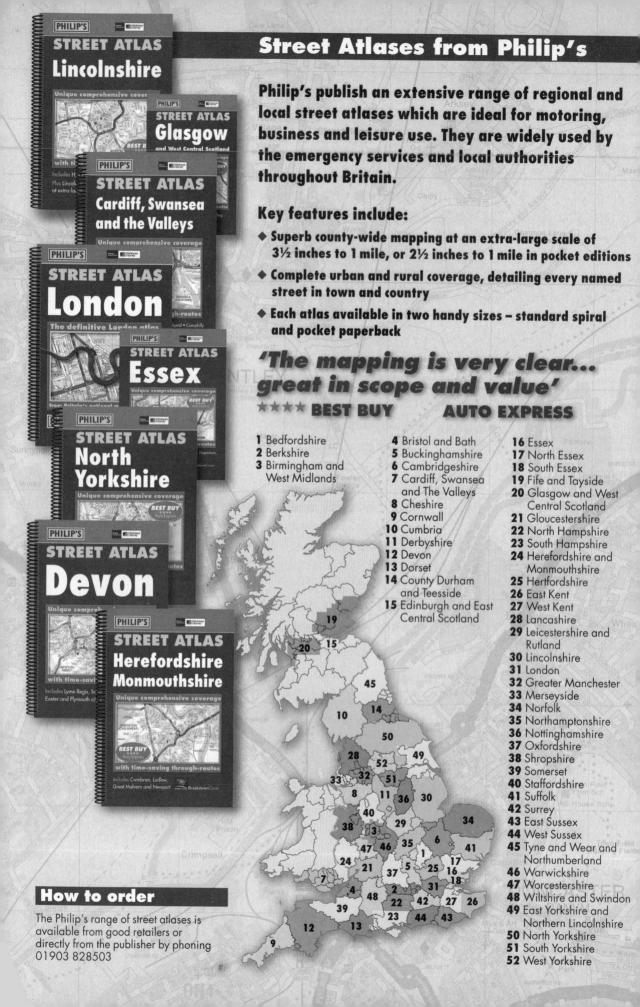

Street Atlases from Philip's

Philip's publish an extensive range of regional and local street atlases which are ideal for motoring, business and leisure use. They are widely used by the emergency services and local authorities throughout Britain.

Key features include:

◆ Superb county-wide mapping at an extra-large scale of 3½ inches to 1 mile, or 2½ inches to 1 mile in pocket editions

◆ Complete urban and rural coverage, detailing every named street in town and country

◆ Each atlas available in two handy sizes – standard spiral and pocket paperback

'The mapping is very clear... great in scope and value'

★★★★ BEST BUY   AUTO EXPRESS

1 Bedfordshire
2 Berkshire
3 Birmingham and West Midlands
4 Bristol and Bath
5 Buckinghamshire
6 Cambridgeshire
7 Cardiff, Swansea and The Valleys
8 Cheshire
9 Cornwall
10 Cumbria
11 Derbyshire
12 Devon
13 Dorset
14 County Durham and Teesside
15 Edinburgh and East Central Scotland
16 Essex
17 North Essex
18 South Essex
19 Fife and Tayside
20 Glasgow and West Central Scotland
21 Gloucestershire
22 North Hampshire
23 South Hampshire
24 Herefordshire and Monmouthshire
25 Hertfordshire
26 East Kent
27 West Kent
28 Lancashire
29 Leicestershire and Rutland
30 Lincolnshire
31 London
32 Greater Manchester
33 Merseyside
34 Norfolk
35 Northamptonshire
36 Nottinghamshire
37 Oxfordshire
38 Shropshire
39 Somerset
40 Staffordshire
41 Suffolk
42 Surrey
43 East Sussex
44 West Sussex
45 Tyne and Wear and Northumberland
46 Warwickshire
47 Worcestershire
48 Wiltshire and Swindon
49 East Yorkshire and Northern Lincolnshire
50 North Yorkshire
51 South Yorkshire
52 West Yorkshire

How to order

The Philip's range of street atlases is available from good retailers or directly from the publisher by phoning 01903 828503

Symbol	Description
22a	**Motorway** with junction number
	Primary route - dual carriageway and single
	A road - dual carriageway and single
	B road - dual carriageway and single
	Minor road - dual carriageway and single
	Other minor road - dual carriageway and single
	Road under construction
	Pedestrianised area
DY7	**Postcode boundaries**
	County and Unitary Authority boundaries
	Railway
	Tramway, miniature railway
	Rural track, private road or narrow road in urban area
	Gate or obstruction to traffic (restrictions may not apply at all times or to all vehicles)
	Path, bridleway, byway open to all traffic, road used as a public path
	The representation in this atlas of a road, track or path is no evidence of the existence of way
126 / 94	**Adjoining page indicators**

Symbol	Description
Walsall	**Railway station**
	London Underground station
	Private railway station
	Bus, coach station
◆	**Ambulance station**
◆	**Coastguard station**
◆	**Fire station**
◆	**Police station**
✚	**Accident and Emergency entrance to hospital**
H	**Hospital**
+	**Places of worship**
i	**Information Centre** (open all year)
P	**Parking**
P&R	**Park and Ride**
PO	**Post Office**
⋏	**Camping site**
	Caravan site
►	**Golf course**
⊠	**Picnic site**
Prim Sch	**Important buildings, schools, colleges, universities and hospitals**
River Medway	**Water name**
	Stream
	River or canal - minor and major
	Water
	Tidal water
	Woods
	Houses
House	**Non-Roman antiquity**
VILLA	**Roman antiquity**

Allot Gdns	**Allotments**	Meml	**Memorial**
Acad	**Academy**	Mon	**Monument**
Cemy	**Cemetery**	Mus	**Museum**
C Ctr	**Civic Centre**	Obsy	**Observatory**
CH	**Club House**	Pal	**Royal Palace**
Coll	**College**	PH	**Public House**
Crem	**Crematorium**	Recn Gd	**Recreation Ground**
Ent	**Enterprise**	Resr	**Reservoir**
Ex H	**Exhibition Hall**	Ret Pk	**Retail Park**
Ind Est	**Industrial Estate**	Sch	**School**
Inst	**Institute**	Sh Ctr	**Shopping Centre**
Ct	**Law Court**	TH	**Town Hall/House**
L Ctr	**Leisure Centre**	Trad Est	**Trading Estate**
LC	**Level Crossing**	Univ	**University**
Liby	**Library**	Wks	**Works**
Mkt	**Market**	YH	**Youth Hostel**

■ The dark grey border on the inside edge of some pages indicates that the mapping does not continue onto the adjacent page

■ The small numbers around the edges of the maps identify the 1 kilometre National Grid lines

The scale of the maps is 5.52 cm to 1 km
3¹/₂ inches to 1 mile 1: 18103

0	¼	½	³/₄	1 mile
0	250m 500m 750m	1 kilometre		

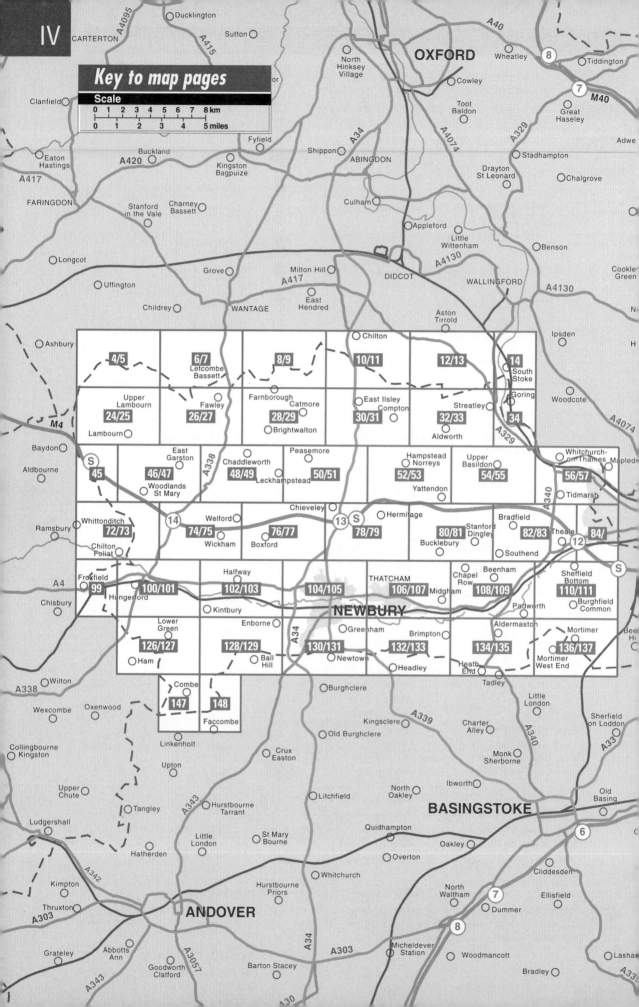

Key to map pages

Scale

| 0 | 1 | 2 | 3 | 4 | 5 | 6 | 7 | 8 km |
| 0 | | 1 | | 2 | | 3 | | 4 | 5 miles |

CARTERTON
Ducklington
Sutton
A4095
A4115
Clanfield
A420
Buckland
Kingston Bagpuize
Fyfield
Shippon
ABINGDON
North Hinksey Village
OXFORD
Cowley
Toot Baldon
Great Haseley
Wheatley
Tiddington
M40
Stadhampton
Adwe
Drayton St Leonard
Chalgrove
Cookley Green
Eaton Hastings
A417
FARINGDON
Stanford in the Vale
Charney Bassett
Culham
Appleford
Little Wittenham
Benson
Longcot
Uffington
Grove
Milton Hill
A417
Childrey
WANTAGE
East Hendred
DIDCOT
WALLINGFORD
A4130
A4130
A4074
Ipsden
Ashbury
Chilton
Aston Tirrold
4/5
6/7 Letcombe Bassett
8/9
10/11
12/13
14 South Stoke
Woodcote
Goring
M4
Upper Lambourn
Fawley
Farnborough
Catmore
East Ilsley
Compton
Streatley
24/25
26/27
28/29
Brightwalton
30/31
32/33 Aldworth
34
A329
Baydon
Lambourn
East Garston
Chaddleworth
Peasemore
Hampstead Norreys
Upper Basildon
Whitchurch-on-Thames
Mapled
Aldbourne
S **45**
46/47
Woodlands St Mary
48/49
Leckhampstead
50/51
52/53
Yattendon
54/55
56/57
Tidmarsh
A338
A340
Ramsbury
Whittonditch
Chieveley
Hermitage
Bradfield
72/73
14
Welford
74/75
Wickham
76/77
Boxford
13 **S**
78/79
80/81
Stanford Dingley
Bucklebury
82/83
Theale
84/
Chilton Foliat
Southend
12
S
A4
Froxfield
Halfway
THATCHAM
Chapel Row
Beenham
Sheffield Bottom
99
Hungerford
100/101
102/103
104/105
106/107
Midgham
108/109
110/111
Burghfield Common
Chisbury
Kintbury
NEWBURY
Padworth
Lower Green
Enborne
Greenham
Brimpton
Aldermaston
Mortimer
Bee
Hi
126/127
Ham
128/129
Ball Hill
A34
130/131
Newtown
Headley
132/133
Heath End
134/135
Tadley
Mortimer West End
136/137
Wilton
A338
Wexcombe
Oxenwood
Combe
147
148
Faccombe
Burghclere
Little London
Sherfield on Loddon
A33
Collingbourne Kingston
Linkenholt
Upton
Kingsclere
Old Burghclere
A339
Charter Alley
Monk Sherborne
A340
Upper Chute
Litchfield
North Oakley
Ibworth
Old Basing
Tangley
Hurstbourne Tarrant
North Waltham
BASINGSTOKE
6
Ludgershall
A343
Little London
St Mary Bourne
Quidhampton
Oakley
Cliddesden
Wexcombe
Hatherden
Overton
Kimpton
A342
Hurstbourne Priors
Whitchurch
7
Ellisfield
Thruxton
A303
ANDOVER
A34
North Waltham
Dummer
8
Grateley
Abbotts Ann
Goodworth Clatford
A3057
Barton Stacey
A303
Micheldever Station
Woodmancott
Bradley
Lasha
A343
A30

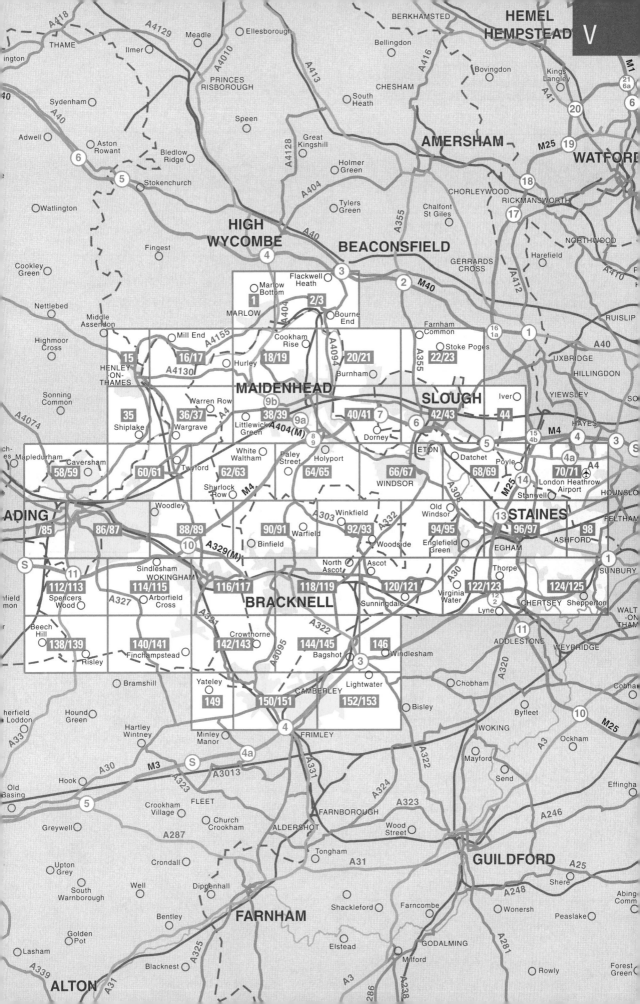

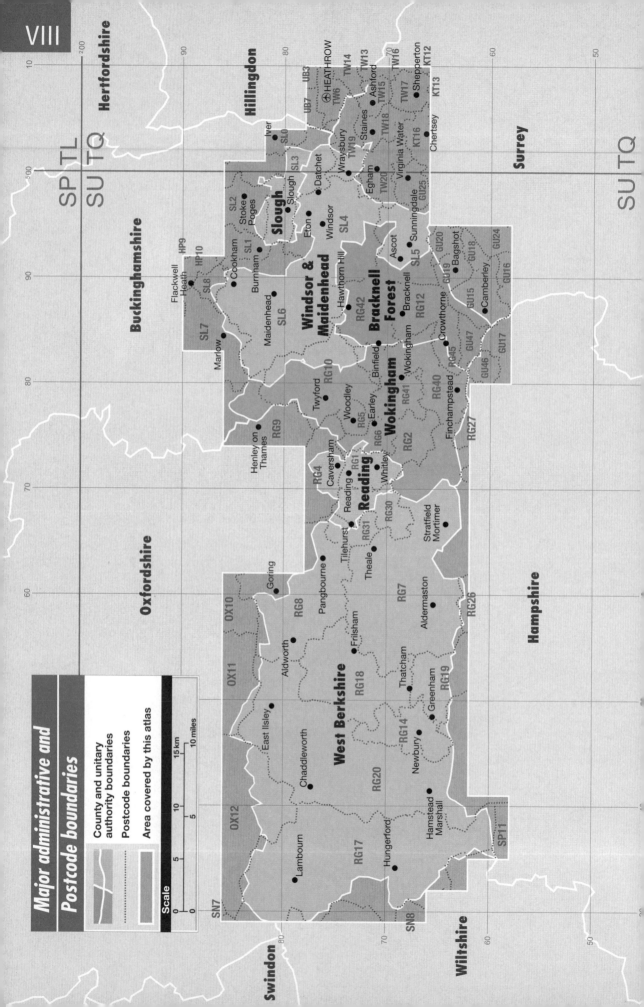

Major administrative and
Postcode boundaries

County and unitary
authority boundaries

Postcode boundaries

Area covered by this atlas

Scale

0   5   10   15 km
0   5   10 miles

SP TL
SU TQ

SU TQ

Hertfordshire

Hillingdon

Surrey

Buckinghamshire

Oxfordshire

Hampshire

Wiltshire

Swindon

West Berkshire

Slough

Windsor &
Maidenhead

Bracknell
Forest

Wokingham

Reading

HEATHROW

Flackwell
Heath

HP9
HP10
SL8
SL7
SL1
SL2
SL0
SL3
SL6
SL4
SL5

Marlow
Cookham
Burnham
Maidenhead
Stoke
Poges
Iver
Slough
Eton
Datchet
Windsor
Hawthorn Hill
Ascot

UB3
UB7
TW6
TW14
TW13
TW15
TW18
TW19
TW20
TW16
TW17
KT12
KT16
KT13

Wraysbury
Staines
Ashford
Shepperton
Egham
Virginia Water
Sunningdale
Chertsey

GU25
GU20
GU19
GU18
GU15
GU16
GU17
GU46
GU47
GU24
Bagshot
Camberley
Crowthorne

RG42
RG12
RG45
RG40
RG41
RG2
RG30
RG27
RG26
RG7
RG1
RG4
RG10
RG5
RG6
RG9
RG8
RG31
RG14
RG18
RG19
RG20
RG17

Bracknell
Binfield
Wokingham
Finchampstead
Caversham
Reading
Whitley
Twyford
Woodley
Earley
Henley on
Thames
Goring
Pangbourne
Tilehurst
Theale
Frilsham
Stratfield
Mortimer
Aldermaston
Thatcham
Newbury
Greenham
Aldworth
East Ilsley
Chaddleworth
Lambourn
Hungerford
Hamstead
Marshall

OX10
OX11
OX12
SP11
SN7
SN8

200
90
80
70
60
50

10
500
90
80
70
60

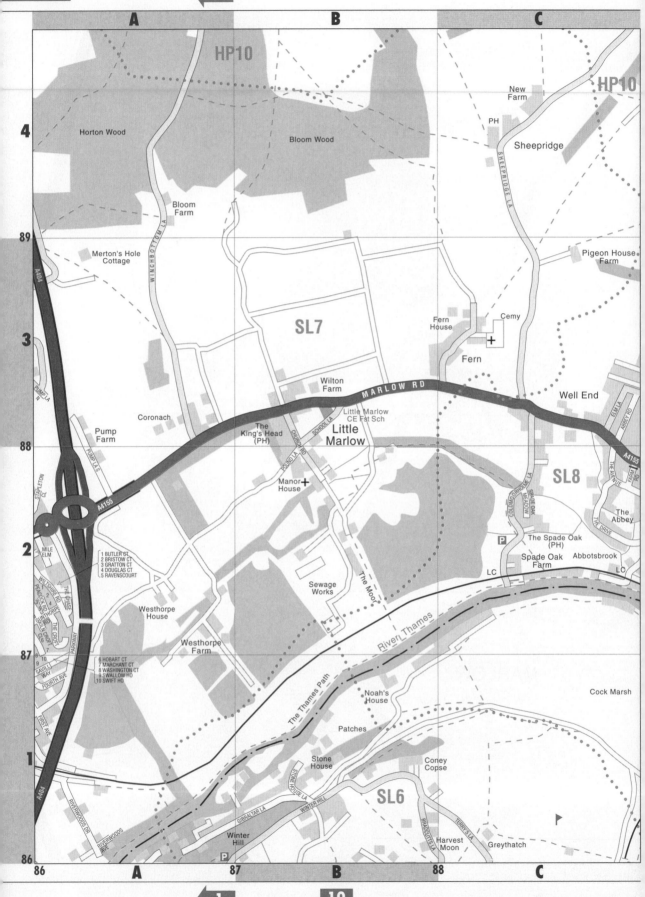

HP10

Horton Wood

Bloom Wood

HP10

New Farm

PH

Sheepridge

SL8

Bloom Farm

Merton's Hole Cottage

WINCHBOTTOM LA

89

A404

SL7

Fern House

Cemy

Pigeon House Farm

Fern

PUMP LA N

3

Wilton Farm

MARLOW RD

Well End

Coronach

SCHOOL LA

Little Marlow CE Fst Sch

Pump Farm

PUMP LA S

The King's Head (PH)

CHURCH RD

POUND LA

Little Marlow

STAPLETON CL

88

A4155

Manor House

ELM LA

ABBEY RD

SL8

THE AVENUE

The Abbey

A4155

THE DRIVE

COLDMOORHOLME LA

SPADE OAK MEADOW

P

The Spade Oak (PH)

Abbotsbrook

2

MILE ELM

1 BUTLER ST
2 BRISTOW CT
3 GRATTON CT
4 DOUGLAS CT
5 RAVENSCOURT

Sewage Works

The Moor

Spade Oak Farm

LC

LC

WILTSHIRE RD

PEACOCK RD

GUNTHORPE RD

SAVILL CROFT

THE CROFT

Westhorpe House

PARKWAY

River Thames

Westhorpe Farm

87

SAVILL WAY

FOURTH AVE

6 HOBART CT
7 MARCHANT CT
8 WASHINGTON CT
9 SWALLOW HO
10 SWIFT HO

The Thames Path

Noah's House

Cock Marsh

FIRST AVE

Patches

1

A404

Stone House

Coney Copse

RIVERWOODS DR

RIVERWOODS AVE

GIBRALTAR LA

STONE HOUSE LA

WINTER HILL

SL6

BRADCUTTS LA

TERRY'S LA

Winter Hill

P

Harvest Moon

Greythatch

86

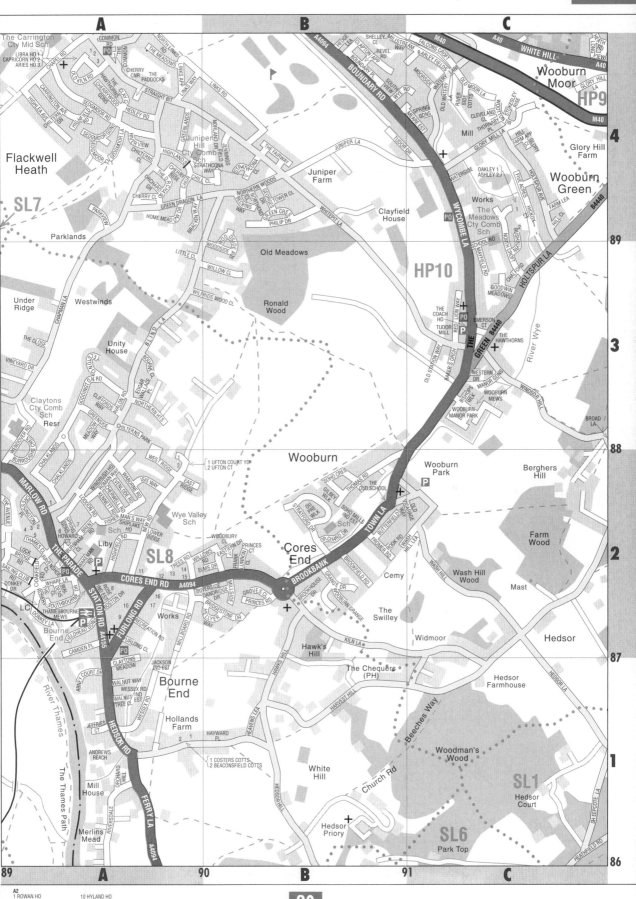

A2
1 ROWAN HO
2 COKERS CT
3 RUSSELL HO
4 RAY HO
5 GRANT HO
6 ORCHARD HO
7 BAILEY HO
8 BOURNE END BSNS CTR
9 EGHAMS CT

10 HYLAND HO
11 FARRIER CT
12 MOUNT PLEASANT COTTS
13 SYCAMORE CL
14 THE WILLOWS
15 THE MAPLES
16 MEADOW BANK
17 THE COURTYARD

Ridgeway

SN7

Uffington
Down

Long
Plantation

4

Woolstone Hill
Barn

SN6

Pingoose
Covert

85

Idlebush
Barrow

Kingston
Warren

OX12

Gallops

Kingston Warren Down

Gallops

Gallops

Gallops

3

Woolstone
Down

84

Compton
Close

Gallops

2

Knighton
Down

Whit
Coombe

Wellbottom
Down

Gallops

83

Knighton Bushes
Plantation

RG17

Lambourn Valley Way

Baldback
Covert

1

Gallops

Post Down

Postdown
Border

82

Parkfarm Down

MADDLE RD

Maddle
Farm

Weathercock
Hill

29

30

31

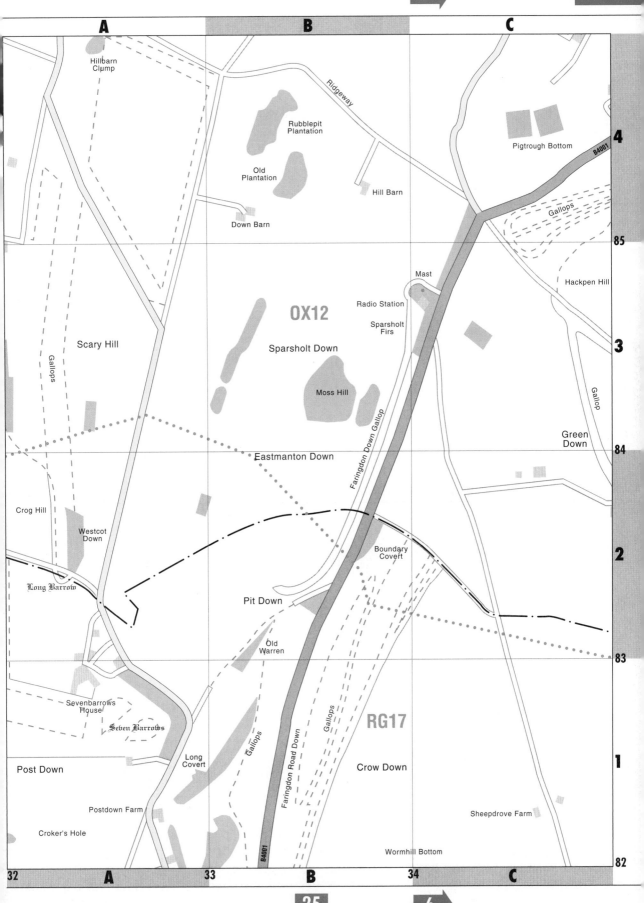

A

B

C

Hillbarn
Clump

Ridgeway

Rubblepit
Plantation

Old
Plantation

Hill Barn

Down Barn

Pigtrough Bottom

B4001

4

Gallops

85

Mast

Hackpen Hill

OX12

Radio Station

Sparsholt
Firs

Scary Hill

Gallops

Sparsholt Down

Moss Hill

Faringdon Down Gallop

Gallop

Green
Down

3

84

Eastmanton Down

Crog Hill

Westcot
Down

Boundary
Covert

2

Long Barrow

Pit Down

Old
Warren

83

Sevenbarrows
House

Seven Barrows

Gallops

Faringdon Road Down

Gallops

RG17

Crow Down

1

Post Down

Long
Covert

Postdown Farm

Sheepdrove Farm

Croker's Hole

B4001

Wormhill Bottom

82

32

A

33

B

34

C

5

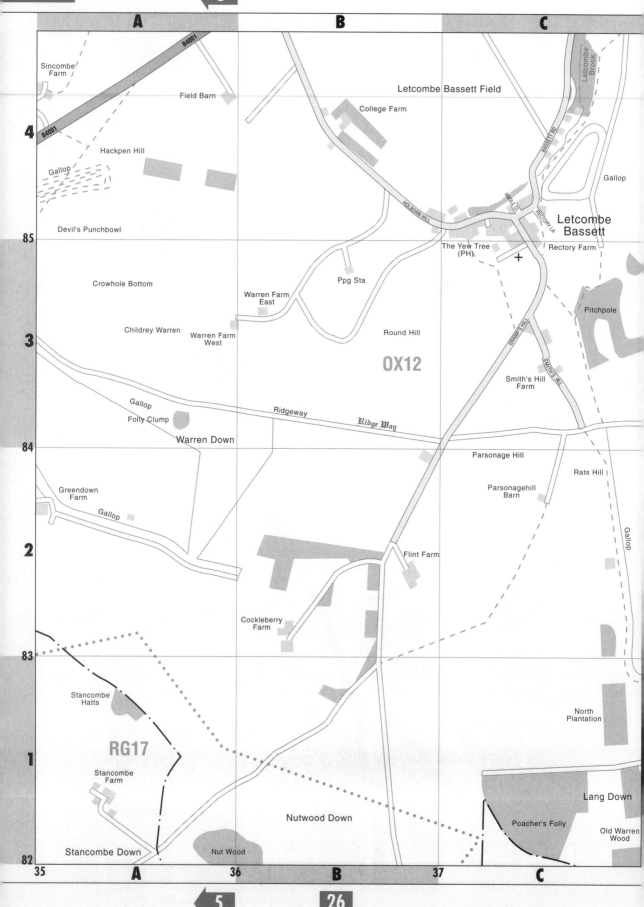

A

B

C

Sincombe Farm

B4001

B4001

Field Barn

Letcombe Bassett Field

College Farm

4

Hackpen Hill

Gallop

Gallop

HOLBORN HILL

BASSETT RD

KNOLL CL

RECTORY LA

Letcombe Bassett

Gallop

85

Devil's Punchbowl

The Yew Tree (PH)

Rectory Farm

+

Crowhole Bottom

Ppg Sta

Pitchpole

Warren Farm East

Round Hill

Childrey Warren

OX12

GRAMP'S HILL

SMITH'S HILL

3

Warren Farm West

Smith's Hill Farm

Gallop

Ridgeway

Ridge Way

Folly Clump

Warren Down

Parsonage Hill

84

Rats Hill

Greendown Farm

Parsonagehill Barn

Gallop

Gallop

2

Flint Farm

Cockleberry Farm

83

Stancombe Hatts

North Plantation

RG17

1

Stancombe Farm

Lang Down

Poacher's Folly

Old Warren Wood

Nutwood Down

Stancombe Down

Nut Wood

82

35   **A**   36   **B**   37   **C**

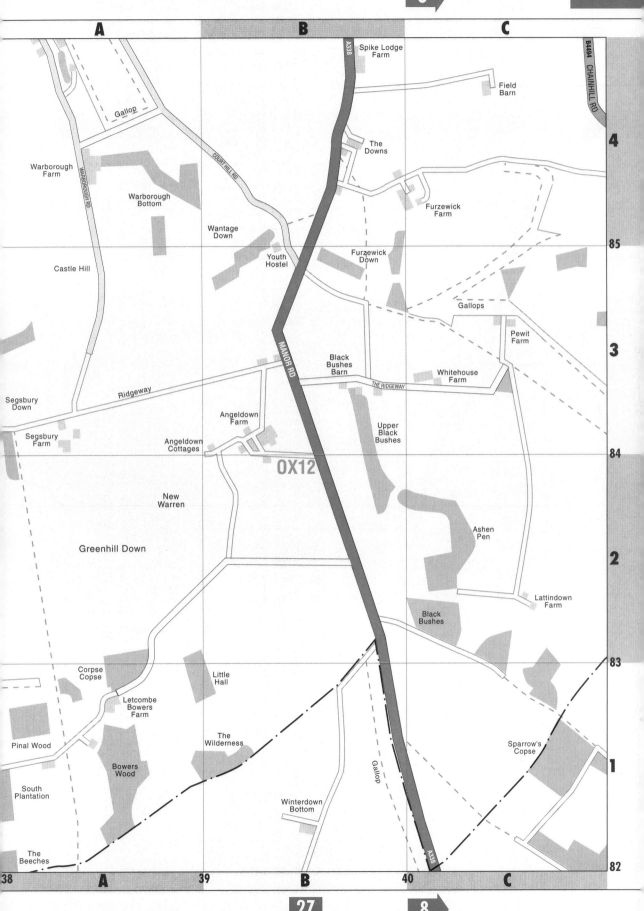

A B C

4
85
3
84
2
83
1
82

Spike Lodge Farm
Field Barn
The Downs
Furzewick Farm
Furzewick Down
Gallops
Pewit Farm
Whitehouse Farm
Black Bushes Barn
THE RIDGEWAY
Upper Black Bushes
Ashen Pen
Lattindown Farm
Black Bushes
Sparrow's Copse

Warborough Farm
Warborough Bottom
Wantage Down
Youth Hostel
Castle Hill
Ridgeway
Segsbury Down
Segsbury Farm
Angeldown Farm
Angeldown Cottages
OX12
New Warren
Greenhill Down
Corpse Copse
Little Hall
Letcombe Bowers Farm
Pinal Wood
The Wilderness
Bowers Wood
South Plantation
Winterdown Bottom
Gallop
The Beeches

Gallop
WARBOROUGH RD
COURT HILL RD
MANOR RD
A338
B4494 CHAINHILL RD

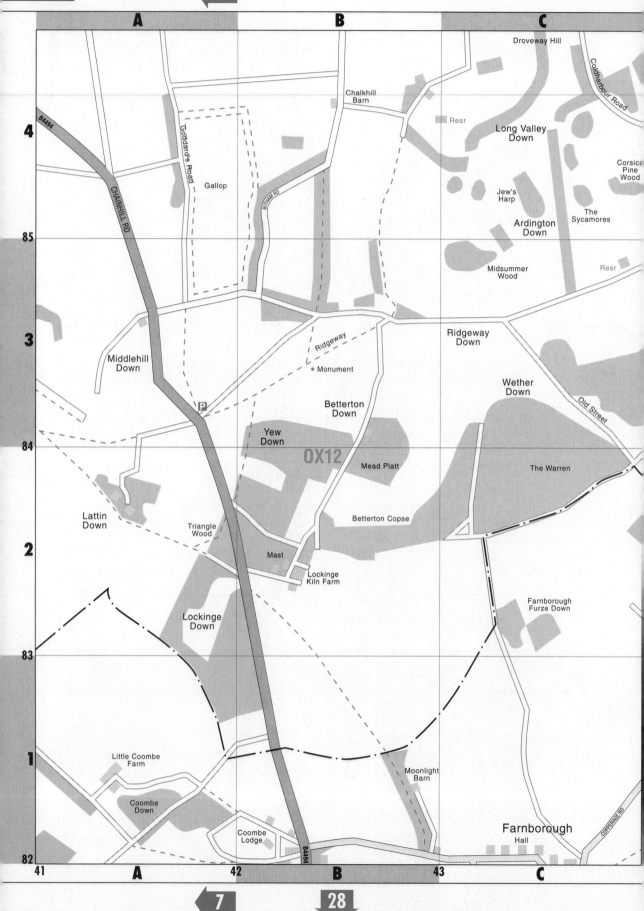

A   B   C

Droveway Hill

Coldharbour Road

Chalkhill Barn

Resr

Long Valley Down

Corsica Pine Wood

4

B4494

Goddard's Road

BITHAM RD

Gallop

Jew's Harp

The Sycamores

CHAINHILL RD

Ardington Down

85

Midsummer Wood

Resr

3

Ridgeway

Ridgeway Down

Middlehill Down

Monument

Wether Down

Old Street

Betterton Down

P

Yew Down

OX12

84

Mead Platt

The Warren

Lattin Down

Triangle Wood

Betterton Copse

2

Mast

Lockinge Kiln Farm

Farnborough Furze Down

Lockinge Down

83

Little Coombe Farm

Moonlight Barn

1

Coombe Down

Farnborough Hall

COPPERAGE RD

Coombe Lodge

B4494

82

41   A   42   B   43   C

A B C

Diamond Jubilee Wood

White Way

Coldharbour Barn

Tile Barn

Knob Down

Fore Down

Foredown Plantation

Coldharbour Road

East Ginge Down

Cuckhamsley Hill
P

Ridgeway

East Hendred Down

OX11

Scutchamer Knob

85

Lew's Barn

West Ginge Down

Johnson's Farm

Upper Plantation

Gallop

Abbot's Heath

Sheep Down

3

Down Barn

Kilman Knoll Down

Gallops

Middle Plantation

OX12

Big Allens

84

Little Allens

Gallops

Cow Down

Curlew

Old Street

Lands End

Knollend Down

RG20

2

83

Copperage Rd

Old Street

Old Down

Starveall Farm

Harcourt Farm

1

Catmore Rd

Hernehill Down

82

44 A 45 B 46 C

Silleway Road

PLANTATION RD
MEADHILL WAY
PROTO RD
LIDO RD
DIDO RD
DOWNS WAY
STRAITS

HARWELL INT BSNS CTR

4

85

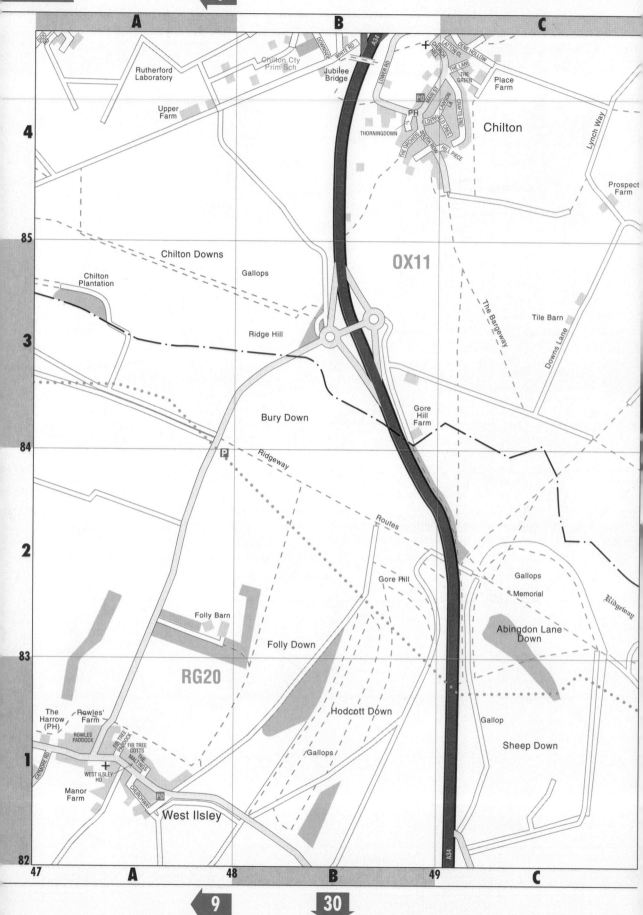

A   B   C

Rutherford
Laboratory

Chilton Cty
Prim Sch

Jubilee
Bridge

DOWNSIDE

WHITE RD

LOWER RD

A34

DENE HOLLOW

LATTON CL

THE LANE

THE
GREEN

Place
Farm

CHURCH
HILL

MAIN ST

ELDENE LA

LAWSON
LA

CRAFTS END

Chilton

Lynch Way

Upper
Farm

PO

PH

THORNINGDOWN

THE ORCHIDS

SOUTH ROW

HILL PIECE

4

Prospect
Farm

85

Chilton Downs

Gallops

OX11

Chilton
Plantation

The Bargeway

Tile Barn

Downs Lane

Ridge Hill

3

Bury Down

Gore
Hill
Farm

84

P

Ridgeway

Routes

Gore Hill

Gallops

Memorial

Ridgeway

2

Folly Barn

Abingdon Lane
Down

Folly Down

83

RG20

Hodcott Down

Gallop

The
Harrow
(PH)

Rowles'
Farm

Sheep Down

ROWLES
PADDOCK

FIR TREE
PADDOCK

FIR TREE
COTTS

THE
MALTINGS

Gallops

CATMORE RD

WEST ILSLEY
HO

1

Manor
Farm

CHURCHWAY

PO

West Ilsley

82

47   48   49

A   B   C

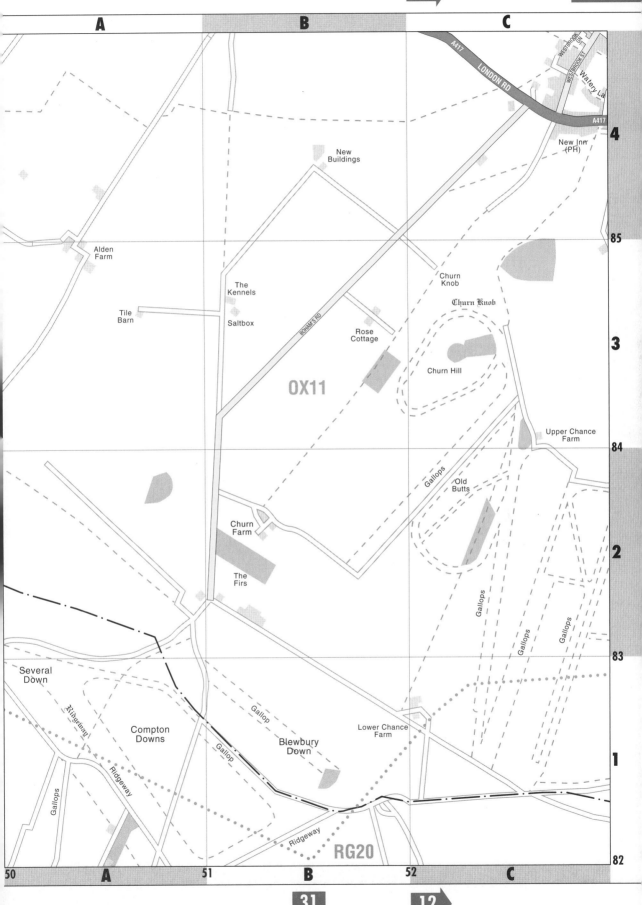

A   B   C

4

85

3

84

2

83

1

82

A417

LONDON RD

WESTBROOK ST

Watery La

A417

New Inn
(PH)

New
Buildings

Churn
Knob

Churn Knob

Alden
Farm

The
Kennels

BOHAM'S RD

Churn Hill

Tile
Barn

Saltbox

Rose
Cottage

OX11

Upper Chance
Farm

Gallops

Old
Butts

Churn
Farm

The
Firs

Gallops

Gallops

Gallops

Gallops

Several
Down

Ridgeway

Gallop

Compton
Downs

Gallop

Blewbury
Down

Lower Chance
Farm

Gallops

Ridgeway

Ridgeway

RG20

50   A   51   B   52   C

A   **B**   **C**

Blewbury

Aston
Tirrold

Church End   Watt's La
Church Rd   South St   Eastfield   Bessel's Way
Robinson Cl
Chapel La   Rumsey's La
Dir Ley's
PH
A417   LONDON RD
Treble Ho Terr

4

Copsestile
Farm

Rectory La
The
Close
Downs
View
PO
Baker St
Aston St

BLEWBURY HILL   B4016

Blewbury
Barn

Spring La

Chalk Hill

A4

Hunt's
Grave

Golf Driving
Range

Downside
Farm

Woodway Rd

Baldon Hill

Lid's Down

Gallop

Carrimers
Farm

85

White Shoot

Riddle Hill

Chalk Hill Bottom

3

OX11

Sheepcot
Farm

Lower Hill
Barn

Woodway
Hostel

Hogtrough
Bottom

Woodway

84

Gallop

Upper Hill
Barn

Oven Bottom

Langdon
Hill

Big Bull
Hill

Gallop

The
Plantation

2

Gallops

Aston Upthorpe
Downs

83

The Fair Mile

Unhill Bottom

Gallops

Fuller's Firs

1

RG20

Lowbury
Hill

RG8

Dean's Bottom

Ridgeway

82

A   **B**   **C**

53   54   55

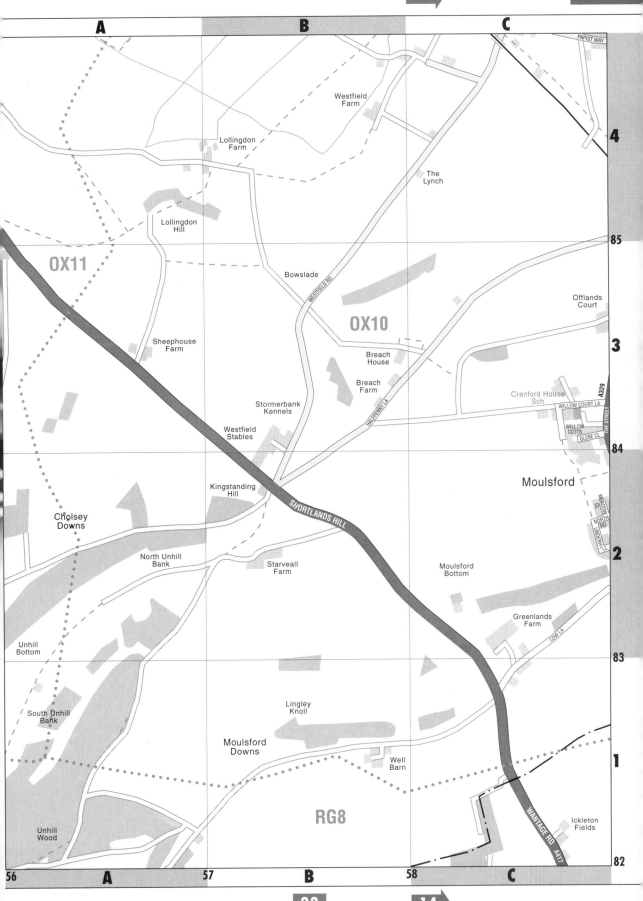

14

PAPIST WAY

A   B   C

Westfield
Farm

Lollingdon
Farm

The
Lynch

4

Lollingdon
Hill

85

OX11

Bowslade

WESTFIELD RD

Offlands
Court

OX10

Sheephouse
Farm

Breach
House

3

Breach
Farm

HALFPENNY LA

Cranford House
Sch

A329

Stormerbank
Kennels

WILLOW COURT LA

Westfield
Stables

WILLOW
COTTS

THE STREET

GLEBE CL

84

Kingstanding
Hill

Moulsford

SHORTLANDS HILL

MEADOW CL

Cholsey
Downs

NORTH RD

UNICORN

North Unhill
Bank

Starveall
Farm

Moulsford
Bottom

2

Unhill
Bottom

Greenlands
Farm

COW LA

83

South Unhill
Bank

Lingley
Knoll

Moulsford
Downs

Well
Barn

1

RG8

WANTAGE RD

Ickleton
Fields

Unhill
Wood

A417

82

56   A   57   B   58   C

33
14

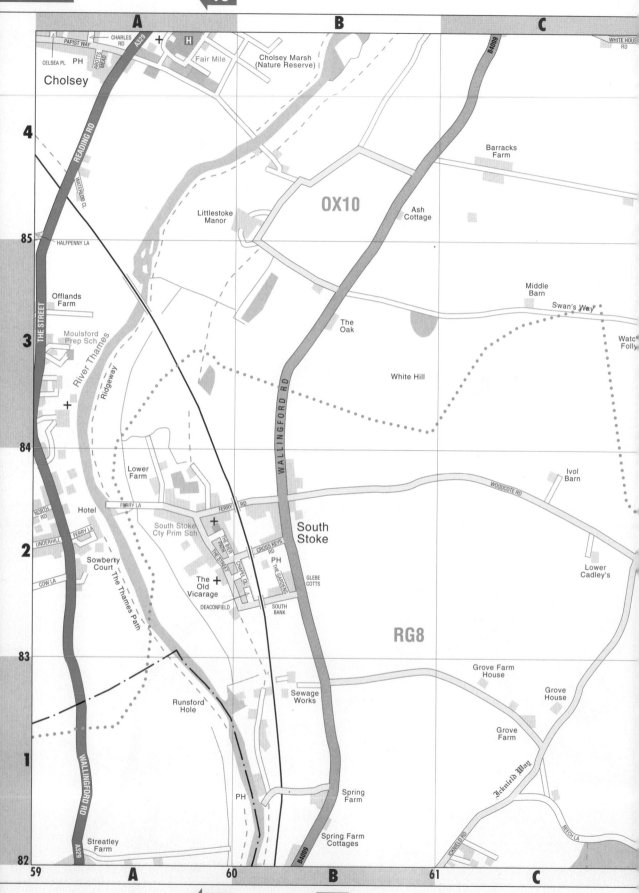

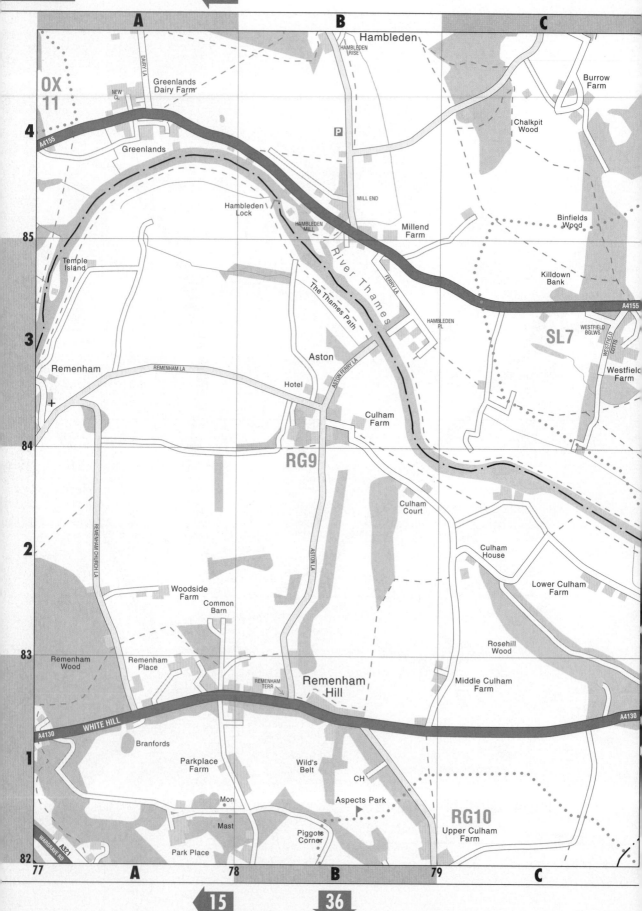

A B C

Hambleden

OX 11

HAMBLEDEN RISE

Burrow Farm

NEW CL

DAIRY LA

Greenlands Dairy Farm

Chalkpit Wood

4 A4155

Greenlands

P

MILL END

Binfields Wood

85

Hambleden Lock

HAMBLEDEN MILL

Millend Farm

Killdown Bank

River Thames

FERRY LA

Temple Island

The Thames Path

HAMBLEDEN PL

SL7

WESTFIELD BGLWS

WESTFIELD COTTS

3

Remenham

REMENHAM LA

Aston

ASTON FERRY LA

Westfield Farm

Hotel

Culham Farm

84

RG9

REMENHAM CHURCH LA

Culham Court

2

ASTON LA

Culham House

Woodside Farm

Common Barn

Lower Culham Farm

Rosehill Wood

83

Remenham Wood

Remenham Place

REMENHAM TERR

Remenham Hill

Middle Culham Farm

A4130

WHITE HILL

A4130

Branfords

1

Parkplace Farm

Wild's Belt

CH

WARGRAVE RD

A321

Mon

Aspects Park

RG10

Mast

Piggots Corner

Upper Culham Farm

82

Park Place

77 A 78 B 79 C

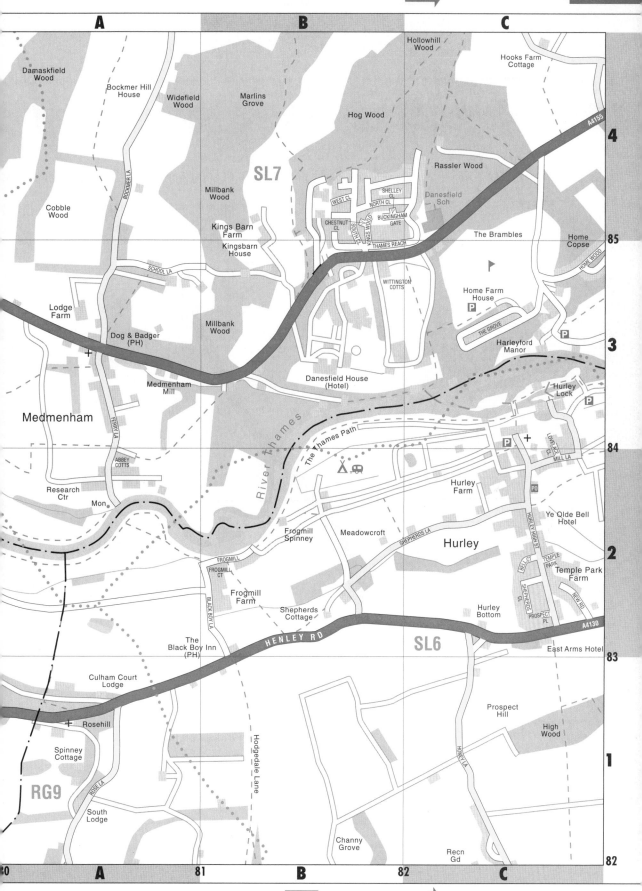

Damaskfield Wood
Bockmer Hill House
Widefield Wood
Marlins Grove
Hollowhill Wood
Hooks Farm Cottage
A4155
Hog Wood
4
SL7
Millbank Wood
Rassler Wood
Danesfield Sch
Cobble Wood
Kings Barn Farm
WEST CL
SHELLEY CL
NORTH CL
BUCKINGHAM GATE
The Brambles
Home Copse
HOME WOOD
85
Kingsbarn House
CHESTNUT CL
SOUTH CL
THAMES REACH
KINGS WOOD
Lodge Farm
SCHOOL LA
WITTINGTON COTTS
Home Farm House
P
THE GROVE
P
Dog & Badger (PH)
Millbank Wood
Harleyford Manor
3
Hurley Lock
Medmenham Mill
Danesfield House (Hotel)
P
Medmenham
FERRY LA
ABBEY COTTS
River Thames
The Thames Path
P
LOVELACE CL
MILL LA
84
Research Ctr
Mon
Hurley Farm
PO
Ye Olde Bell Hotel
Frogmill Spinney
Meadowcroft
SHEPHERDS LA
Hurley
HURLEY HIGH ST
2
FROGMILL
FROGMILL CT
BELL CT
TEMPLE PARK
Temple Park Farm
BLACK BOY LA
Frogmill Farm
Shepherds Cottage
Hurley Bottom
SHEPHERDS CL
PROSPECT PL
NEW RD
The Black Boy Inn (PH)
HENLEY RD
SL6
A4130
East Arms Hotel
83
Culham Court Lodge
Rosehill
Prospect Hill
High Wood
Spinney Cottage
ROSE LA
Hodgedale Lane
HOME LA
1
RG9
South Lodge
Channy Grove
Recn Gd
82

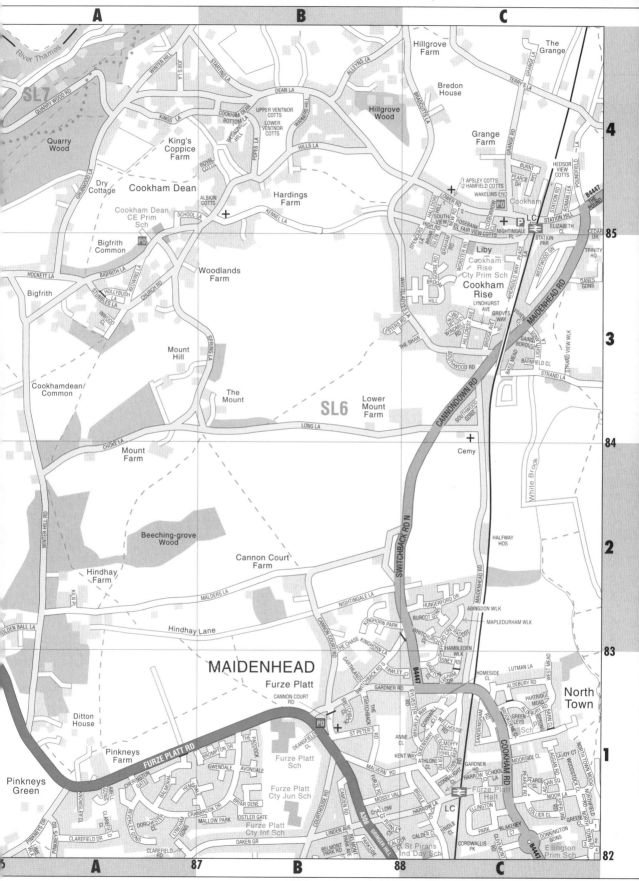

A B C

River Thames

SL7

Quarry Wood

Cookham Dean

Dry Cottage

King's Coppice Farm

GRUBWOOD LA

QUARRY WOOD RD

WINTER HILL

STARTINS LA

KINGS LA

COOKHAM DEAN BOTTOM LA

WESSONS HILL

WARNERS HILL

DEAN LA

UPPER VENTNOR COTTS

LOWER VENTNOR COTTS

HILLS LA

ALLEYNS LA

Hillgrove Wood

Hillgrove Farm

Bredon House

The Grange

GRANGE LA

TERRY'S LA

Grange Farm

GRANGE RD

BRADCUTTS LA

Cookham Dean CE Prim Sch

SCHOOL LA

ROYAL COTTS

POPES LA

ALBION COTTS

KENNEL LA

Hardings Farm

Bigfrith Common

Woodlands Farm

BIGFRITH LA

BENWINS LA

HOCKETT LA

STUBBLES LA

HOLLYBUSH LA

CHURCH RD

INWOOD CL

Bigfrith

Mount Hill

SPRING LA

The Mount

SL6

Lower Mount Farm

LONG LA

CHOKE LA

Mount Farm

Cookhamdean Common

WINTER HILL RD

Beeching-grove Wood

Hindhay Farm

KILN PL

MALDERS LA

Cannon Court Farm

Hindhay Lane

NIGHTINGALE LA

GOULDEN BALL LA

MAIDENHEAD

Furze Platt

CANNON COURT RD

Ditton House

Pinkneys Farm

FURZE PLATT RD

Pinkneys Green

Furze Platt Cty Jun Sch

Furze Platt Sch

Furze Platt Cty Inf Sch

CANNONDOWN RD

SWITCHBACK RD N

MAIDENHEAD RD

Cookham

Cookham Rise Cty Prim Sch

Cookham Rise

STATION HILL

STATION RD

North Town

COOKHAM RD

B4447

A308

Cemy

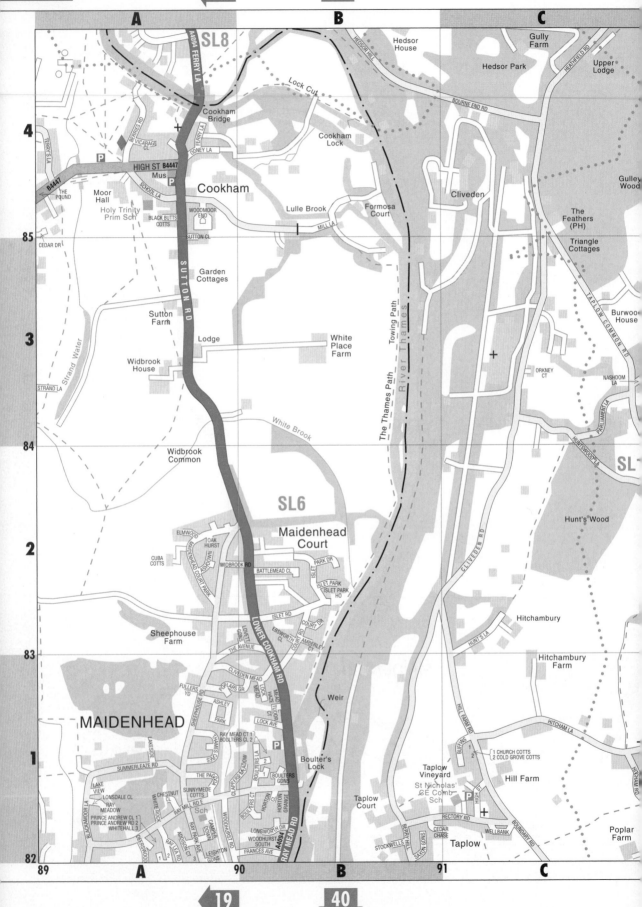

SL8

Gully Farm

Hedsor House

Hedsor Park

Upper Lodge

HEATHFIELD RD

Lock Cut

HEDSOR HILL

BOURNE END RD

Cookham Bridge

4

VICARAGE CL

BERRIES RD

ODNEY LA

FERRY LA

A4094 FERRY LA

Cookham Lock

Gulley Wood

Cliveden

The Feathers (PH)

HIGH ST B4447

Mus

TERRY'S LA

B4447

THE POUND

Moor Hall

SCHOOL LA

Cookham

WOODMOOR END

Lulle Brook

Formosa Court

Triangle Cottages

Holy Trinity Prim Sch

BLACK BUTTS COTTS

MILL LA

85

CEDAR DR

SUTTON CL

Garden Cottages

TAPLOW COMMON RD

Burwood House

SUTTON RD

Sutton Farm

Lodge

White Place Farm

Strand Water

Widbrook House

The Thames Path

Towing Path

River Thames

ORKNEY CT

NASHDOM LA

3

STRAND LA

HUNTSWOOD LA

PARLIAMENT LA

SL

White Brook

84

Widbrook Common

Hunt's Wood

SL6

ELMWOOD

OAK HURST

Maidenhead Court

HUNT'S LA

CLIVEDEN RD

Hitchambury

CUBA COTTS

WIDBROOK RD

BATTLEMEAD CL

PARK DR

ISLET PARK

ISLET PARK HO

MAIDENHEAD COURT PARK

2

Sheephouse Farm

ISLET RD

EBSWORTH CL

COURT RD

COURT DR

AMBERLEY CT

Hitchambury Farm

LOWER COOKHAM RD

THE AVENUE

LOWEN GDNS

HILL FARM RD

HITCHAM LA

83

CLIVEDEN MEAD

POPLARS GR

Weir

FULLERS YD

SHEEPHOUSE RD

ASHLEY PARK

HAZEL MEAD

MEAD CT

TUDOR CL

BUFFINS

1 CHURCH COTTS
2 COLD GROVE COTTS

LOCK AVE

P

Boulter's Lock

BERRY HILL

Taplow Vineyard

1
2

Hill Farm

MAIDENHEAD

SUMMERLEAZE RD

LAKESIDE

WHITE ROCK

RAY MEAD CT 1
BOULTERS CL 2

JAMES ST

P

BOULTERS GDNS

St Nicholas' CE Comb Sch

HIGH ST

LAKE VIEW

LONSDALE CL

CHESTNUT

THE PAG

CLAPPERS MEADOW

BOULTERS CT

HORTON CL

SUNNYMEDE COTTS

Sch

Taplow Court

RECTORY RD

CEDAR CHASE

WELLBANK

P

BOUNDARY RD

1

RAY MEADOW

RAY MILL RD E

BOULTERS RD

WOODHURST RD

HORTON GRANGE

Poplar Farm

BLACKAMOOR LA

PRINCE ANDREW CL 1
PRINCE ANDREW RD 2
WHITEHALL 3

RAY PARK AVE

CAMDER DUNN

LEIGHTON GDNS

LONGWORTH DR

WOODHURST SOUTH

FRANCES AVE

A4094

RAY MEAD RD

STOCKWELLS

SINGLE

BERRY HILL

SPINES

Taplow

82

89

A

90

B

91

C

A   B   C

Whitespark Wood

SL2

Root Mound

Abbey Wood

Littleworth Corner

Beeches Way

Dorney Wood

4

HORSESHOE HILL

Brook End Farm

Lower Brook End

Kilnwood

PARK LA

Tower Wood

Cabrook

CURRIERS LA

Towerwood

Burnham Beeches

85

Little Barns Wood

P

CH Lambournes Wood

Dorney Wood

PUMPKIN HILL

Victoria Drive

Lord Mayors Drive

Juniper Grove

Wymers Wood

DROPMORE RD

DORNEY WOOD RD

Pumpkin Hill Cottage

PH

HAWTHORN LA

THOMPKINS LA

3

NASHDOM LA

Fox Den

Pumpkin Hill

NIGHTINGALE PARK

ROSE HILL

Rose Hill House

Longmead

LONGMEAD LA

Longmead

Hunts Wood Farm

84

Rose Hill

Poyle Cottages

CHALK PIT

Snowball Farm

SL1

Rose Hill Farm

INTSWOOD LA

BRICKFIELD LA

Westalls

Hotel

High Meadow

GREEN LA

CH

GROVE RD

Burnham Grove

ALLERDS RD

Cant's Hill

CROW PIECE LA

Bottom Waltons

2

TAPLOW COMMON RD

Grovefield Hotel

WYMERS WOOD RD

REDWOOD

POYLE LA

ASHCROFT CT

PINK LA

BOWMANS CL

Burnham

HAZELHURST RD

BEETLEY PARK

Grove Wood

WALTON LA

BOTTOM WALTONS CARAVAN SITE

SL2

83

Hitcham Park

OXFORD AVE

WILLOW WOOD CL

CAMBRIDGE AVE

WYNDHAM CRES

NORTH BURNHAM

GRENVILLE CL

WALTHAM NDS DR

HALL MEADOW

LINKSWOOD RD

THE FAIRWAY

PIPERS CL

PIPERS CT

KNAPERS DR

Court Farm

COURT LA

DOVE HOUSE CRES

FARNHAM LA

FARNHAM LA

ROKESBY RD

SAMPSONS GN

MASCOLL PATH

ROKESBY RD

LILAC CT

TRAVIC RD

MARINDEN

CHILWICK RD

1

Hitcham House Farm

HITCHAM LA

HAMILTON GDNS

TOOKLEY WAY

BREWARD CL

GORE RD

THE GORE

MINNIECROFT RD

OLD FIVES CT

WILMOT RD

SUMMERS

ALMOND CT

BAKER TREE LA

BALDWIN RD

FAIRFIELD RD

LONG DR

PIPERS CT

JENNERY LA

BRITWELL RD

1 THE GRANGE
2 GREEN LANE CT

Grenville Court

DOVE HOUSE CRES

LYNCH HILL LA

GAVESTON RD

GARRARD RD

CECIL WAY

DOWNING PATH

WINTOUN PATH

LONG FURLONG DR

RINGTO N CL

PERRYMAN WAY

GOODWIN RD

 PRIEL WAY

SKYDMORE PATH

SLOUGH

Sch

UMB

1

New Cut

HITCHAM HOUSE

Hitcham Park

Lent

CLEARES PASTURE

BURN WLK

MIDDLE WAY

CHURCH ST

PO

P

DAWES EAST RD

HOGFAIR LA

HATCHGATE GDNS

THE POUND

Burnham Gram Sch

LOWER BRITWELL RD

LOWER BRITWELL RD

WOODSWORTH RD

STRAFFORD RD

BARTELOTTS RD

NEWPORT RD

Cross

COVERDALE WAY

VAUGHAN WAY

BASSETT WAY

EGERTON RD

PEMBERTON RD

KESTREL PATH

MAGPIE WAY

TENNYSON WAY

VERMONT RD

FOSTERS PATH

Britwell

New Cut

ORCHARDVILLE RD

BURLINGTON RD

THE GREEN

EIGHT ACRES

LENT RISE RD

ALICE LA

Orchardville

ST PETER'S CL

PERRY HO

PERRYFIELDS

STOMP RD

WINDSOR LA

Liby

WINDSOR CL

Sch

The Priory

PRIORY RD

SHENSTONE DR

MICHAEL'S CT

HAYMILL RD

PORTLAND CL

KINGSLEY PATH

BLUNFIELD CRES

WHITTAKER RD

LITTLE

NORTHMEAD RD

LOVEGROVE DR

NEWCHURCH RD

MARESCROFT RD

SCAFELL RD

TEESDALE RD

82

2   A   93   B   94   C

21

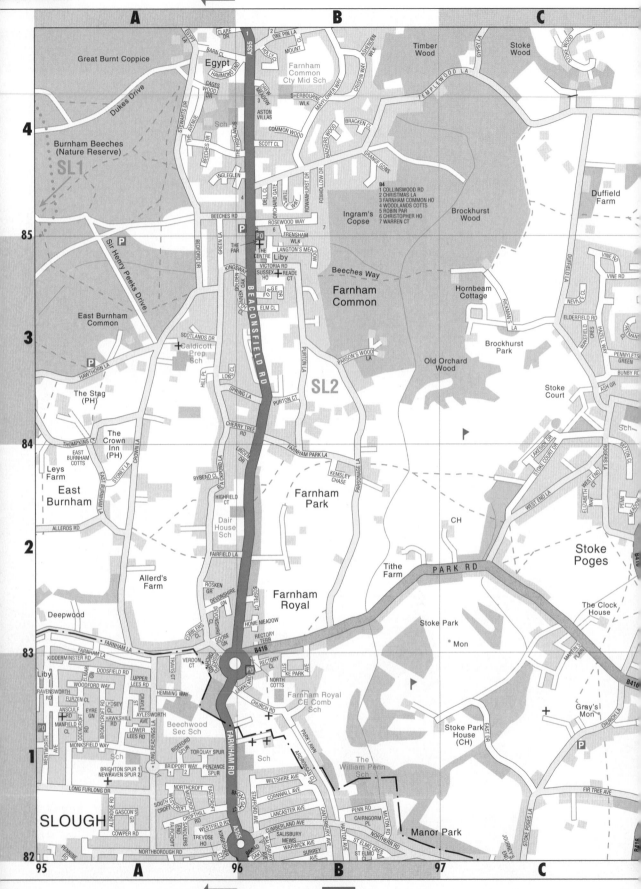

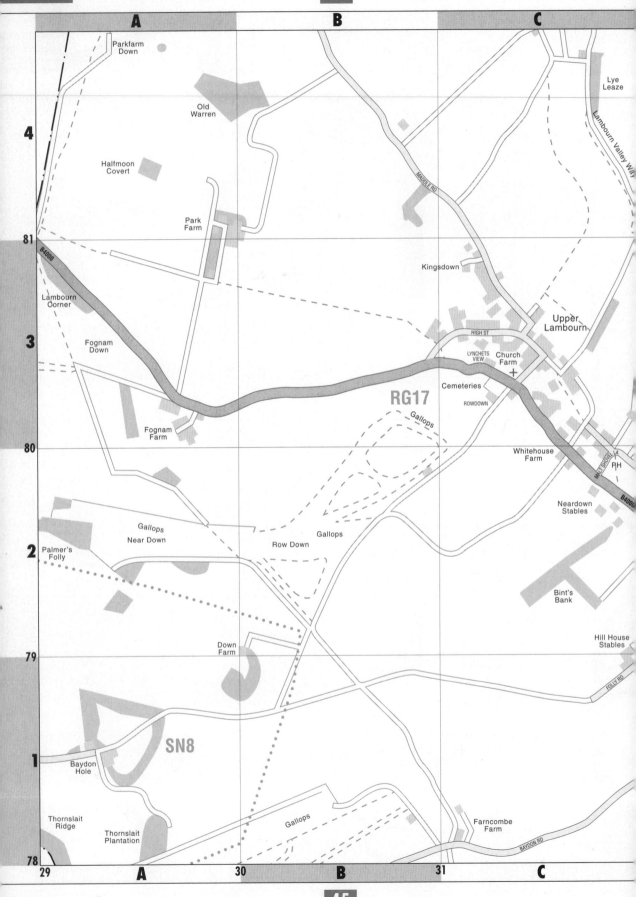

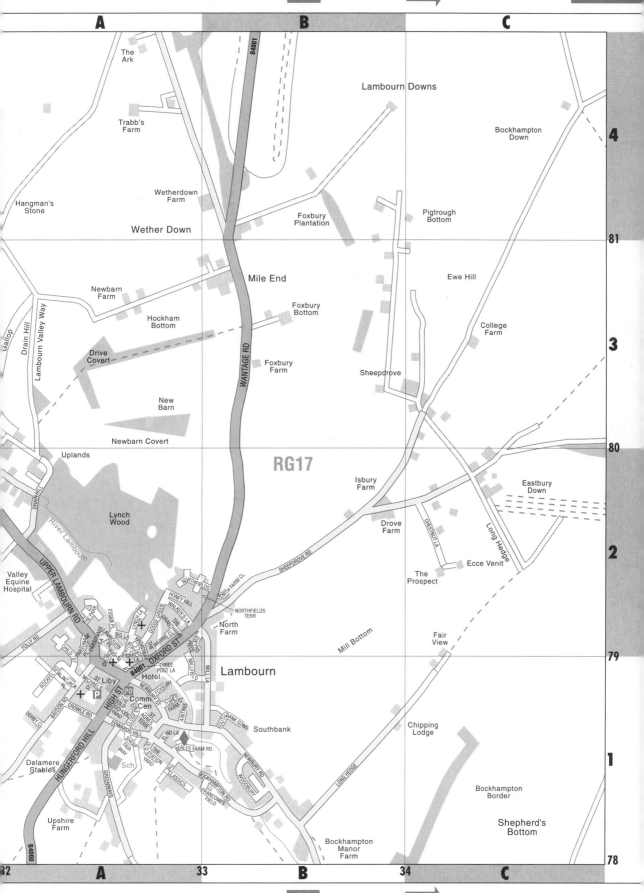

A   B   C

↑ 5   26 →

The Ark

Trabb's Farm

Lambourn Downs

Bockhampton Down

4

Hangman's Stone

Wetherdown Farm

Foxbury Plantation

Pigtrough Bottom

Wether Down

81

Mile End

Ewe Hill

Newbarn Farm

Hockham Bottom

Foxbury Bottom

College Farm

3

Drive Covert

Foxbury Farm

Sheepdrove

Gallop

Drain Hill

Lambourn Valley Way

WANTAGE RD

New Barn

Newbarn Covert

80

Uplands

RG17

Isbury Farm

Eastbury Down

Lynch Wood

Drove Farm

Long Hedge

2

River Lambourn

Sheepdrove Rd

CHESTNUT LA

Ecce Venit

Valley Equine Hospital

UPPER LAMBOURN RD

NORTHFIELDS

HONEY HILL

WALKER'S LA

NORTH FARM CL.

The Prospect

FOLLY RD

CHILD ST

ESSEX PL

PARSONAGE

LAMBURG

BIG LA

THE PARK

GOOSE GREEN

GRANTHAMS

NORTHFIELDS TERR

North Farm

Fair View

79

ROCKET RD.

DERBY CL.

BAYDON RD

CROWLE RD.

FLINT JACK

ST. MICHAEL'S

ST. Liby

HIGH ST

PD

P

COMM Cen

NEWBURY RD

FOXBURY

THREE POST LA

MILLFIELD

MILL LA

Hotel

Lambourn

Mill Bottom

Chipping Lodge

Delamere Stables

Sch

EDWARDS HILL

SHEEP FAIR WAY

HUNGERFORD HILL

GREENWAYS

THE STATION YARD

BEALES FARM RD

BOCKHAMPTON RD

NEWBURY RD

WOODBURY

Southbank

Long Hedge

1

Bockhampton Border

Upshire Farm

B4000

FRANCOMES FIELD

Bockhampton Manor Farm

Shepherd's Bottom

78

25
6

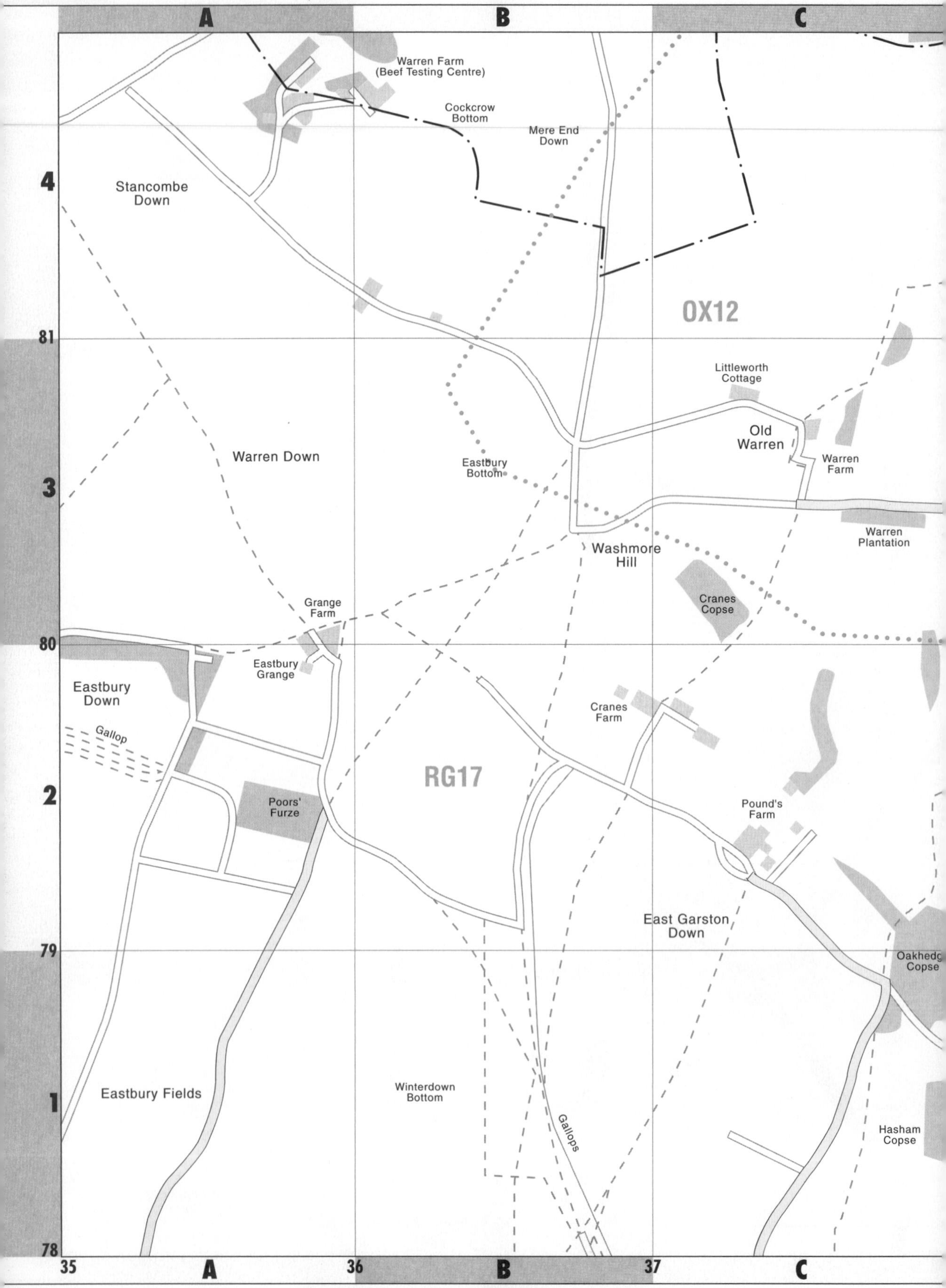
A
B
C
4
81
3
80
2
79
1
78
35
36
37
Warren Farm
(Beef Testing Centre)
Cockcrow
Bottom
Mere End
Down
Stancombe
Down
OX12
Littleworth
Cottage
Old
Warren
Warren
Farm
Warren Down
Eastbury
Bottom
Warren
Plantation
Washmore
Hill
Grange
Farm
Cranes
Copse
Eastbury
Grange
Eastbury
Down
Gallop
Cranes
Farm
RG17
Poors'
Furze
Pound's
Farm
East Garston
Down
Oakhedg
Copse
Eastbury Fields
Winterdown
Bottom
Gallops
Hasham
Copse

25
47

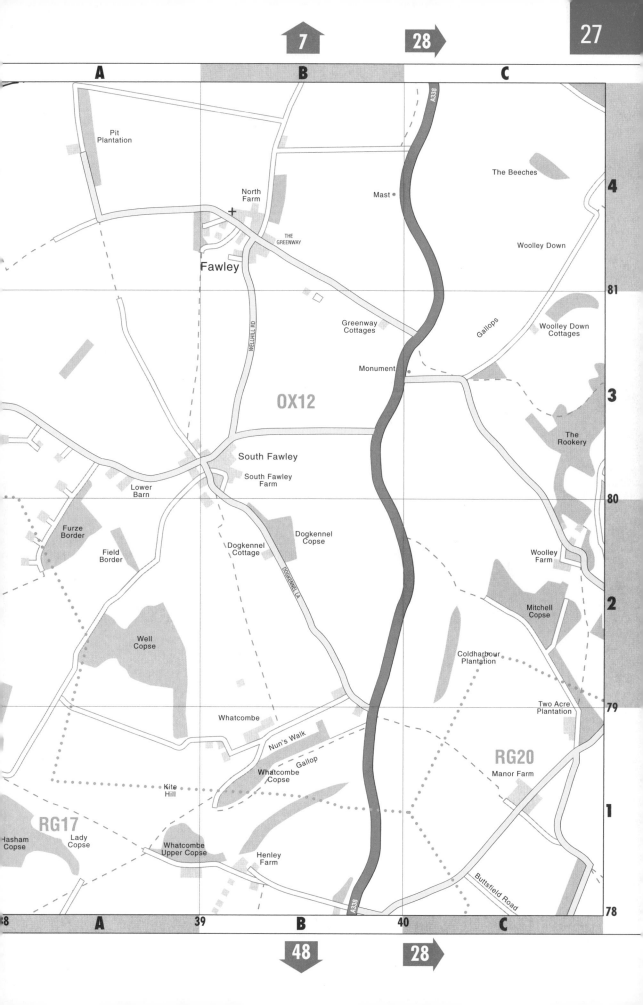

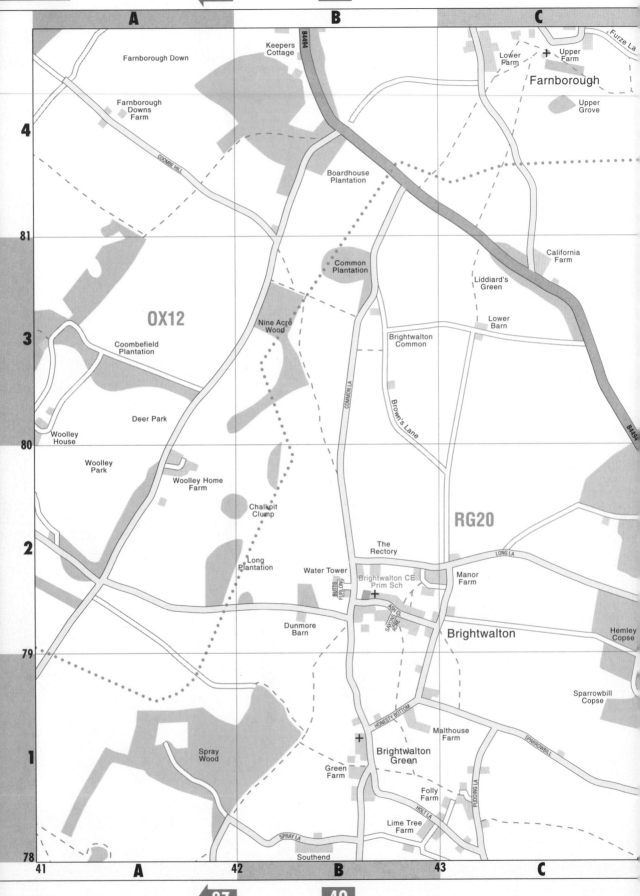

A　　　　B　　　　C

4

81

OX12

3

Farnborough Down

Keepers
Cottage

Lower
Farm

Upper
Farm

Farnborough

Furze La

Farnborough
Downs
Farm

COOMBE HILL

Boardhouse
Plantation

B4494

Common
Plantation

California
Farm

Liddiard's
Green

Lower
Barn

Coombefield
Plantation

Nine Acre
Wood

Brightwalton
Common

Deer Park

Brown's Lane

COMMON LA

B4494

Woolley
House

80

Woolley
Park

Woolley Home
Farm

Chalkpit
Clump

RG20

2

Long
Plantation

The
Rectory

Water Tower

Brightwalton CE
Prim Sch

LONG LA

Manor
Farm

BUTTS
FURLONG

ASH CL

SAXONS
ACRE

Brightwalton

Hemley
Copse

79

Dunmore
Barn

Sparrowbill
Copse

1

Spray
Wood

Honesty Bottom

Malthouse
Farm

SPARROWBILL

Green
Farm

Brightwalton
Green

Folly
Farm

PUDDING LA

Lime Tree
Farm

HOLT LA

SPRAY LA

Southend

78

41　　　A　　　42　　　B　　　43　　　C

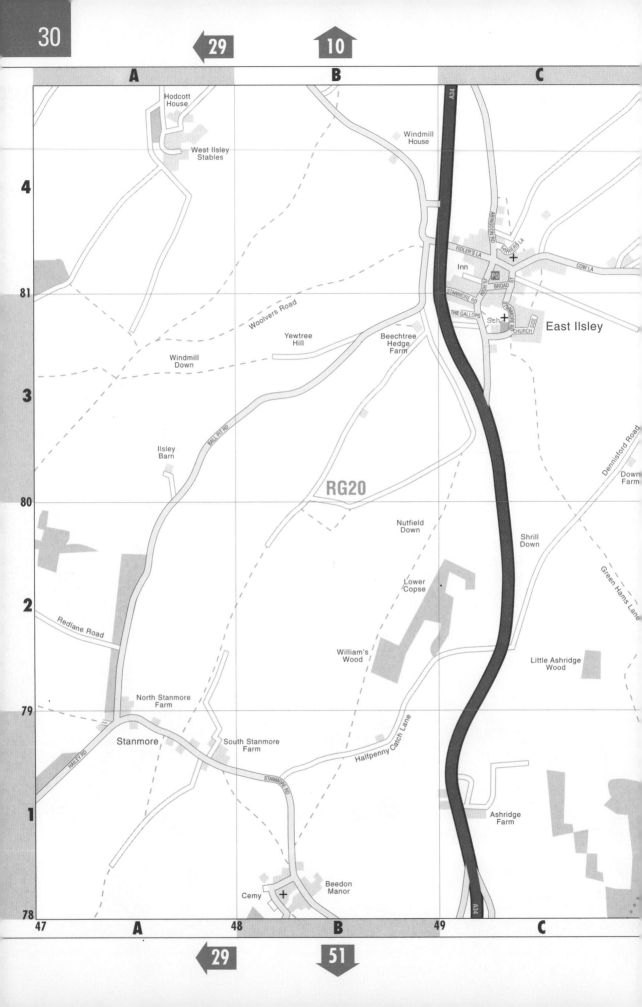

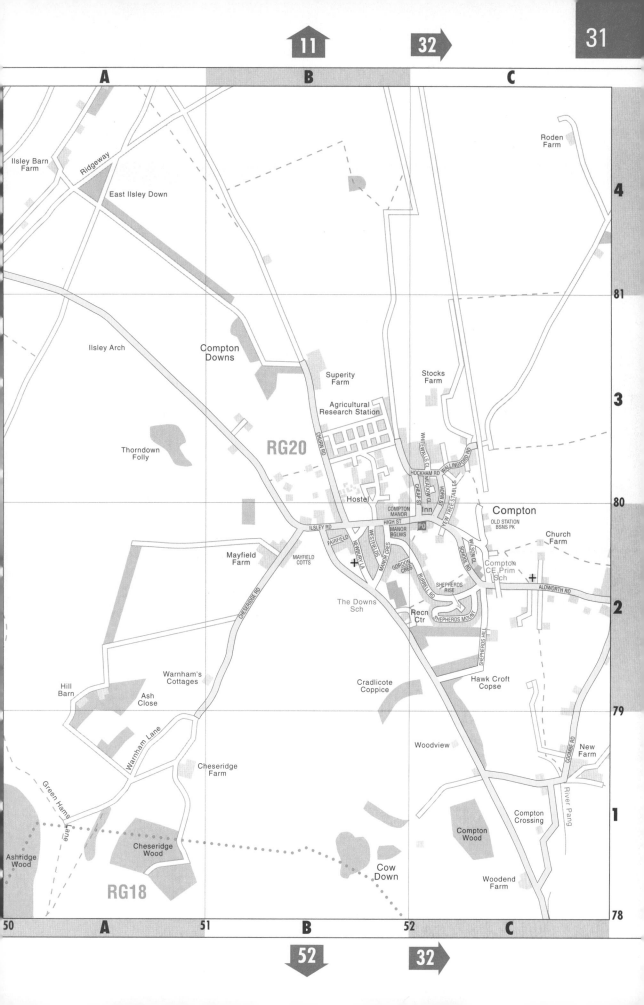

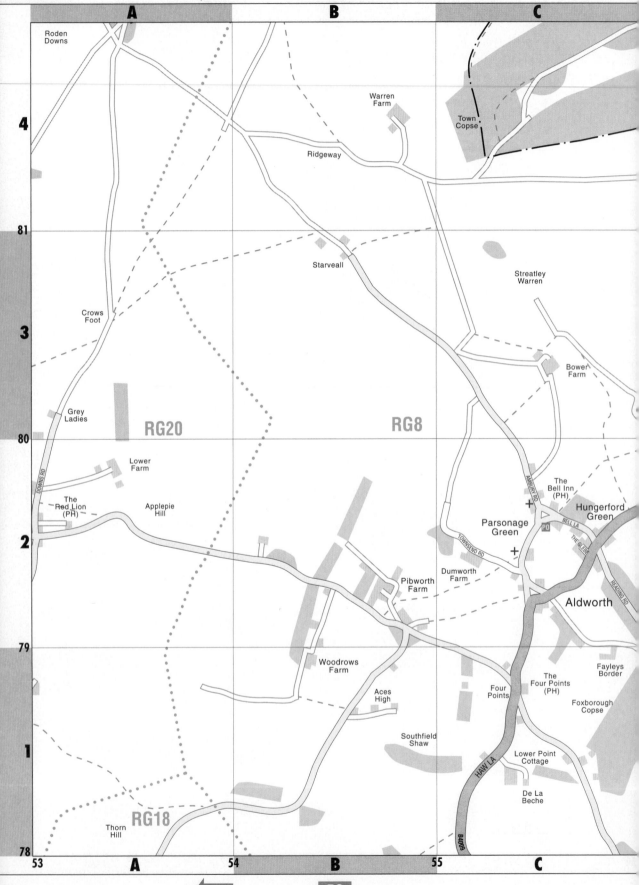

A
B
C

Roden
Downs

Warren
Farm

Town
Copse

4

Ridgeway

81

Starveall

Streatley
Warren

Crows
Foot

3

Bower
Farm

Grey
Ladies

RG20

RG8

80

Lower
Farm

The
Bell Inn
(PH)

The
Red Lion
(PH)

Applepie
Hill

Parsonage
Green

Hungerford
Green

PO

2

Pibworth
Farm

Dumworth
Farm

Aldworth

79

Woodrows
Farm

Fayleys
Border

Aces
High

Four
Points

The
Four Points
(PH)

Foxborough
Copse

Southfield
Shaw

1

Lower Point
Cottage

De La
Beche

RG18

Thorn
Hill

78
53
A
54
B
55
C

DOWNS RD
AMBURY RD
TOWNSEND RD
BELL LA
THE GLEBE
READING RD
HAW LA
B4009

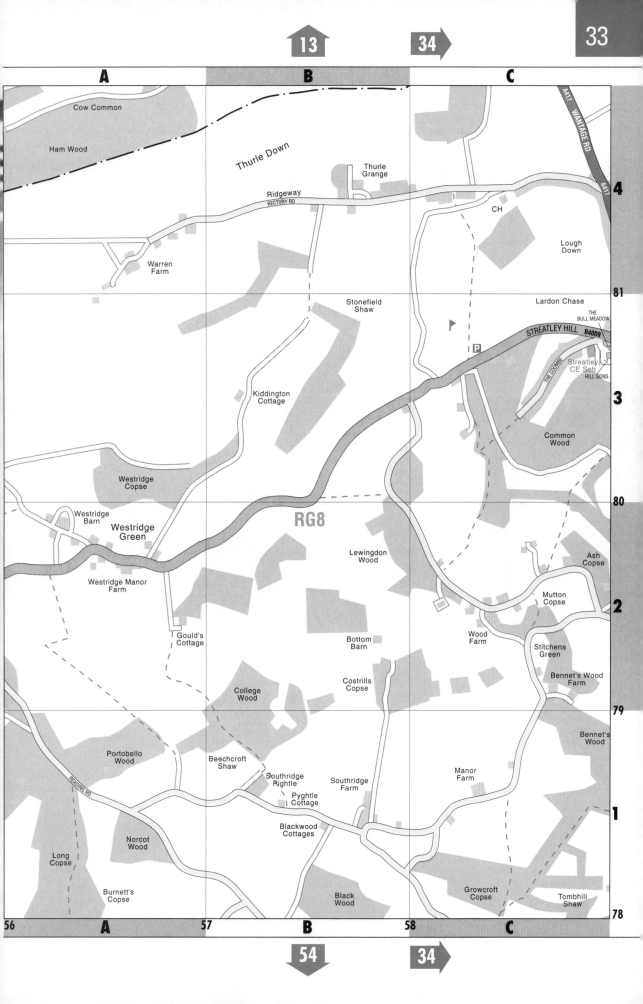

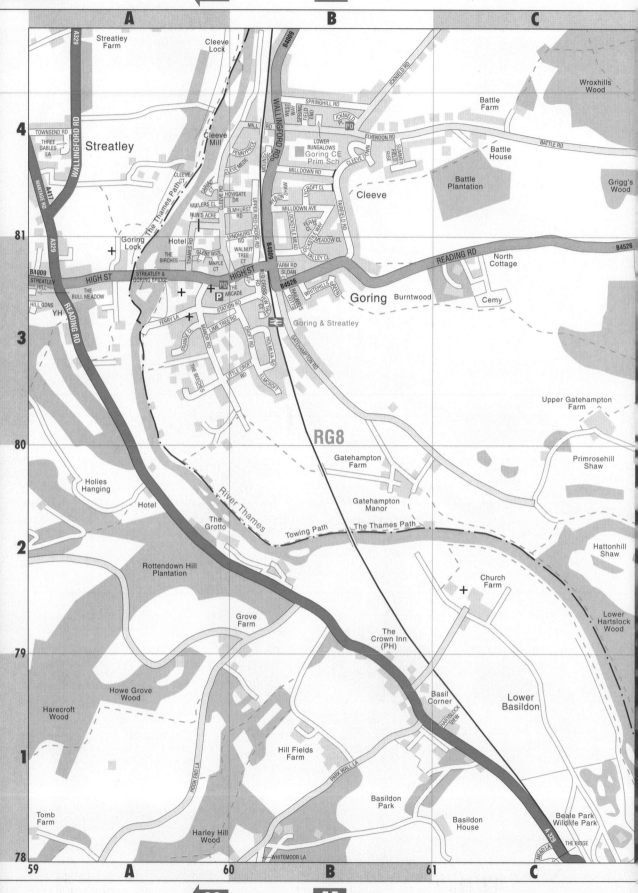

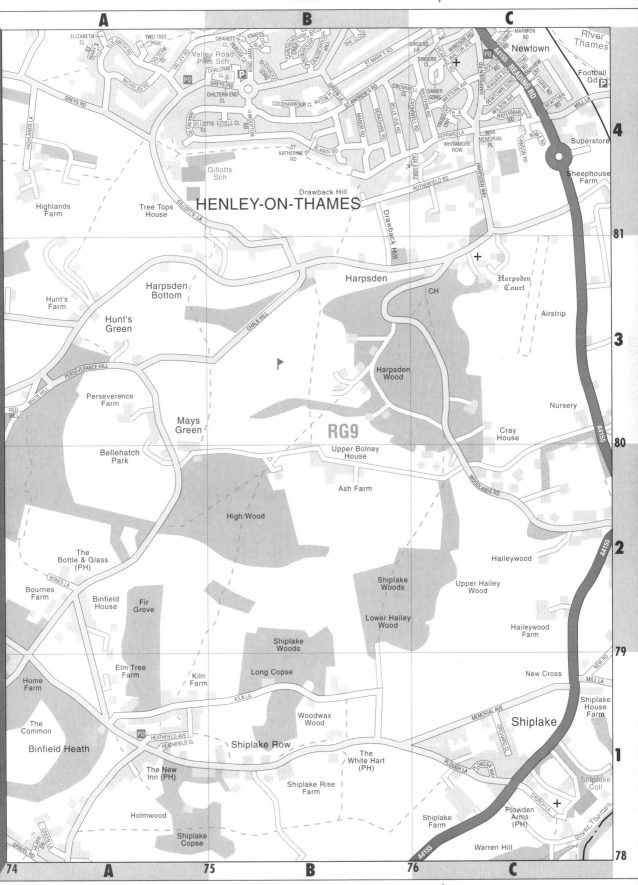

A B C

Elizabeth CL
MARY'S CL
TWO TREE HILL
ELIZABETH RD
CHILTERN RD
VALLEY RD
GRAVETT CL
KNAPPE CL
GAINSBOROUGH CRES
GAINSBOROUGH HILL
GAINSBOROUGH RD
THE CLOSE
ST MARK'S RD
SINGERS LA
VICARAGE RD
WINDSOR RD
WALTON AVE
QUEBEC RD
MARMION RD
Newtown
River Thames

Valley Road Prim Sch
PO
NICHOLAS RD
MARY'S CL
ELIZABETH RD
PERIAM CL
KING JAMES WAY
STERWOOD GDNS
GREEN LA
SINGERS CL
WESTERN AVE
SOUTH A
NIAGARA RD
NEWTOWN GDNS
WILSON AVE
WATERMAN'S RD
NOBLE RD
VINSON RD
NEWTOWN RD
FARM RD
FAIRVIEW RD
READING RD

GREYS RD
CHALCRAFT CL
GREYS RD
P
COLDHARBOUR CL
ST ANDREW'S RD
CROMWELL CL
WESTERN RD
CROMWELL RD
DAMER GDNS
PEPPARD LA
WAR MEMORIAL PL
Football Gd
P

CHILTERN END CL
GILLOTTS CL
LOVELL CL
HAKINS RD
WOOTTON
MANOR RD
BERKSHIRE RD
BELLE VUE RD
BLANDY RD
ST KATHERINE'S RD
WHITAMORE ROW
HARPSDEN WAY
Superstore
Sheephouse Farm

HIGHLANDS LA
Gillotts Sch
CARLESSILL PL
ROTHERFIELD RD
4

Highlands Farm
Tree Tops House
GILLOTT'S LA
Drawback Hill
HENLEY-ON-THAMES
Drawback Hill
81

Hunt's Farm
Harpsden Bottom
CHALK HILL
Harpsden
CH
Harpsden Court
Airstrip

Hunt's Green
PERSEVERANCE HILL
WHITE HILL
RED HILL
Perseverence Farm
Harpsden Wood
Nursery
3

Mays Green
RG9
Upper Bolney House
Cray House
80

Bellehatch Park
Ash Farm
WOODLANDS RD

High Wood
The Bottle & Glass (PH)
BONES LA
Haileywood
2

Bournes Farm
Binfield House
Fir Grove
Shiplake Woods
Upper Hailey Wood
Haileywood Farm

Home Farm
Elm Tree Farm
Kiln Farm
Long Copse
Lower Hailey Wood
Shiplake Woods
New Cross
MILL LA
NEW RD
Shiplake House Farm
79

The Common
Binfield Heath
PO
HEATHFIELD AVE
HEATHFIELD CL
KILN LA
Woodwax Wood
Shiplake Row
MEMORIAL AVE
ORCHARD CL
Shiplake
1

The New Inn (PH)
The White Hart (PH)
PLOUGH LA
PLOWDEN WAY
CHURCH LA
Shiplake Coll

Holmwood
Shiplake Rise Farm
Shiplake Farm
Plowden Arms (PH)
River Thames

GREEN LA
GRAVEL LA
HEATH DR
Shiplake Copse
A4155
Warren Hill
Plowden LA
78

74 A 75 B 76 C

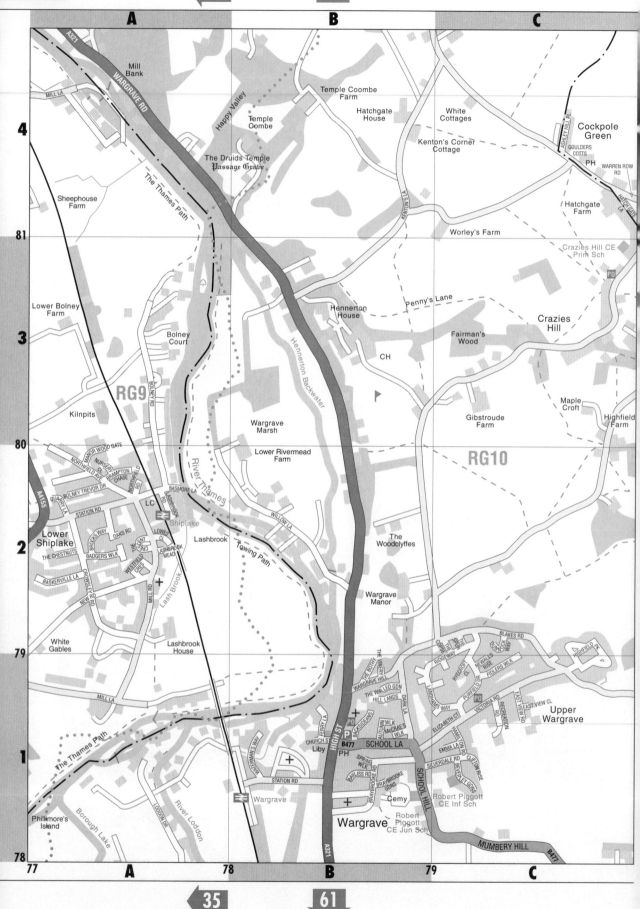

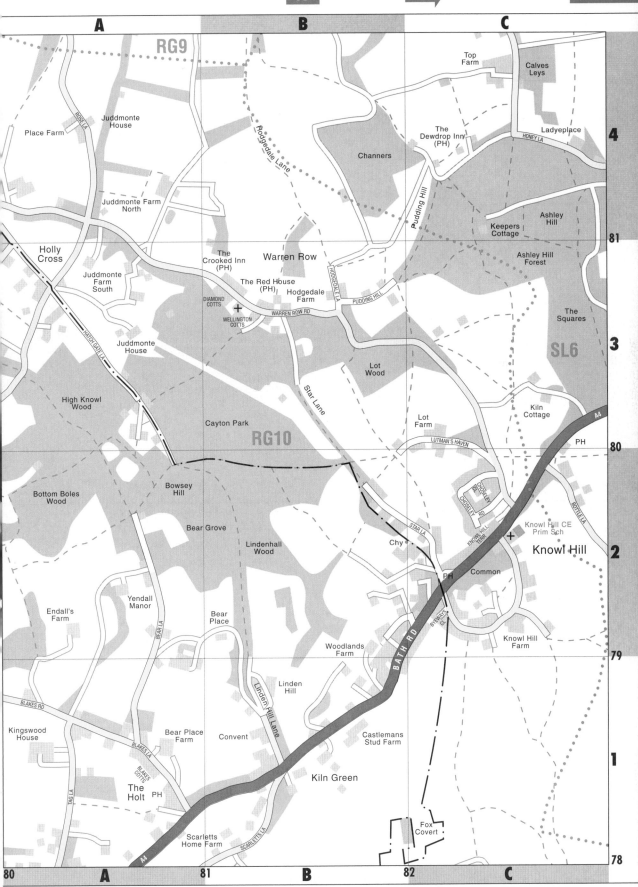

17
38

A B C

RG9

Place Farm

Juddmonte House

Juddmonte Farm North

ROSE LA

Hodgedale Lane

Channers

Top Farm

Calves Leys

The Dewdrop Inn (PH)

Ladyeplace

HONEY LA

4

Pudding Hill

Keepers Cottage

Ashley Hill

81

Holly Cross

Juddmonte Farm South

The Crooked Inn (PH)

Warren Row

The Red House (PH)

Hodgedale Farm

DIAMOND COTTS

WELLINGTON COTTS

WARREN ROW RD

HODGEDALE LA

PUDDING HILL

Ashley Hill Forest

The Squares

SL6

HATCH GATE LA

Juddmonte House

Lot Wood

3

High Knowl Wood

Cayton Park

RG10

Star Lane

Lot Wood

Lot Farm

Kiln Cottage

A4

LUTMAN'S HAVEN

PH

80

Bottom Boles Wood

Bowsey Hill

Bear Grove

Lindenhall Wood

STAR LA

Chy

STAR LA

CHOSELEY RD

CHOSELEY RD

KNOWL HILL TERR

BOTTLE LA

Knowl Hill CE Prim Sch

Knowl Hill

2

Yendall Manor

BEAR LA

Bear Place

PH

Common

Endall's Farm

Woodlands Farm

BATH RD

BYEWAYS CL

Knowl Hill Farm

79

Kingswood House

BLAKES RD

BLAKES LA

Bear Place Farm

Linden Hill Lane

Linden Hill

Convent

Castlemans Stud Farm

1

BLAKES COTTS

TAG LA

The Holt

PH

Kiln Green

A4

Scarletts Home Farm

SCARLETTS LA

Fox Covert

78

80 A 81 B 82 C

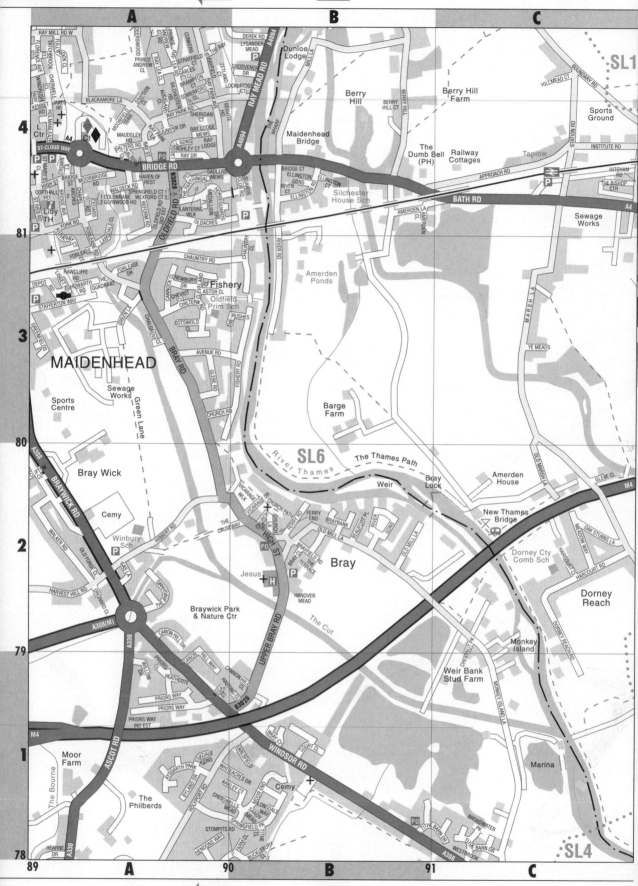

C3
1 SHERIDAN CT   7 MOLYNS MEWS
2 SELWYN PL
3 BOWER CT
4 LEWINS FARM CT
5 WATERMAN CT
6 BIDDLES CL

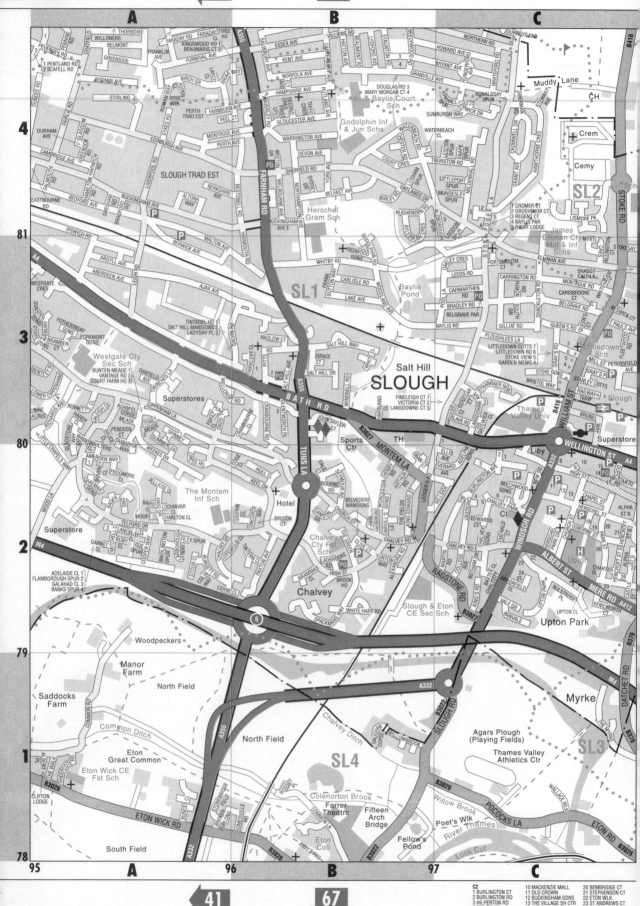

C2
1 BURLINGTON CT
2 BURLINGTON RD
3 HILPERTON RD
4 TOWER HO
5 ASHBOURNE HO
6 SHAFTESBURY CT
7 MOORSTOWN CT
8 PRUDENTIAL BLDGS
9 MACKENZIE ST
10 MACKENZIE MALL
11 OLD CROWN
12 BUCKINGHAM GDNS
13 THE VILLAGE SH CTR
14 LEOPOLD MALL
15 CURZON MALL
16 CHANDOS MALL
17 TOWN SQ
18 VICTORIA ST
19 BISHAM CT
20 BEMBRIDGE CT
21 STEPHENSON CT
22 ETON WLK
23 ST ANDREWS CT
24 LINCOLN CT
25 LOCKSLEY CT
26 SPRUCE CT
27 DARTMOUTH CT
28 ALBERT CL
29 MANOR CT

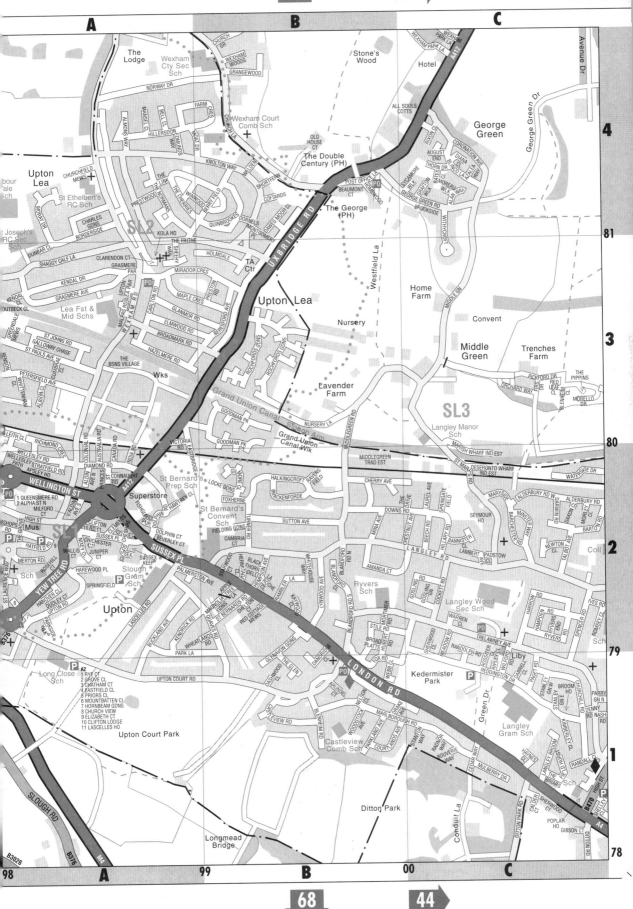

SN8

Farncombe Down

Gallops

Gallops

Gallops

Windmill Farm

Farn Combe

B4000

Hatchets Corner

Lodge Down

Dean Stubbing Copse

Coppington Down

4

Lodge Farm

Lodge Copse

Kingwood House

The Kingwood Stud

77

Woodlands Lodge

Rookery

PLATT LA

Gallop

Brickkiln Copse

Great West Wood

Little West Wood

Great Noakes Copse

Hadley Farm

ERMIN ST

Lambourn Woodlands

3

Common Barn Copse

Fox Farm

oneygre Copse

Mast

Membury Service Area

Batten's Farm

Badger Hole

RG17

76

Baydon Wood

St John's Green

Works

Works

The Hare and Hounds (PH)
Lyedowns

B4000

HILLDROP LA

Copse Ground Wood

Membury Airfield (disused)

Dixon's Farm

M4

Paxlet Plantation

Walls Copse

AERIAL BSNS PK

Works

2

Hillier's Copse

Membury

Cuckoo Copse

75

SN8

Membury

Petteville Copse

Marridge Hill Chicken Farm

Membury Farm

Leigh Farm

Membury House

Moon's Copse

Lyckweed Farm

HALF MILE RD

1

Balak Farm

White House

Membury Lodge

Pit Cottage

Ballard's Copse

Marridge Hill Wood

Witcha Copse

Pit (dis)

74

A B C

4

Hungerford Gap

Coppington Hill

White Shute

Lambourn Valley Way

River Lambourn

THE HERMITAGE

Hall

Eastbury

Manor Farm

The Plough (PH)

DOWNS CL

Boldstart Farm

Boldstart Copse

Thorn Hill

Thornhill Copse

77

HAYFIELD C

Willis Farm

Ox Wood

Gifford's Copse

Clapper Border

Cleeve Wood

Shrags Hill

3

Dance's Cottage

Lord's Wood

Alms Wood

Haycroft Hill

Berry's Wood

Cleeve Hill

RG17

76

Great Park Wood

Household Copse

Rooksnest

Patch Copse

Pebblehill Copse

Cymbalcroft Copse

Lambourn Woodlands

Leyatt Copse

STRAIGHT LA

Danesfield Copse

Stony Lane

Watchcroft Copse

2

Lyedown Copse

HILLDROP LA

Hilldrop Farm

B4000

B4001

Burgess's Farm

Peaks Copse

Bushyleaze Border

M4

75

ERMIN ST

EASTBURY SHUTE

May's Copse

Hall

Lye Farm Cottages

Woodlands St Mary

1

Riverwood Border

Kimber's Border

HALF MILE RD

Carols Acre

Breach Border

Holt Copse

B4000

B4001

M4

LOODOMBE

74

32 A 33 B 34 C

A
B
C

Winterdown Barn

Jimmy's Farm

Lone Barry Farm

Coldborough Hill

Furze Border

4

Lambourn Valley Way

Manor Farm

77

Rose Farm

Coldborough Farm

ROGERS'S LA

DOWNLANDS

STATION RD

THE WALDRONS

BURFORD'S

SCHOOL LA

BACK ST

FRONT ST

HUMPHREY'S LA

HILLSIDE

PD

COLLEGE

Westfield Farm

East Garston

3

Queen's Arms (PH)

STRAIGHT LA

River Lambourn

Parsonage Farm

Maidencourt Farm

Peake's Border

RG17

76

Gold Hill

River Mead

Bottom Copse

GOODINGS LA

2

Dore's Farm

Manor Farm

Goodings

East Garston Woodlands

Gallop

75

Fairchild's Farm

Grasscroft Copse

Greenlands Copse

Potter's Cottage

South Hidden Farm

A338

1

HUNGERFORD HILL

Fieldridge Copse

Fieldridge Lane

Coldridge Copse

A338

ROMAN ROAD

ERMIN ST

B4000

74

35
A
36
B
37
C

A
B
C

Buttsfield Road

Butt's Plantation

4

Lodge Copse

Trindledown Border

Head's Farm

BOTMOOR WAY

A338

Trindledown Farm

77

Trindledown Copse

Buckham Hill

Hillside Stud

WANTAGE RD

3

Northfield Farm

76

Carters Piece Farm

Mount Pleasant

RG17

RG20

Elton Wood

Shefford CE Sch

CHERRY ORCH

SPRING MDWS

DOWNSHIRE

PENEY FIELDS

HAWTHORNE WY

2

Manor Farm

THE MALLARDS

RIVERWAY

STATION RD

MILLER'S FIELD

THE BROAD

PETTY PLACE

PO

Great Shefford

HUNTERS MOW

CHURCH ST

THE CLOSE

SCHOLARS CL

The Stag (PH)

75

Boot Farm

River Lambourn

East Shefford House

Elton Lane

A338 HUNGERFORD HILL

NEWBURY RD

Lambourn Valley Way

1

Daldridge Wood

Elton Farm

Sewage Works

74

38
A
39
B
40
C

A

B

C

Hailey Copse

Old Street L

PEASEMORE HILL

Eastley Copse

Little Hailey Copse

HAILEY LA

FIELD RD

4

B4494

Lower Hailey Copse

Eastley House

WEST VIEW

HATT CL

PALMER CL

Fox and Hounds (PH)

Drake's Farm

HILLGREEN LA

BOLTON ROW

MEAD CL

Peasemore

THE ROOKERY

Nightingale Farm

77

Prince's Farm

Peasemore House

PRINCE'S LA

Widows' Farm

Old Street Lane

3

Egypt

Bushy Leaze

MUD LA

Hillgreen House

Hillgreen

Woods Folly Bungalow

Windmill Place

Gidley Farm

76

Chapel Farm

RG20

Prior's Wood

Gidley Copse

2

New Road

Gidley Lane

Chapel Wood

75

Ward's Copse

Hazelhanger Farm

1

North Heath Farm

North Heath

Pope's Wood

SCHOOL RD

Green Lane

Penclose Wood

Blue Boar Inn (PH)

74

B4494

44

A

45

B

46

C

A **B** **C**

Perborough Castle

RG20

Floodcross Cottage

Little Ridge Copse

Northfield Row

Banterwick Farm

4

Ramsworth Cottages

Milkhill Farm

Uplands

Green Hams La

77

Allen's Row

New Copse

Middle Barn

Five Ways

River Pang

3

Oakhouse Farm

Laycroft Wood

HILLCREST

Hampstead Norreys

STATION
THE OLD SCHOOL
WEST VIEW COTTS
SCOTTALLS LA
THE CLOSE
WATER ST
THE CUTHINGS
PENDALS
B4009

Bothampstead Farm

Oakhouse Cottages

Hollingsworth

NEWBURY HILL
CHURCH S

Hampstead Norreys CE Prim Sch

76

RG18

Park Wood

Westbroc Copse

Bothampstead

Malthouse

Trumpletts Farm

Down Wood

2

New Cottages

Hatchgate Cottages

The Thatched Cottage

Eling

Elingpark Copse

Eling Farm

75

Four Elms

1

Oareborough La

Pimbus Shaw

EVERINGTON LA

Sand Pit

Common Barn Cottages

Heather Piece

Spring Plantation

Everington Hill

M4

Newhouse Farm

B4009

Furze Hill

74

50

A

51

B

52

C

M4

53
33

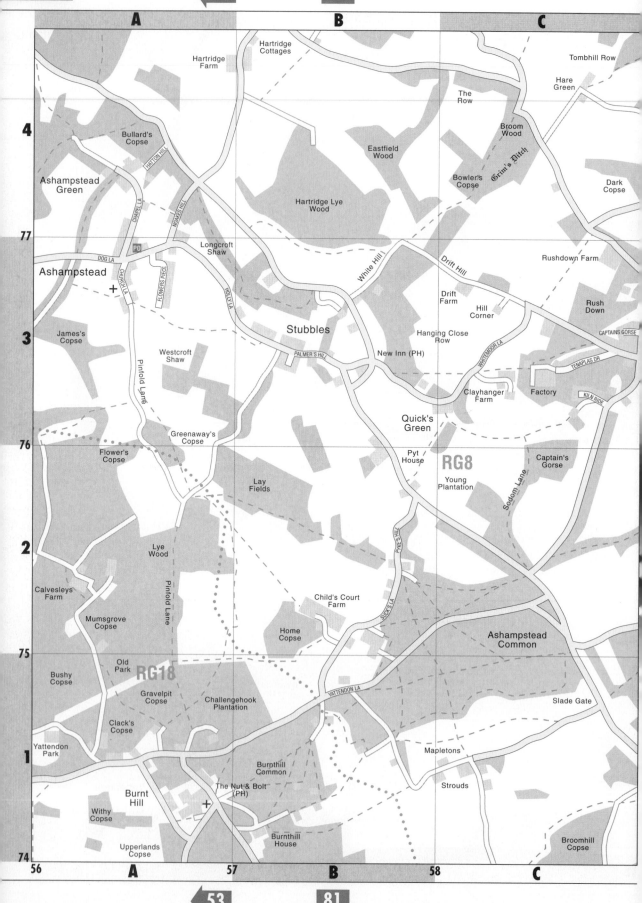

53
81

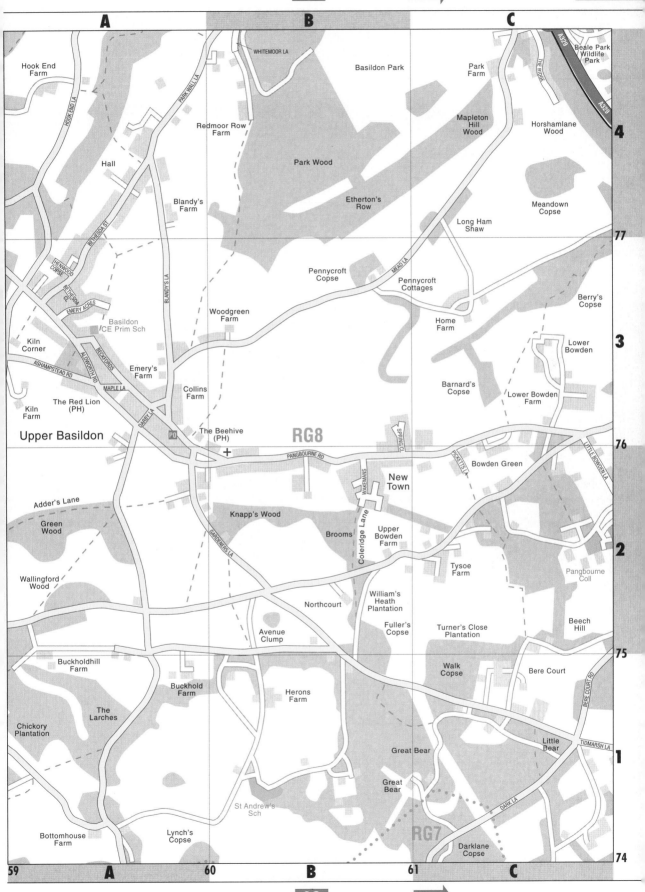

A B C

WHITEMOOR LA

Hook End
Farm

Basildon Park

Park
Farm

Beale Park
Wildlife
Park

4

Redmoor Row
Farm

Mapleton
Hill
Wood

Horshamlane
Wood

A329

THE RIDGE

Hall

Park Wood

Etherton's
Row

Meandown
Copse

PARK WALL LA

Blandy's
Farm

Long Ham
Shaw

77

HENWOOD
COPSE

BETHESDA ST

Pennycroft
Copse

MEAD LA

Pennycroft
Cottages

Berry's
Copse

BETHESDA
CL

EMERY ACRES

Basildon
CE Prim Sch

Woodgreen
Farm

Home
Farm

Lower
Bowden

3

Kiln
Corner

BLANDY'S LA

BECKFORDS

Emery's
Farm

Barnard's
Copse

Lower Bowden
Farm

ASHAMPSTEAD RD

ALDWORTH RD

MAPLE LA

Collins
Farm

SPRING CL

LITTLE BOWDEN LA

Kiln
Farm

The Red Lion
(PH)

DARK LA

RG8

PICKETTS LA

76

Upper Basildon

PO

The Beehive
(PH)

Bowden Green

PANGBOURNE RD

WAKEMANS

New
Town

Adder's Lane

Knapp's Wood

Coleridge Lane

Upper
Bowden
Farm

Pangbourne
Coll

2

Green
Wood

Brooms

Tysoe
Farm

GARDENERS LA

Beech
Hill

Wallingford
Wood

Northcourt

William's
Heath
Plantation

Fuller's
Copse

Turner's Close
Plantation

75

Avenue
Clump

Walk
Copse

Bere Court

Buckholdhill
Farm

BERE COURT RD

Buckhold
Farm

Herons
Farm

The
Larches

Little
Bear

TIDMARSH LA

1

Chickory
Plantation

Great Bear

Great
Bear

DARK LA

Bottomhouse
Farm

Lynch's
Copse

St Andrew's
Sch

RG7

Darklane
Copse

74

59 A 60 B 61 C

55

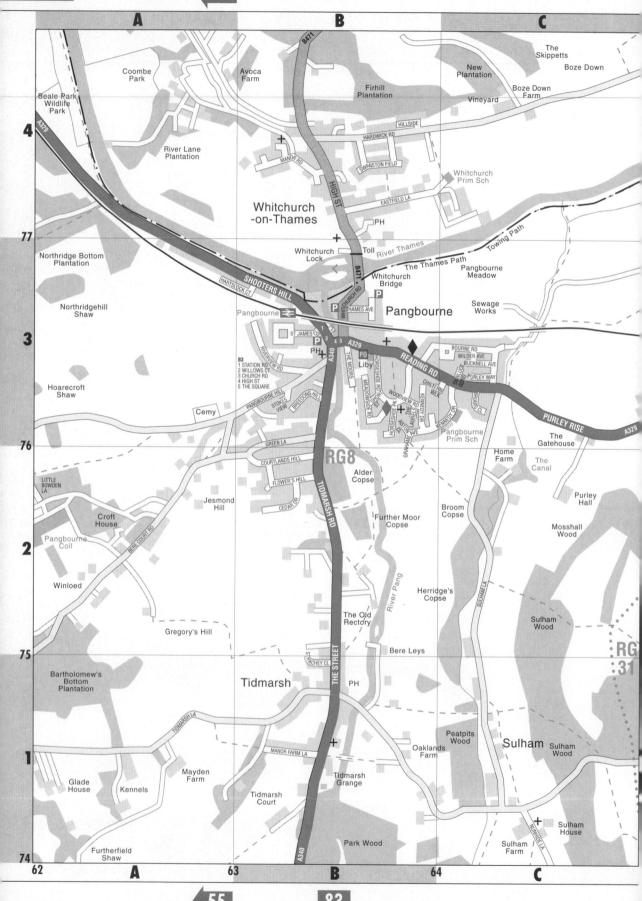

A   B   C

The Skippetts
Boze Down
Coombe
Park
Avoca
Farm
New
Plantation
Vineyard
Boze Down
Farm
Beale Park
Wildlife Park
Firhill
Plantation
Hillside
4
River Lane
Plantation
Hardwick Rd
Whitchurch Prim Sch
Manor Rd
Swanston Field
Eastfield La
Whitchurch
-on-Thames
77
PH
Northridge Bottom
Plantation
River Thames
Towing Path
Whitchurch
Lock
Toll
Pangbourne
Meadow
Hartslock Ct
Shooters Hill
Whitchurch
Bridge
The Thames Path
Northridgehill
Shaw
Pangbourne
P
P
Pangbourne
Sewage
Works
St James Cl
P
Reading Rd
Bourne Rd
Wilder Ave
Bucknell Ave
3
PH
Liby
PO
Purley Way
Riverview Rd
B3
1 Station Rd
2 Willows Ct
3 Church Rd
4 High St
5 The Square
The Moors
Chiltern
Wlk
Hoarecroft
Shaw
Stokes
View
Breedons Hill
Woodview Rd
Meadowside Rd
Horseshoe Pk
Pangbourne
Prim Sch
The
Gatehouse
76
Cemy
Pangbourne Hill
Green La
RG8
The Canal
Courtlands Hill
Home
Farm
Purley Rise
A329
Little
Bowden
La
Flower's Hill
Alder
Copse
Purley
Hall
Jesmond
Hill
Cedar Dr
The
Canal
Croft
House
Further Moor
Copse
Broom
Copse
Mosshall
Wood
2
Pangbourne
Coll
Tidmarsh Rd
Bere Court Rd
Winloed
River Pang
Herridge's
Copse
Sulham La
Sulham
Wood
RG
31
Gregory's Hill
The Old
Rectory
Bere Leys
75
Bartholomew's
Bottom
Plantation
Tidmarsh
The Street
PH
Peatpits
Wood
Sulham
Tidmarsh La
Mayden
Farm
Manor Farm La
Oaklands
Farm
Sulham
Wood
1
Glade
House
Kennels
Tidmarsh
Court
Tidmarsh
Grange
Sulham
House
A340
Furtherfield
Shaw
Park Wood
Sulham
Farm
Nunhide La

74

62   A   63   B   64   C

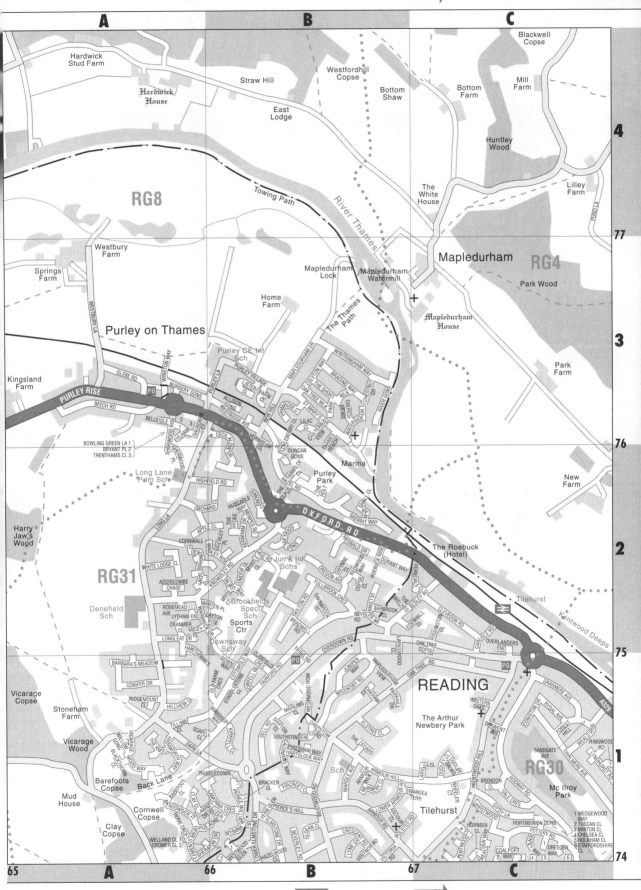

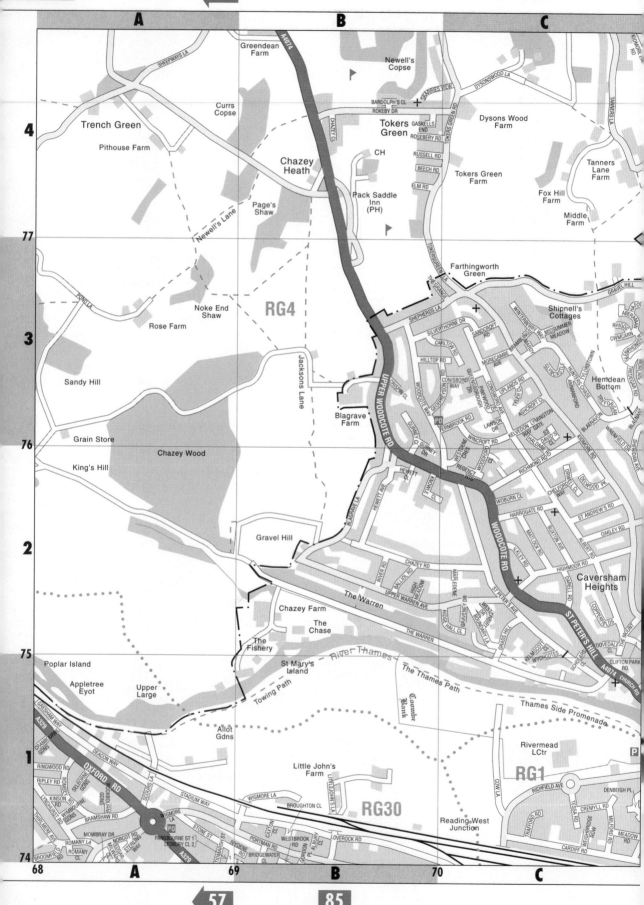

57

A B C

4

Trench Green
Pithouse Farm

Greendean Farm

Currs Copse

Newell's Copse

Chazey Heath

Tokers Green
CH

Pack Saddle Inn (PH)

BARDOLPH'S CL
ROKEBY DR
SKARRIES VIEW

DYSONSWOOD LA

Dysons Wood Farm

GASKELLS END
ROSEBERY RD
RUSSELL RD
BEECH RD
ELM RD

Tokers Green Farm

Tanners Lane Farm

Fox Hill Farm

Middle Farm

77

Newell's Lane

Page's Shaw

RG4

Farthingworth Green

THE GRANGE

Shipnell's Cottages

GRAVEL HILL

3

Noke End Shaw

Rose Farm

Sandy Hill

Jacksons Lane

Blagrave Farm

SHEPHERDS LA
SILVERTHORNE DR
CARLTON RD
HILLTOP RD
CONISBORO WAY
QUEENSBOROUGH WAY
PINEWOOD
UPLANDS RD
CONISBORO AVE
ASHCROFT RD
LAWSON DR
WINCROFT RD
WOODFORD CL
KELVEDON
LYMINGTON
WAY GATE
HALDANE RD
ST DAVID'S CL
REGENCY HTS
RICHMOND RD

SANDCROFT RD
BRAMBLINGS WAY
MIDSUMMER MEADOW
WINTERBURY WAY

Hemdean Bottom

76

Grain Store

King's Hill

Chazey Wood

UPPER WOODCOTE RD

BLAGRAVE LA

HEWETT CL
HEWETT LA
KNOWLE CL

WOBURN CL
HARROGATE RD

CHELFORD CT
ORWELL CL
WAY
FREWOOD PK

ST ANDREW'S RD
OAKLEY RD

2

Gravel Hill

RIVER RD
BALLIOL RD
CHAZEY RD
HIGH MEADOW
UPPER WARREN AVE
MAPLEDENE
GRAVENEY DR
RIDGE HALL CL

The Warren

WOODCOTE RD

BUXTON AVE
ILKLEY RD
MATLOCK RD
HIGHMOOR RD
ST PETER'S AVE

ALBERT RD
DARELL RD

Caversham Heights

COPPER CL

75

Poplar Island

Appletree Eyot

Upper Large

Chazey Farm

The Chase

The Fishery

St Mary's Island

River Thames

Towing Path

THE WARREN

GRASS HILL
KELMSCOTT CL
WYCH-COTES
KELMSCOTT CL

ST PETER'S HILL

The Thames Path

Coombe Bank

Thames Side Promenade

SCHOLARS CL
DOVEDALE CL
CLIFTON PARK
CHURCH RD
A4074
THE MOUNT

1

GRESHAM WAY
A329
CRANBOURN GDNS
RINGWOOD RD
RIPLEY RD
ROMSEY RD
SELBOURNE GDNS
KINSON RD
LYNDHURST RD
WIMBORNE GDNS
OXFORD RD
DEACON WAY
ROCKBOURNE GDNS
SCOURS LA

Allot Gdns

Little John's Farm

WIGMORE LA
BROUGHTON CL
LITTLE JOHN'S LA

RG30

Rivermead LCtr

RG1

RICHFIELD AVE
COW LA

Reading West Junction

TRAFFORD RD
CARDIFF RD
WEIGHBRIDGE ROW
TESSA RD
CREMYLL RD
MILFORD RD
DENBEIGH PL
MEADOW RD

74

THIRLMERE AVE
BROOMFIELD
ROMANY LA
ROMANY CL
MOWBRAY DR
NORCOT RD
STERLING WAY
WIGMORE LA
PANGBOURNE ST 1
LEDBURY CL 2
A329
STADIUM WAY
STONE ST
TIDMARSH ST
IVYDENE RD
BRIDGEWATER CL
WESTBROOK RD
CAXTON RD
PORTMAN RD
GORDON PL
ALBURY
LOVEROCK RD

68 A 69 B 70 C

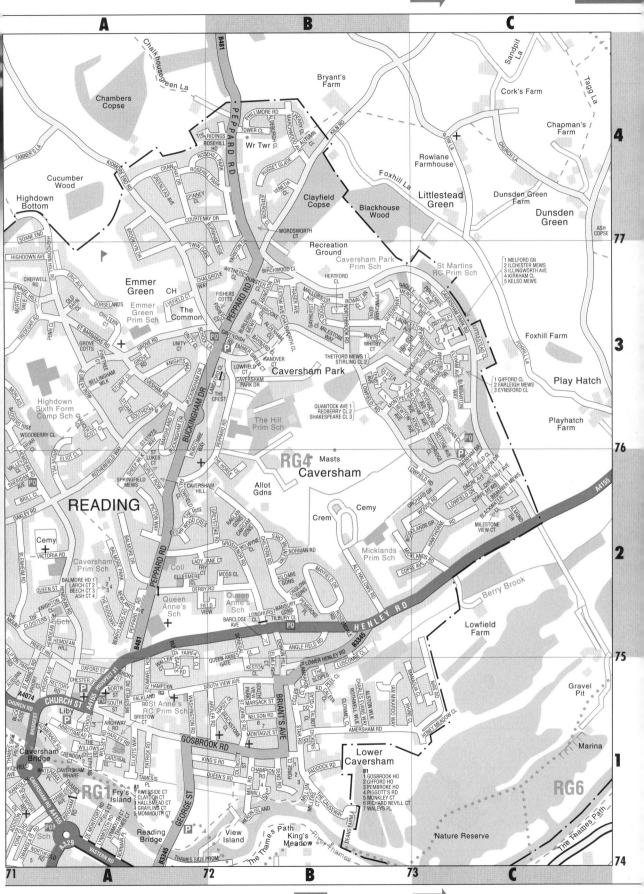

A   **B**   **C**

A4155

The Warren

The Lynch

Hampstead Farm

Hampstead Hill

HENLEY RD

Hampstead Bottom

Hallsmead Ait

Bint's Farm

4

RG9

Round Wood

The Firs

Ash Copse

Spanhill Copse

Buck Ait

Dunsden Farmhouse

SPAN HILL

Dunsden Green

Berry Brook

St Patrick's Stream

77

St Patrick's Bridge

The Flowing Spring (PH)

MILESTONE AVE

RG10

THAMES DR

Botany Bay

SPRING LA

The Thames Path

3

River Thames

Broadmoor La

Play Hatch

FOXHILL LA

A4155

PLAYHATCH RD

FOXHILL CL

Sonning Eye

Hotel

B478

B478

PH

76

RG4

Aquatic Research Ctr

Gravel Works

Frizers Farm

P

Sonning Bridge

Sonning

A4155

Marsh La

Mill

Hotel

OLD WELL CT

CHARVIL LA

THAMES ST

+

HIGH ST

2

Sonning Lock

Sonning Farm

PO

A4

Holme Park

B4446

PEARSON RD

GLEBE GDNS

LITTLE GLEBE

GARD RD

Reading Blue Coat Sch

Sonning CE Prim Sch

PARKWAY DR

GLEBE LA

PADDICK CL

HAWTHORN WAY

SONNING LA

HOLMERIDOR DR

75

Nature Reserve

ROUND LA

CH

Duffields Bridge

RG6

Holme Park Farm

BATH RD

WEST DR

(OLD BATH RD)

MUSTARD LA

COPSE MEAD

1

THAMES VALLEY BSNS PK

HOLME PARK FARM LA

WEST CT

Buttshill Bridge

HIGHCLIFFE CL

RG5

Big Gogs

SONNING MDWS

B4446

OLD BATH RD

WEST DR

ALDERLEY CL

DUFFIELD RD

SANDFORD CL

RETFORD CL

SOUTH DR

THETFORD RD

WILCROSS LA

Willow Bank Jun & Int Schs

SHEPHERDS HILL

LONDON RD

HAMWOOD CL

WYNDHAM CRES

WARREN RD

RYECROFT CL

WESTERN AVE

GODSTOW CL

ROCHESTER AVE

FRIMLEY CL

RAVENSBOURNE DR

RADCOT CL

FRAMPTON CL

BINGLEY GRN

BRUNEL DR

UPPINGHAM DR

ROTHWELL GDNS

WALMER RD

TELFORD CRES

74

ORACLE PARKWAY

74   **A**   **75**   **B**   **76**   **C**

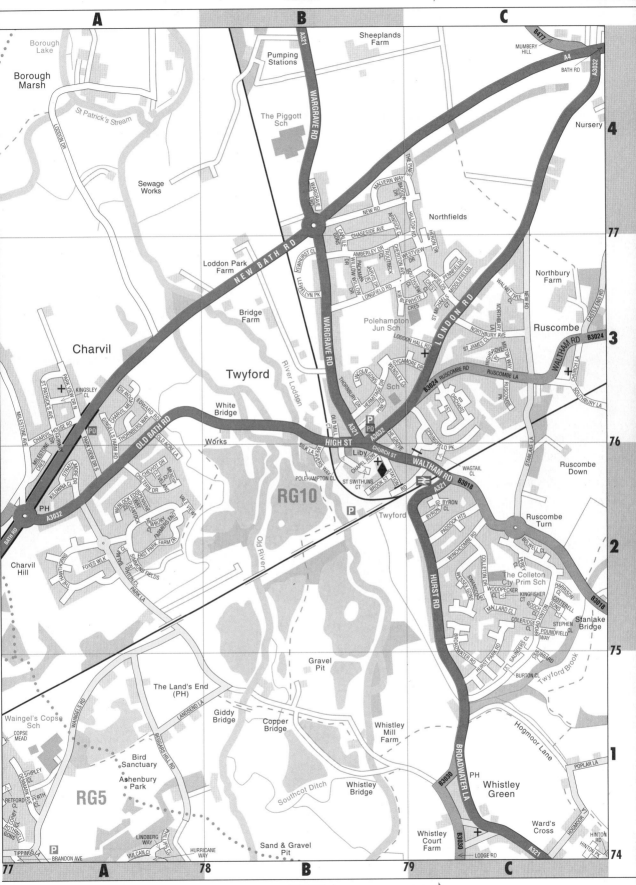

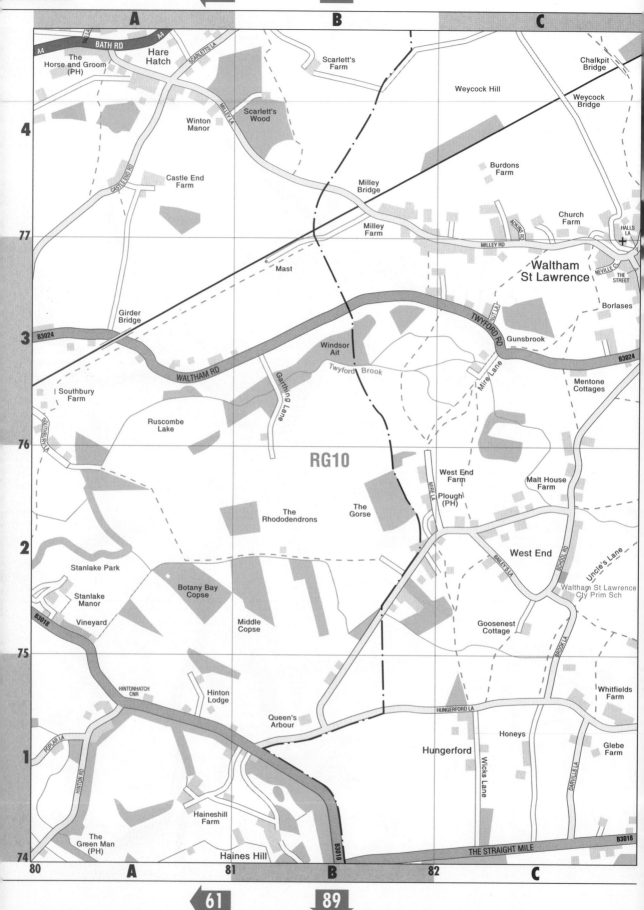

A B C

4

The Horse and Groom (PH)

BATH RD

A4

A4

TEAL LA

Hare Hatch

SCARLETTS LA

Scarlett's Farm

Weycock Hill

Chalkpit Bridge

Weycock Bridge

Winton Manor

Scarlett's Wood

MILLEY LA

Burdons Farm

Castle End Farm

CASTLE END RD

Milley Bridge

ADKINS RD

Church Farm

HALLS LA

77

Milley Farm

MILLEY RD

Waltham St Lawrence

NEVILLE C

THE STREET

Mast

Girder Bridge

3

B3024

WALTHAM RD

Windsor Ait

Twyford Brook

TWYFORD RD

Gunsbrook

MILL LA

Borlases

B3024

Southbury Farm

SOUTHBURY LA

Garthing Lane

MIRE LANE

Mentone Cottages

76

Ruscombe Lake

RG10

West End Farm

Malt House Farm

The Rhododendrons

The Gorse

MIRE LA

Plough (PH)

2

Stanlake Park

Botany Bay Copse

BAILEY'S LA

West End

SCHOOL RD

Uncle's Lane

Waltham St Lawrence Cty Prim Sch

Stanlake Manor

Vineyard

B3018

Middle Copse

Goosenest Cottage

BROOK LA

75

HINTONHATCH CNR

Hinton Lodge

Whitfields Farm

1

POPLAR LA

HINTON RD

Queen's Arbour

HUNGERFORD LA

Honeys

DARVILLS LA

Glebe Farm

Hungerford

WICKS LANE

Haineshill Farm

The Green Man (PH)

74

Haines Hill

B3018

THE STRAIGHT MILE

B3018

80 A 81 B 82 C

A · B · C

4

Airfield

Sewage Works

GROVE PK

Refuse Tip

White Waltham CE Prim Sch

White Waltham

Waltham Place

Shottesbrooke Park

The Beehive (PH)

BRAEMAR

WALGROVE GDNS

Shottesbrooke Park

77

Halls Farm

HALLS LA

Burringham Wood

South Wood

BROADMOOR LA

PUNDLES LA

SL6

Littlefield Green

Marsh Down

Great Wood

3

THE STREET

PO PH

POOL LA

Refuse Tip

DOWNFIELD LA

Smewins Farm

76

DOWNFIELD RD

RG10

Crockford's Bridge

Twyford Brook

Pond Wood

Pondwood Farm

Uncle's La

Crockford's Copse

Long Wood

The Cut

2

Beenham's Farm

CALLINS LA

MARE LA

Old Malt House (Hill Farm)

Beenham's Heath

75

The Royal Oak (PH)

Great Martins

Little Hazes

Pope's Farm

HUNGERFORD LA

RG42

HOWE LA

Buck Farm

The Manor

Great Hazes

Furze Ground

1

Shurlock Row

The Plantation

Mare La

Yate's Farm

The White Hart (PH)

PO

Foxley PNEU Sch

Mast

Spinningwheel La

Benhams Copse

Jolly Farmer (PH)

WESTLEY MILL

THE STRAIGHT MILE

B3018

74

83 · A · 84 · B · 85 · C

A **B** **C**

4

M4

THRIFT LA

Belmont Farm

Thimble Farm

MEADOW VIEW LA

ROLLS LA

STURT GREEN

A330

Stud Green

ASCOT RD

Bartletts Lane

Paddock Wood

Foxley Green Farm

Holyport Manor Sch

77

Paley Street Farm

PALEY ST

The Jolly Gardener (PH)

B3024

FOREST GREEN RD

Longchase Farm

Little Foxley

Gadbridge Farm

Win Agins Inn (PH)

Short Lane Farm

3

M4

Whitehouse Farm

Whites Farm

B3024

A330

Touchen-end

LONG LA

The Bourne

B3024

LITTLEFIELD GREEN

Duell Farm

+

Paley Street

Littlefield Farm

The Royal Oak (PH)

The Bridge House (PH)

GREEN LA

SL6

Long Lane Farm

76

How Lane Farm

SHEEPCOTE LA

The Cut

Windmills

HOWE LA

Howlane Bridge

LONG LA

Hay Hill Farm

Blackbird La

2

Braywoodside

Braywood Farm

75

DRIFT RD

Hornbuckle Farm

Silver Springs Farm

CRUCH LA

CH

1

RG42

Fernygrove Copse

Hawthorn Hill

Cruchfield Manor House

Lordland's Farm

Hazelwood La

Pendry's La

A3095

MAIDENHEAD RD

A330

ASCOT RD

74

86   **A**   **87**   **B**   **88**   **C**

A B C

Water Oakley

WINDSOR RD

A308

PH

HEARNE DR
PAMELA ROW
ASCOT RD A330

HOLYPORT ST
SSAN CL
MANOR WAY
HOLYPORT RD
LINDEN CL
STOMPITS RD
NEW RD
STOMPITS RD

PO

Holyport
CE Prim
Sch

STROUD FARM RD

LANGWORTHY
END
TRENCHARD RD
REEVE RD
LINDORES RD

FERNDALE PARK

The Guild
House

The Queen's Head
(PH)

John
Gays
House

LANGWORTHY LA
GAYS LA

Stroud
Farm

4

Holyport

BARTLETTS LA
THE
FIELDINGS
DAIRY CT
IVY CL
MONEYROW GREEN

Primrose Lane

Moneyrow
Green

FIFIELD RD
THE RETREAT

MANOR GR

The Retreat
Farm

77

Old Beams

Green Lane

Fifield

✚

The Hare and Hounds
(PH)

CONINGSBY LA

Coningsby
Farm

Grove
House

MEADOW WAY

SL6

FOREST VIEW
COTTS

STEWART CL

Pond Farm

Fifield
House

Braywood
CE Fst
Sch

3

Blackbird Lane

The Rising Sun
(PH)

FOREST GREEN RD

Ledger
Farm

LEDGER LA

FIFIELD
COTTS

OAKLEY GREEN RD

✚

Kimbers
Farm

B3024

Mount Scipett
Copse

Banham
Farm

76

Longfields
Farm

Mount Scipett
Farm

FIFIELD LA

Braywood
House

2

Haws Hill
Farm

The Bourne

Lakeside
Farm

Nobbscrook

The
Royal Foresters
(PH)

Wakers
Farm

SL4

DRIFT RD

New Lodge
Farm

New
Lodge

75

Chawridge Bourne

Foliejon
Park

Darkhole Ride

Hogoak Lane

Lawn
Hill

Windsor
Hill

Nobbscrook
Copse

Nobbscrook
Farm

1

Chawridge
Gorse

Home
Farm

Home
Covert

RG42

74

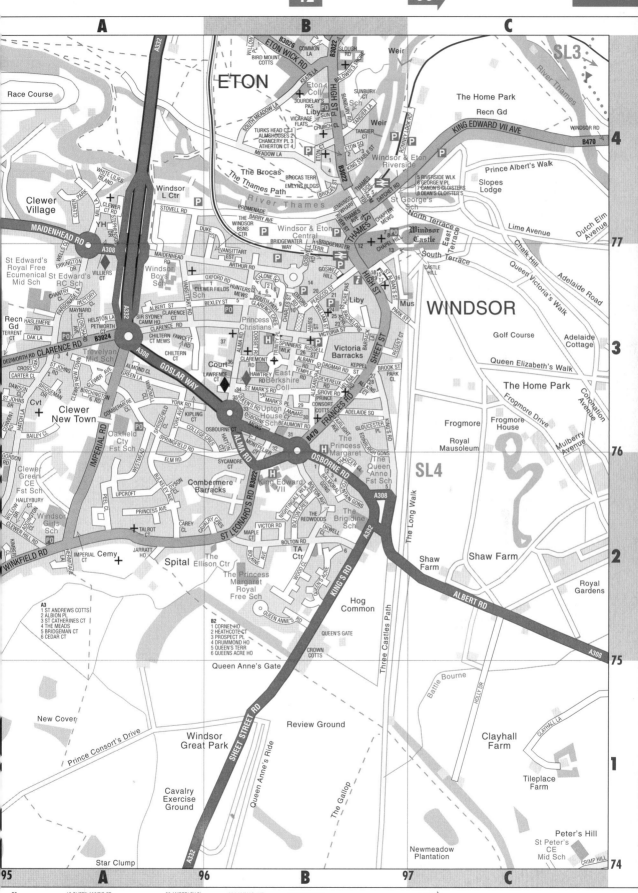

ETON

WINDSOR

SL3

SL4

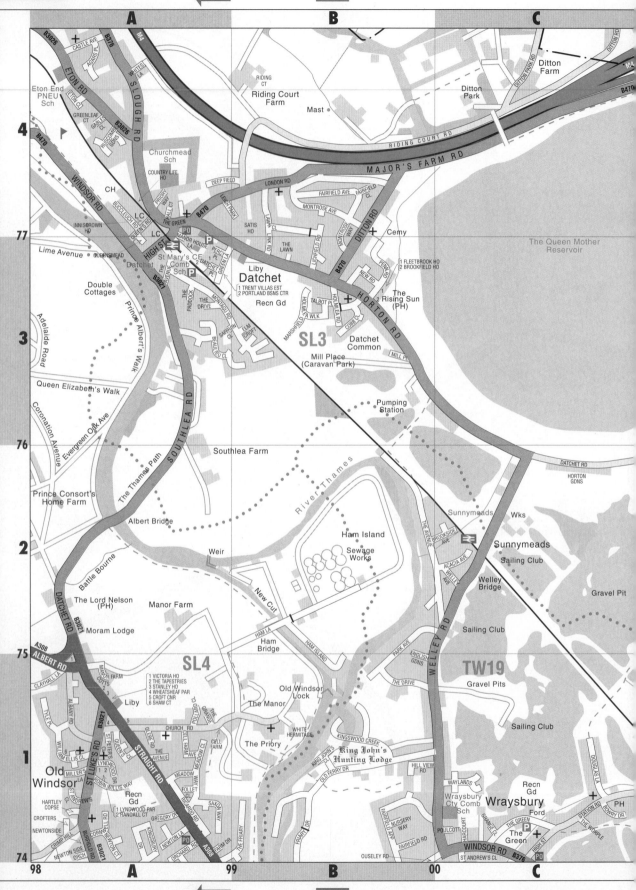

A B C

M4

B3026
CASTLE AVE
AGARS LA
B376
ETON RD
B3026
Eton End
PNEU
Sch
GREENLEAF
CT
ETON CL
GABLES CT
RUSCOMBE
GDNS
WINDSOR RD
CH
INNISCROWN
HO
SLOUGH RD
WHITES LA
Churchmead
Sch
COUNTRY LIFE
HO
PRIORY
WAY
HALL CT
THE GREEN
MANOR HOUSE LA
LC
LC
QUEENS RD
HIGH ST
BUCCLEUCH RD
PO
P
B470

RIDING
CT
Riding Court
Farm
Mast

Ditton
Park
DITTON PARK RD
Ditton
Farm
Ditton
Park
B470
M4

4

RIDING COURT RD

MAJOR'S FARM RD

DEEP FIELD
LONDON RD
FAIRFIELD AVE
FAIRFIELD
CL
MONTROSE AVE
MONTROSE
WAY
DITTON RD
Cemy
B470
1 Fleetbrook Ho
2 Brookfield Ho

77

Lime Avenue
QUEENSMEAD
Datchet
St Mary's CE
Comb Sch
P
THE AVENUE
THE DRIVE
THE PADDOCK
MONTAGU RD
DATCHET PL
GREEN LA
PERCY PL
SATIS
HO
THE GREEN
LIGHT PATH
LAWN
CL
LINK RD
THE LAWN
LYCHFIELD RD
MARSHFIELD
HOLMLEA WLK
TALBOT PL
COBB CL
HOLMLEA RD
NEW RD
PENN RD
The Rising Sun
(PH)
HORTON RD
Liby
Datchet
1 TRENT VILLAS EST
2 PORTLAND BSNS CTR
Recn Gd
SAFFRON CL
ELM CROFT
BEAULIEU CL

Double
Cottages

Prince Albert's Walk

Adelaide
Road

Queen Elizabeth's Walk

Coronation Avenue

Evergreen Oak Ave

SL3

Datchet
Common

Mill Place
(Caravan Park)
MILL PL

3

Prince Consort's
Home Farm

The Thames Path

SOUTHLEA RD

Southlea Farm

River Thames

Pumping
Station

DATCHET RD
HORTON
GDNS

76

Albert Bridge

Battle Bourne

Weir

New Cut

Ham Island

Sewage
Works

Sunnymeads
BROOKSIDE AVE
THE AVENUE
ACACIA AVE
WELLEY AVE
Wks
Sunnymeads
Sailing Club
Welley
Bridge
WELLEY RD
Gravel Pit

2

DATCHET RD
B3021
The Lord Nelson
(PH)
Moram Lodge

Manor Farm

HAM LA
Ham
Bridge
HAM LA
HAM ISLAND

Old Windsor
Lock

Sailing Club

Sailing Club

A308
ALBERT RD
75

SL4

MANOR FARM
COTTS
Liby
1 VICTORIA HO
2 THE TAPESTRIES
3 STANLEY HO
4 WHEATSHEAF PAR
5 CROFT CNR
6 SHAW CT
CLAYHALL LA
B3021
ALBANY RD
TYLE PL
WILLIAM
ELLIS CL
POLLARD RD
CHURCH RD
CELL FARM
MEADOW LA
THE GRANGE

The Manor
WHITE
HERMITAGE

The Priory

KINGSWOOD CREEK
King John's
Hunting Lodge
KING JOHN'S
CL
OLD FERRY DR
HILL VIEW
RD

PARK AVE
ENGLISH
GDNS
THE DRIVE

TW19
Gravel Pits

1

Old
Windsor
HARTLEY
COPSE
CROFTERS
NEWTONSIDE
CRIMP HILL
NEWTON SIDE
ORCH
B3021
MILLER'S LA
ST LUKE'S RD
ST PETER'S CL
LYNDWOOD RD
QUEEN'S RD
ST ANDREW'S
ROBIN WILLIS WAY
STRAIGHT RD
GLEBE RD
THE AVENUE
MEADOW
FOLLET
SAXON WAY
RICHARD RD
GREGORY DR
YE FRIARY
CORNELL CL
NEWTON LA
KINGSBURY
BURFIELD RD
B3021
ORCHARD RD
FARM LA
PO
A308
Recn
Gd
1 LYNDWOOD PAR
2 RANDALL CT
CELL
FARM

FRIARY DR
FAIRFIELD APP
NURSERY
WAY
FAIRFIELD RD
Wraysbury
Cty Comb
Sch
POULCOTT
Ford
WAYLANDS

Recn
Gd
Wraysbury
DOUGLAS LA
STATION RD
THE WORPLE
BOWRY DR
PH
PO
THE GREEN
HIGH ST
HARCOURT
GRANGER

74

WINDSOR RD
B376
OUSELEY RD
ST ANDREW'S CL

98 A 99 B 00 C

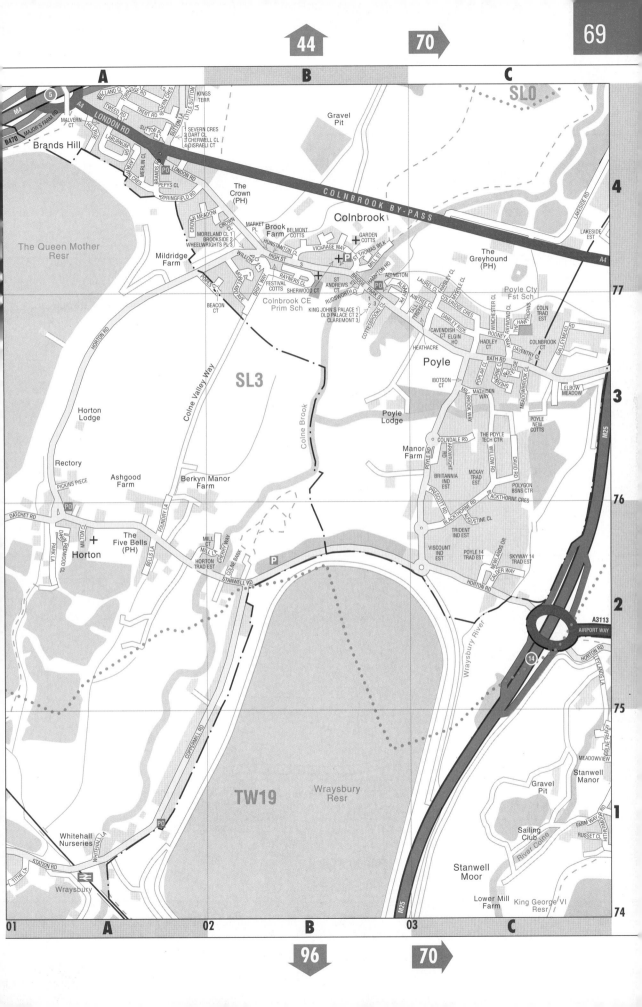

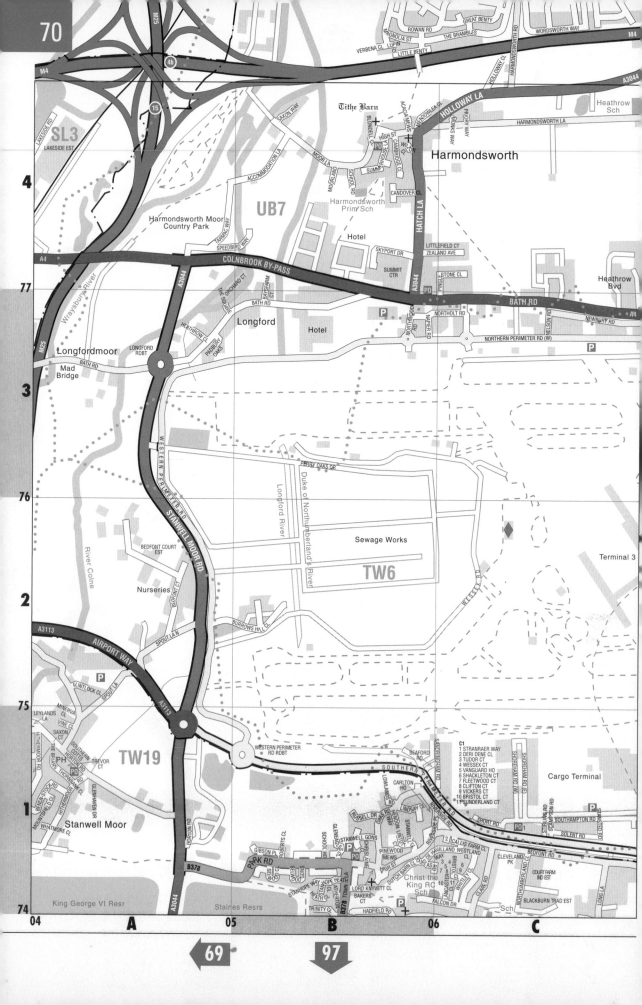

SL3
LAKESIDE RD
LAKESIDE EST

4

UB7

Tithe Barn

ROWAN RD   GREAT BENTY
MAGNOLIA ST   THE BRAMBLES   WORDSWORTH WAY
VERBENA CL   LUPIN   LITTLE BENTY   M4

HOLLOWAY LA
HARMONDSWORTH LA
Heathrow Sch

A3044

SAXON WAY
BLONDELL
HIGH ST
ACACIA MEWS
CAMBRIDGE CL
MONKS WAY
PRIORY WAY
HOLLOWAY CL

Harmondsworth

MOOR LA
MOORLAND
SCHOOL RD
SUMMI
CANDOVER CL

Harmondsworth Moor
Country Park

ACCOMMODATION LA

Harmondsworth
Prim Sch

HATCH LA

TARMAC WAY
SPEEDBIRD WAY

Hotel

SKYPORT DR
SUMMIT
CTR

LITTLEFIELD CT
ZEALAND AVE
Heathrow
Bvd

A4   COLNBROOK BY-PASS

A3044

STONE CL
PIGMIL

77

Wraysbury River

THE SQUARE
HEATHROW CL
BATH RD
BAYSFARM CT
THE ORCHARD CT

Longford

Hotel

BATH RD
NORTHOLT RD
NORTHWOOD RD
NAPIER RD
P
NEWBURY RD
A4

A3044
PO

M25

Longfordmoor
Longford
RDBT
BATH RD
PADBURY
OAKS

P

NORTHERN PERIMETER RD (W)

NELSON RD

P

3

Mad
Bridge

WESTERN PERIMETER RD

PERRY OAKS DR

Duke of Northumberland's River

76

River Colne

STANWELL MOOR RD

BEDFONT COURT
EST

Longford River

Sewage Works

TW6

Terminal 3

Nurseries

BEDFONT RD

BURROWS HILL CL

WESSEX RD

2

A3113   AIRPORT WAY

SPOUT LAN

A3113

P

C1
1 STRANRAER WAY
2 DERI DENE CL
3 TUDOR CT
4 WESSEX CT
5 VANGUARD HO
6 SHACKLETON CT
7 FLEETWOOD CT
8 CLIFTON CT
9 VICKERS CT
10 BRISTOL CT
11 SUNDERLAND CT

75

LEYLANDS
LA
MINERVA
CL
VINE CL
SAXON
CT
FLINTLOCK CL   SPOUT LA

WESTERN PERIMETER
RD RDBT

SEAFORD
RD
SANDRINGHAM RD

SHOREHAM RD (E)
SHOREHAM RD (W)

Cargo Terminal

SOUTHERN PERIMETER

CARLTON
HO

P

P

STIRLING RD
SCAMPTON RD
SOUTHAMPTON RD
STANSTED RD

P

THE BRIARS
HITHERMOOR RD
SOUTHERN PERIM
TREVOR
CT
PH
PO
GLENHAVEN DR

TW19

HORTON RD

LOWLANDS
LINDSAY CL
RUSSELL DR
OAKS RD
HERDON
STANWELL
RIVERDENE RD
PINEWOOD
MEWS

SHORT RD
PO 1

SOLENT RD

BENBOW CL
MOUNTSIDE CL
WHATMORE CL

Stanwell Moor

B378

PARK RD

GIBSON PL
ROBERTS CL
SCHOOL RD
SOUTH
STANWELL GDNS
CHRISLAINE
CALLIS FARM CL
DE HAVILLAND
WESTLAND
BRISTOL
2

CLEVELAND CL
CLEVELAND
PK
BEDFONT RD

COURT FARM
IND EST

1

A3044

King George VI Resr

B378

Staines Resrs

STANHOPE WAY
HOPE
HEATH
LORD KNYVETT CL
ATHERTON
TRINITY CL
HADFIELD RD

DUTCH BARN CL
B378   TOWN LA
BAKERS
CT
FALCON DR

Christ the
King RD Sch
Sch

CLARE RD
WHITLEY CL
LONG CL
BLACKBURN TRAD EST
LONG LA

74

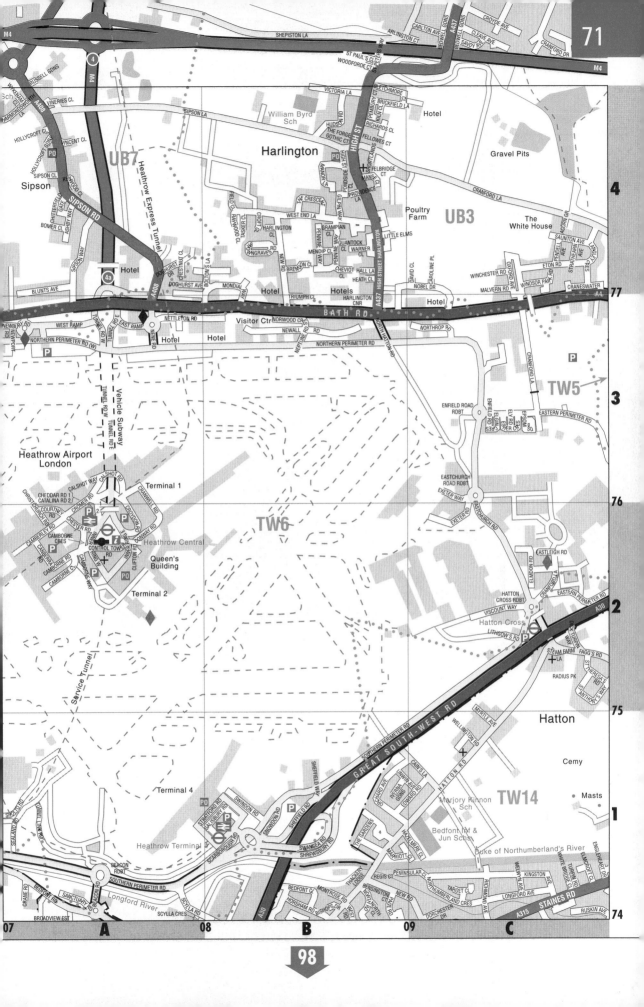

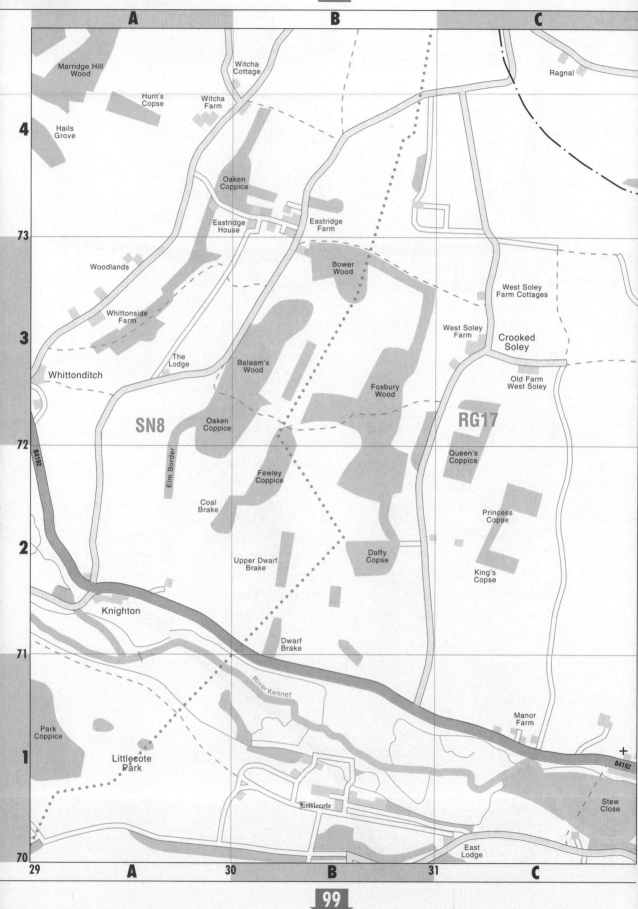

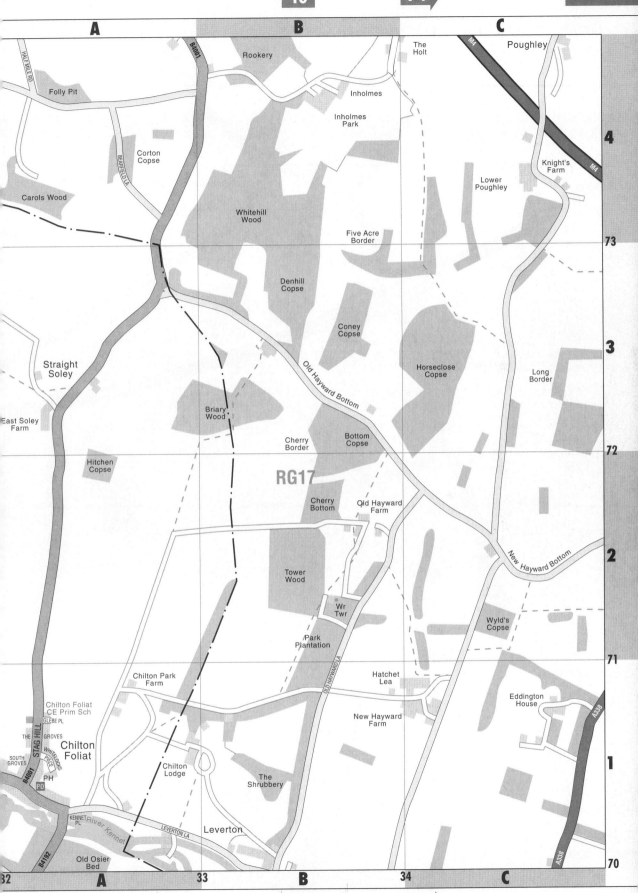

73
47

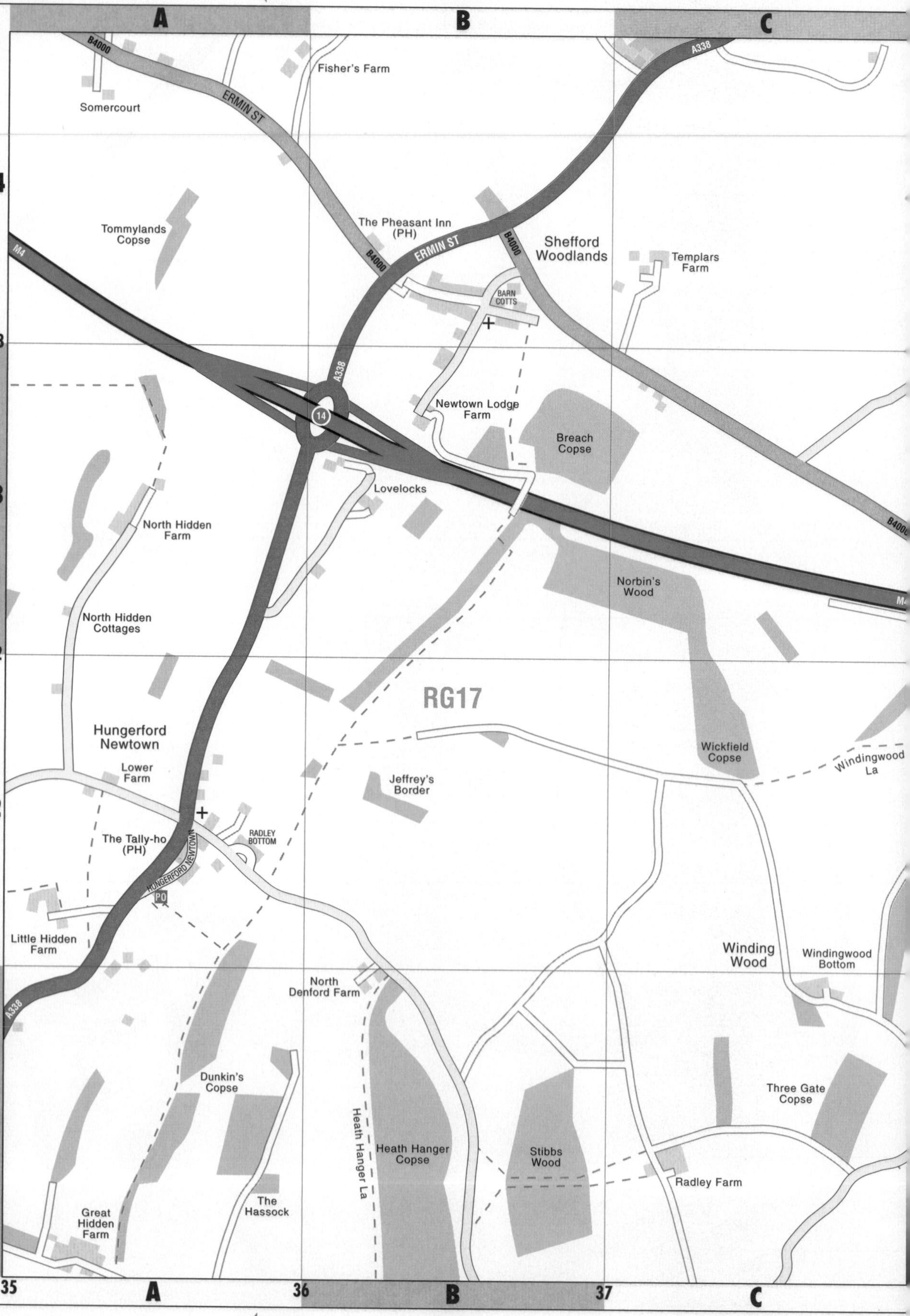

A **B** **C**

B4000

Somercourt

ERMIN ST

Fisher's Farm

A338

4

Tommylands
Copse

The Pheasant Inn
(PH)

B4000

ERMIN ST

B4000

Shefford
Woodlands

Templars
Farm

M4

BARN
COTTS

73

A338

14

Newtown Lodge
Farm

Breach
Copse

3

North Hidden
Farm

Lovelocks

Norbin's
Wood

B4000

M4

North Hidden
Cottages

72

RG17

Wickfield
Copse

Windingwood
La

Hungerford
Newtown

Lower
Farm

Jeffrey's
Border

2

The Tally-ho
(PH)

RADLEY
BOTTOM

HUNGERFORD NEWTOWN

PO

Little Hidden
Farm

North
Denford Farm

Winding
Wood

Windingwood
Bottom

71

A338

Dunkin's
Copse

Three Gate
Copse

1

Heath Hanger La

Heath Hanger
Copse

Stibbs
Wood

Radley Farm

Great
Hidden
Farm

The
Hassock

70

35 **A** **36** **B** **37** **C**

75
49

A **B** **C**

4

73

3

Bradleywood
Farm

Grove
Corner

M4

M4

Tullock
Bottom

Easton
Farm

Westbrook
Farm

Borough
Copse

Easton

River Lambourn

Welford
Farm

Welford

ROOD HILL

Westbrook

Knapps
Farm

72

EASTON HILL

RG20

Lambourn Valley Way

SHEPHERD'S
HILL

Boxford
Farm

2

Sole
Border

+

+

SCHOOL LA

WINTERBOURNE RD

The Bell
Inn
(PH)

−

Sole
Farm

SOUTHFIELDS

Boxford

High Street
Farm

Woodmansfield
Cottages

Hoar
Hill

71

HIGH ST

Moorbridge
Farm

Sole
Plantation

Ownham
Old Farm

1

B4000

Upper
Farm

Ownham

ERMIN ST

B4000

Ownham
Plantation

Ownham
Lower Farm

COOMBESBURY LA

Coombesbury
Farm

William's
Copse

Jannaways

Hunt's
Green

70

41 **A** 42 **B** 43 **C**

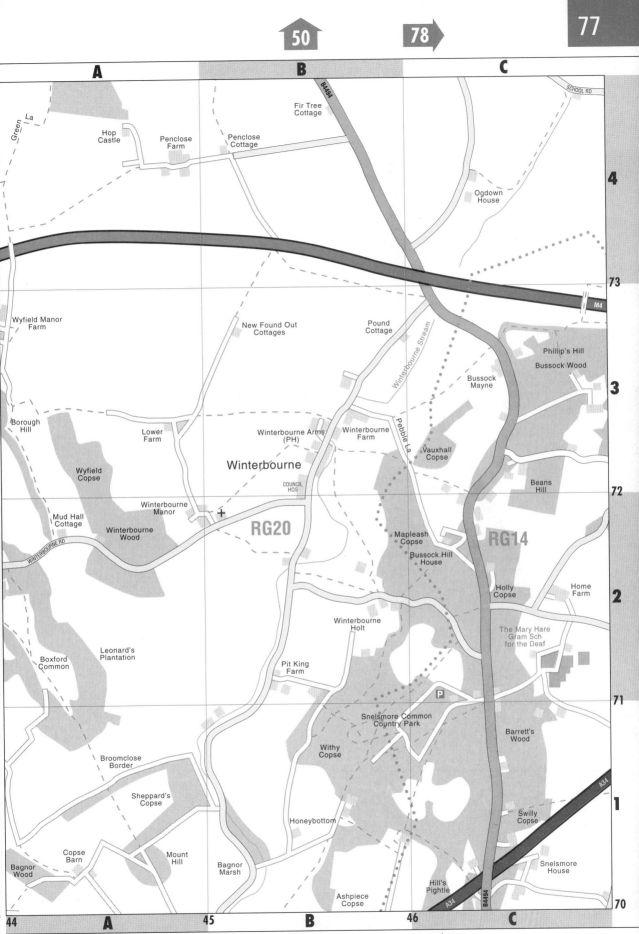

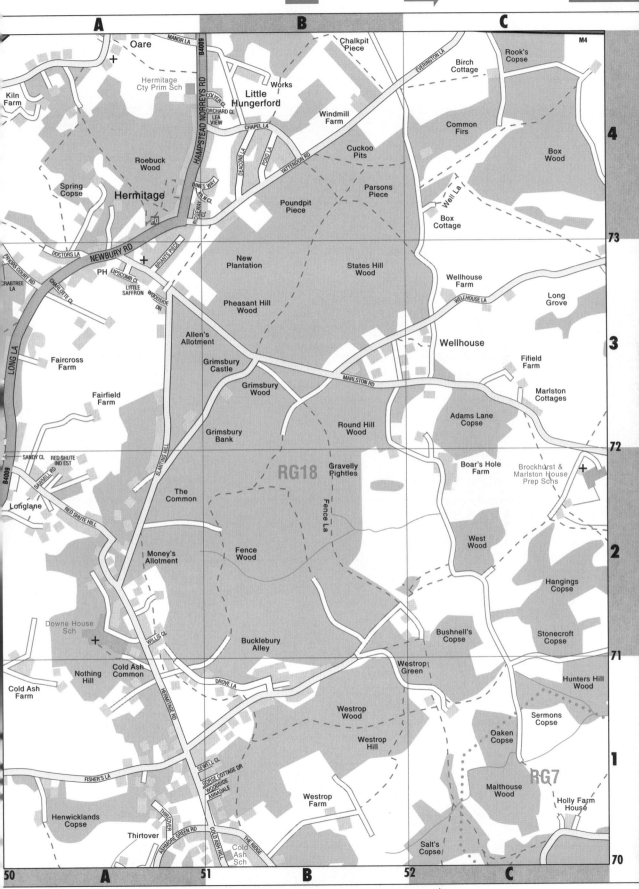

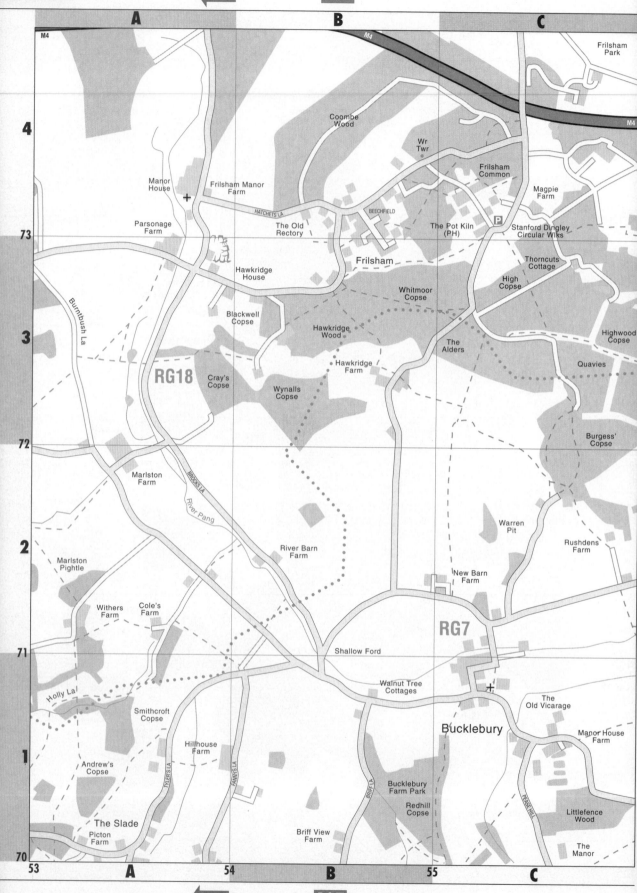

Chalkangles
Copse

Tanner's
Copse

Birchlands
Copse

Lambden's
Bottom

RG8

Beard's
Hill

M4

Gravel
Copse

New
Fields

Stone
Copse

Broomhill
Copse

Coxland
Cottages

The
Gravels

4

RG18

Timber Copse

Collier's
Copse

Owlpit
Copse

Cook's
Copse

Oxley's
Shaw

Hangers
Copse

Miram's
Copse

SCRATCHAGE LA

Round
Copse

73

Rushall
Farm

Mazelands
Farm

Quill
Copse

Long
Copse

Bradfield
House

Mazelands
Copse

House
Leas

Rushall Manor
Farm

3

New
Common

Rushall
Copse

Mounthill
Copse

Nightingale's
Green

Manor
Farm

BACK LA

Frogmoor
Farm

72

Pangfield
Farm

RG7

NEW
BLDGS

Bradfield
Hall

Severals
Farm

Manor Farm

River Pang

Kimberhead
Farm

Rotten Row

2

Stanford Dingley

The Bull
(PH)

ROTTEN ROW HILL

Jewell's
Farm

Bradfield
Farm

BISHOPS RD

The Old
Boot Inn
(PH)

CASEY CT

Jennetshill
Wood

GREEN LA

Jewell's Spring

Jennetts
Hill

JENNETTS LA

Tutts Clump

71

Clay Hill

COCK LA

King's
Copse

The
Travellers Rest
(PH)

HUNGERFORD LA

1

Bushnells
Green

Hillfoot
Farm

Acres
Farm

SOUTH END RD

Hillfoot

Nine Elms

St Crispins Farm

70

A | B | C

RG8 RG8

M4

Bottingham
Shaw

M

Red
Hill

RG8

Greathouse
Wood

Maidenhatch
Farm

The
Tidmarsh Stud

4

Hewins
Wood

DARK LA

Hogmoor
Copse

Greathouse
Cottages

Hewinswood
Farm

Barn Elms
Farm

Maidenhatch Brook

Hewins
Wood Farm

ASHAMPSTEAD RD

Bradfield
Plantation

Thuja
Wood

River Pang

73

Greathouse Wlk

Home
Farm

ST ANDREWS
CL

Back Lane
Plantation

BACK LA

RIVERSIDE

Sports
Ctr

Hill
Plantation

3

Bradfield
Coll

The House
on the Hill

Old
Deerpark
Wood

Old
Deer
Park

Bradfield

Folly
Bridge

The
Old Rectory

Malthouse
Farm

72

Sherwood
House

Wayland's
Copse

Bradfield
Hall
Farm

Horse
Leas

RG7

Bennett's
Copse

Dainty
Land

WAYLANDS CL

Bournefield
Farm

COMMON HILL

Fisher's
Copse

Buscot
Gully

UNION RD

Englefield Common
Wood

Ham
Copse

2

BISHOPS RD

Sewage
Works

Copyhold
Farm

River Bourne

MARINERS LA

Berry's
Farm

Clays
Copse

Potash

71

Bradfield
CE Prim Sch

THE LASFORDS

ASH
GR

Southend
Farm

Berry's
Shaw

Andrew's
Copse

COCK LA

Somerwells

PH

Mayridge
Farm

SANDBROOK

HEATH RD

NEW WAY

SOUTH END RD

STRETTON CL

Culham
Shaw

1

Southend

WELLINGTON GDNS

Admoor
Copse

ADMOOR LA

Cold Hill

Ufton
Wood

PO

Cripps
Farm

Holly
Copse

WEBBS LA

LAMBDENS HILL

The
Lambden's

70

59 | A | 60 | B | 61 | C

A | B | C

4

73

3

72

2

71

1

70

Flobrigham's Copse

River Pang

Hogmoor Bridge

Withy Eyot

Moor Copse

RG8

Wigley Copse

Horsemoor Wood

Alder Copse

River Bourne

Chalkpit Farm

Chalkpit Cottages

Horns Copse

Malpas Farm

Pond Farm

Malpas

Sluice Copse

RG31

Nunhide Farm

Dovecot

Beech Hill Wood

PH

North Street

Blossomsend Copse

Englefield

THE STREET

ST MARK'S CL

PO

Englefield CE Prim Sch

North Street Farm

Works

RG7

Englefield House

Wickcroft

Englefield Park (Deer Park)

Cranemoor Lake

Theale

KATHLEEN SAUNDERS CT

CHESTNUT

WOODFIELD WAY

ALDERFIELD CL

ROTHERFIELD CL

THE CRESCENT

THE ORCHARD

BLOSSOM LA

ELLERTON CL

MORTON PL

WORSLEY PL

SWALLOWFIELD GDNS

ENGLEFIELD RD

PLAY PLAT

BLOSSOM AVE

THE COURTYARD

CROWN LA

HIGH ST

P

12

M4

A4

P

Parker's Corner

Wigmore Wood

Theale Green Com Sch

DEADMAN'S LA

CHURCH STREET MEWS

LAMBFIELDS

Theale CE Prim Sch

CLOISTERS

THE MEWS

ST ANDREWS CL

CHURCH ST

TRINITY CL

ROUNDHEAD RD

PO

JAMES BUTCHER DR

STATION RD

WATERSIDE DR

EXETER WAY

ELY RD

BRUNEL RD

Liby

MEADOW WAY

MILL BERRY WAY

MYTON WLK

CANAL CL

MUSTWELL

Haywards Farm

THE MARKHAM CENTRE TRAD EST

ARROWHEAD RD

Theale

Kennet and Avon Canal

BOSTOCK LA

Gravel Pit Cottages

BATH RD

THE GREEN

ST IVES CL

VOLUNTEER RD

A340

WIGMORE LA

A4

Mill

Swing Bridge

P

Draper's Osier Bed Stream

River Kennet

Milehouse Cottages

A4

2 | 63 | 64

A | B | C

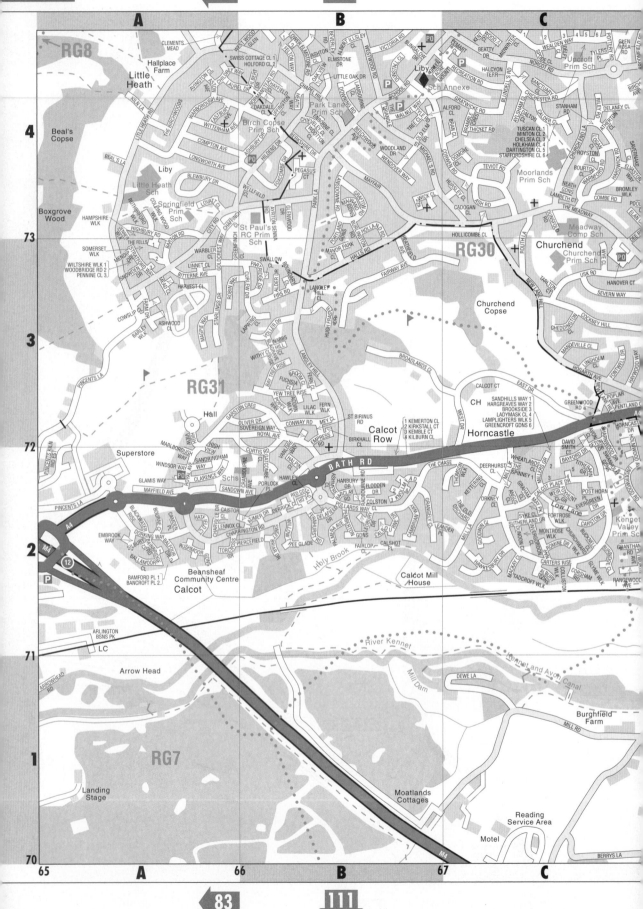

C4
1 CAMBRIDGE ST
2 LITTLE ST
3 CANNON ST
4 FOXGLOVE GDNS
5 STANLEY GR
6 MASON CT

7 CAROLINE ST
8 MALTHOUSE LA
9 STRATHEDEN PL
10 VINCENT HO
11 BURFORD CT
12 BRUNSWICK LODGE
13 TAYLOR CT

58

C4
14 TETBURY CT
15 BELLEVUE TERR
16 WINDSOR CT
17 ALLISON CT
18 CHERWELL CRES
19 BRANKSOME CT

86

C4
20 NATHAN CT
21 FRANKLIN CT
22 MULLION CT
23 NICHOLAS CT
24 ALEXANDER CT
25 CHANCERY MEWS

26 SEAFIELD CT
27 HERITAGE CT

85

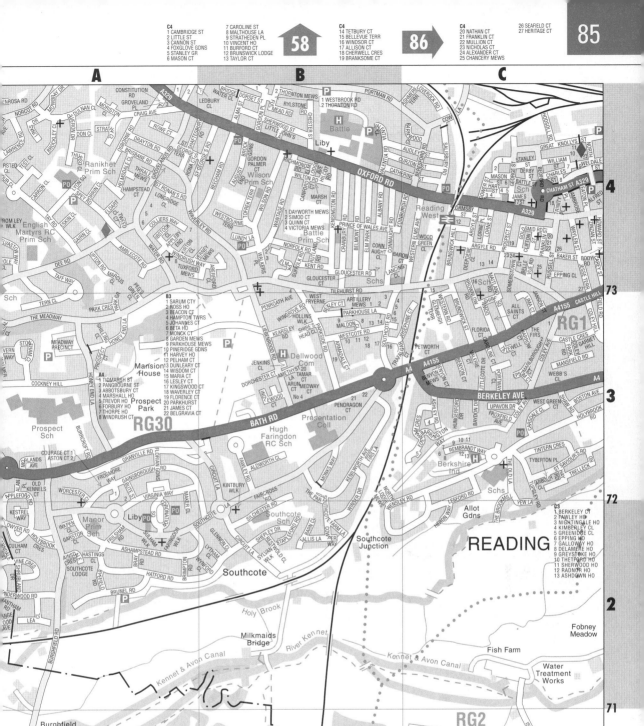

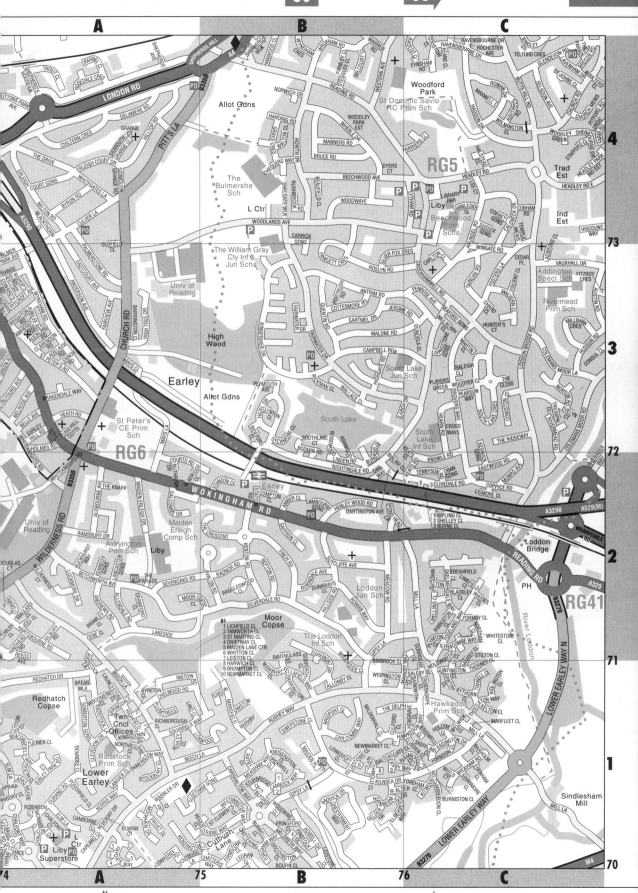

A1
1 WARNSHAM CL
2 SHARPETHORPE CL
3 BERSTEAD CL
4 WATERSFIELD CL
5 RUSTINGTON CL

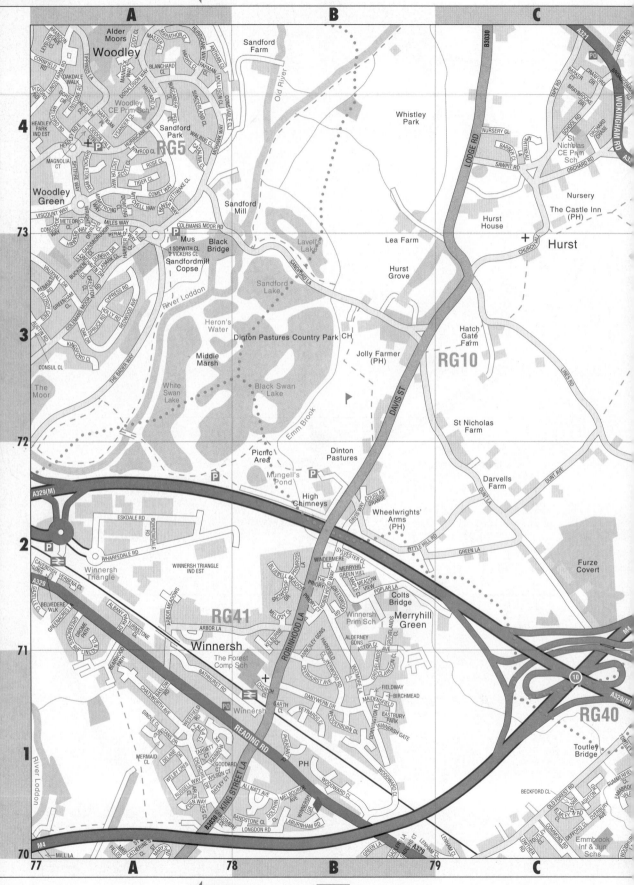

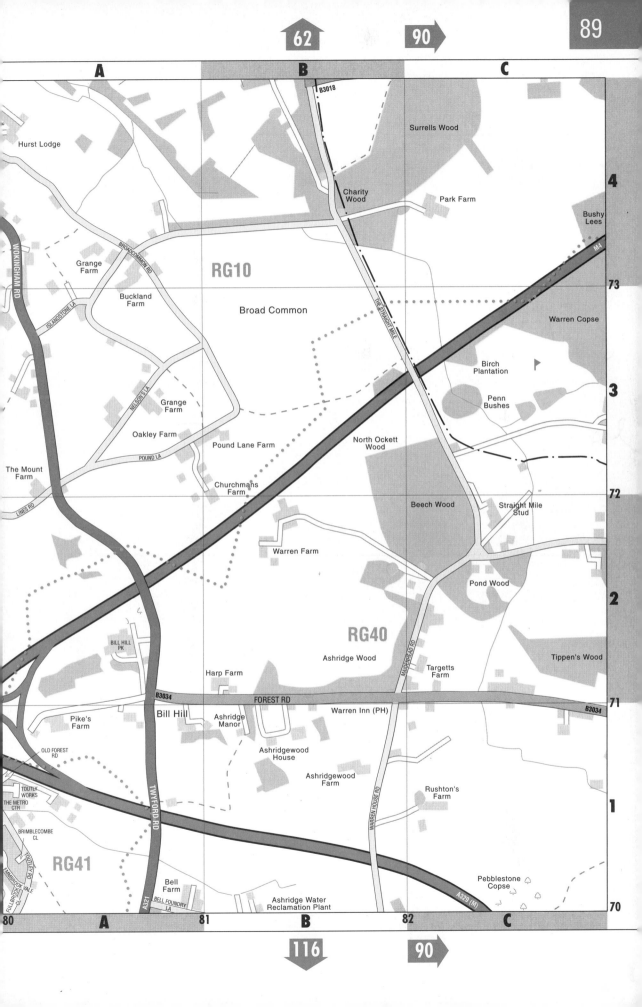

A
B
C

B3018

Hurst Lodge

Surrells Wood

Charity Wood

Park Farm

4

Bushy Lees

M4

BROADCOMMON RD

Grange Farm

RG10

73

WOKINGHAM RD

ISLANDSTONE LA

Buckland Farm

Broad Common

THE STRAIGHT MILE

Warren Copse

Birch Plantation

NELSON'S LA

Grange Farm

Penn Bushes

3

Oakley Farm

Pound Lane Farm

North Ockett Wood

POUND LA

The Mount Farm

Churchmans Farm

Beech Wood

72

Straight Mile Stud

LINES RD

Warren Farm

Pond Wood

2

BILL HILL PK

RG40

Ashridge Wood

Tippen's Wood

MAIDENHEAD RD

Harp Farm

Targetts Farm

B3034

FOREST RD

71

B3034

Pike's Farm

Bill Hill

Ashridge Manor

Warren Inn (PH)

OLD FOREST RD

TOUTLY WORKS
THE METRO CTR

Ashridgewood House

TWYFORD RD

Ashridgewood Farm

WARREN HOUSE RD

Rushton's Farm

BRIMBLECOMBE CL

1

TOUTLEY RD

RG41

Bell Farm

Ashridge Water Reclamation Plant

Pebblestone Copse

A329 (M)

FINCHBROOK VALE

FULLBROOK CL

A321

BELL FOUNDRY LA

70

80

A

81

B

82

C

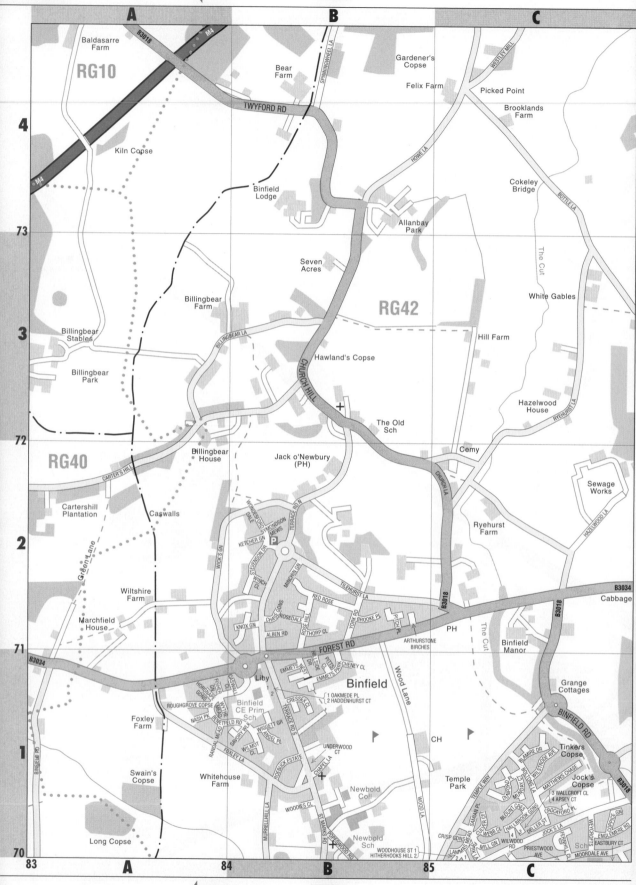

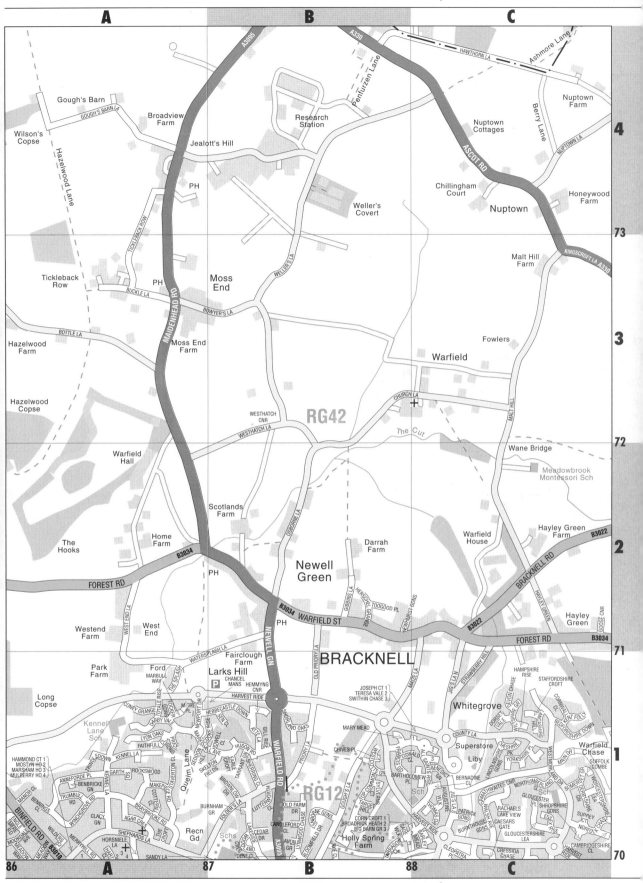

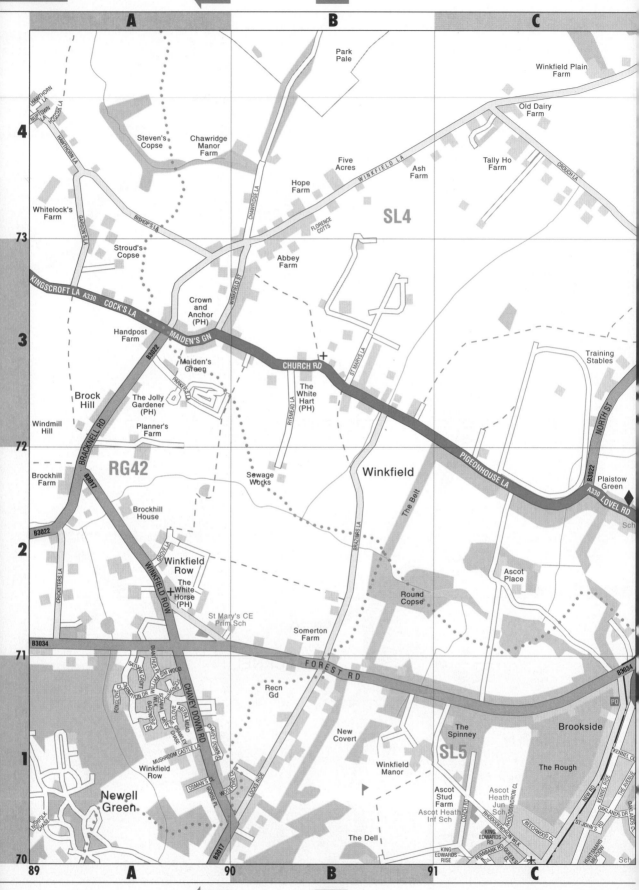

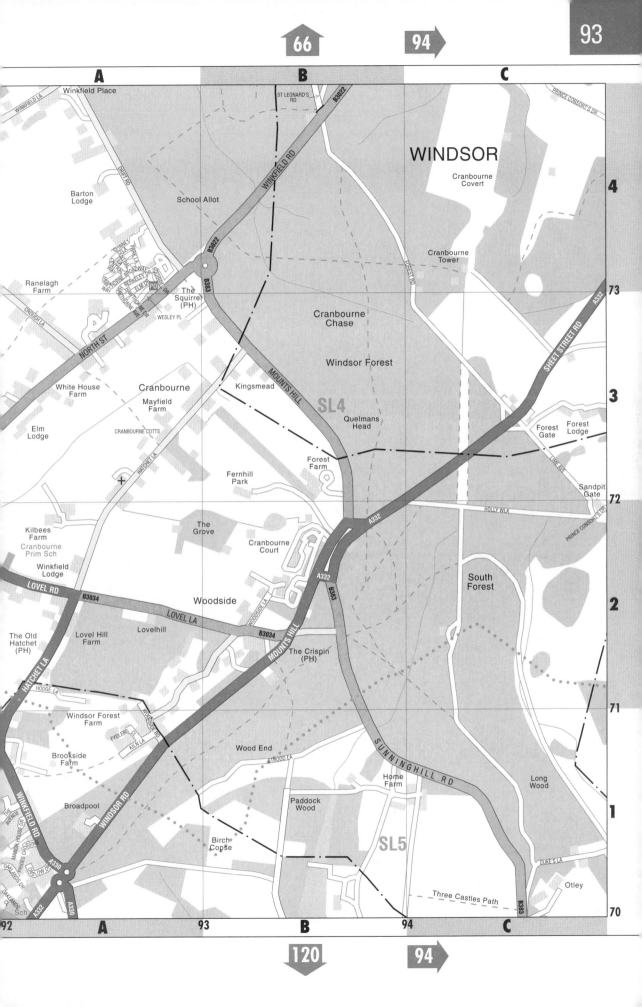

66
94

A
B
C

Winkfield Place
St LEONARD'S RD
B3022

WINDSOR

PRINCE CONSORT'S DR

Barton
Lodge

School Allot

Cranbourne
Covert

4

DRIFT RD

WINKFIELD RD

B3022

SPINNEY

PARK CL

Ranelagh
Farm

HAWTHORNE BROADWAY

SQUIRREL DR

BERKELEY DR

ELM DR

WINDSOR

Cranbourne
Tower

FOREST RD

73
A332

PO
The
Squirrel
(PH)

WESLEY PL

B3383

CROUCH LA

NORTH ST

Cranbourne
Chase

SHEET STREET RD

White House
Farm

Cranbourne

Kingsmead

Windsor Forest

SL4

Forest
Gate

Forest
Lodge

3

MOUNTS HILL

Mayfield
Farm

Quelmans
Head

Elm
Lodge

CRANBOURNE COTTS

HATCHET LA

Fernhill
Park

Forest
Farm

LIME AVE

Sandpit
Gate

72

The
Grove

HOLLY WLK

PRINCE CONSORT'S DR

Kilbees
Farm

Cranbourne
Prim Sch

Cranbourne
Court

A332

South
Forest

Winkfield
Lodge

LOVEL RD

B3034

Woodside

A332

2

LOVEL LA

WOODSIDE LA

B3383

The Old
Hatchet
(PH)

Lovel Hill
Farm

Lovelhill

B3034

MOUNTS HILL

HATCHET LA

HODGE LA

The Crispin
(PH)

71

Windsor Forest
Farm

WOODSIDE RD

FYDLERS

KILN LA

Wood End

STROOD LA

SUNNINGHILL RD

Long
Wood

Brookside
Farm

Home
Farm

WINKFIELD RD

WINDSOR RD

Broadpool

Paddock
Wood

1

THE AVENUE

MANOR HOUSE DR

PRIDES CROSSING

Birch
Copse

SL5

DUKE'S LA

B3383

A330

OAKLANDS DR

A332

A330

Otley

Three Castles Path

70

120
94

A **B** **C**

Flemish Farm

A332

SHEET STREET RD

Pickleherring Pond

4

Ranger's Lodge

Beehive Hill

PRINCE CONSORT'S DR

A332

73

Russel's Pond

Fiddle Covert

Bear's Rails

Cemy

CRIMP HILL

Rush Pond

Prince of Wales Pond

Battle Bourne

The Gallop

Seymours Plantation

The Long Walk

Bear's Rails Pond

BEARS RAILS PK

Statue

Snow Hill

Spring Hill

Cookes Hill

SL4

Three Castles Path

BISHOPSGATE

3

RICHARDSON'S LAWN COTTS

THE VILLAGE

QUEEN ANNE'S CL

Richardson's Lawn

PO

Isle of Wight Pond

The Village

Poets Lawn

Deepstrood

Royal Lodge

The Fox Hounds (PH)

72

Queen Anne's Ride

Windsor Great Park

Dark Wood

The Royal Prim Sch

Cow Pond

Bishopsgate

Chapel Wood

PARK CLOSE COTTS

2

DUKE'S LA

Hilton's Covert

MEZEL HILL COTTS

CUMBERLAND LODGE

The Sun (PH)

Mezel Hill

Park Close

WICK LA

RHODODENDRON RIDE

Square Covert

Wilderness

71

The Savill Gardens

Parkside House

Leiper Hill

Slans Hill

Great Meadow Pond

TW20

1

Temple Hill

Mill Pond

Smith's Lawn

Obelisk

SL5

Norfolk Plantation

Norfolk Farm

Statue

P

Rosy Bottom

Obelisk Pond

70

Polo Gds

95 **A** **96** **B** **97** **C**

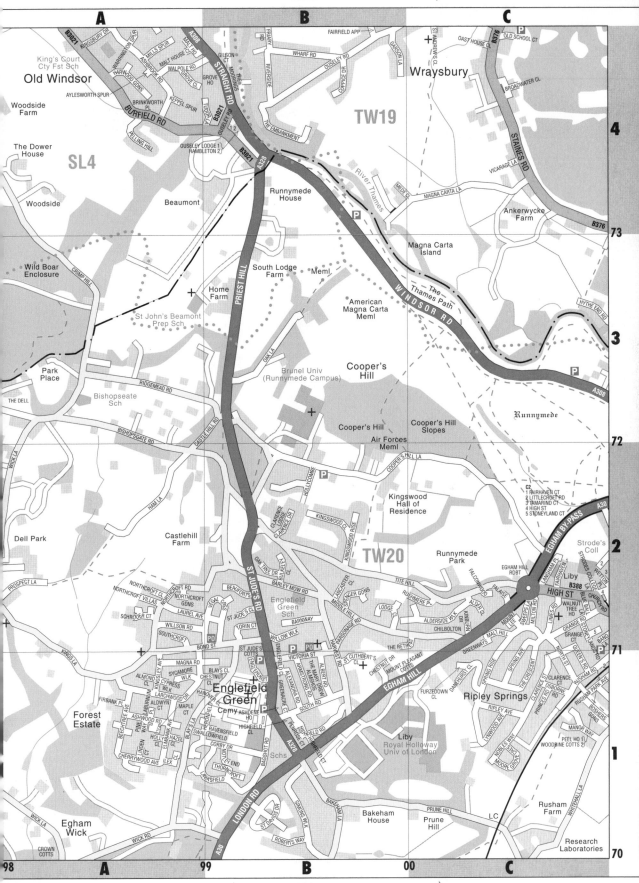

A B C

Wraysbury Resr

TW19

River Colne

Bone Head

Wks

RUNNYMEDE COTTS

Staines Moor

4

Colne Brook

Sailing Club

Colne Valley Way

Bonehead Ditch

73

B376

STAINES RD

Hythe End

B376

13

YEOVENEY CL

The Moor

BERKELEY CL

Wraysbury River

Church Lammas

STAINES BY-PASS

A30

SARSBY DR
FEATHERS LA

BELL WEIR
CL

FERRY LA

HYTHE END RD

RIVERSIDE

A30

A30

COLNE WAY

LAMMAS RD

W R A Y S B U R Y   R D

GLOUCESTER DR

ANNIE
BROOKS CL
MANOR
PK

MEDE CT

KINGACRE CT
VICTORIA RD

MEADOW
GREEN PK

MARLEY
CROFT

PLOVER CL

River Ash

A30

STAINES

72

WINDSOR RD

A308

A2
1 BAND LA
2 HERITAGE CT
3 NICHOLSON WLK
4 CADDY CL
5 STATION RD N

Hotel

RUNNYMEDE
RDBT

Queensmead Lake
(Resr)

Holm Island

LAMMAS DR

DUNCROFT
MANOR

BINBURY
ROW

CAMBRIA CT
CHURCH ST

ISLAND
CL

HALE ST

THE
MALTINGS

BRIDGE
ST

ALDOUS
HO

TWO RIVERS
SH CTR

MUSTARD MILL RD

TILLY'S LA

NORRIS
RD

ROBIN
WAY

WATERS DR

KINGFISHER
DR

THE
OAKS

LARK
AVE

KESTREL CL

SWALLOW

HAWKSWAY

NORMEDE CRES

FAIRFIELD AVE

MILL RD

HIGH
ST

A308

PO

ST GEORGE
PATTON CT

EGHAM

EGHAM BY-PASS

A30

THE GLANTY

A308

THE AVENUE

GREEN LA

WOODHAW

Wks

River Thames

Wks

THE GREEN
BSNS CTR
CAUSEWAY
EST

LOVE'T

A308

THE CAUSEWAY

RIVER PARK
AVE

The Thames Path

KINGSBURY
CRES

The Watermans
BSNS PK

CLARENCE ST

COLNEBRIDGE CL
MARKET SQ

PO

TH

THE
ELMSLEIGH
CTR

THE
CYGNETS

OAST
CT

2

STRODE ST

MANDEVILLE CT

B388

RUNNYMEDE
CL

ALBANY PL

HIGH

KINGS RD

PARK
RD

HUMER ST

CEDAR CT

BENHAM RD

CROWN CL

Mus

PO

WREN
CT

THE
PRECINCT

GREEN LA

VICARAGE
CRES

HAWTHORNE RD

NEW RD

FOXLEIGH

Ind Est

CHANDOS CL

CLAREMONT RD

AVENUE RD

BLENHEIM RD

Superstore

B376

FARMERS
WAY

THE FERRERS

RIVERSIDE

A320

SIMMONS RD

FELIX
LA

HYTHE

CHERTSEY LA

LC

HYTHE
CL

Mus

Liby

Westbrook

SOUTH ST

THAMES ST

PROSPECT PL

BEECHEN CL

Island

RICHMOND CL

GRESHAM RD

TROSTED CT

B376

MATTHEW ARNOLD CL

MANOR VARMOR
CT

MANOR FARM CT

B388 CHURCH RD

ST JOHNS CT

SCHOOL LA

AVONDALE

GROVE
GDNS

CLARE
GDNS

GROVE
CL

SPINS CRES

RD

ALEXANDER RD

POOLEY AVE

RHODES CL

MULLENS RD

TOWN AVE

MONS
WLK

CENTURY RD

WENDOVER RD

CUMBERLAND RD

Railway Terr

LC

BOLEYN CL

PINE TREES
BSNS PK

A320

BOWES RD

COPERS CL

MONSELL
GDNS

TIMSWAY

LALEHAM RD

LANGLEY RD

FELTHAM RD

EDGELL RD

RIVERFIELD RD

THAMES SIDE

Riverbank

BARRINGTON CT
ARGOSY GDNS

1

P

Egham

LC

ELWELL CL

DE PARS

WESLEY DR

FITZROBERT PL

Sports
Ctr

Glenville Farm

MANOR
LEAZE

VICARAGE AVE

VICARAGE CT

COLLEGE AVE

POOLEY GREEN CL

WOLSEY RD

HOLBROOK

CHAFFA

RD

MEAD RD

WOLBOROUGH

MEAD
RD

CHAUCER CT

1 ST NAZAIRE CL
2 RHODES CT
3 FLANDERS CT
4 NORMANDY WLK

Hythe
Cty Prim
Sch

GORING RD

MILLER'S LA

WENDOVER RD

FIELD
VIEW

ARGENT CL

GLEBE RD

MEADOW GDNS

THE PARADE

ST PAUL'S RD

WASHOTT

CORNWALL
WAY

THORPE RD

BRACKLEY HO 1
CRESCENT CT 2
LAZARE CT 3
ABBEY LO 4
REGATTA HO 5
BOSSINGTON CT 6
LAUDERDALE HO 7
AMBER CT 8
THE CYGNETS 9
IFFLEY CT 10

BUNDY'S WAY

MAYFIELD GDN

PENTON RD

DUNCOMBE
CT

SWANDRIFT

ONSLOW LO
WYTHEGATE

PENTON RD

RISKIN
CT

CARLYLE
RD

MEADWAY

71

Manorcroft Sch

1 RUSHAM PARK AVE
2 BRAYWOOD AVE

TW20

BOSHERS
GDNS

Priory CT

VICARAGE CT

3 WINDERMERE CL
4 CONISTON WAY
5 BORROWDALE CL
6 BUTTERMERE WAY
7 GRASMERE CL
8 HELVELLYN CL

Pooley
Green
Sch

PO

HARCOURT RD

TEMPEST RD

HEDLAKE RD

HIGH
ST

Magna Carta
Sch

Egham
Hythe

BISHOPS WAY

HYTHE FIELD AVE

Thorpe Lea
Prim Sch

RIVERSIDE DR

ST IVES CL

GLEN CT

NUTBOURNE
CT

WHEATSHEAF LA

MEADWAY

Lodge

Milton
Park

STROUDE RD

NEW WICKHAM LA

Nurseries

Thorpe
Lea

B3376

THORPE LEA RD

PRIORY CT

COLLEGE AVE

LANGTON WAY

STEPHEN CL

DEVIL ST LA

PARK AVE

CROSSWAYS

MALET CL

BAAKNIGHTS

HUNTINGFIELD WAY

TW18

FERRY AVE

A320

1

WICKHAM LA

CLOCKHOUSE LA W

CLOCKHOUSE LA E

B388

AYEBRIDGES AVE

Mead Lake Ditch

SOUTH AVE

OAK AVE

WAVENDENE AVE

ASHLEIGH AVE

WARWICK AVE

M25

PENTON RD

70

01 A 02 B 03 C

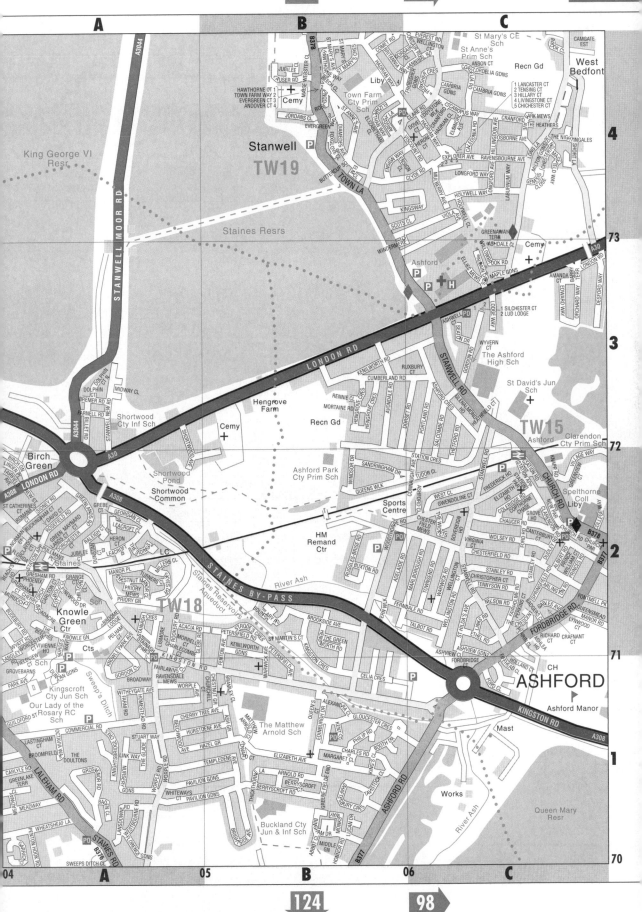

C1
1 TASMAN CT
2 WILLOW CT
3 CATLE CL
4 KILLIGREW HO
5 GRANTHAM HO
6 ASH LODGE
7 LIME LODGE
8 OAK LODGE
9 ELM CT

10 WILLOW LODGE
11 SYCAMORE LODGE
12 ISOBEL HO
13 PRISCILLA HO
14 SUNBURY CROSS CTR

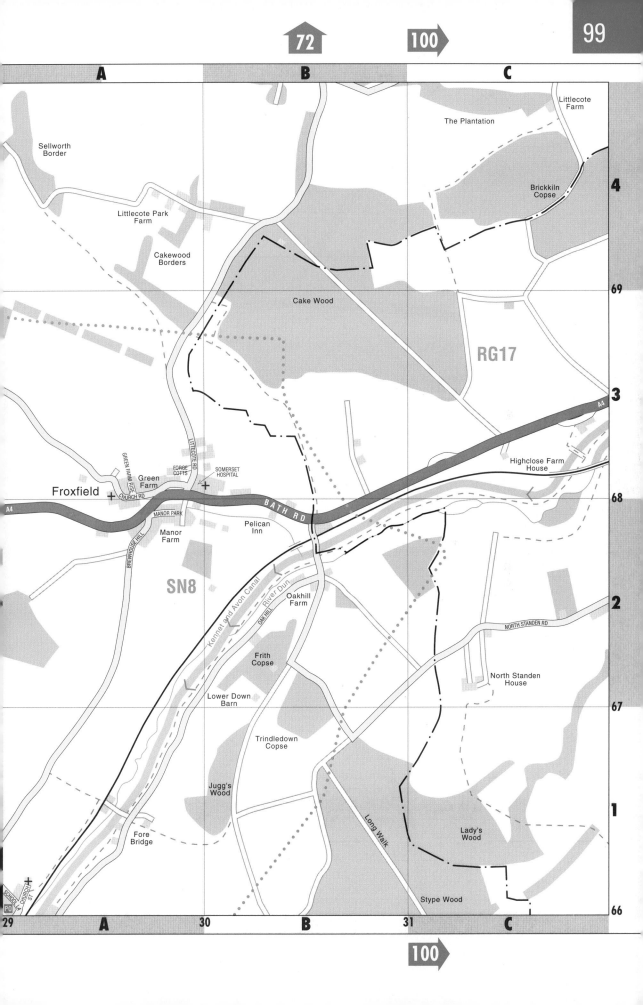

A B C

Littlecote Farm

The Plantation

Sellworth Border

4

Brickkiln Copse

Littlecote Park Farm

Cakewood Borders

69

Cake Wood

RG17

3

A4

LITTLECOTE RD

GREEN FARM RISE

Green Farm

FORGE COTTS

SOMERSET HOSPITAL

Highclose Farm House

Froxfield

CHURCH RD

BATH RD

68

A4

MANOR PARK

Pelican Inn

BREWHOUSE HILL

Manor Farm

SN8

Kennet and Avon Canal

River Dun

OAKHILL

Oakhill Farm

NORTH STANDEN RD

2

Frith Copse

North Standen House

Lower Down Barn

67

Trindledown Copse

Jugg's Wood

Long Walk

Lady's Wood

1

Fore Bridge

SCHOOL

CHURCH ST

PO

Stype Wood

66

29 A 30 B 31 C

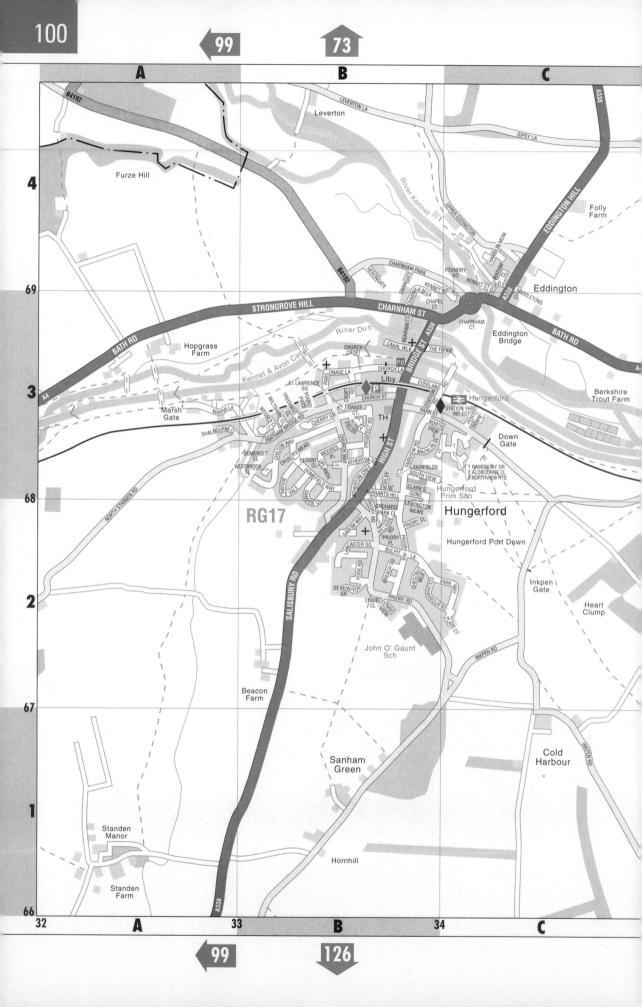

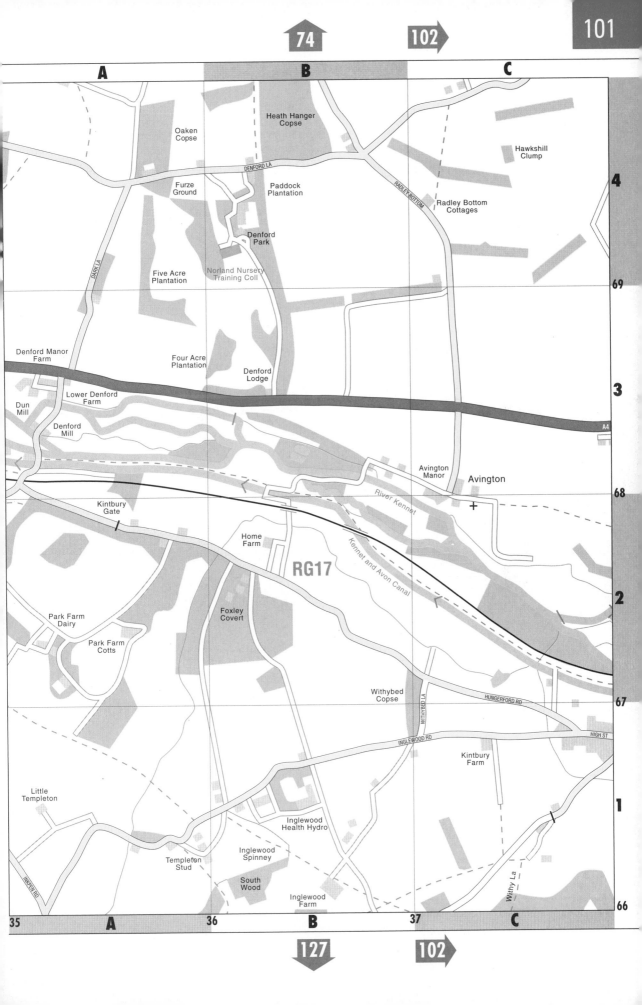

A   B   C

Heath Hanger
Copse

Oaken
Copse

Hawkshill
Clump

DENFORD LA

Furze
Ground

Paddock
Plantation

RADLEY BOTTOM

Radley Bottom
Cottages

4

Denford
Park

DARK LA

Five Acre
Plantation

Norland Nursery
Training Coll

69

Four Acre
Plantation

Denford Manor
Farm

Denford
Lodge

Lower Denford
Farm

3

Dun
Mill

A4

Denford
Mill

Avington
Manor

Avington

River Kennet

68

Kintbury
Gate

Home
Farm

RG17

Kennet and Avon Canal

2

Park Farm
Dairy

Foxley
Covert

Park Farm
Cotts

Withybed
Copse

HUNGERFORD RD

67

WITHYBED LA

HIGH ST

INGLEWOOD RD

Little
Templeton

Kintbury
Farm

1

Inglewood
Health Hydro

Templeton
Stud

Inglewood
Spinney

WITHY LA

South
Wood

Inglewood
Farm

66

INKPEN RD

35   A   36   B   37   C

101
75

A **B** **C**

Clapton Farm

Lower Farm

Lip La

Rowland's Copse

Hoe Benham

4

Elcot Farm

Elcot

Field's Copse

Highcroft Copse

Elcot Park Hotel

Pound's Border

Hoe Benham La

69

Bottom Barn

The Halfway (PH)

Halfway Manor Farm

3

A4

Halfway Farm

A4

Lodges

Board La

Little Wawcott

Richen's Cottage

RG17

68

RG20

Wawcott Farm

River Kennet

Barton Court

Barton Holt

The Wilderness

2

Dreweat's Lock

Kintbury

LC

Shepherd's Bridge

Irish Hill Copse

67

P

PH

Sewage Works

Kennet and Avon Canal

Irish Hill

The Croft

Mill Bank

St Mary's CE Prim Sch

Kintbury Park Farm

Church St

Station Rd

Forge Cl

Kintbury Sq

Newbury St

Elizabeth Gdns

High St

Titcombe Way

PO

Barn Cl

Great Severalls

Gainsborough Ave

Gladstone Cl

Irish Hill Rd

Holt Rd

Harold Rd

Irish Hill Cottages

Wallingtons Rd

Lawrence Mead

Fennel Cl

Ashton Pl

Burtons Hill

Long Cl

Craven Way

The Pentlands

1

The Haven

Inkpen Rd

Bratle Cl

Craigie Cl

Queens Way

Peartree Cottage

Illwills Border

The Crescent

Oxen Cres

Old La

Kintbury

Laylands Gn

The Green

Barrymore Lodge

Dongall's Wood

Horn Copse

Hamstead Holt Farm

Hankin's La

Blandys Hill

66

38 **A** **39** **B** **40** **C**

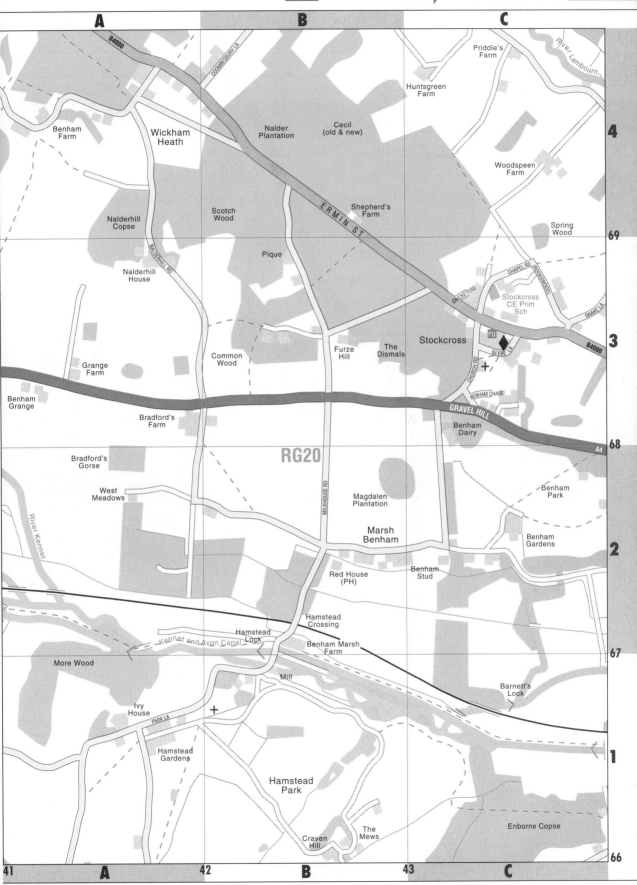

76
104
129
104

A   B   C

River Lambourn

B4000

Benham Farm

Wickham Heath

COOMBESBURY LA

Priddle's Farm

Huntsgreen Farm

Nalder Plantation

Cecil (old & new)

4

Woodspeen Farm

Nalderhill Copse

Scotch Wood

ERMIN ST

Shepherd's Farm

Spring Wood

69

NALDERHILL RD

Nalderhill House

Pique

CRICKETERS

CHAPEL RD (ROOKSWOOD)

Stockcross CE Prim Sch

SNAKE LA

Common Wood

Furze Hill

The Dismals

Stockcross

PO

GLEBE LA

B4000

3

Grange Farm

CHURCH RD

Benham Grange

Bradford's Farm

BENHAM CHASE

GRAVEL HILL

Benham Dairy

A4

68

Bradford's Gorse

RG20

Magdalen Plantation

Benham Park

West Meadows

MILKHOUSE RD

Marsh Benham

Benham Gardens

2

River Kennel

Red House (PH)

Benham Stud

Hamstead Crossing

Kennet and Avon Canal

Hamstead Lock

Benham Marsh Farm

Barnett's Lock

67

More Wood

Mill

Ivy House

PARK LA

Hamstead Gardens

Hamstead Park

1

Enborne Copse

Craven Hill

The Mews

66

41   A   42   B   43   C

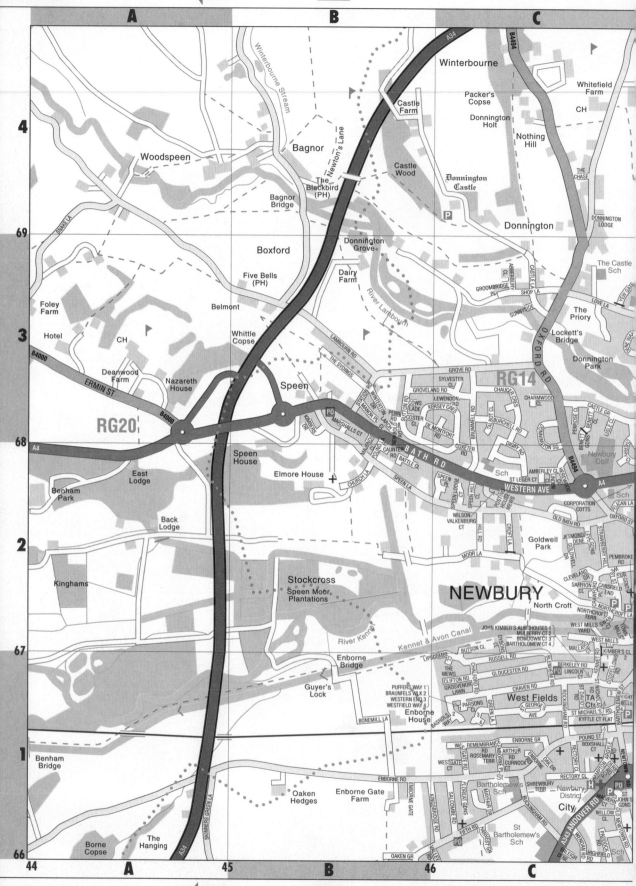

103
77

A   B   C

Winterbourne Stream

4

Woodspeen

Bagnor

Newton's Lane

Winterbourne

Castle Farm

Packer's Copse

Whitfield Farm

CH

Donnington Holt

Nothing Hill

THE CHASE

The Blackbird (PH)

Castle Wood

Bagnor Bridge

Donnington Castle

THE CHASE

P

Donnington

Donnington Lodge

69

Boxford

Donnington Grove

DONNINGTON

The Castle Sch

Five Bells (PH)

Dairy Farm

River Lambourn

GROOMBRIDGE PL

ABERBURY CL

CASTLE LA

SHOP LA

LOVE LA

YEW GATE

The Priory

Foley Farm

Belmont

SUNNYSIDE

Lockett's Bridge

Hotel

CH

Whittle Copse

LAMBOURN RD

THE SYDINGS

GROVE RD

RG14

CHARMWOOD CL

OXFORD RD

Donnington Park

3

B4000

Deanwood Farm

Nazareth House

ERMIN ST

Speen

SYLVESTER CL

GROVELAND RD

CHAUCER CRES

CASTLE GR

PENROSE CL

BENETT GDNS BENETT CL

LISLE CL

STATION RD

COWS LADE

LEWENDON RD

KERSEY CRES

CHARMWOOD CL

RG20

B4000

MARSHALLS CT

WINTERTON DR

MANOR PL

PENN RD

SUTTON RD

COSTER CL

DE MONTFORT RD

BRUMMELL RD

TALBOT CL

BURCHELL RD

CONNINGTON RD

Newbury Coll

68

A4

Speen House

KNIGHTS

Elmore House

CHURCH LA

CAUNTER CT

POUND

BATTLE CL

BATH RD

COXETER RD

DIGBY RD

Sch

AMBERLEY CL

ST LEGER CT

HEREWARD RD

B4494

Newbury Coll

Benham Park

East Lodge

SPEEN LA

Speen Hill

SPEEN HILL CL

POSITIVO HOUSE MEWS

WESTERN AVE

A4

Sch

PECAN LA

Oxford St

CORPORATION COTTS

2

Kinghams

Back Lodge

WILSON VALKENBURG CT

HILL RD

MOOR LA

CROFT LA

OLD BATH RD

Goldwell Park

GOLDWELL DR

JESMOND DENE

CLEVELAND GR

SAFFRON CL

CANSFIELD CT END

STRAWBERRY HILL

LES GDNS

PEMBROKE RD

Stockcross

Speen Moor Plantations

CRAWFORD CL

NORTHCROFT TERR

P

NEWBURY

North Croft

NORTHCROFT LA

WEST MILLS SQ

P

River Kennet

Kennet & Avon Canal

JOHN KIMBER'S ALMSHOUSES 1
MULBERRY CT 2
BOWDOWN CT 3
BARTHOLOMEW CT 4

WEST MILLS YARD

WEST MILLS

KIMBER'S CL

MALLARD

67

Enborne Bridge

BUTSON CL

DYSONS CL

LIPSCOMBE

LOWER WAY

The Mews

Guyer's Lock

Enborne House

PUFFERS WAY 1
BRAUNFELS WLK 2
WESTERN END 3
WESTFIELD WAY 4

RUSSELL RD

CLIFTON RD

GROSVENOR LAWN

CHALFORD RD

GLOUCESTER RD

CRAVEN RD

PARSONS ST

BAGNOLS WAY

GREEN LA

ST MICHAEL'S RD

BERKELEY RD

LINCOLN

ROCKINGHAM RD

West Fields

GEORGE AVE

TA Ctr

KYFTLE CT FLAT

BONEMILL LA

1

Benham Bridge

ENBORNE RD

ENBORNE GATE

Enborne Gate Farm

KINGSBRIDGE RD

SALCOMBE RD

FLOREAT GDNS

WESTGATE RD

REMEMBRANCE RD

ROSEMARY TERR

ARTHUR RD

CURNOCK

ENBORNE GR

OAK DR

RECTORY CL

BOXSHALL

POUND ST

ARGYLE

WESTGATE CT

St Bartholomew's Sch

SHREWBURY TERR

MAYFAIR DR

RECTORY CL

Newbury District City

H

P

JOHN'S RD

MALVERN RD

WILLOW

NEWTOWN RD

HAMPTON RD

66

Borne Copse

The Hanging

SKINNERS GREEN LA

A34

Oaken Hedges

OAKEN GR

ENBORNE GATE

Enborne Gate Farm

BUCKINGHAM RD

FIFTH RD

St Bartholemew's Sch

P

HARVEST CL

VALLEY RD

A343 ANDOVER RD

WENDAN RD

HIGHFIELD RD

PADDOCK

BLEIGH

44   A   45   B   46   C

103
130

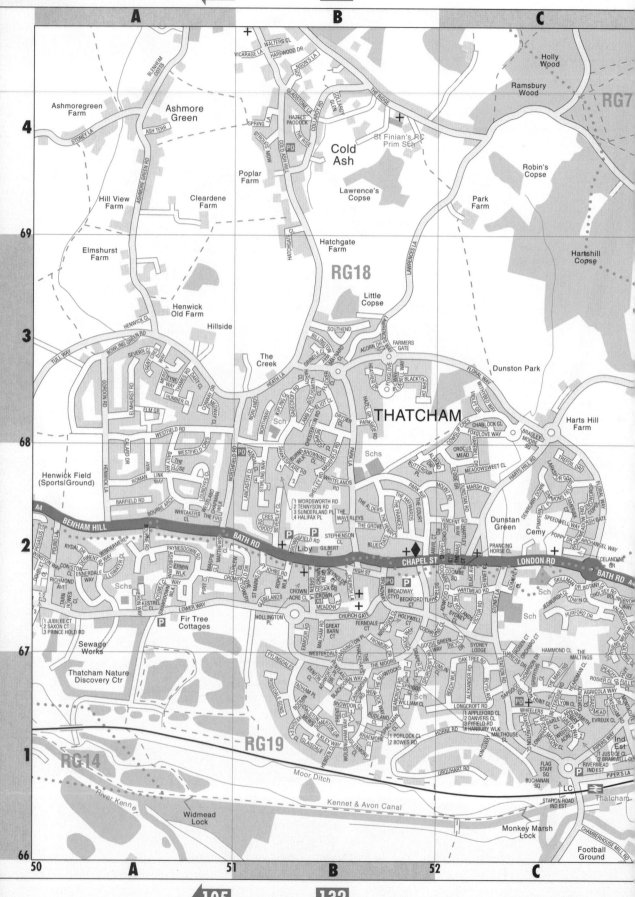

A	**B**	**C**

The Slade
Hopgood's Farm
Winchcombe Farm
Sewage Works
Vanners
Woodground Shaw
Lodge Copse

Briff Farm
Sadgrove Farm

Upper Common
Miles's Green
Osgood's Gully

Turner's Green
Workhouse Gn
Buckleybury Common

Burdens Heath
Roundfield
Upper Bucklebury
PH

Burden's Heath Plantation
Hart's Hill
Harts Hill Rd
Wimble's Wood
Long Gr
Blacklands Rd
Broad La
Woodside Cl
Tomlins

RG7

Hockett Wood

Upper Hartshill Farm
Big Gully
Bucklebury CE Prim Sch
Blacklands Copse
The Grange
Midgham Wood
Wootten's

Long Grove Copse
Kent's Down Gully
Webb's Farm

RG18
Ouzel Gully
King's Farm
Birds La

Siege Cross Farm
Colthrop Manor
Nursery Copse
Midgham

Meadowside
Westend Farm
The Berkshire Arms
Coach and Horses (PH)

RG19
Industrial Estate
Enterprise Way
Colthrop Way
Daytona Dr
Gables Way
BATH RD
Church Hill
Goddard Dr
School Hill
Carbinswood La

Pipers Ct
Aylesford Way
Colthrop Mill
Colthrop
LC
Midgham Marsh
Brimpton Rd
Midgham Bridge
LC

Kennet and Avon Canal
Midgham Lock

River Kennet
River Kennet

A	**B**	**C**

107
81

A B C

Scotland

Chapelrow
Common

St Annes
Farm

Gunnells
Farm

Hilliers

PO

The
Blade Bone
(PH)

Chapel Row

Beenham
Hatch

The
Bourne

The Bourne

4

Lower
Common

Long Gully

PARADISE WAY

HATCH CL

Paradise La

Withy
Copse

Awbery's
Farm

Middle Wood

Ironmongers
Copse

69

HATCH LA

Copyhold
Farm

Greyfield
Wood

Six Bells
(PH)

TPO

Beenham Cty Prim
Sch

CLAY LA

THE STROUDS

Reading's Gully

Horn's
Copse

Kiff Green

Beenham

3

CARBINSWOOD LA

High Wood

Old
Copse

Bucklebury
Place

WINDMILL LA

Channel
Wood

Douai Abbey
(Benedictine)

Ferrises

Oakwood
Farm

Douai Sch

68

SCHOOL HILL

Midgham
Green

RG7

Lodge

Malthouse
Farm

Gravelpit
Copse

Webcroft
Copse

Woolhampton
CE Prim Sch

Upper
Woolhampton

Beenham
Lodge

2

Midgham Park

NEW ROAD HILL

Elstree
Sch

Hallcourt
Farm

The
Court

Home
Farm

Jennings's
Copse

Woolhampton Park

67

Great Mounts
Copse

HILL CRES

WOOLHAMPTON HILL

Inn

ORCHARD CL

Woolhampton

PO

BATH RD

Gateways

Midgham

STATION RD

WATERMILL CT

Rising Sun
(PH)

RAILSIDE

A4

Oxlease
Bridge

ANGEL MEAD

LC

P

1

Heales Lock

Woolhampton
Lock

Kennet & Avon Canal

Woolhampton Bridge

River Kennet

Swing-bridge

River Enborne

Froud
Bridg
Mari

Gravel
Pit

66

56 A 57 B 58 C

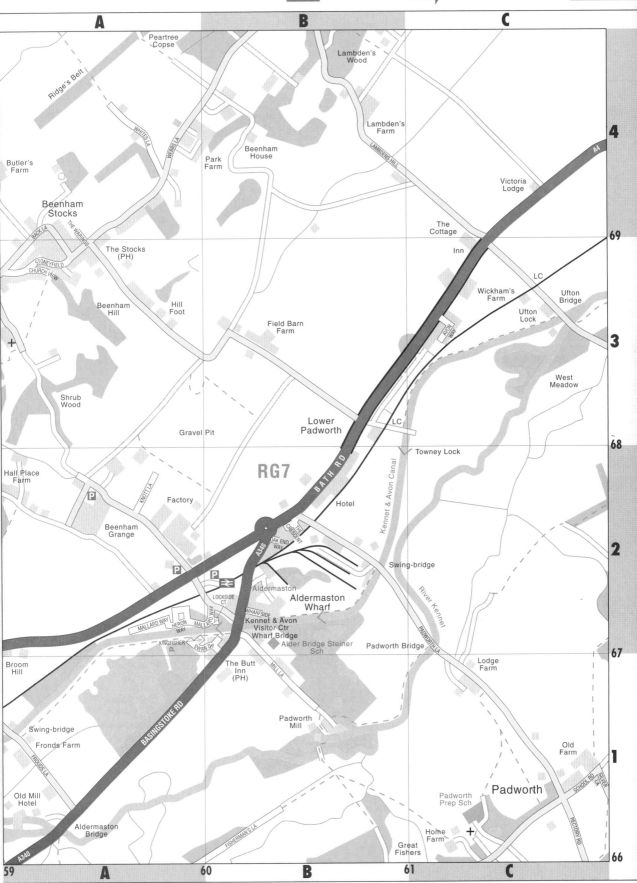

A **B** **C**

A4

Milehouse
Farm

Woolwichgreen
Farm

PH

Kennet & Avon Canal

Sulhamstead
Lock

Sheffield Bottom

BATH RD

The
Mile House

River Kennet

Sulhamstead
Swing-bridge

BOTTOM LA

Malthouse
Copse

4

A4

Sulhamstead House
(Police Training Sch)

Brick Kiln
Copse

Tyle
Mill

Tylemill
Bridge
(swing)

Brazenhead
Copse

NORTH
DR

SOUTH
DR

SOUTH
DR

SOUTH

Ford
Bridge

69

Kennet & Avon Canal

Folly Farm

Home
Farm

Mast

JAQUESS LA

Sulhamstead

Whitehouse
Green

SULHAMSTEAD HILL

Field
Farm

KINGSTON LA

3

Sulhamstead Bannister
Upper End

Meales
Farm

Boarmoor
Wood

FOLLY LA

HART'S LA

Uftongreen
Farm

Ufton
Green

RG7

WHITE'S HILL

68

Sulhamstead
Abbots

CHURCH LA

Middle
Farm

SULHAMSTEAD RD

Seward's Gully

Sulhamstead
& Ufton Nervet
Prim Sch

Glebe Farm

Shortheath
House

Omer's Gully

SHORTHEATH LA

2

Ufton Nervet

HUNTER'S HILL

BLUEBELL DR

ABBEY PARK

OMER'S RISE

Ashen
Wood

ALDER GLADE

CLAYHILL RD

SCHOOL LA

BIRCH RD

WISE'S FIRS

WOODMAN'S
LA

KIRKWOOD
CRES

BOWOOD RD

Island
Farm

Benham's
Farm

HOLYBUSH LA

ABBOT'S RD

JORDAN'S LA

67

GREEN LA

BANNISTER
RD

Burghfield
Common

The
Willink
Sch

BLAND'S
OAK RD

Normoor Copse

Shootersbrook La

ISLAND FARM RD

Church
Plantation

CAMP RD

Firlands
Farm

GARLANDS
CL

Ufton Court

TANNERS CL

ALISON
CL

TOTTERDOWN

1

SILVER LA

Pennsylvania
Wood

Poor's
Allotments

THREE FIRS WAY

BROOKS
RD

NORMOOR
RD

READING LA

PADWORTH RD

Brickcroft

Ufton Park

Park Piece

BRACKEN
WOOD

66

62 **A** 63 **B** 64 **C**

Old Park

A   B   C

Knight's Farm

BERRYS LA

Kirtons Farm Country Club

Works

M4

AMNERS FARM RD

RG30

Pingewood

PINGEWOOD RD S

Moores Farm

4

Small Mead Farm

BROOK DR

Madejski Stadium

HOOPS WAY

ROYAL WAY

SHOOTERS WAY

BOOT END

BISCUIT WAY

HURST WAY

RG2

LONG WATER DR

SOUTH OAK WAY

Brewery

M4

69

Pinge Wood

BURNTHOUSE LA

Amner's Wood

Burghfield Brook

Hopkiln Farm

Hartley Court Farm

Hartley Court

HARTLEY COURT RD

3

Burnthouse Farm

KYBES LA

Great Lea Farm

Works

Burnthouse Bridge

RIDER'S LA

68

RG7

Foudry Brook

A33

MEREOAK LA

FULLER'S LA

Manor Farm

Grazeley Court Farm

Poundgreen Farm

Gravelly Bridge Farm

2

PALMER'S LA

Bell Copse

Poundgreen

Gravelly Bridge

The Old Bell (PH)

Rapleys

67

Shepherdton La

PUMP LA

Grazeley

BLOOMFIELDHATCH LA

The Wheatsheaf (PH)

Lambwoodhill Common

Grazeley Parochial Prim Sch

Highlands

Woodcock Lane

1

GOODBOYS LA

Lambwoodhill Farm

LAMBWOOD HILL

Diddenham Manor Farm

Thurley Farm

A33

66

BROOMFIELDHATCH LA

68   A   69   B   70   C

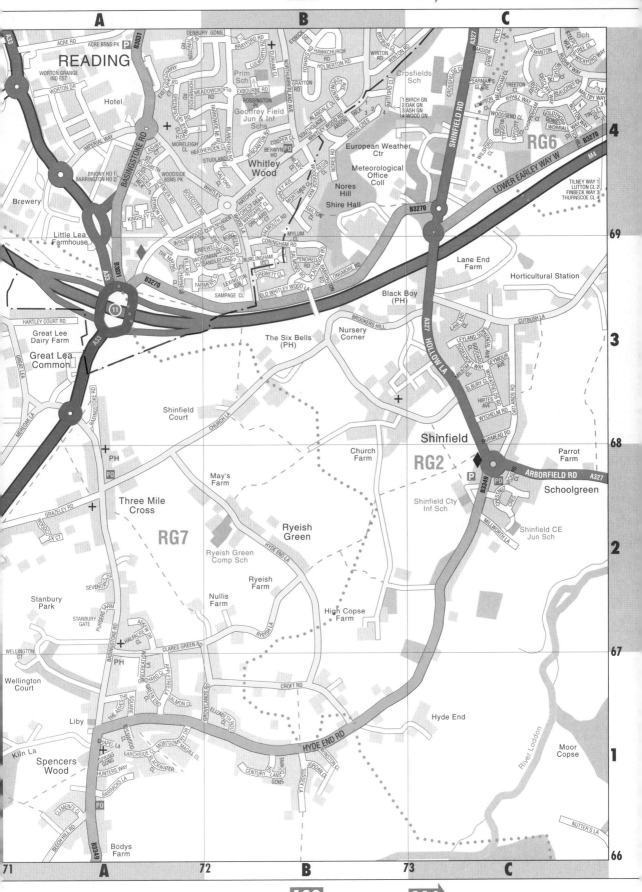

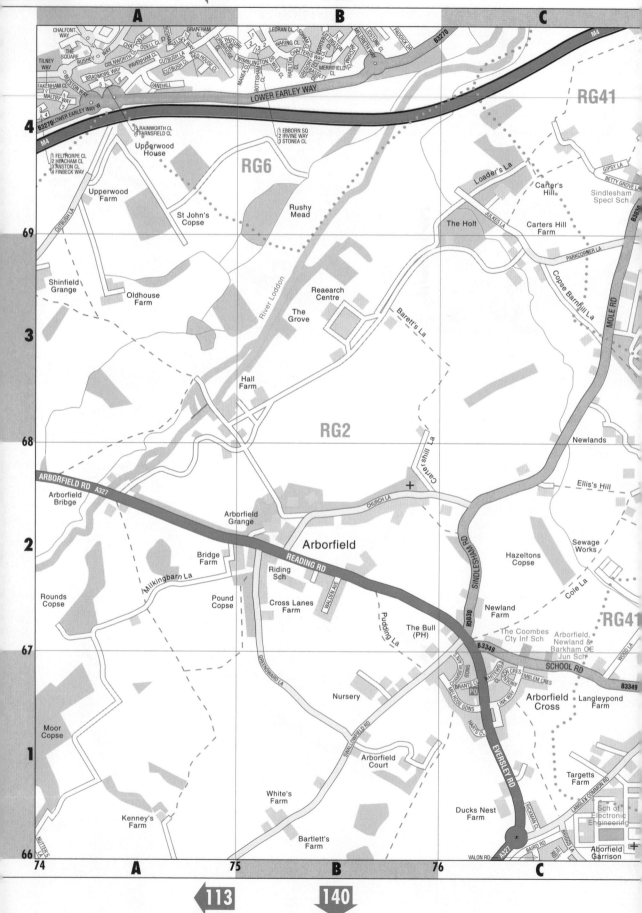

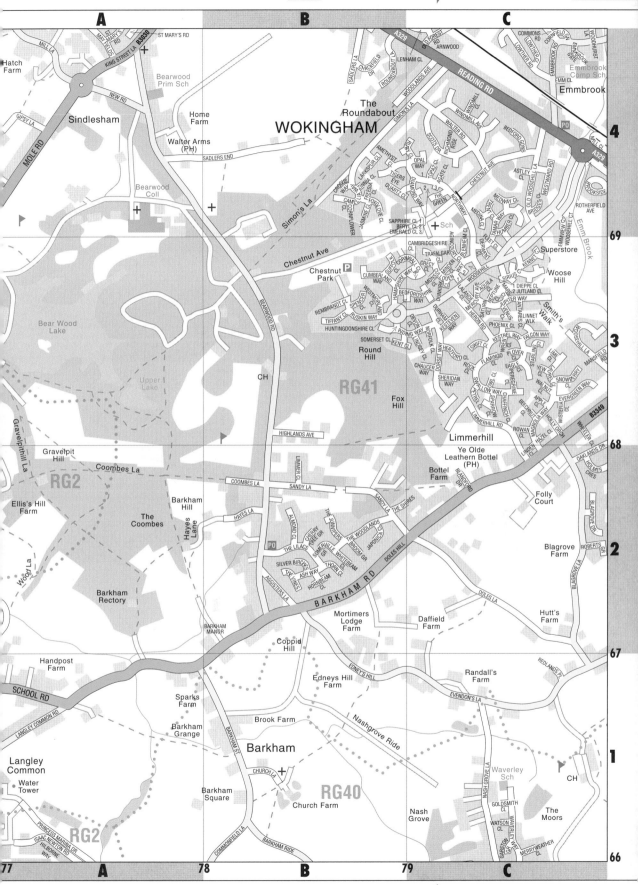

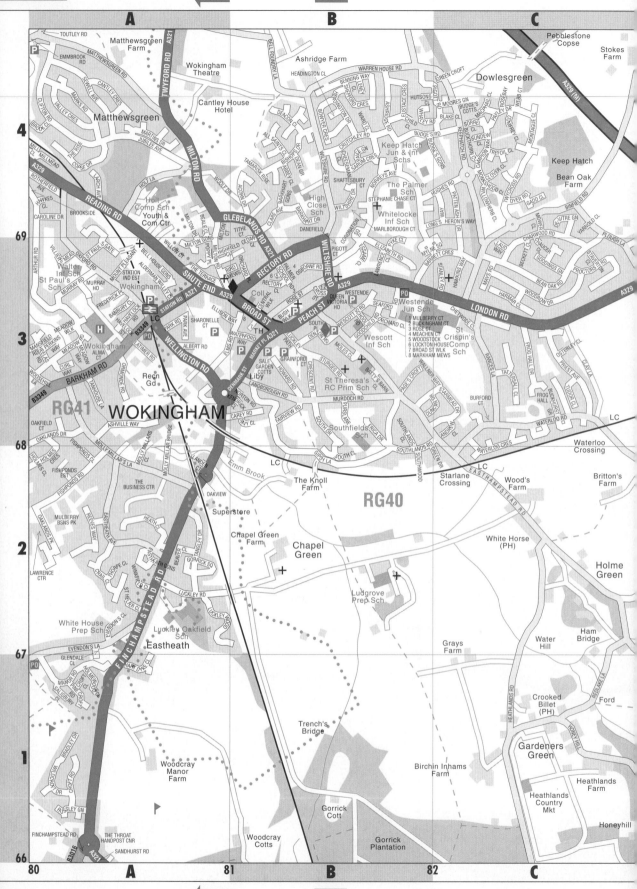

A   B   C

Stokes Farm

Top Copse

Pockets Copse

Murrellhill Grange

Popes Manor

MURRELLHILL LA

PROSPECT COTTS

POPESWOOD RD

WOOD LA

JOCK'S LA

Priestwood

Sch

YORK HO

STUART HO

WINDLESHAM RD

RG42

WOKINGHAM RD

B3408

4

Popeswood

Springfield RD

MILWARD GDNS

PHOENIX BSNS PK

JACOB CL

ARKWRIGHT DR

BOMFIELD DALE

COVES FARM WOOD

POCKET CL

Amen Corner

AMEN CORNER BSNS PK

LONGSHOT IND EST

1 HITHERHOOKS ST
2 WOODHOUSE ST
3 CAMPION HO
4 BRYONY HO
5 BROADLANDS CT
6 HAWKSWOOD HO
7 HOMBROOK HO

THE WESTERN CTR

WESTERN IND AREA

THE BRACKNELL BSNS CTR

DOWNMILL RD

LONDON RD

Hotel

Leisure-Sport Complex

JOHN NIKE WAY

B3408

Mast

LONDON RD   A329

A329 (M)

A329

69

A329

Rose Farm

Buckhurst Moors

Peacock Farm

PEACOCK LA

BERKSHIRE WAY

Wykery Copse

DONCASTLE RD

OLDBURY

SOUTHERN IND AREA

WILLOUGHBY RD

A3095

Plough Farm

Hotel

RG12

ELLESFIELD AVE

LOVELACE RD

MILL LA

Mill Pond

3

Big Wood

Peacock Cotts

BILTON IND EST

Northerams (Nature Reserve)

A3095

68

West Garden Copse

BRACKNELL

Big Wood House

WATERLOO RD

Lock's House

Easthampstead Park

Easthampstead Park Sch

RINGMEAD

Great Hollands Jun & Inf Schs

Liby

Great Hollands

2

RG40

Con Ctr

PENWOOD GDNS

WICKHAM VALE

HATCHGATE COPSE

FLEXFORD GN

LONGMORE RD

KINGSBURY DR

ST ANDREWS

UNDERWOOD

GREAT HOLLANDS RD

HIGHFIELD

HOLBECK

ULLSWATER

67

Six Oaks

EASTHAMPSTEAD RD

OLD WOKINGHAM RD

GLENEAGLES HO 1
MOOR PARK HO 2
MUIRFIELD HO 3

TURNBERRY

CARNOUSTIE

TREVELYAN

STAPLEHURST

HOLLAND PINES

CROWTHORNE RD

A3095

Sutton Court Farm

WEST RD

CH

Cemy

Crem

Woodenhill Cty Prim Sch

SYLVANUS

WOODENHILL

SPINIS

SOUTHWOLD

SARUM

RINGMEAD

Sch

PRESCOTT

PEMBROKE

1

HONEY HILL

Newlands

PH

Meteorological Off Experimental Site

STRATFIELD

NINE MILE RIDE

B3430

FORESTERS WAY

66

B3430

A   84   B   85   C

118

A4
1 PRIESTWOOD SQ
2 SALTIRE GDNS
3 WINDLEBROOK GN
4 APPLETREE PL
5 PORTMAN CL

6 HART CL
7 BIRCHETTS CL
8 ASHRIDGE GN

B4
1 LYNWOOD CHASE
2 DENE CL
3 LAKESIDE
4 EDMONDS CT

◄ **117**

91 ▲

A B C

Chavey Down

Big Wood

MAIN DR

Pump Rough

WINDSOR FOREST CT

WOODEND CL
KING EDWARDS RISE
QUEENS CL
KING EDWARDS CL

ROYAL HUNT HO
OAK LEAF CT

CH PO

North Ascot

Liby

Pappleweck Sch

RG 42

SANDY LA

THE GROVE

MILL

NORTH RD

BIRCH LA

LONG HILL RD

CHURCH RD

Ascot Priory

Cemy

GREEN WOOD
FERRARD CL

RANELAGH CRES

BRACKEN BANK

St CHRISTOPHERS GDNS

WENTWORTH WAY

FERNBANK PL

WENTWORTH AVE

GOATERS RD

NAPPER CL

THE CLOSE

NORTH LODGE DR

ASKET DR

WHITELANDS DR

GOLD CUP

MANSFIELD CL

DARWALL DR

ELLIOT RISE

PRINCE ANDREW WAY

BLACKMOOR WOOD

BLACKMOOR CL

New Meadow

WASH LA

JONES CMP

LANGDALE DR

PRUSTON WAY

VERNON CL

SEFERS RIDE

HEATHWAY

BURLEIGH RD

BURLEIGH LA

ANCASTER DR

BYTHERWOOD LA

1 MARSTON WAY
2 CHERINGTON WAY

THE LINKS

HERMITAGE DR

ASCOT TOWERS

WINDSOR RD

JUBILEE AVE

JUBILEE GDNS

KENNEL AVE

DAWNAY DR

WALTON DR

CHURCHILL RD

A332

KENNEL RIDE

KENNEL WOOD

HUNTSMAN'S

NURSERY LA

WOOLCOTE PL

CROCKER CT

4

Mast

P

HARVEST RIDE

LILY HILL RD

MILMAN CL

HAWKINS CL

B3430

Heathfield Sch

Hotel

The Brackens

LILY HILL GN

CLAYHILL CL

NEW FOREST RIDE

BOG LA

LAVENDER PK

FOREST CL

Licensed Victuallers Sch

AUDLEY WAY

THE LAWNS

LONDON RD

HALLEY DR

GAINSBOROUGH DR

LOCKTON CHASE

Ascot Race Course

HIGH ST A329

69

Hereford House

P

Englemere Pond Nature Trail

Woodstock

Englemere Pond

KING'S RIDE

GRASMERE PK

Englemere

LC

H

Heatherwood

3

Whitmoor Bog

RG12

Sewage Wks

Three Castles Path

B3017

WINDSOR RIDE

PRINCE CONSORT DR

SL5

King's Ride House

PRINCE ALBERT DR

Green Acres

CARROLL CRES

BEAUMONT CT

BOULDISH FARM RD

KINROSS CT

LIDDELL WAY

KINGS RD

68

Icehouse Hill

Blacksmith's Hill

SWINLEY RD

Passmore's Plantation

CROWN COTTS

Kingsride

WOODLANDS RIDE

WOODLANDS CL

P

2

Swinley Park

BLANE'S LA

67

Blane's Allotment

Tower Hill

Buttersteep Hill

Buttersteep Allotments

Swinley Forest

CH

BODENS RIDE

TINNAIR DR

1

Bright's Allotment

A332

BUTTERSTEEP RISE

Buttersteep House

66

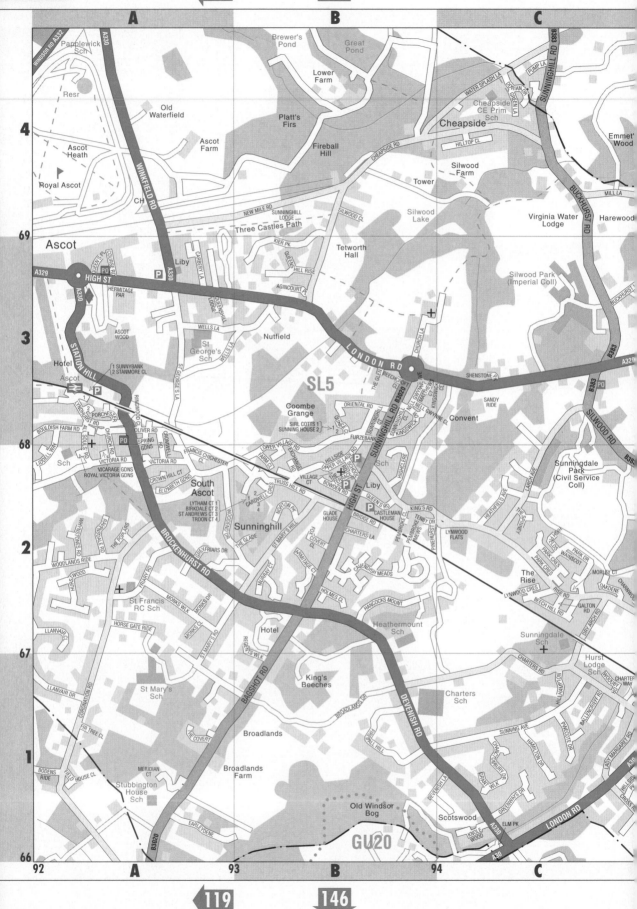

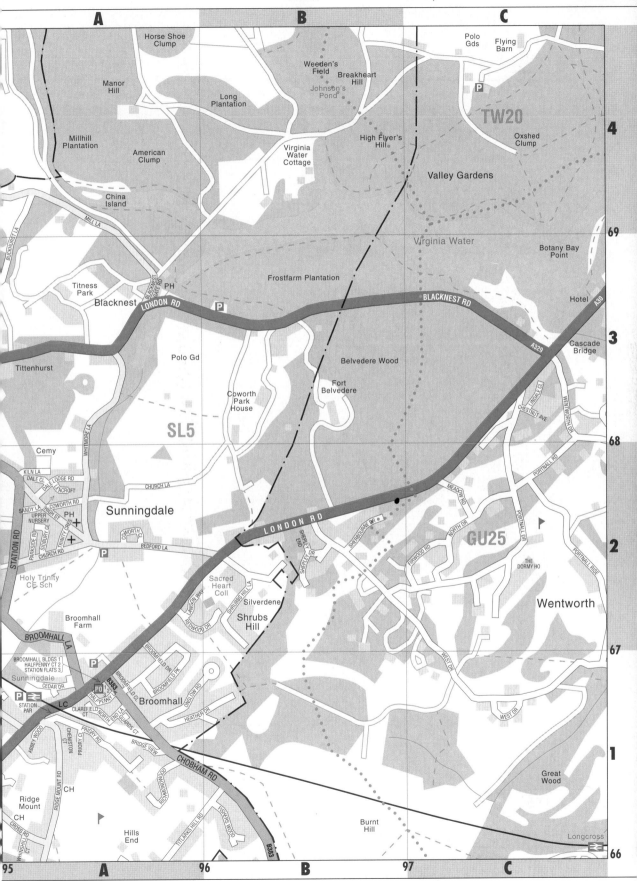

A B C

TW20

Egham Wick
Plantations

Wick
Pond

Totem
Pole

4

Woodlee

Virginia Water
Plantations

American
Comm Sch

GLENWOOD

WOODLEE
CL

Callow
Hill

Great
Wood

Whitehall
Farm

Stroude

The
Dell

Highmoor
Farm

69

The Clockcase

Christchurch
CE Fst Sch

CHRISTCHURCH
COTTS

VIRGINIA
BEECHES

HOLLOW LA

Merlewood

PIPER'S END

Stroude
Farm

Allot
Gdns

The
Royal Standard
(PH)

3

Virginia
Water

GORSE HILL RD

HEATH RISE

HEATH CL

TROTSWORTH AVE

St Ann's
Heath

Home
Farm

WOODSIDE WAY

STUART WAY

WAVERLEY DR

QUENTIN WAY

SPRING WOODS

OW LA

WOODLANDS RD W

WOODLANDS RD

WOODLANDS AVE

CHRISTCHURCH RD

MORELLA CL

Virginia Water
Prep Sch

TROTSWORTH
CT

GORSE

Generals
Copse

PINEWOOD RD

STAYNE END

LAKE RD

ABBEY DR

BROCK WAY

VIRGINIA DR

FRIARS RD

STATION APP

MONKS RD

ABBEY RD

STATION

Liby

68

Broom
Hill

Wentworth
Club

CH

WENTWORTH DR

KEEPERS
TERR

BADGERS HILL

VIRGINIA
AVE

OAKWOOD RD

NUNS WLK

KEEPERS WLK

THE CLOSE

St Ann's
Heath
Cty Mid Sch

GU25

The Bourne

Virginia
Water

IMPERIAL
HOUSE

Waterloo
Bridge

2

HEATHERSIDE DR

EAST DR

WOODSTONE CL

WELLINGTON AVE

BACON CRES

HARPESFORD AVE

CABRERA AVE

HILLSIDE

CABRERA CL

Trumps Green
Cty Fst Sch

RICHMOND

BEECHMONT AVE

BOURNE RD

1 FAIRVIEW COTTS
2 THE PARADE

M3

67

Harpesford

CROWN RD

TITHE CL

TRUMPSGREEN RD

THE MOUNT

CROWN LA

FURNIVAL

MOUNT CL

Trumps
Green

LYNE RD

BRIDGE LA

LYNE CL

HARROW BOTTOM RD

The
Stag & Hounds
(PH)

OAK TREE CL

PORTNALL RISE

BOURNESIDE

WEST DR

SOUTH DR

Knowle
Hill

KNOWLE GROVE CL

KNOWLE GR

KNOWLE HILL

CORVE GDNS

Knowle
Grove

Trumps
Farm

LYNE PLACE
MANOR

LYNE
CT

1

Westwood

BEECHWOOD RD

Beech
Wood

Knowle
Hill

KT16

Hersham
Copse

66

Works

Longcross
Bridge

CHOBHAM LA

KITSMEAD LA

Works

M3

Works

98 A 99 B 00 C

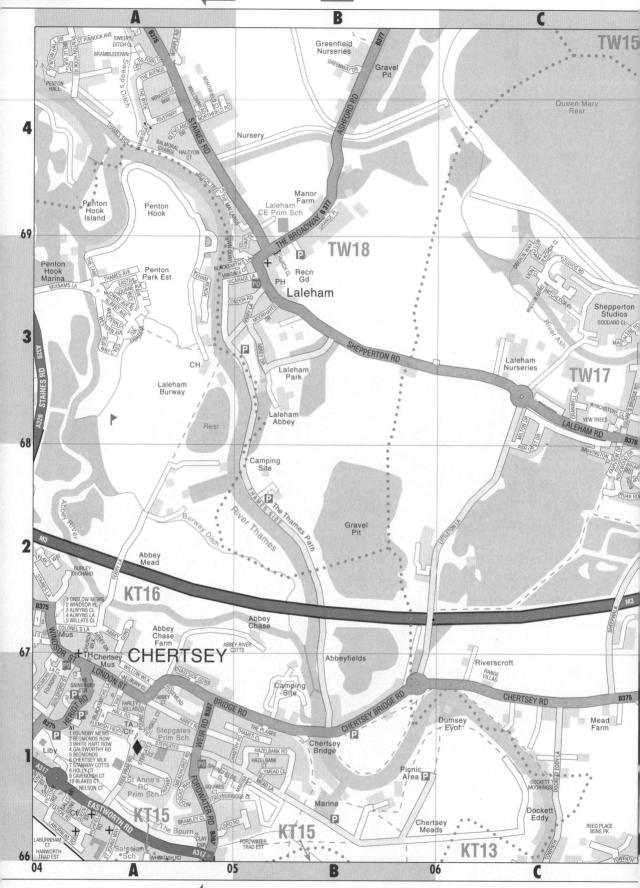

TW15

A B C

Greenfield
Nurseries

Gravel
Pit

Queen Mary
Resr

4

Nursery

Manor
Farm

Laleham
CE Prim Sch

69

TW18

Laleham

Shepperton
Studios

GODDARD CL

Recn
Gd

PH

3

Laleham
Nurseries

TW17

CH

SHEPPERTON RD

Laleham
Burway

Laleham
Park

LALEHAM RD

B376

Resr

Laleham
Abbey

68

Camping
Site

The Thames Side

Gravel
Pit

2

M3

Abbey
Mead

M3

KT16

Abbey Chase

Abbey
Chase
Farm

ABBEY RIVER COTTS

67

1 ONSLOW MEWS
2 WINDSOR PL
3 ALWYNS CL
4 ALWYNS LA
5 WILLATS CL

CHERTSEY
Mus

Abbeyfields

Camping
Site

Riverscroft

RANGE
VILLAS

CHERTSEY

LONDON ST

BRIDGE RD

CHERTSEY BRIDGE RD

CHERTSEY RD

B375

Dumsey
Eyot

Mead
Farm

1 FOUNDRY MEWS
2 BEOMONDS ROW
3 WHITE HART ROW
4 GALSWORTHY RD
5 BEOMONDS
6 CHERTSEY WLK
7 STANWAY COTTS
8 HOLLY CT
9 CAVENDISH CT
10 BLAKES CT

Liby

Stepgates
Prim Sch

TA Ctr

Chertsey
Bridge

Picnic
Area

DOCKETT
MOORINGS

Dockett
Eddy

1

St Anne's
RC
Prim Sch

Marina

Chertsey
Meads

REED PLACE
BSNS PK

A317

EASTWORTH RD

KT15

The Bourn

KT15

KT13

Salesian
Sch

FORDWATER
TRAD EST

TOWPATH

66

04 A 05 B 06 C

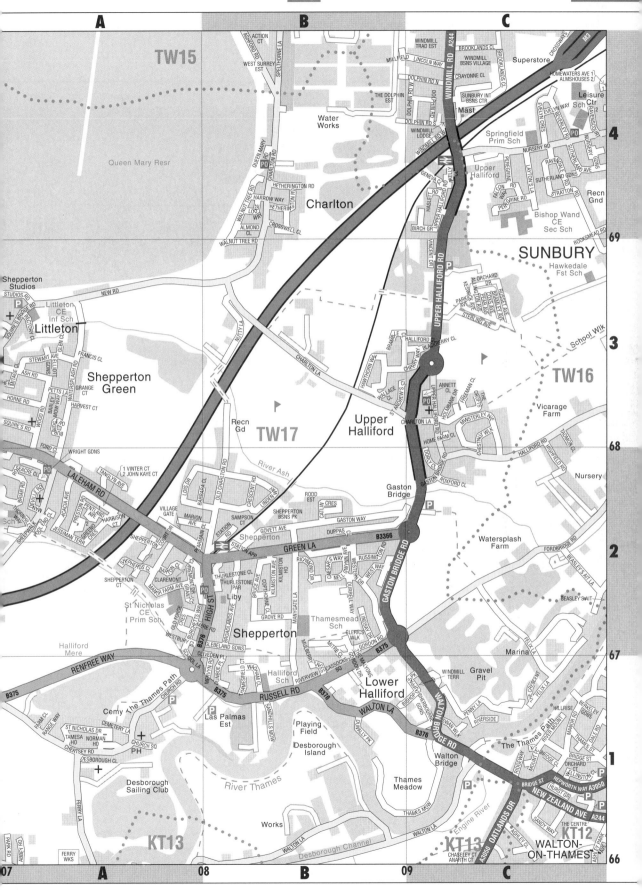

A   B   C

A338

Anvilles

Upper Slope End Farm

Upper Slope End

Hightree Copse

Elm Copse

Totterdown House

Prosperous Home Farm

Lower Slope End Farm

The Heath

The Gully

Middle Copse

RG17

Kiln Copse

Anville's Copse

Great Sadler's Copse

SADLERS RD

SIX ACRE LA

A338

Daniel's La

SN8

Mount Prosperous

Bitham La

BITHAM LA

CUTTING HILL

CUTTING HILL

Happy Valley Nursery

Lower Spray Farm

Cowley's Copse

Lower Spray Copse

HAM RD

THE SEVERALLS

SPRAY RD

Dove's Farm

ACORN COTTS

Ham Spray Farm

Field La

Crown & Anchor (PH)

SN8

Ham Spray House

63

CHURCH RD

Manor House

Ham

The Lynch

Eastcourt Farm

Inwood Copse

Manor Farm

Ham Hill

A
B
C

4

65

3

64

63

1

62

35
A
36
B
37
C

Totterdown Copse

INKPEN RD

Templeton Border

High Trees

St Cassian's

Catmore Copse

Winterly Copse

WINTERLY LA

Titcomb Manor

New Templeton Gorse

Cherrytree Copse

Pond Close

Follygully Copse

Titcomb

BACK LA

Little Common

The Firs

SADLERS RD

Finch's Copse

Balsdon Farm

Blandy's Corner

Pondgully Wood

Holly Copse

Titcomb Farm

Sadlers

Clayground Copse

CRAVEN RD

Moss Farm

Vale Farm

The Swan Inn (PH)

Northcroft Farm

The Folly

The Folly

Inkpen Prim Sch

WEAVERS LA

KINTBURY RD

Fox Hill

FOLLY RD

ROBINS HILL

BRACKEN COPSE

THE OLD SAWMILLS

Gully Copse

The Plantation

Great Plantation

Lower Green

Sands Dro

Manor Farm

Inkpen

POTTERY LA

POST OFFICE RD

THE FIRS

BITHAM LA

RG17

Wergs Barn

The Wansdyke

The Drove

SPRAY RD

BUNGUM LA

Ingles Edge

Rolf's Farm

PH

Trapshill

Upper Green

Kirby Farm

BELL LA

Rookery Copse

Kirby House

Red Woods

Oldlands Copse

SN8

Gallows Down

Combe Gibbet

Little Rivar Copse

Inkpen Hill

Test Way

Wayfarers Wlk

RG20

Rivar Copse

P

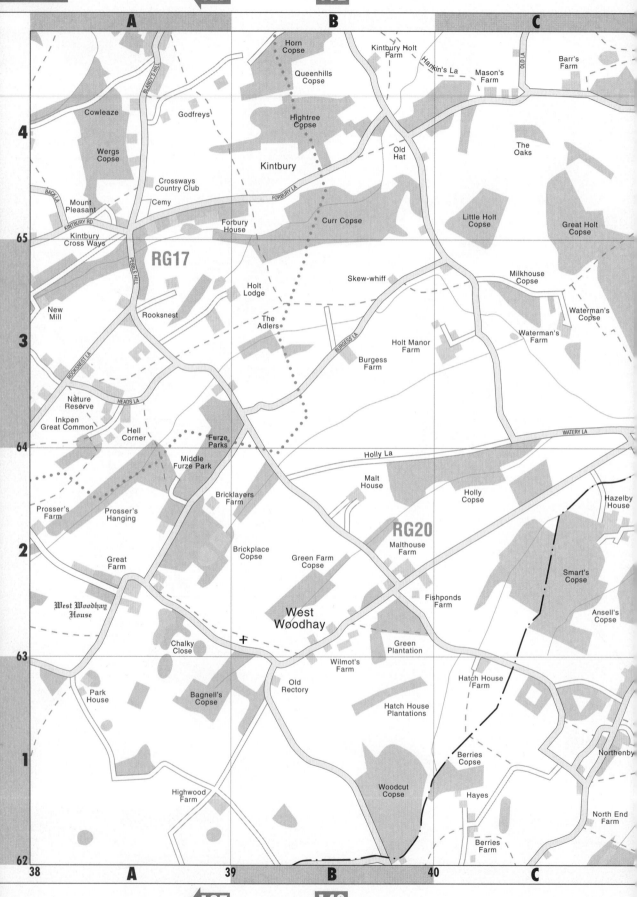

A **B** **C**

Horn Copse

Kintbury Holt Farm

Hankin's La

Mason's Farm

Old La

Barr's Farm

Queenhills Copse

Cowleaze

Godfreys

Hightree Copse

The Oaks

4

Wergs Copse

Old Hat

BACK LA

Crossways Country Club

Kintbury

FORBURY LA

Little Holt Copse

Great Holt Copse

Mount Pleasant

Cemy

KINTBURY RD

Forbury House

Curr Copse

65

Kintbury Cross Ways

Skew-whiff

Milkhouse Copse

PEBBLE HILL

RG17

Holt Lodge

Waterman's Copse

New Mill

Rooksnest

The Adlers

BURGESS LA

Holt Manor Farm

Waterman's Farm

Waterman's Farm

3

ROOKSNEST LA

Burgess Farm

HEADS LA

Nature Reserve

Inkpen Great Common

Hell Corner

Furze Parks

WATERY LA

64

Middle Furze Park

Holly La

Malt House

Hazelby House

Bricklayers Farm

Holly Copse

Prosser's Farm

Prosser's Hanging

Brickplace Copse

Green Farm Copse

RG20

Malthouse Farm

Smart's Copse

2

Great Farm

Ansell's Copse

West Woodhay House

West Woodhay

Fishponds Farm

Chalky Close

Green Plantation

63

Wilmot's Farm

Hatch House Farm

Park House

Bagnell's Copse

Old Rectory

Hatch House Plantations

Northenby

1

Berries Copse

Highwood Farm

Woodcut Copse

Hayes

North End Farm

Berries Farm

62

38   **A**   39   **B**   40   **C**

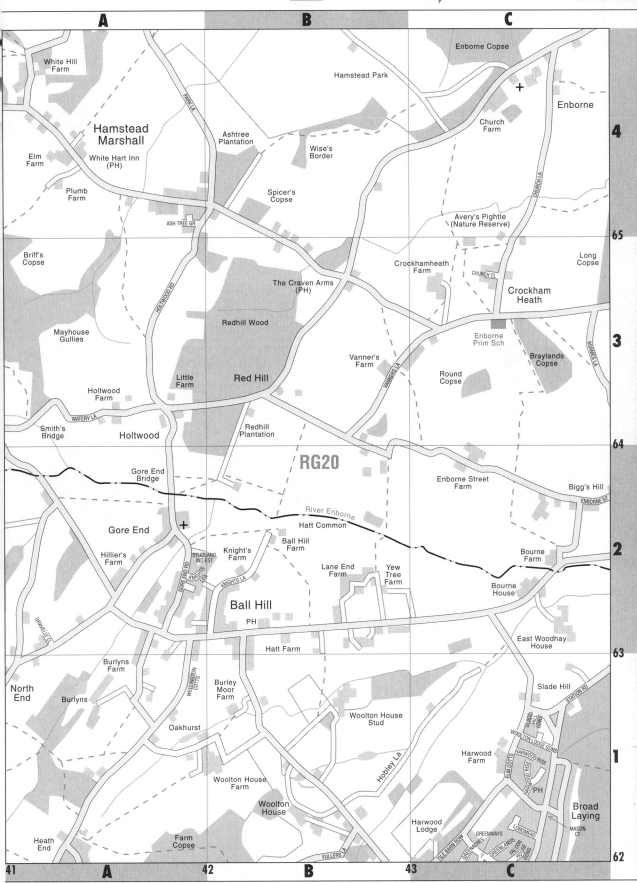

White Hill Farm

Hamstead Park

Enborne Copse

Enborne

Hamstead Marshall

Church Farm

Ashtree Plantation

Elm Farm

White Hart Inn (PH)

Wise's Border

4

Plumb Farm

Spicer's Copse

ASH TREE GR

Avery's Pightle (Nature Reserve)

Long Copse

65

Briff's Copse

Crockhamheath Farm

CHURCH CL

The Craven Arms (PH)

Crockham Heath

Mayhouse Gullies

HOLTWOOD RD

Redhill Wood

Enborne Prim Sch

Braylands Copse

3

CHURCH LA

Little Farm

Red Hill

Vanner's Farm

VANNERS LA

Round Copse

BOAMES LA

Holtwood Farm

WATERY LA

HoltwoodRedhill Plantation

Smith's Bridge

Holtwood

Redhill Plantation

64

RG20

Gore End Bridge

Enborne Street Farm

Bigg's Hill

ENBORNE ST

River Enborne

Hatt Common

Gore End

Ball Hill Farm

Bourne Farm

2

Hillier's Farm

STUDLAND IND EST

GORE END RD

KNIGHTS LA

Knight's Farm

Lane End Farm

Yew Tree Farm

Bourne House

GRAVELLY CL

Ball Hill

PH

East Woodhay House

63

North End

Burlyns Farm

WELLINGTON COTTS

Hatt Farm

Slade Hill

STATION RD

Burlyns

Burley Moor Farm

SLADE HILL GDNS

WOOLTON LODGE GDNS

Oakhurst

Woolton House Stud

HARWOOD RISE

Harwood Farm

HARWOOD RISE

ELM COTTS

PH

1

Woolton House Farm

Hobley La

Harwood Lodge

LONGMEAD

Broad Laying

MASON CT

Heath End

Farm Copse

Woolton House

Harwood Lodge

TILE BARN ROW

GREENACRES

GREENWAYS

GREENLANDS

FALCON HOUSE GDNS

62

FULLERS LA

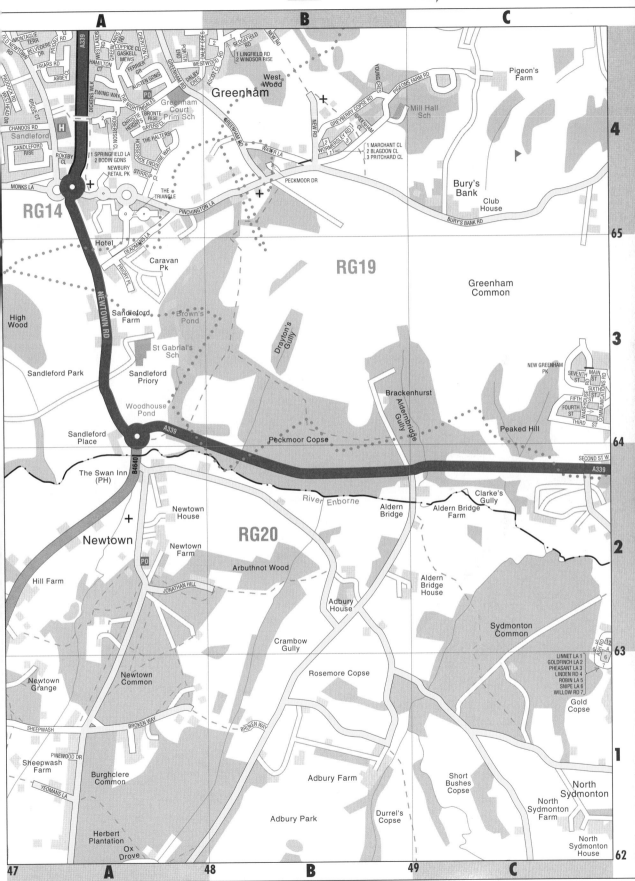

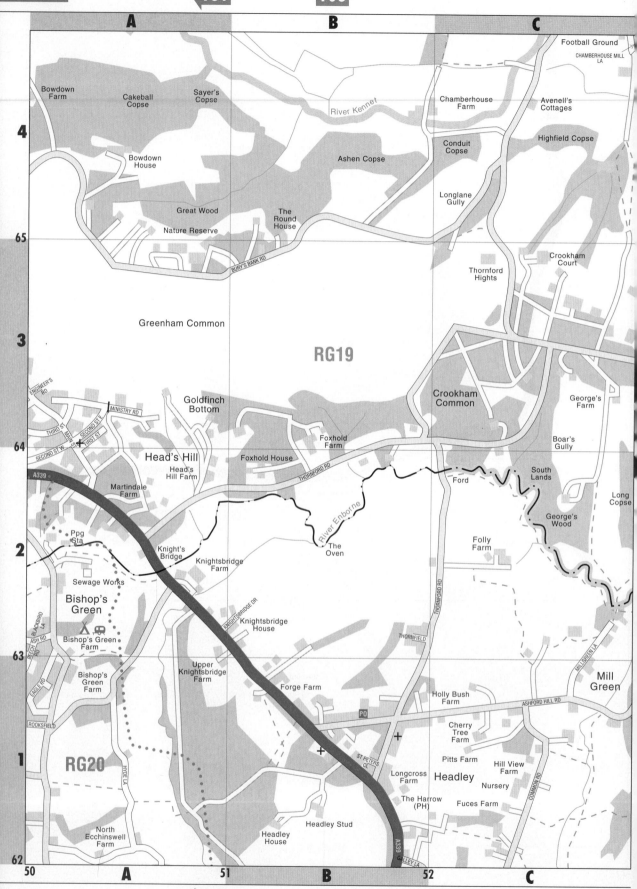

A · B · C

Football Ground
CHAMBERHOUSE MILL LA

Bowdown Farm
Cakeball Copse
Sayer's Copse
Chamberhouse Farm
Avenell's Cottages

4

Bowdown House
Highfield Copse

River Kennet
Ashen Copse
Conduit Copse

Longlane Gully

65

Great Wood
Nature Reserve
The Round House
Crookham Court

Thornford Hights

BURY'S BANK RD

Greenham Common
Thornford Hights

3

RG19
Crookham Common

George's Farm

ENGINEER'S RD
Goldfinch Bottom
Boar's Gully

MINISTRY RD
SECOND ST E
FIRST ST
THIRD ST
MAIN ST
SECOND ST
Foxhold Farm

64

SECOND ST W
Head's Hill
Foxhold House
THORNFORD RD
Ford
South Lands

Head's Hill Farm
Long Copse

A339
Martindale Farm
George's Wood

Ppg Sta
River Enborne
Folly Farm

2

Sewage Works
Knight's Bridge
Knightsbridge Farm
The Oven
THORNFORD RD

BLACKBIRD LA
Bishop's Green
KNIGHTSBRIDGE DR
Knightsbridge House
THORNFIELD

ASH RD
Bishop's Green Farm
MILL GREEN LA

63

BEECH RD
Upper Knightsbridge Farm
Mill Green

EAGLE RD
Bishop's Green Farm
Forge Farm
Holly Bush Farm
ASHFORD HILL RD

ROOKSFIELD
PO
Cherry Tree Farm
COMMON RD

1

RG20
HYDE LA
ST PETERS CL
Pitts Farm
Hill View Farm

Longcross Farm
Headley
Nursery

North Ecchinswell Farm
The Harrow (PH)
Fuces Farm

62

Headley House
Headley Stud
A339
GALLEY LA

50 · A · 51 · B · 52 · C

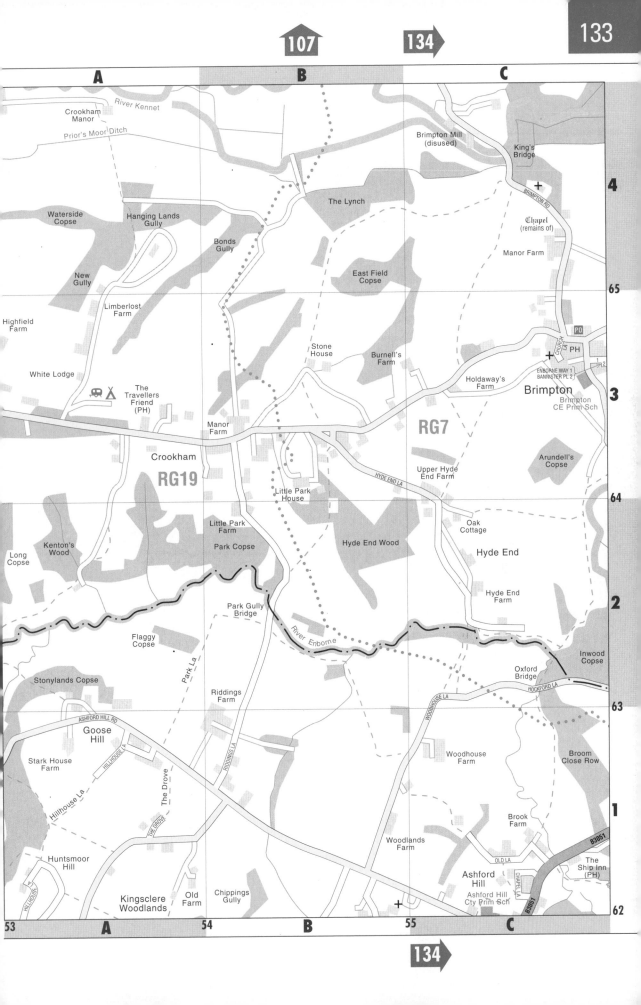

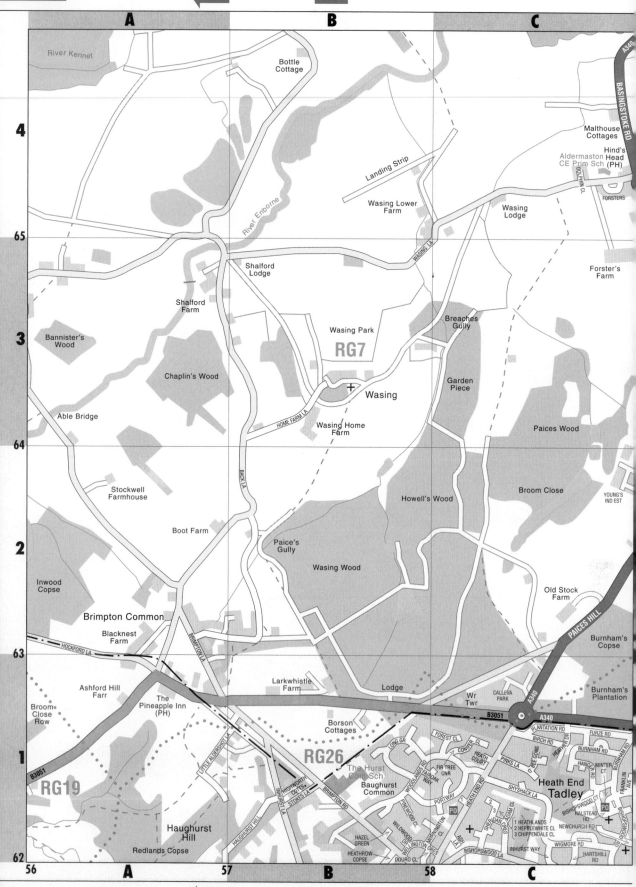

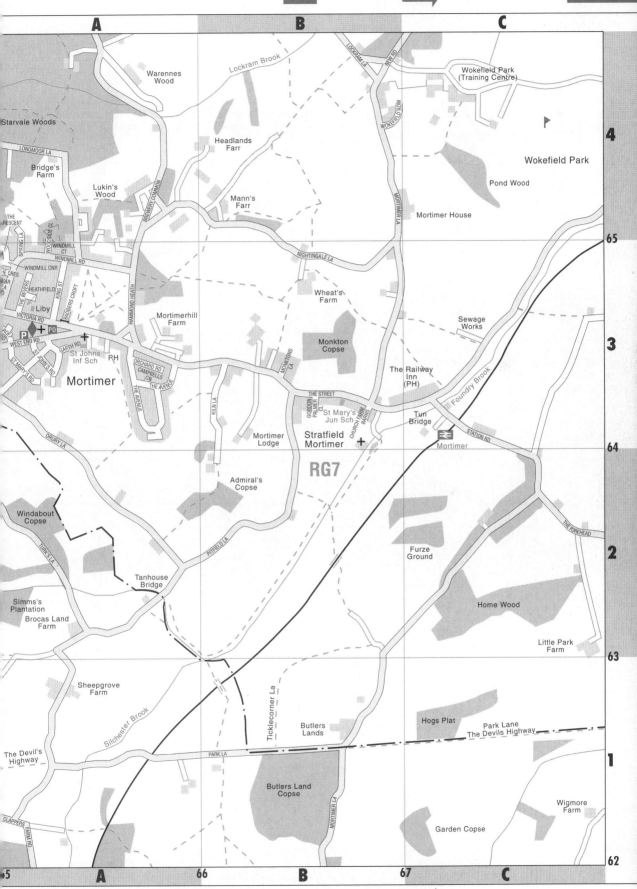

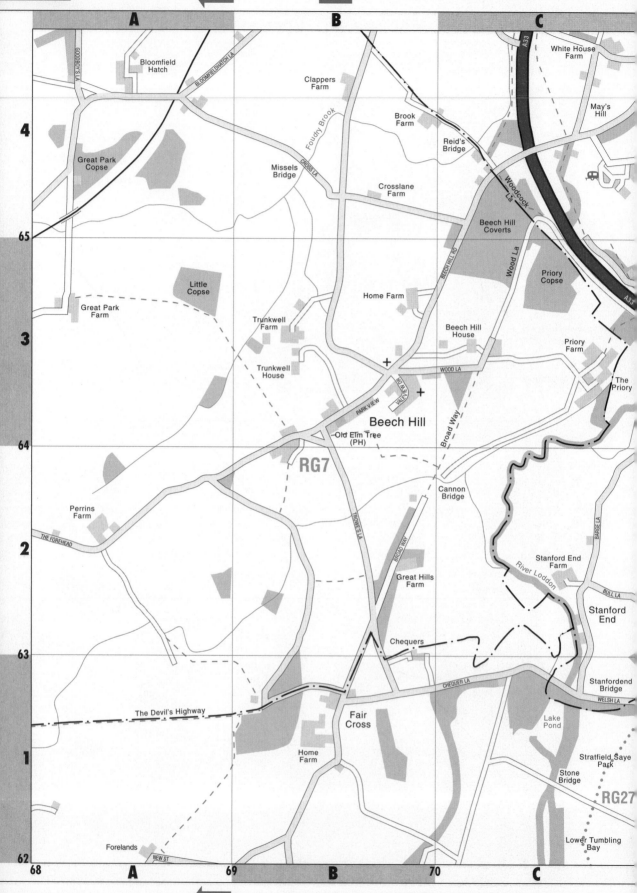

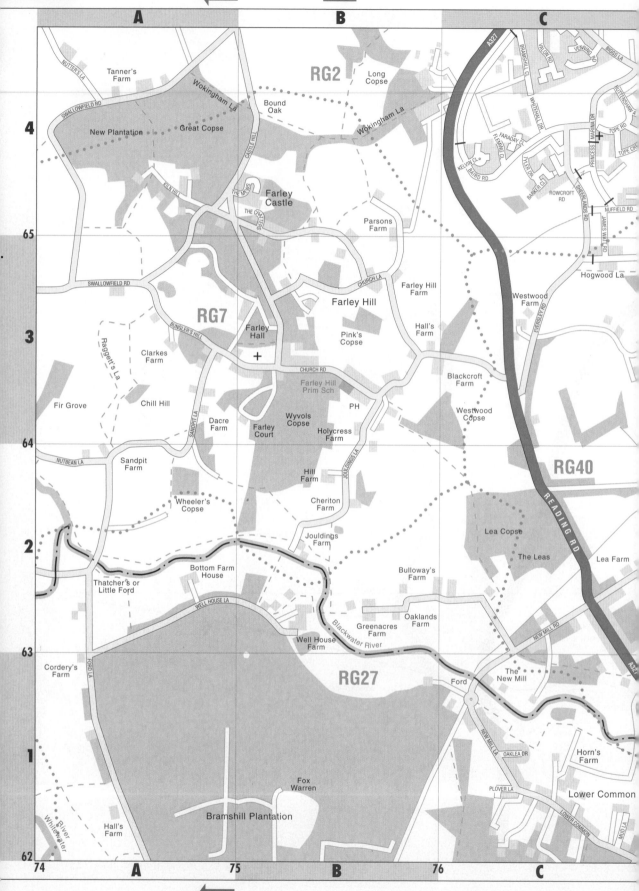

A   B   C

RG2

Long Copse

Tanner's Farm

Nutter's La

Wokingham La

Bound Oak

Swallowfield Rd

New Plantation

Great Copse

4

Castle Hill

Kiln Hill

The Veins

Farley Castle

The Chalets

Wokingham La

A327

Bramshill Cl

Valom Rd

Venning Rd

Biggs La

Buttenshaw A

Whitehall Dr

Faraday Cl

Fleming Cl

Princes Rd

Marina Dr

Tope Rd

Tope Cres

65

Parsons Farm

Kelvin Cl

Baird Rd

Barker Cl

Tyler Dr

Rowcroft Rd

Sherlands Rd

James Watt Rd

Nuffield Rd

Church La

Farley Hill Farm

Swallowfield Rd

RG7

Raggett's La

Bungler's Hill

Farley Hill

Hall's Farm

Hogwood La

Westwood Farm

Eversley Rd

3

Clarkes Farm

Farley Hall

Pink's Copse

Blackcroft Farm

+

Church Rd

Chill Hill

Sandpit La

Fir Grove

Dacre Farm

Farley Hill Prim Sch

Farley Court

Wyvols Copse

Holycross Farm

PH

Westwood Copse

64

Nutbean La

Sandpit Farm

Hill Farm

Jouldings La

RG40

READING RD

Wheeler's Copse

Cheriton Farm

Lea Copse

2

Jouldings Farm

The Leas

Lea Farm

Bottom Farm House

Thatcher's or Little Ford

Bulloway's Farm

Well House La

Blackwater River

Greenacres Farm

Oaklands Farm

New Mill Rd

63

Cordery's Farm

Well House Farm

RG27

Ford

The New Mill

New Mill La

A321

Ford La

Oaklea Dr

Horn's Farm

1

Plover La

Lower Common

Fox Warren

Mill La

River Whitewater

Hall's Farm

Bramshill Plantation

Lower Common

62

74   75   76

A   B   C

A   B   C

Model
Farm

Rook's Nest
Farm

Rifle Range

Mus

RG2

Arborfield
Garrison

Moor
Farm

Windmill
Farm

California Country
Park

Long Moor
Bog

Longmoor
Lake

Long Moor

Longmoor
Farm

Coleshill
Farm

Gorse Ride
Cty Jun Sch

Briarwood

Greenacres
Farm

Nine Mile Ride

Warren La

Warren
Lodge

Nine Mile Ride
Prim Sch

Hogwood
Farm

Industrial
Estate

Shepperlands
Copse

Wheatlands
Farm

Furze
Hill

White Horse La

RG40

Larchwood
Farm

Church
Farm

PH

Ridge
Farm

Wick Hill La

64

The Devil's Highway

West Court

Manor
House

North
Court

Wheatlands
Manor

Church La

B3348

2

Park
Farm

Rectory
Farm

East
Court

Manor
Farm

Finchampstead
CE Prim Sch

PH

ROMAN
MILESTONE

Banisters
Farm

Agates
Meadow

THE VILLAGE

Longwater La

63

FLEET HILL

Fleet Copse

Finchampstead

Reading Rd

The Rise

B3348

The Tally Ho
(PH)

Fleet La

Fleethill
Farm

Longwater La

Longwater Rd

Burnmoor Mdw

Lower
Sandhurst
Rd

1

Eversley
Bridge

Eversley St

Eversley

Long Water

Finchampstead
Bridge

Dray Stables
Farm

Warbrook La

Blackwater River

RG27

62

7   78   A   B   79   C

141 116

141 149

A **B** **C**

A322

Gormoor
Farm

Penny
Hill

Gravel
Hill

Caesar's
Camp

Pudding
Hill

Mill
Pond

4

Three Castles Path

RG12

New England
Hill

65

Wickham
Bushes

Roman Star
or
Upper Star Post

The Devil's Highway

3

DANGER AREA

Windsor Ride

DANGER AREA

GU19

FORESTERS WAY

A3095

Lower Star
Post

64

RG45

DANGER AREA

Wishmoor
Cross

2

Poppy
Hills

Deer Rock
Hill

DANGER AREA

GU15

63

Paschal
Wood

Windsor Bottom

GU47

Olddean
Common

1

DANGER AREA

WINDSOR RIDE

Saddleback
Hill

P

HIGHVIEW CRES
WIMBLEDON CL
BERKSHIRE RD
WAVERLEY RD
BRACKNE
CL

The Devil's
Pound

MATTHEWS RD
KING'S RIDE
QUEEN ELIZABETH RD
DUKE OF CORNWALL
AVE

Sch

62

86 **A** 87 **B** 88 **C**

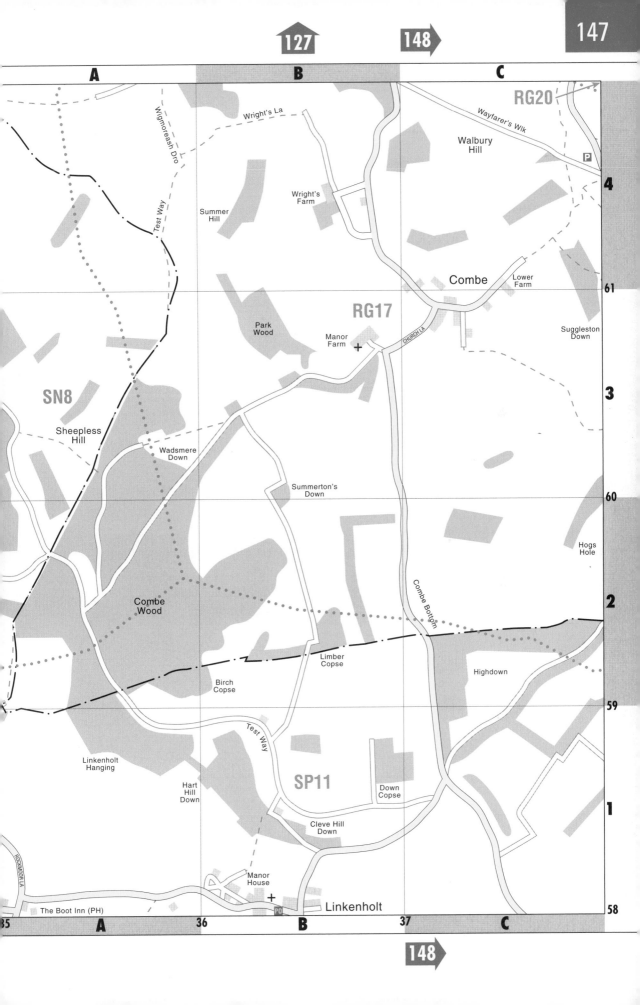

A B C

RG20

Wayfarer's Wlk

Wright's La

Wigmoreash Dro

Test Way

Walbury
Hill

P

4

Summer
Hill

Wright's
Farm

Combe

Lower
Farm

61

RG17

Park
Wood

Manor
Farm

CHURCH LA

Suggleston
Down

SN8

Sheepless
Hill

Wadsmere
Down

3

Summerton's
Down

60

Combe
Wood

Hogs
Hole

Combe Bottom

2

Limber
Copse

Highdown

Birch
Copse

59

Test Way

Linkenholt
Hanging

SP11

Down
Copse

Hart
Hill
Down

1

Cleve Hill
Down

ROCKMOOR LA

Manor
House

The Boot Inn (PH)

PO

Linkenholt

58

A B C

35 36 37

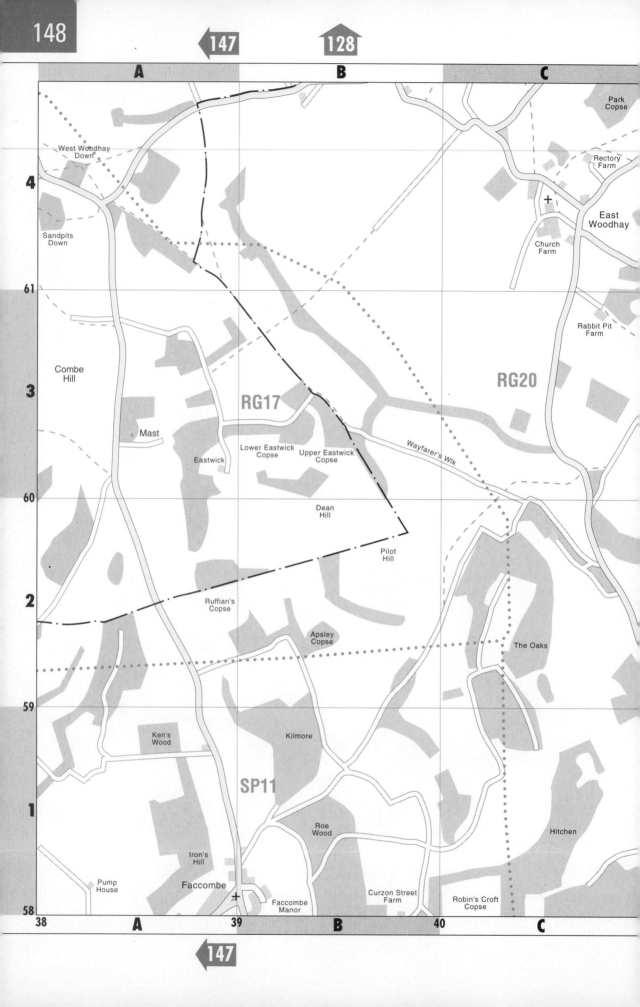

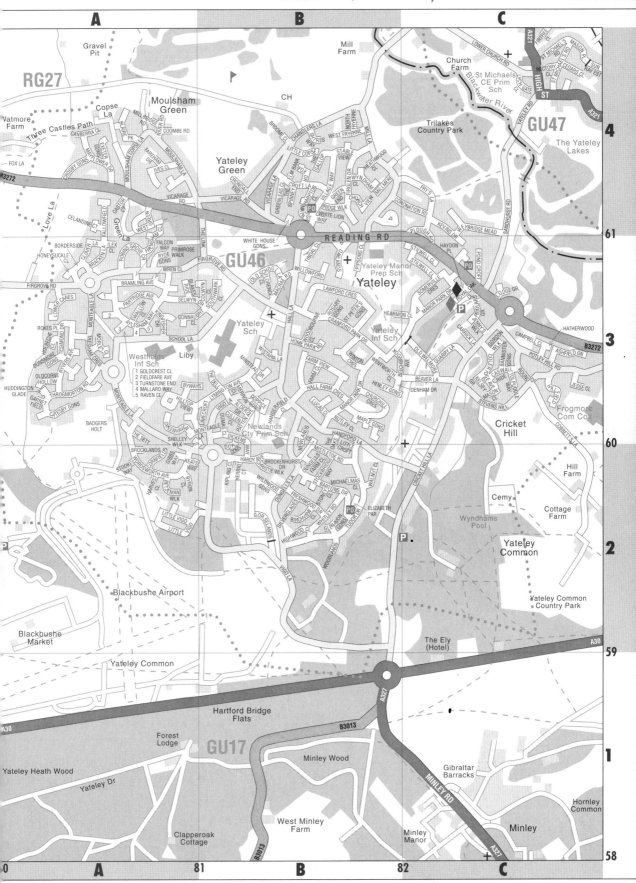

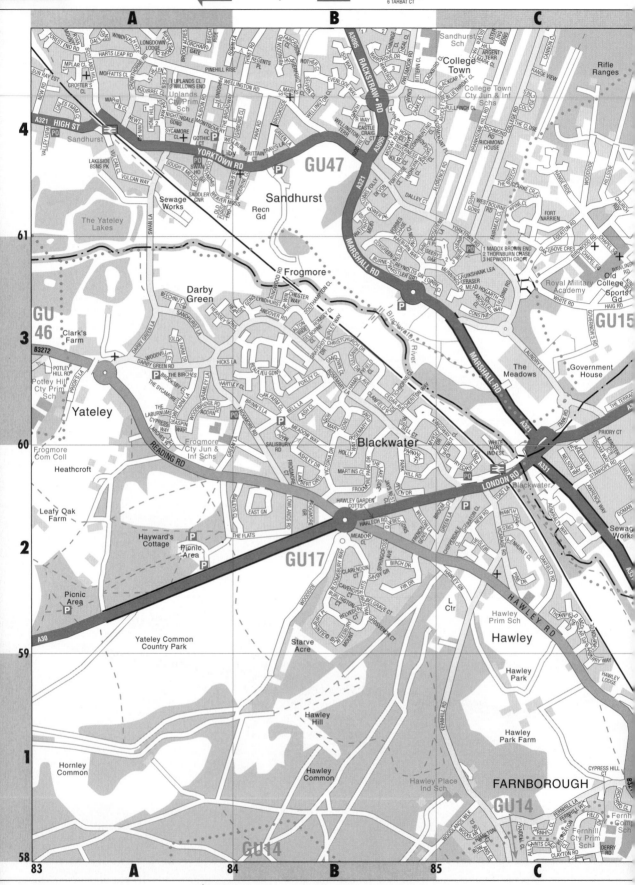

149
143

B4
1 MULBERRY CL
2 MAY CL
3 SHRIVENHAM CL
4 CENTURION CL
5 CHAFFINCH CL
6 TARBAT CT
7 ROCKFIELD WAY
8 BALINTORE CT

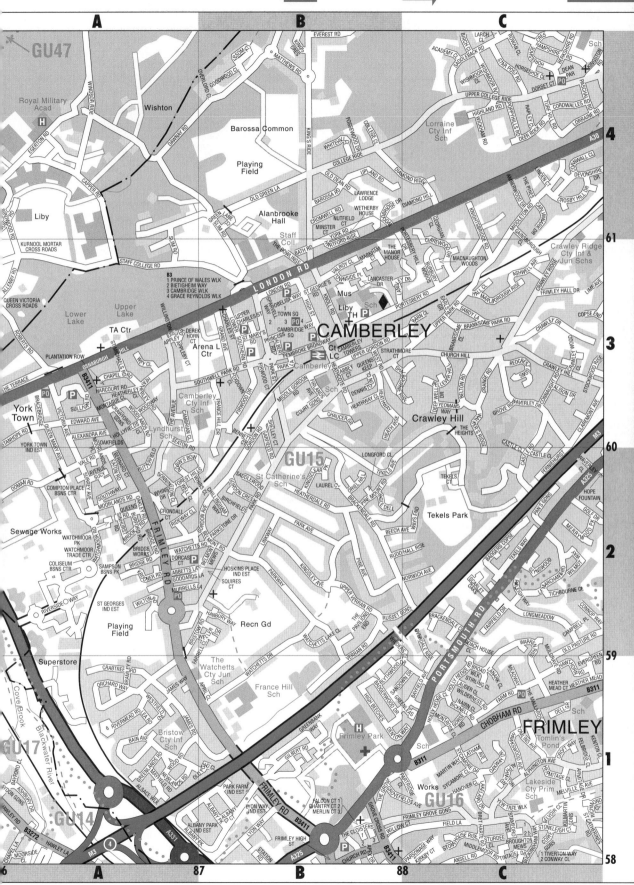

A   B   C

FOX COVERT
CLASPRINGS
MALLARDS
MACDONALD RD
RIDGEWAY PL
RYDAL PL
OAKLEIGH
RIVERSIDE AVE
WYCHELM
PARNHAM
AVE
MANSWOOD DR

MAPLE
DR
AMBLESIDE RD
CK DR
DERWENT
LIGHTWATER RD
SPRINGFIELD
BLACKSTROUD LA
SUNDEW CL
Brooklands
Farm

BLACKSTROUD LA E

HOOKSTONE LA
Halebourne
Farm

OAKWOOD
MYRTLE
CL
COLVILLE GDNS
GUILDFORD RD
HERONSCOURT

A319

OSBORNE DR
NORTHEY
LIGHTWATER MDW
Turf
Hill
Windlemere
Golf Ctr.
CH

DEER LEAP
BLUEBELL
RISE
BURDOCK
COLDHARBOUR
LA
BAGSHOT RD
WINDLESHAM RD
STREETS HEATH RD
BENNER WAY

4

RED RD
B311
A319
A322
COUNCIL
COTTS
FAIRFIELD LA

DANGER AREA
GU18
New
England
Sandpit
Hill
Gordon's
Sch
STREETS HEATH
OLDACRE
HATHOUSE LA
COMMONFIELDS

Grayspot
Hill
Cuckoo
Hill
TANGLEWOOD RIDE
PO
61

DANGER
AREA
BIRCH LA
PH
FENNSCOMBE CT
OAKCROFT
West
End

Westend Common
ASHLEY WAY
CUCKOO VALE
BROADFORD LA
BROAD ST
BRENTMOOR RD
RUBUS CL
RIBGENIA
KERRIA
CAMELLIA
CT
ACER DR
FIELD
END
WILLOW
GN
FELLOW GN
SEFTON CL

Pirbright Ranges
Donkey
Town
BIRCH PLATT
ROUNCE LA
HOLLY
RIDGE
BURNET
ROSA4
VIBURNUM
FUCHSIA WY
FENNS LA
MAHONIA CL
KINGS
RD

HOOK LA
Rounce
Farm
Fenns
Farm
3

Hagthorn Bog
PRIEST LA
Trulley Brook
Lucas
Green
Nurseries

Dog Hill
GU24
Lucas Green
FORD RD
SCHOOL CL
60

Strawberry
Bottom
Works
White Cott
Farm
Lucas Green
Farm
Hall
CHURCH LA
P

Brock
Hill
LUCAS GREEN
Bisley
Nursery

Straight
Oak
Peatmoor
Pond
PO
2

GU15
Bayfield
SHAFTESBURY RD
COTTS OF CL
ARETHUSA WAY
SOUTH RD

Round
Butt
DANGER AREA
Furze
Farm
HM Prison
59

Colony
Bog
Bullhousen
Farm

DANGER AREA
Pirbright Common
Bisley
Common
Miles
Green

GU16
Bisley
Ranges
Polledoak
Slade
DANGER
AREA
GU21
Chaseley
1

Mainstone Bottom
DANGER AREA
Hog
Lees
Staffordlake
STAFFORD LAKE
58

92   A   93   B   94   C

Index

Street names are listed alphabetically and show the locality, the Postcode District, the page number and a reference to the square in which the name falls on the map page

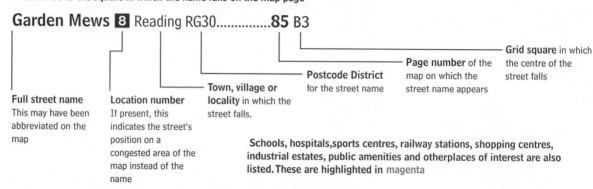

Schools, hospitals, sports centres, railway stations, shopping centres, industrial estates, public amenities and other places of interest are also listed. These are highlighted in magenta

Abbreviations used in the index

App	Approach	Cl	Close	Espl	Esplanade	N	North	S	South
Arc	Arcade	Comm	Common	Est	Estate	Orch	Orchard	Sq	Square
Ave	Avenue	Cnr	Corner	Gdns	Gardens	Par	Parade	Strs	Stairs
Bvd	Boulevard	Cotts	Cottages	Gn	Green	Pk	Park	Stps	Steps
Bldgs	Buildings	Ct	Court	Gr	Grove	Pas	Passage	St	Street, Saint
Bsns Pk	Business Park	Ctyd	Courtyard	Hts	Heights	Pl	Place	Terr	Terrace
Bsns Ctr	Business Centre	Cres	Crescent	Ind Est	Industrial	Prec	Precinct	Trad	Trading Est
Bglws	Bungalows	Dr	Drive		Estate	Prom	Promenade	Wlk	Walk
Cswy	Causeway	Dro	Drove	Intc	Interchange	Ret Pk	Retail Park	W	West
Ctr	Centre	E	East	Junc	Junction	Rd	Road	Yd	Yard
Cir	Circus	Emb	Embankment	La	Lane	Rdbt	Roundabout		

Town and village index

Aldermaston	135 A3	Chilton	10 B4	Harlington	71 A1
Aldworth	32 A2	Chilton Foliat	73 A4	Harmondsworth	70 A2
Arborfield	114 B1	Cholsey	14 A4	Hatton	71 B1
Ascot	120 A1	Cold Ash	106 A4	Headley	132 C1
Ashampstead	54 A3	Colnbrook	69 A3	Henley-on-T	15 A2
Ashford	97 A3	Combe	147 C3	Hermitage	79 A1
Aston Tirrold	12 C4	Compton	31 B2	Holyport	65 A4
Bagshot	145 B1	Cookham	20 A3	Horton	69 A1
Ball Hill	129 C1	Crowthorne	143 A3	Hungerford	100 A2
Barkham	115 A1	Datchet	68 A3	Hungerford Newtown	74 A2
Beech Hill	138 A1	Dorney	41 A2	Hurley	17 A1
Beedon	51 B4	Earley	87 A1	Hurst	88 B2
Beenham	108 C3	East Bedfont	98 A3	Inkpen	127 B2
Binfield	90 A1	East Garston	47 A2	Iver	44 A3
Bisham	18 A1	East Isley	30 A3	Iver Heath	23 B1
Bisley	153 C2	Egham	96 A1	Kintbury	102 A1
Blackwater	150 A2	Englefield Green	95 A1	Knowl Hill	37 A3
Blewbury	12 A3	Eton	67 B4	Laleham	124 A4
Bourne End	3 A1	Farnborough (Berks)	28 A4	Lambourn	25 A1
Boxford	76 A1	Farnborough (Hants)	150 C1	Leckhampstead	49 C3
Bracknell	118 B2	Farnham Common	22 A1	Letcombe Bassett	6 B4
Bradfield	82 A1	Fawley (Berks)	27 B2	Lightwater	152 C4
Brands Hill	69 A4	Fawley (Bucks)	15 A3	Linkenholt	147 A1
Brightwalton	28 B1	Feltham	98 B2	Little Marlow	2 A2
Brimpton	133 C3	Finchampstead	141 A1	Littleton	125 A2
Bucklebury	80 A1	Flackwell Heath	3 A3	Littlewick Green	38 A2
Burchett's Green	38 A3	Frimley	151 B1	Lower Basildon	34 A1
Burghfield Common	110 B1	Froxfield	99 A1	Lower Halliford	125 A1
Burnham	21 A1	Fulmer	23 A3	Lyne	123 A1
Camberley	151 A1	Goring	34 A3	Maidenhead	39 A1
Caversham	59 A1	Great Shefford	48 A1	Mapledurham	57 C3
Chaddleworth	49 A2	Greenham	131 B4	Marlow	1 A1
Charlton	125 B4	Ham	126 A1	Marlow Bottom	1 A3
Charvil	61 A1	Hambleden	16 A4	Medmenham	17 A2
Chertsey	124 A1	Hampstead Norreys	52 C3	Mortimer	137 A3
Chieveley	51 A1	Hamstead Marshall	129 A4	Moulsford	13 B2

Newbury	104 B1	Theale	83 A1
Newell Green	92 A3	Thorpe	123 A3
Newtown	131 C1	Thorpe Lea	96 A1
North Ascot	119 C4	Tidmarsh	56 A1
Oakley Green	66 A1	Twyford	61 A3
Old Windsor	95 A3	Upper Basildon	55 A3
Padworth	109 B2	Upper Halliford	125 B3
Pangbourne	56 A1	Virginia Water	122 A2
Peasemore	50 A4	Waltham St Lawrence	62 A4
Poyle	69 B3	Walton-on-T	125 C1
Purley on T	57 A1	Wargrave	36 B1
Reading	86 A2	Wentworth	121 A1
Remenham Hill	16 A1	West End	153 C3
Sandhurst	150 A4	West Ilsley	10 A1
Shefford Woodlands	74 B4	West Woodhay	128 A3
Shepperton	125 A1	Whitchurch-on-T	56 B4
Shinfield	113 A1	White Waltham	63 A3
Shiplake	35 A1	Wickham	75 B2
Silchester	136 A1	Windlesham	146 A2
Slough	42 A3	Windsor	67 A2
Sonning	60 C1	Winkfield	92 A1
South Stoke	14 A2	Winnersh	88 A1
Staines	96 B3	Winterbourne	77 B3
Stanford Dingley	81 B2	Wokingham	116 A1
Stanwell	97 A3	Wooburn Green	3 B2
Stockcross	104 A4	Wooburn Moor	3 C4
Stoke Poges	22 C1	Woodley	88 A3
Streatley	34 A3	Woolhampton	108 B1
Sulham	56 C3	Wraysbury	68 A3
Sulhamstead	110 B1	Yateley	149 A2
Sunbury	125 C3	Yattendon	53 A1
Sunningdale	121 A1		
Swallowfield	139 A1		
Tadley	134 A1		
Taplow	20 C1		
Thatcham	106 A1		

3 Acre Mobile Home Pk SL0 ......44 A4

A

Abattoirs Rd RG1 ......86 A4
Abberbury Cl RG14 ......104 C3
Abbetts La GU15 ......151 A2
Abbey Cl Bracknell RG12 ......118 B2
　Newbury RG14 ......131 A4
　Slough SL1 ......41 C3
　Wokingham RG40 ......116 B4
Abbey Cotts SL7 ......17 A2
Abbey Ct Camberley GU15 ......151 B3
　Chertsey KT16 ......124 A1
Abbey Dr TW18 ......124 A1
Abbey Gdns KT16 ......124 A2
Abbey Gn KT16 ......124 A2
Abbey Jun Sch RG1 ......86 B3
Abbey Lodge TW18 ......96 C2
Abbey Pk RG7 ......110 C2
Abbey Rd Bourne End SL8 ...2 C3
　Chertsey KT16 ......124 A1
　Lower Halliford TW17 ......125 A1
　Virginia Water GU25 ......122 B3
Abbey River Cotts KT16 ......124 B2
Abbey Sq RG1 ......86 A4
Abbey St RG1 ......86 A4
Abbey Way SL7 ......18 B3
Abbey Wood SL5 ......121 A1
Abbot Cl TW18 ......97 B1
Abbot's Wlk SL4 ......66 C3
Abbots Dr GU25 ......122 B3
Abbots Rd
　Burghfield Common RG7 ......110 C1
　Newbury RG14 ......105 A1
Abbots Way KT16 ......123 C1
Abbots Wlk RG1 ......86 A4
Abbotsbury RG12 ......117 C2
Abbotsbury Ct 3 RG30 ......85 A4
Abbotsmead Pl RG4 ......59 A1
Abbotts Way SL1 ......41 B3
Abelia Cl GU24 ......153 C3
Abell Gdns SL6 ......19 A1
Aberaman RG4 ......58 C3
Aberdeen Ave SL1 ......42 A3
Aberford Cl RG30 ......85 B4
Abex Rd RG14 ......105 B2
Abingdon Cl RG12 ......118 C2
Abingdon Dr RG4 ......59 B3
Abingdon Rd
　East Isley RG20 ......30 C4
　Sandhurst GU47 ......143 B1
Abingdon Wlk SL6 ......19 C2
Abington SL3 ......69 B4
Abney Court Dr SL8 ......3 A1
Abotts Mead OX10 ......14 A4
Abrahams Rd RG9 ......15 B2
Acacia RG9 ......15 B2
Acacia Ave Littleton TW17 ......125 A2
　Sandhurst GU47 ......143 B1
　Wraysbury TW19 ......68 C2
Acacia Ct RG12 ......118 A3
Acacia Mews UB7 ......70 B4
Acacia Rd Reading RG1 ......86 B3
　Staines TW18 ......97 A2
Academy Cl GU15 ......151 C4
Accommodation La UB7 ...70 B4
Acer Dr GU24 ......153 C3
Ackrells Mead GU47 ......142 C1
Acorn Cotts SN8 ......126 B2
Acorn Dr Thatcham RG18 ......106 B3
　Wokingham RG40 ......116 B4
Acorn Gr UB3 ......71 C4
Acorn Rd GU17 ......150 A3
Acorn Wlk RG31 ......84 B3
Acre Bsns Pk RG2 ......113 A4
Acre Pas SL4 ......67 B3
Acre Rd RG2 ......113 A4
Acre The SL7 ......1 C1
Action Ct TW15 ......125 B4
Adam Cl Slough SL1 ......42 A3
　Tadley RG26 ......134 C1
Adam Ct RG9 ......15 C1
Adams Way RG6 ......86 C1
Addington Cl SL4 ......67 A2
Addington Rd RG1 ......86 B3
Addington Specl Sch RG5 .87 C3
Addiscombe Chase RG31 ..57 A2
Addiscombe Rd RG45 ......143 B2
Addison Cl SL0 ......44 C3
Addison Ct SL6 ......20 C1
Addison Rd RG1 ......59 A1
Adelaide Cl SL1 ......42 A2
　Reading RG30 ......87 A3
Adelaide Rd Ashford TW15 ......97 B2
Adelaide Sq SL4 ......67 B3
Adelphi Gdns SL1 ......42 C2
Adey's Cl RG14 ......105 A1
Adkins Rd RG10 ......62 C4
Admirals Ct RG2 ......86 A3
Admiralty Way GU15 ......150 C2
Admoor La RG7 ......82 B1
Adwell Dr RG6 ......87 B1
Adwell Sq RG9 ......15 B1
Adwood Ct RG19 ......106 C1
Aeriel Bsns Pk RG17 ......45 C2
Agar Cres RG42 ......91 A1
Agars Pl SL3 ......68 A4
Agate Cl RG41 ......115 C4
Aggisters La RG41 ......115 B2
Agincourt Cl RG41 ......115 C3
Agincourt Pl SL5 ......120 B3
Agricola Way RG19 ......106 C1

Ainsdale Cres RG30 ......85 A2
Aintree RG12 ......118 A4
Aintree Cl Newbury RG14 ......105 B1
　Poyle SL3 ......69 C3
Air Forces Meml TW20 ......95 B2
Airport Way TW19 ......70 A2
Aisne Rd GU16 ......152 C1
Ajax Ave SL1 ......42 A3
Alan Pl RG30 ......85 A3
Alan Way SL3 ......43 C4
Alandale Cl RG2 ......113 B4
Albain Cres TW15 ......97 C3
Albany Park Dr RG14 ......88 C2
Albany Park Ind Est GU15 ......151 B1
Albany Pk Frimley GU15 ......151 B1
　Poyle SL3 ......69 B4
Albany Rd Old Windsor SL4 ...68 A1
　Reading RG30 ......85 A4
　Windsor SL4 ......67 B3
Alben Rd RG42 ......90 B2
Albert Ave KT16 ......124 B2
Albert Cl 28 SL1 ......42 C2
Albert Illsley Cl RG31 ......84 B4
Albert Pl SL4 ......42 A1
Albert Rd Ashford TW15 ......97 C2
　Bagshot GU19 ......145 C1
　Bracknell RG42 ......118 A4
　Camberley GU15 ......151 B3
　Caversham RG4 ......58 C2
　Crowthorne RG45 ......143 A3
　Englefield Green TW20 ......95 B1
　Henley-on-T RG9 ......15 C1
　19 Newbury RG14 ......105 A2
　Windsor SL4 ......67 C2
　Wokingham RG40 ......116 A3
Albert St Maidenhead SL6 ...39 C4
　Slough SL1 ......42 C2
　Windsor SL4 ......67 A3
Albert Wlk RG45 ......143 A3
Albion SL3 ......44 A1
Albion Cl SL2 ......43 A3
Albion Cotts SL6 ......19 B4
Albion Pl 2 SL4 ......67 A3
Albion Rd GU47 ......150 A4
Albion Terr RG1 ......86 B4
Albury Cl RG30 ......58 B1
Albury Gdns RG31 ......84 C2
Alcot Cl RG45 ......143 A2
Aldborough Spur SL1 ......42 C4
Aldbourne Ave RG6 ......87 A2
Aldbourne Cl RG17 ......100 B3
Aldbourne Rd SL1 ......41 A4
Aldeburgh Cl RG4 ......59 B4
Aldebury Rd SL6 ......19 C1
Alden View SL4 ......66 B3
Aldenham Cl RG4 ......59 B3
Aldenham Terr RG12 ......118 B2
Alder Bridge Steiner Sch RG7 ......109 B2
Alder Cl
　Englefield Green TW20 ......95 C2
　Newbury RG14 ......105 B2
　Slough SL1 ......41 C3
Alder Ct RG12 ......118 A3
Alder Dr Earley RG6 ......87 B1
　Reading RG31 ......84 B3
Alder Glade RG7 ......110 C2
Alder Gr GU46 ......149 B3
Alderbourne La SL3 ......23 C4
Alderbrook Cl RG45 ......142 C2
Alderbury Rd SL3 ......43 C2
Alderbury Rd W SL3 ......43 C2
Alderley Cl RG5 ......60 C1
Alderman Willey Cl RG41 ......116 A3
Aldermaston CE Prim Sch RG7 ......134 C4
Aldermaston Sta RG7 ......109 B2
Alderney Ct 27 RG1 ......86 B4
Alderney Gdns RG41 ......88 B1
Alders The RG18 ......106 B2
Alderside Wlk TW20 ......95 C2
Aldin Ave N SL1 ......43 A2
Aldin Ave S SL1 ......43 A2
Aldous Ho TW18 ......96 C1
Aldridge Rd SL2 ......22 A1
Aldryington Prim Sch RG6 ......87 A2
Aldwick Dr SL6 ......39 B3
Aldwick Cl
　Bracknell RG12 ......118 A3
　Reading RG30 ......85 B3
Aldworth Gdns RG45 ......143 A3
Aldworth Rd
　Compton RG20 ......31 C2
　Upper Basildon RG8 ......55 A3
Aldwyn Ct TW20 ......95 A1
Alexander Ct 41 RG1 ......85 C4
Alexander Fst Sch SL4 ...66 B2
Alexander Rd Egham TW20 ......96 B2
　Thatcham RG19 ......106 C1
Alexander Wlk RG12 ......118 A2
Alexandra Ave GU15 ......151 A3
Alexandra Cl Ashford TW15 ...98 B1
　Staines TW18 ......97 B1
Alexandra Ct TW15 ......98 B1
Alexandra Rd
　Ashford TW15 ......98 C1
　Englefield Green TW20 ......95 B1
　Maidenhead SL6 ......39 B4
　Reading RG1 ......86 B3
　Slough SL1 ......42 B2
　Windsor SL4 ......67 B3
Alford Cl RG30 ......84 B4

Alfred Davis Ct SL7 ......1 B2
Alfred St RG1 ......85 C4
Alfred Sutton Prim Sch RG1 ......86 C3
Alice Gough Memorial Homes RG12 ......118 A3
Alice La SL1 ......21 A1
Alison Cl RG7 ......110 C1
Alison Dr GU15 ......151 C3
All Hallows Rd RG4 ......59 B2
All Saints' Ave SL6 ......39 B4
All Saints CE Inf Sch RG1 .85 C4
All Saints CE Jun Sch SL6 .39 B3
All Saints Cl RG40 ......116 B4
All Saints Cres GU14 ......150 C4
All Saints Rd RG30 ......85 C3
All Saints Rd GU18 ......146 B1
All Saints Rise RG42 ......91 C1
All Souls Cotts SL3 ......43 C4
All Souls' Rd SL5 ......120 A3
Allanson Rd SL7 ......1 C2
Allcot Cl TW14 ......98 C4
Allcroft Rd RG1 ......86 B3
Allenby Rd Maidenhead SL6 ...39 A4
　Sandhurst GU15 ......151 A3
Allendale Cl GU47 ......143 A1
Allendale Rd RG6 ......87 A2
Allerds Rd SL2 ......22 A2
Allhusen Gdns SL3 ......23 C4
Alleyns La SL6 ......19 B4
Alliance Ct TW15 ......98 B2
Allington Ave TW17 ......125 C3
Allington Cl SL2 ......42 C3
Allison Ct 17 RG1 ......85 C4
Allison Gdns RG8 ......57 B3
Allkins Ct SL4 ......67 B3
Allnatt Ave RG41 ......88 B1
Allonby Rd RG6 ......87 B1
Allsmoor La RG12 ......118 C3
Allyn Cl TW18 ......96 C1
Alma Ct Burnham SL1 ......21 B1
　Eton SL4 ......41 C1
　Wokingham RG41 ......116 A3
Alma Rd Eton SL4 ......41 C1
　Windsor SL4 ......67 B3
Alma St RG30 ......85 B4
Almners Rd KT16 ......123 A1
Almond Ave RG14 ......105 A3
Almond Cl Charlton TW17 ......125 B4
　Englefield Green TW20 ......95 A1
　Windsor SL4 ......67 A3
　Wokingham RG41 ......115 B2
Almond Dr Caversham RG4 ...59 C2
　Thatcham RG18 ......106 B2
Almond Rd SL1 ......21 B1
Almons Way SL2 ......23 A4
Almshouses Eton SL4 ......67 B4
　Reading RG1 ......86 A4
　Sunbury TW16 ......125 C4
Almswood Rd RG26 ......135 A1
Alpha Ho 4 RG1 ......86 B3
Alpha St N SL1 ......43 A2
Alpha St S SL1 ......42 C2
Alpha Way TW20 ......123 B4
Alphington Ave GU16 ......151 C1
Alphington Gn GU16 ......151 C1
Alphington Rd RG2 ......113 A4
Alpine St RG1 ......86 A3
Alsace Wlk GU15 ......151 A1
Alsford Cl GU18 ......152 C4
Alston Gdns SL6 ......39 C4
Alston Mews RG19 ......106 B1
Alston Wlk RG4 ......59 B1
Altmore SL6 ......38 C2
Alton Ct TW18 ......123 C4
Alton Ride GU17 ......150 B3
Altona Way SL1 ......42 A4
Altwood Bailey SL6 ......39 A3
Altwood CE Comp Sch SL6 ......39 A3
Altwood Cl
　Maidenhead SL6 ......39 A3
　Slough SL1 ......41 C4
Altwood Dr SL6 ......39 A3
Altwood Rd SL6 ......39 A3
Alvista Ave SL6 ......41 A4
Alwyn Inf Sch SL6 ......39 A4
Alwyn Rd SL6 ......39 A4
Alwyns Cl KT16 ......124 A2
Alwyns La KT16 ......124 A2
Alyson Ct 2 RG1 ......19 C1
Amanda Ct Ashford TW15 ...97 C3
　Slough SL3 ......43 B2
Ambarrow Cres GU47 ......142 C1
Ambarrow La GU47 ......142 C1
Ambassador RG12 ......117 C2
Amber Cl RG7 ......87 B2
Amber Ct TW18 ......96 C2
Amber Hill GU15 ......152 A2
Amberley Cl RG14 ......104 C2
Amberley Cl SL6 ......20 B2
Amberley Dr RG10 ......61 B3
Amberley Pl 20 SL4 ......67 B3
Amberley Rd SL2 ......41 C4
Amberwood Dr GU15 ......151 C4
Amblecote Rd RG30 ......85 A3
Ambleside Cl RG5 ......87 C4
Ambleside Dr TW14 ......98 C4
Ambleside Rd GU18 ......153 A4
Ambleside Way TW20 ......96 A1
Ambrook Rd RG2 ......113 A4
Ambrose Pl RG1 ......85 C4
Ambury Rd RG8 ......32 C2
Amen Corner Bsns Pk RG12 ......117 B4
Amerden Cl SL6 ......40 B4
Amerden La SL6 ......40 B4
Amerden Way SL1 ......42 A2

American Comm Sch GU25 ......122 B4
American Magna Carta Meml TW20 ......95 B3
American Sch in Switzerland (English Branch) The TW20 ......123 B3
Amersham Rd RG4 ......59 B1
Amethyst Cl RG41 ......115 B4
Amethyst La RG30 ......85 B3
Amherst Rd RG6 ......87 A3
Amity Rd RG1 ......86 C4
Amity St RG1 ......86 C4
Ammanford RG4 ......58 C3
Amners Farm Rd RG30 ......112 A4
Ampere Rd RG14 ......105 A2
Anarth Ct KT13 ......125 C1
Ancaster Dr SL5 ......119 C4
Ancastle Gr RG9 ......15 B1
Andermans SL4 ......66 B3
Anderson Ave RG6 ......87 A3
Anderson Cres RG2 ......114 C1
Anderson Dr TW15 ......98 B2
Anderson Pl GU19 ......145 C2
Andover Cl
　East Bedfont TW14 ......98 C4
　Reading RG31 ......57 B1
Andover Ct TW19 ......97 B4
Andover Dro RG20 ......130 A2
Andover Rd
　Blackwater GU17 ......150 B3
　Newbury RG14 ......130 B3
Andrew Cl RG40 ......116 C3
Andrews Cl RG7 ......83 C2
Andrews Rd RG6 ......87 A2
Andrews Reach SL8 ......3 A1
Andrews Way SL7 ......1 B4
Angel Ct 2 RG14 ......105 A2
Angel Mead RG7 ......108 B1
Angel Pl RG42 ......90 C1
Angers Cl GU15 ......152 A2
Angle Field Rd RG4 ......59 B2
Anglers Way RG1 ......86 B4
Anglesey Cl TW15 ......98 A3
Angus Cl RG31 ......84 C2
Annadale RG18 ......79 B1
Anne Cl SL6 ......19 C1
Anneforde Pl RG42 ......91 A1
Anners Cl TW20 ......123 B3
Annesley Gdns RG41 ......88 B2
Annett Cl TW17 ......125 B4
Annie Brookes Cl TW18 ...96 B3
Ansculf Rd SL2 ......22 A1
Ansell Rd GU16 ......151 C1
Anslow Pl SL1 ......41 B4
Anson Cres RG2 ......113 B4
Anson Ct TW15 ......97 C4
Anson Wlk RG2 ......113 B4
Anstey Pl RG7 ......111 A2
Anstey Rd 6 RG1 ......86 A4
Anston Ct RG6 ......114 A4
Antares Cl RG41 ......115 C3
Anthian Cl RG5 ......88 A4
Anthony Wall RG42 ......118 C4
Anthony Way SL1 ......41 B3
Antrim Rd RG5 ......87 B3
Anvil Ct Slough SL3 ......44 A1
　Thatcham RG18 ......106 B2
Apex Dr GU16 ......151 B1
Aplin Way GU18 ......146 A1
Apple Cl Purley on T RG31 ...57 A2
　Wokingham RG41 ......115 C3
Apple Tree La RG14 ......130 C4
Apple Tree Way GU47 ......143 B1
Appleby Ct GU15 ......151 A3
Appleby End RG30 ......85 A4
Appleby Gdns TW14 ......98 C4
Applecroft SL6 ......39 B4
Appledore RG12 ......117 C2
Appleford Cl RG19 ......106 B1
Appleford Rd RG30 ......85 A3
Appleton Ho 34 RG1 ......86 B4
Appletree La Shinfield RG7 ......113 A1
　Slough SL3 ......43 B2
Appletree Pl 4 RG42 ......118 A4
Appley Dr GU15 ......151 A3
Approach Rd
　Ashford TW15 ......98 B1
　Taplow SL6 ......40 C4
April Cl GU15 ......151 B1
Apsey Ct RG42 ......90 C1
Apsley Cotts SL6 ......19 C4
Apsley Ho SL1 ......43 A4
Aquila Ct RG7 ......110 C3
Aragon Cl TW16 ......98 C1
Aragon Ct RG12 ......118 B3
Arbor La RG41 ......88 A2
Arbor Mdws RG41 ......88 B2
Arborfield Cl SL1 ......42 C2
Arborfield, Newland & Barkham CE Jun Sch RG2 ......114 C1
Arborfield Rd RG2 ......113 C2
Arbour Cl RG1 ......85 C3
Arbour Vale Sch SL2 ......42 C4
Arc The RG1 ......86 A4
Arcade The Goring RG8 ......34 B3
　Newbury RG14 ......105 A2
Archangel Way RG18 ......106 C2
Archer Cl SL6 ......39 B4
Archway Rd RG4 ......59 A2
Arden Cl RG12 ......119 A4
Ardingly RG12 ......118 A2
Ardler Rd RG4 ......59 B1
Ardossan Ave GU15 ......152 A3
Ardrossan Cl SL2 ......22 A1
Ardwell Cl RG45 ......142 C3

Arena L Ctr GU15 ......151 B3
Arena The RG12 ......118 A4
Arenal Dr RG45 ......143 B2
Arethusa Way GU24 ......153 C2
Argent Cl TW20 ......96 A2
Argent Terr GU47 ......150 C4
Argosy Gdns TW18 ......96 C1
Argosy La TW19 ......97 B4
Argyle Rd Newbury RG14 ......104 C1
　Reading RG1 ......85 C4
Argyle St RG1 ......85 C4
Argyll Ave SL1 ......42 A3
Aries Ho HP10 ......3 A4
Arkle Ave RG19 ......105 C3
Arkley Ct SL3 ......40 B1
Arkwright Dr RG42 ......117 B4
Arkwright Rd Poyle SL3 ......69 C3
　Reading RG2 ......86 A2
Arlington Bsns Pk RG7 ......84 C4
Arlington Cl
　Bracknell RG42 ......118 A4
　Maidenhead SL6 ......39 A4
Arlington Rd TW15 ......97 C3
Arlington Sq RG12 ......118 A4
Armadale Ct RG30 ......85 B3
Armitage Ct SL5 ......120 B2
Armitage Dr GU16 ......151 C1
Armour Hill RG31 ......57 B1
Armour Rd RG31 ......57 B1
Armour Wlk RG31 ......57 B1
Armstrong Rd TW20 ......95 B1
Armstrong Way RG5 ......88 A4
Arncliffe RG12 ......118 A2
Arndale Way TW20 ......96 A2
Arnett Ave RG40 ......141 B4
Arnewood Ave RG26 ......135 B1
Arnhem Rd RG14 ......105 A2
Arnold Rd TW18 ......97 B1
Arnside Cl RG10 ......61 B4
Arnwood RG41 ......115 C4
Arrowhead Rd RG7 ......83 C1
Arrowsmith Way RG19 ......106 C1
Artemis Ho RG14 ......105 A2
Arthur Cl GU19 ......145 C1
Arthur Pl RG1 ......86 B4
Arthur Rd Newbury RG14 ......104 C1
　Slough SL1 ......42 B2
　Windsor SL4 ......67 B3
　Wokingham RG41 ......116 A3
Arthurstone Birches RG42 .90 B2
Artillery Mews RG30 ......85 B3
Arun Cl RG41 ......88 A1
Arun Ct RG30 ......85 B3
Arundel Cl SL6 ......39 A4
Arundel Ct SL3 ......43 B1
Arundel Rd Frimley GU15 ......152 B2
　Woodley RG5 ......87 C4
Ascot Heath Inf Sch SL5 .92 C1
Ascot Heath Jun Sch SL5 .92 C1
Ascot Race Course SL5 ...119 C3
Ascot Rd
　East Bedfont TW14 ......98 A3
　Holyport SL6 ......65 A4
　Newell Green RG42 ......91 C4
Ascot Sta SL5 ......120 A3
Ascot Twrs SL5 ......119 C4
Ascot Wood SL5 ......120 A3
Ash Cl Blackwater GU17 ......150 B3
　Brightwalton RG20 ......28 B2
　Slough SL3 ......44 A2
Ash Copse RG4 ......59 C4
Ash Ct Ashford TW15 ......98 B2
　Caversham RG4 ......59 A2
　18 Newbury RG14 ......105 A2
Ash Gate RG18 ......106 C2
Ash Gn RG2 ......113 B4
Ash Gr Bradfield RG7 ......82 A3
　East Bedfont TW14 ......98 C4
　Staines TW18 ......97 B1
　Stoke Poges SL2 ......22 C3
Ash La
　Burghfield Common RG7 ......111 A2
　Tadley RG26 ......134 C1
　Windsor SL4 ......66 B3
Ash Lodge 6 TW16 ......98 C1
Ash Rd Littleton TW17 ......125 B4
　Newtown RG20 ......131 C1
　Reading RG30 ......84 C4
Ash Terr RG18 ......106 A4
Ash Tree Gr RG20 ......129 A4
Ash Way RG41 ......115 C2
Ashampstead Rd
　Bradfield RG7 ......82 A4
　Reading RG30 ......85 A2
　Upper Basildon RG8 ......55 A3
Ashbourne RG12 ......117 C2
Ashbourne Cl SL6 ......39 B2
Ashbourne Ho 5 SL1 ......42 C4
Ashbourne Way RG19 ......106 A2
Ashbrook Rd SL4 ......95 A4
Ashburton Rd RG2 ......86 B1
Ashbury Dr
　Farnborough (Hants) GU17 ......151 A1
　Reading RG31 ......84 B4
Ashby Ct RG2 ......113 C4
Ashby Way UB7 ......71 A4
Ashcombe Cl RG4 ......58 C3
Ashcroft Cl SL1 ......21 A2
Ashcroft Rd SL6 ......39 C4
Ashdale Cl TW19 ......97 C3
Ashdale Pk RG40 ......142 B3
Ashdene Cl TW15 ......98 B1
Ashdene Ho RG30 ......95 B1
Ashdown SL6 ......20 A2
Ashdown Cl RG12 ......119 A4

Ashdown Ho 13 RG30 ... 85 C3
Ashen Cross SL3 ... 44 A4
Ashenden Wlk SL2 ... 22 B4
Asher Dr SL5 ... 119 B4
Ashes The RG7 ... 113 A1
Ashfield Gn GU46 ... 149 C3
Ashford Ave TW15 ... 98 A1
Ashford CE Prim Sch TW15 ... 98 A1
Ashford Cl TW15 ... 97 C2
Ashford Cres TW15 ... 97 C3
Ashford High Sch The TW15 ... 97 C3
Ashford Hill Cty Prim Sch RG19 ... 133 C1
Ashford Hill Rd RG19 ... 132 C1
Ashford Hospl TW15 ... 97 C3
Ashford Ind Est TW15 ... 98 B2
Ashford La SL4 ... 41 A2
Ashford Manor Golf Club TW15 ... 97 C1
Ashford Park Cty Prim Sch TW15 ... 97 B2
Ashford Rd
Feltham TW13, TW15 ... 98 C3
Littleton TW15 ... 98 B1
Staines TW18 ... 124 B4
Ashford Sta TW15 ... 97 C3
Ashgrove Rd TW15 ... 98 B2
Ashlea Ho TW15 ... 97 C2
Ashleigh Ave TW20 ... 96 B1
Ashley HP10 ... 3 C4
Ashley Cl Earley RG6 ... 87 A1
Walton-on-T KT12, KT13 ... 125 C1
Ashley Ct SL6 ... 40 A4
Ashley Dr GU17 ... 150 B2
Ashley Hill Pl RG10 ... 36 C4
Ashley Park Ave KT12 ... 125 C1
Ashley Pk SL6 ... 20 A1
Ashley Rd RG1 ... 85 C3
Ashley Way GU24 ... 153 B3
Ashman Rd RG19 ... 107 A2
Ashmead Sch RG2 ... 86 B1
Ashmere Cl RG31 ... 84 B2
Ashmere Terr RG30 ... 85 C4
Ashmore Green Rd RG18 ... 106 A4
Ashmore Rd RG2 ... 86 B1
Ashridge Ct 7 RG14 ... 105 A1
Ashridge Gn 3 RG42 ... 118 A4
Ashridge Rd RG40 ... 116 B4
Ashton Cl RG31 ... 84 B4
Ashton Pl Kintbury RG17 ... 102 A1
Maidenhead SL6 ... 39 A3
Ashton Rd Newbury RG14 ... 105 A1
Wokingham RG41 ... 88 C1
Ashtree Ct TW15 ... 98 A2
Ashtrees Rd RG5 ... 87 C4
Ashurst Dr TW17 ... 124 C3
Ashview Cl TW15 ... 97 C2
Ashview Gdns TW15 ... 97 C2
Ashville Way RG41 ... 116 A3
Ashwell Ave GU15 ... 151 C3
Ashwell Ct TW15 ... 97 C3
Ashwood RG5 ... 87 B2
Ashwood Cl RG31 ... 84 A3
Ashwood Dr RG14 ... 105 B2
Ashwood Rd TW20 ... 95 A1
Ashworth Dr RG19 ... 106 B1
Askew Dr RG7 ... 113 A2
Aspect Park Golf Ctr RG9 ... 16 B1
Aspen Cl Slough SL2 ... 42 A4
Staines TW18 ... 96 C3
Aspen Gdns TW15 ... 98 B2
Aspin Way GU17 ... 150 A3
Astleham Rd TW17 ... 124 C3
Astley Cl RG41 ... 115 C4
Aston Ave RG31 ... 84 A4
Aston Cl RG8 ... 56 B3
Aston Ct RG30 ... 85 A3
Aston Ferry La RG9 ... 16 B3
Aston La RG9 ... 16 B2
Aston Mead SL4 ... 66 C3
Aston St OX11 ... 12 C4
Aston Villas SL2 ... 22 B4
Astor Cl Maidenhead SL6 ... 40 A3
Winnersh RG41 ... 88 B2
Astra Mead RG42 ... 92 A1
Atfield Gr GU20 ... 146 B2
Atherton Cl Reading RG30 ... 84 C4
Stanwell TW19 ... 70 B1
Atherton Cres RG17 ... 100 B3
Atherton Ct SL4 ... 67 B4
Atherton Pl RG17 ... 25 A2
Atherton Rd RG17 ... 100 B3
Athlone Cl SL6 ... 19 C1
Atrebatti Rd GU47 ... 143 B1
Atte La RG42 ... 91 B1
Attebrouche Ct RG12 ... 118 B1
Auburn Ct RG4 ... 59 A1
Auckland Cl SL6 ... 40 A4
Auckland Rd RG6 ... 87 A3
Auclum Cl RG7 ... 111 A1
Auclum La RG7 ... 111 A1
Audley Cl RG14 ... 105 B3
Audley Dr SL6 ... 39 A3
Audley St RG30 ... 85 C4
Audley Way SL5 ... 119 B3
Augur Cl TW18 ... 96 C2
August End Reading RG30 ... 85 B4
Slough SL3 ... 43 C4
Augustine Cl SL3 ... 69 C2
Augustine Wlk RG42 ... 91 C1
Augustus Gdns GU15 ... 152 B3
Austen Gdns RG14 ... 131 A4
Austin Rd RG5 ... 87 C3
Austins Gate SL6 ... 38 C4
Australia Ave SL6 ... 39 C4
Australia Rd SL1 ... 43 A2
Auton Pl RG9 ... 35 B4
Autumn Cl Caversham RG4 ... 59 B4
Slough SL1 ... 41 C3
Autumn Wlk
Maidenhead SL6 ... 39 A3
Wargrave RG10 ... 36 B1
Avalon Rd Bourne End SL8 ... 3 A3
Earley RG6 ... 87 B2
Avebury Bracknell RG12 ... 118 A2
Slough SL1 ... 42 A3
Avebury Sq RG1 ... 86 B3
Aveley Wlk 26 RG1 ... 86 A3
Avenue Rd Egham TW18 ... 96 B2
Feltham TW13 ... 98 C3
Maidenhead SL6 ... 40 A3
Avenue Sch The RG2 ... 86 B2
Avenue Sucy GU15 ... 151 A2
Avenue The Bourne End SL8 ... 3 A2
Camberley GU15 ... 151 A3
Crowthorne RG45 ... 143 A3
Datchet SL3 ... 68 A3
Egham TW20 ... 96 A2
Farnham Common SL2 ... 22 A4
Lightwater GU18 ... 146 A1
Maidenhead SL6 ... 20 B2
Mortimer RG7 ... 137 A3
North Ascot SL5 ... 92 C1
Old Windsor SL4 ... 68 A1
Staines TW18 ... 124 A4
Wraysbury TW19 ... 68 B2
Averil Ct SL6 ... 41 B4
Avery Cl RG40 ... 141 C3
Avington Cl RG31 ... 84 A4
Avocet Cres GU47 ... 150 C4
Avocet Ct 4 RG1 ... 86 A3
Avon Cl Reading RG31 ... 84 C3
Slough SL1 ... 41 C3
Avon Gr RG12 ... 91 B1
Avon Pl RG1 ... 86 B4
Avon Rd TW16 ... 98 C1
Avon Way RG7 ... 109 C3
Avondale SL6 ... 19 B1
Avondale Ave TW18 ... 96 C1
Avondale Rd TW15, TW19 ... 97 B3
Avonway RG14 ... 105 B2
Axbridge RG12 ... 118 C2
Axbridge Rd RG2 ... 86 B1
Ayebridges Ave TW20 ... 96 B1
Aylesbury Cres SL1 ... 42 B4
Aylesford Way RG19 ... 107 A1
Aylesham Way GU46 ... 149 A3
Aylesworth Ave SL2 ... 22 A1
Aylesworth Spur SL4 ... 95 A4
Aylsham Cl RG30 ... 84 C4
Aymer Cl TW18 ... 123 C4
Aymer Dr TW18 ... 123 C4
Ayrton Senna Rd RG31 ... 84 B4
Aysgarth RG12 ... 118 A2
Aysgarth Pk SL6 ... 40 A1
Azalea Cl RG41 ... 88 A1
Azalea Way Frimley GU15 ... 152 A3
Slough SL3 ... 43 C4

B

Babbington Rd RG2 ... 113 B3
Bachelors Acre SL4 ... 67 B3
Back La Beenham RG7 ... 109 A4
Brimpton RG7 ... 134 B2
Kintbury RG17 ... 127 C4
Shinfield RG7 ... 139 A4
Silchester RG7 ... 136 B2
Stanford Dingley RG7 ... 81 C2
Back St RG17 ... 47 B3
Backsideans RG10 ... 36 B1
Bacon Cl GU47 ... 150 B3
Bad Godesberg Way SL6 ... 39 C4
Baden Cl TW18 ... 97 A1
Bader Gdns SL1 ... 42 A2
Bader Way The RG5 ... 88 A3
Badgebury Rise SL7 ... 1 B4
Badgemoor La RG9 ... 15 B2
Badgemore Cty Prim Sch RG9 ... 15 B1
Badger Cl SL6 ... 39 B2
Badger Dr
Lightwater GU18 ... 146 A1
Twyford RG10 ... 61 B4
Badgers Cl TW15 ... 97 C2
Badgers Copse GU15 ... 151 C2
Badgers Croft RG7 ... 137 A3
Badgers Glade RG7 ... 111 A1
Badgers Hill GU25 ... 122 B2
Badgers Holt GU46 ... 149 A3
Badgers Ridge RG20 ... 130 B2
Badgers Rise RG4 ... 59 A3
Badgers Sett RG45 ... 142 C3
Badgers Way
Bracknell RG12 ... 118 C4
Marlow Bottom SL7 ... 1 B4
Badgers Wlk RG9 ... 36 A2
Badgers Wood SL2 ... 22 B4
Badgerwood Dr GU16 ... 151 B1
Badminton Rd SL6 ... 39 A3
Bagnols Way RG14 ... 104 C1
Bagshot Cty Inf Sch GU19 ... 145 C1
Bagshot Gn GU19 ... 145 C2
Bagshot Rd Ascot SL5 ... 120 B1
Bracknell RG12 ... 118 B2
Englefield Green TW20 ... 95 B1
West End GU24 ... 153 C4
Bagshot Sta GU19 ... 145 C2
Baigents La GU20 ... 146 B2
Bailey Cl Maidenhead SL6 ... 39 C4
Windsor SL4 ... 67 A3
Bailey Ho 7 SL8 ... 3 A2
Bailey's La RG10 ... 62 C2
Baileys Cl GU17 ... 150 B2
Baily Ave RG18 ... 106 A2
Bain Ave GU15 ... 151 A1
Bainbridge Rd RG31 ... 84 A2
Bainhurst Cotts SL6 ... 38 A3
Baird Cl SL1 ... 42 A2
Baird Rd RG2 ... 140 C4
Bakeham La TW20 ... 95 B1
Baker St Aston Tirrold OX11 ... 12 C4
Reading RG1 ... 85 C4
Baker's Orch HP10 ... 3 C3
Bakers Ct TW19 ... 70 B1
Bakers La SL6 ... 38 C4
Baldwin Rd SL1 ... 21 B1
Baldwin's Shore SL4 ... 67 B4
Balfour Cres
Bracknell RG12 ... 118 A2
Newbury RG14 ... 130 B3
Balfour Dr RG31 ... 84 A2
Balfour Pl SL7 ... 1 B2
Balintore Ct 8 GU47 ... 150 B4
Ball Pit Rd RG20 ... 30 A3
Ballamoor Cl RG31 ... 84 A2
Ballard Ct GU15 ... 152 A4
Ballard Gn SL4 ... 66 C4
Ballard Rd GU15 ... 152 A4
Ballencrieff Rd SL5 ... 120 C1
Balliol Rd RG4 ... 58 B2
Balliol Way GU47 ... 143 C1
Balme Cl RG10 ... 61 A2
Balmoral SL6 ... 19 A1
Balmoral Cl SL1 ... 41 C4
Balmoral Gdns SL4 ... 67 B2
Balmoral Grange TW18 ... 124 A4
Balmore Dr RG4 ... 59 A2
Balmore Ho RG4 ... 59 A2
Balmore Pk RG4 ... 59 A2
Bamburgh Cl RG2 ... 86 B2
Bamford Pl RG31 ... 84 A2
Banbury RG12 ... 118 C1
Banbury Ave SL1 ... 41 C4
Banbury Cl RG41 ... 116 A3
Banbury Gdns RG4 ... 59 B2
Bancroft Cl TW15 ... 98 A2
Bancroft Pl RG31 ... 84 A2
Band La 1 TW20 ... 96 A2
Bangors Cl SL0 ... 44 C4
Bangors Rd S SL0 ... 44 C4
Bank Side RG40 ... 141 C3
Banks Spur SL1 ... 42 A2
Bankside Cl RG2 ... 86 B1
Bannard Rd SL6 ... 39 A3
Bannister Cl SL3 ... 43 C2
Bannister Gdns GU46 ... 149 C3
Bannister Pl RG7 ... 133 C3
Bannister Rd RG7 ... 110 C1
Barbara Cl TW17 ... 125 A2
Barbaras Mdw RG31 ... 57 A1
Barbel Cl RG6 ... 87 A4
Barber Cl RG10 ... 88 C4
Barberry Way GU17 ... 150 C1
Barbon Cl GU15 ... 152 B2
Barbrook Cl RG31 ... 57 B1
Barchester Rd SL3 ... 43 C2
Barclay Rd RG31 ... 84 B2
Barclose Ave RG4 ... 59 B2
Bardney Cl SL6 ... 39 B2
Bardolphs Cl RG4 ... 58 B4
Bardown RG20 ... 51 A1
Barefoot Cl RG31 ... 57 A1
Barfield Rd RG18 ... 106 A2
Barge La RG7 ... 139 A3
Bargeman Rd SL6 ... 39 C3
Barholm Cl RG6 ... 87 C1
Barkby RG6 ... 87 B1
Barker Cl RG2 ... 140 C4
Barker Ct RG10 ... 88 C4
Barker Gn RG12 ... 118 A2
Barker Rd KT16 ... 123 C1
Barkham Manor RG41 ... 115 B2
Barkham Rd
Barkham RG41 ... 115 B2
Wokingham RG41 ... 116 A3
Barkham Ride
Barkham RG40 ... 115 B1
Wokingham RG40 ... 141 C4
Barkham St RG40 ... 115 B1
Barkhart Dr RG40 ... 116 B4
Barkhart Gdns RG40 ... 116 B4
Barkis Mead GU47 ... 143 C1
Barkwith Cl RG6 ... 87 C1
Barley Cl RG19 ... 106 C1
Barley Fields HP10 ... 3 C4
Barley Mead RG42 ... 91 C1
Barley Mow Rd TW20 ... 95 B2
Barley Mow Way TW17 ... 125 A3
Barley Way 6 SL7 ... 1 B1
Barley Wlk RG31 ... 84 A3
Barn Cl Ashford TW15 ... 98 A2
Bracknell RG12 ... 118 B4
Camberley GU15 ... 151 C3
Farnham Common SL2 ... 22 A4
Kintbury RG17 ... 102 A1
Maidenhead SL6 ... 19 C1
Reading RG30 ... 85 B2
Barn Cotts RG17 ... 74 B4
Barn Cres RG14 ... 130 B4
Barn Dr SL6 ... 39 A2
Barn La RG9 ... 15 B2
Barn Owl Way RG7 ... 111 A2
Barnard Cl RG4 ... 59 B3
Barnards Hill SL7 ... 1 B1
Barnes Way SL0 ... 44 C3
Barnett Ct RG12 ... 118 B4
Barnett Gn RG12 ... 118 A2
Barnett La GU18 ... 152 C4
Barnfield Iver SL0 ... 44 C4
Slough SL1 ... 41 B3
Barnfield Cl SL6 ... 19 C3
Barnhill Cl SL7 ... 1 B2
Barnhill Gdns SL7 ... 1 B2
Barnhill Rd SL7 ... 1 B2
Barnsdale Rd RG2 ... 86 B2
Barnway TW20 ... 95 B2
Barnwood Cl RG30 ... 85 C4
Baroma Way RG9 ... 15 C1
Baron Ct RG30 ... 85 C4
Barons Mead RG9 ... 15 B1
Barons Way TW20 ... 96 B1
Barossa Rd GU15 ... 151 B4
Barr's Rd SL6 ... 41 A4
Barracane Dr RG45 ... 143 A3
Barrack La SL4 ... 67 B3
Barracks La RG7 ... 113 A1
Barrett Cres RG40 ... 116 C3
Barrington Cl RG6 ... 87 A3
Barrington Ct TW18 ... 96 C1
Barrington Ho RG2 ... 113 A4
Barrington Way RG30 ... 85 C3
Barry Ave SL4 ... 67 B4
Barry Pl RG1 ... 86 A4
Barry Sq RG12 ... 118 B1
Barry Terr TW15 ... 97 C3
Barry View SL4 ... 66 B3
Bartelotts Rd SL2 ... 21 C1
Bartholemew Pl RG42 ... 91 C1
Bartholomew Ct RG14 ... 104 C1
Bartholomew St RG14 ... 104 C1
Bartlemy Cl RG14 ... 130 C4
Bartlemy Rd RG14 ... 130 C4
Bartletts La SL6 ... 65 A4
Barton Cl TW17 ... 125 A2
Barton Rd Reading RG31 ... 84 A4
Slough SL3 ... 43 C2
Bartons Dr GU46 ... 149 B2
Barwell Cl RG45 ... 142 C2
Basemoors RG12 ... 118 C4
Basford Way SL4 ... 66 B2
Basil Cl RG6 ... 86 C1
Basildon CE Prim Sch RG8 ... 55 A3
Basingstoke Rd
Aldermaston RG7 ... 109 A1
Reading RG2 ... 86 A2
Swallowfield RG7 ... 139 B3
Baskerville La RG9 ... 36 A2
Baslow Rd RG41 ... 88 A1
Basmore La RG9 ... 36 A2
Bass Mead SL6 ... 19 C3
Bassett Cl RG6 ... 114 B4
Bassett Rd OX12 ... 6 C4
Bassett Way SL2 ... 21 C1
Batcombe Mead RG12 ... 118 C1
Bates Cl SL3 ... 43 C4
Bath Ct SL6 ... 39 B3
Bath Rd Camberley GU15 ... 151 B3
Froxfield SN8, RG17 ... 99 B2
Harlington TW6, UB3 ... 71 B3
Harmondsworth TW6, UB7 ... 70 C3
Hungerford RG17 ... 100 C4
Knowl Hill RG10 ... 37 B2
Littlewick Green SL6 ... 38 B3
Maidenhead SL6 ... 39 B3
Newbury RG14 ... 104 B2
Poyle SL3, UB7 ... 69 C3
Reading RG30, RG31 ... 85 B3
Slough SL1, SL6 ... 41 B3
Sonning RG4 ... 60 C1
Thatcham RG7, RG19 ... 107 B1
Woolhampton RG7 ... 108 B1
Bathurst Cl SL0 ... 44 C2
Bathurst Rd RG41 ... 88 A1
Bathurst Wlk SL0 ... 44 C2
Battery End RG14 ... 130 B3
Battle Cl RG14 ... 104 B2
Battle Hospl RG30 ... 85 B4
Battle Prim Sch RG30 ... 85 B4
Battle Rd Goring RG8 ... 34 C4
Newbury RG14 ... 130 B3
Battle St RG1 ... 85 C4
Battlemead Cl SL6 ... 20 B2
Batty's Barn Cl RG40 ... 116 B3
Baxendales The RG14 ... 105 B1
Baxter Cl SL1 ... 42 C2
Bay Cl RG6 ... 86 C1
Bay Dr RG12 ... 118 C4
Bay Rd RG12 ... 118 C4
Bay Tree Ct SL1 ... 21 B1
Bay Tree Rise RG31 ... 84 B3
Baydon Dr RG1 ... 85 C3
Baydon Rd RG17 ... 24 C1
Bayfield Ave GU16 ... 151 C1
Bayford Cl GU17 ... 151 A1
Bayford Dr RG31 ... 84 C2
Bayley Cres SL1 ... 41 A4
Bayley Ct RG41 ... 88 A1
Baylis Court Sch SL1, SL2 ... 42 B4
Baylis Par SL1 ... 42 C4
Baylis Rd SL1 ... 42 C3
Bayliss Rd RG10 ... 36 B1
Baysfarm Ct TW6, UB7 ... 70 B3
Beach's Ho TW18 ... 97 A2
Beacon Ct Colnbrook SW3 ... 69 B4
3 Reading RG30 ... 85 B3
Beacon Rd TW19, TW6 ... 71 A1
Beacon Rdbt TW6 ... 71 A1
Beaconsfield Cotts SL8 ... 3 A1
Beaconsfield Rd SL2 ... 22 B3
Beaconsfield Way RG6 ... 87 A1
Beacontree Plaza RG2 ... 86 A1
Beal's La RG31 ... 84 A4
Beale Cl RG40 ... 116 A4
Beale Park Wildlife Pk RG8 ... 55 C4
Beales Farm Rd RG17 ... 25 A1
Bean Oak Rd RG40 ... 116 C3
Beancroft Rd RG19 ... 106 B1
Bear La Newbury RG14 ... 105 A2
Wargrave RG10 ... 37 A2
Beard's Rd TW15 ... 98 C1
Bearfield La RG17 ... 73 A4
Bears Rails Pk SL4 ... 94 C4
Bearwater RG17 ... 100 B3
Bearwood Coll RG41 ... 115 A4
Bearwood Path RG41 ... 88 A1
Bearwood Prim Sch RG41 ... 115 A4
Bearwood Rd RG41 ... 115 B3
Beasley's Ait TW16, TW17 ... 125 C2
Beasley's Ait La TW16, TW17 ... 125 C2
Beattie Cl TW14 ... 98 C4
Beatty Dr RG30 ... 84 C4
Beauchief Cl RG6 ... 113 C4
Beaufield Cl RG5 ... 87 B4
Beaufort Cl SL7 ... 1 C1
Beaufort Gdns Marlow SL7 ... 1 C1
North Ascot SL5 ... 119 C4
Beaufort Pl SL6 ... 40 B2
Beauforts TW20 ... 95 B2
Beaufront Cl GU15 ... 152 A4
Beaufront Rd GU15 ... 152 A4
Beaulieu Cl
Bracknell RG12 ... 119 A3
Datchet SL3 ... 68 A3
Beaulieu Gdns GU17 ... 150 B3
Beaumaris Ct SL1 ... 42 B4
Beaumont Cl SL6 ... 39 A2
Beaumont Cotts 1 SL4 ... 67 B3
Beaumont Ct Ascot SL5 ... 119 C3
Slough SL3 ... 43 B4
Beaumont Dr TW15 ... 98 B2
Beaumont Gdns RG12 ... 118 C2
Beaumont Rd Slough SL2 ... 42 B4
Windsor SL4 ... 67 B3
Beaumont Rise SL7 ... 1 C1
Beaver Cl RG41 ... 116 A2
Beaver La GU46 ... 149 C3
Beaver Way RG5 ... 88 A4
Beavers Cl RG26 ... 135 A1
Beck Ct RG1 ... 86 B3
Beckett Cl RG40 ... 116 C3
Beckford Ave RG12 ... 118 A2
Beckford Cl RG41 ... 88 C1
Beckford Ct RG19 ... 106 B2
Beckfords RG8 ... 55 A3
Beckins Way HP10 ... 3 B4
Bede Wlk RG2 ... 86 B2
Bedfont Cl TW14 ... 71 B1
Bedfont Court Est TW19 ... 70 A2
Bedfont Ct TW19 ... 70 A2
Bedfont Green Cl TW14 ... 98 B4
Bedfont Ho TW14 ... 98 C4
Bedfont Ind Pk N TW15 ... 98 B3
Bedfont Inf Sch TW14 ... 71 C1
Bedfont Jun Sch TW14 ... 71 C1
Bedfont La TW14, TW13 ... 98 C4
Bedfont Lakes Ctry Pk TW14 ... 98 B3
Bedfont Rd
Feltham TW13, TW14 ... 98 B3
Stanwell TW19 ... 70 C1
Bedford Ave SL1 ... 42 A4
Bedford Cl Maidenhead SL6 ... 39 A2
Newbury RG14 ... 130 B3
Bedford Dr SL2 ... 22 A3
Bedford Gdns RG41 ... 115 C4
Bedford La SL5 ... 121 A2
Bedford Rd RG1 ... 85 C4
Bedfordshire Down RG42 ... 91 C1
Bedfordshire Way RG41 ... 115 C3
Bedwins La SL6 ... 19 A3
Beech RG9 ... 15 B1
Beech Ave GU15 ... 151 B2
Beech Cl Ashford TW15 ... 98 B2
Burghfield Common RG30 ... 111 A2
Hampstead Norreys RG18 ... 53 A3
Maidenhead SL6 ... 39 A4
Stanwell TW19 ... 97 B4
Beech Ct Caversham RG4 ... 59 A2
1 Marlow SL7 ... 1 C1
15 Newbury RG14 ... 105 A2
Beech Dr GU17 ... 150 B2
Beech Glen RG12 ... 118 A3
Beech Hill Rd
Beech Hill RG7 ... 138 C3
Sunningdale SL5 ... 120 C2
Beech La RG6 ... 87 A1
Beech Lodge TW18 ... 96 C2
Beech Rd
East Bedfont TW14 ... 98 C4
Mapledurham RG4 ... 58 B4
Newtown RG20 ... 132 A2
Purley on T RG8 ... 57 A3
Reading RG2 ... 86 C1
Slough SL3 ... 43 C2
Beech Ride GU47 ... 143 A1
Beech Tree La TW18 ... 124 A4
Beech Wlk RG19 ... 106 C1
Beecham Rd RG30 ... 85 B4
Beechbrook Ave GU46 ... 149 B3
Beechcroft RG18 ... 53 A3
Beechcroft Cl SL5 ... 120 B3
Beechcroft Ct RG12 ... 118 A3
Beeches Dr SL2 ... 22 A4
Beeches Rd SL2 ... 22 A4
Beeches The Goring RG8 ... 34 A3
Reading RG31 ... 57 B2
Staines TW18 ... 97 A2

Beechfield RG18 . . . . .80 B4
Beechingstoke [4] SL7 . . . . . .1 C2
Beechmont Ave GU25 . . . .122 B2
Beechnut Cl RG41 . . . . . . .115 C3
Beechnut Dr GU17 . . . . . .150 A3
Beechtree Ave
  Englefield Green TW20 . . .95 A1
  Marlow Bottom SL7 . . . . . .1 B3
Beechwood Ave
  Reading RG31 . . . . .84 B4
  Staines TW18 . . . . .97 A1
  Woodley RG5 . . . . .87 B4
Beechwood Cl SL5 . . . . . . .92 C1
Beechwood Dr
  Maidenhead SL6 . . . . .39 A3
  Marlow SL7 . . . . .18 A4
Beechwood Gdns SL1 . . . . .42 C2
Beechwood Prim Schs
  RG5 . . . . .87 C4
Beechwood Rd Slough SL2 . .42 A4
  Wentworth GU25 . . . . . . .122 A1
Beechwood Sec Sch SL2 . . .22 A1
Beedon CE Prim Sch
  RG20 . . . . .51 B4
Beedon Dr RG12 . . . . . . .117 C2
Beehive La RG12 . . . . . . .117 A4
Beehive Rd
  Bracknell RG12, RG42 . . . .117 B4
  Staines TW18 . . . . .96 C2
Beenham Cty Prim Sch
  RG7 . . . . .108 C3
Beeston Way RG6 . . . . . . .114 A4
Beggars Hill RG10 . . . . . . .61 A1
Beighton Cl RG6 . . . . .113 C4
Belfast Ave SL1 . . . . .42 B4
Belford Ct [18] RG1 . . . . . . .86 A3
Belgrave Ct GU17 . . . . . . .150 B2
Belgrave Par SL1 . . . . .42 C3
Belgrave Rd SL1 . . . . .42 C3
Belgravia [22] RG30 . . . . . .85 B3
Bell Bridge Rd KT16 . . . . . .123 C1
Bell Bsns Ctr SL6 . . . . .39 C3
Bell Cl SL2 . . . . .43 A4
Bell Cnr KT16 . . . . .123 C1
Bell Ct SL6 . . . . .17 C2
Bell Foundry La RG40 . . . . .116 B4
Bell Hill RG14 . . . . .130 A2
Bell Holt RG14 . . . . .130 B3
Bell House Gdns RG41 . . . .116 A3
Bell La Aldworth RG8 . . . . . .32 C2
  Blackwater GU17 . . . . . . .150 B3
  Eton SL4 . . . . .41 C1
  Henley-on-T RG9 . . . . . . .15 C1
  Inkpen RG17 . . . . .127 B2
Bell Pl GU19 . . . . .145 C2
Bell St Henley-on-T RG9 . . .15 C1
  Maidenhead SL6 . . . . .39 C3
Bell View SL4 . . . . .66 C3
Bell View Cl SL4 . . . . .66 C3
Bell Weir Cl TW19 . . . . .96 A3
Belle Ave RG6 . . . . .87 A3
Belle Vue Cl TW18 . . . . . . .124 A4
Belle Vue Rd
  Henley-on-T RG9 . . . . . . .35 B4
  Reading RG1 . . . . .85 C4
Belleisle RG8 . . . . .57 A3
Bellever Hill GU15 . . . . . . .151 C3
Bellevue Terr [15] RG1 . . . . .85 C4
Bellingham Cl GU15 . . . . . .152 B2
Bellingham Wlk RG4 . . . . . .59 A3
Bellman Ct [1] RG1 . . . . . . .86 A4
Bells Hill SL2 . . . . .23 A2
Bells Hill Gn SL2 . . . . .23 A3
Bells La SL3 . . . . .69 A2
Bellsfield Cl SL1 . . . . .41 C1
Bellswood La SL0 . . . . .44 A4
Belmont SL2 . . . . .42 A4
Belmont Cotts SL3 . . . . .69 B4
Belmont Cres SL6 . . . . .39 B4
Belmont Dr SL6 . . . . .39 B4
Belmont Mews GU15 . . . . . .151 B2
Belmont Park Ave SL6 . . . . .39 B4
Belmont Park Rd SL6 . . . . . .39 B4
Belmont Rd
  Camberley GU15 . . . . . . .151 B2
  Crowthorne RG45 . . . . . . .143 A3
  Maidenhead SL6 . . . . .39 B4
  Reading RG30 . . . . .85 B4
Belmont Vale SL6 . . . . .39 B4
Belton Rd GU15 . . . . .151 C3
Belvedere Ct SL2 . . . . .150 B2
Belvedere Dr RG14 . . . . . . .131 A4
Belvedere Mans SL1 . . . . . .42 B2
Belvedere Wlk RG41 . . . . . .88 A2
Belvoir Cl GU16 . . . . .151 C1
Bembridge Ct [20] SL1 . . . . .42 C2
Bembridge Pl RG1 . . . . .86 B4
Benbricke Gn RG42 . . . . . . .91 A1
Bence The TW20 . . . . .123 A3
Bencombe Rd SL7 . . . . .1 C3
Benedict Dr TW14 . . . . .98 B4
Benedict Gn RG42 . . . . .91 A1
Benen-Stock Rd TW19 . . . . .70 A1
Benetfeld Rd RG42 . . . . . . .90 A1
Benett Cl SL1 . . . . .104 C3
Benett Gdns RG14 . . . . . . .104 C3
Benham Chase RG20 . . . . . .103 C3
Benham Hill
  Newbury RG18 . . . . .105 C2
  Thatcham RG18 . . . . .106 A2
Benham La RG7 . . . . .139 B2
Benhams La RG9 . . . . .15 C4
Benjamin Ct TW15 . . . . . . .98 B1
Benner La GU24 . . . . .153 A4
Bennet Ct RG2 . . . . .86 A1
Bennet Rd RG2 . . . . .86 A1
Bennett Cl GU15 . . . . .151 B3
Bennetts Cl SL1 . . . . .42 B4

Bennetts Hill RG7,RG30 . . .111 B4
Benning Cl SL4 . . . . .66 B2
Bennings Cl RG42 . . . . .91 A1
Bensington Ct TW14 . . . . . .71 B1
Benson Cl Reading RG2 . . . .86 B2
  Slough SL2 . . . . .43 A3
Benson Rd RG45 . . . . .142 C3
Bentley Copse GU15 . . . . . .152 A2
Bentley Pk SL2 . . . . .21 B2
Bentley Rd SL1 . . . . .42 A3
Benyon Ct RG1 . . . . .85 C3
Benyon Mews RG1 . . . . . . .85 C3
Beomonds [5] KT16 . . . . . . .124 A1
Beomonds Row [2] KT16 . . . .124 A1
Bere Court Rd RG8 . . . . . . .56 A2
Bere Rd RG12 . . . . .118 C2
Beresford Ave SL2 . . . . .43 B3
Beresford Rd RG30 . . . . . . .85 C4
Bergenia Ct GU24 . . . . . . .153 C3
Berkeley Ave RG1 . . . . .85 C3
Berkeley Cl TW19 . . . . .96 B3
Berkeley Ct [1] RG1 . . . . . . .85 C3
Berkeley Dr SL4 . . . . .93 A4
Berkeley Gdns KT12 . . . . . .125 C1
Berkeley Mews SL7 . . . . . . .1 C1
Berkeley Rd RG14 . . . . .104 C1
Berkley Cl SL6 . . . . .39 A4
Berkshire Ave SL1 . . . . .42 A4
Berkshire Bsns Ctr RG19 . .107 A1
Berkshire Coll
  of Agriculture SL6 . . . . . . .18 A1
Berkshire Coll
  of Agriculture
  (Hall Place) SL6 . . . . .38 A4
Berkshire Dr Reading RG31 . .84 B4
  Thatcham RG19 . . . . .107 A1
Berkshire Ind Hospl RG1 . . .85 C3
Berkshire Lodge [1] SL6 . . . .39 C3
Bernadine Ct RG2 . . . . .91 C1
Bernard Ct GU15 . . . . .151 A2
Berners Cl SL1 . . . . .41 C3
Bernersh Cl GU47 . . . . . . .143 B1
Berries Rd SL6 . . . . .20 A4
Berry Field SL2 . . . . .43 B4
Berry Hill SL6 . . . . .40 B4
Berry Hill Ct SL6 . . . . .40 B4
Berrybank GU47 . . . . .150 C3
Berrycroft RG12 . . . . .118 B4
Berrys La RG30 . . . . .85 A1
Berrys Rd RG7 . . . . .107 B3
Berryscroft Ct TW18 . . . . . .97 B1
Berryscroft Rd TW18 . . . . . .97 B1
Berstead Cl [3] RG6 . . . . . . .87 A1
Berwick Ave SL1 . . . . .42 A3
Berwick Cl SL7 . . . . .1 B1
Berwick La SL7 . . . . .1 B1
Berwick Rd SL7 . . . . .1 B2
Berwyn Ho RG2 . . . . .113 B4
Beryl RG41 . . . . .115 C2
Bessels Way OX11 . . . . . . .12 A4
Bestobell Rd SL1 . . . . .42 B4
Beswick Gdns RG12 . . . . . .118 C4
Beta Ho [6] RG30 . . . . .85 B3
Beta Way TW20 . . . . .123 B4
Betam Rd RG1 . . . . .86 B4
Betchworth Ave RG6 . . . . . .87 B4
Bethany Waye TW14 . . . . . .98 C4
Bethesda Cl RG8 . . . . .55 A3
Bethesda St RG8 . . . . .55 A4
Betjeman Wlk GU46 . . . . . .149 A2
Betteridge Rd RG19 . . . . . .106 C1
Betty Grove La RG41 . . . . . .114 C4
Beverley Cl Frimley GU15 . . .152 B3
  Marlow SL7 . . . . .1 A1
  Thatcham RG18 . . . . .106 B2
Beverley Ct SL1 . . . . .43 A2
Beverley Gdns
  Maidenhead SL6 . . . . .19 A1
  Wargrave RG10 . . . . .36 C1
Beverley Rd Reading RG31 . .57 B1
  Sunbury TW16 . . . . .125 C4
Bevers The RG7 . . . . .137 A3
Bexley Ct RG30 . . . . .85 B3
Bexley St SL4 . . . . .67 B3
Bibury Rd RG5 . . . . .87 B2
Bicknell Rd GU16 . . . . .151 C1
Biddles Cl [6] SL1 . . . . .41 C3
Bideford Cl RG5 . . . . .87 B3
Bideford Spur SL2 . . . . . . .22 A1
Bietigheim Way [2] GU15 . . .151 B3
Big Barn Gr RG42 . . . . .91 B1
Big La RG17 . . . . .25 A2
Bigbury Gdns RG2 . . . . . . .86 B2
Bigfrith La SL6 . . . . .19 A3
Biggs La RG2,RG40 . . . . . .141 A4
Bill Hill Pk RG41 . . . . .89 A2
Billet La SL3 . . . . .44 A4
Billet Rd TW18, TW19 . . . . .97 A3
Billing Ave RG40 . . . . .141 C3
Billingbear La RG42 . . . . . .90 A3
Billington Way RG18 . . . . . .106 B3
Bilton Ind Est RG12 . . . . . .117 C3
Binbrook Cl RG6 . . . . .87 B1
Binbury Row SL1 . . . . .41 A4
Binfield CE Prim Sch
  RG42 . . . . .90 B1
Binfield Park Hospl RG42 . . .90 B2
Binfield Rd
  Bracknell, Priestwood RG42 .91 A1
  Wokingham RG40 . . . . . . .116 C4
Bingham Dr TW18 . . . . .97 B1
Bingham Rd SL1 . . . . .41 A4

Binghams The SL6 . . . . .40 A2
Bingley Gr RG5 . . . . .60 C1
Binsted Dr GU17 . . . . .150 B3
Birch Ave RG30 . . . . .85 A4
Birch Cl GU15 . . . . .151 C4
Birch Copse Prim Sch
  RG31 . . . . .84 B4
Birch Dr GU17 . . . . .150 B3
Birch Gn Reading RG2 . . . . .113 B4
  Staines TW18 . . . . .97 A2
Birch Gr Bracknell RG12 . . . .118 B3
  Slough SL2 . . . . .42 A4
  Upper Halliford TW17 . . . .125 C4
  Windsor SL4 . . . . .66 B3
Birch Hill Prim Sch
  RG12 . . . . .118 A1
Birch Hill Rd RG12 . . . . . . .118 A1
Birch La Mortimer RG7 . . . .136 C3
  West End GU24 . . . . .153 B4
  Winkfield GU12, SL5 . . . . .119 A4
Birch Platt GU24 . . . . .153 B3
Birch Rd
  Burghfield Common RG7 . .111 A2
  Tadley RG26 . . . . .134 C1
  Windlesham GU20 . . . . . .146 C2
  Wokingham RG40 . . . . . . .142 A4
Birch Side RG45 . . . . .143 A4
Birch Tree View GU18 . . . . .146 A1
Birch View 86 C1
Birches The
  Blackwater GU17 . . . . . . .150 A3
  Goring RG8 . . . . .34 A3
Birchetts Cl [2] RG42 . . . . . .118 A4
Birchfields GU15 . . . . .151 B2
Birchington Rd SL4 . . . . . . .67 A3
Birchland Ct RG7 . . . . .136 C3
Birchlands Ct GU47 . . . . . . .143 C1
Birchmead RG41 . . . . .88 B1
Birchview Cl GU46 . . . . . . .149 B2
Birchwood Cl RG4 . . . . .59 B3
Birchwood Dr GU18 . . . . . .146 B1
Birchwood Rd RG4 . . . . . . .105 B2
Birchwoods The RG31 . . . . .84 A4
Bird Mews RG40 . . . . .116 A3
Bird Mount Cotts SL4 . . . . .67 A4
Birdhill Ave RG2 . . . . .86 B1
Birds La RG7 . . . . .107 C2
Birdwood Rd
  Maidenhead SL6 . . . . .39 A4
  Sandhurst GU15 . . . . .150 C3
Birkbeck Pl GU47 . . . . .143 C1
Birkdale GU47 . . . . .150 C3
Birkdale Ct SL5 . . . . .120 B2
Birkhall Cl RG31 . . . . .84 B3
Birley Rd SL1 . . . . .42 B4
Biscuit Way RG2 . . . . .112 C4
Bisham Abbey National
  Sports Ctr SL7 . . . . .18 A4
Bisham CE Prim Sch SL7 . . .18 A4
Bisham Ct Bisham SL7 . . . . .18 C3
  [19] Slough SL1 . . . . .42 C2
Bisham Gn SL7 . . . . .18 C2
Bishop Cl SL6 . . . . .39 B3
Bishop Ctr The SL6 . . . . . . .40 A2
Bishop Duppas Pk TW17 . . .125 C1
Bishop Wand CE Sec Sch
  TW16 . . . . .125 C4
Bishop's La SL4 . . . . .92 A4
Bishopdale RG12 . . . . .118 A3
Bishops Cl RG26 . . . . .135 A1
Bishops Ct TW16 . . . . .98 C1
Bishops Dr
  East Bedfont TW14 . . . . . .71 B1
  Wokingham RG40 . . . . . . .116 B4
Bishops Farm Cl SL4 . . . . . .66 B3
Bishops Gr GU20 . . . . .146 B2
Bishops Orch SL2 . . . . .22 A1
Bishops Rd Bradfield RG7 . . .81 C2
  Reading RG6 . . . . .87 A3
Bishops Way TW20 . . . . . . .96 B1
Bishops Wlk HP10 . . . . .3 C3
Bishopsgate Rd TW20 . . . . .95 A3
Bishopswood Ct RG26 . . . . .134 C1
Bishopswood La RG26 . . . . .134 C1
Bishopswood Rd RG26 . . . . .134 C1
Bispham Ct [2] RG1 . . . . . . .86 B3
Bissley Dr SL6 . . . . .39 A2
Bitham La Hart RG17 . . . . . .126 A3
  Inkpen RG17 . . . . .127 A3
Bitham Rd OX12 . . . . .8 A4
Bittern Cl GU47 . . . . .150 B4
Bitterne Ave RG31 . . . . . . .84 A3
Bix Hill RG9 . . . . .15 A3
Bix La SL6 . . . . .38 C4
Black Boy La SL6 . . . . .17 B2
Black Horse Cl SL4 . . . . . . .66 B3
Black Lake Cl TW20 . . . . . .123 A4
Black Park Ctry Pk SL3 . . . .23 C2
Black Park Rd SL3 . . . . .23 C2
Blackberry Cl TW17 . . . . . .125 C3
Blackbird Cl
  Burghfield Common RG7 . .111 A2
  Sandhurst GU47 . . . . .150 B4
Blackbird La RG20 . . . . . . .132 C3
Blackburn Trad Est TW19 . . .70 C1
Blackcap Ct GU47 . . . . . . .150 C4
Blackdown Way RG19 . . . . .106 B1
Blackett Cl TW18 . . . . .123 C4
Blacklands Rd RG7 . . . . . . .107 B3
Blackley Cl RG6 . . . . .87 C2
Blackmeadows RG12 . . . . . .118 B3
Blackmoor Cl SL5 . . . . .119 B4
Blackmoor Wood SL5 . . . . .119 B4
Blacknest Gate Rd SL5 . . . .121 A3
Blacknest Rd GU25, SL5 . . .121 C3
Blackpond La SL2 . . . . .22 A2

Blacksmith Row SL3 . . . . . .44 A1
Blacksmith's La TW18 . . . . .124 B3
Blacksmiths La KT16 . . . . . .124 A1
Blackstroud La E
  GU18, GU24 . . . . .153 C4
Blackstroud La W GU18 . . . .153 C4
Blackthorn Cl Earley RG6 . . .87 A2
  Purley on T RG31 . . . . . . .57 C1
Blackthorn Dell SL3 . . . . . . .43 B2
Blackthorn Dr
  Lightwater GU18 . . . . .153 C4
  Thatcham RG18 . . . . .106 B3
Blackthorne Cres SL3 . . . . . .69 C4
Blackthorne Rd SL3 . . . . . . .69 C4
Blackwater Cl
  Caversham RG4 . . . . .59 C2
  Shinfield RG7 . . . . .113 A1
Blackwater Rise RG31 . . . . .84 A2
Blackwater Sta GU17 . . . . .150 C2
Blaenant RG4 . . . . .58 C3
Blaenavon RG4 . . . . .58 C3
Blagdon Cl RG19 . . . . .131 B4
Blagdon Rd RG2 . . . . .86 B1
Blagrave La RG4 . . . . .58 B2
Blagrave Rise RG31 . . . . . . .84 B3
Blagrave St RG1 . . . . .86 A4
Blagrove La RG41 . . . . .115 C2
Blagrove La RG41 . . . . .115 C2
Blair Rd SL1 . . . . .42 A3
Blaire Pk GU46 . . . . .149 C4
Blake Cl Crowthorne RG45 . .143 B2
  Wokingham RG40 . . . . . . .116 C4
Blakeney Cl SL6 . . . . .19 C1
Blakeney Fields RG17 . . . . .48 C3
Blakes Cotts Reading RG1 . . .86 A1
  Wargrave RG10 . . . . .37 A1
Blakes Ct [10] KT16 . . . . . . .124 A1
Blakes La Tadley RG26 . . . . .135 B1
  Wargrave RG10 . . . . .37 A1
Blakes Lock Mus RG1 . . . . .86 B4
Blakes Rd RG10 . . . . .36 C2
Blakes Ride GU46 . . . . .149 A3
Blamire Dr RG42 . . . . .90 C1
Blanchard Cl RG5 . . . . .88 A4
Blandford Cl SL3 . . . . .43 B2
Blandford Dr RG41 . . . . . . .115 C2
Blandford Rd RG2 . . . . .113 B4
Blandford Rd N SL3 . . . . . . .43 B2
Blandford Rd S SL3 . . . . . . .43 B2
Blands Cl RG7 . . . . .110 C1
Blandy Rd RG9 . . . . .35 B4
Blandys Hill RG17 . . . . .128 A4
Blandys La RG8 . . . . .55 A3
Blane's La RG12 . . . . .119 B2
Blatchs Cl RG7 . . . . .83 B2
Blay's La TW20 . . . . .95 A1
Blays Cl TW20 . . . . .95 A1
Bledlow Cl RG14 . . . . .130 B3
Blenheim Cl Slough SL3 . . . .43 C1
  Wokingham RG41 . . . . . . .115 C2
Blenheim Cotts SL6 . . . . . . .106 A4
Blenheim Gdns RG1 . . . . . . .86 C3
Blenheim Rd
  Caversham RG4 . . . . .59 A2
  Maidenhead SL6 . . . . .39 A4
  Newbury RG14 . . . . .104 C1
  Reading RG1 . . . . .86 C3
  Slough SL3 . . . . .43 B1
Blenheim Terr [1] RG1 . . . . .86 A3
Bletchmore Cl UB3 . . . . . . .71 B4
Blewburton Wlk RG12 . . . . .118 C3
Blewbury Dr RG31 . . . . .84 A4
Blewbury Hill OX11 . . . . . . .12 A4
Blinco La SL3 . . . . .43 C4
Blind La
  Bourne End HP10, SL8 . . . .3 A3
  Lambourn RG17 . . . . .25 A1
  Taplow SL6 . . . . .40 C4
  Wooburn Green HP10 . . . . .3 B4
Blomfield Dale RG42 . . . . . .117 B4
Blondell Cl UB7 . . . . .70 A4
Bloomfield Dr RG12 . . . . . . .91 B1
Bloomfield Rd SL6 . . . . .39 B1
Bloomfieldhatch La
  Beech Hill RG7 . . . . .138 A4
  Shinfield RG7 . . . . .112 C1
Bloomsbury Way GU17 . . . .150 B2
Blossom Ave RG7 . . . . .83 C2
Blossom La RG7 . . . . .83 C2
Blount Cres RG42 . . . . .90 C1
Bloxworth Cl [17] RG12 . . . .118 C3
Blue Ball La TW20 . . . . .95 C1
Blue Coat Wlk RG12 . . . . . .118 B2
Bluebell Dr RG7 . . . . .110 C4
Bluebell Hill RG12 . . . . .118 C4
Bluebell Mdw RG41 . . . . . . .88 B2
Bluebell Rise SL5 . . . . .119 A4
Bluebell Way RG18 . . . . . . .106 B3
Bluecoats RG18 . . . . .106 B3
Bluethroat Cl GU47 . . . . . . .150 C4
Blumfield Cres SL1 . . . . . . .41 C4
Blumfield Ct SL1 . . . . .21 B1
Blundell's Rd RG30 . . . . . . .84 C4
Blunden Dr SL3 . . . . .44 B1
Blunts Ave UB7 . . . . .71 A4
Blyth Ave RG19 . . . . .106 A1
Blyth Wlk [5] RG1 . . . . .86 A3
Blythe Cl SL6 . . . . .44 C1
Blythewood La SL5 . . . . . . .119 C4
Blythwood Dr GU16 . . . . . .151 B1
Boames La RG20 . . . . .129 C3
Boarlands Cl SL1 . . . . .41 C3
Boathouse Reach RG9 . . . . .15 C1
Bobgreen Ct RG2 . . . . .113 B3
Bobmore La SL7 . . . . .1 C2
Bockhampton Rd RG17 . . . .25 B1
Bockmer La SL7 . . . . .17 A4
Bodens Ride SL5 . . . . .119 C1

Bodin Gdns RG14 . . . . .131 A4
Bodmin Ave SL2 . . . . .42 A4
Bodmin Cl RG19 . . . . .106 C3
Bodmin Rd RG5 . . . . .87 B3
Body Rd RG1 . . . . .85 C4
Bog La RG12 . . . . .119 A3
Bohams Rd OX11 . . . . .11 B3
Bold's Ct SL2 . . . . .23 A4
Bolding House La GU24 . . . .153 C4
Boldrewood RG7 . . . . .110 C1
Boleyn Cl TW18 . . . . .96 C2
Bolingbroke Way RG19 . . . .106 C2
Bolney Rd RG9 . . . . .36 A3
Bolney Trevor Dr RG9 . . . . .36 A2
Bolton Ave SL4 . . . . .67 B2
Bolton Cres SL4 . . . . .67 B2
Bolton Rd SL4 . . . . .67 B2
Bolton Row RG20 . . . . .50 B4
Bolton's La UB3 . . . . .71 B4
Boltons La RG42 . . . . .90 C1
Bolwell Cl RG10 . . . . .61 C2
Bomer SL7 . . . . .71 A4
Bomford Cl RG18 . . . . .78 C3
Bond St TW20 . . . . .95 B2
Bone La RG14 . . . . .105 A2
Bonemill La RG20 . . . . .104 C3
Bones La RG9 . . . . .35 A2
Boot End RG2 . . . . .112 C4
Booth Dr TW18 . . . . .97 B1
Borderside Slough SL2 . . . . .43 A4
  Yateley GU46 . . . . .149 A4
Borrowdale Cl TW20 . . . . . .96 A1
Borrowdale Gdns GU15 . . . .152 B2
Borrowdale Rd RG41 . . . . . .88 C2
Boscombe Cl TW20 . . . . . . .123 B4
Boscowen Way RG19 . . . . . .107 A1
Bosham Cl RG6 . . . . .114 A4
Boshers Gdns TW20 . . . . . .95 C1
Bosman Dr GU20 . . . . .146 A3
Bossington Ct TW18 . . . . . .96 C3
Bostock La RG7 . . . . .83 A1
Boston Ave RG6 . . . . .85 C3
Boston Dr SL8 . . . . .3 A2
Boston Gr SL1 . . . . .42 B4
Boston Rd RG9 . . . . .35 C4
Bosworth Gdns RG5 . . . . . .87 C2
Botany Cl RG19 . . . . .106 C2
Botham Dr SL1 . . . . .42 C2
Bothy The RG10 . . . . .36 B1
Botmoor Way RG20 . . . . . . .48 C3
Bottisham Cl RG6 . . . . .114 B4
Bottle La Knowl Hill SL6 . . . .38 A1
  Newell Green RG42 . . . . . .91 A3
Bottom La RG7 . . . . .110 B4
Bottom Waltons
  Caravan Site SL2 . . . . . . .21 C2
Bouldish Farm Rd SL5 . . . . .120 A3
Boult St RG1 . . . . .86 B4
Boulters Cl
  Maidenhead SL6 . . . . .20 B1
  Slough SL1 . . . . .42 A2
  Woodley RG5 . . . . .87 C4
Boulters Ct SL6 . . . . .20 B1
Boulters Gdns SL6 . . . . .20 B1
Boulters Ho [3] RG12 . . . . . .118 C3
Boulters La SL6 . . . . .20 B1
Boulton Rd RG2 . . . . .86 B2
Boults Wlk RG2 . . . . .86 B3
Boundary Cl RG31 . . . . .84 B3
Boundary La RG4 . . . . .58 C2
Boundary Pl HP10 . . . . .3 B4
Boundary Rd
  Newbury RG14 . . . . .105 A1
  Staines TW15 . . . . .97 B2
  Taplow SL6 . . . . .40 C4
  Wooburn Green HP10 . . . . .3 B4
Bourn Cl RG6 . . . . .87 B1
Bourne Arch RG18 . . . . . . .106 A2
Bourne Ave
  Chertsey KT16 . . . . .124 A3
  Reading RG2 . . . . .86 A2
  Windsor SL4 . . . . .67 B2
Bourne Cl Bourne End SL8 . .3 A3
  Reading RG31 . . . . .84 A2
Bourne End Bsns Ctr [8]
  SL8 . . . . .3 A2
Bourne End Rd SL6,SL8 . . .20 C4
Bourne End Sta SL8 . . . . . . .3 A2
Bourne Ho TW15 . . . . .98 A2
Bourne Mdw TW20 . . . . . . .123 A3
Bourne Rd Pangbourne RG8 . .56 C3
  Slough SL1 . . . . .23 B2
  Thatcham RG19 . . . . .106 A2
  Wentworth GU25 . . . . . . .122 B3
Bourne- Stevens Cl RG1 . . .86 A4
Bourne Vale RG17 . . . . . . .100 C3
Bourneside GU25 . . . . .122 A1
Bourton Cl RG30 . . . . .84 C4
Boveney Cl SL1 . . . . .42 A2
Boveney Ho [2] RG12 . . . . . .118 C3
Boveney New Rd SL4 . . . . . .41 C1
Boveney Rd SL4 . . . . .41 B1
Bovingdon Hts SL7 . . . . . . .1 A1
Bowden Cl TW14 . . . . .98 C4
Bowden Rd SL5 . . . . .120 B2
Bowdown Ct RG14 . . . . . . .104 C1
Bower Ct [3] SL1 . . . . .41 C4
Bower Way SL1 . . . . .41 C4
Bowes Rd Egham TW18 . . . .96 C1
  Thatcham RG19 . . . . .106 B1
Bowes-Lyon Cl [7] SL4 . . . . .67 B3
Bowfell Cl RG31 . . . . .57 B1
Bowland Dr RG12 . . . . .118 C1
Bowling Ct RG9 . . . . .15 B2

Bowling Green La RG8 ....57 A3
Bowling Green Rd RG18 .106 A4
Bowlings The GU15 .....151 B3
Bowman Ct RG45 ....142 C2
Bowmans Cl SL1 ....21 A2
Bowry Dr TW19 ....68 C1
Bowyer Cres RG40 ......116 B4
Bowyer Dr SL1 ....41 C3
Bowyer Wlk SL5 ....119 C4
Bowyers La RG42 ....91 B3
Boxford Ridge RG12 ....118 A3
Boxshall Ct SL4 ....104 C1
Boyd Ct RG42 ....118 A4
Boyn Hill Ave SL6 ......39 B3
Boyn Hill Cl SL6 ....39 B3
Boyn Hill Rd SL6 ....39 B3
Boyn Valley Rd SL6 .....39 B3
Boyndon Rd SL6 ....39 B4
Boyne Hill CE Inf Sch SL6 .39 B3
Bracebridge GU15 ......151 A4
Bracken Bank SL6 ......119 B4
Bracken Cl Ashford TW16 .98 C1
  Farnham Common SL2 ...22 B4
  Purley on T RG31 ......57 B1
Bracken Copse RG17 ....127 C3
Bracken La GU46 ....149 A3
Bracken Rd SL6 ....39 B2
Bracken Way
  Burghfield Common RG7 ..111 A1
  Flackwell Heath HP10 .....3 A4
Brackendale Cl GU15 ...151 C2
Brackendale Rd GU15 ...151 B2
Brackenforde SL3 ......43 B2
Brackenhale Comp Sch
  RG12 ....118 A3
Brackens The RG45 ....143 A4
Brackenwood
  Burghfield Common RG7 ..110 C1
  Frimley GU15 ....152 B3
Brackenwood Dr RG26 ..135 A1
Brackley Ho TW18 .....96 C2
Bracknell Beeches RG12 .118 A3
Bracknell Bsns Ctr The
  RG12 ....117 C4
Bracknell Cl GU15 .....144 C1
Bracknell Coll
  Bracknell RG12 ....118 A4
  Bracknell, Wick Hill RG12 .118 B4
Bracknell Enterprise Ctr
  RG12 ....118 A4
Bracknell Rd
  Bagshot GU19 ....145 A1
  Camberley GU15 ......145 A1
  Crowthorne RG45 .....143 B3
  Winkfield RG42 ....92 A3
Bracknell Sports & L Ctr
  RG12 ....118 B2
Bracknell Sta RG12 ....118 A3
Brackstone Cl RG4 .....59 B1
Bradbury Gdns SL3 .....23 B4
Bradcutts La SL6 ......19 C4
Bradenham La SL7 .....18 B3
Bradfield CE Prim Sch
  RG7 ....82 A1
Bradfield Coll RG7 .....82 B3
Bradfields RG12 ....118 B2
Bradford Rd SL1 ....42 A4
Brading Way RG8 ......57 B3
Bradley Cl RG17 ....102 A1
Bradley Dr RG40 ....116 A1
Bradley Rd SL1 ....42 C3
Bradley-Moore Sq RG6 .106 C3
Bradmore Way RG6 ....114 A4
Bradshaw Cl SL4 ......66 C3
Bradwell Rd RG31 .....57 B2
Braemar SL6 ....63 B4
Braemar Ct SL7 ....1 B1
Braemar Gdns SL1 .....42 A2
Braemore Cl RG19 .....106 B1
Brakendale Way RG6 ...87 A3
Bramber Ct SL1 ....42 A3
Bramber Mews RG4 ....59 C2
Bramble Cl TW17 ......125 B3
Bramble Cres RG30 ....84 C4
Bramble Dr SL6 ....39 A2
Brambledown TW18 ....124 A4
Bramblegate RG45 .....143 A3
Brambles The
  Crowthorne RG45 .....142 B4
  Newbury RG14 ....130 C4
Bramblings RG4 ......58 C3
Bramcote GU15 ....152 B4
Bramley Ave TW17 ....125 C3
Bramley Chase SL6 ....39 B2
Bramley Cl Chertsey KT16 .124 A1
  Earley RG6 ....87 A2
  Maidenhead SL6 ......39 B2
  Staines TW18 ....97 B1
Bramley Gr RG45 ......142 B3
Bramley La GU17 ......150 A3
Bramley Rd
  Camberley GU15 ......151 A1
  Silchester RG7 ....136 A1
Bramling Ave GU46 ....149 A3
Brammas Cl SL1 ......42 B2
Brampton Chase RG9 ..36 A2
Brampton Ct SL6 ......40 A4
Bramshaw Rd RG30 ....58 A1
Bramshill Cl RG2 ......140 C4
Bramwell Cl RG19 .....106 C1
Bran Cl RG30 ....84 C4
Brandon Ave SL6 ......88 A4
Brandon Cl GU15 ......152 B4
Brands Rd SL3 ....69 A4
Branksome Cl GU15 ...151 C3

Branksome Ct **19**RG1 ....85 C4
Branksome Hill Rd GU47 .150 C4
Branksome Park Rd
  GU15 ....151 C3
Brants Bridge RG12 ....118 C4
Brants Cl RG2 ....114 C1
Braunfels Wlk RG14 ...104 C1
Bravington Cl TW17 ...124 C2
Bray Cl SL6 ....40 B2
Bray Cl SL6 ....40 B1
Bray Rd Maidenhead SL6 ..40 A3
  Reading RG30 ....85 A2
Braybank SL6 ....40 B2
Braybrooke Dr RG10 ...88 C4
Braybrooke Gdns RG10 .36 B1
Braybrooke Rd
  Bracknell RG42 ....91 A1
  Wargrave RG10 ....36 B1
Braye Cl GU47 ....143 B1
Brayfield Rd SL6 ......40 B2
Brayford Rd RG2 ......113 B4
Braywick Park
  & Nature Ctr SL6 .....40 A2
Braywick Rd SL6 ......40 A2
Braywood Ave TW20 ...96 A1
Braywood CE Fst Sch SL4 .65 C3
Braywood Cotts SL6 ...66 A3
Braziers La SL4, SL5 ...92 B2
Breach Sq RG17 ......100 B2
Breadcroft La SL6 .....38 C2
Breadcroft Rd SL6 ....38 C2
Bream Cl SL7 ....18 B4
Brean Wlk RG6 ....87 A1
Brechin Ct **3**RG1 ....86 B3
Brecon Ct SL1 ....42 B2
Brecon Rd RG5 ....87 C4
Bredon Rd RG41 ......88 C1
Bredward Cl SL1 ......21 A1
Breech The GU47 .....150 C4
Breedons Hill RG8 .....56 B3
Bremer Rd TW18, TW19 .97 A3
Brendon Cl Harlington UB3 .71 B4
  Reading RG30 ....57 C1
Brent Cl RG19 ....106 B1
Brent Gdns RG2 ......86 A2
Brent Rd SL8 ....3 A2
Brentmoor Rd GU24 ...153 B3
Brerewood RG6 ......86 C1
Bret Harte Rd GU16 ...151 C1
Brew Tower SL7 ......1 B1
Brewery Comm RG7 ...137 A4
Brewhouse Hill SN8 ...99 A2
Briants Ave RG6 ......59 B1
Briants Piece RG18 ....79 A3
Briar Ave GU18 ......153 A4
Briar Cl Burnham SL6 ...41 A4
  Caversham RG4 ....59 A2
Briar Dene SL6 ....19 B1
Briar Glen SL6 ....19 C3
Briar Rd TW17 ....125 A2
Briar Way SL2 ....42 A4
Briarlea Rd RG6 ......136 C3
Briars Cl RG8 ....56 C3
Briars The Slough SL3 ..43 C1
  Stanwell TW19 ....70 A1
Briarwood RG40 ......141 C3
Briarwood Cl TW13 ...98 C3
Brickfield La Burnham SL1 .21 A2
  Harlington UB3 ....71 B4
Brickfields Ind Ctr RG12 .118 A4
Bridge Ave Cookham SL6 .19 C3
  Maidenhead SL6 ......40 A4
Bridge Cl Slough SL1 ...41 C3
  Staines TW18 ....96 C2
  Walton-on-T KT12 ....125 C1
Bridge Ct SL6 ....40 A4
Bridge End GU15 .....151 A2
Bridge Gdns TW15 ....98 B1
Bridge La GU25, KT16 ..122 C2
Bridge Rd Ascot SL5 ...120 B2
  Bagshot GU19 ....145 C2
  Camberley GU15 ......151 A2
  Chertsey KT16 ....124 A1
  Maidenhead SL6 ......40 A4
Bridge St Caversham RG4 .59 A1
  Colnbrook SL3 ....69 B4
  Hungerford RG17 .....100 B3
  Maidenhead SL6 ......40 A4
  Newbury RG14 ....105 A2
  Reading RG1 ....86 A4
  Staines TW18 ....96 C2
  Walton-on-T KT12 ....125 C1
Bridge View SL5 .....121 A1
Bridge Walk GU46 ....149 B4
Bridge Works GU15 ...151 A1
Bridgeman Ct **5**SL4 ..67 A2
Bridgeman Dr SL4 ....67 A3
Bridges Cl RG41 ......115 C4
Bridges The RG7 .....136 B3
Bridgestone Dr SL8 ...3 B2
Bridgewater Cl RG30 ..58 B3
Bridgewater Ct SL3 ...44 A1
Bridgewater Terr SL4 ..67 A2
Bridgwater Wlk SL4 ...67 B3
Bridle Cl SL6 ....19 B1
Bridle Rd SL6 ....19 C1
Bridlepath Way TW14 .98 C4
Bridlington Spur SL1 ..41 C2
Bridport Cl RG6 ......87 B1
Bridport Way SL2 ....22 A1
Brierley Pl RG31 ......57 B2
Briff La RG7 ....107 B4
Brigham Rd RG1 .....59 A1
Brighton Rd RG6 .....87 A3
Brighton Spur SL2 ....22 A1
Brightside Ave TW18 ..97 B1
Brightwalton CE Prim Sch
  RG20 ....28 B2

Brigidine Sch The SL4 ...67 B2
Brill Cl Caversham RG4 ..59 A2
  Maidenhead SL6 ......39 B2
  Marlow SL7 ....1 B1
Brimblecombe Cl RG41 .89 A1
Brimpton CE Prim Sch
  RG7 ....133 C3
Brimpton La RG7 .....134 B2
Brimpton Rd
  Brimpton RG7 ....133 C4
  Reading RG30 ....85 A4
  Tadley RG26 ....134 B1
Brinkworth Pl SL4 .....95 A4
Brinn's La GU17 ......150 B3
Briony Ho RG2 ....113 A4
Brisbane Rd RG30 ....85 A4
Bristol Cl TW19 ......70 C1
Bristol Ct **10**TW19 ...70 C1
Bristol Way SL1 ......42 C3
Bristow Ct Caversham RG4 .59 A1
  Marlow SL7 ....2 A2
Bristow Cty Inf Sch
  GU15 ....151 A1
Bristow Rd GU15 .....151 A2
Britannia Ind Est SL3 ..69 C3
Britannia Way TW19 ...97 B4
Brittain Ct GU47 .....150 B4
Britwell Rd SL1 ......21 B1
Brixham Rd RG2 .....86 A3
Broad Hinton RG10 ...61 C2
Broad La Bracknell RG12 .118 B3
  Bucklebury RG7 ....107 B3
  Wooburn Green HP10 ..3 C3
Broad Ley's SL4 ......66 C4
Broad Oak Ashford TW16 .98 C1
  Slough SL2 ....22 B1
Broad Oak Ct SL2 ....22 B1
Broad Platts SL3 .....43 B2
Broad St East Isley RG20 .30 C4
  Reading RG1 ....86 A4
  West End GU24 ......153 B3
  Wokingham RG40 .....116 B3
Broad St Wlk RG40 ...116 B3
Broad Street Mall The
  RG1 ....86 A4
Broad Way RG42 .....138 B2
Broad Wlk GU16 .....151 C1
Broadacre TW18 .....97 A2
Broadcommon Rd RG10 .89 A4
Broadhalfpenny La RG26 .135 B1
Broadlands Ave TW17 .125 B2
Broadlands Cl RG31 ...84 B3
Broadlands Ct GU47 ..117 C4
Broadlands Dr SL5 ....120 B1
Broadley Gn GU20 ...146 B2
Broadmark Rd SL2 ...43 A3
Broadmeadow End
  RG18 ....106 C2
Broadmoor Cty Prim Sch
  RG45 ....143 C3
Broadmoor Hospl RG45 .143 C3
Broadmoor La RG10, SL6 .63 A3
Broadrick Heath RG42 .91 C1
Broadview TW19 .....98 A4
Broadwater Cl TW19 ..95 C4
Broadwater La RG10 ..61 C1
Broadwater Pk SL6 ...40 C1
Broadwater Rd RG10 ..61 C2
Broadway Bracknell RG12 .118 B4
  Maidenhead SL6 ......39 C4
  Staines TW18 ....97 A1
  Thatcham RG19 ......106 B2
  Winkfield SL4 ....93 A4
Broadway Ctyd RG19 ..106 B2
Broadway Mall **6**SL6 ..39 C4
Broadway Rd GU18,GU20 .146 B2
Broadway The
  Laleham TW18 ....124 B4
  Lambourn RG17 ......25 A2
  12Newbury RG14 ...105 A2
  Sandhurst GU47 .....150 A4
Brocas Rd RG7 ......110 C1
Brocas St SL4 ....67 B4
Brocas Terr SL4 .....67 B4
Brock Gdns RG30 ....85 B4
Brock La SL6 ....39 C4
Brock La Mall **7**SL6 ..39 C4
Brock Way GU25 .....122 B3
Brockenhurst Dr GU46 .149 B3
Brockenhurst Rd
  Ascot SL5 ....120 A2
  Bracknell RG12 ......119 A3
Brockhurst & Marlston
  House Prep Schs RG18 .79 C2
Brocklands GU46 .....149 A2
Brockley Cl RG30 .....85 A4
Brocks La RG7 & RG18 .80 A2
Brocks Way RG9 .....36 A2
Brockway SL3 ....44 A1
Broken Furlong SL4 ..42 A1
Broken Way RG20 ....131 A1
Bromley Wlk RG30 ...84 C4
Brompton Cl **9**RG6 ..87 B1
Brompton Dr SL6 ....19 B1
Bromycroft Rd SL2 ...22 A1
Bronte Rise RG14 ....131 A4
Brook Cl Sandhurst GU47 .143 C1
  Stanwell TW19 ......97 C4
  Wokingham RG41 ....116 A4
Brook Cres SL1 ......41 C4
Brook Dr Ashford TW16 .98 C1
  Bracknell RG12 ......118 C3
  Reading RG30 ......112 C4
Brook Gn RG42 ......117 C4
Brook Ho SL1 ....42 B4
Brook La RG10 ......62 C1
Brook Path SL1 .....41 C4

Brook Rd Bagshot GU19 .145 C1
  Camberley GU15 .....151 A2
Brook St Twyford RG10 ..61 B2
  Windsor SL4 ....67 B3
Brook St W RG1 .....86 A3
Brookbank HP10 .....3 B2
Brookdene Cl SL6 ....19 C1
Brooke Furmston Pl SL7 .1 C2
Brooke Pl RG42 ......90 B2
Brookers Cnr RG45 ...143 B3
Brookers Hill RG2 ....113 B3
Brookers Row RG45 ..143 B3
Brookfield Ho SL3 ....68 B3
Brookfield Rd HP10 ...3 B1
Brookfields Specl Sch
  RG31 ....57 B2
Brookhouse Dr HP10 ..3 B2
Brooklands Cl TW16 ..125 C4
Brooklyn Dr RG4 .....59 A3
Brookmill The RG1 ...85 C3
Brooks Rd RG18 .....106 C2
Brooksby Cl GU17 ...150 A3
Brooksby Rd RG31 ...57 B1
Brookside Chertsey KT16 .123 C1
  Colnbrook SL3 ....69 B4
  Reading RG31 ....84 C2
  Sandhurst GU47 .....150 B4
  Slough SL3 ....43 C4
  Wokingham RG41 ....115 C4
Brookside Ave
  Staines TW15 ....97 B3
  Wraysbury TW19 .....68 C2
Brookside Cl RG6 ....87 B1
Brookway RG14 .....105 C1
Broom Acres GU47 ..143 A1
Broom Cl
  Blackwater GU17 ....150 C2
  Reading RG31 ....84 B3
Broom Field RG18 ...153 A4
Broom Gr RG41 .....115 B2
Broom Hill Cookham SL6 .19 C3
  Stoke Poges SL2 .....23 A3
Broom Ho SL3 ....43 C1
Broome Cl GU46 .....149 A4
Broome Ct RG12 .....118 A3
Broome Lodge TW18 ..97 A2
Broomfield TW18 ....97 A1
Broomfield Cl SL5 ...121 A1
Broomfield Dr SL5 ...121 A1
Broomfield Pk SL5 ...121 A1
Broomfield Rd RG30 ..84 C4
Broomhall Bldgs SL5 .121 A1
Broomhall La SL5 ....121 A1
Broomsquires Rd GU19 .145 C1
Broughton Cl RG30 ...58 B3
Broughton Mews GU16 .151 C1
Brownfield Gdns SL6 ..39 C3
Browngraves Rd UB3 .71 B4
Browning Cl
  Frimley GU15 ....152 B3
  Thatcham RG18 .....106 B2
Brownlow Dr RG42 ...91 B1
Brownlow Rd RG1 ....85 C4
Brownrigg Cres RG12 .118 C4
Brownrigg Rd TW15 ..98 A3
Browns Cl SL1 ......41 C3
Brownsfield Rd RG18 .106 B2
Bruan Rd RG14 .....130 C4
Bruce Ave TW17 ....125 B3
Bruce Cl SL1 ....42 A3
Bruce Rd RG5 ......87 B4
Bruce Wlk SL4 .....66 B3
Brucewood Par SL7 ..1 C3
Brudenell SL4 ......66 C2
Brummell Rd RG14 ..104 C3
Brunel Cl SL6 ......39 C3
Brunel Ctr SL6 .....39 B3
Brunel Dr
  Crowthorne RG45 ...143 B4
  Woodley RG5 ......60 C1
Brunel Rd Maidenhead SL6 .39 B3
  Reading RG30 ....85 A2
  Theale RG7 ....83 C1
Brunel Ret Pk RG2 ..86 A2
Brunel Univ (Runnymede
  Campus) TW20 .....95 B3
Brunel Way SL1 .....42 C3
Brunswick RG12 ....118 A1
Brunswick Hill RG1 ..85 C4
Brunswick Lodge **12**RG1 .85 C4
Brunswick St RG1 ...85 C4
Bruton Way RG12 ...118 C1
Bryant Ave SL2 .....42 C4
Bryants La RG18 ....53 C1
Bryants Pl RG8 .....57 A3
Brybur Cl RG2 ......113 B4
Bryer Pl SL4 ....66 B2
Bryony Ho RG12 ....117 C4
Bryony Way SL6 ....98 C1
Bsns Village The SL2 ..43 A3
Buccaneer Cl RG5 ...88 A4
Buccleuch Rd SL3 ...68 A4
Buchan The SL5 .....152 A4
Buchanan Dr RG40 ..141 C4
Buchanan Sq RG19 ..106 C1
Buck Side RG4 ......59 A1
Buckden Cl RG5 .....88 A3
Buckfield Ct SL0 .....44 C2
Buckham Hill
  RG17 & RG20 ....48 B3
Buckhurst Gr RG40 ..116 C3
Buckhurst Hill RG12 .118 C3
Buckhurst La SL5 ...121 A1
Buckhurst Moors RG12 .117 C3
Buckhurst Rd SL5 ...120 C4
Buckhurst Way RG6 ..87 A2
Buckingham Ave SL1 .42 A4
Buckingham Ave E SL1 .42 B4

Buckingham Ct
  Staines TW18 ....97 A2
  Wokingham RG40 ....116 B3
Buckingham Dr RG4 ..59 A3
Buckingham Gate SL7 .17 B4
Buckingham Gdns **12**SL1 .42 C2
Buckingham Ho **4**SL6 .39 C3
Buckingham Rd RG14 .104 C1
Buckingham Way GU16 .151 C1
Buckland Ave SL2 ...43 A2
Buckland Cres SL4 ...66 C3
Buckland Cty Jun
  & Inf Sch TW18 .....97 B1
Buckland Gate SL3 ..23 A1
Buckland Rd RG2 ...86 A2
Buckle La RG42 .....91 A3
Bucklebury RG12 ...118 A1
Bucklebury CE Prim Sch
  RG7 ....107 B3
Bucklebury Cl SL6 ...40 B1
Bucklebury Farm Pk RG7 .80 B1
Bucknell Ave RG8 ...56 C3
Bucknell Cl RG31 ...84 C2
Buckthorn Cl RG40 ..116 C4
Budebury Rd TW18 ..97 A2
Budge's Cotts RG40 .116 C4
Budge's Gdns RG40 .116 C4
Budge's Rd RG40 ...116 C4
Budham Way RG12 ..118 A2
Buffins SL6 ....20 C1
Bulbrook Row RG12 .118 C4
Bulkeley Ave SL4 ...67 A2
Bulkeley Cl TW20 ...95 B2
Bull La Bracknell RG42 .118 A4
  Swallowfield RG7 ....139 A2
Bull Meadow The RG8 .33 C3
Bullbrook Dr RG12 ..118 C4
Bullfinch Cl GU47 ...150 C4
Bulmershe Rd RG1 ..86 C3
Bulpit La RG17 .....100 B2
Bulstrode Pl SL1 ....42 C2
Bunby Rd SL2 ......22 C3
Bunces Cl SL4 .....42 A1
Bunces La RG7 .....111 A1
Bundy's Way TW18 ..96 C1
Bungalow Dr RG31 ..84 B4
Bunglers Hill RG7 ...140 A3
Bunkers Hill RG14 ..130 B3
Bunten Meade SL1 ..42 A3
Bunyan Ct **2**RG1 ..86 A3
Burbage Gn RG12 ...118 C2
Burbidge Cl RG31 ...84 C2
Burbidge Rd TW17 ..125 A3
Burbury Woods GU15 .151 C3
Burchell Rd RG14 ...104 C3
Burchett Copse RG40 .141 C4
Burchett's Green
  CE Inf Sch SL6 .....38 A4
Burchett's Green La SL6 .38 B3
Burchetts Green Rd SL6 .38 A4
Burchetts Way TW17 .125 A3
Burcombe Way RG4 ..59 A2
Burcot Gdns SL6 ....19 C2
Burdens Heath RG7 ..107 A3
Burdett Ct RG2 .....86 B2
Burdock Cl
  Burghfield Common RG7 .111 A1
  Lightwater GU18 ....153 A4
Burfield Rd SL4, TW19 .95 A4
Burford Cl SL7 .....1 A4
Burford Ct **11**Reading RG1 .85 C4
  Wokingham RG40 ...116 C3
Burford Cty Comb Sch SL7 .1 B3
Burford Gdns SL1 ...41 B4
Burford Rd GU15 ...151 A2
Burfords RG17 .....47 B3
Burges Way TW18 ..97 A2
Burgess Cl RG5 .....87 B2
Burgess La RG17,RG20 .128 B3
Burgett Rd SL1 .....42 A2
Burghead Cl GU47 ..150 B4
Burghfield Rd RG30 ..85 A2
Burghfield St Mary's CE
  Prim Sch RG30 .....111 B3
Burgoyne Rd
  Ashford TW16 ......98 C1
  Camberley GU15 ....152 A3
Burleigh Gdns TW15 ..98 B2
Burleigh La SL5 ....119 C4
Burleigh Mews RG4 ..59 B3
Burleigh Rd SL5 ...119 C4
Burlingham Cl RG2 ..113 C4
Burlings The SL5 ...119 C4
Burlington Ave SL1 ..42 C2
Burlington Cl TW14 ..98 B4
Burlington Ct
  Blackwater GU17 ...150 B2
  1Slough SL1 .....42 C2
Burlington Rd
  Burnham SL1 ....21 A1
  Reading RG30 ......84 B4
  2Slough SL1 .....42 C2
Burlsdon Way RG12 .118 C4
Burn Moor Chase RG12 .118 C1
Burn Wlk SL1 ......21 A2
Burne-Jones Dr GU47 .150 B3
Burnet Cl GU24 ....153 C3
Burnetts Rd SL4 ....66 C3
Burney Bit RG26 ...135 C2
Burnham Beeches
  (Nature Reserve) SL2 ..22 A4
Burnham CE Bourne End SL8 .3 A2
  Windsor SL4 ....66 B3
Burnham Copse Jun &
  Inf Schs RG26 .....135 A1

Burnham Gr RG42 91 B1
Burnham Gram Sch SL1 21 B1
Burnham La SL1 41 C4
Burnham Manor GU15 152 A4
Burnham Rd RG26 134 C1
Burnham Rise RG4 59 B4
Burnham Sta SL1 41 B4
Burnham Upper Sch SL1 41 A4
Burniston Cl RG6 87 C1
Burnmoor Mdw RG27 141 C1
Burns Cl RG5 87 C2
Burns Wlk RG18 106 B2
Burnt Oak Cookham SL6 19 C4
Wokingham RG40 141 C4
Burnt Pollard La GU18 146 C1
Burnthouse Gdns RG42 91 C1
Burnthouse La RG7,RG30 112 A3
Burrcroft Rd RG30 85 A3
Burrell Rd RG20 31 C2
Burroughs Cres SL8 3 A2
Burroway Rd SL3 44 A2
Burrows Hill Cl
TW19, TW6 70 B2
Burrows The RG26 135 A1
Burton Cl Twyford RG10 61 C1
Windlesham GU20 146 B2
Burton Way SL4 66 C2
Burtons Hill RG17 102 A1
Burway Cres KT16 124 A3
Burwell Cl RG6 87 B1
Burys Bank Rd RG19 132 B3
Bush Rd TW17 124 C2
Bush Wlk RG40 116 B3
Business Ctr The RG41 116 A2
Butchers La SL6 63 B4
Bute St RG30 85 A3
Butler Ct 5 SL7 1 C2
Butler Rd Bagshot GU19 145 C1
Crowthorne RG45 143 A3
Butlers Cl SL4 66 B3
Butson Cl RG14 104 C2
Buttenshaw Ave RG2 141 A4
Buttenshaw Cl RG2 141 A4
Butter Market RG1 86 A4
Buttercup Cl RG40 117 A3
Buttercup Pl RG18 106 B2
Buttercup Sq TW19 97 B4
Butterfield
Camberley GU15 151 A2
Wooburn Green HP10 3 B2
Buttermere Ave SL1 41 B4
Buttermere Cl TW14 98 C4
Buttermere Dr GU15 152 B2
Buttermere Gdns RG12 118 B3
Buttermere Way TW20 96 A1
Buttersteep Rise
GU20, SL5 119 B1
Butts Furlong RG20 28 B2
Butts Hill Rd RG5 87 C4
Buxton Ave RG4 58 C2
Buxton Rd TW15 97 B2
Bybend Cl SL2 22 A2
Byefield Rd RG30 85 A2
Byeways Cl RG10 37 C2
Byland Dr SL6 40 A1
Byreton Cl RG6 87 A1
Byron SL3 44 A1
Byron Ave GU15 152 A2
Byron Cl 6 Marlow SL7 1 C2
Newbury RG14 130 C4
Twyford RG10 61 C2
Yateley GU46 149 A2
Byron Dr RG45 143 A2
Byron Rd Earley RG6 87 A4
Twyford RG10 61 C2
Bythorn Cl RG6 87 C1
Byways Burnham SL1 41 A4
Yateley GU46 149 A3
Bywood RG12 118 A1
Byworth Cl RG2 113 A4

C

Cabin Moss RG12 118 C1
Cabrera Ave GU25 122 B2
Cabrera Cl GU25 122 B2
Cadbury Cl TW16 98 C1
Cadbury Rd TW16 98 C1
Caddy Cl 4 TW20 96 A2
Cadogan Cl Holyport SL6 65 A4
Reading RG30 84 C4
Cadwell Dr SL6 39 B2
Caesar's Camp Rd GU15 152 A4
Caesar's Cl GU15 152 A4
Caesar's Way TW17 125 B2
Caesars Gate RG42 91 C1
Caesers Ct GU15 152 A4
Cages Wood Dr SL2 22 A4
Cain Rd RG12, RG42 117 C4
Cain's La TW14 71 C1
Cairn Cl GU15 152 A2
Cairngorm Pl SL2 22 B1
Cairngorm Rd RG19 106 B1
Caistor Cl RG31 84 A2
Calard Dr RG18 106 A3
Calbourne Dr RG31 84 B2
Calbroke Rd SL2 21 C1
Calcot Ct RG31 84 C3
Calcot Place Dr RG31 84 C2
Caldbeck Dr RG5 87 C4
Calder Cl Maidenhead SL6 19 C1
Reading RG30 84 C4
Calder Ct Maidenhead SL6 19 B1
Slough SL3 43 C1
Calder Way SL3 69 C2
Caldicott Prep Sch SL2 22 A3
Caldwell Rd GU20 146 B3
Caledonia Rd TW19 97 C4
Caleta Cl RG4 59 B1
Calfridus Way RG12 118 C3
California Ctry Pk RG2 141 B4
Calleva Mus RG7 136 A1
Calleva Pk RG7 134 C1
Calleva Roman Town
RG7 136 B1
Callington Rd RG2 86 B1
Callins La RG10 63 A2
Callis Farm Cl TW19 70 C1
Callow Hill GU25, TW20 122 B4
Calshot Pl RG31 84 B2
Calshot Rd TW6 71 A3
Calshot Way TW6 71 A3
Calvin Cl GU15 152 A2
Camberley Cty Inf Sch
GU15 151 B3
Camberley Heath
Golf Course GU15 152 A3
Camberley Rd TW6 71 A2
Camberley Sta GU15 151 B3
Camberley Towers GU15 151 B3
Camborne Cl Earley RG6 87 A1
Harmondsworth TW6 71 A2
Camborne Cres TW6 71 A2
Camborne Rd TW6 71 A2
Camborne Way TW6 71 A2
Cambria Ct Slough SL3 43 B2
Staines TW18 96 C2
Cambria Gdns TW19 97 C4
Cambrian Cl GU15 151 A3
Cambrian Way
Reading RG31 84 B2
Wokingham RG40 142 A4
Cambridge Ave
Burnham SL1 21 A2
Slough SL1 42 A4
Cambridge Cl UB7 70 B4
Cambridge Ho 2 SL4 67 B3
Cambridge Rd
Crowthorne RG45 143 B2
Littleton TW15 98 B1
Marlow SL7 1 B1
Sandhurst GU47 143 C1
Cambridge Sq GU15 151 B3
Cambridge St 1 RG1 85 C4
Cambridge Wlk 3 GU15 151 B3
Cambridgeshire Cl
Bracknell RG42 91 C1
Wokingham RG41 115 C3
Camden Pl Bourne End SL8 3 A2
Reading RG31 84 A2
Camden Rd SL6 19 B1
Camelford Cl RG2 86 A1
Camellia Ct GU24 153 C3
Camellia Way RG41 115 B4
Camgate Est TW19 97 C4
Camilla Cl TW16 98 C1
Camley Gdns SL6 39 A4
Camley Park Dr SL6 38 C4
Camm Ave SL4 66 C2
Camp Rd RG7 110 B1
Campbell Cl GU46 149 C3
Campbell Pl GU16 151 C2
Campbell Rd RG5 87 B3
Campbells Gn RG7 137 A3
Camperdown SL6 20 A1
Camperdown Ho 38 SL4 67 B3
Campion Cl GU17 150 C2
Campion Ho RG42 117 C4
Campion Way RG40 116 C4
Canada Rd SL1 43 A2
Canal View Rd RG14 105 B2
Canal Walk RG17 100 B3
Canal Way RG1 86 B4
Canal Wharf SL3 44 A2
Canberra Cl GU46 149 A4
Canberra Rd TW6 71 A2
Candleford Cl RG12 91 B1
Candover Cl UB7 70 B4
Canford Ct RG30 85 B4
Cannock Cl SL6 40 A3
Cannock Way RG6 87 B1
Cannon Cl GU47 150 C4
Cannon Court Rd SL6 19 B2
Cannon Hill RG12 118 B2
Cannon Hill Cl SL6 40 B1
Cannon La SL6 38 C2
Cannon St 3 RG1 85 C4
Cannondown Rd SL6 19 C3
Canon Hill Dr SL6 40 A2
Canon Hill Way SL6 40 A1
Canon's Cloisters SL4 67 B4
Canopus Way TW19 97 C4
Cansfield End RG14 104 C2
Canterbury Ave SL2 22 B1
Canterbury Ct TW15 97 C2
Canterbury Rd RG2 86 B2
Cantley Cres RG41 116 A4
Cantley House Hotel
RG40 116 A4
Cape Villas SL0 44 C4
Capper Rd GU15 151 A4
Capricorn Ho HP10 3 A4
Captains Gorse RG8 54 C3
Caraway Rd RG6 87 A1
Carbery La SL5 120 A3
Carbinswood La RG7 108 A3
Cardiff Rd RG1 58 C1
Cardigan Cl SL1 41 C3
Cardigan Gdns RG1 86 C3
Cardigan Rd RG1 86 C3
Cardinal Cl RG4 59 A1
Cardinal's Wlk TW16 98 C1
Cardinals Wlk SL6 41 B4
Cardwell Cres SL5 120 B2
Carew Rd TW15 98 B1
Carey Cl SL4 67 A2
Carey Rd RG40 116 B3
Carey St RG1 85 C4
Cariad Ct RG8 34 A4
Carisbrooke Cl
Caversham RG4 59 B3
Maidenhead SL6 39 B3
Carisbrooke Ct SL1 42 C3
Carland Cl RG6 87 A1
Carlesgill Pl RG9 35 C4
Carlile Gdns RG10 61 B3
Carlinwark Dr GU15 151 C4
Carlisle Rd Reading RG31 57 C2
Slough SL1 42 B3
Carlton Cl Frimley GU15 152 A2
Woodley RG5 87 C3
Carlton Ct TW18 97 A2
Carlton Ho TW19 70 B1
Carlton Rd Ashford TW16 98 C1
Caversham RG4 58 C3
Slough SL2 43 A3
Carlyle Ct RG45 143 B3
Carlyle Rd TW18 97 A1
Carmarthen Rd SL1 42 C3
Carmela Ct TW15 98 B1
Carnarvon Rd RG1 86 C3
Carnation Cl RG45 143 A4
Carnation Dr RG42 92 A1
Carnegie Rd RG14 105 A1
Carnoustie RG12 117 C1
Carnoustie Ct 23 RG1 86 B4
Carolina Pl RG40 141 C4
Caroline Ct Ashford TW15 98 A1
Marlow SL7 1 C2
Caroline Dr RG41 116 A4
Caroline Pl UB3 71 C4
Caroline St 7 RG1 85 C4
Carrick Gdns RG5 87 B4
Carrick La GU46 149 C3
Carrington Ave HP10 3 A4
Carrington Cty Mid Sch The
HP10 3 A4
Carrington Rd SL1 42 C3
Carroll Cres SL5 119 C3
Carron Cl RG30 85 A4
Carsdale Cl RG1 85 C3
Carshalton Rd GU15 145 A1
Carshalton Way RG6 87 B1
Carston Gr RG31 84 C2
Carter Cl SL4 67 A3
Carters Hill RG40 & RG42 90 A2
Carters Rise RG31 84 C2
Cartmel Dr RG5 87 B3
Carwarden House Sch
GU15 152 A2
Cary Cl RG14 130 B3
Casey Ct RG7 81 B2
Cassia Dr RG6 86 C1
Cassiobury Ave TW14 98 C4
Cassocks Sq TW17 125 B1
Castle Ave SL3 68 A4
Castle Cl 3 Charlton TW16 98 C1
Frimley GU15 151 C2
Castle Cres RG1 85 C3
Castle Ct SL6 39 B4
Castle Dr SL6 39 B4
Castle End Rd RG10 62 A4
Castle Farm Caravan Site
SL4 66 B3
Castle Gr RG14 104 C3
Castle Hill Maidenhead SL6 39 C4
Reading RG1 85 C3
Swallowfield RG7 140 B4
Windsor SL4 67 C3
Castle Hill Rd TW20 95 B3
Castle Hill Terr SL6 39 C4
Castle Ind Pk RG14 105 B3
Castle La RG14 104 C3
Castle Lodge SL6 39 C4
Castle Mews SL6 39 C4
Castle Rd GU15 151 C2
Castle St Reading RG1 86 A4
Slough SL1 42 C2
Castlecraig Ct GU47 150 B4
Castleman Ho SL5 120 B2
Castleton Ct SL7 1 C1
Castleview Comb Sch
SL3 43 B1
Castleview Ho 11 SL4 67 B3
Castleview Rd SL3 43 B1
Castor Ct GU46 149 A4
Caswall Cl RG42 90 B1
Caswall Ride GU46 149 C3
Catalina Cl RG5 88 A4
Catalina Rd TW6 71 A2
Catcliffe Way RG6 113 C4
Catena Rise GU18 146 A1
Catesby Gdns GU46 149 A3
Catherine Dr TW16 98 C1
Catherine Rd RG14 105 A1
Catherine St RG30 85 C4
Catlin Cres TW17 125 B2
Catmore Rd RG20 29 B4
Caunter Rd RG14 104 B2
Causeway Est TW20 96 B2
Causeway The
Caversham RG4 59 B1
Egham TW18, TW20 96 B2
Maidenhead SL6 40 B2
Marlow SL7 1 C1
Causmans Way RG31 57 B1
Cavalier Cl Newbury RG14 105 B3
Theale RG7 83 B1
Cavalier Ct TW15 98 B1
Cavalry Cres SL4 67 B2
Cavendish Cl
Ashford TW16 98 C1
Burnham SL6 41 A4
Cavendish Ct
Ashford TW16 98 C1
Blackwater GU17 150 B2
9 Chertsey KT16 124 A1
Newbury RG14 105 C3
Poyle SL3 69 C3
Cavendish Gdns RG41 88 A2
Cavendish Meads SL5 120 B2
Cavendish Rd
Ashford TW16 98 C1
Caversham RG4 59 B3
Caversham Hill RG4 59 A2
Caversham Park Dr RG4 59 B3
Caversham Park Prim Sch
RG4 59 B3
Caversham Park Rd RG4 59 C3
Caversham Prim Sch
RG4 59 A2
Caversham Rd RG1 59 A1
Caversham Wharf RG1 59 A1
Caves Farm Cl GU47 150 A4
Cawcott Dr SL4 66 C3
Cawsam Gdns RG4 59 B2
Caxton Cl RG30 58 B1
Caxton Ct RG9 15 C1
Cecil Aldin Dr RG31 57 B2
Cecil Cl TW15 98 B1
Cecil Rd Ashford TW15 98 B1
Iver SL0 44 C4
Cecil Way SL2 21 C1
Cedar RG9 15 B1
Cedar Ave GU17 150 B3
Cedar Chase SL6 20 B1
Cedar Cl Bagshot GU19 145 C2
Laleham TW18 124 B3
Wokingham RG40 116 B3
Cedar Ct Egham TW20 96 A2
Maidenhead SL6 39 B4
Marlow SL7 1 C1
6 Windsor SL4 67 A3
Cedar Dr Bracknell RG42 91 B1
Cookham SL6 19 C4
Marlow Bottom SL7 1 B4
Pangbourne RG8 56 B2
Sunningdale SL5 121 A1
Cedar Gr RG19 106 B2
Cedar Ho TW16 98 C1
Cedar Mount RG14 130 C4
Cedar Pl RG5 87 C3
Cedar Rd
East Bedfont TW14 98 B4
Reading RG2 86 C1
Cedar Way Charlton TW16 98 C1
Slough SL3 43 C1
Cedar Wood Cres RG4 59 A2
Cedars 10 RG12 118 C3
Cedars Cl GU47 149 C4
Cedars Rd SL6 40 A4
Cedars The RG31 57 B1
Celandine Cl RG45 143 B3
Celandine Ct GU46 149 A4
Celandine Gr RG18 106 C2
Celia Cres TW15 97 B1
Cell Farm SL4 68 A1
Cell Farm Ave SL4 68 A1
Celsea Pl OX10 14 A4
Cemetery La TW17 125 A1
Centenary Bsns Pk RG9 15 C1
Central Dr SL1 41 C3
Central Est SL6 39 C4
Central La SL4 93 A4
Central Way SL4 93 A4
Central Wlk RG40 116 B3
Centre The
Farnham Common SL2 22 B3
Walton-on-T KT12 125 C1
Centurion Cl Reading RG1 86 A3
4 Sandhurst GU47 150 B4
Century Dr RG7 113 B1
Century Rd TW20 96 B2
Cerotus Pl KT16 123 C1
Chackfield Dr RG41 115 B4
Chaddleworth St Andrews
CE Prim Sch
RG20 49 A4
Chaffinch Cl Reading RG31 84 A4
5 Sandhurst GU47 150 B4
Wokingham RG41 115 C3
Chagford Rd RG2 86 A1
Chain St RG1 86 A4
Chainhill Rd Ox12 8 A4
Chalcott SL1 42 C2
Chalcraft Cl RG9 35 B4
Chalfont Cl RG6 87 A1
Chalfont Ct RG6 87 A1
Chalfont Way RG6 87 A1
Chalford HP10 3 C3
Chalford Rd RG14 104 C1
Chalgrove Cl SL6 40 A3
Chalgrove Way RG4 59 A3
Chalk Hill
Aston Tirrold OX11 12 C4
Shiplake RG9 35 B3
Chalk Pit La SL1 21 A2
Chalklands SL8 3 A2
Chalkpit La SL7 1 A2
Challenge Rd TW15 98 B3
Challenor Cl RG40 141 C4
Challis Pl RG42 117 C4
Challow Ct SL6 19 B1
Chalmers Rd TW15 98 A2
Chalmers Rd E TW15 98 B2
Chalvey Cty Fst Sch SL1 42 B2
Chalvey Gdns SL1 42 C2
Chalvey Gr SL1 42 A2
Chalvey Pk SL1 42 C2
Chalvey Rd E SL1 42 C2
Chalvey Rd W SL1 42 B2
Chamberhouse Mill Rd
RG19 106 C1
Chamberlains Gdns RG2 114 C1
Chambers The 20 RG1 86 A4
Champion Rd RG4 59 B1
Chancel Mans RG42 91 B1
Chancellors Way The
RG6 86 C2
Chancery Mews 25 RG1 85 C4
Chancery Pl SL4 67 B4
Chanctonbury Dr SL5 120 C1
Chandlers Cl TW14 98 C4
Chandlers La GU46 149 B4
Chandos Mall 16 SL1 42 C2
Chandos Rd Egham TW18 96 B2
Newbury RG14 131 A4
Chantry Cl SL4 67 A3
Chantry Ct GU16 151 B1
Chantry Mead RG17 100 B3
Chantry Rd Bagshot GU19 145 B1
Chertsey KT16 124 B1
Chapel Arches SL6 40 A4
Chapel Cl Bracknell RG12 118 B3
South Stoke RG8 14 B2
Chapel Ct
Hungerford RG17 100 B3
Maidenhead SL6 39 B2
18 Reading RG1 86 A4
Thatcham RG18 106 C2
Chapel Hill Reading RG31 84 B4
Windsor SL4 67 B3
Chapel La
Ashampstead RG8 54 A4
Bagshot GU19 145 B1
Binfield RG42 90 B1
Blewbury OX11 12 A4
Farnborough (Hants) GU14 151 A1
Headley RG19 133 C1
Hermitage RG18 79 B4
Hermitage, Curridge RG18 78 C2
Lambourn RG17 25 A2
Shinfield RG7 113 A1
Silchester RG7 135 C3
Stoke Poges SL2 23 A3
Swallowfield RG7 139 B2
Yattendon RG18 53 C1
Chapel Rd
Camberley GU15 151 A3
Flackwell Heath HP10 3 A4
Silchester RG7 136 B3
Stockcross RG20 103 C3
Chapel Row RG10 61 B2
Chapel Sq
Sandhurst GU15 150 C3
Virginia Water GU25 122 C3
Chapel St Marlow SL7 1 C1
Slough SL1 42 C2
Thatcham RG18 106 B2
Chapels Cl SL1 41 C3
Chaplain's Hill RG45 143 B2
Chaplin Cres TW16 98 C1
Chapman La HP10, SL8 3 A3
Chapman Wlk RG18 106 A2
Chapter Mews SL4 67 B4
Charadon Cl RG2 86 A3
Chard Cl RG5 87 C3
Charfield Ct RG1 86 C4
Charlbury Cl 15 RG12 118 C3
Charlecombe Ct TW18 97 A2
Charles Ct TW15 98 B2
Charles Evans Way RG4 59 B1
Charles Gdns SL2 43 A4
Charles Ho 9 SL4 67 B3
Charles Pl 26 RG1 86 B4
Charles Rd Cholsey OX10 14 A4
Staines TW18 97 B1
Charles Sq RG12 118 B4
Charles St Chertsey KT16 123 C1
Newbury RG14 130 B3
Reading RG1 85 C4
Windsor SL4 67 B3
Charlock Cl RG18 106 C3
Charlotte Cl RG18 79 A3
Charlton SL4 66 B3
Charlton Cl SL1 42 A2
Charlton Ct GU47 143 B1
Charlton La
Swallowfield RG7 139 B3
Upper Halliford TW17 125 B3
Charlton Pl
Newbury RG14 105 A2
2 Windsor SL4 66 B3
Charlton Rd TW17 125 B4
Charlton Row 5 SL4 66 B3
Charlton Sq 4 SL4 66 B3
Charlton Way SL4 66 B3
Charlton Wlk 3 SL4 66 B3
Charlville Dr RG31 84 A2
Charmwood Cl RG14 104 C3
Charnham Ct RG17 100 C3
Charnham La RG17 100 B3
Charnham Pk RG17 100 B4
Charnham St RG17 100 B3
Charnwood SL5 120 C2
Charrington Rd RG31 84 B2
Charta Rd TW20 96 B2
Charter Cl SL1 42 C2
Charter Rd Newbury RG14 130 C4
Slough SL1 41 C3
Charterhouse Cl RG12 118 C2
Charters La SL5 120 B2
Charters Rd SL5 120 C1
Charters Sch SL5 120 B1
Charters Way SL5 120 C1
Charvil House Rd RG10 61 A3

Charvil La RG4 .60 C2
Charvil Meadow Rd RG10 .61 A3
Charwood Rd RG40 .116 C4
Chase Gdns RG42 .90 B2
Chase The
Crowthorne RG45 .143 A3
Maidenhead SL6 .19 B2
Marlow SL7 .2 A2
Newbury RG14 .104 C4
Reading RG31 .84 B2
Chaseley Ct KT13 .125 C1
Chaseside Ave RG10 .61 B4
Chaseside Gdns KT16 .124 A1
Chatfield SL2 .42 A4
Chatham Ct 3 SL1 .43 A2
Chatham St RG1 .85 C4
Chatsworth Ave RG41 .88 A1
Chatsworth Cl
Caversham RG4 .59 B3
Maidenhead SL6 .39 B3
Chatsworth Hts GU15 .152 A4
Chatteris Way RG6 .114 B4
Chattern Ct TW15 .98 A2
Chattern Hill TW15 .98 A2
Chattern Rd TW15 .98 B2
Chatters The RG7 .140 B4
Chatton Cl RG6 .114 A4
Chaucer Cl Caversham RG4 .59 A3
Windsor SL4 .67 B2
Wokingham RG40 .116 C3
Chaucer Cres RG14 .104 C3
Chaucer Ct TW18 .96 B2
Chaucer Gr GU15 .151 B3
Chaucer Rd Ashford TW15 .97 C2
Crowthorne RG45 .143 A2
Chaucer Way RG41 .115 C3
Chauntry Cl SL6 .40 B3
Chauntry Rd SL6 .40 A3
Chavey Down Rd RG42 .92 A1
Chawridge La SL4 .92 B4
Chazey Cl RG4 .58 B4
Chazey Rd RG4 .58 B2
Cheam Cl RG12 .118 B2
Cheap St Compton RG20 .31 C3
Newbury RG14 .105 A1
Cheapside RG1 .86 A4
Cheapside CE Prim Sch
SL5 .120 C4
Cheapside Rd SL5 .120 B4
Cheddar Rd TW6 .71 A3
Cheddington Cl RG30 .84 C3
Cheeseman Cl RG40 .116 B4
Chelford Way RG4 .58 C2
Chelmsford Ct 35 SL4 .67 B3
Chelsea Cl RG30 .84 C4
Chelwood Dr GU47 .142 C1
Chelwood Rd RG6 .87 A1
Cheney Cl RG42 .90 B1
Cheniston Ct SL5 .121 A1
Cheniston Gr SL6 .38 C4
Chepstow Rd RG31 .57 B1
Chequer La RG7 .138 C1
Chequers Orch SL0 .44 C4
Chequers Way RG5 .87 B4
Cherbury Cl RG12 .118 C3
Cherington Gate SL6 .19 A1
Cherington Way SL5 .119 C4
Cheriton Ave RG10 .61 B3
Cheriton Cl RG14 .131 A4
Cheriton Ct 2 RG1 .86 A3
Cheriton Way GU17 .150 B3
Cherries The SL2 .43 A4
Cherry Ave SL3 .43 B2
Cherry Cl Caversham RG4 .59 B4
Flackwell Heath HP10 .3 A4
Newbury RG14 .104 C2
Cherry Cnr HP10 .3 A4
Cherry Garden La SL6 .38 C2
Cherry Gr RG17 .100 B3
Cherry Orch
Great Shefford RG17 .48 A2
Staines TW18 .97 A2
Stoke Poges SL2 .23 A3
Cherry Rise HP10 .3 A4
Cherry Tree Ave TW18 .97 A1
Cherry Tree Cl GU47 .143 B1
Cherry Tree Dr RG12 .118 B3
Cherry Tree Gr RG41 .115 B2
Cherry Tree La SL3 .23 C3
Cherry Tree Rd SL2 .22 B3
Cherry Way Horton SL3 .69 B2
Upper Halliford TW17 .125 C3
Cherrydale Rd GU15 .152 B3
Cherrygarden La SL6 .63 C4
Cherrywood Ave TW20 .95 A1
Cherrywood Gdns HP10 .3 A4
Chertsey Bridge Rd
KT16, TW18 .124 B1
Chertsey Bvd KT16 .123 C1
Chertsey La TW18 .96 C1
Chertsey Mus KT16 .124 A1
Chertsey Rd
Ashford TW15 &TW16 .98 B1
Feltham TW13 &TW16 .98 C2
Lower Halliford TW17 .125 A1
Shepperton TW17 .124 C1
Windlesham GU20 .146 C3
Chertsey Sta KT16 .123 C1
Chertsey Wlk 6 KT16 .124 A1
Chervil Way RG7 .111 A1
Cherwell Cl Brands Hill SL3 .69 A4
Maidenhead SL6 .40 A4
Cherwell Cres 18 RG1 .85 C4
Cherwell Rd Bourne End SL8 .3 A2
Caversham RG4 .59 A3
Cheseridge Rd RG20 .31 B2
Cheshire Ct SL1 .43 A2
Cheshire Pk RG42 .91 B1
Chessholme Ct TW16 .98 C1
Chessholme Rd TW15 .98 B1
Chester Cl Ashford TW15 .98 C2
Newbury RG14 .105 B1
Chester Rd Harlington TW6 .71 A2
Slough SL1 .42 B4
Chester St Caversham RG4 .59 A1
Reading RG30 .85 B4
Chesterblade La RG12 .118 C1
Chesterfield Mews TW15 .97 C2
Chesterfield Rd
Ashford TW15 .97 C2
Newbury RG14 .105 A1
Chesterman St RG1 .86 A3
Chesterment Way RG6 .87 B1
Chesters Rd GU15 .152 A3
Chesterton Dr TW19 .97 C4
Chesterton Rd RG18 .106 B3
Chestnut Ave
Camberley GU15 .152 A3
Caversham RG4 .59 C2
Slough SL3 .43 C2
Wentworth GU25 .121 C3
Wokingham RG41 .115 C4
Chestnut Cl
Ashford, Chattern Hill TW15 .98 A2
Ashford, Felthamhill TW16 .98 C1
Blackwater GU17 .150 C2
Englefield Green TW20 .95 B1
Harlington UB7 .71 A4
Maidenhead SL6 .20 A1
Medmenham SL7 .17 B4
Theale RG7 .83 C2
Chestnut Cres
Newbury RG14 .105 A2
Shinfield RG2 .113 C2
Chestnut Ct 17 RG14 .105 A2
Chestnut Dr
Burghfield Common RG30 .111 A2
Englefield Green TW20 .95 B1
Windsor SL4 .66 C2
Chestnut Gr
Purley on T RG8 .57 B3
Staines TW18 .97 B1
Chestnut La RG17 .25 C2
Chestnut Manor Cl TW18 .97 A2
Chestnut Pk SL4 .40 C2
Chestnut Rd TW15 .98 A2
Chestnut Wlk
Hungerford RG17 .100 B2
Upper Halliford TW17 .125 C3
Chestnuts The RG9 .36 A2
Chetwode Cl RG40 .116 C3
Cheveley Gdns SL1 .21 B2
Cheviot Cl Frimley GU15 .152 B2
Harlington UB3 .71 B4
Maidenhead SL6 .40 A3
Newbury RG14 .130 B3
Cheviot Dr RG10 .61 A2
Cheviot Rd
Sandhurst GU47 .142 C1
Slough SL3 .44 A1
Chewter Cl GU19 .145 C2
Chewter La GU20 .146 A3
Cheylesmore Dr GU16 .152 B2
Cheyne Rd TW15 .98 B1
Chichester Ct Slough SL1 .43 A2
Stanwell TW19 .97 C4
Chichester Rd RG30 .84 C4
Chicory Cl RG6 .86 C1
Chieveley Cl RG31 .84 B4
Chieveley Prim Sch RG20 .78 A4
Chilbolton TW20 .95 C2
Chilcombe Way RG6 .87 B1
Child Cl RG40 .116 B4
Child St RG17 .25 A2
Childrey Way RG31 .84 A4
Chillingham Way GU15 .151 B2
Chilsey Green Rd KT16 .123 C1
Chiltern Cl
Henley-on-T RG9 .35 A4
Newbury RG14 .130 B3
Staines TW18 .97 A2
Chiltern Coll The RG4 .59 A2
Chiltern Cres RG6 .87 A4
Chiltern Ct Caversham RG4 .59 A3
Windsor SL4 .67 A3
Chiltern Ct Mews SL4 .67 A3
Chiltern Dr RG10 .61 A2
Chiltern End Cl RG9 .35 B4
Chiltern Gn HP10 .3 A4
Chiltern Rd Burnham SL1 .41 A4
Caversham RG4 .59 B2
Maidenhead SL6 .40 A3
Marlow SL7 .1 B1
Sandhurst GU47 .142 C1
Chiltern View RG8 .57 B3
Chiltern Wlk RG8 .56 C3
Chilterns Cl HP10 .3 A4
Chilterns Pk SL8 .3 A3
Chilton Ct SL6 .41 B4
Chilton Cty Prim Sch
OX11 .10 B4
Chilton Foliat CE Prim Sch
RG17 .73 A1
Chilton Way RG17 .100 B3
Chilwick Rd SL2 .21 C1
Chippendale Cl
Blackwater GU17 .150 C2
Tadley RG26 .134 C1
Chippenham Cl RG6 .113 C4
Chisbury Cl RG12 .118 C2
Chiswick Lodge 2 SL7 .1 B1
Chitterfield Gate UB7 .71 A4
Chittering Cl RG6 .87 B1
Chive Rd RG6 .87 A1
Chivers Dr RG40 .141 C4
Chives Pl RG42 .91 B1
Chobham La GU25 .122 A1
Chobham Rd
Frimley GU16 .151 C1
Sunningdale SL5 .121 A1
Choke La SL6 .19 A2
Cholmeley Pl RG1 .86 C4
Cholmeley Rd RG1 .86 C4
Cholmeley Terr RG1 .86 C4
Cholsey Rd RG19 .106 C2
Choseley Cl RG10 .37 C2
Choseley Rd RG10 .37 C2
Chrislaine Cl TW19 .70 B1
Christ the King
RC Prim Sch RG2 .113 B4
Christ the King RC Sch
TW19 .70 C1
Christchurch CE Fst Sch
GU25 .122 A3
Christchurch Cotts
GU25 .122 A3
Christchurch Ct 10 RG1 .86 B3
Christchurch Dr GU17 .150 B3
Christchurch Gdns RG2 .86 B3
Christchurch Rd
Harlington TW6 .71 A2
Reading RG2 .86 B3
Virginia Water GU25 .122 B3
Christian Sq SL4 .67 B3
Christie Cl GU18 .146 B1
Christie Hts RG14 .131 A4
Christie Wlk GU46 .149 B2
Christmas La 2 SL2 .22 B4
Christopher Ct
Ashford TW15 .97 C2
Newbury RG14 .105 A1
Christopher Ho 6 SL2 .22 B4
Chudleigh Gdns RG2 .86 B1
Church App TW20 .123 B3
Church Ave RG9 .15 C1
Church Cl Eton SL4 .67 B4
Hamstead Marshall RG20 .129 C3
Laleham TW18 .124 B3
Lambourn RG17 .25 A1
Maidenhead SL6 .39 B3
Winnersh RG41 .88 B1
Church Cotts SL6 .20 C1
Church Croft RG17 .100 B3
Church Dr SL6 .40 B2
Church End La RG30 .84 C4
Church Farm Barns RG7 .137 B3
Church Gate RG19 .106 B2
Church Gr SL3 .43 B4
Church Hams RG40 .141 B3
Church Hill Binfield RG42 .90 B3
Camberley GU15 .151 C3
Chilton OX11 .10 B4
Hurst RG10 .88 C3
Woolhampton RG7 .107 C2
Church Hill House Hospl
RG12 .118 A2
Church La Arborfield RG2 .114 B2
Ascot SL5 .120 B3
Ashampstead RG8 .54 A3
Barkham RG40 .115 B1
Binfield RG42 .90 B2
Bisley GU24 .153 C2
Brimpton RG7 .133 C3
Burghfield Common RG30 .111 C3
Caversham RG4 .59 C4
Chieveley RG20 .51 A1
Combe RG17 .147 C3
Finchampstead RG40 .141 C2
Hamstead Marshall RG20 .129 C4
Hungerford RG17 .100 B3
Maidenhead SL6 .40 B2
Newbury RG14 .104 B2
Newell Green RG42 .91 B3
Padworth RG7 .110 B2
Reading RG2 .113 B3
Shiplake RG9 .35 C1
Silchester RG7 .136 C1
Slough SL2, SL3 .43 B4
Stoke Poges SL2 .22 C1
Sunningdale SL5 .121 A2
Swallowfield RG7 .140 B3
Thatcham RG19 .106 B2
Twyford RG10 .61 C3
17 Windsor SL4 .67 B3
Yattendon RG18 .53 C1
Church Mews
Purley on T RG8 .57 B3
Woodley RG5 .87 C4
Church Par TW15 .97 C2
Church Path SL6 .40 B2
Church Rd
Aldermaston RG7 .135 A4
Arborfield RG7 .140 B3
Ascot SL5 .120 A3
Ashford TW15 .97 C2
Bagshot GU19 .145 B2
Blewbury OX11 .12 A4
Bracknell RG12 .118 B4
Caversham RG4 .59 A1
Cookham SL6 .19 A3
Earley RG6 .87 A3
Egham TW20 .96 A2
Farnham Common SL2 .22 B1
Frimley GU16 .151 B1
Froxfield SN8 .99 A3
Ham SN8 .126 B1
Little Marlow SL7 .2 B3
Lower Halliford TW17 .125 A1
Maidenhead SL6 .40 A3
Newbury RG14 .105 A3
Old Windsor SL4 .68 A1
Church Rd *continued*
Pangbourne RG8 .56 B3
Sandhurst GU15 .150 C4
Sandhurst,
Owlsmoor GU47 .143 C1
Silchester RG26 .135 C1
Stockcross RG20 .103 C3
Sunningdale SL5 .121 A2
Swallowfield RG7 .139 B3
West End GU24 .153 C4
Windlesham GU20 .146 B2
Winkfield SL4 .92 B3
Winkfield, Chavey Down SL5 119 A4
Woodley RG5 .87 C4
Church Rd E RG45 .143 A3
Church Row SL3 .23 B4
Church Side RG20 .30 C3
Church Sq TW17 .125 A1
Church St
Burnham SL1 .21 B1
Caversham RG4 .59 A1
Crowthorne RG45 .143 A2
Froxfield SN8 .99 A1
Great Shefford RG17 .48 A2
Hampstead Norreys RG18 .52 C3
Henley-on-T RG9 .15 B1
Hungerford RG17 .100 B3
Kintbury RG17 .102 A1
Reading RG1 .86 A3
Slough SL1 .42 B2
Slough, Upton Park SL1 .42 C2
Staines TW18 .96 C2
Theale RG7 .83 B2
Twyford RG10 .61 B2
Wargrave RG10 .36 B1
15 Windsor SL4 .67 B3
Church Street Mews RG7 .83 B2
Church Terr
8 Reading RG1 .86 A3
Windsor SL4 .66 C3
Church View
Beenham RG7 .109 A3
8 Slough SL1 .43 A2
White Waltham SL6 .63 C4
Yateley GU46 .149 B4
Church Views SL6 .39 C4
Church Way RG17 .100 B3
Church Wlk KT16 .124 A2
Churchend Prim Sch
RG30 .84 C3
Churchfield Mews SL2 .43 A4
Churchill Cl
East Bedfont TW14 .98 C4
Flackwell Heath HP10 .3 A4
Reading RG2 .86 A1
Churchill Cres GU46 .149 B3
Churchill Ct TW18 .97 B1
Churchill Dr Marlow SL7 .1 C2
Winnersh RG41 .88 A1
Churchill Rd
North Ascot SL5 .119 C4
Slough SL3 .43 C1
Churchmead Sch SL3 .68 A4
Churchward Wlk RG31 .84 C2
Churchway RG20 .10 A1
Churn Rd RG20 .31 B3
Cinnamon Cl RG6 .86 C1
Cintra Ave RG2 .86 B3
Cintra Cl RG1 .86 B3
Cippenham Inf Sch SL1 .41 B3
Cippenham La SL1 .42 A3
Cippenham Mid Sch SL1 .41 C3
Circle Hill Rd RG45 .143 B3
Circuit La RG30 .85 B3
City Rd RG31 .84 A4
Clacy Gn RG42 .91 A1
Claires Court Sch SL6 .20 A1
Clandon Ave TW20 .96 B1
Clanfield Cres RG31 .57 B1
Clanfield Ride GU17 .150 B3
Clappers Farm Rd RG7 .136 C1
Clappers Mdw SL6 .20 B1
Clapps Gate Rd RG26 .135 C1
Clapton App HP10 .3 B4
Clare Ave RG40 .116 B4
Clare Dr SL2 .22 A4
Clare Gdns TW20 .96 A2
Clare Rd Maidenhead SL6 .39 B3
Slough SL6 .41 B4
Stanwell TW19 .97 C4
Clare Wlk RG14 .130 B3
Claredon Cl RG41 .88 B1
Clarefield Cl SL6 .19 A1
Clarefield Ct SL5 .121 A1
Clarefield Dr SL6 .19 A1
Claremont Poyle SL3 .69 B3
Shepperton TW17 .125 A2
Claremont Ave GU15 .151 C3
Claremont Dr TW17 .125 A2
Claremont Gdns SL7 .1 C1
Claremont Rd
Egham TW18 .96 B2
Marlow SL7 .1 C1
Windsor SL4 .67 B3
Clarence Cres SL4 .67 B3
Clarence Ct Egham TW20 .95 C1
Maidenhead SL6 .39 C4
Windsor SL4 .67 A3
Clarence Dr
Camberley GU15 .152 A4
Englefield Green TW20 .95 B2
Clarence Lodge TW20 .95 B2
Clarence Rd
Henley-on-T RG9 .15 B1
Windsor SL4 .67 A3
Clarence St Egham TW20 .95 C1
Staines TW18 .96 C2
Clarence Way RG31 .84 A2
Clarendon Ct
Blackwater GU17 .150 B2
Slough SL2 .43 A3
Clarendon Cty Prim Sch
TW15 .97 C2
Clarendon Gdns RG14 .105 A2
Clarendon Rd
Ashford TW15 .97 C2
Reading RG6 .87 A3
Clares Green Rd RG7 .113 A2
Clarewood Dr GU15 .151 C3
Clarke Cres GU15 .150 C4
Clarks Gdns RG17 .100 B3
Classics The RG17 .25 A1
Claverdon RG12 .118 A1
Clay Cl Flackwell Heath HP10 .3 A4
Purley on T RG31 .57 A1
Clay Cnr KT16 .124 A1
Clay Hill Cres RG14 .105 B3
Clay La Beenham RG7 .108 C3
Wokingham RG40 .116 C3
Claycots Inf Sch SL2 .22 A1
Claycots Jun Sch SL2 .22 A1
Claydon Ct
2 Caversham RG4 .59 A1
Staines TW18 .97 A2
Claydon Gdns GU17 .151 A1
Clayhall La SL4 .67 C1
Clayhill Cl RG12 .119 A3
Clayhill Rd RG7,RG30 .111 A2
Clayton Ct SL3 .44 A2
Clayton Gr RG12 .118 C4
Clayton Rd GU14 .150 C1
Clayton Wlk RG2 .86 B2
Claytons Cty Comb Sch
SL8 .3 A3
Claytons Mdw SL8 .3 A2
Cleares Pasture SL1 .21 A1
Clearsprings GU18 .153 A4
Cleeve Ct TW14 .98 C4
Cleeve Down RG8 .34 B4
Cleeve Ho 6 RG12 .118 C3
Cleeve Rd RG8 .34 A4
Clements Cl Shinfield RG7 .113 A1
Slough SL1 .43 A2
Clements Mead RG31 .57 A1
Clements Rd RG9 .15 B2
Clent Rd RG2 .86 A2
Cleopatra Pl RG42 .91 C1
Clerewater Pl RG19 .105 C2
Clerics Wlk TW17 .125 B2
Cleve Ct RG8 .34 A4
Clevedon Dr RG6 .87 A1
Clevedon Rd RG31 .57 C2
Clevehurst Cl SL2 .23 A3
Cleveland RG10 .61 A2
Cleveland Cl
Maidenhead SL6 .40 A3
Wooburn Green HP10 .3 C4
Cleveland Dr TW18 .124 A4
Cleveland Gr RG14 .104 C2
Cleveland Pk TW19 .70 C1
Clevemede RG8 .34 B4
Cleves Ct SL4 .66 C2
Cleves Way TW16 .98 C1
Clewborough Dr GU15 .152 A3
Clewborough House Sch
GU15 .152 A3
Clewer Ave SL4 .67 A3
Clewer Ct Rd SL4 .67 A4
Clewer Fields SL4 .67 B3
Clewer Green CE Fst Sch
SL4 .67 A2
Clewer Hill Rd SL4 .66 C2
Clewer New Town SL4 .67 A3
Clewer Pk SL4 .67 A4
Clifford Gr TW15 .98 A2
Clifford Way SL8 .3 A3
Clifton Cl SL6 .40 A2
Clifton Ct 8 TW19 .70 C1
Clifton Lodge Eton SL4 .42 A1
10 Slough SL1 .43 A2
Clifton Park Rd RG4 .59 A1
Clifton Rd Harlington TW6 .71 A2
Newbury RG14 .104 C1
Slough SL1 .43 A2
Wokingham RG41 .116 A4
Clifton Rise
Wargrave RG10 .36 C1
Windsor SL4 .66 B3
Clifton St RG1 .85 C4
Clintons Gn RG42 .118 A4
Clive Ct SL1 .42 B2
Clive Gn RG12 .118 A2
Clivedale Rd RG5 .87 C2
Cliveden SL6 .20 C4
Cliveden Mead SL6 .20 B1
Cliveden Pl TW17 .125 B2
Cliveden Rd SL6 .20 C2
Clivemont Rd SL6 .39 C4
Clockhouse La
TW14, TW15 .98 A3
Clockhouse La E TW20 .96 A1
Clockhouse La W TW20 .96 A1
Cloister Mews RG7 .83 C2
Cloisters The
Caversham RG4 .59 A2
Frimley GU16 .151 B1
Clonmel Cl RG4 .59 B1
Clonmel Way SL1 .21 A1
Close End RG17 .25 A1
Close The
Aston Tirrold OX11 .12 C4
Bourne End SL8 .3 A3
Bracknell RG12 .118 B3
Burghfield Common RG7 .111 A2
Burnham SL1 .41 B3
Great Shefford RG17 .48 A2

Close The continued
Hampstead Norreys RG18 ..**52** C3
Henley-on-T RG9 ....**35** B4
Lightwater GU18 ......**146** A1
North Ascot SL5 ....**119** B4
Sandhurst GU47 ....**150** C4
Thatcham RG18 ....**106** A2
Virginia Water GU25 ...**122** B2
Woodley RG5 ....**87** C3
Clough Dr RG18 ....**78** C3
Clove Cl RG6 ....**86** C1
Clover Cl RG40 ....**116** C4
Clover La GU46 ....**149** A3
Club La GU46 ....**149** A3
Clumps The TW13,TW15 ..**98** B2
Clyde Rd TW19 ....**97** C4
Clyve Way TW18 ......**123** C4
Coach Ho The HP10 .....**3** C3
Coach House Cl GU16 ...**151** C2
Coach Rd SL5 ....**92** C1
Coach Ride SL7 ....**1** B2
Coachman's Lodge 28 SL4 .**67** B3
Coachmans Ct RG14 ...**105** A2
Coachmans Way SL1,SL6 ..**41** A4
Coalport Way RG30 .....**57** C1
Cobb Cl SL3 ....**68** B3
Cobbetts La GU46,GU7 ..**149** C3
Cobblers Cl SL2 ....**22** A2
Cobham Cl SL1 ....**41** C3
Cobham Rd RG5 ....**87** C4
Cochrane Cl RG19 .....**106** C2
Cochrane Pl GU20 .....**146** B3
Cock La RG7 ....**82** A1
Cock's La RG42, SL4 ....**92** A3
Cock-A-Dobby GU47 ...**143** A1
Cockett Rd SL3 ....**43** C2
Cockney Hill RG30 ......**84** C3
Cody Cl RG5 ....**88** A4
Coe Spur SL1 ....**42** A2
Coftards SL2 ....**43** B4
Cokers Ct 2 SL8 ....**3** A2
Cold Ash Hill RG18 ....**106** B4
Cold Ash St Mark's
CE Prim Sch RG18 .....**79** B1
Cold Grove Cotts SL6 ...**20** C1
Coldharbour Cl
Henley-on-T RG9 ....**35** B4
Thorpe TW20 ....**123** B3
Coldharbour La
Thorpe TW20 ....**123** B3
West End GU24 ....**153** C4
Coldharbour Rd RG17 ...**100** B2
Coldicutt St RG4 ....**59** B1
Coldmoorholme La SL8 ..**2** C2
Colemans Moor La RG5 ..**87** C3
Colemans Moor Rd RG5 ..**88** A3
Colenorton Cres SL4 ....**41** C1
Coleridge Ave GU46 ...**149** C3
Coleridge Cl
Crowthorne RG45 .....**143** B2
Twyford RG10 ....**61** C1
Coleridge Cres SL3 .....**69** C3
Coleridge Rd TW15 .....**97** C2
Coley Ave RG1 ....**85** C3
Coley Hill RG1 ....**85** C3
Coley Park Prim Sch RG1 .**85** C3
Coley Park Rd RG1 ......**85** C3
Coley Pl RG1 ....**86** A3
Coley Prim Sch RG1 .....**86** A3
Colin Way SL1 ....**42** A2
Coliseum Bsns Ctr GU15 .**151** A2
Collaroy Glen RG18 ....**106** B4
Collaroy Rd RG18 .....**106** B4
College Ave Egham TW20 ..**96** A1
Maidenhead SL6 ......**39** C4
Slough SL1 ....**42** C2
College Cl GU15 ......**151** B4
College Cres
Sandhurst GU47 ....**150** C4
Windsor SL4 ....**67** B3
College Glen SL6 ....**39** B4
College Piece RG7 .....**136** C3
College Rd
Bracknell RG12 ....**118** B3
Maidenhead SL6 ......**39** C4
Reading RG6 ....**86** C3
Sandhurst GU47 ....**150** C4
Slough SL1 ....**41** C3
College Ride
Bagshot GU19 ....**145** B1
Camberley GU15 .....**151** B4
College Rise SL6 ....**39** B4
College Town Cty Inf Sch
GU47 ....**150** C4
College Town Cty Jun Sch
GU47 ....**150** C4
College Way Ashford TW15 .**97** C2
East Garston RG17 .....**47** B3
Colleton Cty Prim Sch The
RG10 ....**61** C2
Colleton Dr RG10 ....**61** C2
Collier Cl SL6 ....**19** C1
Colliers Way RG30 .....**85** C4
Collingwood Coll GU15 ..**152** A4
Collingwood Grange Cl
GU15 ....**152** A4
Collingwood Mount
GU15 ....**152** A3
Collingwood Pl GU15 ...**152** A4
Collingwood Rise GU15 ..**152** A4
Collingwood Wlk RG31 ..**84** A4
Collins Cl RG14 ....**105** A2
Collins Dr RG18 ....**78** C3
Collinswood Rd 1 SL2 ..**22** B4
Collis St RG2 ....**86** A3
Colliston Wlk RG31 .....**84** C2
Collum Green Rd SL2 ...**23** A4

Coln Cl SL6 ....**39** C4
Coln Trad Est SL3 ......**69** C3
Colnbrook By-Pass
Colnbrook SL3, UB7 ....**69** B4
Harmondsworth UB7 ...**70** B4
Colnbrook CE Prim Sch
SL3 ....**69** B4
Colnbrook Ct SL3 ......**69** C3
Colndale Rd SL3 ......**69** B3
Colne Bank SL3, TW19 ...**69** B2
Colne Orch SL0 ....**44** C3
Colne Reach TW19 .....**69** C1
Colne Way TW19 ......**96** A3
Colnebridge Cl TW18 ...**96** C2
Colnworth Cl RG6 .....**114** A4
Colonial Rd
East Bedfont TW14 ....**98** C4
Slough SL1 ....**43** A2
Colonnade SL6 ....**40** A4
Colony Gate GU16 ....**152** B1
Colston Cl RG31 ....**84** B2
Colthrop La RG19 .....**107** A1
Colthrop Way RG19 ...**107** A1
Coltsfoot Cl RG7 ......**111** A2
Columbia Ct RG40 ....**141** C4
Colville Gdns GU18 ...**153** C4
Colwyn Cl GU46 ......**149** B3
Colyer Cl RG18 ....**79** B4
Colyton Way RG8 ......**57** C3
Combe Rd RG30 ....**84** C4
Combe View RG17 ....**100** B3
Combermere Cl SL4 ....**67** A3
Comet Rd TW19 ....**97** B4
Comet Way RG5 ....**88** A4
Comfrey Cl RG40 .....**116** C4
Commercial Rd
Reading RG2 ....**86** A1
Staines TW18 ....**97** A1
Common Hill RG7 ......**82** C2
Common La
Brightwalton RG20 ....**28** B3
Eton SL4 ....**42** B1
Common Rd Dorney SL4 .**41** B1
Eton SL4 ....**42** A1
Flackwell Heath HP10 ...**3** A4
Headley RG19 ....**132** C1
Slough SL3 ....**44** A1
Common The HP10 ....**3** A4
Common Wood SL2 .....**22** B4
Commonfield La RG40 ..**141** A4
Commonfields GU24 ...**153** C3
Commons Rd RG41 .....**88** C1
Communications Rd
RG19 ....**131** C2
Compton Ave RG31 .....**84** A4
Compton CE Prim Sch
RG20 ....**31** C2
Compton Cl
Bracknell RG12 ....**117** C2
Earley RG6 ....**87** B2
Sandhurst GU47 ....**143** B1
Compton Ct SL1 ....**41** C4
Compton Dr SL6 ....**39** A4
Compton Manor RG20 ..**31** B2
Compton Place Bsns Ctr
GU15 ....**151** A2
Comsaye Wlk RG12 ....**118** B2
Concorde Rd SL6 ......**39** B2
Concorde Way Slough SL1 .**42** B2
Woodley RG5 ....**88** A4
Condor Cl RG31 ....**57** B2
Condor Rd TW18 ......**124** B3
Conegar Ct SL1 ....**42** C3
Coney Grange RG42 ....**91** A1
Coneygree Ct RG66 ....**87** A1
Congreve Cl RG7 ......**135** A4
Conifer Cl RG26 ......**134** C1
Conifer Crest RG14 ....**130** B2
Conifer Dr
Camberley GU15 .....**152** A3
Purley on T RG31 .....**57** A1
Conifer La TW20 ....**96** B2
Conifers The
Crowthorne RG45 .....**143** A4
Maidenhead SL6 ......**39** A4
Coningham Rd RG2 ...**113** B3
Coningsby RG12 ......**118** A3
Coningsby Cl SL6 ......**39** B2
Coningsby La SL6 ......**65** B3
Conisboro Ave RG4 ....**58** C3
Conisboro Way RG4 ....**58** C3
Coniston Cl Frimley GU15 .**152** B2
Thatcham RG19 ......**106** A2
Woodley RG5 ....**87** C3
Coniston Cres SL1 ......**41** B4
Coniston Ct
Lightwater GU18 .....**146** A1
18 Newbury RG14 ....**105** A2
Coniston Dr RG30 ......**57** C1
Coniston Way TW20 ....**96** A1
Conkers SL6 ....**40** A4
Connaught Ave TW15 ...**97** C2
Connaught Cl
Crowthorne RG45 .....**142** C2
Maidenhead SL6 ......**19** C1
Reading RG30 ....**85** B4
Yateley GU46 ....**149** A3
Connaught Cty Mid Sch
GU19 ....**145** C1
Connaught Rd
Bagshot GU19 ....**145** B2
Camberley GU15 .....**151** B2
Newbury RG14 ....**105** A2
Reading RG30 ....**85** B4
Slough SL1 ....**43** A2
Conniston Cl SL7 ....**1** A1
Connop Way GU16 ....**151** C2

Consort Dr GU15 ......**152** B4
Constable Cl RG5 ......**88** A4
Constitution Rd RG30 ...**85** A4
Consul Cl RG5 ....**88** A3
Control Tower Rd TW6 ..**71** A2
Convent Lodge TW15 ...**98** A2
Convent Rd Ashford TW15 .**98** A1
Windsor SL4 ....**67** A3
Conway Cl GU16 ......**151** C1
Conway Dr Ashford TW15 ..**98** B1
Thatcham RG18 ......**106** B3
Conway Rd Burnham SL6 ..**41** A4
Harlington TW6 ....**71** A2
Reading RG31 ....**84** B3
Cooke Rise RG42 ....**91** A1
Cookham Cl GU47 .....**143** B1
Cookham Dean Bottom La
SL6 ....**19** B4
Cookham Dean
CE Prim Sch SL6 ......**19** A4
Cookham Lodge 15 SL6 .**39** C3
Cookham Rd
Bracknell RG12 ....**117** C4
Maidenhead SL6 ......**19** C2
Cookham Rise Cty Prim Sch
SL6 ....**19** C3
Cookham Sta SL6 ......**19** C4
Coolarne Rise GU15 ...**152** A3
Coolgardie Rd TW15 ....**98** B2
Coombe Cl RG19 ......**106** C2
Coombe Hill OX12 .....**28** A4
Coombe Pine RG12 ....**118** B2
Coombe Rd Compton RG20 .**31** C1
Yateley GU46 ....**149** A4
Coombe Sq RG19 .....**106** C2
Coombe The RG8 ....**33** C3
Coombes Cty Inf Sch The
RG2 ....**114** C2
Coombes La RG41 .....**115** B2
Coombesbury La RG20 ..**76** B1
Cooper Cl RG2 ....**113** B4
Cooper Rd Henley-on-T RG9 .**15** B1
Windlesham GU20 ....**146** B2
Cooper Way SL1 ....**42** A2
Cooper's Hill La TW20 ..**95** B2
Coopers Cl TW18 ......**96** C2
Coopers Cres RG18 ....**106** B2
Cope Cl SL6 ....**39** B4
Cope Hall La RG14 .....**130** B4
Copeland Cl RG2 ......**113** B4
Copelands GU15 ......**152** B2
Copenhagen Cl RG2 ...**113** B4
Copenhagen Wlk RG45 ..**143** A2
Copped Hall Dr GU15 ..**152** B3
Copped Hall Way GU15 ..**152** B3
Copper Beech Cl SL4 ...**66** B3
Copperage Rd OX12 .....**9** A1
Copperdale Cl RG6 ......**86** C2
Copperfield Ave GU47 ..**143** C1
Copperfields
Ashford TW16 ....**98** C1
Reading RG4 ....**58** C2
Coppermill Rd TW19 ....**69** A1
Coppice Cl RG14 ......**131** C2
Coppice Dr TW19 ......**95** B4
Coppice Gdns
Crowthorne RG45 .....**142** C3
Yateley GU46 ....**149** B3
Coppice Gn RG42 ......**90** C1
Coppice Rd RG5 ....**87** C2
Coppice The TW15 .....**98** A1
Coppins La SL0 ....**44** C4
Copse Ave RG4 ....**59** C2
Copse Cl Camberley GU15 ..**152** A3
Marlow SL7 ....**1** B1
Purley on T RG31 .....**57** B2
Slough SL1 ....**41** C3
Copse Dr RG41 ....**116** A4
Copse End GU15 ......**152** A3
Copse Mead RG5 ....**60** C1
Copse The RG10 ......**36** C3
Copse Way RG40 .....**141** C4
Copthall Ho SL6 ....**40** A4
Copthorn Cl SL6 ....**39** A2
Copthorne Chase TW15 ..**97** C2
Copthorne Cl TW17 ....**125** B2
Copthorne Dr GU18 ...**146** A1
Corbett Dr GU18 ......**152** C4
Corbett Gdns RG5 ......**87** C4
Corbridge Rd RG2 ......**86** B2
Corby Cl RG5 ....**61** A1
Corby Dr TW20 ....**95** B1
Cordelia Croft RG42 ...**118** C4
Cordelia Gdns TW19 ....**97** C4
Cordelia Rd TW19 ......**97** C4
Corderoy Cl RG19 .....**106** C1
Corderoy Pl KT16 ......**123** C2
Cordwalles Cty Jun Sch
GU15 ....**151** C4
Cordwalles Rd GU15 ...**151** C4
Cordwallis Est SL6 ......**39** C4
Cordwallis Pk SL6 ......**39** C4
Cordwallis Rd SL6 ......**39** C4
Cordwallis St SL6 ......**39** C4
Cores End Rd SL8 ....**3** A2
Corfe Gdns Frimley GU16 .**151** C1
Slough SL1 ....**42** A3
Corfe Mews RG4 ......**59** C2
Corfe Pl SL6 ....**39** B2
Corfield Cl RG40 ......**141** C2
Coriander Way RG6 ....**86** C1
Corinne Cl RG2 ....**86** A1
Cormorant Pl GU47 ...**150** C4
Corn Croft RG42 ....**91** C1
Cornbunting Cl GU47 ..**150** B4
Cornel Ho 1 SL4 ....**67** B4
Cornerside TW15 ......**98** B1
Cornfield Gn RG41 ....**115** C4

Cornfield Rd RG5 ....**88** A4
Cornfields GU46 ......**149** A2
Cornflower Cl RG41 ...**115** C4
Cornwall Ave SL2 ......**22** B1
Cornwall Cl Bracknell RG42 .**91** C1
Camberley GU15 .....**151** C4
Eton SL4 ....**41** C1
Maidenhead SL6 ......**19** C1
Purley on T RG31 .....**57** A2
Wokingham RG41 ....**115** B3
Cornwall Lodge 11 SL6 ..**39** C3
Cornwall Way TW18 ....**96** C1
Cornwell Rd SL4 ....**68** A1
Cornwood Gdns RG2 ...**86** B2
Coronation Ave SL3 ....**43** C3
Coronation Rd Ascot SL5 .**120** A1
Littlewick Green SL6 ...**38** A3
Yateley GU46 ....**149** C4
Coronation Sq
Reading RG30 ....**85** A2
Wokingham RG40 ....**116** B4
Corporation Cotts 1
RG14 ....**105** A2
Corrie Gdns GU25 ....**122** B1
Corsair Cl TW19 ....**97** C4
Corsair Rd TW19 ....**97** C4
Corsham Rd RG31 ......**84** C2
Corsham Way RG45 ...**143** A3
Corwen Rd RG30 ....**84** C4
Coster Cl RG14 ....**104** B3
Costers Cotts SL8 ....**3** A1
Cotswold Cl
Maidenhead SL6 ......**40** A3
Slough SL1 ....**42** A2
Staines TW18 ....**97** A2
Cotswold Rd GU47 ....**142** C1
Cotswold Way RG31 ....**57** B1
Cottage Farm Way TW20 .**123** B3
Cottage La RG30 ....**85** B1
Cotterell Cl RG42 ......**91** A1
Cotterell Gdns RG10 ...**61** C2
Cottesbrooke Cl SL3 ....**69** B3
Cottesloe Cl GU24 ....**153** C2
Cottesmore RG12 .....**118** A1
Cottesmore Rd RG5 ....**87** B3
Cottage Farm Way ...
Cottage La RG30 ....**85** B1
Country Life Ho SL3 ....**68** A4
County La RG42 ....**91** C1
Courage Ct RG30 ....**85** A4
Courage Shire Horse Ctr
SL6 ....**38** C3
Course Rd SL5 ....**120** A3
Court Cl SL6 ....**40** B1
Court Cres SL1 ....**42** B4
Court Dr SL6 ....**20** B2
Court Farm Rd SL1 .....**42** A3
Court Garden L Complex
SL7 ....**1** B1
Court Gdns GU15 .....**151** B3
Court Hill Rd OX12 ......**7** B4
Court La Burnham SL1 ...**21** B4
Dorney SL4 ....**41** A2
Iver SL0 ....**44** C3
Court Rd SL6 ....**20** B2
Court The RG18 ......**106** B2
Courtenay Dr RG4 ......**59** A4
Courtfield Dr SL6 ....**39** B3
Courtfield Rd TW15 ....**98** A1
Courthouse Cty Jun Sch
SL6 ....**39** A4
Courthouse Rd SL6 .....**39** B4
Courtlands 14 SL6 ......**39** C3
Courtlands Ave SL3 ....**43** B1
Courtlands Hill RG8 .....**56** B2
Courtlands Rd RG14 ...**105** A4
Courtney Rd TW6 ......**71** A2
Courts Rd RG6 ....**87** A2
Courtyard The
17 Bourne End SL8 .....**3** A2
Theale RG7 ....**83** C2
Coventry Rd RG1 ....**86** C4
Coverdale Way SL2 ....**21** C1
Covert La RG12 ....**118** A3
Covert The SL5 ....**120** A1
Coves Farm Wood RG42 .**117** B4
Cow La East Isley RG20 ...**30** C4
Moulsford OX10 ....**13** C3
Reading RG1 ....**58** C1
Cowley Ave KT16 .....**123** C1
Cowley La KT16 ....**123** C1
Coworth Cl SL5 ....**121** A2
Coworth Rd SL5 ....**121** A2
Cowper Cl KT16 ....**123** C2
Cowper Rd SL2 ....**22** A1
Cowper Way RG30 .....**85** B2
Cowslade RG14 ....**104** B3
Cowslip Cl RG31 ....**84** A3
Cowslip Cres RG18 ....**106** C3
Cox Green Comp Sch SL6 .**39** A2
Cox Green La SL6 ......**39** B2
Cox Green Rd SL6 ......**39** B2
Coxborrow Cl SL6 ......**19** C4
Coxeter Rd RG14 ......**104** C4
Coxgreen GU47 ......**150** B3
Coxs Ave TW17 ....**125** C1
Coxs La RG7 ....**107** B2
Crabtree Ct RG18 ....**78** C3
Crabtree Cnr TW20 ...**123** A4
Crabtree La RG18 ....**78** C3
Crabtree Office Village
TW20 ....**123** B4
Crabtree Rd
Camberley GU15 .....**151** A1
Thorpe TW20 ....**123** B4
Craddock Rd RG2 ......**86** A2

Clo-Cri **161**
Crafnant Ct TW15 ......**97** C2
Crafts End OX11 ....**10** C4
Craig Ave RG30 ....**85** A4
Craigwell Cl TW18 ....**123** C4
Crail Cl RG41 ....**116** A2
Crake Pl GU47 ....**150** B4
Cramond Ct TW14 .....**98** C4
Cranbourne Ave
Reading RG31 ....**84** B2
Windsor SL4 ....**66** C3
Cranbourne Cl SL1 .....**42** B3
Cranbourne Cotts SL4 ..**93** A3
Cranbourne Gdns RG30 .**58** A1
Cranbourne Prim Sch
SL5 ....**93** A2
Cranbrook Dr SL6 ......**19** B1
Cranbury Rd RG30 .....**85** B4
Crane Ct GU47 ....**150** B4
Crane Rd TW19 ....**71** A1
Crane Wharf 14 RG1 ...**86** A4
Craneswater UB3 ......**71** C4
Cranford Ave TW19 ....**97** C4
Cranford Cl Hurst RG10 ..**88** C3
Stanwell TW19 ....**97** C4
Cranford House Sch
OX10 ....**13** C3
Cranford La
Harlington TW6 ....**71** C3
Harlington UB3 ....**71** C4
Hatton TW6 ....**71** C4
Cranford Mews 10 RG1 ..**86** A3
Cranford Park Dr GU46 .**149** B3
Cranleigh Rd TW13 ....**98** C2
Cranmer Cl RG31 ......**57** A2
Cranwell Gr
Lightwater GU18 .....**152** C3
Littleton TW17 ......**124** C3
Cranwell Rd TW6 ......**71** A3
Craufurd Ct SL6 ......**39** C4
Craufurd Rise SL6 ......**39** C4
Craven Cl RG17 ....**102** A1
Craven Dene RG14 ....**105** A2
Craven Rd Inkpen RG17 ..**127** A3
Newbury RG14 ....**104** C1
Reading RG1 ....**86** B3
Craven Way RG17 .....**102** A1
Crawford Cl RG6 ....**87** A2
Crawford Gdns GU15 ..**151** B2
Crawford Pl RG14 .....**104** C2
Crawley Chase RG42 ...**92** A1
Crawley Dr GU15 .....**151** C3
Crawley Hill GU15 ....**151** C3
Crawley Ridge GU15 ...**151** C4
Crawley Ridge
Cty Inf Sch GU15 .....**151** C4
Crawley Ridge
Cty Jun Sch GU15 ....**151** C4
Crawley Wood Cl GU15 .**151** C4
Crawshay Dr RG4 ......**59** A4
Crayle St SL2 ....**22** A4
Crayonne Cl TW16 ....**125** C2
Crazies Hill CE Prim Sch
RG10 ....**36** C3
Crecy Cl RG41 ....**115** C3
Crediton Cl RG5 ....**88** A4
Cree's Mdw GU20 ....**146** B2
Creighton Ct RG2 ......**86** B2
Cremyll Rd RG1 ....**58** C1
Crendon Ct RG4 ....**59** A1
Crescent Cl TW18 ......**96** C2
Crescent Dale SL6 ......**39** C3
Crescent Dr SL6 ....**39** C4
Crescent Rd
Reading, Tilehurst RG31 ..**57** A3
Reading, Whiteknights RG1 ..**86** C3
Shepperton TW17 ....**125** B2
Wokingham RG40 ....**116** B3
Crescent The
Ashford TW15 ....**97** C2
Bracknell RG12 ......**118** B3
Chertsey KT16 ....**124** A3
Earley RG6 ....**87** B2
Egham TW20 ....**95** C1
Harlington UB3 ....**71** B4
Kintbury RG17 ......**102** A1
Lower Halliford TW17 .**125** C1
Maidenhead SL6 ......**39** C4
Mortimer RG7 ....**137** A3
Padworth RG7 ....**109** B2
Shiplake RG9 ....**36** A2
Slough SL1 ....**42** C2
Theale RG7 ....**83** C2
Crescent Villas 5 SL4 ...**67** B3
Cress Rd SL1 ....**42** A2
Cressex Cl RG42 ....**90** B1
Cressida Chase RG42 ...**91** C1
Cressingham Rd RG2 ....**86** B1
Cressington Pl SL8 ......**3** A2
Cresswell Rd RG14 ....**105** B2
Cresswell Row SL7 ......**1** B1
Cresswells Mead SL6 ...**40** B1
Crest Cl RG10 ....**61** C2
Crest Ho TW15 ....**98** A2
Crest The RG4 ....**59** B3
Creswell Cl RG2 ......**113** B3
Cricket Field Gr RG45 ..**143** B2
Cricket Hill La
GU17,GU46 ....**149** C2
Cricketers RG20 ......**103** B3
Cricketers La
Windlesham GU20 ....**146** B2
Winkfield RG42 ....**92** A2
Crimp Hill SL4, TW20 ...**95** A3
Crisp Gdns RG42 ....**90** C1

Crisp Rd RG9 . . . . 15 B2
Crispin Cl RG4 . . . . .58 B3
Crispin Way SL2 . . . . .22 B4
Crocker Cl SL5 . . . . .119 C4
Crockford Pl RG42 . . . . .90 C1
Crockhamwell Rd RG5 . . . .87 C3
Crocus Mead RG18 . . . . . .106 C2
Crocus Way RG41 . . . . . . .115 B4
Croft Cl Harlington UB3 . . . .71 B4
  Wokingham RG41 . . . . . .116 A1
Croft Cnr SL4 . . . . .68 A1
Croft La Newbury RG14 . . . .104 C2
  Yateley GU46 . . . . .149 B4
Croft Rd Goring RG8 . . . . . .34 B3
  Hungerford RG17 . . . . . .100 B3
  Mortimer RG7 . . . . .136 C3
  Newbury RG14 . . . . .130 B3
  Shinfield RG7 . . . . .113 B1
  Wokingham RG40 . . . . . .116 A1
Croft The Bracknell RG42 . . .91 A1
  Kintbury RG17 . . . . .102 A1
  Maidenhead SL6 . . . . . . .39 B3
  Marlow SL7 . . . . .2 A2
Croft Way GU16 . . . . .151 C4
Crofter's Cl GU47 . . . . . . .150 A4
Crofters SL4 . . . . .68 A1
Crofthill Rd SL2 . . . . .22 A1
Crofton Cl RG12 . . . . .118 C2
Crofts The TW17 . . . . . . .125 C3
Cromer Cl RG31 . . . . .57 B1
Cromer Ct SL1 . . . . .42 C4
Cromer Rd TW6 . . . . .71 A3
Cromwell Cl RG9 . . . . .35 C4
Cromwell Dr SL1 . . . . .42 C4
Cromwell Gdns SL7 . . . . . . .1 C4
Cromwell Pl 21 RG14 . . . .105 A2
Cromwell Rd Ascot SL5 . . .120 A2
  Camberley GU15 . . . . . . .151 B4
  Caversham RG4 . . . . .59 A1
  Henley-on-T RG9 . . . . . . .35 C4
  Maidenhead SL6 . . . . . . .39 B4
  Marlow SL7 . . . . .1 C1
  Newbury RG14 . . . . .105 B3
Crondall Ct GU15 . . . . . . .151 A2
Crondall End GU46 . . . . . .149 B4
Cropper Cl RG19 . . . . .107 A2
Crosby Gdns GU46 . . . . . .149 A4
Crosby Hill Dr GU15 . . . . .151 C4
Crosfields Sch RG2 . . . . . .113 C4
Cross Fell RG12 . . . . .118 A3
Cross Gates SL1 . . . . .42 C4
Cross Keys Rd RG8 . . . . . . .14 B2
Cross La RG7 . . . . .138 B4
Cross Oak SL4 . . . . .67 A3
Cross Rd SL5 . . . . .121 A4
Cross St Reading RG1 . . . . .86 A4
  Wokingham RG40 . . . . . .116 B3
Crossfields Cl RG2 . . . . . .113 C4
Crossland Rd RG1 . . . . . . .86 A4
Crossway RG12 . . . . .118 B4
Crossways Charlton TW16 . .98 C4
  Egham TW20 . . . . .96 B1
  Woodley RG5 . . . . .87 C3
Crossways SL4 . . . . .67 B3
Crosswell Cl TW17 . . . . . .125 B4
Crosthwaite Way SL1 . . . . .41 B4
Crouch La SL4 . . . . .92 C4
Crow Piece La SL2 . . . . . . .21 C2
Crowfield Dr RG19 . . . . . .106 A2
Crowle Rd RG17 . . . . .25 C1
Crown Acre Cl RG19 . . . . .106 B2
Crown Cl SW3 . . . . .69 B4
Crown Colonnade RG1 . . . .86 C4
Crown Cotts
  Bracknell SL5 . . . . .119 B2
  Englefield Green TW20 . . .95 A1
  Windsor SL4 . . . . .67 B4
Crown Ct RG19 . . . . .106 B2
Crown Hill Ct SL4 . . . . . . .120 C4
Crown La Burnham SL2 . . . .22 A4
  Maidenhead SL6 . . . . . . .40 A4
  Marlow SL7 . . . . .1 B1
  Theale RG7 . . . . .83 C2
  Wentworth GU25 . . . . . .122 B2
Crown Mdw SL3 . . . . .69 A4
Crown Mead RG19 . . . . . .106 B2
Crown Pl Reading RG1 . . . . .86 B3
  Sandhurst GU47 . . . . . . .143 C1
Crown Rd Marlow SL7 . . . . .1 B1
  Wentworth GU25 . . . . . .122 B2
Crown Rise KT16 . . . . . . .123 C1
Crown Row RG12 . . . . . . .118 B2
Crown St Egham TW20 . . . .96 A2
  Reading RG1 . . . . .86 A3
Crown Wood
  Cty Prim Sch RG12 . . . . .118 C2
Crowsley Rd RG9 . . . . .36 A2
Crowthorne CE Sch
  RG45 . . . . .143 B3
Crowthorne Lodge RG12 .118 A3
Crowthorne Rd
  Bracknell RG40, RG12 . . .117 C1
  Bracknell,
  Easthampstead RG12 . . . .118 A3
  Sandhurst GU47 . . . . . . .143 A1
Crowthorne Rd N RG12 . . .118 A3
Crowthorne Sta RG45 . . . .142 C4
Croxley Rise SL6 . . . . .39 B3
Croydon Rd TW6 . . . . .71 A2
Cruikshank Lea GU47 . . . .150 C4
Crummock Cl SL1 . . . . . . .41 B4
Crutchley Rd RG40 . . . . . .116 B4
Cuba Cotts SL6 . . . . .20 A2
Cuckoo La GU24 . . . . .153 B3
Cuckoo Vale GU24 . . . . . .153 B3

Culford Cl RG6 . . . . .87 B1
Culham Cl RG30 . . . . .85 A2
Culham Dr SL6 . . . . .19 C1
Culham Ho 8 RG12 . . . . .118 C3
Cullen Cl GU46 . . . . .149 B3
Cullern's Pass SL6 . . . . . . .39 C4
Culley Way SL6 . . . . .39 A2
Culloden Way RG41 . . . . . .115 C3
Culver Croft RG42 . . . . . . .90 C1
Culver La RG6 . . . . .87 A4
Culver Rd Newbury RG14 . .130 C4
  Reading RG6 . . . . .86 C3
  Sandhurst GU47 . . . . . . .143 B1
Cumberland Ave SL2 . . . . .22 B1
Cumberland Dr RG12 . . . .118 C4
Cumberland Lodge SL4 . . . .94 B2
Cumberland Rd
  Ashford TW15 . . . . .97 B3
  Frimley SL6 . . . . .152 B2
  Reading RG1 . . . . .86 C4
Cumberland St TW18 . . . . .96 B2
Cumberland Way RG41 . . .115 B4
Cumbernauld Gdns TW16 .98 C2
Cumbrae Cl SL2 . . . . .43 A3
Cumbria Cl SL6 . . . . .39 B2
Cumnor Way RG12 . . . . . .118 C3
Cunworth Ct RG12 . . . . . .117 C2
Curfew Bell Rd KT16 . . . . .123 C1
Curl Way RG41 . . . . .116 A3
Curlew Cl RG19 . . . . .106 B2
Curlew Dr RG31 . . . . .84 B3
Curley Hill Rd GU18 . . . . .152 C4
Curleys Way RG7 . . . . . . .139 B3
Curling Way RG14 . . . . . .105 B2
Curls La SL6 . . . . .39 C2
Curls Rd SL6 . . . . .39 C2
Curnock Ct RG14 . . . . . . .104 C1
Curridge Gn RG18 . . . . . . .78 C2
Curridge Piece RG18 . . . . .78 C3
Curridge Prim Sch RG18 . .78 B2
Curridge Rd RG18 . . . . . . .78 B2
Curriers La SL1 . . . . .21 B4
Curtis Cl GU15 . . . . .152 B4
Curtis Rd RG31 . . . . .84 B2
Curzon Mall 16 SL1 . . . . .42 C2
Curzon St RG30 . . . . .85 C4
Cutbush Cl RG6 . . . . .114 A4
Cutbush La RG2 & RG6 . . .114 A4
Cutting Hill SN8, RG17 . . .126 A2
Cuttings The RG18 . . . . . . .52 C3
Cwmcarn RG4 . . . . .58 C3
Cygnet Ct RG19 . . . . .106 A2
Cygnets The TW18 . . . . . . .96 C2
Cypress Cl RG40 . . . . .142 A4
Cypress Hill GU14 . . . . . .150 C1
Cypress Ho SL3 . . . . .44 A1
Cypress Rd RG5 . . . . .88 A3
Cypress Way GU17 . . . . . .150 A3
Cypress Wlk TW20 . . . . . . .95 A3

D

Dacre Ave RG4 . . . . .59 C2
Dagmar Rd SL4 . . . . .67 B3
Dair House Sch SL2 . . . . . .22 B2
Dairy Ct SL6 . . . . .65 A4
Dairy La RG9 . . . . .16 A4
Dalby Cres RG14 . . . . .131 A4
Dalcross RG12 . . . . .118 C2
Dale Cl SL5 . . . . .121 A2
Dale Ct SL1 . . . . .42 B2
Dale Gdns GU47 . . . . .150 A4
Dale Lodge Rd SL5 . . . . . .121 A2
Dale Rd Ashford TW16 . . . .98 C1
  Reading RG2 . . . . .86 A3
  Walton-on-T KT12 . . . . . .125 C1
Daleham Ave TW20 . . . . . .96 A1
Dalley Ct GU47 . . . . .150 B4
Dalston Cl GU15 . . . . .152 B2
Dalton Cl RG30 . . . . .84 C4
Damask Cl GU47 . . . . .153 C3
Damer Gdns RG9 . . . . .35 C4
Damson Gr SL1 . . . . .42 B2
Dandridge Cl SL3 . . . . .43 B1
Dandridge Dr SL8 . . . . .3 B2
Dane Rd TW15 . . . . .98 B1
Danefield RG40 . . . . .116 B3
Danehill RG6 . . . . .114 A4
Danehurst TW20 . . . . .95 C1
Danes Ct SL6 . . . . .39 B4
Danes Gdns SL6 . . . . .19 C3
Danesfield Sch SL7 . . . . . . .17 C4
Danvers Cl RG19 . . . . .106 B2
Danywern Dr RG41 . . . . . . .88 B1
Darby Green La GU17 . . . .150 A3
Darby Green Rd GU17 . . . .150 A3
Darby La SL6 . . . . .55 A3
Darby Vale RG42 . . . . .91 A1
Darell Rd SL4 . . . . .58 C2
Dark La Bradfield RG7 . . . . .82 B4
  Purley on T RG31 . . . . . . .57 A1
  Wargrave RG10 . . . . .36 B1
  Wickham RG17 . . . . .101 A4
Darleydale Cl GU47 . . . . . .143 B1
Darling's La SL6 . . . . .18 C1
Darracott Cl GU15 . . . . . . .152 A4
Darrell Cl SL3 . . . . .43 C1
Dart Cl Brands Hill SL3 . . . .69 A4
  Thatcham RG18 . . . . . . .106 A3
  Wokingham RG40 . . . . . .141 C3
Dartington Ave RG5 . . . . . .87 B2
Dartington Cl RG30 . . . . . .84 C4
Dartmouth Cl RG12 . . . . . .118 C3
Dartmouth Ct 27 SL1 . . . . .42 C2
Dartmouth Terr 1 RG1 . . .86 B3
Darvill's La SL1 . . . . .41 B2
Darvills La RG10 . . . . .62 C1

Darwall Dr SL5 . . . . .119 B4
Darwin Cl RG2 . . . . .86 A1
Darwin Rd SL3 . . . . .43 C2
Dashwood Cl
  Bracknell RG12 . . . . .118 B4
  Slough SL3 . . . . .43 B1
Datchet Rd SL3 . . . . .68 A3
Datchet Rd Horton SL3 . . . .68 C2
  Old Windsor SL4 . . . . . . .68 A2
  Slough SL3 . . . . .42 C1
  Windsor SL4 . . . . .67 B4
Datchet Sta SL3 . . . . .68 A3
Dauntless Rd RG7 . . . . . . .111 A2
Davenport Rd RG12 . . . . . .118 C4
Daventry Cl SL3 . . . . .69 C3
Daventry Ct RG42 . . . . . . .118 A4
David Cl UB3 . . . . .71 C4
David Ct TW18 . . . . .97 A2
David Rd SL3 . . . . .69 C3
David Smith Ct RG31 . . . . .84 C3
Davis Cl SL1 . . . . .1 C1
Davis Gdns GU47 . . . . . . .150 C4
Davis St RG10 . . . . .88 B3
Davis Way RG10 . . . . .88 B2
Davy Cl RG40 . . . . .116 B3
Dawes East Rd SL1 . . . . . . .21 B1
Dawes Moor Cl SL2 . . . . . .43 B4
Dawley Ride SL3 . . . . .69 C3
Dawlish Rd RG2 . . . . .86 B1
Dawn Redwood Cl SL3 . . . .69 C2
Dawnay Cl SL5 . . . . .119 C4
Dawnay Rd GU15 . . . . . . .151 A4
Daws Cl SL0 . . . . .44 C4
Dawsmere Cl GU15 . . . . . .152 B3
Dawson Cl SL4 . . . . .67 A3
Daytona Dr RG19 . . . . . . .107 A1
Dayworth Mews RG41 . . . . .85 B4
De Beauvoir Rd RG1 . . . . . .86 C3
De Bohun Rd RG1 . . . . .86 A4
De Havilland Way TW19 . . .70 C1
De Montfort Gr RG17 . . . .100 B3
De Montfort Rd
  Newbury RG14 . . . . .104 C3
  Reading RG1 . . . . .59 A1
De Ros Pl TW20 . . . . .96 A1
De-Vitre Gn RG40 . . . . . . .116 C3
Deacon Cl RG40 . . . . .116 B4
Deacon Ct SL4 . . . . .66 B3
Deacon Way RG30 . . . . . . .58 A1
Deaconfield RG8 . . . . .14 C2
Deacons La RG18 . . . . .79 B4
Deadman's La RG7 . . . . . . .83 B2
Deadmans La RG14, RG19 131 A3
Deadmoor La RG20 . . . . . .130 C1
Deal Ave SL1 . . . . .41 C4
Dean Cl SL4 . . . . .66 B2
Dean Gr RG40 . . . . .116 B4
Dean La SL6 . . . . .19 B4
Dean Par GU15 . . . . .151 C4
Dean St SL7 . . . . .1 B1
Dean's Cloisters SL4 . . . . . .67 B4
Deanfield Ave RG9 . . . . . . .15 B1
Deanfield Cl SL7 . . . . .1 B2
Deanfield Rd RG9 . . . . .15 B1
Deans Cl SL2 . . . . .23 A2
Deans Ct GU20 . . . . .146 B2
Deans Farm RG4 . . . . .59 B1
Deansfield Cl SL6 . . . . .19 B1
Deansgate RG12 . . . . .118 A1
Deansgate Rd RG1 . . . . . . .86 A3
Decies Way SL2 . . . . .23 A2
Dedmere Ct SL7 . . . . .1 C1
Dedmere Rd SL7 . . . . .1 C1
Dedmere Rise SL7 . . . . .1 C1
Dedworth Dr SL4 . . . . .66 C3
Dedworth Green Fst Sch
  SL4 . . . . .66 C3
Dedworth Manor SL4 . . . . .66 C3
Dedworth Mid Sch SL4 . . . .66 C3
Dedworth Rd SL4 . . . . .66 B3
Dee Rd RG30 . . . . .85 A4
Deena Cl SL1 . . . . .41 C3
Deep Field SL3 . . . . .68 A4
Deep Well Dr GU15 . . . . . .151 C3
Deepcut Bridge Rd
  GU16 . . . . .152 B1
Deepdale RG12 . . . . .118 A3
Deepdene Cl RG1 . . . . .85 C4
Deepfield Rd RG12 . . . . . .118 B4
Deer Leap GU18 . . . . .153 A4
Deer Rock Hill RG12 . . . . .118 B2
Deer Rock Rd GU15 . . . . . .151 C4
Deerhurst Ave RG41 . . . . . .88 B1
Deerhurst Cl RG31 . . . . . . .84 C2
Deerswood SL6 . . . . .20 A1
Defford Cl RG41 . . . . .88 C1
Delafield Dr RG31 . . . . . . .84 B2
Delaford Cl SL0 . . . . .44 C4
Delamere Ho 8 RG1 . . . . . .85 C3
Delamere Rd RG6 . . . . .87 A4
Delane Dr RG41 . . . . .88 A1
Delaney Cl RG30 . . . . .84 C4
Delft Cl RG30 . . . . .84 C4
Dell Cl SL2 . . . . .22 B4
Dell Gr GU16 . . . . .151 C1
Dell Rd
  Finchampstead RG40 . . . .142 A2
  Purley on T RG31 . . . . . . .57 B1
Dell The
  Englefield Green TW20 . . .95 A3
  Maidenhead SL6 . . . . . . .38 C4
  9 Reading RG1 . . . . .86 B4
  Yateley GU46 . . . . .149 B3
Deller St RG42 . . . . .90 C1
Dellwood Com Hospl
  RG30 . . . . .85 B3
Delph The RG6 . . . . .87 B1
Delta Way TW20 . . . . .123 B4

Delwood Pk RG4 . . . . .58 C2
Denbeigh Pl RG1 . . . . .58 C1
Denborough Cres SL6 . . . . .39 B3
Denbury Gdns RG2 . . . . . .113 B4
Denby Way RG30 . . . . .57 C1
Dencliffe TW15 . . . . .98 A2
Dene Cl 2 Bracknell RG12 .118 B4
  Earley RG6 . . . . .87 A2
Dene Hollow OX11 . . . . . . .10 C4
Dene Way RG14 . . . . .105 A3
Denefield Sch RG31 . . . . . .57 A2
Denford La RG17 . . . . .101 B4
Denham Cl SL6 . . . . .39 B3
Denham Dr GU46 . . . . . . .149 B3
Denham Gr RG12 . . . . . . .118 B2
Denham Rd TW20 . . . . .96 A3
Denison Rd TW13 . . . . .98 C2
Denly Way GU18 . . . . .146 B1
Denman Dr TW15 . . . . .98 A1
Denmark Ave RG5 . . . . . . .61 A1
Denmark Rd
  Newbury RG14 . . . . .105 A2
  Reading RG1 . . . . .86 B3
Denmark St
  Maidenhead SL6 . . . . . . .39 C4
  Wokingham RG40 . . . . . .116 B3
Denmead Ct RG12 . . . . . . .118 C2
Dennis Cl TW15 . . . . .98 B1
Dennis Way SL1 . . . . .41 B3
Dennistoun Cl GU15 . . . . .151 B3
Dennose Cl RG6 . . . . .87 A1
Denny Rd SL3 . . . . .43 C1
Denton Cl RG19 . . . . .106 B1
Denton Ct SL7 . . . . .1 C1
Denton Rd RG40 . . . . .116 B3
Denton Way GU16 . . . . . . .151 B1
Depot Rd SL6 . . . . .40 A3
Derby Cl RG17 . . . . .25 A1
Derby Rd Caversham RG4 . .59 A2
  Newbury RG14 . . . . .104 C1
Derby St RG1 . . . . .85 C4
Derbyshire Gn RG42 . . . . . .91 C1
Derek Horn Ct GU15 . . . . .151 A3
Derek Rd SL6 . . . . .40 B4
Deri Dene Cl 2 TW19 . . . . .70 C1
Derrick Cl RG31 . . . . .84 B2
Derry Rd GU14 . . . . .150 C1
Derwent Ave RG30 . . . . . . .57 C1
Derwent Cl
  East Bedfont TW14 . . . . . .98 C4
  Wokingham RG41 . . . . . .115 C3
Derwent Dr Burnham SL1 . .41 B4
  Maidenhead SL6 . . . . . . .39 B4
Derwent Rd
  Lightwater GU18 . . . . . . .153 A4
  Thatcham RG19 . . . . . . .106 A2
  Thorpe Lea TW20 . . . . . .96 A1
Desborough Cl TW17 . . . . .125 A1
Desborough Sch SL6 . . . . . .39 C3
Deseronto Wharf Ind Est
  SL3 . . . . .43 C2
Desford Way TW15 . . . . . . .97 C3
Devenish La SL5 . . . . .120 B1
Devenish Rd SL5 . . . . .120 B1
Devereux Al SL4 . . . . .67 B3
Deverills Way SL3 . . . . .44 B1
Deveron Dr RG30 . . . . .85 A4
Devil's La GU20 . . . . .96 B1
Devils Highway The
  RG45 . . . . .142 C3
Devitt Cl RG2 . . . . .86 C1
Devon Ave SL1 . . . . .42 B4
Devon Chase RG42 . . . . . . .91 C1
Devon Cl Sandhurst GU47 .150 B4
  Wokingham RG41 . . . . . .115 C3
Devon Dr RG4 . . . . .59 C2
Devonshire Cl SL2 . . . . .22 A2
Devonshire Dr GU15 . . . . .151 C4
Devonshire Gdns RG31 . . . .57 A4
Devonshire Gn SL2 . . . . . . .22 A2
Devonshire Lodge 10 SL6 . .39 C3
Devonshire Pk RG2 . . . . . . .86 C1
Dewberry Down RG18 . . . .106 C2
Dewe La RG30 . . . . .84 C1
Dhoon Rise SL6 . . . . .39 C3
Diamedes Ave TW19 . . . . . .97 B4
Diamond Cotts RG10 . . . . . .37 B3
Diamond Hill GU15 . . . . . .151 C4
Diamond Rd SL1 . . . . .43 A2
Diamond Ridge GU15 . . . .151 C4
Diamond Way RG41 . . . . . .115 C4
Diana Cl SL3 . . . . .43 C4
Dianthus Cl KT16 . . . . . . .123 C1
Dianthus Pl RG42 . . . . .92 A1
Dick Turpin Way TW14 . . . .71 C2
Dickens Cl RG4 . . . . .59 B1
Dickens Way GU46 . . . . . .149 B3
Dickens Wlk RG14 . . . . . . .131 A4
Dido Rd OX11 . . . . .9 C4
Dieppe Cl RG41 . . . . .115 C3
Digby Rd RG14 . . . . .104 C2
Dines Way RG18 . . . . .79 B4
Dingle Rd TW15 . . . . .98 A2
Dinton Pastures Ctry Pk
  RG10 . . . . .88 B3
Disraeli Ct SL3 . . . . .69 A4
Ditchfield La RG40 . . . . . . .141 C4
Ditchling RG12 . . . . .118 A1
Ditton Park Rd SL3 . . . . . . .68 C4
Ditton Rd Datchet SL3 . . . . .68 B4
  Slough SL3 . . . . .68 C4
Dittons The RG40 . . . . . . .141 C3
Divine Mercy Coll RG9 . . . .15 C3
Dobson's La RG9 . . . . .15 B4
Dockett Eddy La TW17 . . . .124 C1
Dockett Moorings KT16 . . .124 C1
Doctors La RG18 . . . . .79 A3
Doddington Cl RG6 . . . . . . .87 B1

Dodsells Well RG40 . . . . . .141 C4
Dodsfield Rd SL2 . . . . .22 A1
Dog La RG8 . . . . .54 A3
Doghurst Ave UB3 . . . . . . .71 C4
Doghurst Dr UB7 . . . . .71 A4
Dogkennel La OX12 . . . . . . .27 B3
Doles Hill RG41 . . . . .115 B2
Doles La RG41 . . . . .115 C2
Dolman Rd RG14 . . . . .105 A2
Dolphin Cl Brimpton RG7 . .134 C4
  Winnersh RG41 . . . . .88 B1
Dolphin Ct Bracknell RG12 .118 B3
  Slough SL1 . . . . .43 A2
  Stanwell TW19 . . . . .97 A3
Dolphin Ct N TW19 . . . . . . .97 A3
Dolphin Est The TW16 . . . .125 B4
Dolphin Rd
  Charlton TW16 . . . . .125 C4
  Slough SL1 . . . . .43 A2
Dolphin Rd N TW16 . . . . . .125 C4
Dolphin Rd S TW16 . . . . . .125 C4
Dolphin Rd W TW16 . . . . . .125 C4
Doman Rd GU15 . . . . .151 A2
Domoney Cl RG19 . . . . . . .106 C2
Don Cl RG30 . . . . .85 A4
Donaldson Way RG5 . . . . . .88 A4
Doncastle Rd RG12 . . . . . .117 C3
Donegal Cl RG4 . . . . .59 B2
Donkey Dr SL8 . . . . .3 A2
Donkey La SL8 . . . . .3 A2
Donkin Hill RG4 . . . . .59 B2
Donnington Castle RG14 . .104 C4
Donnington Cl
  Bucklebury RG7 . . . . . . .108 B4
  Camberley GU15 . . . . . . .151 A2
Donnington Gdns
  Maidenhead SL6 . . . . . . .19 C1
  Reading RG1 . . . . .86 C3
Donnington Lodge RG14 . .104 C4
Donnington Pl RG41 . . . . . .88 B1
Donnington Rd RG1 . . . . . .86 B3
Donnington Sq RG14 . . . . .104 C3
Donnybrook RG12 . . . . . . .118 A1
Dorcas Ct GU15 . . . . .151 A2
Dorchester Cl SL6 . . . . .19 A1
Dorchester Ct
  Reading RG30 . . . . .85 B3
  Staines TW18 . . . . .97 A2
Dorchester Dr TW14 . . . . . .71 C1
Dorian Dr SL5 . . . . .120 C4
Doris Rd TW15 . . . . .98 B1
Dorking Way RG31 . . . . . . .84 A2
Dorly Cl TW17 . . . . .125 C2
Dormer Cl
  Crowthorne RG45 . . . . . .143 A3
  Newbury RG14 . . . . .130 C3
Dormy Ho The GU25 . . . . .121 C2
Dornels SL2 . . . . .43 B4
Dorney Cl SL4 . . . . .41 A2
Dorney Cty Comb Sch
  SL4 . . . . .40 C2
Dorney Lake Rowing Ctr
  SL4 . . . . .66 A4
Dorney Reach Rd SL4 . . . . .40 C4
Dorney Wood Rd SL1 . . . . .21 B3
Dorothy Ct RG14 . . . . .105 B2
Dorothy St 20 RG1 . . . . . . .86 A3
Dorset Cl GU15 . . . . .151 C4
Dorset Lodge 9 SL6 . . . . . .39 C3
  Windsor SL4 . . . . .67 B3
Dorset St RG30 . . . . .85 B4
Dorset Vale RG42 . . . . .91 C1
Dorset Way RG41 . . . . .115 C3
Douai Sch RG7 . . . . .108 C3
Doublet Cl RG19 . . . . .106 A2
Douglas Ct Earley RG6 . . . . .87 A2
  Marlow SL7 . . . . .2 A2
Douglas Grange RG10 . . . . .88 B2
Douglas La TW19 . . . . .68 C1
Douglas Rd
  Caversham RG4 . . . . .59 B1
  Slough SL2 . . . . .42 B4
  Stanwell TW19 . . . . .70 B1
Doultons The TW18 . . . . . . .97 A1
Douro Cl RG26 . . . . .134 B1
Dove Cl RG6 . . . . .113 C4
Dove Ct TW19 . . . . .97 C4
Dove House Cres SL2 . . . . . .21 C1
Dovecote Rd RG2 . . . . . . .113 A4
Dovedale Cl
  Caversham RG4 . . . . .58 C2
  Sandhurst GU47 . . . . . . .143 B1
Dover Rd SL1 . . . . .41 C4
Dover St RG1 . . . . .86 A3
Doveton Way RG14 . . . . . .105 A2
Dowding Ct RG5 . . . . .88 A4
Dowding Ct RG45 . . . . . . .143 B3
Dower Pk SL4 . . . . .66 C2
Down Pl SL4 . . . . .66 A4
Downe House Sch RG18 . . .79 A2
Downend La RG20 . . . . .51 A1
Downfield La SL6 . . . . .63 B3
Downfield Rd RG10 . . . . . . .63 A2
Downham Ct RG2 . . . . .86 C1
Downing Path SL2 . . . . .21 C1
Downing Rd RG31 . . . . .84 B4
Downlands RG17 . . . . .47 B3
Downmill Rd RG12 . . . . . . .117 C4
Downs Cl RG17 . . . . .46 C4
Downs Rd Aldworth RG20 . .32 A2
  Slough SL3 . . . . .43 B2
Downs Sch The RG20 . . . . .31 B2
Downs View OX11 . . . . .9 C4
Downs Way Chilton OX11 . . .9 C4
  Purley on T RG31 . . . . . . .57 B1
Downshire Cl RG17 . . . . . . .48 A2
Downshire Sq RG1 . . . . . . .85 C4

Downshire Way
Bracknell, Priestwood RG12 118 A3
Bracknell, Skimpedhill
RG12, RG42 118 A4
Downside OX11 10 B4
Downsway Sch RG31 57 B2
Doyle Gdns GU46 149 B2
Drain Hill RG17 25 A2
Drake Ave Slough SL3 43 B1
Staines TW18 96 C2
Drake Cl Bracknell RG12 118 A2
Wokingham RG40 141 C4
Draper Cl RG19 106 B1
Draycott RG12 118 C2
Drayhorse Dr GU19 145 C1
Drayton Cl RG12 118 B4
Drayton Rd RG30 85 A4
Dresden Way RG30 57 C1
Drew Mdw SL2 22 B4
Drewett Cl RG2 113 B3
Drift Rd Holyport SL4,SL6 65 B2
Oakley Green SL4 66 A1
Drift Way SL3 69 B4
Driftway Cl 4 RG6 87 B1
Drill Hall Rd KT16 124 A1
Drive The Ashford TW15 98 B1
Bourne End SL8 2 C2
Datchet SL3 68 A3
Earley RG6 87 A4
Newbury RG14 130 C4
Slough SL3 43 C2
Virginia Water GU25 122 C2
Wraysbury TW19 68 B1
Droitwich Cl RG12 118 C3
Dromepath RG41 88 A2
Dropmore Rd SL1 21 B3
Drove La RG18 79 B1
Drove The RG19 133 A1
Drovers Way
Bracknell RG12 118 C3
Woodley RG5 87 C3
Druce Way RG19 106 B2
Druce Wood SL5 119 C4
Drummond Cl RG12 118 C4
Drummond Ho 4 SL4 67 B2
Drury La RG7 137 A3
Dry Arch Rd SL5 120 C2
Dryden RG12 118 A1
Dryden Cl RG18 106 B3
Du Pre Wlk HP10 3 B2
Duchess Cl RG45 143 A4
Duchess St SL1 41 C3
Dudley Cl RG31 57 C1
Dudley Ct SL1 43 A2
Dudley Mews RG31 57 C1
Dudley Rd Ashford TW15 97 C2
East Bedfont TW14 98 B4
Duffield La SL2 22 C3
Duffield Pk SL2 23 A1
Duffield Rd RG5 60 C1
Dugdale Ho TW20 96 B2
Duke Of Cornwall Ave
GU15 144 B1
Duke St Eton SL4 67 B4
Henley-on-T RG9 15 C1
Reading RG1 86 A4
Duke's Hill GU19 145 C3
Duke's La
Old Windsor SL4, SL5 94 A2
Winkfield SL5 93 C1
Duke's Ride RG45 143 A3
Dukes Cl TW15 98 B2
Dukes Covert GU19 145 C3
Dukes Pl SL7 1 B1
Dukes Ride RG7 136 A1
Dukes Wood RG45 143 A3
Dukeshill Rd RG42 118 A4
Dulnan Cl RG30 85 A4
Dulverton Gdns RG2 86 B1
Dumas Cl GU46 149 B3
Dumbarton Way RG4 59 C3
Dunally Pk TW17 125 B1
Dunaways Cl RG6 87 B2
Dunbar Cl SL2 43 A3
Dunbar Dr RG5 88 A3
Dunboe Pl TW17 125 B1
Duncan Dr RG40 116 C3
Duncan Gdns
Purley on T RG8 57 B2
Staines TW18 97 A1
Duncan Rd RG5 87 C3
Duncannon Cres SL4 66 B2
Duncombe Ct TW18 96 C1
Duncroft SL4 66 C2
Duncroft Manor TW18 96 C3
Dundaff Cl GU15 152 A3
Dundas Cl RG12 118 A3
Dundee Rd SL1 42 A4
Dundela Cl RG5 87 C3
Dunford Pl RG42 90 C1
Dungells Farm Cl GU46 149 B2
Dungells La GU46 149 B2
Dungrovehill La SL6 18 B2
Dunholme Cl RG6 87 C1
Dunholme End SL6 39 B2
Dunkirk Cl RG41 115 C3
Dunleary Ct 13 RG30 85 B3
Dunluce Gdns RG8 56 C3
Dunn Cres RG17 102 A1
Dunnock Way RG10 36 C2
Dunoon Cl RG31 84 C2
Dunsfold Rd RG30 84 C4
Dunsmore Gdns GU46 149 A3
Dunstable Ho 11 SL7 1 C1
Dunstall Cl RG31 84 B4
Dunstan Ct TW18 97 A2
Dunstan Park Inf Sch
RG18 106 B2
Dunstan Rd RG18 106 C2
Dunstans Dr RG41 88 A1
Dunster Cl RG4 59 B3
Dunster Gdns SL1 42 A3
Dunt Ave RG10 88 C2
Dunt La RG10 88 C2
Dunwood Ct SL6 39 B3
Duppas Cl TW17 125 B2
Dupre Cl SL1 41 C2
Durand Rd RG6 87 A1
Durant Way RG31 57 B2
Durham Ave SL1 42 A4
Durham Cl Reading RG2 113 B4
Wokingham RG41 115 C3
Durham Rd GU47 143 C1
Durley Mead RG12 118 C2
Durrell Way TW17 125 B2
Dutch Barn Cl TW19 70 B1
Dutton Way SL0 44 C4
Duval Pl GU19 145 C2
Dwyer Rd RG30 85 A2
Dyer Straits OX12 9 C4
Dyers Ct RG5 87 B4
Dyson Cl SL4 67 A2
Dysons Cl RG14 104 C2
Dysonswood La RG4 58 C4

E

Eagle Cl Crowthorne RG45 143 A4
Wokingham RG41 115 C3
Eagle House Sch GU47 143 A1
Eagle Rd RG20 132 A1
Eagles Nest GU47 143 A1
Earle Croft RG42 91 B1
Earley Hill Rd RG6 87 A3
Earley Pl RG1 86 A4
Earley Sta RG6 87 B2
Earleydene SL5 120 A1
Earls Gr GU15 151 C3
Earls La SL1 41 C3
Earlsfield SL6 40 B1
Earlsfield Cl RG4 59 C2
Earlswood RG12 118 A1
Easby La RG6 87 B1
Easington Dr RG6 87 C1
East Berkshire Coll
Maidenhead SL6 39 B3
Slough SL3 44 A2
Windsor SL4 67 B3
East Burnham Cotts SL2 22 A2
East Burnham La SL2 22 A2
East Cres SL4 66 C3
East Dr Reading RG31 84 C3
Stoke Poges SL2 22 C1
Wentworth GU25 122 A2
East Gn GU17 150 B2
East La RG20 51 A1
East Paddock SL6 18 C3
East Park Farm Dr RG10 61 A2
East Ramp TW6 71 A3
East Rd East Bedfont TW14 98 B4
Maidenhead SL6 39 C4
East Ridge SL8 3 A2
East St RG1 86 A4
East Stratton Cl RG12 118 C2
East View Cl RG10 36 C1
East View Rd RG10 36 C1
Eastbourne Rd SL1 42 A4
Eastbridge SL2 43 A3
Eastbury Ave RG31 84 A4
Eastbury Ct RG42 90 C1
Eastbury Pk RG41 88 B1
Eastbury Shute RG17 46 C1
Eastchurch Rd TW6 71 C2
Eastchurch Road Rdbt
TW6 71 C3
Eastcourt Ave RG6 87 A3
Eastcroft SL2 22 A1
Eastern Ave
Chertsey KT16 124 A3
Reading RG1 86 C3
Eastern Dr SL8 3 B2
Eastern Ind Area RG12 118 B4
Eastern La RG45 143 C2
Eastern Perimeter Rd
Hatton TW14 71 C2
Hatton TW6 71 C3
Eastern Rd RG12 118 B4
Eastfield OX11 12 A4
Eastfield Cl 4 SL1 43 A2
Eastfield La RG8 56 B4
Eastfield Rd SL1 41 A4
Easthampstead Park Sch
RG12 117 B2
Easthampstead Rd
Bracknell RG12 118 A4
Wokingham RG40 116 C2
Eastheath Ave RG41 116 A2
Eastheath Gdns RG41 116 A2
Eastleigh Rd TW6 71 C2
Eastlyn Rd RG26 135 C1
Easton Hill RG20 76 A2
Eastwood Ct 1 SL7 1 C2
Eastwood Rd RG5 87 C2
Eastworth Rd KT15, KT16 124 A1
Eaton Pl RG1 85 C4
Eaton Rd GU15 151 A2
Ebborn Sq RG6 114 B4
Ebsworth Cl SL6 20 B2
Eccles Cl RG4 59 B1
Echelford Cty Mid Sch
TW15 98 A2
Echelforde Dr TW15 98 A2
Eddington Hill RG17 100 C4
Eddington Rd RG12 117 C2
Eddystone Wlk TW19 97 C4
Eden Cl SL3 44 A1
Eden Way RG41 88 A1
Edenhall Cl RG31 57 B2
Edenham Cl RG6 87 C1
Edenham Cres RG1 85 C3
Edgar Milward Cl RG30 58 A1
Edgar Wallace Pl SL8 3 A3
Edgbarrow Rise GU47 143 A1
Edgbarrow Sch RG45 143 B2
Edgbarrowhill Star
RG45 143 A2
Edgcumbe Park Dr
RG45 143 A3
Edgecombe La RG14 105 B3
Edgedale Cl RG45 143 A3
Edgehill St RG1 86 A3
Edgell Cl GU25 122 C3
Edgell Rd TW18 96 C2
Edgemoor Rd GU16 152 B2
Edgewood Cl RG45 143 A4
Edinburgh Ave SL1 42 A4
Edinburgh Dr TW18 97 B1
Edinburgh Rd
Maidenhead SL6 19 C1
Marlow SL7 1 C2
Reading RG30 85 C4
Edith Rd SL6 39 A4
Edmonds Ct 4 RG12 118 B4
Edmunds Way SL2 43 A4
Edneys Hill RG41 115 B1
Edward Ave GU15 151 A3
Edward Ct TW18 97 B1
Edward Pauling Ho TW14 98 C4
Edward Pauling Prim Sch
TW13 98 C3
Edward Pl 25 RG1 86 B4
Edward Rd Hatton TW14 71 C1
Twyford RG10 61 A3
Windlesham GU20 146 B2
Edward Way TW15 97 C3
Edwards Ct SL1 42 C2
Edwards Hill RG17 25 A1
Edwin Cl RG19 106 C2
Eeklo Pl RG14 105 A1
Egerton Rd Reading RG2 86 C1
Sandhurst GU15 150 C4
Slough SL2 21 C1
Egham By-Pass TW20 96 A2
Egham Hill TW20 95 B1
Egham Hill Rdbt TW20 95 C2
Egham Mus TW20 96 A2
Egham Sta TW20 96 A2
Eghams Ct 9 SL8 3 A2
Egremont Dr RG6 87 B2
Egremont Gdns SL1 42 A3
Egypt La SL2 22 A4
Eight Acres SL1 21 A1
Eight Bells RG14 104 C1
Eisenhower Ave RG20 49 A2
Elan Cl RG30 84 C4
Elbow Mdw SL3 69 C3
Eldart Cl RG30 85 A4
Elder Cl RG31 57 B1
Elderberry Way RG6 87 B1
Elderfield Cres OX11 10 B4
Elderfield Rd SL2 22 C3
Eldon Pl RG1 86 B4
Eldon Rd RG1 86 B4
Eldon Sq RG1 86 B4
Eldon St RG1 86 B4
Eldon Terr RG1 86 B4
Eldrick Ct TW14 98 B4
Elford Cl RG6 87 B1
Elgar Ave RG45 143 A4
Elgar Rd RG2 86 A3
Elgar Rd S RG2 86 A2
Elgarth Dr RG40 141 C4
Elgin Ave TW15 98 B1
Elgin Cres TW6 71 C3
Elgin Ho SL3 69 C3
Eliot Cl Camberley GU15 152 A4
Caversham RG4 59 A2
Thatcham RG18 106 B3
Elizabeth Ave
Bagshot GU19 145 C1
Newbury RG14 130 B4
Staines TW18 97 B1
Elizabeth Cl
Bracknell RG12 118 B3
Cookham SL6 19 C4
Henley-on-T RG9 35 A4
Elizabeth Ct 9 Slough SL1 43 A2
Wargrave RG10 36 C1
Elizabeth Gdns Ascot SL5 120 A2
Kintbury RG17 102 A1
Elizabeth Ho TW15 97 C2
Elizabeth Mews 18 RG1 86 A3
Elizabeth Par GU46 149 B2
Elizabeth Rd
Henley-on-T RG9 35 A4
Marlow SL7 1 C2
Wokingham RG40 116 B3
Elizabeth Rout Cl RG7 113 B1
Elizabeth Way SL2 22 C2
Elizabeth Wlk 28 RG1 86 A3
Elizabethan Cl TW19 97 B4
Elizabethan Way TW19 97 B4
Ellenborough Cl RG12 118 B4
Ellerton Cl RG7 83 C2
Ellesfield Ave RG12 117 C3
Ellesmere Cl RG4 59 A2
Ellies Mews TW15 97 C3
Elliman Ave SL2 42 C3
Ellington Ct SL6 40 B4
Ellington Gdns SL6 40 B4
Ellington Pk SL6 19 C1
Ellington Prim Sch SL6 19 C1
Ellington Rd Feltham TW13 98 C2
Ellington Rd *continued*
Taplow SL6 40 B4
Elliot Dr SL7 1 C2
Elliot Rise SL5 119 B4
Elliots Way RG4 59 A1
Elliott Gdns TW17 125 A3
Ellis Ave SL1 42 C2
Ellis Rd RG45 143 A3
Ellison Cl SL4 66 C2
Ellison Ho 23 SL4 67 B3
Ellison Way RG40 116 A3
Elm Bank GU46 149 B4
Elm Cl
Farnham Common SL2 22 B3
Stanwell TW19 97 B4
Elm Cotts RG20 129 C1
Elm Croft SL3 68 B3
Elm Ct 9 Charlton TW16 98 C1
Sandhurst GU47 143 C1
Elm Dr
Burghfield Common RG30 111 A3
Winkfield SL4 93 A4
Elm Gr Maidenhead SL6 39 C4
Elm La Bourne End SL8 2 C3
Earley RG6 86 C1
Elm Lodge Ave RG30 85 B4
Elm Park Rd RG30 85 B4
Elm Pk Reading RG30 85 B4
Sunningdale SL5 120 C1
Elm Rd Earley RG2 & RG6 86 C1
East Bedfont TW14 98 B4
Mapledurham RG4 58 B4
Windsor SL4 67 A2
Elm Tree Cl TW15 98 A2
Elmar Gn SL2 22 A1
Elmbank Ave TW20 95 A1
Elmcroft RG8 34 B3
Elmcroft Cl TW14 71 C1
Elmcroft Dr TW15 98 A2
Elmdon Rd TW6 71 C2
Elmhurst Ballet Sch
GU15 151 B3
Elmhurst Ct SL3 44 A2
Elmhurst Rd Goring RG8 34 B4
Reading RG1 86 B3
Slough SL3 44 A2
Thatcham RG18 106 A3
Elmleigh Ct RG4 59 B2
Elmley Cl RG41 88 C1
Elms Ave RG19 106 C2
Elms Dr SL8 3 B2
Elms Rd RG40 116 A3
Elms The TW15 98 A2
Elmshott La SL1 41 C3
Elmsleigh Ctr The TW18 96 C2
Elmsleigh Rd TW18 96 C2
Elmslie Ct SL6 39 C4
Elmstone Dr RG31 57 B1
Elmsway TW15 98 A2
Elmwood SL6 20 A2
Elmwood Rd SL2 43 A3
Elsenwood Cres GU15 152 A3
Elsenwood Dr GU15 152 A4
Elsinore Ave TW19 97 C4
Elsley Rd RG31 57 C2
Elstow Ave RG4 59 B3
Elstree Cl RG31 57 B1
Elstree Sch RG7 108 B2
Elsworth Cl TW14 98 C4
Eltham Ave Caversham RG4 59 C3
Slough SL1 41 C2
Elton Dr SL6 39 B4
Elvaston Way RG30 85 A4
Elveden Cl RG6 87 C1
Elvendon Rd RG8 34 B4
Elwell Cl TW20 96 A1
Ely Ave SL1 42 B4
Ely Rd Hatton TW6 71 C3
Theale RG7 83 C2
Embankment The TW19 95 B4
Ember Rd SL3 44 A2
Emblem Cres RG2 114 C1
Embrook Way RG31 84 A2
Emerald Cl RG41 115 C4
Emerald Ct SL1 42 C2
Emerson Ct HP10 3 C3
Emery Acres RG8 55 A3
Emery Down Cl RG12 119 A3
Emlyns Bldgs SL4 67 B4
Emm Cl RG41 115 C4
Emma La RG10 36 C1
Emmbrook Comp Sch
RG41 115 C4
Emmbrook Ct RG2 86 C1
Emmbrook Gate RG41 115 C4
Emmbrook Inf Sch RG41 88 C1
Emmbrook Jun Sch RG41 88 C1
Emmbrook Rd RG41 115 C4
Emmbrook Vale RG41 89 A1
Emmer Green Ct RG4 59 B3
Emmer Green Prim Sch
RG4 59 A3
Emmets Nest RG42 90 B1
Emmets Pk RG42 90 B1
Emmview Cl RG41 115 C4
Empress Rd RG31 84 B3
Enborne Cl RG31 84 B4
Enborne Gate RG14 104 B1
Enborne Gdns RG12 91 B1
Enborne Gr RG14 104 C1
Enborne Lodge Sch
RG14 130 A3
Enborne Pl RG14 104 C1
Enborne Prim Sch RG20 129 C3
Enborne Rd RG14 104 B1
Enborne St
Hamstead Marshall RG20 130 A2
Enborne St *continued*
Newbury RG14 130 B3
Enborne Way RG7 133 C3
Enfield Rd TW6 71 C3
Enfield Road Rdbt TW6 71 C3
Engineers Rd RG19 132 A3
Englefield CE Prim Sch
RG7 83 A2
Englefield Cl TW20 95 B1
Englefield Green Sch
TW20 95 B2
Englefield Rd RG7 83 B2
Engleheart Dr TW14 71 C1
Englehurst TW20 95 B1
Englemere Pk SL5 119 B3
Englemere Pond
Nature Trail SL5 119 B3
Englemere Rd RG42 90 C1
Englesfield GU15 152 B3
English Gdns TW19 68 B1
English Martyrs
RC Prim Sch RG30 85 A4
Enid Wood Ho RG12 118 B4
Ennerdale RG12 118 A3
Ennerdale Cl TW14 98 C4
Ennerdale Cres SL1 41 B4
Ennerdale Rd RG2 86 B2
Ennerdale Way RG19 106 A2
Ensign Cl TW19 97 B4
Ensign Way TW19 97 B4
Enstone Rd RG5 88 A4
Enterprise Way RG19 107 A1
EP Collier Prim Sch RG1 59 A1
Epping Cl RG1 85 C4
Epping Ho 6 RG1 85 C3
Epping Way RG12 118 C3
Epsom Cl GU15 151 B4
Epsom Cres RG14 105 A1
Epsom Ct RG1 85 C3
Epsom Sq TW6 71 C3
Equine Way RG14 131 A4
Eric Ave RG4 59 A3
Erica Cl Slough SL1 41 C3
West End GU24 153 C3
Erica Dr RG40 116 B3
Eriswell Cl RG6 87 C1
Erkenwald Cl KT16 123 C2
Erleigh Court Dr RG6 87 A4
Erleigh Court Gdns RG6 87 A4
Erleigh Dene RG14 104 C1
Erleigh Rd RG1 86 B3
Ermin St Lambourn RG17 46 B1
Stockcross RG20 103 B4
Wickham RG20 75 B2
Ermin Wlk RG19 106 A2
Errington Dr SL4 67 A3
Erskine Cl RG26 135 C1
Escot Rd TW16 98 C1
Esher Cres TW6 71 C3
Esher Rd GU15 145 A1
Eskdale Gdns SL6 40 A1
Eskdale Rd RG41 88 A2
Eskdale Way GU15 152 B2
Eskin Cl RG30 85 A4
Essame Cl RG40 116 B3
Essex Ave SL2 42 B4
Essex Pl RG17 25 A2
Essex Rise RG42 91 C1
Essex St Newbury RG14 130 B4
Reading RG2 86 A3
Ethel Rd TW15 97 C2
Eton Cl SL3 68 A4
Eton Coll SL4 67 B4
Eton Ct Eton SL4 67 B4
Staines TW18 96 C2
Eton End PNEU Sch SL3 68 A4
Eton Pl SL7 1 B1
Eton Porny CE Comb Sch
SL4 67 B4
Eton Rd Datchet SL3 68 A4
Harlington UB3 71 C4
Eton Sq SL4 67 B4
Eton Wick CE Fst Sch SL4 42 A1
Eton Wick Rd SL4 42 A1
Eton Wlk 22 SL1 42 C2
European Weather Ctr
RG2 113 B4
Eustace Cres RG40 116 B4
Evedon RG12 118 A1
Evelyn Cres TW16 125 C4
Evelyn Ct RG5 87 C3
Evelyn Way TW16 125 C4
Evendon's Cl RG41 116 A2
Evendon's La
Barkham RG41 115 C1
Wokingham RG41 116 A2
Evenlode SL6 39 C4
Evenlode Rd SL8 3 A2
Evenlode Way GU47 150 B4
Everard Ave SL1 42 C2
Everest Rd
Camberley GU15 151 B4
Crowthorne RG45 143 A3
Stanwell TW19 97 C4
Evergreen Ct TW19 97 B4
Evergreen Dr RG31 84 C2
Evergreen Rd GU16 152 A2
Evergreen Way
Stanwell TW19 97 B4
Wokingham RG41 115 C3
Everington La RG18 53 A1
Everland Rd RG17 100 B3
Eversley Rd
Arborfield RG2 114 C1
Barkham RG40 140 C3

Eversley St RG27 ....141 A1
Eversley Way TW20 .....123 B4
Evesham Rd RG4 ....59 A3
Evesham Wlk GU47 .....143 B1
Evreham Rd SL0 ....44 C4
Evreux Cl RG19 ....106 C1
Ewing Way RG14 ....131 A4
Exbourne Rd RG2 ....113 B4
Exchange Rd SL5 ....120 B2
Exeforde Ave TW15 ....98 A2
Exeter Ct RG4 ....113 A4
Exeter Gdns GU46 ....149 A4
Exeter Rd TW6 ....71 C2
Exeter Way Hatton TW6 ..71 C3
  Theale RG7 ....83 C2
Exmoor Rd RG19 ....106 B2
Explorer Ave TW19 ....97 C4
Expressway RG14 ....105 C1
Exwick Sq RG2 ....113 B4
Eylham RG8 ....57 A3
Eynsford Cl RG4 ....59 C3
Eynsham Rd RG5 ....87 C4
Eyre Gn SL2 ....22 A1

F

Fagg's Rd TW14 ....71 C2
Fair Close Ho **1** RG14 ...105 A1
Fair Lawn Gn RG2 ....86 C1
Fair Mile RG9 ....15 B2
Fair Mile Hospl OX10 .....14 A4
Fair View Cotts SL6 ....19 C4
Fairacre SL6 ....39 B3
Fairacres Ind Est SL4 .....66 B3
Faircroft SL2 ....22 A1
Faircross RG12 ....118 A3
Faircross Quarters RG1 ...78 C3
Faircross Rd RG30 ....85 B3
Fairfax RG42 ....118 A4
Fairfax Cl RG4 ....59 A2
Fairfax Pl RG13 ....105 C3
Fairfield RG20 ....31 B2
Fairfield App TW19 ....68 B1
Fairfield Ave Datchet SL3 ..68 B4
  Farnham Common SL2 .....22 A2
  Staines TW18 ....96 C2
Fairfield Cl SL3 ....68 B4
Fairfield Dr GU16 ....151 C2
Fairfield La GU24 ....153 C4
Fairfield Rd Burnham SL1 ..21 B1
  Goring RG8 ....34 B4
  Wraysbury TW19 ....68 B1
Fairfields RG17 ....100 B3
Fairford Rd
  Maidenhead SL6 ....39 C4
  Purley on T RG31 ....57 B1
Fairhaven TW20 ....95 C2
Fairhaven Ct **1** TW20 ....95 C3
Fairholme TW14 ....98 C4
Fairholme Jun & Inf Schs
  TW14 ....98 B4
Fairholme Rd TW15 ....97 C2
Fairlawn Pk SL4 ....66 C2
Fairlawns Cl TW18 ....97 A1
Fairlea SL6 ....39 A2
Fairlie Rd SL6 ....42 A4
Fairlight Ave SL4 ....67 B4
Fairlop Cl RG31 ....84 B1
Fairmead Cl GU47 ....150 C4
Fairmead Rd RG2 ....113 C4
Fairmile Ct RG9 ....15 B2
Fairoak Way RG26 ....134 B1
Fairsted Cl RG30 ....85 A4
Fairview RG14 ....130 C4
Fairview Ave RG6 ....87 A3
Fairview Cotts GU25 ....122 B2
Fairview Ct TW15 ....98 A2
Fairview Dr TW17 ....124 C2
Fairview Est RG9 ....35 C4
Fairview Rd Burnham SL6 ..41 A4
  Hungerford RG17 ....100 B3
  Slough SL2 ....21 C1
  Wokingham RG40 ....116 B3
Fairwater Dr RG5 ....87 B3
Fairway KT16 ....124 A1
Fairway Ave RG30 ....84 B3
Fairway Dr RG10 ....61 A3
Fairway Hts GU15 ....152 B3
Fairway The Burnham SL1 ..21 B2
  Flackwell Heath HP10 ......3 B4
  Frimley GU15 ....152 A2
  Maidenhead SL6 ....39 A2
Fairways TW15 ....98 A1
Faithfull Cl RG42 ....91 A1
Fakenham Cl RG6 ....114 A4
Fakenham Way GU47 ....143 B1
Falaise TW20 ....95 C2
Falcon Ave RG2 ....86 C1
Falcon Cl GU18 ....152 C4
Falcon Ct GU16 ....151 B1
Falcon Dr TW19 ....70 C1
Falcon Fields RG26 .....135 A1
Falcon House Gdns
  RG20 ....129 C1
Falcon Way
  Sunbury TW16 ....95 C3
  Wokingham RG41 ....115 C3
  Yateley GU46 ....149 A3
Falcons Croft HP10 ....3 C4
Falconwood TW20 ....95 C2
Falkland Dr RG14 ....130 B4
Falkland Garth RG14 ....130 B4
Falkland Ho SL6 ....39 C4
Falkland Prim Sch RG14 .130 B3

Falkland Rd
  Caversham RG4 ....59 A1
  Newbury RG14 ....130 B3
Fallowfield GU46 ....149 A4
Fallowfield Cl RG4 ....59 A2
Falmouth Cl GU15 ....152 A2
Falmouth Rd
  Reading RG2 ....113 B4
  Slough SL1 ....42 A4
Falmouth Way RG19 .....106 C2
Falstaff Ave RG6 ....86 C1
Fane Way SL6 ....39 B3
Fanes Cl RG42 ....117 C4
Fannys La RG7 ....80 B1
Faraday Cl Arborfield RG2 .140 C4
  Slough SL2 ....42 A4
Faraday Rd
  Newbury RG14 ....105 A2
  Slough SL2 ....42 A4
Farcrosse Cl GU47 ......150 B4
Fareham Dr GU46 ....149 A4
Faringdon Cl GU47 ......143 B1
Faringdon Dr RG12 ......118 B2
Faringdon Wlk RG30 .....85 A2
Farleigh Mews RG4 ....59 C3
Farley Copse RG42 ......117 C4
Farley Hill Prim Sch
  RG7 ....140 B3
Farley Moor RG42 ....117 B4
Farley Villas KT16 ....124 A1
Farm Cl Ascot SL5 ....120 B2
  Bracknell RG42 ....117 C4
  Crowthorne RG45 ....143 B4
  Egham TW18 ....96 C2
  Lower Halliford TW17 ....125 A1
  Lyne KT16 ....123 A2
  Maidenhead SL6 ....40 B1
  Maidenhead, Highway SL6 ..39 B3
  Purley on T RG8 ....57 B3
  Yateley GU46 ....149 B3
Farm Cres SL2 ....43 B4
Farm Dr Old Windsor SL4 ..68 A1
  Reading RG31 ....84 A1
Farm Lea HP10 ....3 C4
Farm Rd Bourne End SL8 ...2 C2
  Burnham SL6 ....41 A3
  Frimley GU16 ....151 C1
  Goring RG8 ....34 B3
  Henley-on-T RG9 ....35 C4
  Maidenhead SL6 ....39 A4
  Staines TW18 ....97 A1
Farm View RG9 ....149 B3
Farm Way TW19 ....69 C1
Farm Yd SL4 ....67 B4
Farman Cl RG5 ....88 A4
Farmer's Rd TW18 ....96 C2
Farmers End RG10 ....61 A2
Farmers Gate RG18 .....106 B3
Farmers Way SL6 ....39 A2
Farmiloe Cl RG8 ....57 B2
Farnburn Ave SL1 ....42 A4
Farnell Rd TW18 ....97 A3
Farnham Cl RG12 ....118 B4
Farnham Common
  Cty Inf Sch SL2 ....22 A4
Farnham Common
  Cty Jun Sch SL2 ....22 A4
Farnham Common Ho **3**
  SL2 ....22 B4
Farnham Dr RG4 ....59 C2
Farnham La SL2 ....22 A2
Farnham Park La SL2 .....22 B2
Farnham Rd SL1, SL2 ....42 B4
Farningham RG12 ....118 C2
Farningham Ho RG12 ....118 C2
Farnsfield Cl RG6 ....114 A4
Farrell Cl GU15 ....151 B2
Farrer Theatre SL4 ....42 B1
Farrier Ct **11** SL8 ....3 A2
Farriers Cl RG5 ....87 C4
Farriers La RG20 ....30 C4
Farrowdene Rd RG2 .....113 B4
Farthing Green La SL2 ....23 A2
Farthingales The SL6 .....40 A4
Fatherson Rd RG1 ....86 B4
Faulkner Pl GU19 ....145 C2
Faversham Rd GU47 ....143 B1
Fawcett Cres RG5 ....87 B3
Fawcett Rd SL4 ....67 A3
Fawler Mead RG12 ......118 C3
Fawley Bottom Rd RG9 ...15 A4
Fawley Cl SL6 ....19 B1
Fawley Ct RG9 ....15 C3
Fawley Mews **2** RG1 ......85 C3
Fawley Rd RG30 ....85 B3
Fawns Manor Cl TW14 ...98 B4
Fawns Manor Rd TW14 ..98 B4
Fawsley Cl SL3 ....69 C4
Faygate Way RG6 ....87 A1
Feathers La TW19 ....96 A3
Felbridge Cl GU16 ....151 C1
Felbridge Ct UB3 ....71 B4
Felix La TW17 ....125 C2
Felixstowe Ct RG6 ....87 B1
Fellow Gn GU24 ....153 C4
Fellow Green Rd GU24 ..153 C3
Fellowes Ct UB3 ....71 B4
Fells The RG31 ....84 A3
Felstead Ct RG6 ....86 C2
Feltham Hill
  Jun & Inf Schs TW13 .....98 C3
Feltham Hill Rd TW15 ....98 B1
Feltham Rd TW15 ....98 B2
Felthorpe Cl RG6 ....114 A4
Felton Way RG31 ....84 B4
Fencote RG12 ....118 B2

Fennel Cl Earley RG6 .....86 C1
  Newbury RG14 ....105 B3
Fenns La GU24 ....153 C3
Fennscombe Ct GU24 ...153 C3
Fenton Ave TW18 ....97 B2
Fern Cl Crowthorne RG45 .143 A4
  Frimley GU16 ....152 B2
  Reading RG31 ....84 B3
Fern Dr SL6 ....41 A4
Fern Glen RG31 ....57 B1
Fern Wlk Ashford TW15 ...97 B3
  Reading RG31 ....84 B3
Fernbank RG40 ....141 B4
Fernbank Cres SL5 ......119 B4
Fernbank Pl SL5 ....119 B4
Fernbank Rd SL5 ....119 B4
Fernbrook Rd RG4 ....58 C3
Ferndale Ave RG30 ....85 A2
Ferndale Cl RG31 ....57 C2
Ferndale Ct RG19 ....106 C2
Ferndale Pk SL6 ....65 C4
Ferndale Rd TW15 ....97 C2
Ferne Cl RG8 ....34 A4
Fernery The SL6 ....40 A1
Fernhill Cl Bracknell RG42 ..90 C1
  Farnborough (Hants) GU17 .150 C1
Fernhill Comp Sch
  GU14 ....150 C1
Fernhill Cty Prim Sch
  GU14 ....150 C1
Fernhill La GU17 ....150 C1
Fernhill Rd GU14,GU17 ..150 C1
Fernhill Wlk GU17 ....150 C1
Fernhurst Rd
  Ashford TW15 ....98 B2
  Reading RG30 ....84 B2
Ferniehurst GU15 ....151 C2
Fernley Ct SL6 ....19 B1
Ferrard Cl SL5 ....119 B4
Ferrers Cl SL1 ....41 C3
Ferriby Ct RG12 ....118 B4
Ferrier Gr RG14 ....131 A4
Ferry Ave TW18 ....96 C1
Ferry End SL6 ....40 B2
Ferry La Bourne End SL8 ....3 A1
  Chertsey KT16 ....124 A2
  Cookham SL6 ....20 A4
  Goring RG8 ....34 A3
  Hambleden RG9 ....16 B1
  Laleham TW18 ....96 A1
  Lower Halliford TW16,TW17 .125 A1
  Medmenham SL7 ....17 A3
  South Stoke RG8 ....14 A2
  Wargrave RG10 ....36 B1
  Wraysbury TW19 ....96 A3
Ferry Rd Maidenhead SL6 ..40 B2
  South Stoke RG8 ....14 B2
Ferry Wks TW17 ....125 A1
Festival Cotts SL3 ....69 B4
Fettiplace RG17 ....48 A3
Fidlers La RG20 ....30 C4
Fidlers Wlk RG10 ....36 C1
Field Cl
  Burghfield Common RG7 .111 A1
  Harlington UB3 ....71 C4
Field End GU24 ....153 C3
Field House Cl SL5 ......120 A1
Field Hurst SL3 ....43 C1
Field La GU16 ....151 C1
Field Pk RG12 ....118 B4
Field Rd
  Farnborough (Hants) GU14 .150 C1
  Peasemore RG20 ....29 B1
  Reading RG1 ....86 A3
Field View Caversham RG4 .59 A2
  Egham TW20 ....96 B2
  Feltham TW13 ....98 B3
Fielden Pl RG12 ....118 B4
Fieldfare Ave GU46 .....149 A3
Fieldhead Gdns SL8 ....3 A2
Fieldhouse Ind Est SL7 ....1 C1
Fieldhouse La SL7 ....1 C1
Fieldhouse Way SL7 ....1 C1
Fielding Gdns
  Crowthorne RG45 ....143 A2
  Slough SL3 ....43 B2
Fielding Rd
  Maidenhead SL6 ....39 A4
  Sandhurst GU47 ....150 C3
Fieldings The SL6 ....65 A4
Fieldridge RG41 ....105 B3
Fields The SL1 ....42 B2
Fieldview Ct TW18 ....97 A1
Fieldway RG41 ....88 B1
Fifehead Cl TW15 ....97 C1
Fifield Cotts SL6 ....65 B3
Fifield La SL4,SL6 ....65 C3
Fifield Rd SL6 ....65 B4
Fifth Rd RG14 ....104 C1
Fifth St RG19 ....131 C1
Filbert Dr RG31 ....84 B4
Filey Rd RG1 ....86 C4
Filey Spur SL1 ....42 A2
Filmer Rd SL4 ....66 C4
Finbeck Way RG6 ....113 C4
Finch Ct SL6 ....39 B3
Finch Rd RG6 ....87 B2
Finch Way RG7 ....111 A2
Fincham End Dr RG45 ..142 C2
Finchampstead
  CE Prim Sch RG40 ....141 C4
Finchampstead Rd
  Finchampstead RG40 ....141 B4
  Finchampstead RG40 ....142 A4
  Wokingham RG41, RG40 ..116 A2
Findhorn Cl GU47 ....150 B4
Fineleigh Ct SL1 ....42 C4
Finmere RG12 ....118 B1

Finney Dr GU20 ....146 B2
Finstock Cl RG6 ....87 B1
Finstock Gn RG12 ....118 C3
Fir Cottage Rd RG40 ....141 C4
Fir Dr GU17 ....150 B2
Fir Tree Ave SL2 ....22 C1
Fir Tree Cl SL5 ....120 A1
Fir Tree Cnr RG26 ....134 C1
Fir Tree Cotts RG20 ......10 A1
Fir Tree La RG14 ....105 C2
Fir Tree Paddock RG20 ..10 A1
Fir Tree Pl TW15 ....98 A2
Fir Tree Prim Sch RG14 .105 C2
Firbank Pl TW20 ....95 A1
Fircroft Cl Reading RG31 ..57 B1
  Stoke Poges SL2 ....23 C3
Fireball Hill SL5 ....120 B1
Firglen Dr GU46 ....149 B4
Firgrove Rd RG27,GU46 .149 B3
Firlands RG12 ....118 B2
Firlands Ave GU15 ......151 B3
Firmstone Cl RG6 ....87 B1
Firs Ave SL4 ....66 C2
Firs Cl RG40 ....141 C4
Firs Dr SL3 ....43 C3
Firs End RG7 ....111 A3
Firs La Maidenhead SL6 ...38 C2
  Reading RG30 ....85 B3
Firs Rd RG31 ....84 A3
Firs The **14** Bracknell RG12 .118 C3
  Inkpen RG17 ....127 C3
  Maidenhead SL6 ....39 C4
  Reading RG30 ....85 C3
  Thatcham RG18 ....106 A2
First Ave Marlow SL7 ......2 A1
  Tadley RG7 ....135 B1
First Cres SL1 ....42 B4
First St RG19 ....132 A3
Firtree Cl GU47 ....142 C1
Firview Cl SL7 ....1 C1
Firwood Ct GU15 ....151 B3
Firwood Dr GU15 ....151 B3
Firwood Rd GU25 ....121 C2
Fisher Gn RG42 ....90 A1
Fisherman's Way SL8 .....3 A2
Fishermans La RG7 ......135 A4
Fishermans Retreat SL7 ...1 C1
Fishers Cotts RG4 ....59 B3
Fishers Ct RG4 ....59 B3
Fishers La RG18 ....79 A1
Fishers Wood SL5 ....121 B1
Fishery Rd SL6 ....40 B3
Fishguard Spur SL1 ....43 A2
Fishponds Cl RG41 .....116 A2
Fishponds Est RG41 ....116 A2
Fishponds Rd RG41 ....116 A2
Fitzrobert Pl TW20 ....96 A1
Fitzroy Cres RG5 ....88 A3
Five Acre RG2 ....87 A1
Five Acres HP10 ....3 C4
Flag Staff Sq RG19 ......106 C1
Flambards RG4 ....59 B1
Flamborough Cl RG6 ....87 C1
Flamborough Spur SL1 ...42 A2
Flamingo Cl RG41 ....115 C3
Flanders Ct TW20 ....96 B2
Flats The GU17 ....150 B2
Flaxman Cl RG6 ....86 C1
Flecker Cl RG18 ....106 A3
Fleet Cl RG41 ....115 C3
Fleet Hill RG40 ....141 B1
Fleet La RG40 ....141 A1
Fleetbrook Ho SL3 ....68 B3
Fleetham Gdns RG6 .....87 B1
Fleetway TW20 ....123 B3
Fleetwood Cl RG14 .....105 B3
Fleetwood Ct **7** TW19 ...70 C1
Fleetwood Rd SL2 ....42 C3
Fleming Cl RG2 ....140 C4
Fleming Rd RG14 ....105 A2
Flemish Fields KT16 ....124 A1
Fletcher Gdns RG42 ....117 B4
Flexford Gn RG12 ....117 C2
Flintgrove RG12 ....118 B4
Flintjack Pl RG17 ....25 A1
Flintlock Ct TW19 ....70 A2
Flodden Dr RG31 ....84 B2
Floral Ho KT16 ....123 C1
Floral Way KT16 ....106 C3
Floreat Gdns RG14 .....104 C1
Florence Ave SL6 ....40 A4
Florence Cl GU46 ....149 B3
Florence Cotts SL4 ....92 B4
Florence Ct **19** RG30 .....85 B3
Florence Gdns TW18 .....97 A1
Florence Rd GU47 ......150 C4
Florence Wlk RG1 ....86 B4
Florian Gdns RG30 ....85 A3
Florida Ct Reading RG30 ..85 C3
  Staines TW18 ....97 A2
Flowers Hill RG8 ....56 B2
Flowers Piece RG8 ....54 A3
Fobney St RG1 ....86 A4
Fokerham Rd RG19 .....106 C1
Folder's La RG42 ....91 B1
Foliejohn Way SL6 ....38 C1
Follet Cl SL4 ....68 A1
Folly La RG7,RG30 ......110 C3
Folly Rd Inkpen RG17 ...127 C3
  Lambourn RG17 ....25 A2
Folly The RG14 ....105 A1
Fontmell Pk TW15 ....98 A2
Fontwell Cl SL6 ....40 A4
Fontwell Dr RG30 ....84 C3
Fontwell Rd RG14 ......105 A1
Forbes Chase GU47 ....150 B4

Forbury Ho **6** RG30 .....85 B4
Forbury La RG17,RG20 ..128 B3
Forbury Rd RG1 ....86 B4
Forbury Ret Pk RG1 ......86 B4
Forbury The RG1 ....86 B4
Ford Cl Ashford TW15 ....97 C1
  Littleton TW17 ....125 C2
Ford La RG7 ....140 A1
Ford Rd Ashford TW15 ...97 C1
  Bisley GU24 ....153 C2
  Chertsey KT16 ....124 A1
Fordbridge Ct TW15 .....97 C1
Fordbridge Rd
  Ashford TW15 ....97 C2
  Upper Halliford
  TW16, TW17 ....125 C2
Fordham Way RG6 ....87 B1
Fordingbridge Cl KT16 ..124 A1
Fordwater Rd KT15, KT16 .124 A1
Fordwater Trad Est
  KT16 ....124 B1
Fordwells Dr RG12 ......118 C3
Forehead The RG7 ......137 C2
Forest Cl Bracknell SL5 ..119 B3
  Tadley RG26 ....134 C1
Forest Comp Sch The
  RG41 ....88 B1
Forest Dean RG2 ....113 B4
Forest Dr TW16 ....98 C1
Forest End GU47 ....150 A4
Forest Gn RG12 ....118 B4
Forest Green Rd SL6 .....65 B3
Forest Hill RG30 ....57 C1
Forest Hills GU15 ....151 A2
Forest Rd Binfield RG42 ...90 B2
  Crowthorne RG45 ....143 B3
  Windsor SL4 ....93 C4
  Windsor, Dedworth SL4 ...66 C3
  Winkfield RG42, SL5 ......92 B1
Forest View Cotts SL6 ....65 B3
Foresters Sq RG12 ......118 C3
Foresters Way RG45 ....143 C4
Forge Cl Caversham RG4 ..59 B1
  Kintbury RG17 ....102 A1
Forge Cotts SN8 ....99 A3
Forge Dr SL2 ....22 B3
Forge Hill RG18 ....53 A3
Forge The Harlington UB3 ..71 B4
  Hungerford RG17 ....100 B1
Forlease Cl SL6 ....40 A3
Forlease Dr SL6 ....40 A3
Forlease Rd SL6 ....40 A3
Formby Cl Earley RG6 ....87 C2
  Slough SL3 ....44 B1
Forndon Cl RG6 ....87 C1
Forsters RG7 ....134 C4
Fort Narrien GU15 ......150 C4
Fortrose Cl GU47 ....150 B4
Fortrose Wlk RG31 ....84 C2
Forty Green Dr SL7 ....1 A1
Fosseway RG45 ....143 A3
Fossewood Dr GU15 ....151 B4
Foster Ave SL4 ....66 C2
Fosters Gr GU20 ....146 A3
Fosters La RG5 ....87 C3
Fosters Path SL2 ....21 C1
Fotherby Ct SL6 ....40 A4
Fotheringay Gdns SL1 ...42 A3
Foundation Pk SL6 ....38 C2
Foundry Ct KT16 ....124 A1
Foundry Ho RG17 ....100 C4
Foundry La SL3 ....69 A2
Foundry Mews **1** KT16 .124 A1
Foundry Pl **1** RG1 ....86 A4
Fountain Gdns SL4 ....67 B2
Fountains Garth RG12 ..118 A3
Fourth Ave SL7 ....2 A1
Fourth St RG19 ....131 C3
Fowler Cl RG6 ....87 A2
Fowlers La RG42 ....118 A4
Fox Cl RG7 ....111 A2
Fox Covert GU18 ....153 A4
Fox Covert Cl SL5 ....120 B2
Fox Dr GU46 ....149 B4
Fox Hill Prim Sch RG12 .118 A3
Fox La RG27 ....149 A4
Fox La N KT16 ....123 C1
Fox La S KT16 ....123 C1
Fox Rd Bracknell RG12 ..118 B3
  Slough SL3 ....43 B1
Foxborough RG7 ....139 B3
Foxborough Cl SL3 ....44 A1
Foxborough Ct SL6 ....39 C2
Foxborough Prim Sch
  SL3 ....44 A1
Foxbury RG17 ....25 A1
Foxcombe Dr RG31 ......84 B4
Foxcote RG40 ....142 A4
Foxdown Cl GU15 ......151 B3
Foxes Piece SL7 ....1 C2
Foxes Piece Comb Sch SL7 .1 C2
Foxes Wlk RG10 ....61 A2
Foxglove Cl Stanwell TW19 .97 B4
  Winkfield RG42 ....92 A1
  Wokingham RG41 ....115 B4
Foxglove Gdns **4** RG1 ...85 C2
Foxglove Way
  Thatcham RG18 ....106 B3
  Thatcham RG18 ....106 C3
Foxhays Rd RG2 ....113 B4
Foxheath RG12 ....118 C2
Foxherne SL3 ....43 B2
Foxhill Cl RG4 ....60 A3
Foxhill Cres GU15 ....152 A4
Foxhill La RG4 ....59 C3
Foxhill Rd RG1 ....86 C3
Foxhollow Dr SL2 ....22 A4
Foxhunt Gr RG31 ....84 C2

Foxhunter Way RG19 . . . . .105 C2
Foxleigh Ct TW18 . . . . . . .96 B2
Foxley Cl GU17 . . . . .150 B3
Foxley La RG42 . . . . .90 B1
Foxley PNEU Sch RG10 . . .63 A1
Framewood Manor SL2 . . . .23 B3
Framewood Rd SL2, SL3 . . .23 B3
Framlingham Dr RG4 . . . . .59 C3
Frampton Cl RG5 . . . . .60 C1
France Hill Dr GU15 . . . . .151 B3
France Hill Dr GU15 . . . . .151 B1
Frances Ave SL6 . . . . .20 B1
Frances Rd SL4 . . . . .67 B3
Frances The RG18 . . . . . . .106 B2
Francis Baily Prim Sch
    RG19 . . . . .106 C2
Francis Chichester Cl
    SL5 . . . . .120 A2
Francis Cl TW17 . . . . .125 A3
Francis Gdns RG42 . . . . . . .91 B1
Francis St RG1 . . . . .86 A3
Francis Way Burnham SL1 . .41 B3
    Frimley GU15 . . . . .152 B2
Francomes Field RG17 . . . .25 B1
Frank Lunnon Cl SL8 . . . . . .3 B2
Frank Sutton Way SL1 . . . .42 A3
Franklin Ave Slough SL2 . . .42 A4
    Tadley RG26 . . . . .135 A1
Franklin Ct 21 RG1 . . . . . .85 C4
Franklin St RG1 . . . . .85 C4
Franklyn Cres SL4 . . . . . . .66 B2
Frascati Way SL6 . . . . .39 C4
Fraser Ave RG4 . . . . .59 B3
Fraser Mead GU47 . . . . . .150 C3
Fraser Rd RG42 . . . . .118 A4
Frederick Ho TW15 . . . . . .97 C2
Frederick Pl RG41 . . . . . . .116 A4
Free Prae Rd KT16 . . . . . .124 A1
Freeborn Way RG12 . . . . .118 C4
Freeman Cl TW17 . . . . . . .125 C3
Freemans Cl
    Hungerford RG17 . . . . . .100 B3
    Stoke Poges SL2 . . . . . . .23 A3
Freemantle Rd GU19 . . . .145 C2
Freemantles Sch
    (Specl Sch) KT16 . . . . . .123 C1
Freesia Cl RG41 . . . . .115 B4
French Gdns GU15 . . . . . .150 B2
Frenchum Gdns SL1 . . . . . .41 C3
Frensham RG12 . . . . .118 B2
Frensham GU46 . . . . .149 A3
Frensham Gn RG2 . . . . . . .86 C1
Frensham Rd RG45 . . . . . .143 C4
Frensham Wlk SL2 . . . . . . .22 B3
Freshfield Cl RG6 . . . . .87 C2
Freshfields La RG20 . . . . . .51 A1
Freshwater Rd RG1 . . . . . .86 C4
Freshwood Dr GU46 . . . . .149 B2
Friar St RG1 . . . . .86 A4
Friars Keep RG12 . . . . . . .118 A4
Friars Rd Newbury RG14 . . .131 A4
    Virginia Water GU25 . . . .122 B3
Friars Way KT16 . . . . .124 A1
Friars Wlk 3 RG1 . . . . . . .86 A4
Friary Dr TW19 . . . . .68 B1
Friary Rd Ascot SL5 . . . . .120 A2
    Wraysbury TW19 . . . . . . .95 B4
Friary The SL4 . . . . .68 B1
Friday St RG9 . . . . .15 C1
Friendship Way RG12 . . . .118 A3
Frieth Cl RG6 . . . . .87 A1
Frilsham Rd RG30 . . . . . . .85 A2
Frimley Cl RG5 . . . . .87 B4
Frimley Grove Gdns
    GU16 . . . . .151 C1
Frimley Hall Dr GU15 . . . .151 C3
Frimley High St GU16 . . . .151 B1
Frimley Park Hospl
    GU16 . . . . .151 B1
Frimley Rd
    Camberley GU15 . . . . . .151 A2
    Frimley GU15, GU16 . . . .151 B1
Fringford Cl RG6 . . . . .87 B1
Frith Hill Rd GU16 . . . . . .152 A1
Frithe The SL4 . . . . .43 A4
Frithwald Rd KT16 . . . . . .123 C1
Frobisher RG12 . . . . .118 B1
Frobisher Cres TW19 . . . . .97 C4
Frobisher Gdns TW19 . . . .97 C4
Frodsham Way GU47 . . . .143 C1
Frog Hall RG40 . . . . .116 C3
Frog Hall Dr RG40 . . . . . .116 C3
Frog La RG12 . . . . .118 A3
Frogmill SL6 . . . . .17 B2
Frogmill Ct SL6 . . . . .17 B2
Frogmore Cl SL1 . . . . .42 A4
Frogmore Com Coll
    GU46 . . . . .149 C3
Frogmore Gr GU17 . . . . . .150 B2
Frogmore Cty Inf Sch
    GU17 . . . . .150 A3
Frogmore Cty Jun Sch
    GU17 . . . . .150 A3
Frogmore Gr GU17 . . . . . .150 B2
Frogmore Park Dr GU17 . .150 B2
Frogmore Rd GU17 . . . . . .150 B3
Frogmore Way RG30 . . . . .85 A2
Fromer Rd HP10 . . . . .3 B2
Fromont Dr RG19 . . . . . . .106 C2
Fromow Gdns GU20 . . . . .146 B2
Front St RG7 . . . . .47 B3
Frouds Bridge Marina
    RG7 . . . . .108 C1
Frouds La RG7 . . . . .109 A1
Froxfield Ave RG1 . . . . . . .85 C3
Froxfield Down 6 RG12 . .118 C2
Fruen Rd TW14 . . . . .98 C4
Fry Cl RG4 . . . . .59 A2

Frymley Hill SL4 . . . . .66 B3
Frys La GU46 . . . . .149 C4
Fuchsia Cl RG31 . . . . .84 B3
Fuchsia Way GU24 . . . . . .153 C3
Fullbrook Cl
    Maidenhead SL6 . . . . . . .40 A4
    Wokingham RG41 . . . . . .89 A1
Fullbrook Cres RG31 . . . . .57 B2
Fuller Cl RG19 . . . . .106 C1
Fullers La Ball Hill RG20 . . .129 B1
    Burghfield Common RG7 . .112 A2
Fullers Yd SL6 . . . . .20 A1
Fulmead Rd RG30 . . . . . . .85 B4
Fulmer Chase SL3 . . . . . . .23 B4
Fulmer Cl RG6 . . . . .87 A1
Fulmer Common Rd SL3 . .23 C3
Fulmer Cty Fst Sch SL3 . .23 C4
Fulmer Rd SL3 . . . . .23 C4
Furlong Cl SL8 . . . . .3 A2
Furlong Rd SL8 . . . . .3 A2
Furness SL4 . . . . .66 B3
Furness Pl 8 SL4 . . . . . . .66 B3
Furness Row 9 SL4 . . . . . .66 B3
Furness Sq 6 SL4 . . . . . . .66 B3
Furness Way SL4 . . . . .66 B3
Furness Wlk 7 SL4 . . . . . .66 B3
Furnival Ave SL2 . . . . .22 A4
Furnival Cl GU25 . . . . . . .122 A2
Furrow Way SL6 . . . . .39 A2
Furse Cl GU15 . . . . .152 B2
Furse Hill Cres RG45 . . . .143 B2
Furze Platt Cty Inf Sch
    SL6 . . . . .19 B1
Furze Platt Cty Jun Sch
    SL6 . . . . .19 B1
Furze Platt Halt SL6 . . . . .19 A1
Furze Platt Rd SL6 . . . . . .19 A1
Furze Platt Sch SL6 . . . . . .19 A1
Furze Rd Maidenhead SL6 . .19 B1
    Tadley RG26 . . . . .134 C1
Furzebank SL5 . . . . .120 B3
Furzedown Cl TW20 . . . . . .95 C1
Furzemoors RG12 . . . . . . .118 A2
Furzen Cl SL2 . . . . .22 A1
Fuzzens Wlk SL4 . . . . .66 C3
Fydlers Cl SL5 . . . . .93 A1
Fyfield Cl GU17 . . . . .150 B3
Fyfield Rd RG19 . . . . .106 B1
Fylingdales RG19 . . . . . . .106 B1

G

Gables Ave TW15 . . . . .97 C2
Gables Cl Datchet SL3 . . . .68 A4
    Maidenhead SL6 . . . . . . .40 A4
Gables Way RG19 . . . . . . .107 B1
Gabriel Dr GU15 . . . . .152 A2
Gabriels The RG14 . . . . . .130 B3
Gage Cl SL6 . . . . .39 C2
Gainsborough
    Bracknell RG12 . . . . . . .118 B2
    Cookham SL6 . . . . .19 C3
Gainsborough Ave RG17 . .102 A1
Gainsborough Cl
    Camberley GU15 . . . . . .151 C4
    Woodley RG5 . . . . .88 B3
Gainsborough Cres RG9 . .35 B4
Gainsborough Dr
    Maidenhead SL6 . . . . . . .39 B2
    North Ascot SL5 . . . . . . .119 B4
Gainsborough Hill RG9 . . .35 B4
Gainsborough Rd
    Henley-on-T RG9 . . . . . .35 B4
    Reading RG30 . . . . .85 A3
Gairn Cl RG30 . . . . .85 A4
Galahad Cl SL1 . . . . .42 A2
Gale Dr GU18 . . . . .146 A1
Galley La RG19 . . . . .132 B1
Galleymead Rd SL3 . . . . . .69 C3
Gallop The GU46 . . . . .149 B4
Gallops The RG20 . . . . .30 C3
Galloway Chase SL2 . . . . . .43 A3
Galloway Ho 7 RG1 . . . . . .85 C3
Gallys Rd SL4 . . . . .66 B3
Galsworthy Dr RG4 . . . . . .59 C3
Galsworthy Rd 4 KT16 . . .124 A1
Galton Rd SL5 . . . . .120 C2
Galvin Rd SL1 . . . . .42 B3
Garde Rd RG4 . . . . .60 C2
Garden Cl Ashford TW15 . . .98 B1
    Maidenhead SL6 . . . . . . .39 A4
Garden Close La RG14 . . . .130 B2
Garden Cotts SL3 . . . . .69 B4
Garden Mews
    8 Reading RG30 . . . . . . .85 B3
    Slough SL1 . . . . .42 C3
Gardeners La RG8 . . . . . . .55 B2
Gardenia Dr GU24 . . . . . .153 C3
Gardens The Hatton TW14 . .71 B1
    South Stoke RG8 . . . . . . .14 B2
Gardner Ho SL6 . . . . .19 C1
Gardner Rd SL6 . . . . .19 C1
Gardners Rd RG42 . . . . . . .92 A1
Garfield Pl 20 SL4 . . . . . . .67 B3
Garfield Rd GU15 . . . . . . .151 B1
Garford Cres RG14 . . . . . .130 B4
Garlands Cl RG7 . . . . .111 A1
Garlands Cl RG7 . . . . .111 A1
Garnet Cl SL1 . . . . .42 A2
Garnet Ct SL7 . . . . .1 B1
Garnet Field GU46 . . . . . .149 A3
Garnet Hill 7 RG1 . . . . . . .86 A3
Garnet St RG1 . . . . .86 A3
Garrard Rd SL2 . . . . .21 C1
Garrard St RG1 . . . . .86 A4
Garrett Rd RG40 . . . . .141 C4

Garrick Cl TW18 . . . . .97 A1
Garson La TW19 . . . . .95 B4
Garson's La SL4 . . . . .92 A4
Garston Cl RG30 . . . . .85 A3
Garston Cres RG31 . . . . . .84 A3
Garston Gr RG40 . . . . .115 C3
Garswood RG12 . . . . .118 B2
Garth Cl RG41 . . . . .88 B1
Garth Rd RG7 . . . . .137 A3
Garth Sq RG42 . . . . .91 A1
Gas La SL6 . . . . .40 A2
Gas Works Rd RG1 . . . . . . .86 B4
Gascon's Gr SL2 . . . . .22 A1
Gaskell Mews RG14 . . . . .131 A4
Gaskells End RG4 . . . . .58 B4
Gaston Bridge Rd
    Shepperton TW17 . . . . . .125 B2
    Upper Halliford TW17 . . . .125 C2
Gaston Way TW17 . . . . . . .125 B2
Gatcombe Cl RG31 . . . . . .84 B2
Gatehampton Rd RG8 . . . . .34 B3
Gatewick Cl SL1 . . . . .42 C3
Gatward Ave SL6 . . . . .39 A2
Gaveston Rd SL2 . . . . .21 C1
Gayhurst Cl RG4 . . . . .59 B3
Gays La SL6 . . . . .65 A4
Gaywood Dr RG14 . . . . . .105 A2
Gazelle Cl RG41 . . . . .88 A2
Geffers Ride SL5 . . . . .119 C4
Gelder Dr RG6 . . . . .87 B1
Genesis Cl TW19 . . . . .97 C4
Geneva Cl TW17 . . . . .125 C1
Geoffrey Field
    Jun & Inf Schs RG2 . . . .113 B4
Geoffreyson Rd RG4 . . . . .58 C3
George Cl SL7 . . . . .1 C2
George Green Rd SL3 . . . .43 C4
George Palmer Inf Sch
    RG2 . . . . .86 B2
George Palmer Jun Sch
    RG2 . . . . .86 B2
George St Caversham RG4 . .59 A1
    Reading RG1 . . . . .85 C4
    Staines TW18 . . . . .96 C2
George V Pl SL4 . . . . .67 B4
Georgeham Rd GU47 . . . .143 B1
Georges Dr HP10 . . . . .3 B4
Georgian Cl
    Camberley GU15 . . . . . .151 C4
    Staines TW18 . . . . .97 A2
Geranium Cl RG45 . . . . . .143 A4
Gerrards Cross Rd SL2 . . .23 A4
Gervaise Cl SL1 . . . . .41 C3
Gibbet La GU15 . . . . .152 A3
Gibbins La RG42 . . . . .91 B2
Gibbons Cl GU47 . . . . . . .150 B4
Gibbs Cl RG40 . . . . .141 C3
Gibbs Way GU46 . . . . .149 A2
Gibraltar La SL6 . . . . .2 B1
Gibson Cl SL3 . . . . .43 C1
Gibson Pl TW19 . . . . .70 B1
Gifford Cl RG4 . . . . .59 C3
Gifford Ho 2 RG4 . . . . . . .59 B1
Gilbert Cl RG18 . . . . .106 B2
Gilbert Rd GU15 . . . . .151 B1
Gilbert Way RG40 . . . . . . .141 C4
Gilbey Wlk HP10 . . . . .3 B2
Gilchrist Way RG5 . . . . . . .38 A3
Giles Travers Cl TW20 . . .123 B3
Gill Rise SL4 . . . . .66 B2
Gillette Way RG2 . . . . .86 A1
Gilliat Rd SL1 . . . . .42 C3
Gilliatt Cl SL0 . . . . .44 C4
Gillotts Cl RG9 . . . . .35 A4
Gillotts La RG9 . . . . .35 A4
Gillotts Sch RG9 . . . . .35 A4
Gilman Cres SL4 . . . . .66 B2
Gilmore Cl SL3 . . . . .43 B2
Gilmore Cres TW15 . . . . . .98 A1
Gilpin Way UB3 . . . . .71 B4
Gilroy Cl RG14 . . . . .130 B3
Gilson Ct SL4 . . . . .95 B4
Gingells Farm Rd RG10 . . .61 A3
Gipsy La Arborfield RG41 . . .114 C4
    Bracknell RG12 . . . . . . .118 B4
    Earley RG6 . . . . .87 B2
    Hungerford RG17 . . . . . .100 C3
    Reading RG30 . . . . .57 C1
    Wokingham RG40 . . . . . .116 B2
Wokingham,
    Sindlesham RG41 . . . . . .115 A4
Girton Cl GU47 . . . . .143 C1
Glade Ho Ascot SL5 . . . . .120 B2
    3 Marlow SL7 . . . . .1 C1
Glade Rd SL7 . . . . .1 C1
Glade The Ascot SL5 . . . . .120 B2
    Newbury RG14 . . . . .130 C4
    Purley on T RG8 . . . . .57 B2
    Staines TW18 . . . . .97 A1
Gladridge Cl RG6 . . . . .87 B2
Gladstone Cl RG17 . . . . . .102 A1
Gladstone Ind Est SL6 . . .39 C4
Gladstone La RG18 . . . . . .106 B4
Gladstone Way SL1 . . . . . .42 A3
Glaisdale RG12 . . . . .118 B1
Glamis Way RG31 . . . . . . .84 A2
Glanmor Rd SL2 . . . . .43 A3
Glanty The TW20 . . . . .96 A2
Glasgow Rd SL1 . . . . .42 A4
Glassonby Wlk GU15 . . . .152 B3
Glebe Cl Dorney SL6 . . . . .40 C2
    Moulsford OX10 . . . . .13 C4
Glebe Cotts RG8 . . . . .14 B2
Glebe Field RG20 . . . . .49 A4
Glebe Gdns RG4 . . . . .60 C2
Glebe La Sonning RG4 . . . .60 C2

Glebe La continued
    Stockcross RG20 . . . . . . .103 C3
Glebe Pl RG41 . . . . .73 A1
Glebe Rd Egham TW20 . . . .96 B1
    Maidenhead SL6 . . . . . . .40 A3
    Old Windsor SL4 . . . . . . .68 A1
    Purley on T RG8 . . . . .57 A3
    Reading RG2 . . . . .86 B3
    Staines TW18 . . . . .97 A2
Glebe Ride SL8 . . . . .3 A2
Glebe Ride RG8 . . . . .34 A3
Glebe The Aldworth RG8 . . .32 C3
    Blackwater GU17 . . . . . .150 C2
Glebefields RG14 . . . . . . .105 A3
Glebeland Gdns TW17 . . . .125 B2
Glebeland Rd GU15 . . . . . .150 C2
Glebelands RG19 . . . . . . .106 B2
Glebelands Rd RG40 . . . . .116 A4
Glebewood RG12 . . . . . . .118 B2
Glen Ave TW15 . . . . .98 A2
Glen Ct TW18 . . . . .96 C1
Glen Innes GU47 . . . . .143 C1
Glen The Ascot SL5 . . . . . .120 B3
    Silchester RG26 . . . . . . .135 C1
    Slough SL3 . . . . .43 B1
Glenalmond Ho TW15 . . . .97 C3
Glenapp Grange RG7 . . . .136 C3
Glenavon Gdns Slough SL3 . .43 B2
    Yateley GU46 . . . . .149 B2
Glenbeigh Terr RG1 . . . . . .85 C3
Glendale Ave RG14 . . . . . .130 B3
Glendale Cl RG41 . . . . . . .116 A2
Glendale Rd RG26 . . . . . . .135 A1
Glendevon Rd RG5 . . . . . . .87 C4
Gleneagles Cl TW19 . . . . . .70 B1
Gleneagles Ct 32 RG1 . . . .86 B4
Gleneagles Ho RG12 . . . . .117 C2
Glenfield Ho RG12 . . . . . . .118 B3
Glenfield Rd TW15 . . . . . . .98 B1
Glenhaven Dr TW19 . . . . . .70 A1
Glenhurst Cl GU17 . . . . . .150 C3
Glenmore Cl RG19 . . . . . .106 B1
Glenn Miller Ct RG20 . . . . .49 A3
Glennon Cl RG30 . . . . .85 B2
Glenrhondda RG4 . . . . .58 C3
Glenrosa Rd RG30 . . . . . . .85 A4
Glentworth Pl SL1 . . . . . . .42 B3
Glenwood Bracknell RG12 . .118 B3
    Virginia Water GU25 . . . .122 B4
Glenwood Dr RG31 . . . . . .84 B4
Globe Farm La GU17 . . . . .150 A3
Glory Cl HP10 . . . . .3 C4
Glory Hill La HP9 . . . . .3 C4
Glory Mill La HP10 . . . . .3 C4
Gloucester Ave SL1 . . . . . .42 B4
Gloucester Cres TW18 . . . .97 B1
Gloucester Ct RG30 . . . . . .85 B4
Gloucester Dr TW18, TW19 . .96 B1
Gloucester Gdns GU19 . . .145 C2
Gloucester Pl
    Bracknell RG42 . . . . .91 C1
    Windsor SL4 . . . . .67 B3
Gloucester Rd
    Bagshot GU19 . . . . .145 C2
    Maidenhead SL6 . . . . . . .19 C1
    Newbury RG14 . . . . .104 C1
    Reading RG30 . . . . .85 B4
Gloucestershire Lea RG42 . .91 C1
Glyme Wlk RG31 . . . . .84 C2
Glyncastle RG4 . . . . .58 C3
Glynswood GU15 . . . . . . .151 C2
Glynwood Ho SL6 . . . . .40 A4
Goaters Rd SL5 . . . . .119 B4
Goddard Cl
    Littleton TW17 . . . . .124 C3
    Shinfield RG2 . . . . .113 C3
Goddard Ct RG41 . . . . .88 A1
Goddard Dr RG7 . . . . .107 C2
Goddards La GU15 . . . . . .151 A2
Goddington Rd SL8 . . . . . . .3 A2
Godfrey Cl GU47 . . . . .150 B4
Godolphin Inf Sch SL1 . . .42 B4
Godolphin Jun Sch SL1 . .42 B4
Godolphin Rd SL1 . . . . . . .42 B3
Godstow Cl RG5 . . . . .87 C4
Goffs Rd TW15 . . . . .98 B1
Gogmore Farm Cl KT16 . . .123 C1
Gogmore La KT16 . . . . . . .124 A1
Gold Cup La SL5 . . . . .119 B4
Goldcrest Cl GU46 . . . . . .149 A3
Goldcrest Way RG31 . . . . .84 A3
Golden Ball La SL6 . . . . . . .19 C4
Golden Oak SL2 . . . . .22 B4
Golden Orb Wood RG42 . .117 B4
Goldfinch La RG20 . . . . . .131 C2
Golding Cl RG19 . . . . .106 C2
Goldney Rd GU15 . . . . . . .152 B2
Goldsmid Rd RG1 . . . . .85 C4
Goldsmith Cl
    Thatcham RG18 . . . . . . .106 B3
    Wokingham RG40 . . . . . .115 C1
Goldsmith Way RG45 . . . .143 A4
Goldsworthy Way SL1 . . . .41 B4
Goldthorpe Gdns RG6 . . . .113 C4
Goldwell Dr RG14 . . . . . . .104 C2
Golf Dr GU15 . . . . .151 C2
Goodboys La RG7 . . . . . . .112 A1
Goodings Gn RG40 . . . . . .116 C3
Goodings La RG17 . . . . . . .47 C2
Goodliffe Gdns RG31 . . . . .57 B2
Goodman Pk SL2 . . . . .43 B3
Goodman Pl TW18 . . . . . . .96 C2
Goodrich Cl RG4 . . . . .59 C3
Goodways Dr RG12 . . . . . .118 B4
Goodwin Cl RG31 . . . . .84 C2
Goodwin Mdws HP10 . . . . .3 C4

Goodwin Rd SL2 . . . . .21 C1
Goodwin Wlk RG14 . . . . . .130 B3
Goodwood Cl
    Burghfield Common RG7 . .111 A1
    Camberley GU15 . . . . . .151 B4
Goodwood Rise SL7 . . . . . . .1 B4
Goodwood Way RG14 . . . .105 B3
Goose Cnr RG42 . . . . .91 C2
Goose Gn
    Farnham Common SL2 . . .22 A2
    Lambourn RG17 . . . . .25 A4
Goose Green Way RG19 . . .106 B2
Goose La RG20 . . . . .49 C3
Gordon Ave GU15 . . . . . . .151 B2
Gordon Cl TW18 . . . . .97 A1
Gordon Clifford Ct RG42 . .118 A4
Gordon Cres
    Camberley GU15 . . . . . .151 B2
    Compton RG20 . . . . .31 B2
Gordon Ct 8 RG14 . . . . . .105 A1
Gordon Dr TW17 . . . . .125 B2
Gordon Palmer Cl RG7 . . .137 B3
Gordon Palmer Ct RG30 . .85 B4
Gordon Pl RG30 . . . . .85 B4
Gordon Rd Ashford TW15 . .97 C3
    Camberley GU15 . . . . . .151 B3
    Crowthorne RG45 . . . . . .143 B2
    Maidenhead SL6 . . . . . . .39 B4
    Newbury RG14 . . . . .105 A1
    Shepperton TW17 . . . . . .125 B2
    Thatcham RG18 . . . . . . .106 A3
    Windsor SL4 . . . . .66 C3
Gordon Wlk GU46 . . . . . . .149 C3
Gordon's Sch GU24 . . . . .153 C4
Gore End Rd RG20 . . . . . .129 A2
Gore Rd SL1 . . . . .21 A1
Gore The SL1 . . . . .21 A1
Goring CE Prim Sch RG8 . .34 B4
Goring La RG7 . . . . .111 A1
Goring Rd TW18 . . . . .96 C2
Goring & Streatley Sta
    RG8 . . . . .34 B3
Gorrick Sq RG41 . . . . .116 A2
Gorse Bank GU18 . . . . . . .153 A4
Gorse Cottage Dr RG18 . . .79 B1
Gorse Dr RG5 . . . . .88 A4
Gorse Hill La GU25 . . . . . .122 B3
Gorse Hill Rd GU25 . . . . . .122 B3
Gorse Meade SL1 . . . . .42 A3
Gorse Pl RG42 . . . . .92 A1
Gorse Rd Cookham SL6 . . .19 C3
    Frimley GU16 . . . . .151 C1
Gorse Ride Cty Jun Sch
    RG40 . . . . .141 C4
Gorse Ride N RG40 . . . . . .141 C4
Gorse Ride S RG40 . . . . . .141 C4
Gorselands
    Caversham RG4 . . . . .59 A3
    Newbury RG14 . . . . .130 B3
    Tadley RG26 . . . . .135 B1
    Yateley GU46 . . . . .149 B2
Gosbrook Ho 1 RG4 . . . . . .59 B1
Gosbrook Rd RG4 . . . . .59 A1
Gosden Rd GU24 . . . . .153 C3
Gosforth Cl RG6 . . . . .87 B1
Goslar Way SL4 . . . . .67 A3
Gosling Gn SL3 . . . . .43 C2
Gosling Rd SL3 . . . . .43 C2
Gosnell Cl GU16 . . . . .152 B2
Gossmore Cl SL7 . . . . .1 C1
Gossmore La SL7 . . . . .1 C1
Gossmore Wlk SL7 . . . . .1 C1
Goswell Hill SL4 . . . . .67 B3
Goswell Rd SL4 . . . . .67 B3
Gothic Ct Harlington UB3 . . .71 B4
    Sandhurst GU47 . . . . . . .150 A4
Gough's La
    Bracknell RG12 . . . . . . .118 B4
    Newell Green RG42 . . . . .91 B1
Gough's Mdw GU47 . . . . .150 A4
Goughs Barn La RG42 . . . .91 A4
Gould Cl RG14 . . . . .105 A2
Gould Rd TW14 . . . . .98 C4
Goulders Cotts RG10 . . . . .36 C4
Governor's Rd GU15 . . . . .150 C2
Govett Ave TW17 . . . . . . .125 B2
Govett Gr GU20 . . . . .146 B4
Gower Pk GU47 . . . . .150 B4
Gower St RG1 . . . . .85 C4
Gower The TW20 . . . . .123 B3
Gowings Gn SL1 . . . . .41 C2
Grace Ct SL1 . . . . .42 B3
Grace Reynolds Wlk 4
    GU15 . . . . .151 B3
Graces La RG20 . . . . .78 A4
Graffham Cl RG6 . . . . .114 A4
Grafton Cl Maidenhead SL6 . .19 C1
    Slough SL3 . . . . .43 C4
Grafton Ct TW14 . . . . .98 C4
Grafton Rd RG30 . . . . .84 B4
Graham Cl Blewbury OX11 . .12 A4
    Maidenhead SL6 . . . . . . .39 B3
    Reading RG31 . . . . .84 C2
Graham Rd Cookham SL6 . .19 C3
    Windlesham GU20 . . . . . .146 B2
Grahame Ave RG8 . . . . . . .56 B3
Grainford Ct RG40 . . . . . . .116 B3
Grampian Cl UB3 . . . . .71 C4
Grampian Rd GU47 . . . . . .143 A1
Grampian Way SL3 . . . . . . .44 A1
Gramps Hill OX12 . . . . .6 C3
Granby Ct RG1 . . . . .86 C4
Granby End RG7 . . . . .111 A2
Granby Gdns RG1 . . . . .86 C4
Grand Ave GU15 . . . . .151 B3

Grange Ave
Crowthorne RG45 ....**143** A3
Reading RG6 ....**87** A3
Grange Cl Goring RG8 ....**34** A3
Wraysbury TW19 ....**68** C1
Grange Ct Earley RG6 ....**87** A4
Egham TW20 ....**95** C2
Littleton TW17 ....**125** A3
Newbury RG14 ....**105** A1
Staines TW18 ....**97** A2
Grange Dr HP10 ....**3** B2
Grange Gdns SL2 ......**22** B4
Grange La SL6 ....**19** C4
Grange Pl TW18 ......**124** B4
Grange Rd Bracknell RG12 .**118** B4
Camberley GU15 ......**151** C3
Cookham SL6 ....**19** C4
Egham TW20 ....**95** C2
Henley-on-T RG9 ....**15** C1
Grange The Burnham SL1 .**21** B1
Caversham RG4 ....**58** B3
Newbury RG14 ....**130** B3
Old Windsor SL4 ......**68** A1
Grange Way SL0 ....**44** C4
Grangely Cl RG31 ......**84** B2
Grangewood SL3 ....**43** B4
Grant Ave SL1 ....**42** C4
Grant Cl TW17 ....**125** A2
Grant Ho ⑤ SL8 ....**3** A2
Grant Rd RG45 ....**143** B2
Grant Wlk SL5 ....**120** C1
Grantham Cl GU47 .....**143** C1
Grantham Ho ⑥ TW16 ...**98** C1
Grantham Rd RG30 ....**84** C2
Granthams The RG17 ...**25** A2
Grantley Hts ③ RG1 ....**86** B4
Granville Ave SL2 ......**42** B4
Granville Rd RG30 ......**85** A3
Grasholm Way SL3 .....**44** B1
Grasmere Ave
Reading RG30 ....**57** C1
Slough SL2 ....**43** A3
Grasmere Cl
East Bedfont TW14 ......**98** C4
Thorpe Lea TW20 ....**96** A1
Grasmere Par SL2 ......**43** A3
Grasmere Rd GU18 ....**146** A1
Grass Hill RG4 ....**58** C2
Grassington Pl RG19 ...**106** B2
Grassmead RG19 ......**106** C1
Grassmere Cl RG41 .....**88** A1
Grassy La SL6 ....**39** C4
Grattan Ct SL7 ....**2** A2
Gratton Rd RG2 ....**113** B4
Gratwicke Rd RG30 .....**84** C4
Gravel Hill Caversham RG4 .**59** A3
Henley-on-T RG9 ....**15** B1
Stockcross RG20 ....**103** C3
Gravel Rd RG9 ....**35** A1
Gravelly Cl RG20 ......**129** A2
Graveney Dr RG4 ....**58** C2
Gravett Cl RG9 ....**35** B4
Gray Ct SL4 ....**66** B3
Gray's Mon SL2 ....**22** C1
Gray's Pl SL2 ....**42** C3
Gray's Rd SL1 ....**42** C3
Grayling Cl SL7 ....**18** C2
Grayling Ct ④ RG1 .....**59** A1
Grays Cres RG5 ....**87** B4
Grays La TW15 ....**98** A2
Grays Park Rd SL2 ......**23** A1
Grayshot Dr GU17 ....**150** B3
Grazeley Parochial
Prim Sch RG7 ....**112** C1
Grazeley Rd RG7 ......**113** A2
Great Auclum Pl RG7 ...**111** A1
Great Barn Ct RG19 ...**106** B2
Great Hill Cres SL6 .....**39** B3
Great Hollands
Jun & Inf Sch RG12 ....**117** C2
Great Hollands Rd RG12 .**117** C2
Great Hollands Sq RG12 .**117** C2
Great Knollys St RG1 ....**85** C4
Great Lea RG7 ....**113** A3
Great Marlow Sch SL7 ...**1** C2
Great Severals RG17 ...**102** A1
Great South-West Rd
East Bedfont TW14 ......**98** B4
Hatton TW14 ....**71** B1
Grebe Ct TW18 ....**97** A2
Green Acre Mount RG30 .**84** B4
Green Bsns Ctr TW20 ...**96** B2
Green Cl Burnham SL6 ....**41** A4
Maidenhead SL6 ....**19** C1
Green Cres HP10 ....**3** B4
Green Croft RG40 .....**116** C4
Green Ct TW16 ....**98** C1
Green Dr RG40 ....**116** C2
Green Dragon La HP10 ...**3** A4
Green End GU46 ......**149** B4
Green End Cl RG7 .....**113** A1
Green Farm Rd GU19 ...**145** C2
Green Farm Rise SN8 ...**99** A3
Green Finch Cl RG45 ...**142** C4
Green Hill Cl GU15 ....**152** B3
Green Hill Rd GU15 ....**152** B3
Green La Ascot SL5 ....**120** C4
Ashford TW16 ....**98** C1
Bagshot GU19 ....**145** C1
Blackwater GU17 ......**150** A2
Blackwater, Hawley GU17 .**150** C4
Bradfield RG7 ....**81** C2
Burghfield Common RG30 .**85** A1

Green La continued
Burnham SL1 ....**21** B2
Caversham RG4 ....**35** A1
Chieveley RG20 ....**78** A4
Datchet SL3 ....**68** A3
Egham TW20 ....**96** A2
Farnham Common SL2 ...**22** A3
Henley-on-T RG9 ....**35** B4
Holyport SL6 ....**64** A3
Hurst RG10 ....**88** C2
Littlewick Green SL6 ....**38** A3
Maidenhead SL6 ....**40** A3
Newbury RG14 ....**104** C1
Padworth RG7 ....**110** B1
Pangbourne RG8 ....**56** B3
Sandhurst GU47 ......**150** B4
Shepperton TW17 .....**125** B2
Thatcham RG19 ......**106** B2
Thorpe TW18 ....**123** C4
Windsor SL4 ....**67** A3
Wokingham RG41 ....**88** B1
Green Lane Cl GU15 ...**151** B4
Green Lane Ct SL1 ......**21** B1
Green Leas TW16 ....**98** C1
Green Leas Cl TW16 ....**98** C1
Green Leys SL6 ....**19** C1
Green Pk TW18 ....**96** C3
Green Rd Reading RG6 ...**87** A3
Thorpe TW20 ....**123** A3
Green The
Bracknell RG12 ....**118** A3
Burnham SL1 ....**21** A1
Chilton OX11 ....**10** C4
Datchet SL3 ....**68** A4
Kintbury RG17 ....**102** A1
Slough SL1 ....**42** B2
Staines TW18 ....**97** B2
Theale RG7 ....**83** B1
Wokingham RG41 .....**115** C4
Wooburn Green HP10 ....**3** C3
Wraysbury TW19 ....**68** C1
Green Verges SL7 ....**1** C2
Green Wood SL5 ......**119** B4
Greenacre SL4 ....**66** C3
Greenacre Ct TW20 .....**95** B1
Greenacres RG20 .....**129** C1
Greenacres Ave RG41 ...**88** A2
Greenacres La RG41 ....**88** A2
Greenaway Terr TW19 ...**97** C4
Greenbank Way GU15 ..**151** B1
Greencroft Gdns RG30 ..**84** C2
Greendale Mews SL2 ....**43** A3
Greene Fielde End TW18 .**97** B1
Greenfern Ave SL1 ......**41** B4
Greenfield Way RG45 ..**143** A4
Greenfields SL6 ....**40** A3
Greenfields Rd RG2 ....**113** A4
Greenfinch Cl RG31 .....**84** A3
Greenham Cl
Greenham RG19 ....**131** B4
Woodley RG5 ....**88** A3
Greenham Court
Prim Sch RG14 ....**131** B4
Greenham Mill RG14 ...**105** A2
Greenham Rd RG14 ....**105** A1
Greenham Wood RG12 ..**118** B2
Greenhaven GU46 .....**149** A3
Greenholme GU15 .....**152** B3
Greenhow RG12 ......**118** A3
Greenidge Ct ⑥ RG1 ....**85** C3
Greenlake Terr TW18 ....**97** A1
Greenlands Ball Hill RG20 .**129** C1
Flackwell Heath HP10 ....**3** A4
Greenlands Ct
Maidenhead SL6 ....**39** A4
Staines TW18 ....**97** A2
Greenlands Rd
Camberley GU15 ......**151** A1
Newbury RG14 ....**105** A1
Staines TW18 ....**97** A2
Greenleaf Ct SL3 ....**68** A4
Greenleas GU15 ......**151** C1
Greenleas Ave RG4 .....**59** A4
Greenleas Cl GU46 ....**149** B4
Greenleaves Ct TW15 ...**98** A2
Greeno Cres TW17 ....**125** A2
Greenock Rd SL1 ....**42** A4
Greenside Bourne End SL8 .**3** A3
Crowthorne RG45 .....**142** C3
Slough SL2 ....**42** A4
Greensward La RG12 ...**114** B1
Greenview Ct TW15 .....**97** C2
Greenway Dr TW18 ....**124** B4
Greenway The
Fawley OX12 ....**27** B4
Slough SL1 ....**42** C3
Greenways Ball Hill RG20 .**129** C1
Egham TW20 ....**95** C2
Lambourn RG17 ....**25** A1
Sandhurst GU47 ......**143** A1
Greenways Dr
Maidenhead SL6 ....**39** A4
Sunningdale SL5 ......**120** C1
Greenwood ⑫ RG12 ...**118** C3
Greenwood Gr RG41 ....**88** B2
Greenwood Rd
Crowthorne RG45 .....**143** A3
Reading RG30 ....**84** C3
Gregory Cl RG6 ....**114** B4
Gregory Dr SL4 ....**68** A1
Grenfell Ave SL6 ....**39** C3
Grenfell Cl SL6 ....**39** C3
Grenfell Pl SL6 ....**39** C3
Grenville Cl SL1 ....**21** A2
Gresham Ct TW18 ......**97** A2
Gresham Rd Slough SL1 ..**42** A4
Staines TW18 ....**97** A2
Gresham Way RG30 .....**58** A1

Greyberry Copse Rd
RG19 ....**131** B4
Greyfriars Dr SL5 ......**120** A2
Greyfriars Rd RG1 ......**86** A4
Greys Ct ⑥ RG1 ....**86** B4
Greys Hill RG9 ....**15** B1
Greys Rd RG9 ....**15** B1
Greystoke Ct RG45 ....**143** A2
Greystoke Ho ⑨ RG1 ....**85** C3
Greystoke Rd
Caversham RG4 ....**59** B2
Slough SL2 ....**41** C4
Griffin Cl Maidenhead SL6 .**39** C3
Slough SL1 ....**42** B2
Griffiths Ct RG19 ......**106** C1
Grindle Cl RG18 ......**106** B3
Gringer Hill SL6 ....**39** C4
Groombridge Pl RG14 ..**104** C3
Grosvenor Ct
Blackwater GU17 .....**150** B2
Slough SL1 ....**42** C4
Grosvenor Dr SL6 ......**40** B4
Grosvenor Lawn RG14 ..**104** C1
Grosvenor Rd
Caversham RG4 ....**59** B2
Staines TW18 ....**97** A1
Grove Cl Old Windsor SL4 .**95** A4
② Slough SL1 ....**43** A2
Wokingham RG40 ....**142** C4
Grove Cotts RG4 ....**59** A3
Grove Cross Rd GU16 ...**151** B1
Grove Ct Egham TW20 ...**96** A2
Maidenhead SL6 ....**39** B4
Newbury RG14 ....**131** A4
Grove La RG42 ....**92** A2
Grove Pk SL6 ....**63** C4
Grove Rd Burnham SL1 ...**21** C2
Camberley GU15 ......**151** C3
Caversham RG4 ....**59** A3
Chertsey KT16 ....**123** C2
Henley-on-T RG9 ......**15** C1
Maidenhead SL6 ....**39** C4
Newbury RG14 ....**104** C3
Shepperton TW17 ....**125** B2
Windsor SL4 ....**67** B3
Grove The Egham TW20 ..**96** A2
Frimley GU16 ....**151** B1
Medmenham SL7 ....**17** C3
North Ascot SL5 ......**119** B4
Reading RG1 ....**86** B4
Slough SL1 ....**43** A2
Thatcham RG18 ......**106** B2
Twyford RG10 ....**61** B3
Grovebarns TW18 ......**97** A1
Grovefields Ave GU19 ..**145** C3
Groveland Pl RG30 ......**85** A4
Groveland Rd RG14 ....**104** C3
Grovelands Ave RG41 ...**88** B1
Grovelands Cl RG41 .....**88** B2
Grovelands Rd
Reading RG30 ....**85** A4
Shinfield RG7 ....**113** B1
Groveley Rd TW13, TW16 .**98** C2
Groves Cl SL8 ....**3** B2
Groves Lea RG7 ....**136** C3
Groves The RG17 ....**73** A1
Groves Way SL6 ....**19** C3
Grovestile Waye TW14 ..**98** B4
Grubwood La SL6 ......**19** A4
Guards Club Rd SL6 .....**40** B4
Guards Ct SL5 ....**121** A1
Guards Rd SL4 ....**66** B3
Guards Wlk ❶ SL4 ......**66** B3
Guerdon Pl RG12 ......**118** B1
Guildford Ave TW13 ....**98** C3
Guildford Rd
Bagshot GU19 ....**145** C1
Bagshot GU19 ....**145** C2
Bisley GU24 ....**153** C2
Chertsey KT16 ....**123** C1
Lightwater GU18 .....**146** A1
West End GU24 ......**153** C4
Guildford St
Chertsey KT16 ....**124** A1
Staines TW18 ....**97** A1
Gullane St ⑨ RG1 ......**86** B4
Gun St RG1 ....**86** A4
Gunthorpe Rd SL7 ....**2** A2
Gurney Cl RG4 ....**58** B3
Gurney Dr RG4 ....**58** B3
Gwendale SL6 ....**19** B1
Gwendoline Ct TW15 ...**97** C2
Gweneth Ct SL7 ....**1** B2
Gwent Cl SL6 ....**39** C2
Gwyn Cl RG14 ....**130** C3
Gwynne Cl
Purley on T RG31 ......**57** B2
Windsor SL4 ....**66** C3
Gwyns Piece RG17 ......**25** A2
Gypsy La Marlow SL7 ....**1** C2
Stoke Poges SL2 ....**22** C4

H

Habershon Dr GU16 ...**152** B1
Haddenhurst Ct RG42 ...**90** B1
Haddon Dr RG5 ....**87** C4
Haddon Rd SL6 ....**39** B3
Hadfield Rd TW19 ....**70** B1
Hadleigh Rise RG4 ......**59** C3
Hadley Cl SL3 ....**69** C3

Hadlow Ct SL1 ....**42** B3
Hadrian Cl TW19 ....**97** C4
Hadrian Way TW19 .....**97** B4
Hadrian Wlk E RG2 ......**86** B2
Hadrian Wlk W RG2 .....**86** B2
Hafod SL4 ....**58** C3
Hag Hill La SL6 ....**41** A4
Hag Hill Rise SL6 ....**41** A4
Hagley Rd RG2 ....**86** A2
Haig Dr SL1 ....**42** A2
Haig Rd GU15 ....**150** C3
Hailey La RG20 ....**29** C1
Haileybury Cl SL4 ....**67** A2
Hailsham Cl GU47 .....**143** B1
Halcyon Ct TW18 ......**124** A4
Halcyon Terr RG30 .....**84** C4
Haldane Rd RG4 ....**58** C3
Hale SL4 ....**66** C3
Hale End RG12 ....**118** C3
Hale St TW18 ....**96** C2
Halewood RG12 ....**117** C2
Half Mile Rd RG17 ......**46** A1
Half Moon St GU19 ....**145** C2
Halfacre Ct RG7 ....**113** A2
Halfpenny Ct SL5 ......**121** A1
Halfpenny La Cholsey OX10 .**13** B3
Sunningdale SL5 ......**121** A1
Halfway Hos SL6 ....**19** C2
Halifax Cl SL6 ....**39** A4
Halifax Pl RG18 ....**106** B3
Halifax Rd SL6 ....**39** A4
Halifax Way SL6 ....**39** A4
Halkingcroft SL3 ....**43** B2
Hall Cl GU15 ....**151** C3
Hall Ct SL3 ....**68** A4
Hall Farm Cres GU46 ..**149** B3
Hall Grove (Sch) GU19 .**146** A3
Hall La Harlington UB3 ...**71** B4
Yateley GU46 ....**149** B3
Hall Mdw SL1 ....**21** A3
Hall Place La SL6 ....**38** A4
Hallbrook Gdns RG42 ...**90** C1
Halldore Hill SL6 ....**19** C4
Halley Dr SL5 ....**119** B4
Hallgrove Bottom GU19 .**145** C3
Halliford Cl TW17 .....**125** C3
Halliford Rd TW16, TW17 .**125** C3
Halliford Sch TW17 ...**125** B1
Hallmark Cl GU47 .....**150** C4
Halls La Earley RG6 .....**87** A4
Waltham St Lawrence RG10 .**63** A4
Halls Rd RG30 ....**84** B3
Hallsmead Ct ③ RG1 ....**59** A1
Halpin Cl RG31 ....**84** B2
Halstead Cl RG5 ....**87** C4
Halstead Ho RG26 .....**134** C1
Halters The RG14 .....**131** A4
Ham Island SL4 ....**68** B2
Ham La
Englefield Green TW20 ...**95** A2
Old Windsor SL4 ......**68** B2
Ham Rd SN8 ....**126** A2
Hamble Ave GU17 .....**150** B3
Hamble Ct ⑯ RG1 ......**86** A3
Hambleden Ct RG12 ...**118** C3
Hambleden Mill RG9 ....**16** B4
Hambleden Pl RG9 ......**16** B3
Hambleden Rise RG9 ....**16** B4
Hambleden Wlk RG9 ....**19** C1
Hambledon Cl RG6 ......**87** C1
Hambleton TW19 ....**95** B4
Hambleton Cl GU16 ...**152** A2
Hamblin Mdw RG17 ...**100** C4
Hambridge Rd RG14 ...**105** B3
Hamfield Cotts SL6 .....**19** C4
Hamilton Ave RG9 ......**15** C1
Hamilton Cl TW13 ......**98** C2
Hamilton Cl GU19 ....**145** C2
Hamilton Cl KT16 .....**123** C1
Hamilton Ct
Farnborough (Hants) GU17 .**150** A4
Newbury RG14 ....**131** A4
Hamilton Dr SL5 ......**120** C1
Hamilton Gdns SL1 .....**21** A1
Hamilton Pk SL6 ....**39** A3
Hamilton Rd Feltham TW13 .**98** C2
Reading RG1 ....**86** C3
Slough SL1 ....**42** A4
Wargrave RG10 ....**36** C1
Hamlet St RG42 ....**118** C4
Hammond Cl RG19 ....**106** C1
Hammond Ct RG42 .....**91** A1
Hammond End SL2 .....**22** A4
Hammond Jun Sch
GU18 ....**146** A1
Hammond Way GU18 ..**146** A1
Hammonds Heath RG7 .**137** A3
Hampden Cl SL2 ....**23** A1
Hampden Rd
Caversham RG4 ....**59** A1
Maidenhead SL6 ....**39** A4
Slough SL3 ....**43** C2
Hampdens The RG14 ...**130** B3
Hampshire Ave SL1 .....**42** B4
Hampshire Lodge ⑧ SL6 .**39** C3
Hampshire Rd GU15 ...**151** C4
Hampshire Rise RG42 ...**91** C1
Hampshire Way RG41 ..**115** B3
Hampshire Wlk RG31 ...**84** A4
Hampstead Ct RG30 .....**85** A4
Hampstead Hill RG9 .....**60** B4
Hampstead Norreys
CE Prim Sch RG18 .....**52** C3
Hampstead Norreys Rd
RG18 ....**79** A4
Hampton Ho SL3 ....**69** B4
Hampton Rd RG14 .....**104** C1
Hampton Twrs ④ RG30 ..**85** B3

Hanbury Cl SL1 ....**41** A3
Hanbury Dr RG31 ....**84** B2
Hanbury Way GU15 ...**151** B2
Hanbury Wlk RG19 ....**106** B1
Hancocks Mount SL5 ..**120** B2
Hancombe Rd GU47 ...**143** A1
Handford La GU46 ....**149** B3
Hanger Rd RG26 ......**134** C1
Hangerfield Cl GU46 ...**149** B3
Hangmans Stone La RG20 .**49** A3
Hanley Cl SL4 ....**66** B3
Hannibal Rd TW19 ......**97** C4
Hanningtons Way RG7 .**111** B2
Hanover Cl
Englefield Green TW20 ...**95** B1
Frimley GU16 ....**151** C1
Slough SL1 ....**43** A2
Windsor SL4 ....**66** C3
Hanover Ct Caversham RG4 .**59** B2
Reading RG30 ....**84** C3
Hanover Gdns RG12 ...**117** C3
Hanover Mead
Maidenhead SL6 ....**40** B2
Newbury RG14 ....**130** B3
Hanover Way SL4 ....**66** C3
Hanson Cl GU15 ......**152** A4
Hanwood Cl RG5 ....**87** B4
Hanworth Cl RG12 ....**118** B2
Hanworth La KT16 ....**123** C1
Hanworth Rd RG12 ....**118** A1
Hanworth Trad Est KT16 .**123** C1
Harborough Cl SL1 ......**41** B3
Harbury Ct RG14 ......**105** A1
Harcourt TW19 ....**68** C1
Harcourt Cl Dorney SL4 ..**40** C2
Egham TW20 ....**96** B1
Henley-on-T RG9 ....**15** B1
Harcourt Dr RG6 ....**86** C2
Harcourt Rd
Bracknell RG12 ....**118** A2
Camberley GU15 ......**151** A3
Dorney SL4 ....**40** C2
Windsor SL4 ....**66** C3
Hardell Cl TW20 ....**96** A2
Harding Rd RG5 ....**87** B4
Hardwell Way RG12 ...**118** C3
Hardwick Cl SL6 ....**39** A4
Hardwick La KT16 .....**123** B1
Hardwick Rd Reading RG30 .**84** C4
Whitchurch-on-T RG8 ...**56** B4
Hardy Ave GU46 ......**149** B3
Hardy Cl Caversham RG4 ..**59** B1
Slough SL1 ....**42** A3
Thatcham RG18 ......**106** B3
Hardy Gn RG45 ....**143** A2
Hare Shoots SL6 ....**39** C3
Harebell Dr RG18 .....**106** C3
Harefield Cl RG41 ....**88** B1
Harefield Rd SL6 ....**39** A4
Harewood Dr RG18 ....**106** B4
Harewood Pl SL1 ....**43** A2
Hargrave Rd RG2 ....**86** A2
Hargreaves Way RG31 ..**84** C2
Harkness Rd SL1 ....**41** A4
Harlech Ave RG4 ....**59** B3
Harlech Rd GU17 .....**150** B2
Harley Rd RG4 ....**59** A1
Harlington Cl UB3 ....**71** B4
Harlington Cnr UB3 ......**71** B3
Harlton Cl RG6 ....**114** B4
Harmans Water
Cty Inf Sch RG12 ......**118** C2
Harmans Water
Cty Jun Sch RG12 .....**118** C2
Harmans Water Rd RG12 .**118** B2
Harmar Ct RG40 ......**116** C3
Harmondsworth La UB7 ..**70** C4
Harmondsworth Prim Sch
UB7 ....**70** B4
Harness Cl RG2 ....**113** A3
Harold Rd RG17 ......**102** A1
Harpesford Ave GU25 ..**122** B2
Harpsden Rd RG9 ....**35** C4
Harpsden Way RG9 .....**35** C4
Harpton Cl GU46 ......**149** B4
Harrier Cl RG5 ....**88** A3
Harrington Cl Earley RG6 .**87** B1
Newbury RG14 ....**105** C3
Windsor SL4 ....**66** C2
Harris Arc ⑤ RG1 ....**86** B4
Harris Cl Lambourn RG17 ..**25** A2
Woodley RG5 ....**88** A4
Harrison Cl RG10 ....**61** C2
Harrison Ct TW17 .....**125** A4
Harrison Way SL1 ....**41** B3
Harrogate Ct SL3 ....**44** A1
Harrogate Rd RG4 ......**58** C2
Harrow Bottom Rd GU25 .**122** C2
Harrow Cl SL6 ....**19** C1
Harrow Ct RG1 ....**85** C3
Harrow La SL6 ....**19** C1
Harrow Mkt The SL3 ....**44** A2
Harrow Rd
Ashford TW14, TW15 ...**98** A3
Slough SL3 ....**43** C2
Harrow Way TW17 ....**125** B4
Harry Tee Ct ⑪ RG1 .....**86** B4
Hart Cl ⑥ RG42 ....**118** A4
Hart Dene Cl GU19 ....**145** C2
Hart Dyke Cl RG41 ....**116** A1
Hart St Henley-on-T RG9 ..**15** C1
Reading RG1 ....**85** C4
Hartford Rise GU15 ...**151** B3
Hartigan Pl RG5 ....**88** A4
Hartland Cl SL1 ....**42** B3
Hartland Rd RG2 ....**86** B1
Hartley Cl
Blackwater GU17 .....**150** A4

Hartley Cl *continued*
Stoke Poges SL3 .23 B2
Hartley Copse SL4 .68 A1
Hartley Court Rd RG7 .112 C3
Hartley Way RG18 .106 C2
Hartmead Rd RG19 .106 C2
Harts Cl RG2 .114 C1
Harts Hill Rd RG18 .106 C2
Harts La RG7 .110 B3
Harts Leap Cl GU47 .143 A1
Harts Leap Rd GU47 .150 A4
Hartsbourne Rd RG6 .87 A2
Hartshill Rd RG26 .134 C1
Hartslock Ct RG8 .56 A3
Hartslock View RG8 .34 C1
Hartslock Way RG31 .57 B1
Hartvale Ct GU15 .152 A4
Harvard Cl RG5 .88 A4
Harvard Rd GU47 .143 C1
Harvest Cl Reading RG31 .84 A3
Yateley GU46 .149 A2
Harvest Ct TW17 .125 A3
Harvest Gn RG14 .104 C1
Harvest Hill SL8 .3 B1
Harvest Hill Rd SL6 .39 C2
Harvest Rd TW20 .95 B1
Harvest Ride
Bracknell RG42 .91 B1
Winkfield RG12, RG42, SL5 .119 A4
Harvey Ho 11 RG30 .85 B3
Harvey Rd SL3 .44 A2
Harwell Int Bsns Ctr OX11 .9 C4
Harwich Cl 8 RG6 .87 B1
Harwich Rd SL1 .42 A4
Harwood Gdns SL4 .95 A4
Harwood Rd SL7 .1 B1
Harwood Rise RG20 .129 C1
Haslemere Cl GU16 .152 B2
Haslemere Rd SL4 .67 A3
Haslett Rd TW17 .125 C4
Hasting Cl SL6 .40 B1
Hastings Mdw SL2 .23 A2
Hatch Cl RG7 .108 B4
Hatch End GU20 .146 B2
Hatch Gate La RG10 .37 A3
Hatch La Bucklebury RG7 .108 B4
Burghfield Common RG30 .111 B3
Harmondsworth TW6, UB7 .70 B4
Windsor SL4 .67 A3
Hatch Ride
Crowthorne RG45 .143 A4
Wokingham RG40 .142 C4
Hatch Ride Cty Prim Sch
RG45 .143 A4
Hatch The SL4 .66 B4
Hatchet La SL4, SL5 .93 A3
Hatchets La RG18 .80 B4
Hatchett Rd TW14 .98 B4
Hatchgate Cl RG18 .106 B4
Hatchgate Copse RG12 .117 C2
Hatchgate Gdns SL1 .21 B1
Hatchley RG2 .113 B4
Hatfield Cl SL6 .39 B3
Hatfield Ct RG31 .84 A2
Hatfield Rd SL1 .43 A2
Hatford Rd RG30 .85 A2
Hatherley Rd RG1 .86 C3
Hatherwood GU46 .149 C3
Hatt Cl RG20 .50 B4
Hatton Ave SL2 .22 B1
Hatton Cross Rdbt TW6 .71 C2
Hatton Cross Sta TW6 .71 C2
Hatton Ct SL4 .67 B3
Hatton Hill
Ashampstead RG8 .54 A4
Windlesham GU20 .146 B3
Hatton Rd
East Bedfont TW14 .98 B4
Hatton TW14, TW6 .71 C1
Haughurst Hill RG26 .134 B1
Havelock Cres SL6 .39 A4
Havelock Rd
Maidenhead SL6 .39 A4
Wokingham RG41 .116 A3
Havelock St RG41 .116 A3
Haven Ct 21 RG1 .86 B4
Haven Of Rest SL6 .40 A4
Haven Rd TW15 .98 A3
Haven The RG17 .102 A1
Haversham Dr RG12 .118 A2
Haw La Aldworth RG8 .32 C1
Ashampstead RG8, RG18 .53 C4
Hawk La RG12 .118 B3
Hawkchurch Rd RG2 .113 B4
Hawkedale Fst Sch
TW16 .125 C3
Hawkedon Prim Sch RG6 .87 C1
Hawkedon Way RG6 .87 C1
Hawker Ct SL3 .44 A2
Hawker Way RG5 .88 A4
Hawkes Cl RG41 .116 A4
Hawkes Leap GU20 .146 A3
Hawkesbury Dr RG31 .84 C2
Hawkesworth Dr GU19 .145 C1
Hawkins Cl RG12 .119 A4
Hawkins Way RG40 .116 C3
Hawkridge Ct RG12 .118 C3
Hawks Hill SL8 .3 B1
Hawkshill Rd SL2 .22 A1
Hawksway TW18 .96 C3
Hawkswood Ave GU16 .151 C1
Hawkswood Ho RG42 .117 C4
Hawkswood La SL9 .23 C4
Hawksworth Rd RG7 .111 A2
Hawley Cl RG31 .84 B2
Hawley Garden Cotts
GU17 .150 B2
Hawley Gn GU17 .150 C2
Hawley La GU14, GU17 .151 A1
Hawley Lodge GU17 .150 C1
Hawley Place Ind Sch
GU17 .150 C1
Hawley Prim Sch GU17 .150 C2
Hawley Rd GU17 .150 C2
Hawley Way TW15 .98 A2
Hawthorn Cl
Bracknell RG42 .118 A4
Marlow SL7 .1 C2
Hawthorn Gdns RG2 .86 C1
Hawthorn La Burnham SL2 .22 A3
Newell Green, Hawthorn Hill
RG42 .91 C4
Newell Green,
Nuptown RG42 .92 A4
Hawthorn Rd
Frimley GU16 .151 C1
Newbury RG14 .105 A2
Hawthorn Way
Sonning RG4 .60 C2
Upper Halliford TW17 .125 B3
Hawthorne Ave SL4 .93 A3
Hawthorne Cres
Blackwater GU17 .150 C2
Slough SL1 .42 C4
Hawthorne Ct TW19 .97 B4
Hawthorne Dr SL4 .93 A4
Hawthorne Rd
Caversham RG4 .59 C2
Egham TW20 .96 B2
Hawthorne Way
Great Shefford RG17 .48 A2
Stanwell TW19 .97 B4
Winkfield SL4 .93 A4
Hawthornes RG31 .57 A2
Hawthorns Prim Sch The
RG41 .115 C4
Hawthorns The
Charvil RG10 .61 A2
Flackwell Heath HP10 .3 A4
Poyle SL3 .69 C3
Wooburn Green HP10 .3 C3
Hawtrey Cl SL1 .43 A2
Hawtrey Rd SL4 .67 B3
Hay La SL3 .23 B4
Hay Rd RG1 .85 C3
Haydon Ct SL6 .39 C3
Haydon Pl GU46 .149 C3
Hayes La RG41 .115 B2
Hayes Pl SL7 .1 B1
Hayfield Cl RG31 .84 B4
Hayfield Ct RG17 .46 C3
Hayley Gn RG42 .91 C2
Haymill Rd SL1, SL2 .21 B1
Haynes Cl SL3 .43 C1
Hayse Hill SL4 .66 B3
Hayward Pl SL8 .3 B1
Haywards Cl RG9 .15 B1
Haywards Mead SL4 .41 C1
Haywards The RG18 .106 B2
Haywood RG12 .118 B1
Haywood Ct RG1 .86 C4
Haywood Way RG30 .84 C3
Hazel Cl
Burghfield Common RG30 .111 A3
Englefield Green TW20 .95 A1
Marlow Bottom SL7 .1 B3
Wokingham RG41 .115 C3
Hazel Cres RG2 .86 C1
Hazel Dr RG5 .87 B3
Hazel Gn RG26 .134 B1
Hazel Gr Staines TW18 .97 B1
Thatcham RG18 .106 B3
Hazel Rd RG8 .57 B2
Hazelbank RG40 .141 C3
Hazelbank Ct KT16 .124 B1
Hazelbank Rd KT16 .124 B1
Hazeldene RG20 .51 A1
Hazelhurst Rd SL1 .21 B2
Hazell Cl SL6 .39 C4
Hazell Hill RG12 .118 B3
Hazell Way SL2 .22 C3
Hazelmere Cl TW14 .71 C1
Hazelmere Rd SL2 .43 A3
Hazels Paddock RG18 .106 B4
Hazelwood Cl RG31 .57 B1
Hazelwood La RG42 .90 C2
Heacham Cl RG6 .114 A4
Headington Cl
Maidenhead SL6 .39 A4
Wokingham RG40 .116 B4
Headington Dr RG40 .116 B4
Headington Rd SL6 .39 A4
Headley Cl RG5 .88 A4
Headley Park Ind Est RG5 .87 C4
Headley Rd RG5 .87 C4
Headley Rd E RG5 .88 A4
Heads La RG17 .128 A3
Heardman Cl RG19 .106 C1
Hearmon Cl GU46 .149 C3
Hearn Rd RG5 .87 C3
Hearn Wlk RG12 .118 C4
Hearne Dr SL6 .40 A1
Hearsey Gdns GU17 .150 B3
Heath Cl Harlington UB3 .71 B4
Stanwell TW19 .70 B1
Virginia Water GU25 .122 B3
Wokingham RG41 .116 A2
Heath Cnr GU15 .152 A2
Heath Ct RG26 .134 C1
Heath Dr RG9 .35 A1
Heath End Rd RG26 .134 C1
Heath Gr TW16 .98 C1
Heath Hill Rd N RG45 .143 A3
Heath Hill Rd S RG45 .143 A2
Heath La RG18 .106 B3
Heath Rd Bagshot GU19 .145 C2
Heath Rd *continued*
Bradfield RG7 .82 A1
Reading RG6 .87 A3
Silchester RG26 .135 C1
Wooburn Moor HP9 .3 C4
Heath Ride RG40, RG45 .142 B3
Heath Rise
Camberley GU15 .151 B3
Virginia Water GU25 .122 B3
Heathacre SL3 .69 C3
Heathcote SL6 .40 A1
Heathcote Ct 2 SL4 .67 B2
Heathcote Rd GU15 .151 B3
Heathcroft Ave TW16 .98 C1
Heather Cl RG40 .141 C4
Heather Dr
Sunningdale SL5 .121 A1
Tadley RG26 .134 C1
Thatcham RG18 .106 B3
Heather Gdns RG14 .130 C4
Heather Mead GU16 .151 C1
Heather Mead Ct GU16 .151 C1
Heather Ridge Arc GU15 .152 B2
Heather Ridge
Cty Inf Sch GU15 .152 B2
Heatherdale Rd GU15 .151 B2
Heatherden Cl RG2 .113 B4
Heatherdene Ave RG45 .142 C2
Heatherley Cl GU15 .151 A3
Heatherley Rd GU15 .151 A3
Heathermount 4 RG12 .118 C3
Heathermount Dr RG45 .143 A3
Heathermount Sch SL5 .120 B2
Heathers The TW19 .97 C4
Heatherside Dr GU25 .122 A2
Heatherway RG45 .143 A3
Heatherwood Hospl SL5 .119 C3
Heathfield RG7 .137 A3
Heathfield Ave Ascot SL5 .120 C2
Reading RG30 .84 B3
Shiplake RG9 .35 A1
Heathfield Cl RG9 .35 A1
Heathfield Ct TW15 .97 C3
Heathfield Rd SL1 .3 C1
Heathfield Sch SL5 .119 A4
Heathfields RG20 .78 A4
Heathlands RG26 .134 C1
Heathlands Country Mkt
RG40 .116 C1
Heathlands Ct RG40 .142 C4
Heathlands Dr SL6 .39 A3
Heathlands Rd RG40 .116 C1
Heathmoors RG12 .118 B2
Heathpark Dr GU20 .146 C2
Heathrow Airport London
TW6 .71 A3
Heathrow Airport Visitor Ctr
TW6 .71 B3
Heathrow Bvd UB7 .70 C4
Heathrow Central Sta
TW6 .71 A2
Heathrow Cl TW6 .70 A3
Heathrow Copse RG26 .134 B1
Heathrow Sch UB7 .70 C4
Heathrow Terminal 4 Sta
TW6 .71 B1
Heathside Pk GU15 .152 B4
Heathway
Camberley GU15 .151 B3
North Ascot SL5 .119 C4
Reading RG31 .84 B4
Heathway Cl GU15 .151 B3
Heathwood Cl GU46 .149 B4
Heavens Lea SL8 .3 B1
Hebbecastle Down RG42 .91 B1
Hebden Cl RG19 .106 B1
Hedge Lea HP10 .3 B4
Hedgeway RG14 .105 B2
Hedingham Mews SL6 .39 B4
Hedley Rd HP10 .3 A4
Hedsor Hill SL8 .3 B1
Hedsor La HP10, SL1 .3 C1
Hedsor Rd SL8 .3 A1
Hedsor View Cotts SL6 .19 C4
Heelas Rd RG41 .116 A3
Heights The
Camberley GU15 .151 C3
Marlow SL7 .18 A4
Helen Cotts SL4 .66 B3
Helena Rd SL4 .67 B3
Helgiford Gdns TW16 .98 C1
Helksham Cl GU47 .143 B1
Hellyer Way SL8 .3 B2
Helmsdale RG12 .118 C2
Helmsdale Cl RG30 .85 A4
Helston Gdns RG2 .86 A1
Helston La SL4 .67 A3
Helvellyn Cl TW20 .96 A1
Hemdean Hill RG4 .59 A2
Hemdean House Sch RG4 .59 A2
Hemdean Rd RG4 .59 A2
Hemdean Rise RG4 .59 A2
Hemming Way SL2 .22 A1
Hemmyng Cnr RG42 .91 B1
Hempson Ave SL3 .43 B2
Hemsdale SL6 .19 A1
Hemwood Rd SL4 .66 B2
Hencroft St N SL1 .42 C2
Hencroft St S SL1 .42 C2
Hendon Terr TW15 .98 B1
Hendon Way TW19 .70 B1
Hendons Way SL6 .40 A1
Hengrave Cl RG6 .87 C1
Hengrove Cres TW15 .97 B3
Henley Coll The
(Deanfield Bldgs) RG9 .15 B1
Henley Coll The
(Rotherfield Bldgs) RG9 .15 B1
Henley Coll The
(Southfield Bldgs) RG9 .15 B1
Henley Gdns GU46 .149 B3
Henley Lodge 12 SL6 .39 C3
Henley Rd Bisham SL6 .18 A1
Caversham RG9 .59 B2
Hurley SL6 .17 B2
Marlow SL7 .18 A4
Shiplake RG9 .60 B4
Slough SL1 .41 C4
Henley Trinity Prim Sch
RG9 .15 B1
Henley Wood Rd RG6 .87 B2
Henley-on-Thames Sta
RG9 .15 C1
Henry Ct 24 RG1 .86 B4
Henry Rd SL1 .42 B2
Henry St RG1 .86 A3
Henrys The RG18 .106 B2
Henshaw Cres RG14 .130 B4
Hensworth Rd TW15 .97 B2
Henwick Cl RG18 .106 A3
Henwick La RG18 .106 A2
Henwood Copse RG8 .55 A3
Hepplewhite Cl RG26 .134 C1
Hepworth Croft GU47 .150 C3
Hepworth Way KT12 .125 C1
Herald Way RG5 .88 A3
Herbert Cl RG12 .118 A2
Hereford Cl TW18 .124 A4
Herewood Cl RG14 .104 C2
Heriot Rd KT16 .124 A1
Heritage Ct 2
Egham TW20 .96 A2
27 Reading RG1 .85 C4
Hermitage Cl
Frimley GU16 .151 C1
Littleton TW17 .125 A3
Slough SL3 .43 B2
Hermitage Ct TW18 .96 C2
Hermitage Cty Prim Sch
RG18 .79 A4
Hermitage Dr
North Ascot SL5 .119 C4
Twyford RG10 .61 B3
Hermitage La SL4 .67 A2
Hermitage Par SL5 .120 A3
Hermitage Rd RG18 .79 A1
Hermitage The
Feltham TW13 .98 C3
Lambourn RG17 .46 C4
Hermits Cl RG7 .111 A2
Hermits Hill RG7, RG30 .111 B2
Herndon Cl TW20 .96 A2
Heroes Wlk RG2 .113 A4
Heron Cl SL5 .119 B4
Heron Ct Staines TW18 .97 A2
Stanwell TW19 .97 C4
Heron Dr Slough SL3 .44 A1
Twyford RG10 .61 C3
Heron Ho RG14 .105 B2
Heron Island RG4 .59 B1
Heron Rd RG41 .115 C3
Heron Shaw RG8 .34 B4
Heron Way
Burghfield Common RG1 .85 C2
Padworth RG7 .109 A2
Thatcham RG19 .106 A2
Heron's Way RG40 .116 C4
Herondale RG12 .118 B1
Heronfield TW20 .95 B1
Herongate RG17 .100 B4
Herons Pl SL7 .1 C2
Heronscourt GU18 .153 B4
Herrick Cl GU16 .152 B2
Herrings La GU20 .146 B2
Herriot Ct GU46 .149 B2
Herschel Gram Sch SL1 .42 B4
Herschel Grange RG42 .91 B2
Herschel Park Dr SL1 .42 C2
Herschel St SL1 .42 C2
Hertford Cl Caversham RG4 .59 B3
Wokingham RG41 .115 C3
Hetherington Cl SL2 .21 C1
Hetherington Rd TW17 .125 B4
Hever Cl SL6 .39 B3
Hewett Ave RG4 .58 B2
Hewett Cl RG4 .58 B2
Hewgate Ct RG9 .15 C1
Hewlett Pl GU19 .145 C2
Hexham Cl GU47 .143 B1
Hexham Rd RG2 .86 B2
Heynes Gn SL6 .39 A2
Heywod Dr GU19 .145 B2
Heywood Ave SL6 .39 A1
Heywood Court Cl SL6 .39 A1
Heywood Gdns SL6 .39 A1
Hibbert Rd SL6 .40 A2
Hibbert's Alley 25 SL4 .67 B3
Hickox Ct HP10 .3 C4
Hicks La GU17 .150 A3
Higgs La GU19 .145 B2
High Beech RG12 .118 C3
High Beeches GU16 .151 B1
High Close Sch RG40 .116 B4
High Fields SL5 .120 C2
High Heavens Wood SL7 .1 B4
High Mdw RG4 .58 B2
High Meadow Pl KT16 .123 C2
High Rd SL6 .19 C3
High St Ascot SL5 .120 A3
Ascot, Sunninghill SL5 .120 B2
Bagshot GU19 .145 C2
Boxford RG20 .76 A1
Bracknell RG12 .118 A4
Burnham SL1 .21 B1
Camberley GU15 .151 B3
Chieveley RG20 .51 A1
High St *continued*
Colnbrook SL3 .69 B4
Compton RG20 .31 B2
Cookham SL6 .20 A4
Crowthorne RG45 .143 B2
Datchet SL3 .68 A3
East Isley RG20 .30 C4
4 Egham TW20 .95 C2
Eton SL4 .67 B4
Feltham TW13 .98 C3
Goring RG8 .34 B3
Harlington UB3 .71 B4
Harmondsworth UB7 .70 B4
Hungerford RG17 .100 B3
Iver SL0 .44 C4
Kintbury RG17 .102 A1
Lambourn RG17 .25 A1
Lambourn, Upper
Lambourn RG17 .24 C3
Maidenhead SL6 .40 B2
Marlow SL7 .1 C1
Pangbourne RG8 .56 B3
Reading RG1 .86 A4
Sandhurst GU47 .149 C4
Sandhurst,
Little Sandhurst GU47 .143 A1
Shepperton TW17 .125 B2
Slough, Langley SL3 .44 A1
Slough, Upton SL1 .42 C2
Sonning RG4 .60 B2
Staines TW18 .96 C2
Stanwell TW19 .70 B1
Streatley RG8 .34 A3
Sunningdale SL5 .121 A2
Taplow SL6 .20 C1
Thatcham RG19 .106 B2
Theale RG7 .83 C2
Twyford RG10 .61 B2
Wargrave RG10 .36 B1
West End GU24 .153 C4
Whitchurch-on-T RG8 .56 B4
Windsor SL4 .67 B3
Wraysbury TW19 .68 C1
High St Mall 1 SL6 .39 C4
High Street Harlington
UB3 .71 B4
High Town Rd SL6 .39 C4
High Tree Dr RG6 .87 A3
High View Cl SL7 .1 B4
High View Rd GU18 .152 C4
Highbeeches Cl SL7 .1 B4
Highbridge Cl RG4 .59 C3
Highbridge Wharf 18 RG1 .86 A4
Highbury Cres GU15 .152 A4
Highbury Rd RG31 .84 A4
Highclere SL5 .120 B2
Highclere Cl RG12 .118 C4
Highclere Dr GU15 .152 A4
Highcliffe Cl RG5 .60 C1
Highdown Ave RG4 .59 A3
Highdown Hill Rd RG4 .59 A3
Highdown Sixth Form
Comp Sch RG4 .59 A3
Higher Alham RG12 .118 C1
Highfield Bracknell RG12 .117 C2
Earley RG6 .87 A1
Highfield Ave RG14 .105 A1
Highfield Cl
Englefield Green TW20 .95 B1
Wokingham RG40 .116 A3
Highfield Ct
Burghfield Common RG7 .111 A2
Burnham SL2 .22 A2
Englefield Green TW20 .95 B1
Highfield La SL6 .39 A2
Highfield Pk Marlow SL7 .1 A1
Wargrave RG10 .36 C2
Highfield Rd Bourne End SL8 .3 A2
Chertsey KT16 .124 A1
Englefield Green TW20 .95 B1
Flackwell Heath HP10 .3 A4
Maidenhead SL6 .39 A4
Newbury RG14 .104 C1
Purley on T RG31 .57 B2
Upper Halliford TW16 .125 C2
Windsor SL4 .66 C2
Highgate Rd RG5 .87 B3
Highgrove Pk SL6 .39 C4
Highgrove Pl RG10 .61 C3
Highgrove St RG1 .86 B3
Highgrove Terr RG1 .86 A3
Highland Pk TW13 .98 C2
Highland Rd GU15 .151 C4
Highlands HP10 .3 A4
Highlands Ave RG41 .115 B3
Highlands La RG9 .35 A4
Highlands Sch The RG31 .57 B1
Highlands The SL2 .22 B4
Highlea Ave HP10 .3 A4
Highmead Cl RG2 .86 C1
Highmoor Rd RG4 .58 C2
Highview GU21 .84 A3
Highview Cres GU15 .144 C1
Highway RG45 .143 A3
Highway Ave SL6 .39 A3
Highway Rd SL6 .39 A3
Highwayman's Ridge
GU20 .146 A3
Highwood Cl
Newbury RG14 .105 A3
Yateley GU46 .149 B2
Highwoods Cl SL7 .1 B4
Highwoods Dr SL7 .1 B4
Highworth Cotts RG26 .134 B1
Highworth Way RG31 .57 A1

Hilary Cl RG2 . . . . .113 B4
Hilary Dr RG45 . . . . .143 A3
Hilary Ho 🔟 RG14 . . . . . .105 A1
Hilborne Way RG2 . . . . . .115 A1
Hilbury Rd RG6 . . . . .87 A2
Hilcot Rd RG30 . . . . .85 B4
Hildens Dr RG31 . . . . .84 B4
Hill Cl Newbury RG14 . . . .130 B4
  Wooburn Green HP10 . . . . .3 C4
Hill Copse View RG12 . . . .118 C4
Hill Cres RG12 . . . . .108 B2
Hill Farm App HP10 . . . . . . .3 C4
Hill Farm Rd
  Marlow Bottom SL7 . . . . . . .1 C3
  Taplow SL6 . . . . .20 C1
Hill Gdns RG8 . . . . .34 A3
Hill Lands RG10 . . . . .36 B1
Hill Piece OX11 . . . . .10 C4
Hill Pl SL2 . . . . .22 A3
Hill Prim Sch The SL4 . . . .59 B3
Hill Rd Arborfield RG2 . . . .114 C1
  Newbury RG14 . . . . .104 C2
Hill Side RG1 . . . . .86 B3
Hill St RG1 . . . . .86 A3
Hill Top Dr SL1 . . . . .1 A1
Hill View Rd TW19 . . . . . . .68 B1
Hillary Ct TW19 . . . . .97 C4
Hillary Rd SL3 . . . . .43 C2
Hillberry RG12 . . . . .118 B1
Hillbrow RG2 . . . . .86 C1
Hillcrest
  Hampstead Norreys RG18 . .52 C3
  Tadley RG26 . . . . .135 A1
Hillcrest Ave SL6 . . . . .19 C3
Hillcrest Rd GU15 . . . . . . .152 A4
Hilldrop La RG17 . . . . .46 A2
Hillersdon SL2 . . . . .43 A4
Hillfield GU46 . . . . .149 C3
Hillgreen La RG20 . . . . . . .50 B4
Hillhouse La RG19 . . . . . .133 A1
Hillingdon Ave TW19 . . . . .97 C4
Hillmead Ct SL6 . . . . .40 C4
Hillrise Hampstead Hill SL3 . .69 A4
  Walton-on-T KT12 . . . . . .125 C1
Hills La SL6 . . . . .19 B4
Hillsborough Pk GU15 . . . .152 B3
Hillside Ascot SL5 . . . . . . .120 B2
  Burghfield Common RG7 . .111 B4
  East Garston RG17 . . . . . .47 B3
  Maidenhead SL6 . . . . .39 B3
  Sandhurst GU15 . . . . . . .150 C4
  Slough SL1 . . . . .42 C2
  Wentworth GU25 . . . . . . .122 B2
  Whitchurch-on-T RG8 . . . .56 B4
Hillside Dr RG42 . . . . .90 B1
Hillside Pk Earley RG2 . . . .86 C1
  Sunningdale SL5 . . . . . . .120 C1
Hillside Rd Earley RG6 . . . .87 B2
  Hungerford RG17 . . . . . .100 B2
  Marlow SL7 . . . . .1 C2
Hilltop Cl SL5 . . . . .120 C4
Hilltop Fst Sch SL4 . . . . . . .66 C2
Hilltop Rd Caversham RG4 . .58 B3
  Earley RG6 . . . . .87 A4
  Twyford RG10 . . . . .61 C4
Hilltop View GU46 . . . . . . .149 A3
Hilmanton RG6 . . . . .113 C4
Hilperton Rd 🔳 SL1 . . . . . .42 C2
Hindhead Rd RG6 . . . . .87 A2
Hinksey Cl SL3 . . . . .44 A2
Hinton Cl RG45 . . . . .143 A4
Hinton Dr RG45 . . . . .143 A4
Hinton Pk RG10 . . . . .61 C1
Hinton Rd Hurst RG10 . . . . .62 A1
  Slough SL1 . . . . .41 C2
Hintonhatch Cnr RG10 . . . .62 A1
Hirstwood RG30 . . . . .57 C1
Hirtes Ave RG2 . . . . .113 C3
Hitcham Ho SL1 . . . . .21 A1
Hitcham La Burnham SL1 . . .21 A1
  Taplow SL1,SL6 . . . . .20 C1
Hitcham Rd SL1,SL6 . . . . . .41 A4
Hitchcock Cl TW17 . . . . . .124 C3
Hitherhooks Hill RG42 . . . .90 C1
Hithermoor Rd TW19 . . . . .70 A1
Hobart Ct SL7 . . . . .2 A2
Hobbis Dr SL6 . . . . .39 A3
Hockett La SL6 . . . . .19 A3
Hockford La RG7 . . . . .134 A2
Hockham Rd RG20 . . . . . . .31 C3
Hockley La SL2 . . . . .23 A3
Hodge La SL5 . . . . .93 A2
Hodgedale La RG10 . . . . . .37 B3
Hodges Cl GU19 . . . . .145 C1
Hodsoll Rd RG1 . . . . .85 C4
Hoe Benham La RG20 . . . .102 C4
Hogarth Ave Ashford TW15 . .98 B1
  Reading RG30 . . . . .84 C3
Hogarth Cl
  Sandhurst GU47 . . . . . . .150 C3
  Slough SL1 . . . . .41 C2
Hogfair La SL1 . . . . .21 B1
Hogmoor La RG10 . . . . . . .61 C1
Hogoak La SL4 . . . . .92 A4
Hogwood La RG40 . . . . . . .141 A4
Hoibeche Cl GU46 . . . . . . .149 A3
Holbeck RG12 . . . . .117 C2
Holberton Rd RG2 . . . . . . .113 B4
Holborn Hill OX12 . . . . .6 B4
Holborne La RG14 . . . . . . .130 B3
Holbrook Ct TW20 . . . . . . .96 B2
Holbrook Mdw TW20 . . . . .96 B1
Holford Cl RG31 . . . . .84 B4

Holkam Cl RG30 . . . . .84 C4
Holkham Rd RG30 . . . . . . .57 C1
Holland Ct TW15 . . . . .97 C1
Holland Gdns TW20 . . . . .123 C4
Holland Pines RG12 . . . . .117 C1
Holland Rd Marlow SL7 . . . .1 C2
  Reading RG30 . . . . .84 B4
Hollands The RG19 . . . . . .106 C2
Hollicombe Cl RG30 . . . . . .84 C4
Hollies The RG14 . . . . .130 B3
Hollington Pl RG19 . . . . . .106 B2
Hollins Wlk RG30 . . . . .85 B3
Hollow Hill La SL0 . . . . . . .44 B3
Hollow La Shinfield RG2 . . .113 C3
  Virginia Water GU25 . . . . .122 B3
Holloway Dr GU25 . . . . . . .122 C3
Holloway La UB7 . . . . .70 C4
Holly Ave GU16 . . . . .152 A2
Holly Cl
  Englefield Green TW20 . . . .95 A1
  Farnham Common SL2 . . . .22 B4
  Yateley GU46 . . . . .149 A3
Holly Cres SL4 . . . . .66 B3
Holly Ct 🖪 KT16 . . . . .124 A1
Holly Dr Maidenhead SL6 . . .39 C4
  Windsor SL4 . . . . .67 C1
Holly Hedge Cl SL4 . . . . . .151 C1
Holly Hedge Rd GU16 . . . .151 C1
Holly La RG12 . . . . .118 A2
Holly Orch RG41 . . . . .115 C3
Holly Rd RG5 . . . . .88 A3
Holly Ridge GU24 . . . . . . .153 C3
Holly Spring Cty Inf Sch
  RG12 . . . . .118 C4
Holly Spring Cty Jun Sch
  RG12 . . . . .118 C4
Holly Spring La RG12 . . . . .118 B4
Holly Way GU17 . . . . .150 B2
Holly Wlk SL4 . . . . .93 C2
Hollybank RG12 . . . . .118 A2
Hollybush Hill SL2 . . . . . . .23 A3
Hollybush La Cookham SL6 . .19 A3
  Iver SL0 . . . . .44 A4
  Sulhamstead RG7 . . . . . . .110 C2
Hollybush Ride
  Windlesham GU19,GU20 . . .145 C3
  Windlesham RG40,RG45 . . .142 B3
Hollycombe TW20 . . . . . . .95 B2
Hollycroft Cl UB7 . . . . .71 A4
Hollycroft Gdns UB7 . . . . . .71 A4
Hollydale Cl RG12 . . . . .86 C1
Hollyfields Cl GU15 . . . . . .151 A3
Hollym Cl RG6 . . . . .87 C1
Holmanleaze SL6 . . . . .40 A4
Holmbank Dr TW17 . . . . . .125 C3
Holmbury Ave RG45 . . . . .143 A4
Holmdale SL2 . . . . .43 B3
Holmdene RG7 . . . . .111 A2
Holme RG45 . . . . .143 A4
Holme Park Farm La RG4 . .60 B1
Holmemoor Dr RG4 . . . . . . .60 C1
Holmes Cl Ascot SL5 . . . . .120 B2
  Wokingham RG41 . . . . . . .116 A2
Holmes Cres RG41 . . . . . .116 A2
Holmes Rd RG6 . . . . .87 A3
Holmewood Rd RG41 . . . . .116 A1
Holmlea Rd Datchet SL3 . . .68 B3
  Goring RG8 . . . . .34 B3
Holmlea Wlk SL3 . . . . .68 B3
Holmsdale Cl SL0 . . . . .44 A4
Holmwood Ave RG30 . . . . .84 C2
Holmwood Cl SL6 . . . . .39 A3
Holsworthy Cl RG6 . . . . . . .87 C2
Holt Comp Sch RG41 . . . . .116 A4
Holt La Brightwalton RG20 . .49 C4
  Wokingham RG41 . . . . . . .116 A4
Holt Rd RG17 . . . . .102 A1
Holt The RG8 . . . . .57 B2
Holton Heath 🔟 RG12 . . . .118 C3
Holtspur Ave HP10 . . . . .3 C4
Holtspur La HP10 . . . . .3 C3
Holtwood Rd RG20 . . . . . .129 A3
Holy Family RC Sch SL3 . . .43 C1
Holy Trinity CE Mid Sch
  SL7 . . . . .1 B2
Holy Trinity CE Sch SL5 . . .121 A2
Holy Trinity Prim Sch
  SL6 . . . . .20 A4
Holybrook Cres RG30 . . . . .85 A2
Holybrook Rd RG1 . . . . . . .85 C3
Holyhook Cl RG45 . . . . . . .143 A3
Holyport CE Prim Sch
  SL6 . . . . .65 A4
Holyport Manor Sch SL6 . . .64 C3
Holyport Rd SL6 . . . . .40 A1
Holyport St SL6 . . . . .65 A4
Holyrood Cl RG4 . . . . .59 B3
Holywell Cl TW19 . . . . .97 C4
Holywell Ct RG19 . . . . . . .106 B2
Holywell Way TW19 . . . . . .97 C4
Hombrook Dr RG42 . . . . . .117 C4
Hombrook Ho RG42 . . . . . .117 C4
Home Croft RG31 . . . . .57 A1
Home Farm Cl
  Reading RG2 . . . . .86 B2
  Upper Halliford TW17 . . . .125 C3
Home Farm La RG7 . . . . . .134 B3
Home Farm Way SL3 . . . . . .23 B2
Home Mdw SL2 . . . . .22 B2
Home Mead Cl RG14 . . . . .130 C4
Home Meadow Dr HP10 . . . .3 A4
Home Park Rd GU46 . . . . .149 B3
Home Wood SL7 . . . . .17 C3
Homefield Way RG17 . . . . .100 B3
Homelands Way RG9 . . . . . .15 B1
Homer Fst Sch SL4 . . . . . . .66 B3
Homers Rd SL4 . . . . .66 B3
Homeside Cl SL6 . . . . .19 C1

Homestead Rd
  Maidenhead SL6 . . . . .39 B2
  Staines TW18 . . . . .97 A1
Homewaters Ave TW16 . . .125 C4
Homewood SL3 . . . . .43 B4
Hone Hill GU47 . . . . .150 A4
Honesty Bottom RG20 . . . .28 B1
Honey End La RG30 . . . . . .85 A3
Honey Hill
  Lambourn RG17 . . . . .25 A2
  Wokingham RG40 . . . . . . .117 A1
Honey La SL6 . . . . .17 C1
Honey Meadow Cl RG4 . . . .59 C1
Honeybottom Rd RG26 . . . .135 A1
Honeyfields RG17 . . . . . . .100 B3
Honeyhill Rd RG42 . . . . . . .118 A4
Honeysuckle Cl
  Crowthorne RG45 . . . . . . .143 A4
  Iver SL0 . . . . .44 B4
  Yateley GU46 . . . . .149 A3
Honister Wlk GU15 . . . . . . .152 B2
Honiton Rd RG2 . . . . .86 B1
Honnor Rd TW18 . . . . .97 B1
Hook End La RG8 . . . . .34 C1
Hook La SL6 . . . . .20 B1
Hook Mill La SL18 . . . . . . .146 B1
Hookstone La GU24 . . . . . .153 C4
Hoops Way RG2 . . . . .112 C4
Hop Gdns RG9 . . . . .15 B1
Hope Ave RG12 . . . . .118 C1
Hope Fountain GU15 . . . . .152 A2
Hopeman Cl GU47 . . . . . . .150 B4
Hopwood Cl RG14 . . . . . . .105 B2
Horatio Ave RG42 . . . . .118 C4
Horewood Rd RG12 . . . . . .118 A2
Horizon West Ind Est
  RG14 . . . . .105 B2
Hormer Cl GU47 . . . . .143 B1
Horn St RG20 . . . . .31 C3
Hornbeam Cl
  Purley on T RG8 . . . . .57 B3
  Sandhurst GU47 . . . . . . .143 B1
  Wokingham RG41 . . . . . . .115 B2
Hornbeam Dr RG6 . . . . .87 B1
Hornbeam Gdns 🖪 SL1 . . . .43 A2
Hornbeam Pightle RG7 . . . .111 A2
Hornbeams RG7 . . . . .139 B3
Hornby Ave RG12 . . . . .118 B1
Horncastle Dr RG30 . . . . . . .84 C3
Horndean Rd RG12 . . . . . .118 C2
Horne Rd Littleton TW17 . . .125 A3
  Thatcham RG19 . . . . .106 C1
Hornsea Cl RG30 . . . . .57 C1
Horris Hill Sch RG20 . . . . .130 C2
Horse Cl The RG4 . . . . .59 B2
Horse Gate Ride SL5 . . . . .120 A2
Horsebrass Dr GU19 . . . . .145 C1
Horseguards Dr SL6 . . . . . .40 A4
Horsell Ct KT16 . . . . .124 A1
Horsemoor Cl SL3 . . . . .44 A1
Horseshoe Cl GU15 . . . . . .151 C4
Horseshoe Cloisters 🔢
  SL4 . . . . .67 B3
Horseshoe Cres
  Burghfield Common RG7 . . .111 A2
  Camberley GU15 . . . . . . .151 C4
Horseshoe End RG14 . . . . .131 A4
Horseshoe Hill SL1 . . . . . . .21 B4
Horseshoe Pk RG8 . . . . . . .56 C3
Horseshoe Rd RG8 . . . . . . .56 B3
Horsham Rd
  East Bedfont TW14 . . . . . .71 B1
  Sandhurst GU47 . . . . . . .143 B1
Horsnape Gdns RG42 . . . . .90 A1
Horsneile La RG42 . . . . . . .118 A4
Horton Cl SL6 . . . . .20 B1
Horton Gdns SL3 . . . . .68 C2
Horton Grange SL6 . . . . . . .20 B1
Horton Rd Datchet SL3 . . . .68 B3
  Horton SL3 . . . . .69 A3
  Poyle SL3, TW19 . . . . .69 C2
  Stanwell TW19 . . . . .70 A1
Horton Trad Est SL3 . . . . . .69 A2
Hose Hill RG7,RG30 . . . . . .111 A4
Hosier St RG1 . . . . .86 A4
Hoskins Place Ind Est
  GU15 . . . . .151 A2
Houlton Ct GU19 . . . . .145 C1
Houston Ct 🖪🖪 SL4 . . . . . . .67 B4
Houston Way RG45 . . . . . .142 B3
Howard Ave SL2 . . . . .42 C4
Howard Cl TW16 . . . . .98 C1
Howard Ct SL8 . . . . .3 C1
Howard Rd
  Newbury RG14 . . . . .105 A1
  Wokingham RG40 . . . . . . .116 B1
Howard St RG1 . . . . .85 C4
Howarth Rd SL6 . . . . .40 A3
Howe La RG42 . . . . .63 C1
Howell Cl RG42 . . . . .91 B1
Howgate Dr RG8 . . . . .34 B4
Howorth Ct 🔟 RG12 . . . . . .118 C3
Howth Dr RG5 . . . . .87 B4
Hoylake Cl SL1 . . . . .41 C2
Hrmondsworth Moor
  Ctry Pk UB7 . . . . .70 A4
Hubbard Cl RG10 . . . . .61 C1
Hubberholme RG12 . . . . . .118 A3
Hubert Rd SL3 . . . . .43 B2
Huckleberry Cl RG8 . . . . . . .57 B2
Huddington Glade GU46 . . .149 A3
Hudson Rd Harlington UB3 . .71 B4
  Woodley RG5 . . . . .87 C3
Hugh Faringdon RC Sch
  (Specl Resource Aspergers
  Syndrome) RG30 . . . . .85 B3
Hugh Fraser Dr RG31 . . . . .84 B3
Hughenden Rd SL1 . . . . . . .42 B4

Hughenden Cl SL6 . . . . . . .39 B3
Hughes Rd Ashford TW15 . . .98 B1
  Wokingham RG40 . . . . . . .116 C4
Hull Cl SL1 . . . . .42 B2
Humber Cl
  Thatcham RG18 . . . . .106 A3
  Wokingham RG41 . . . . . . .115 C4
Humber Way
  Sandhurst GU47 . . . . . . .150 B4
  Slough SL3 . . . . .44 A1
Hummer Rd TW20 . . . . . . .96 A2
Humphreys La RG17 . . . . . .47 B3
Humphries Yd RG12 . . . . . .118 B3
Hungerford Ave SL2 . . . . . .42 C4
Hungerford Cl GU47 . . . . . .150 B4
Hungerford Dr
  Maidenhead SL6 . . . . .19 C2
  Reading RG1 . . . . .85 C3
Hungerford Hill
  East Garston RG17 . . . . . .47 C1
  Lambourn RG17 . . . . .25 A1
Hungerford La
  Bradfield RG7 . . . . .81 C1
  Waltham St Lawrence RG10 . .62 C1
Hungerford Newtown
  RG17 . . . . .74 A2
Hungerford Prim Sch
  RG17 . . . . .100 B3
Hungerford Rd RG17 . . . . .101 C2
Hungerford Sta RG17 . . . . .100 C3
Hunstanton Cl SW3 . . . . . . .69 B4
Hunt's La SL6 . . . . .20 C2
Hunter Ct SL1 . . . . .41 B4
Hunter's Ct RG5 . . . . .87 C3
Huntercombe Cl SL6 . . . . . .41 B4
Huntercombe La N SL6 . . . .41 B4
Huntercombe La S SL6 . . . .41 B3
Hunters Chase RG4 . . . . . . .58 C3
Hunters Hill RG7 . . . . .110 C2
Hunters Mdw RG17 . . . . . . .48 A2
Hunters Mews SL4 . . . . . . .67 B3
Hunters Way
  Shinfield RG7 . . . . .113 A1
  Slough SL1 . . . . .41 C2
Huntingdonshire Cl
  RG41 . . . . .115 B3
Huntingfield Way TW20 . . . .96 B1
Huntington Cl RG6 . . . . .87 C1
Huntley Cl RG1 . . . . .86 C3
Huntsgreen Ct RG12 . . . . .118 B4
Huntsmans Mdw SL5 . . . . .119 C4
Huntsmoor Rd RG26 . . . . .135 A1
Huntswood La SL1,SL6 . . . . .20 C2
Hurford Dr RG19 . . . . .106 C2
Hurley Ct RG12 . . . . .118 C1
Hurley High St SL6 . . . . . . .17 C2
Hurley La SL6 . . . . .18 A2
Hurricane Way Slough SL3 . .44 B1
  Woodley RG5 . . . . .88 A4
Hursley Cl RG30 . . . . .84 C4
Hurst Com Sch The
  RG26 . . . . .134 B1
Hurst Gr KT12 . . . . .125 C1
Hurst La TW20 . . . . .123 A3
Hurst Lodge Sch SL5 . . . . .120 C1
Hurst Park Rd RG10 . . . . . . .61 C1
Hurst Rd Slough SL1 . . . . . .41 B4
  Twyford RG10 . . . . .61 C2
Hurst Way RG2 . . . . .112 C4
Hurstdene Ave TW18 . . . . . .97 A1
Hurstfield Dr SL6 . . . . .41 A4
Hurstwood SL5 . . . . .120 A2
Huscarle Way RG31 . . . . . . .57 B2
Huson Rd RG42 . . . . .91 B1
Hutsons Cl RG40 . . . . .116 B4
Hutton Cl Earley RG6 . . . . . .87 A1
  Newbury RG14 . . . . .105 A2
  Windlesham GU20 . . . . . .146 B2
Hyde Cl TW15 . . . . .98 C1
Hyde End La
  Brimpton RG7 . . . . .133 B3
  Shinfield RG7 . . . . .113 B2
Hyde End Rd RG7 . . . . .113 B1
Hyde Gn SL7 . . . . .1 C1
Hyde La RG20 . . . . .132 A1
Hyde Terr TW15 . . . . .98 C1
Hydes The RG31 . . . . .57 B2
Hyland Ho 🔟 SL8 . . . . .3 A2
Hylle Cl SL4 . . . . .66 C3
Hyperion Way RG2 . . . . . . .86 A2
Hythe Cl RG12 . . . . .118 C2
Hythe Cty Prim Sch TW18 . .96 B2
Hythe End Rd TW19 . . . . . .96 A3
Hythe Field Ave TW20 . . . . .96 B1
Hythe Park Rd TW20 . . . . . .96 B1
Hythe Rd TW18 . . . . .96 B2
Hythe The TW18 . . . . .96 C1

Ian Mikardo Way RG4 . . . . .59 B1
Iberian Way GU15 . . . . . . .152 A2
Ibotson Ct SL3 . . . . .69 C3
Ibstock Ct RG30 . . . . .85 A4
Ibstone Ave RG4 . . . . .59 C3
Icarus Ct 🔢 RG1 . . . . .86 B4
Icknield Pl RG8 . . . . .34 B4
Icknield Rd RG8 . . . . .34 B4
Iden Ct RG14 . . . . .105 A2
Iffley Ct TW18 . . . . .96 C2
Ilbury Ct RG30 . . . . .113 C3
Ilchester Cl SL6 . . . . .39 B3
Ilchester Ct 🖪 RG14 . . . . . .105 A1
Ilchester Mews RG4 . . . . . .59 C3
Ilex Cl
  Englefield Green TW20 . . . .95 A1
  Silchester RG26 . . . . .135 C1

Ilex Cl continued
  Yateley GU46 . . . . .149 A3
Ilfracombe Way RG6 . . . . . .87 C2
Ilkley Rd RG4 . . . . .58 C2
Ilkley Way RG19 . . . . .106 B1
Illingworth SL4 . . . . .66 C2
Illingworth Ave RG4 . . . . . .59 C3
Illingworth Gr RG12 . . . . . .118 C4
Ilsley Prim Sch The RG20 . .30 C3
Ilsley Rd RG20 . . . . .31 B2
Imperial Ct
  Henley-on-T RG9 . . . . .15 C1
  Windsor SL4 . . . . .67 A2
Imperial Ho GU25 . . . . . . .122 C2
Imperial Rd
  East Bedfont TW14 . . . . . .98 C4
  Windsor SL4 . . . . .67 A3
Imperial Way RG2 . . . . . . .113 A4
Impstone Rd RG26 . . . . . . .135 C1
In The Ray SL6 . . . . .40 A4
Inchwood RG12 . . . . .118 B1
India Rd SL1 . . . . .43 A2
Ingle Dell GU15 . . . . .151 B2
Ingle Glen RG40 . . . . .142 A4
Ingleglen SL2 . . . . .22 A4
Ingleside SL3 . . . . .69 C3
Ingleton RG12 . . . . .118 A3
Inglewood Ave GU15 . . . . .152 B3
Inglewood Ct RG30 . . . . . . .85 B3
Inglewood Rd RG17 . . . . . .101 C1
Inhurst La RG26 . . . . .134 B1
Inhurst Way RG26 . . . . . . .134 C1
Inkerman Rd SL4 . . . . .41 C1
Inkpen Cl RG30 . . . . .85 A2
Inkpen Prim Sch RG17 . . . .127 B3
Inkpen Rd
  Hungerford RG17 . . . . . . .100 C2
  Inkpen RG17 . . . . .127 A4
  Kintbury RG17 . . . . .102 A1
Inner Ring E TW6 . . . . .71 A2
Inner Ring W TW6 . . . . .71 A2
Innings La
  White Waltham SL6 . . . . . . .63 B4
  Winkfield RG12 . . . . .118 C4
Inniscrown Ho SL3 . . . . . . .68 A4
Institute Rd Marlow SL7 . . . .1 C1
  Taplow SL6 . . . . .40 C4
Instow Rd RG6 . . . . .87 A1
Invergordon Cl RG31 . . . . . .84 C2
Inverness Way GU47 . . . . . .150 B4
Invicta Cl TW14 . . . . .98 C4
Inwood Cl SL6 . . . . .19 A3
Iona Cres SL1 . . . . .41 C4
Ipswich Rd SL1 . . . . .42 A4
Irish Hill Rd RG17 . . . . . . .102 A1
Irvine Ho SL4 . . . . .66 C3
Irvine Pl GU25 . . . . .122 C2
Irvine Way RG6 . . . . .114 B4
Isaac Newton Rd RG2 . . . .115 A1
Isis Cl RG41 . . . . .88 A1
Isis Ct RG1 . . . . .59 A1
Isis Way Bourne End SL8 . . . .3 A2
  Sandhurst GU47 . . . . . . .150 B4
Island Cl TW18 . . . . .96 C2
Island Farm Rd RG7 . . . . . .110 B1
Island Rd RG2 . . . . .85 C1
Islandstone La RG10 . . . . . .89 A3
Islet Park Dr SL6 . . . . .20 B2
Islet Park Ho SL6 . . . . .20 B2
Islet Pk SL6 . . . . .20 B2
Islet Rd SL6 . . . . .20 B2
Isobel Ho 🔢 TW16 . . . . .98 C1
Ivanhoe Rd RG40 . . . . .141 A3
Iveagh Ct RG12 . . . . .118 B2
Iver Cty Fst Sch SL0 . . . . . .44 C4
Iver Cty Mid Sch SL0 . . . . . .44 C4
Iver Lodge SL0 . . . . .44 C4
Iver Sta SL0 . . . . .44 C2
Iverdale Cl SL0 . . . . .44 B3
Iverna Gdns TW14 . . . . . . .71 B1
Ives Cl GU46 . . . . .149 A4
Ives Rd SL3 . . . . .44 A2
Ivy Cl SL6 . . . . .65 A4
Ivy Cres SL1 . . . . .41 C3
Ivy Dr GU18 . . . . .153 A4
Ivybank RG31 . . . . .57 B1
Ivydene Rd RG30 . . . . .58 B1

Jack Price Ct 🔢 RG1 . . . . . .86 A3
Jack St RG14 . . . . .105 A2
Jackson Cl RG12 . . . . .118 A2
Jackson Ind Est SL8 . . . . . . .3 A1
Jacob Cl Bracknell RG42 . . .117 B4
  Windsor SL4 . . . . .66 C3
Jacob Rd GU15 . . . . .151 A4
Jakes Ho SL6 . . . . .40 A4
James Butcher Dr RG7 . . . .83 C2
James Cl SL7 . . . . .1 C2
James Ct 🔢 RG30 . . . . .85 B3
James Elliman Cty Inf Sch
  SL2 . . . . .42 C4
James Elliman Cty Mid Sch
  SL2 . . . . .42 C4
James Rd GU15 . . . . .151 A1
James St Reading RG1 . . . . .85 C4
  Windsor SL4 . . . . .67 B3
James Watt Rd RG2 . . . . . .140 C4
James Way GU15 . . . . .151 A1
James's La RG7,RG30 . . . . .111 C2
Jameston RG12 . . . . .118 B1
Jamnagar Cl TW18 . . . . . . .96 C1
Janson Ct RG1 . . . . .85 C3
Japonica Cl RG41 . . . . .115 B2
Jaques's La RG7 . . . . .110 C3
Jardine Cotts SL2 . . . . .23 A4

Jarratt Ho SL4 ... 67 A2
Jarry Ct SL7 ... 1 C2
Jarvis Dr RG10 ... 61 B3
Jasmine Cl RG41 ... 115 B4
Jay Cl RG6 ... 87 A1
Jays Nest Cl GU17 ... 150 B2
Jayworth Ho RG1 ... 86 C4
Jedburgh Cl RG19 ... 106 C2
Jefferson Cl
Caversham RG4 ... 59 B4
Slough SL3 ... 44 A1
Jeffries Ct SL8 ... 3 A1
Jellicoe Cl SL1 ... 42 A2
Jenkins Cl RG30 ... 85 B3
Jenkins' Hill London Rd GU19 ... 145 B1
Jenner Wlk RG31 ... 84 A4
Jennery La SL1 ... 21 B1
Jennetts Cl RG7 ... 81 C2
Jennings Field HP10 ... 3 B4
Jennings Wharf SL4 ... 67 B4
Jennys Wlk GU46 ... 149 C3
Jerome Cl SL7 ... 1 C2
Jerome Cnr GU47 ... 143 B2
Jerome Rd RG5 ... 87 C3
Jerrymoor Hill RG40 ... 141 C4
Jesmond Dene RG14 ... 104 C2
Jesse Cl GU46 ... 149 C3
Jesse Terr RG1 ... 85 C4
Jessiman Terr TW17 ... 125 A2
Jevington RG12 ... 118 B1
Jig's La N RG42 ... 91 C1
Jig's La S Bracknell RG42 ... 91 C1
Winkfield RG42 ... 118 C4
Job's La SL6 ... 19 A4
Jock's La Binfield RG42 ... 90 C1
Bracknell RG42 ... 117 C4
Joel Cl RG6 ... 87 A2
Johannes Ct 5 RG30 ... 85 B3
John Balliol Ct 29 RG1 ... 86 B4
John Boys Ho RG14 ... 130 B3
John Childs Cl RG14 ... 105 A1
John Hunt Ct RG19 ... 106 C1
John Kaye Ct TW17 ... 125 A2
John Kimber's Almshouses RG14 ... 104 C2
John Nike Way RG12 ... 117 B4
John Norgate Ho RG18 ... 105 C2
John O'Gaunt Sch RG17 ... 100 B2
John Rankin Cty Inf Sch RG14 ... 130 B4
John Rankin Cty Jun Sch RG14 ... 130 B4
John Taylor Ct SL1 ... 42 B3
Johnson Dr RG40 ... 142 A4
Johnsons La RG18 ... 106 B4
Jonathan Ct SL6 ... 39 C4
Jonathan Hill RG20 ... 131 A2
Jonathan Miller Sch The SL1 ... 41 C4
Jones Cnr SL5 ... 119 C4
Jordan Cl Caversham RG4 ... 59 C3
Shinfield RG7 ... 113 B1
Jordans Cl TW19 ... 97 B4
Jordans La RG7 ... 110 C1
Joseph Ct RG42 ... 91 C1
Josephine Ct RG1 ... 85 C3
Jouldings La RG7 ... 140 B2
Jourdelay's Pas SL4 ... 67 B4
Journeys End SL2 ... 42 C4
Jubilee Ave
North Ascot SL5 ... 119 C4
Wokingham RG41 ... 116 A4
Jubilee Cl
North Ascot SL5 ... 119 C4
Silchester RG26 ... 135 C1
Stanwell TW19 ... 97 B4
Jubilee Ct Bracknell RG12 ... 118 B3
Staines TW18 ... 97 A2
Thatcham RG19 ... 106 A2
Jubilee Rd
Finchampstead RG40 ... 141 C2
Littlewick Green SL6 ... 38 A3
Newbury RG14 ... 105 A1
Reading RG6 ... 87 A3
Jubilee Sq RG1 ... 86 A3
Jubilee Way TW14 ... 98 C4
Judy's Pas SL4 ... 42 B1
Juliet Gdns RG42 ... 118 C4
Julius Hill RG42 ... 118 C4
Julkes La RG2 ... 114 C4
Junction Rd Ashford TW15 ... 98 B2
Lightwater GU18 ... 146 A1
Reading RG1 ... 86 C3
Junction Terr RG14 ... 105 B1
Juniper RG12 ... 118 B1
Juniper Ct SL1 ... 43 A2
Juniper Dr SL6 ... 40 A4
Juniper Gdns TW16 ... 98 C1
Juniper Hill Cty Comb Sch HP10 ... 3 A4
Juniper La HP10 ... 3 B4
Juniper Rd SL7 ... 1 B3
Juniper Way RG31 ... 57 B1
Junnipers The RG41 ... 115 B2
Jupiter Way RG41 ... 115 C3
Justice Cl RG19 ... 106 C1
Jutland Cl RG41 ... 115 C3
Jutland Ho SL4 ... 66 C3
Jutland Pl TW20 ... 96 B2

K

Katesgrove La RG1 ... 86 A3
Katesgrove Prim Sch RG1 ... 86 A3
Kathleen Saunders Ct RG7 ... 83 C2
Kaynes Pk SL5 ... 119 C4
Kaywood Cl SL3 ... 43 B2
Keane Cl RG5 ... 87 C4
Kearsley Rd RG30 ... 85 B3
Keates Gn RG42 ... 118 A4
Keats Cl RG5 ... 87 C2
Keats La SL4 ... 67 B4
Keats Rd RG5 ... 87 C2
Keats Way
Crowthorne RG45 ... 143 A3
Yateley GU46 ... 149 A2
Keble Rd SL6 ... 39 C4
Keble Way GU47 ... 143 C1
Keel Dr SL1 ... 42 B2
Keeler Cl SL4 ... 66 C2
Keep Hatch Inf Sch RG40 ... 116 B4
Keep Hatch Jun Sch RG40 ... 116 B4
Keepers Combe RG12 ... 118 B2
Keepers Farm Cl SL4 ... 66 C3
Keepers Terr GU25 ... 122 A2
Keepers Wlk GU25 ... 122 B2
Keephatch Rd RG40 ... 116 C4
Keighley Cl RG19 ... 106 B1
Kelburne Cl RG41 ... 88 B2
Keldholme RG12 ... 118 A3
Kelly Cl TW17 ... 125 C4
Kelmscott Cl RG4 ... 58 C2
Kelpatrick Rd SL1 ... 41 B4
Kelsey Ave RG40 ... 141 C3
Kelsey Cl SL6 ... 39 B2
Kelsey Gr GU46 ... 149 C3
Kelso Mews RG4 ... 59 C3
Kelton Cl RG6 ... 87 C1
Kelvedon Way RG4 ... 58 C3
Kelvin Cl RG2 ... 140 C4
Kelvin Rd RG14 ... 105 A2
Kemble Ct RG31 ... 84 B2
Kemerton Cl RG31 ... 84 B2
Kemp Ct GU19 ... 145 C1
Kempe Cl SL3 ... 44 B1
Kempton Cl RG14 ... 105 B1
Kemsley Chase SL2 ... 22 B2
Kenavon Dr RG1 ... 86 B4
Kendal Ave Caversham RG4 ... 59 C3
Shinfield RG2 ... 113 C3
Kendal Cl
East Bedfont TW14 ... 98 C4
Slough SL2 ... 43 A3
Thatcham RG18 ... 106 B2
Kendal Dr SL2 ... 43 A3
Kendal Gr GU15 ... 152 B2
Kendrick Cl RG40 ... 116 B3
Kendrick Ct 5 RG1 ... 86 B3
Kendrick Girls' Gram Sch RG1 ... 86 B4
Kendrick Rd
Newbury RG14 ... 130 B3
Reading RG1 ... 86 B3
Slough SL3 ... 43 A2
Kenilworth Ave
Bracknell RG12 ... 118 B4
Reading RG30 ... 85 B3
Kenilworth Ct SL1 ... 42 C2
Kenilworth Gdns TW18 ... 97 B2
Kenilworth Rd TW15, TW19 ... 97 B3
Kenneally SL4 ... 66 B3
Kenneally Cl 11 SL4 ... 66 B3
Kenneally Pl 12 SL4 ... 66 B3
Kenneally Row 13 SL4 ... 66 B3
Kenneally Wlk 10 SL4 ... 66 B3
Kennedy Cl
Farnham Common SL2 ... 22 B3
Maidenhead SL6 ... 39 B3
Marlow SL7 ... 1 C2
Newbury RG14 ... 130 B3
Kennedy Ct TW15 ... 98 B2
Kennedy Dr RG8 ... 56 C3
Kennedy Gdns RG6 ... 87 A2
Kennedy Ho SL1 ... 41 B3
Kennel Ave SL5 ... 119 C4
Kennel Cl SL5 ... 92 C1
Kennel Gn SL5 ... 119 C4
Kennel La Bracknell RG42 ... 91 A1
Cookham SL6 ... 19 B4
Windlesham GU20 ... 146 B3
Kennel Lane Sch RG42 ... 91 A1
Kennel Ride SL5 ... 92 C1
Kennel Wood SL5 ... 119 C4
Kennet & Avon Canal Visitor Ctr RG7 ... 109 B2
Kennet Cl RG19 ... 106 C2
Kennet Ct
Hungerford RG17 ... 100 C4
4 Newbury RG14 ... 105 A1
Wokingham RG41 ... 115 C3
Kennet Ctr The RG14 ... 105 A1
Kennet Pl
Burghfield Common RG7 ... 111 A2
Chilton Foliat RG17 ... 73 A1
10 Newbury RG14 ... 105 A2
Kennet Rd Kintbury RG17 ... 102 A1
Maidenhead SL6 ... 39 C4
Newbury RG14 ... 104 C1
Kennet Sch RG19 ... 106 C2
Kennet Side
Newbury RG14 ... 105 B2
12 Reading RG1 ... 86 B4
Kennet St RG1 ... 86 B4
Kennet Valley Prim Sch RG31 ... 84 C2
Kennet Way RG17 ... 100 C4
Kennett Rd Bourne End SL8 ... 3 A2
Slough SL3 ... 44 A2
Kensington Cl RG6 ... 87 A1
Kensington Rd RG30 ... 85 B4
Kent Ave SL1 ... 42 B4
Kent Cl Staines TW18 ... 97 B1
Wokingham RG41 ... 115 B3
Kent Folly RG42 ... 91 C1
Kent Lodge 6 SL6 ... 39 C3
Kent Rd Reading RG30 ... 85 B4
Windlesham GU20 ... 146 B3
Kent Way SL6 ... 19 C1
Kentigern Dr RG45 ... 143 C3
Kenton Cl Bracknell RG12 ... 118 B4
Frimley GU16 ... 151 C1
Marlow SL7 ... 1 C1
Kenton Rd RG6 ... 87 B2
Kenton's La SL4 ... 66 C3
Kentons La RG10 ... 36 B4
Kentwood Cl RG30 ... 57 C1
Kentwood Hill RG31 ... 57 C1
Kenwood Cl
Harmondsworth UB7 ... 71 A4
Maidenhead SL6 ... 39 A4
Kenworth Gr GU18 ... 146 A1
Keppel Spur SL4 ... 95 A4
Keppel St SL4 ... 67 B3
Kepple Pl GU19 ... 145 C2
Kernham Dr RG31 ... 57 B2
Kerria Way GU24 ... 153 C3
Kerris Way RG6 ... 87 A1
Kersey Cres RG14 ... 104 C3
Kesteven Way RG41 ... 115 C3
Keston Cl RG4 ... 59 B1
Kestrel Ave TW18 ... 96 C3
Kestrel Cl RG19 ... 106 A2
Kestrel Path SL2 ... 21 C1
Kestrel Way
Burghfield Common RG7 ... 111 A2
Reading RG30 ... 85 A2
Wokingham RG41 ... 115 C3
Keswick Ave TW17 ... 125 C3
Keswick Cl Frimley GU15 ... 152 B2
Reading RG30 ... 84 B4
Keswick Ct SL2 ... 42 C3
Keswick Dr GU18 ... 153 A4
Keswick Gdns RG5 ... 87 C3
Keswick Rd TW20 ... 96 A1
Ketcher Gn RG42 ... 90 B2
Kettering Cl RG31 ... 84 C2
Kevins Dr GU46 ... 149 C4
Keynsham Way GU47 ... 143 B1
Keys La SL6 ... 39 C3
Kibble Gn RG12 ... 118 B2
Kibblewhite Cres RG10 ... 61 B3
Kidderminster Rd SL2 ... 22 A1
Kidmore End Rd RG4 ... 59 A4
Kidmore Rd RG4 ... 58 C3
Kidwells Cl SL6 ... 39 C4
Kidwells Park Dr SL6 ... 39 C4
Kielder Wlk GU15 ... 152 B2
Kier Pk SL5 ... 120 B3
Kilburn Cl RG31 ... 84 B2
Kildare Gdns RG4 ... 59 B2
Killarney Dr SL6 ... 39 C4
Killigrew Ho 4 TW16 ... 98 C1
Killross Rd TW14 ... 98 B4
Kilmartin Gdns GU16 ... 151 C1
Kilmington Cl RG12 ... 118 C1
Kilmiston Ave TW17 ... 125 B2
Kilmiston Ho TW17 ... 125 B2
Kilmore Dr GU15 ... 152 A2
Kilmuir Cl GU47 ... 150 B4
Kiln Cl Harlington UB3 ... 71 B4
Hermitage RG18 ... 79 B4
Kiln Croft Cl SL7 ... 2 A2
Kiln Dr RG18 ... 78 C3
Kiln Hill RG7 ... 140 A4
Kiln La Bourne End SL8,HP10 ... 3 B2
Bracknell RG12 ... 118 A4
Mortimer RG7 ... 137 B3
Reading RG31 ... 84 A4
Shiplake RG9 ... 35 B1
Sunningdale SL5 ... 121 A2
Winkfield SL5 ... 93 A1
Kiln Pl SL6 ... 19 A2
Kiln Rd Caversham RG4 ... 59 B4
Newbury RG14 ... 105 B3
Kiln Ride
Upper Basildon RG8 ... 54 C3
Wokingham RG40 ... 142 A4
Kiln Ride Extension RG40 ... 142 A3
Kiln Terr RG18 ... 78 C3
Kiln View Rd RG2 ... 86 B1
Kilnsea Dr RG6 ... 87 B1
Kilowna Cl RG10 ... 61 A2
Kilross Rd TW14 ... 98 C4
Kimber Cl SL4 ... 67 A2
Kimber's Cl RG14 ... 104 C2
Kimber's La SL6 ... 39 C2
Kimberley RG12 ... 118 B1
Kimberley Cl
4 Reading RG1 ... 85 C3
Slough SL3 ... 43 C1
Kimbers Dr Burnham SL1 ... 21 B1
Newbury RG14 ... 104 B3
Kimmeridge RG12 ... 118 C2
Kimpton Cl RG6 ... 113 C4
Kinburn Dr TW20 ... 95 C2
King Acre Ct TW18 ... 96 C3
King Edward Ct 14 SL4 ... 67 B3
King Edward St SL1 ... 42 B2
King Edward VII Ave SL4, SL3 ... 67 C4
King Edward VII Hospl SL4 ... 67 B2
King Edwards Cl SL5 ... 119 C4
King Edwards Rd SL5 ... 119 C4
King Edwards Rise SL5 ... 119 C4
King George Cl TW16 ... 98 C2
King James Way RG9 ... 35 B4
King John's Cl TW19 ... 68 B1
King John's Palace SL3 ... 69 B3
King St Chertsey KT16 ... 124 A1
Maidenhead SL6 ... 39 C3
Mortimer RG7 ... 137 A3
Reading RG1 ... 86 A4
King Stable St SL4 ... 67 B4
King Street La RG41 ... 88 B1
King's Ave TW16 ... 98 C1
King's Cl TW18 ... 97 B1
King's Court Cty Fst Sch SL4 ... 95 A4
King's Gr SL6 ... 39 C3
King's Keep GU47 ... 143 A1
King's Rd Ascot SL5 ... 120 B2
Crowthorne RG45 ... 143 B3
Egham TW20 ... 96 A2
Henley-on-T RG9 ... 15 B1
Slough SL1 ... 42 C2
Windsor SL4 ... 67 B2
Windsor SL4 ... 67 B3
King's Ride Bracknell SL5 ... 119 B3
Camberley GU15 ... 151 B4
King's Road Ho 27 SL4 ... 67 B3
King's Wlk GU15 ... 150 C3
Kingfisher Cl RG7 ... 109 A2
Kingfisher Court Ind Est RG14 ... 105 B2
Kingfisher Ct Slough SL2 ... 22 A1
Twyford RG10 ... 61 C2
Kingfisher Dr
Staines TW18 ... 96 C2
Woodley RG5 ... 87 B3
Yateley GU46 ... 149 A3
Kingfisher Pl RG1 ... 86 A4
Kinghorn La SL6 ... 19 B2
Kinghorn Pk SL6 ... 19 B2
Kings Cl RG9 ... 15 B1
Kings Cres GU15 ... 151 B4
Kings La Cookham SL6 ... 19 A4
Englefield Green TW20 ... 95 A1
Windlesham GU20 ... 146 C3
Kings Mead RG14 ... 130 B3
Kings Meadow Rd RG1 ... 86 A4
Kings Rd Caversham RG4 ... 59 B1
Newbury RG14 ... 105 A1
Reading RG1 ... 86 B4
Silchester RG7 ... 136 A1
West End GU24 ... 153 C3
Kings Rd W RG14 ... 105 A1
Kings Reach Ct 17 RG1 ... 86 A4
Kings Terr SL3 ... 69 A4
Kings Wlk 4
Maidenhead SL6 ... 39 C4
Reading RG1 ... 86 A4
Kings Wood SL7 ... 17 B4
Kingsbridge Cotts RG40 ... 142 C4
Kingsbridge Hill RG7 ... 139 A3
Kingsbridge Rd
Newbury RG14 ... 104 C1
Reading RG2 ... 86 B1
Kingsbury Cres TW18 ... 96 B2
Kingsbury Dr SL4 ... 95 A4
Kingsclear Pk GU15 ... 151 B2
Kingscroft Cty Inf Sch TW18 ... 97 A2
Kingscroft Cty Jun Sch TW18 ... 97 A1
Kingscroft La RG42 ... 92 A3
Kingsdown Cl RG6 ... 87 A1
Kingsfield SL4 ... 66 B3
Kingsford Cl RG5 ... 88 A3
Kingsgate Pl 20 RG1 ... 86 B4
Kingsgate St RG1 ... 86 B4
Kingsland Grange RG14 ... 130 C4
Kingsley Ave
Camberley GU15 ... 151 B2
Englefield Green TW20 ... 95 A1
Kingsley Cl Charvil RG10 ... 61 A3
Crowthorne RG45 ... 143 A2
Newbury RG14 ... 105 A3
Reading RG2 ... 113 A4
Kingsley Dr SL7 ... 1 B3
Kingsley Path SL2 ... 21 B1
Kingsmere Rd RG42 ... 117 C4
Kingston Ave TW14 ... 71 C1
Kingston Cres TW15 ... 97 B1
Kingston Gdns RG2 ... 86 B1
Kingston La RG7 ... 110 B3
Kingston Rd
Ashford TW15, TW17 ... 97 C1
Camberley GU15 ... 145 A1
Staines TW15, TW18 ... 97 A1
Kingsway
Blackwater GU17 ... 150 C3
Caversham RG4 ... 59 C3
Farnham Common SL2 ... 22 B3
Iver SL0 ... 44 C4
Stanwell TW19 ... 97 C4
Thatcham RG19 ... 106 C1
Kingswick Cl SL5 ... 120 B3
Kingswick Dr SL5 ... 120 B3
Kingswood Cl TW20 ... 95 B2
Kingswood Creek TW19 ... 68 B1
Kingswood Ct
Maidenhead SL6 ... 39 C3
17 Reading RG30 ... 85 B3
Kingswood Hall of Residence TW20 ... 95 B2
Kingswood Ho SL1 ... 42 B4
Kingswood Par SL7 ... 1 B3
Kingswood Rise TW20 ... 95 B2
Kinnaird Cl SL1 ... 41 B4
Kinross Ave SL5 ... 119 C2
Kinross Cl TW16 ... 98 C2
Kinross Ct SL5 ... 119 C2
Kinross Dr TW16 ... 98 C2
Kinson Rd RG30 ... 58 A1
Kintbury Rd RG17 ... 127 C3
Kintbury Sq RG17 ... 102 A1
Kintbury Sta RG17 ... 102 A2
Kinver Wlk 30 RG1 ... 86 A3
Kipling Cl Thatcham RG18 ... 106 B3
Woodley RG5 ... 87 C2
Yateley GU46 ... 149 B2
Kipling Ct SL4 ... 67 A3
Kirkby Ct GU16 ... 151 C1
Kirkfell Cl RG31 ... 57 B1
Kirkham Cl Caversham RG4 ... 59 C3
Sandhurst GU47 ... 143 B1
Kirkstall Ct RG31 ... 84 B2
Kirkstone Cl GU15 ... 152 B2
Kirkwall Spur SL1 ... 42 C4
Kirkwood Cres RG7 ... 110 C2
Kirton Cl RG30 ... 85 A4
Kirtons Farm Rd RG2 & RG30 ... 85 B1
Kitsmead La GU25 ... 122 B1
Kittiwake Cl RG5 ... 88 A4
Kitwood Dr RG6 ... 87 C1
Klondyke SL7 ... 1 B1
Knapp Rd TW15 ... 97 C2
Knapp The RG6 ... 87 A2
Knappe Cl RG9 ... 35 B4
Knighton Cl RG4 ... 59 A2
Knights Cl Egham TW20 ... 96 B1
Windsor SL4 ... 66 B3
Knights La RG20 ... 129 B2
Knights Lea RG20 ... 129 A2
Knights Pl 32 SL4 ... 67 B3
Knights Way
Caversham RG4 ... 59 A3
Frimley GU15 ... 152 B2
Knightsbridge Cres TW18 ... 97 A1
Knightsbridge Dr RG19 ... 132 A2
Knightsbridge Rd GU15 ... 151 C4
Knightswood RG12 ... 118 A1
Knole Wood SL5 ... 120 C1
Knoll Cl OX12 ... 6 C4
Knoll Park Rd KT16 ... 123 C1
Knoll Rd GU15 ... 151 B3
Knoll The Chertsey KT16 ... 123 C1
Purley on T RG31 ... 57 A1
Knollmead RG31 ... 84 B2
Knollys Rd RG26 ... 135 C1
Knolton Way SL2 ... 43 B4
Knossington Cl RG6 ... 87 B1
Knott La RG7 ... 109 A2
Knowl Hill CE Prim Sch RG10 ... 37 C2
Knowl Hill Terr RG10 ... 37 C2
Knowle Cl RG4 ... 58 B2
Knowle Gn TW18 ... 97 A2
Knowle Gr GU25 ... 122 B1
Knowle Grove Cl GU25 ... 122 B1
Knowle Hill GU25 ... 122 B1
Knowle Park Ave TW18 ... 97 A2
Knowle Rd RG5 ... 87 C2
Knowles Ave RG45 ... 142 C3
Knowsley Cl SL6 ... 19 A1
Knowsley Rd RG31 ... 57 B2
Knox Gn RG42 ... 90 B2
Kola Ho SL2 ... 43 A3
Korda Cl TW17 ... 124 C3
Krooner Rd GU15 ... 151 A2
Kurnool Mortar Cross Roads GU15 ... 151 A3
Kybes La RG7,RG30 ... 112 B3
Kyftle Court Flat RG14 ... 104 C1
Kyle Cl RG12 ... 118 A3

L

La Roche Cl SL3 ... 43 B2
Laburnham Ct KT16 ... 124 A1
Laburnham Rd
Maidenhead SL6 ... 39 C3
Winnersh RG41 ... 88 B1
Laburnum Cl SL7 ... 1 C2
Laburnum Gdns RG2 ... 86 C1
Laburnum Gr
Brands Hill SL3 ... 69 A4
Newbury RG14 ... 105 A2
Laburnum Pl TW20 ... 95 A1
Laburnum Rd KT16 ... 124 A1
Laburnum Way TW19 ... 97 C4
Laburnums The GU17 ... 150 A3
Lacewood Gdns RG2 ... 86 C1
Lacey Cl TW20 ... 96 B1
Ladbroke Cl RG5 ... 87 C3
Ladbrooke Rd SL1 ... 42 B2
Ladwell Cl RG14 ... 130 B3
Lady Jane Ct RG4 ... 59 B2
Lady Margaret Rd SL5 ... 120 C1
Ladybank RG12 ... 118 A1
Ladyday Pl SL1 ... 42 B3
Ladymask Cl RG31 ... 84 C2
Laffords The RG7 ... 82 A1
Laggan Rd SL6 ... 19 C1
Laggan Sq SL6 ... 19 C1
Laird Ct GU19 ... 145 C1
Lake Ave SL1 ... 42 B3
Lake End Ct SL6 ... 41 A4
Lake End Rd SL4,SL6 ... 41 A3
Lake End Way RG45 ... 143 A2
Lake Rd GU25 ... 122 A3
Lake Side The GU17 ... 150 B2
Lake View SL6 ... 20 A1
Lakeland Dr GU16 ... 151 C1
Lakes The SL7 ... 18 A3
Lakeside
3 Bracknell RG42 ... 118 B4

Lakeside *continued*
Earley RG6 . . . . .87 A2
Maidenhead SL6 . . . . .20 A1
Lakeside Bsns Pk GU47 .150 A4
Lakeside Cty Prim Sch
GU16 . . . . .151 C1
Lakeside Dr SL2 . . . . . . .22 C1
Lakeside Est SL3 . . . . . . .70 A4
Lakeside Rd SL3 . . . . . . .69 C4
Lalande Cl RG41 . . . . . .115 C3
Laleham CE Prim Sch
TW18 . . . . .124 B4
Laleham Rd
Shepperton TW17 . . . . . .125 A2
Staines TW18 . . . . .96 C1
Laleham Reach KT16 . . .124 A3
Laleys Gn RG18 . . . . . . .78 C2
Lamb Cl RG18 . . . . .106 B3
Lambdens Hill RG7 . . . .109 B4
Lambert Ave SL3 . . . . . . .43 C2
Lambert Cres GU17 . . . .150 A2
Lambeth Ct RG30 . . . . . .84 C4
Lambfields RG7 . . . . . . .83 B2
Lambly Hill GU25 . . . . .122 C3
Lamborne Cl GU47 . . . .143 A1
Lambourn Ct RG14 . . . .105 A2
Lambourn Pl RG17 . . . . .25 A2
Lambourn Rd RG20 . . . .104 B3
Lambourne Cl RG31 . . . .84 B3
Lambourne Dr
Bagshot GU19 . . . . .145 B1
Maidenhead SL6 . . . . .39 B2
Lambourne Gdns RG6 . . .87 B2
Lambourne Gr RG12 . . . .118 C4
Lambridge La RG9 . . . . . .15 B2
Lambridge Wood Rd RG9 .15 A2
Lambs La RG7 . . . . .139 A4
Lambs Lane Prim Sch
RG7 . . . . .139 A4
Lambwood Hill RG7 . . . .112 B1
Lamerton Rd RG2 . . . . . .86 B1
Lamesley Ho SL6 . . . . . . .39 C3
Lammas Ave SL4 . . . . . . .67 B3
Lammas Ct Stanwell TW19 .96 B3
Windsor SL4 . . . . .67 B3
Lammas Dr TW18 . . . . . .96 B2
Lammas Mead RG42 . . . .90 C1
Lammas Rd SL1 . . . . .41 B4
Lamorna Cres RG31 . . . . .57 C1
Lamp Acres RG14 . . . . . .105 A3
Lamplighters Wlk RG31 .84 C2
Lamsden Way RG7 . . . . .111 A2
Lanark Cl Frimley GU16 .151 C1
Woodley RG5 . . . . .88 A3
Lancashire Hill RG42 . . . .91 C1
Lancaster Ave SL2 . . . . . .22 B1
Lancaster Cl
Englefield Green TW20 . . . .95 B2
Stanwell TW19 . . . . .70 C1
Thatcham RG18 . . . . .106 A4
Lancaster Ct Reading RG2 .86 C1
Stanwell TW19 . . . . .97 C4
Lancaster Dr GU15 . . . .151 B3
Lancaster Gdns RG6 . . . .87 B2
Lancaster Ho RG12 . . . .118 A2
Lancaster Rd SL6 . . . . . . .39 A4
Lancaster Sq RG17 . . . . .100 C3
Lancastria Mews SL6 . . . .39 B4
Lancelot Cl SL1 . . . . .42 C1
Lanchester Dr RG45 . . . .143 B4
Lancing Cl RG30 . . . . . . .85 B4
Lancing Rd TW13 . . . . . .98 C3
Landen Ct RG40 . . . . . . .116 A2
Landon Way TW15 . . . . .98 A1
Landrake Cres RG2 . . . . .86 B1
Landseer Cl GU47 . . . . . .150 C3
Landsend La RG10 . . . . . .61 C1
Lane End Cl RG2 . . . . . . .113 C3
Lane The Chertsey KT16 . .124 A3
Chilton OX11 . . . . .10 C4
Virginia Water GU25 . . . .122 C3
Laneswood RG7 . . . . . . .136 C3
Langborough Rd RG40 . .116 B3
Langdale Cl SL6 . . . . .40 A3
Langdale Dr SL5 . . . . . . .119 C4
Langdale Gdns RG6 . . . . .86 C1
Langdon Cl GU15 . . . . . .152 B2
Langford Cl RG4 . . . . . . .59 B3
Langham Pl TW20 . . . . . .95 C2
Langhams Way RG10 . . . .36 C1
Langley Broom SL3 . . . . .43 C1
Langley Bsns Ctr SL3 . . . .44 A2
Langley Bsns Pk SL3 . . . .44 A2
Langley Cnr SL3 . . . . . . .23 C2
Langley Common Rd
RG2, RG40 . . . . .114 C1
Langley Cres UB3 . . . . . . .71 C4
Langley Dr GU15 . . . . . .151 B3
Langley Gram Sch SL3 . . .43 C1
Langley Hill RG31 . . . . . .84 B3
Langley Hill Cl RG31 . . . .84 B3
Langley Manor Sch SL3 . .43 C3
Langley Park Rd SL0 . . . .44 B3
Langley Rd Slough SL3 . . .43 C2
Staines TW18 . . . . .96 C1
Langley Sta SL3 . . . . .44 A2
Langley Way SL7 . . . . .1 B1
Langley Wood Sec Sch
SL3 . . . . .43 C2
Langton Cl Maidenhead SL6 .39 B3
Slough SL1 . . . . .41 B3
Langton Way TW20 . . . . .96 B1
Langton's Mdw SL2 . . . . .22 B1
Langworthy End SL6 . . . .65 A4

Langworthy La SL6 . . . . . .65 A4
Laniver Ct RG6 . . . . .87 A1
Lansdowne Ave SL1 . . . . .42 C3
Lansdowne Ct SL1 . . . . . .42 C3
Lansdowne Gdns RG7 . .113 B3
Lansdowne Rd
Reading RG30 . . . . .84 B4
Staines TW18 . . . . .97 A1
Lanterns Wlk SL6 . . . . . .40 A4
Lapwing Cl RG31 . . . . . . .84 B3
Larbert Cotts SL6 . . . . . .38 A3
Larch Ave Ascot SL5 . . . .120 C2
Wokingham RG41 . . . . . .116 A4
Larch Cl
Burghfield Common RG30 .111 A3
Camberley GU15 . . . . . . .151 C4
Newbury RG14 . . . . .104 B3
Slough SL2 . . . . .42 A4
Larch Ct RG4 . . . . .59 A2
Larch Dr RG5 . . . . .87 C3
Larches Way GU17 . . . . .150 A3
Larchfield Prim Sch SL6 . .39 C2
Larchfield Rd SL6 . . . . . .39 C3
Larchside Cl RG31 . . . . . .113 A1
Larchwood 18 RG12 . . . .118 C3
Larchwood Dr TW20 . . . . .95 A1
Larchwood Glade SL5 . . .152 A4
Larges Bridge Dr RG12 . .118 B2
Larges La RG12 . . . . .118 B4
Larissa Cl RG31 . . . . .57 C1
Lark Ave TW18 . . . . .96 C3
Larkham Cl TW13 . . . . . .98 C3
Larkings La SL2 . . . . .23 A2
Larks-Meade RG6 . . . . . .87 A1
Larksfield TW20 . . . . .95 B1
Larkspur Cl RG41 . . . . . .115 B4
Larkspur Gdns RG18 . . . .106 C2
Larkswood Cl
Reading RG31 . . . . .57 B2
Sandhurst GU47 . . . . . . .143 A1
Larkswood Dr RG45 . . . .143 A3
Lascelles Ho 11 SL1 . . . . .43 A2
Lascelles Rd SL3 . . . . .43 A2
Lashbrook Mead RG9 . . . .36 A2
Lashbrook Rd RG9 . . . . . .36 A2
Lassell Gdns SL6 . . . . . . .40 A4
Lastingham Ct TW18 . . . .97 A1
Latham Ave GU16 . . . . . .151 C1
Latimer RG12 . . . . .118 A1
Latimer Dr RG31 . . . . . . .84 B2
Latimer Rd RG41 . . . . . .116 A3
Latton Cl OX11 . . . . .10 C4
Laud Cl Newbury RG14 . .105 B3
Reading RG2 . . . . .86 A3
Laud Way RG40 . . . . . . .116 C3
Laud's Cl RG9 . . . . .15 B1
Lauder Cl GU16 . . . . . . .151 C1
Lauderdale Ho TW18 . . . .96 C2
Launceston Ave RG4 . . . .59 C3
Launceston Cl RG6 . . . . . .87 A1
Laundry La GU47 . . . . . .150 C3
Lauradale RG12 . . . . . . .118 A3
Laurel Ave
Englefield Green TW20 . . . .95 A2
Slough SL3 . . . . .43 C2
Laurel Cl Camberley GU15 .151 B2
Poyle SL3 . . . . .69 C4
Wokingham RG41 . . . . . .115 C3
Laurel Dr RG31 . . . . .84 A4
Laurels The RG8 . . . . . . .56 B3
Laurence Ct SL7 . . . . .1 B1
Laurence Lodge GU15 . .151 B4
Lawrence Mead RG17 . . .102 A1
Lawrence Rd RG30 . . . . . .85 A4
Lawrence Way
Camberley GU15 . . . . . . .150 C2
Slough SL1 . . . . .41 B4
Lawrences La RG18 . . . . .106 B3
Lawrences Way RG18 . . .106 B3
Lawson Dr RG4 . . . . .58 C3
Lawson La OX11 . . . . . . .10 C4
Lawson Rd RG9 . . . . .35 C4
Lawson Way SL5 . . . . . . .121 C2
Laxton Gn SL6 . . . . .39 B2
Layburn Cres SL3 . . . . . .69 A4
Laylands Gn RG17 . . . . . .102 A1
Layton Rise RG31 . . . . . .57 B2
Layton's La TW16 . . . . . .125 A2
Lazare Ct TW18 . . . . .96 C2
Le Marchant Rd
GU15, GU16 . . . . .151 C2
Lea Cl Marlow Bottom SL7 . .1 B3
Reading RG30 . . . . .85 A2
Lea Croft RG45 . . . . .143 A4
Lea Fst Sch SL2 . . . . .43 A3
Lea Mid Sch SL2 . . . . . . .43 A3
Lea Rd GU15 . . . . .151 A1
Lea The Thorpe Lea TW20 . .96 B1
Wokingham RG40 . . . . . .141 B4
Lea View RG18 . . . . .79 B4

Leacroft Staines TW18 . . . .97 A2
Sunningdale SL5 . . . . . . .121 A2
Leacroft Cl TW18 . . . . . . .97 A2
Leacroft Rd SL0 . . . . .44 C4
Leafield Copse RG12 . . . .118 C3
Leaholme Gdns SL1 . . . . .41 B4
Leander Rd RG31 . . . . . . .84 B2
Leas Dr SL0 . . . . .44 C4
Leaver Rd RG9 . . . . .15 B1
Leaves Gn RG12 . . . . . . .118 B2
Ledbury Cl RG30 . . . . . . .58 A1
Ledbury Dr RG31 . . . . . . .84 B2
Ledger La SL6 . . . . .65 B3
Ledger's Rd SL1 . . . . .42 B2
Ledran Cl RG6 . . . . .87 B1
Lee Ct RG5 . . . . .87 C4
Leeds Rd SL1 . . . . .42 C3
Lees Cl SL6 . . . . .39 A3
Lees Gdns SL6 . . . . .39 A3
Lees Wlk SL7 . . . . .1 B1
Leeson Gdns SL4 . . . . . . .41 C1
Legoland Windsor SL4 . . .66 B1
Leicester RG12 . . . . .118 C1
Leicester Cl RG9 . . . . .15 B2
Leigh Field RG7 . . . . . . .136 C3
Leigh Pk SL3 . . . . .68 A4
Leigh Rd SL1 . . . . .42 A3
Leigh Sq SL4 . . . . .66 B3
Leighton Cl RG2 . . . . .86 C2
Leighton Gdns SL6 . . . . . .20 A1
Leighton Ho 9 SL1 . . . . . .42 C3
Leighton Park Sch RG2 . . .86 C2
Leiston Cl 7 RG6 . . . . . . .87 B1
Leiston Spur SL1 . . . . . . .42 C4
Leith Cl Crowthorne RG45 .143 A4
Slough SL1 . . . . .43 A3
Lemart Cl RG30 . . . . .84 C4
Lemington Gr RG12 . . . .118 A2
Leney Cl RG40 . . . . .116 B4
Lenham Cl RG41 . . . . . . .88 C1
Lennox Cl RG31 . . . . .84 A2
Lennox Rd RG6 . . . . .87 A3
Lent Gn SL1 . . . . .21 A1
Lent Green La SL1 . . . . . .21 A1
Lent Rise Cty Comb Sch
SL1 . . . . .41 A4
Lent Rise Rd SL1 . . . . . . .21 A1
Leopold Mall 14 SL1 . . . . .42 C2
Leopold Wlk RG1 . . . . . . .86 B4
Leppington RG12 . . . . . . .118 A1
Lerwick Dr SL1 . . . . .42 C4
Lesford Rd RG1 . . . . .85 C3
Lesley Ct 16 RG30 . . . . . .85 B3
Leslie Southern Ct RG14 .105 A2
Lesters Rd SL6 . . . . .19 B3
Letchworth Ave TW14 . . .98 C4
Letcombe Ct 17 RG1 . . . . .86 A3
Letcombe Pl RG12 . . . . . .118 C3
Letcombe Sq RG12 . . . . .118 C3
Letcombe St RG1 . . . . . . .86 A4
Leverkusen Rd RG12 . . . .118 A2
Leverton La RG17 . . . . . .73 A1
Lewendon Rd RG14 . . . .104 C3
Lewington Mews RG17 . .100 B2
Lewins Farm Ct 4 SL1 . . .41 C3
Lewins Way SL1 . . . . .41 C3
Lewis Wlk RG14 . . . . . . .130 B3
Lewisham Way GU47 . . . .143 B1
Lexington Ave SL6 . . . . . .39 B3
Lexington Gr RG2 . . . . . .113 B3
Leyburn Cl RG5 . . . . .88 A4
Leycester Cl GU20 . . . . . .146 A3
Leyland Gdns RG2 . . . . . .113 C3
Leylands La TW19 . . . . . .70 A1
Leys Gdns RG14 . . . . . . .104 C3
Leyside RG45 . . . . .143 A3
Libra Ho 1 RG40 . . . . .3 A4
Library Par RG5 . . . . .87 C4
Licensed Victuallers Sch
SL5 . . . . .119 B3
Lichfield Cl 1 RG6 . . . . . . .87 B1
Lichfield Ho SL1 . . . . . . .68 B3
Lichfields RG12 . . . . .118 C4
Liddell SL4 . . . . .66 B2
Liddell Cl RG40 . . . . .141 C2
Liddell Pl SL4 . . . . .66 B2
Liddell Sq 15 SL4 . . . . . . .66 B2
Liddell Way Ascot SL5 . . .119 C3
Windsor SL4 . . . . .66 B2
Lido Rd OX11 . . . . .9 C4
Lidstone Cl RG6 . . . . .114 B4
Liebenrood Rd RG30 . . . .85 B3
Lightlands La SL6 . . . . . . .19 C3
Lightwater Ctry Pk GU18 .145 C1
Lightwater Mdw GU18 . .153 A4
Lightwater Rd GU18 . . . .153 B3
Lightwater Village Sch
GU18 . . . . .146 A1
Lightwood RG12 . . . . . . .118 B2
Lilac Cl RG8 . . . . .57 B3
Lilac Ct SL2 . . . . .21 C1
Lilac Wlk RG31 . . . . .84 B3
Lilacs The RG41 . . . . . . .115 B2
Lilley Way SL1 . . . . .41 C3
Lillibrooke Cres SL6 . . . . .39 A2
Lily Hill Dr RG12 . . . . . . .118 C4
Lily Hill Rd RG12 . . . . . . .118 C4
Lima Ct RG1 . . . . .85 C3
Lime Ave Camberley GU15 .152 A3
Winkfield SL4 . . . . .93 C3
Lime Barn 4 SL7 . . . . .1 B1
Lime Cl Newbury RG14 . .105 B2
Wokingham RG41 . . . . . .115 C3
Lime Lo 7 TW16 . . . . .98 C1
Lime Tree Rd RG8 . . . . . .34 C4
Lime Tree Wlk RG45 . . . .143 C2
Lime Wlk Bracknell RG12 .118 B3
Maidenhead SL6 . . . . .39 A4

Limecroft GU46 . . . . . . .149 B3
Limefield Cl RG6 . . . . . . .87 C2
Limerick Cl RG42 . . . . . .118 A4
Limes Cl TW15 . . . . .98 A2
Limes Rd TW20 . . . . .95 C2
Limes The SL4 . . . . .66 B3
Limmer Cl RG41 . . . . . . .115 B2
Limmerhill Rd RG41 . . . .115 C3
Lincoln Cl Frimley GU15 .152 A2
Winnersh RG41 . . . . .88 A2
Lincoln Ct Newbury RG14 .104 C1
24 Slough SL1 . . . . .42 C2
Lincoln Gdns RG10 . . . . .61 B3
Lincoln Hatch La SL1 . . . .21 B1
Lincoln Rd
Maidenhead SL6 . . . . .39 A4
Reading RG2 . . . . .86 B2
Lincoln Way
Charlton TW16 . . . . .125 C4
Slough SL1 . . . . .41 B3
Lincolnshire Gdns RG42 . .91 C1
Lind Cl RG6 . . . . .87 A1
Lindale Cl GU25 . . . . . . .121 C3
Lindberg Way RG5 . . . . . .61 C1
Linden 3 Bracknell RG12 .118 C2
Slough SL3 . . . . .44 A1
Linden Ave SL6 . . . . .19 B1
Linden Cl Holyport SL6 . . .65 A4
Newbury RG14 . . . . .104 C2
Wokingham RG41 . . . . . .115 C2
Linden Ct
Camberley GU15 . . . . . . .151 C4
Englefield Green TW20 . . . .95 A1
Linden Dr SL2 . . . . .22 B2
Linden Pl RG10 . . . . .97 A2
Linden Rd Newtown RG20 .131 C2
Reading RG2 . . . . .86 C1
Woodley RG5 . . . . .87 B2
Linden Way TW17 . . . . . .125 B2
Lindenhill Rd RG42 . . . . .117 C4
Lindores Rd SL6 . . . . .65 A4
Lindsay Cl TW19 . . . . .70 B1
Lindsay Dr TW17 . . . . . . .125 B2
Lindsey Cl RG41 . . . . . . .115 C3
Lindsey Gdns TW14 . . . . .98 B4
Lines Rd RG10 . . . . .88 C3
Ling Dr GU18 . . . . .152 C1
Lingfield Rd RG14 . . . . . .131 C4
Lingholm Cl
Maidenhead SL6 . . . . .39 B3
Reading RG30 . . . . .84 C3
Lingwood RG12 . . . . . . .118 B2
Link Ho 2 RG14 . . . . . . .105 A1
Link Rd Datchet SL3 . . . . .68 B3
East Bedfont TW14 . . . . . .98 C4
Newbury RG14 . . . . .105 A1
Link The Slough SL2 . . . . .43 A4
Yateley GU46 . . . . .149 B4
Link Way Arborfield RG2 . .114 C1
Staines TW18 . . . . .97 A1
Thatcham RG18 . . . . .106 A2
Links Dr RG30 . . . . .85 A4
Links Rd Ashford TW15 . . .97 C2
Flackwell Heath HP10 . . . . .3 B4
Links The SL5 . . . . .119 C4
Links Way HP10 . . . . .3 A4
Linkscroft Ave TW15 . . . .98 A1
Linkswood Rd SL1 . . . . . .21 B1
Linkway Camberley GU15 .151 B2
Crowthorne RG45 . . . . . .142 C3
Linnet Cl RG31 . . . . .84 A3
Linnet La RG20 . . . . .131 C2
Linnet Wlk RG41 . . . . . . .115 C3
Lintott Ct TW19 . . . . .70 B1
Lion Cl TW17 . . . . .124 C3
Lipscomb Cl RG18 . . . . . .79 A3
Lipscombe Ct RG14 . . . . .104 C2
Liquel Cl RG17 . . . . .100 B2
Liscombe RG12 . . . . .118 A1
Liscombe Ho RG12 . . . . .118 A1
Lisle Cl RG14 . . . . .104 C3
Lismore Cl RG5 . . . . .87 C2
Lismore Ct TW18 . . . . . . .97 A2
Lismore Pk SL2 . . . . .42 C4
Lisset Rd SL6 . . . . .40 A3
Lister Cl RG8 . . . . .57 B3
Liston Ct 3 SL7 . . . . .1 B1
Liston Rd SL7 . . . . .1 B1
Litcham Spur SL1 . . . . . . .42 B4
Lithgow's Rd TW14, TW6 . .71 C2
Littington Cl RG6 . . . . . . .114 B4
Little Aldershot La RG26 .134 A1
Little Boltons 7 SL1 . . . . . .1 C1
Little Bowden La RG8 . . . .55 C2
Little Buntings SL4 . . . . . .66 C2
Little Chapels Way SL1 . . .42 A2
Little Cl HP10 . . . . .3 A3
Little Copse GU46 . . . . . .149 B4
Little Croft Rd RG8 . . . . . .34 B3
Little Croft Rd RG8 . . . . . .34 B3
Little Elms UB3 . . . . .71 B4
Little Fryth RG40 . . . . . . .142 B3
Little Glebe RG4 . . . . .60 C2
Little Heath Rd RG31 . . . .84 A4
Little Heath Sch RG31 . . . .84 A4
Little Hill Rd RG10 . . . . . .88 B2
Little Johns La RG30 . . . . .85 B4
Little La RG7 . . . . .107 B3
Little London Rd RG7 . . . .136 A1
Little Marlow CE Fst Sch
SL7 . . . . .1 C2
Little Marlow Rd SL7 . . . . .1 C2
Little Moor GU47 . . . . . . .143 B1
Little Oak Dr RG31 . . . . . .84 B4
Little Paddock GU15 . . . .152 A4
Little Ringdale RG12 . . . .118 C3
Little Saffron RG18 . . . . . .79 A3
Little St 2 RG1 . . . . .85 C4

Little Sutton La
Brands Hill SL3 . . . . .69 A4
Slough, Sutton SL3 . . . . . .44 B1
Little Vigo GU46 . . . . . . .149 A2
Little Woodlands SL4 . . . .66 C2
Littlebrook Ave SL2 . . . . .41 C4
Littlecote Dr RG1 . . . . . . .85 C3
Littlecote Rd SN8 . . . . . . .99 A3
Littlecroft Rd 2 TW20 . . . .95 C2
Littledale Cl RG12 . . . . . .118 C3
Littledown Cotts SL1 . . . . .42 C3
Littledown Rd SL1 . . . . . .42 C3
Littledown Sch SL1 . . . . . .42 C3
Littlefield Cl UB7 . . . . . . .70 B4
Littlefield Gn SL6 . . . . . . .63 C3
Littlejohns La RG30 . . . . .58 B1
Littleport Spur SL1 . . . . . .42 C4
Littlestead Cl RG4 . . . . . .59 C3
Littleton CE Inf Sch
TW17 . . . . .125 A3
Littleton La TW17, TW18 . .124 C2
Littleton Rd TW15 . . . . . .98 A1
Littlewick Green
Montessori Sch SL6 . . . . .38 C2
Litton Rd RG2 . . . . .86 B1
Liverpool Rd Reading RG1 . .86 C4
Slough SL1 . . . . .42 A4
Livery Cl RG1 . . . . .86 A4
Livingstone Ct TW19 . . . .97 C4
Livingstone Gdns RG5 . . .87 C3
Livingstone Rd RG14 . . . .105 A1
Llangar Gr RG45 . . . . . . .143 A3
Llanvair Cl SL5 . . . . .120 A2
Llanvair Dr SL5 . . . . .119 C2
Llewellyn Pk RG10 . . . . . .61 B3
Lochinvar Cl SL1 . . . . .42 A2
Lochinver RG12 . . . . .118 A1
Lock Ave SL6 . . . . .20 B1
Lock Bridge Rd SL8 . . . . . .3 A2
Lock La SL6 . . . . .39 B2
Lock Mead SL6 . . . . .20 B1
Lock Path SL4 . . . . .66 B4
Lock Pl RG1 . . . . .86 B4
Lock Rd SL7 . . . . .1 C1
Lockbridge Ct SL6 . . . . . .40 B4
Locke Gdns SL3 . . . . .43 B2
Lockets Cl SL4 . . . . .66 B3
Lockram La RG7 . . . . . . .111 B1
Locks Ride SL5 . . . . .92 B1
Lockside Ct RG7 . . . . . . .109 B2
Locksley Ct 25 SL1 . . . . . .42 C2
Lockstile Mead RG8 . . . . .34 B3
Lockstile Way RG8 . . . . . .34 B3
Lockton Chase SL5 . . . . .119 B3
Lockton Ho RG40 . . . . . .116 B3
Loddon Bridge Rd RG5 . . .87 C3
Loddon Cl GU15 . . . . . . .152 B3
Loddon Dr Charvil RG10 . . .61 A4
Maidenhead SL6 . . . . .39 B4
Loddon Hall Rd RG10 . . . .61 C3
Loddon Inf Sch The RG6 . .87 B2
Loddon Jun Sch RG6 . . . .87 B2
Loddon Rd SL8 . . . . .3 A2
Loddon Spur SL1 . . . . . . .42 C4
Loddon Vale Ctr RG5 . . . .88 A4
Lodge Cl
Englefield Green TW20 . . . .95 B2
Marlow SL7 . . . . .1 C1
Slough SL1 . . . . .42 B2
Lodge Gr GU46 . . . . .149 C3
Lodge Rd RG10 . . . . .88 C2
Lodge The RG14 . . . . . . .105 A2
Lodge Way Ashford TW15 . .97 C3
Charlton TW17 . . . . .125 B4
Windsor SL4 . . . . .66 C2
Lodgings of the Military
Knights 13 SL4 . . . . .67 B3
Logan Cl RG30 . . . . .84 C4
Lois Dr TW17 . . . . .125 A2
Lomond Ave RG4 . . . . . . .59 C3
London Rd Ascot SL5 . . . .120 B3
Ashford TW15, TW18,
TW19, TW14, ...97 B3
Bagshot GU15,GU19 . . . .145 B1
Blackwater GU15,GU17 . .150 C2
Blewbury OX11 . . . . .11 C4
Bracknell RG12, SL5 . . . .119 B3
Bracknell, Binfield
RG12, RG42 . . . . .117 B4
Brands Hill SL3 . . . . .69 A4
Camberley GU15 . . . . . . .151 B3
Datchet SL3 . . . . .68 B4
Earley RG6 . . . . .87 A4
Englefield Green TW20 . . . .95 B1
Newbury RG14 . . . . .105 B2
Reading RG1 . . . . .86 B4
Slough SL3 . . . . .43 C1
Sunningdale, Blacknest SL5 .121 A3
Sunningdale, Shrubs Hill
SL5, GU25 . . . . .120 C2
Thatcham RG18 . . . . .106 B2
Twyford RG10 . . . . .61 C3
Virginia Water
GU25, TW20 . . . . .122 A4
Windlesham GU19,GU20,SL5,
GU19,GU20,SL5 . . . . . . .146 B4
Woodley RG4,RG5 . . . . . .60 B1
London St Chertsey KT16 . .124 A1
Reading RG1 . . . . .86 B4
Loneacre GU20 . . . . .146 C2
Long Barn La RG2 . . . . . .86 B2
Long Cl
Farnham Common SL2 . . . .22 A3
Kintbury RG17 . . . . .102 A1
Long Close Sch SL3 . . . . .43 A2
Long Dr SL1 . . . . .21 B1
Long Furlong Dr SL2 . . . . .21 C1
Long Gr RG26 . . . . .134 B1

ong Grove RG7 ....107 B3
ong Half Acre SL6 ....38 A2
ong Hedge RG17 ....25 B1
ong Hill Rd RG12, SL5 ...119 A4
ong La Brightwalton RG20 ..28 C2
  Cookham SL6 ....19 B3
  Hermitage RG14, RG18 ......78 C1
  Holyport, Braywoodside SL6 .64 B2
  Holyport, Touchen-end SL6 ..64 C3
  Newbury RG18 ....105 B4
  Purley on T RG31 ....57 A2
  Stanwell TW15, TW19 ......97 C4
ong Lane Prim Sch
  RG31 ....57 A2
ong Mickle GU47 ....143 A1
ong Readings La SL2 ....22 A1
ong Water Dr RG30 ....112 B4
ong Wlk The SL4 ....94 B4
ong's Way RG40 ....116 C4
ongacre RG14 ....130 B4
ongbourne Way KT16 ....123 C2
ongbridge Rd RG19 ....106 C1
ongcroft Rd RG19 ....106 C1
ongcross Sta GU25 ....121 C1
ongdon Rd RG1 ....88 B1
ongdown Lodge GU47 ....150 A4
ongdown Rd GU47 ....143 A1
ongfield Rd RG10 ....61 B3
ongford
  Feltham TW14 ....71 C1
  Stanwell TW19 ....97 C4
ongford Rdbt TW6, UB7 ...70 A3
ongford Sch TW14 ....98 C4
ongford Way TW19 ....97 C4
onghurst Cl RG4 ....59 B2
onglands Way GU15 ......152 B3
ongleat Dr SL4 ....57 A2
ongleat Gdns SL6 ....39 B3
ongleat Way TW14 ....98 B4
ongmead (Ball Hill) RG20 .129 C1
  Windsor SL4 ....66 C3
ongmeadow GU15, GU16 151 C2
ongmoor La RG7 ....137 A4
ongmoors RG42 ....117 C4
ongmore Rd RG2 ....113 B3
ongridge SL6 ....85 A4
Longridge Scout Boating
  Activity Ctr SL7 ....18 C4
ongshot Ind Est RG12 ....117 C4
ongshot La RG12 ....117 C4
ongside Cl TW20 ....123 B4
ongview HP9 ....3 C4
ongwater Dr RG30 ....85 C1
ongwater La RG27, RG40 ..141 C2
ongwater Rd
  Bracknell RG12 ....118 B2
  Finchampstead RG40 .....141 C1
ongworth Ave RG31 ....84 A4
ongworth Dr SL6 ....20 B1
onsdale Cl SL6 ....40 B1
onsdale Way SL6 ....40 B1
Look Out Discovery Ctr
  The RG12 ....118 B1
oosen Dr SL6 ....39 A2
ord Knyvett Cl TW19 ......70 B1
oring Rd SL4 ....66 C3
orne Cl SL1 ....42 A2
orne Pl RG1 ....85 C4
orne St RG1 ....85 C4
Lorraine Cty Inf Sch
  GU15 ....151 C4
orraine Rd GU15 ....151 C4
ory Ridge GU19 ....145 C2
osfield Rd SL6 ....66 C3
oughborough RG12 ......118 C2
oundyes Cl RG18 ....106 A2
ovatt Rd RG31 ....84 A4
Love Green La SL0 ....44 C4
Love Hill La SL3 ....44 A3
Love La Iver SL0 ....44 B4
  Newbury RG14 ....105 A2
ovedean Ct RG12 ....118 C2
ovegrove Dr SL2 ....21 C1
ovejoy La SL4 ....66 B3
ovel La SL5 ....93 A2
ovel Rd SL5 ....93 A2
ovelace Cl SL6 ....17 C2
ovelace Rd RG12 ....117 C3
ovell Cl RG9 ....35 B4
ovells Cl GU18 ....146 A1
overock Rd RG30 ....58 B1
oves Cl RG7 ....111 A2
oves Wood RG7 ....136 C3
ovett Gdns SL6 ....20 B2
ovett Rd TW20 ....96 B2
owbrook Dr SL6 ....39 A2
owbrook Prim Sch SL6 ...39 A2
owbury RG12 ....118 C3
ower Armour Rd RG31 ....57 B1
ower Bglws RG8 ....34 B4
ower Boyndon Rd SL6 ....39 C3
ower Britwell Rd SL2 .....21 B1
ower Broadmoor Rd
  RG45 ....143 B2
ower Brook St RG1 ....86 A3
ower Canes GU46 ....149 A3
ower Charles St GU15 ...151 B3
ower Church Rd SL5 .....120 A3
ower Cippenham La SL1 .41 C2
ower Common RG27 ....140 C1
ower Cookham Rd SL6 ...20 B1
ower Earley Way RG6 ...114 B4
Lower Earley Way (N)
  RG6 ....87 C1
Lower Earley Way (W)
  RG6 ....113 C4

Lower Elmstone Dr RG31 ..57 B1
Lower Farm Ct RG19 .....105 C1
Lower Field Rd RG1 ....86 A3
Lower Henley Rd RG4 ......59 B2
Lower Lees Rd SL2 ....22 A1
Lower Meadow Rd RG2 ....86 B1
Lower Mill Field GU19 ....145 A3
Lower Mount RG1 ....86 B3
Lower Pound La SL7 ....1 C1
Lower Rd Chilton OX11 ....10 B4
  Cookham SL6 ....19 C4
Lower Ridge SL8 ....3 A2
Lower Sandhurst Rd
  RG40, GU47 ....142 A2
Lower Ventnor Cotts SL6 ..19 B4
Lower Village Rd SL5 .....120 B2
Lower Way RG19 ....106 A2
Lower Wokingham Rd
  RG40, RG45 ....142 A2
Lowes Cl RG9 ....36 A2
Lowestoft Cl RG6 ....87 B1
Lowestoft Dr SL1 ....41 B4
Loweswater Wlk GU15 ...152 B2
Lowfield Cl GU18 ....153 A4
Lowfield Ct RG4 ....59 B3
Lowfield Gn RG4 ....59 C2
Lowfield Rd RG4 ....59 B3
Lowlands Rd
  Blackwater GU17 ....150 B2
  Stanwell TW19 ....70 B1
Lowry Cl GU47 ....150 B3
Lowther Cl RG41 ....115 C4
Lowther Rd RG41 ....115 C4
Loxwood RG6 ....87 B1
Loxwood Cl TW14 ....98 C1
Lucan Dr TW18 ....97 B1
Lucas Cl GU46 ....149 B3
Lucas Gn SL4 ....92 A3
Lucas Green Rd GU24 ...153 C3
Lucey Cl RG31 ....57 A2
Lucie Ave TW15 ....98 A1
Luckley Oakfield Sch
  RG40 ....116 A2
Luckley Path RG40 ....116 B3
Luckley Rd RG41 ....116 A2
Luckley Wood RG41 .....116 A2
Luckmore Dr RG6 ....87 A2
Lud Lodge TW15 ....97 C3
Luddington Ave
  GU25, TW20 ....122 C4
Ludgrove Prep Sch
  RG40 ....116 B2
Ludlow RG12 ....118 A1
Ludlow Cl RG14 ....105 C3
Ludlow Ho SL6 ....39 C3
Ludlow Rd SL6 ....39 C3
Luff Cl SL4 ....66 C2
Luker Ave RG9 ....15 C3
Lulworth Rd RG2 ....113 B4
Lunds Farm Rd RG5 ....88 A4
Lundy Ct SL1 ....41 C3
Lundy La RG30 ....85 B4
Lupin Cl GU19 ....145 A3
Lupin Ride RG45 ....143 A4
Lutman La SL6 ....19 C1
Lutmans Haven RG10 .....37 C3
Lutterworth Cl RG42 ......91 B1
Lutton Cl RG6 ....113 C4
Lych Gate Cl GU47 ......149 C4
Lycroft Cl RG8 ....34 B4
Lydbury RG12 ....118 C3
Lydford Ave SL2 ....42 B4
Lydford Rd RG1 ....86 C3
Lydney RG12 ....118 A1
Lydsey Cl SL2 ....22 A1
Lyefield Ct RG4 ....59 B4
Lyell Place E SL4 ....66 B2
Lyell Place W SL4 ....66 B2
Lyell Rd SL4 ....66 B2
Lyell Walk E SL4 ....66 B2
Lyell Walk W SL4 ....66 B2
Lyme Gr RG1 ....57 B1
Lymington Ave GU46 ....149 B3
Lymington Gate RG4 ......58 C2
Lynch Hill La SL2 ....21 C1
Lynch Hill Sch SL2 ....21 C1
Lynch La RG17 ....25 A2
Lynchets View RG17 ....24 C3
Lynden Mews RG2 ....86 A3
Lyndhurst Ave
  Blackwater GU17 ....150 B3
  Cookham SL6 ....19 C3
Lyndhurst Rd Ascot SL5 ..120 A3
  Goring RG8 ....34 B4
  Reading RG30 ....58 A1
Lyndhurst Sch GU15 .....151 A3
Lyndwood Dr SL4 ....68 A1
Lyndwood Par SL4 ....68 A1
Lyne Cl GU25 ....122 C2
Lyne Crossing Rd
  KT16, GU25 ....123 A2
Lyne La KT16, TW20, GU25 ..123 A2
Lyne Place Manor GU25 ..122 C2
Lynegrove Ave TW15 ......98 B2
Lyneham Gdns SL6 ....19 A1
Lyneham Rd RG45 ....143 A3
Lynmouth Ct RG1 ....59 A4
Lynmouth Rd RG1 ....59 A4
Lynton Cl TW15 ....98 B2
Lynton Ct RG5 ....87 B3
Lynton Ct RG14 ....105 A2
Lynton Gn SL6 ....39 C4
Lynwood Ave Egham TW20 .95 C1
  Slough SL3 ....43 B2

Lynwood Chase RG12 ....118 B4
Lynwood Cres SL5 ....120 C2
Lynwood Flats SL5 ....120 C2
Lyon Cl RG19 ....106 C1
Lyon Oaks RG42 ....91 A1
Lyon Rd RG45 ....143 B3
Lyon Sq RG30 ....85 A4
Lyon Way GU16 ....151 B1
Lysander Cl RG5 ....88 A4
Lysander Mead SL6 ....40 B4
Lytchet Minster Cl
  RG12 ....118 C2
Lytham RG12 ....117 C2
Lytham Cl RG30 ....85 B2
Lytham Ct SL5 ....120 B2
Lytham End RG31 ....57 A2
Lytham Rd RG5 ....87 C4

M

Macadam Ave RG45 .....143 B4
Macbeth Ct RG42 ....118 C2
Macdonald Rd GU18 .....153 A4
Mace Cl RG6 ....87 A1
Mackay Cl RG31 ....84 C2
Mackenzie Mall SL1 ....42 C2
Mackenzie St RG1 ....42 C2
Macklin Ct RG17 ....100 B3
Macnaughton Woods
  GU15 ....151 C3
Macphail Cl RG40 ....116 C4
Macrae Rd GU46 ....149 B3
Maddle Rd RG17 ....24 B4
Madeira Pl RG14 ....105 A1
Madejski Stad RG2 ......112 C4
Madingley RG12 ....118 A1
Madox Brown End GU47 .150 C3
Mafeking Rd TW19 ....96 A3
Magdalene Rd
  Littleton SL7 ....124 C3
  Sandhurst GU47 ....143 C1
Magill Cl RG7 ....113 A1
Magna Carta La TW19 .....95 C4
Magna Carta Sch TW18 ..96 B1
Magna Rd TW20 ....95 A1
Magnolia Cl GU47 ....143 B1
Magnolia Ct SL5 ....88 A4
Magnolia Gdns SL3 ....43 B2
Magnolia Way RG41 .....115 C3
Magpie Cl RG19 ....106 A2
Magpie Rd Reading RG31 .84 A3
  Slough SL2 ....21 C1
Maguire Dr GU16 ....152 B2
Mahonia Cl RG17 ....97 C3
Maiden Erlegh Comp Sch
  RG6 ....87 A2
Maiden Erlegh Dr RG6 ...87 A2
Maiden Lane Ctr RG6 .....87 B1
Maiden Pl RG6 ....87 B1
Maiden's Gn SL4 ....92 A3
Maidenhead Coll Claires
  Court Girls SL6 ....39 C4
Maidenhead Court Pk
  SL6 ....20 A2
Maidenhead Office Pk
  SL6 ....38 C1
Maidenhead Rd
  Binfield RG40 ....89 B2
  Cookham SL6 ....19 C3
  Newell Green RG42 ....91 A3
  Windsor SL4 ....66 C4
Maidenhead Sta SL6 ......39 C3
Maidensfield RG41 ....88 B1
Main Dr Bracknell RG42 ..91 C1
  Iver SL0 ....44 C2
  Winkfield RG12, SL5 .....119 A4
Main St Chilton OX11 .....10 B4
  Greenham RG19 ....131 C3
  Newtown RG19 ....132 A3
  Yateley GU46 ....149 B4
Mainprize Rd RG12 ......118 C4
Mainstone Rd GU24 .....153 C2
Maise Webster Cl TW19 ..97 B4
Maitland Rd RG1 ....85 C4
Maiwand Gdns RG31 .....84 B4
Maize La RG42 ....91 C1
Majendie Cl RG14 ....104 B3
Major's Farm Rd
  Brands Hill SL3 ....69 A4
  Datchet SL3 ....68 B4
Makepiece Rd RG42 ....91 A1
Maker Cl RG30 ....85 A1
Makins Rd RG9 ....35 A4
Malders La SL6 ....19 B2
Maldon Cl RG30 ....85 B3
Malet Cl TW20 ....96 B1
Malham Fell RG12 ....118 A4
Malham Rd RG19 ....106 B2
Mallard Cl Earley RG6 .....87 B2
  Twyford RG10 ....61 C2
Mallard Ct RG14 ....104 C2
Mallard Dr SL1 ....41 C3
Mallard Row RG1 ....86 A4
Mallard Way
  Padworth RG7 ....109 A2
  Yateley GU46 ....149 A3
Mallards The
  Frimley GU16 ....151 B1
  Great Shefford RG17 .....48 A2
  Laleham TW18 ....124 A4
Mallards Way GU18 ......153 A3
Mallory Ave RG4 ....59 B3
Mallow Pk SL6 ....19 B1
Mallowdale Rd RG12 ....118 C1
Malone Rd RG5 ....87 B4

Malpas Rd SL2 ....43 A3
Malt Hill Egham TW20 .....95 C2
  Newell Green RG42 ....91 C3
Malt Ho SL4 ....95 A4
Malt House Cl SL4 ....95 A4
Malt Shovel La RG17 ......24 C2
Maltby Way RG6 ....114 A4
Malthouse Cl RG19 ......106 C1
Malthouse La
  Reading RG1 ....85 C4
  West End GU24 ....153 C4
Malthouse Way SL7 ....1 B1
Maltings Pl RG1 ....86 A4
Maltings The Staines TW18 .96 C2
  Thatcham RG19 ....106 C1
  West Ilsley RG20 ....10 A1
Malton Ave SL1 ....42 A3
Malvern Cl RG5 ....87 C3
Malvern Ct Brands Hill SL3 .69 A4
  Newbury RG14 ....104 C1
  Reading RG1 ....86 B3
Malvern Rd Harlington UB3 .71 C4
  Maidenhead SL6 ....19 B1
Malvern Way RG10 ....61 B4
Malyons The TW17 ......125 B2
Man's Hill RG7 ....111 B1
Managua Cl RG4 ....59 C1
Manchester Rd RG1 ......86 C4
Mandarin Ct RG14 ....105 B1
Mandela Ct RG1 ....86 B4
Mandeville Cl SL6 ....84 C3
Mandeville Ct TW20 ......96 A2
Mandeville Rd TW17 .....125 A2
Manea Cl RG6 ....114 B4
Manfield Cl SL2 ....22 A1
Manners Rd RG5 ....87 B4
Mannock Way RG5 ....88 A4
Manor Bglws RG20 ....31 B2
Manor Ct RG42 ....91 A1
Manor Cres RG20 ....31 B2
Manor Farm Ave TW17 ..125 A2
Manor Farm Cl SL4 ....66 C2
Manor Farm Cotts SL4 ...68 A1
Manor Farm Ho SL4 ......66 C2
Manor Farm La
  Egham TW20 ....96 A2
  Tidmarsh RG8 ....56 B1
Manor Farm Rd RG2 ......86 A1
Manor Gdns HP10 ....3 C2
Manor Gr SL6 ....65 B3
Manor House Dr SL5 ......93 A1
Manor House La SL3 ......68 A3
Manor House The GU15 .151 B3
Manor La Chieveley RG20 ..51 A1
  Harlington UB3 ....71 B4
  Hermitage RG18 ....79 A4
  Leckhampstead RG20 ....49 C2
  Maidenhead SL6 ....39 C2
  Newbury RG14 ....105 C3
Manor Leaze TW20 ....96 A2
Manor Park Cl RG30 ......84 B3
Manor Park Dr
  Wokingham RG40 ....141 C3
  Yateley GU46 ....149 B3
Manor Pk Froxfield SN8 ..99 C3
  Staines TW18 ....96 B3
Manor Pl Newbury RG14 ..104 B3
  Staines TW18 ....97 A2
Manor Prim Sch RG30 ....85 A2
Manor Rd Ashford TW15 ..98 A2
  Goring RG8 ....34 A3
  Henley-on-T RG9 ....35 B4
  Letcombe Bassett OX12 ...7 B3
  Maidenhead SL6 ....39 C2
  Walton-on-T KT12 ....125 C1
  Whitchurch-on-T RG8 .....56 B4
  Windsor SL4 ....66 C3
  Wokingham RG41 ....116 A1
Manor Way Bagshot GU19 .145 C2
  Egham TW20 ....95 C1
  Holyport SL6 ....65 A4
Manor Wood Gate RG9 ...36 A2
Manorcroft Sch TW20 .....96 A1
Manorcrofts Rd TW20 ....96 A1
Manse Cl UB3 ....71 B4
Mansel Ct SL4 ....66 C3
Mansell Ct RG2 ....86 C1
Mansell Dr RG14 ....130 B3
Mansfield Cl SL5 ....119 B4
Mansfield Cres RG12 ....118 A2
Mansfield Pl SL5 ....119 B4
Mansfield Rd
  Reading RG1 ....85 C3
  Wokingham RG41 ....116 A3
Mansion House St
  RG14 ....105 A2
Mansion La SL0 ....44 B3
Manston Dr RG12 ....118 B2
Mant Cl RG20 ....75 B3
Manygate La TW17 ......125 B2
Mapel Ct RG12 ....118 C2
Maple Cl Blackwater GU17 .150 B3
  Maidenhead SL6 ....39 B3
  Sandhurst GU47 ....142 C1
  Winnersh RG41 ....88 B2
Maple Cres
  Newbury RG14 ....105 A2
  Slough SL2 ....43 A3
Maple Ct
  Englefield Green TW20 ...95 A1
  Goring RG8 ....34 A3
  Marlow SL7 ....1 C1
  Windsor SL4 ....67 B2

Maple Dr
  Crowthorne RG45 ....143 B4
  Lightwater GU18 ....152 C4
Maple Gdns Reading RG2 .86 C1
  Stanwell TW19 ....97 C3
  Yateley GU46 ....149 B3
Maple La RG8 ....55 A3
Maple Rise SL7 ....1 C2
Mapledene RG4 ....58 C2
Mapledurham Dr RG8 .....57 B3
Mapledurham Ho RG31 ...57 C3
Mapledurham View RG31 .57 B1
Mapledurham Watermill
  RG31 ....57 C3
Mapledurham Wlk SL6 ...19 C1
Maples The SL8 ....3 A2
Maplin Pk SL3 ....44 A2
Marathon Cl RG5 ....88 A4
Marbeck Cl SL4 ....66 B3
Marbull Way RG42 ....91 A1
Marchant Cl RG19 ....131 B4
Marchant Ct SL7 ....2 A2
Marcheria Cl RG12 ......118 A2
Marchwood Ave RG4 ......59 B4
Marcia Ct SL1 ....41 C3
Marconi Rd RG14 ....105 A4
Marcus Cl RG30 ....85 A4
Mardale GU15 ....152 B2
Mardy RG4 ....58 C3
Mare La RG10 ....63 C2
Marefield RG6 ....87 B1
Marefield Rd SL7 ....1 B1
Marescroft Rd SL2 ....21 C1
Mareshall Ave RG42 ......91 A1
Marfleet Cl RG6 ....87 C1
Margaret Cl Reading RG2 .113 B4
  Staines TW18 ....97 B1
Maria Ct RG30 ....85 B3
Marie Davis Ct RG1 ....86 A4
Marigold Cl RG45 ....142 C4
Marina Cl KT16 ....124 B1
Marina Way SL1 ....41 B3
Mariners La RG7 ....82 A2
Marino Way RG40 ....141 A3
Marion Ave TW17 ....125 A2
Marish Cl SL3 ....44 A2
Marish Cty Fst Sch SL3 ...44 A2
Marish Jun Sch SL3 ......44 A2
Marish Wharf Ind Est SL3 .43 C2
Marjory Kinnon Sch
  TW14 ....71 C1
Markby Way RG6 ....87 C1
Market La SL3 ....44 B2
Market Pl Colnbrook SL3 ..69 B4
  Henley-on-T RG9 ....15 B1
  Newbury RG14 ....105 A2
  Reading RG1 ....86 A4
  Wokingham RG40 ....116 B3
Market Sq Marlow SL7 .....1 B1
  Staines TW18 ....96 C2
Market St Bracknell RG12 .118 A4
  Maidenhead SL6 ....39 C2
  Newbury RG14 ....105 A1
  Windsor SL4 ....67 B3
Market Way RG1 ....86 A4
Markham Centre
  Trad Est TW6 ....83 C1
Markham Ct GU15 ....151 B3
Markham Mews RG40 ...116 A3
Marks Rd RG41 ....116 A4
Marlborough Ave RG1 ....86 B3
Marlborough Cl SL6 ....39 A3
Marlborough Ct
  Reading RG1 ....85 C3
  Slough SL1 ....41 C4
  Wokingham RG40 ....116 A3
Marlborough Ho
  Maidenhead SL6 ....39 C3
  Reading RG1 ....86 B3
Marlborough Rd
  Ashford TW15 ....97 C2
  Maidenhead SL6 ....39 A3
  Slough SL3 ....43 C1
Marlborough Rise GU15 .151 C3
Marlborough Way RG31 ..84 A2
Marley Croft TW18 ....96 C3
Marlin Cl TW16 ....98 C1
Marlin Ct SL1 ....1 B1
Marling Cl RG31 ....57 B2
Marlow Bottom SL7 ....1 B3
Marlow Bridge La SL7 .....1 B1
Marlow CE Inf Sch SL7 ....1 B2
Marlow Com Hospl SL7 ...1 C1
Marlow Lodge SL6 ....39 C3
Marlow Mill SL7 ....1 C1
Marlow Rd Bisham SL7 ...18 B4
  Bisham SL6 ....18 C2
  Henley-on-T RG9 ....15 C2
  Little Marlow SL7, SL8 .....2 B3
  Maidenhead SL6 ....39 C4
  Marlow Bottom SL7 ....1 A4
  Marlow Sta SL7 ....1 B3
Marlowes The RG14 .....130 C4
Marlston Rd RG18 ....79 B3
Marmion Rd RG9 ....35 C4
Marquis Pl RG1 ....86 C4
Marriott Cl TW14 ....71 B1
Mars Cl RG41 ....115 C3
Marsack St RG4 ....59 B1
Marsh Ct RG30 ....85 B4
Marsh La
  Hungerford RG17 ....100 A3
  Newbury RG14 ....105 A2
  Taplow SL6 ....40 C3
Marsh Rd RG18 ....106 C1

Marshall Cl Frimley GU16 ..152 B1
 Purley on T RG8 ....57 B2
Marshall Ho 4 RG30 ....85 A4
Marshall Rd GU47 ....150 B3
Marshalls Ct RG14 ....104 B3
Marsham Ho RG42 ....91 A1
Marshaw Ct RG2 ....86 B2
Marshfield SL3 ....68 B3
Marshgate Trad Est SL6 ....41 A4
Marshland Sq RG4 ....59 A3
Marshwood Rd GU18 ....153 B4
Marston Dr RG14 ....105 B3
Marston Way SL5 ....119 C4
Martel Cl GU15 ....152 B4
Marten Pl RG31 ....57 C2
Martin Cl Windsor SL4 ......66 B3
 Woodley RG5 ....87 C3
Martin Rd Maidenhead SL6 ..39 C4
 Slough SL1 ....42 C2
Martin Way GU16 ....151 C1
Martin's Heron Sta
 RG12 ....118 C3
Martin's Plain SL2 ....22 C2
Martindale Ave GU15 ......152 B2
Martineau La RG10 ....88 C4
Martins Cl GU17 ....150 B2
Martins Dr RG41 ....116 A4
Martins La RG12 ....118 C3
Martins The RG19 ....106 C1
Marunden Gn SL2 ....21 C1
Mary Drew Almshouse
 The TW20 ....95 B1
Mary Hare Gram Sch for
 the Deaf The RG18 ....77 C2
Mary Mead RG42 ....91 B1
Mary Morgan Ct SL2 ....42 B4
Maryland RG40 ....141 C4
Maryside SL3 ....43 C2
Mascoll Path SL2 ....21 C1
Masefield Gdns RG45 .....143 A2
Masefield Rd RG18 ....106 B2
Masefield Way TW19 ....97 C4
Mason Cl GU46 ....149 C3
Mason Ct Ball Hill RG20 ...129 C1
 6 Reading RG1 ....85 C4
Mason Pl GU47 ....149 C4
Mason St RG1 ....85 C4
Mason's Ct SL1 ....41 C3
Masonic Hall Rd KT16 .....123 C2
Masons Rd SL1 ....41 C3
Master Cl RG5 ....88 A4
Mathisen Way SL3 ....69 C3
Matlock Rd RG4 ....58 C2
Matson Dr RG9 ....15 C1
Matthew Arnold Cl TW18 ...97 B1
Matthew Arnold Sch The
 TW18 ....97 B1
Matthews Chase RG42 ......90 C1
Matthews Ct RG19 ....106 A2
Matthews Ct SL5 ....120 B3
Matthews La TW18 ....96 C2
Matthews Rd GU15 ....151 B4
Matthewsgreen Rd
 RG41 ....116 A4
Maudsley Ho SL1 ....40 A4
Maultway Cl GU15 ....152 A4
Maultway Cres GU15 ......152 A4
Maultway N GU15 ....145 A1
Maultway The
 GU15, GU16 ....152 B3
Mawbray Cl RG6 ....87 B1
Maxine Cl GU47 ....143 A4
Maxwell Cl RG5 ....87 C4
Maxwell Rd TW15 ....98 B1
May Cl 2 GU47 ....150 B4
May Fields RG41 ....115 A4
May Pk RG31 ....84 C2
May Tree Cl SL7 ....1 B3
May's La RG7 ....136 A4
Maybrick Cl GU47 ....142 C1
Maybury Cl SL1 ....41 B4
Mayfair RG30 ....84 B4
Mayfair Dr RG14 ....104 C1
Mayfield Ave RG41 ....84 A2
Mayfield Cl TW15 ....98 A1
Mayfield Cotts RG20 ....31 B2
Mayfield Dr RG4 ....59 B2
Mayfield Gdns TW18 ....96 C1
Mayfield Rd
 Camberley GU15 ....151 A1
 Wooburn Green HP10 ......3 C3
Mayflower Cl 16 RG1 ....86 A4
Mayflower Dr GU46 ....149 A4
Mayflower Way SL2 ....22 B4
Maynard Ct RG18 ....106 B3
Maynard Ct Staines TW18 ..97 A2
 Windsor SL4 ....67 A3
Mayors La RG14 ....105 A1
Mayow Rd RG19 ....106 C1
Maypole Rd SL6 ....41 A4
Mays Cl RG6 ....87 A3
Mays La RG6 ....87 A3
Mays Rd RG40 ....116 C3
Maywood Dr GU15 ....152 A4
McCarthy Way RG40 ......141 C4
McCraes Wlk RG10 ....36 B1
Mckay Trad Est SL3 ....69 C3
McNair Cl RG6 ....87 A1
Meachen Ct RG40 ....116 B3
Mead Ave SL3 ....44 A2
Mead Cl Egham TW20 ......96 A1
 7 Marlow SL7 ....1 C2
 Peasemore RG20 ....50 B4
 Reading RG31 ....84 A3
 Slough SL3 ....44 A2

Mead Ct TW20 ....96 B1
Mead Haze SL6 ....20 B1
Mead La Chertsey KT16 ...124 B1
 Lower Basildon RG8 ....34 C1
 Upper Basildon RG8 ....55 B3
Mead The RG17 ....48 A2
Mead Way SL1 ....41 B4
Mead Wlk SL3 ....44 A2
Meade Ct GU19 ....145 C2
Meadfield Ave SL3 ....44 A2
Meadfield Rd SL3 ....44 A2
Meadhurst Pk TW16 ....98 C1
Meadhurst Rd KT16 ......124 A1
Meadhurst Sports Club
 TW16 ....98 C2
Meadow Bank 16 SL8 ....3 A2
Meadow Cl
 Blackwater GU17 ....150 B2
 Compton RG20 ....31 C3
 Goring RG8 ....34 B3
 Marlow SL7 ....1 C1
 Moulsford OX10 ....13 C2
 Old Windsor SL4 ....68 A1
 Thatcham RG18 ....106 B2
Meadow Cotts GU24 .....153 C4
Meadow Ct TW18 ....96 C3
Meadow Gdns TW18 ....96 B2
Meadow La SL4 ....67 B4
Meadow Rd Ashford TW15 ..98 B2
 Earley RG6 ....87 B2
 Henley-on-T RG9 ....15 C1
 Newbury RG14 ....130 C4
 Reading RG1 ....58 C1
 Slough SL3 ....43 C2
 Wentworth GU25 ....121 C3
 Wokingham RG41 ....116 A3
Meadow Vale Prim Sch
 Binfield RG42 ....90 C1
 Bracknell RG42 ....117 C4
Meadow View
 Marlow Bottom SL7 ....1 C3
 Winnersh RG41 ....88 B2
Meadow View La SL6 ......64 C4
Meadow Way
 Blackwater GU17 ....150 B3
 Bracknell RG42 ....91 A1
 Dorney SL4 ....40 C2
 Holyport SL6 ....65 B3
 Old Windsor SL4 ....68 A1
 Theale RG7 ....83 B2
 West End GU24 ....153 B3
 Wokingham RG41 ....116 A3
Meadow Wlk RG41 ....116 A3
Meadowbank Rd GU18 ...146 B1
Meadowbrook SL3 ....69 C3
Meadowbrook
 Montessori Sch RG42 ....91 C2
Meadowcroft Rd RG2 ....113 B4
Meadowlea Cl UB7 ....70 B4
Meadows Cty Comb Sch
 The HP10 ....3 C4
Meadows The
 Flackwell Heath HP10 ......3 A4
 Sandhurst GU47 ....150 C3
Meadowside RG31 ....57 A1
Meadowside Rd RG8 ....56 B3
Meadowsweet Cl RG18 ...106 C2
Meadowview TW19 ....69 C1
Meads The 4 SL4 ....67 A3
Meadway Ashford TW15 ...98 A2
 Frimley GU16 ....151 C1
 Staines TW18 ....97 A1
Meadway Cl TW18 ....97 A1
Meadway Comp Sch
 RG30 ....84 C4
Meadway Prec RG30 ....85 A3
Meadway The RG30 ....84 C4
Meare Est HP10 ....3 C4
Mearings The RG30 ....111 C3
Measham Way RG6 ....87 B1
Meashill Way OX11 ....9 C4
Meavy Gdns RG2 ....86 A1
Medallion Pl SL6 ....40 A4
Mede Cl TW19 ....95 B4
Mede Ct TW18 ....96 C3
Medina Cl RG41 ....115 C4
Medlake Rd TW20 ....96 B1
Medlar Dr GU17 ....150 C2
Medway Cl
 Thatcham RG18 ....106 A3
 Wokingham RG41 ....115 C4
Medway Ct RG30 ....85 B3
Melbourne Ave Slough SL1 .42 B4
 Winnersh RG41 ....88 B1
Melbury Cl KT16 ....124 A1
Meldreth Way RG6 ....87 B1
Meldrum Ct RG14 ....130 B3
Melford Gn RG4 ....59 C3
Melksham Cl RG6 ....113 C4
Melling Cl RG6 ....87 C2
Mellor Wlk 27 RG1 ....86 A3
Melody Ct RG41 ....88 B2
Melrose RG12 ....118 A1
Melrose Ave RG6 ....87 A3
Melrose Gdns RG2 ....114 C1
Melton Cl SL6 ....36 C3
Melville Ave GU16 ....151 C1
Membury Wlk RG12 .....118 C3
Memorial Ave RG9 ....35 C1
Mendip Cl Charvil RG10 ....61 A2
 Harlington UB3 ....71 B4
 Slough SL3 ....44 A1
Mendip Dr RG31 ....84 A3
Mendip Rd RG12 ....118 C2
Menpes Rd RG31 ....57 B2
Meon Cl RG26 ....135 A1
Merchants Pl RG1 ....86 A4
Mercia SL6 ....39 B2

Mercian Way SL1 ....41 B3
Mercury Ave RG41 ....115 C3
Mere Cl SL7 ....1 C1
Mere Rd
 Shepperton TW17 ....125 A2
 Slough SL1 ....42 C2
Mereoak La RG7 ....112 C2
Meridian Ct SL5 ....120 A1
Merlewood RG12 ....118 B2
Merlin Cl SL3 ....69 A4
Merlin Clove RG42 ....92 A1
Merlin Ct Frimley GU16 ...151 B1
 Maidenhead SL6 ....39 A4
Mermaid Cl RG41 ....88 C1
Merrifield Cl RG6 ....114 B4
Merron Cl SL6 ....149 B3
Merryhill Green Hill RG41 .88 B2
Merryhill Rd RG42 ....118 A4
Merryman Dr RG45 ......143 A4
Merryweather Cl RG40 ...115 C1
Merrywood Pk GU15 .....151 C2
Mersey Way RG18 ....106 A3
Merthyr Vale RG4 ....59 A3
Merton Cl Maidenhead SL6 .39 B2
 Sandhurst GU47 ....143 C1
Merton Rd SL1 ....43 A2
Merton Rd N RG2 ....86 A1
Merton Rd S RG2 ....86 A1
Mervyn Rd TW17 ....125 B1
Merwin Way SL4 ....66 B2
Metcalf Rd TW15 ....98 A2
Meteor Ct RG5 ....88 A4
Meteorological Off (HQ)
 RG12 ....118 B4
Meteorological Office
 Coll RG2 ....113 B4
Metro Ctr The RG41 ....89 A1
Mews The Newbury RG14 .104 C1
 Reading RG1 ....86 C3
 Swallowfield RG7 ....140 B4
Mey Cl RG31 ....84 B3
Meyrick Dr RG14 ....130 B3
Mezel Hill Cotts SL4 ....94 B2
Michael Rd SL6 ....39 B3
Michaelmas Cl GU46 ....149 B2
Micheldever Way RG12 ...118 C2
Michelet Cl GU18 ....146 A1
Micklands Prim Sch RG4 ..59 B2
Micklands Rd RG4 ....59 C2
Mickle Hill GU47 ....143 A4
Micro Ctr The RG2 ....86 A1
Midcroft SL2 ....22 A1
Middle Cl Frimley GU15 ...152 B3
 Newbury RG14 ....130 B4
Middle Gn Slough SL3 .....43 C3
 Staines TW19 ....97 B1
Middle Gordon Rd GU15 .151 B3
Middle Hill TW20 ....95 B2
Middle Walk SL1 ....21 B1
Middlefields RG10 ....61 C3
Middlegreen Rd SL3 ....43 B3
Middlegreen Trad Est
 SL3 ....43 B2
Middlemoor Rd GU16 ....151 C1
Middleton Ct RG14 ....105 C3
Middleton Rd GU15 ......151 C1
Middletons Cl RG17 ......100 C4
Midsummer Mdw RG4 .....58 C2
Midway Ave
 Chertsey KT16 ....124 A3
 Thorpe TW20 ....123 A3
Midway Ct TW18 ....97 A3
Midwinter Ct RG30 ....84 C3
Milbanke Ct RG12 ....117 C4
Milbanke Way RG12 .....117 C4
Mildenhall Cl RG6 ....87 B3
Mildenhall Rd SL1 ....42 C4
Mile Elm SL7 ....2 A2
Miles Pl GU18 ....152 C4
Miles Way RG5 ....88 A4
Milestone Ave
 Charvil RG10 ....61 A3
 Sonning RG4 ....60 C2
Milestone Cres RG10 ......61 A2
Milestone View Ct RG4 ....59 C2
Milestone Way RG4 ....59 B3
Milford Ct SL1 ....43 A2
Milford Rd RG1 ....58 C1
Milkhouse Rd RG20 ......103 B2
Mill Bank RG17 ....102 A2
Mill Cl Bagshot GU19 .....145 B2
 Wokingham RG41 ....116 A4
Mill Ct SL3 ....69 B2
Mill End RG9 ....16 B4
Mill Farm Ave TW16 ....98 C1
Mill Field GU19 ....145 B2
Mill Gn Binfield RG42 ......90 C1
 Caversham RG4 ....59 B1
Mill Hall Sch RG20 ....131 B4
Mill House La KT16 ......123 A3
Mill La Ascot SL5 ....121 A4
 Bracknell RG12 ....117 C3
 Cookham SL6 ....20 B4
 Earley RG6 ....87 C2
 Earley, Sindlesham RG6 ...87 C1
 Henley-on-T RG9 ....35 C4
 Horton SL3 ....69 B2
 Hurley SL6 ....17 C2
 Lambourn RG17 ....25 B1
 Newbury RG14 ....105 A2
 Padworth RG7 ....109 B1
 Reading RG1 ....86 A4
 Shiplake RG9 ....36 A1
 Taplow SL6 ....40 B4
 Thorpe TW20 ....123 B3
 Windsor SL4 ....67 A4

Mill La continued
 Winnersh RG41 ....87 C1
 Yateley GU46 ....149 B4
Mill Mead TW18 ....96 C2
Mill Pl SL3 ....68 B3
Mill Pond Rd GU20 ......146 A3
Mill Rd
 Burghfield Common RG30 ..84 C1
 Caversham RG4 ....59 B1
 Goring RG8 ....34 B4
 Marlow SL7 ....1 C1
 Shiplake RG9 ....36 A2
Mill Reef Cl RG19 ....105 C2
Mill Ride SL5 ....119 B4
Mill St Colnbrook SL3 ......69 B4
 Slough SL2 ....42 C3
Millbank SL7 ....1 C1
Millbank Cres RG5 ....87 C3
Millboard Rd SL8 ....3 A2
Millbridge Rd GU46 ......149 A4
Millbrook Way SL3 ....69 C3
Milldown Ave RG8 ....34 B4
Milldown Rd RG8 ....34 B4
Miller's Ct TW20 ....96 B1
Miller's La SL4 ....68 A1
Millers Cl Goring RG8 ......34 C4
 Staines TW18 ....97 A2
Millers Ct RG4 ....59 B1
Millers Field RG17 ....48 A2
Millers Gr RG31 ....84 C2
Milley La RG10 ....62 A4
Milley Rd RG10 ....62 C3
Millfield Charlton TW16 ...125 B4
 Lambourn RG17 ....25 A1
Millgreen La RG19 ....132 C1
Millholme Wlk GU15 .....152 B2
Millins Cl GU47 ....143 C1
Millmead RG41 ....116 A4
Millmere GU46 ....149 B4
Mills Spur SL4 ....95 A4
Millside SL8 ....3 B2
Millstream Ho RG14 .....105 B2
Millstream La SL1 ....41 C3
Millstream Way HP10 ......3 C4
Millworth La RG2 ....113 C2
Milman Cl RG12 ....119 A4
Milman Rd RG2 ....86 A3
Milner Rd SL1 ....41 A4
Milsom Ct RG2 ....113 C3
Milton Cl Bracknell RG12 ..118 A2
 Henley-on-T RG9 ....15 B1
 Horton SL3 ....69 A2
Milton Ct RG40 ....116 A4
Milton Dr Littleton TW17 ..124 C3
 Wokingham RG40 ....116 A4
Milton Gdns
 Stanwell TW19 ....97 C4
 Wokingham RG40 ....116 A3
Milton Rd Earley RG6 ......87 A4
 Egham TW20 ....95 C2
 Slough SL2 ....22 B1
 Wokingham RG40, RG41 ..116 A4
Milton Way RG10 ....61 C3
Milverton Cl SL6 ....39 A2
Milward Gdns RG12 .....117 B4
Mina Ave SL3 ....43 B2
Minchin Gn RG42 ....90 B2
Minden Cl RG41 ....115 C3
Minerva Cl TW19 ....70 A1
Ministry Rd RG19 ....132 A3
Minley Rd GU17 ....149 C1
Minniecroft Rd SL1 ....21 A1
Minorca Ave GU16 ......152 C1
Minorca Rd GU16 ....152 C1
Minstead Cl RG12 ....118 C3
Minstead Dr GU46 ......149 B3
Minster Ct
 Camberley GU15 ....151 B4
 Camberley, York
 Town GU15 ....150 C2
Minster St RG1 ....86 A4
Minster Way SL3 ....43 C2
Minsterley Ave
 TW16, TW17 ....125 C3
Mint Cl RG6 ....86 C1
Minter Ct RG26 ....134 C1
Minton Cl RG30 ....84 C4
Minton Rise SL6 ....41 A4
Mirador Cres SL2 ....43 B3
Mire La RG10 ....62 B2
Misbourne Ct SL3 ....44 A1
Missenden Cl TW14 ....98 C4
Missenden Gdns SL1 ......41 A4
Mistletoe Rd GU46 ......149 B2
Mitcham Cl RG2 ....86 B2
Mitcham Rd GU15 ....145 A1
Mitchell Cl SL1 ....42 A2
Mitchell Way RG5 ....88 A4
Mitford Cl RG2 ....113 B4
Mitre Cl TW17 ....125 B2
Mitre Pl RG42 ....91 A1
Mixnams La KT16 ....124 A3
Moat Dr SL2 ....43 B4
Modbury Gdns RG2 ....86 B1
Moffatts Cl GU47 ....150 A4
Moffy Hill SL6 ....19 C1
Mohawk Way RG5 ....88 A4
Mole Rd RG41 ....114 C3
Moles Cl RG40 ....116 B3
Mollison Cl RG5 ....88 A4
Molly Millar Bridge
 RG41 ....116 A2
Molly Millar's La RG41 ...116 A2
Molly Millars Cl RG40 ....116 A2
Molyneux Rd GU20 ......146 B2
Molyns Mews 7 SL1 ....41 C3
Monarch Cl TW14 ....98 C4
Monck Ct 7 RG30 ....85 B3

Mondial Way UB3 ....71 E
Moneyrow Gn SL6 ....65 A
Monkey Island La
 Holyport SL6 ....65 C
 Maidenhead SL6 ....40 C
Monkley Ct 5 RG4 ....59 B
Monks Cl SL5 ....120 A
Monks Dr SL5 ....120 A
Monks Hollow SL7 ....1 C
Monks La RG14 ....130 C
Monks Rd
 Virginia Water GU25 .....122 B
 Windsor SL4 ....66 B
Monks Way
 Harmondsworth UB7 ....70 C
 Reading RG30 ....85 B
 Staines TW18 ....97 B
Monks Wlk SL5 ....120 A
Monksbarn RG2 ....86 B
Monksfield Way SL2 ....22 A
Monkshood Cl RG40 ....116 C
Monkswood Cl RG14 ....130 C
Monkswood Ct 6 SL7 ......1 C
Monktons La RG7 ....137 B
Monmouth Ct 8 RG1 ....59 A
Mons Cl RG41 ....115 C
Mons Wlk TW20 ....96 B
Monsell Gdns TW18 ....96 C
Montacute Dr RG19 ......106 C
Montagu Rd SL3 ....68 A
Montague Cl
 Camberley GU15 ....151 A
 Lightwater GU18 ....146 A
 Wokingham RG40 ....116 C
Montague Ho (Coll)
 RG40 ....116 B
Montague Rd SL1 ....42 C
Montague St
 Caversham RG4 ....59 B
 Reading RG1 ....86 B
Montague Terr RG14 .....131 A
Monteagle La
 Yateley GU46 ....149 A
 Yateley GU46 ....149 B
Montem Inf Sch The SL1 ..42 A
Montem La SL1 ....42 B
Montgomery Cl GU47 ....150 A
Montgomery Dr RG7 .....113 A
Montgomery Pl SL2 ....43 B
Montgomery Rd RG14 ...130 C
Montpelier Ct SL4 ....67 B
Montpelier Dr RG4 ....59 B
Montrose Ave Datchet SL3 .68 B
 Slough SL1 ....42 A
Montrose Cl Ashford TW15 .98 B
 Frimley GU16 ....151 C
Montrose Dr SL6 ....39 A
Montrose Ho 2 RG1 ....86 A
Montrose Rd TW14 ....71 B
Montrose Way SL3 ....68 B
Montrose Wlk RG31 ....84 C
Monument Cl RG14 ......130 B
Monycrower Dr SL6 ....39 C
Moor Cl Sandhurst GU47 ..143 C
 Wokingham RG40 ....141 C
Moor Copse Cl RG6 ....87 A
Moor End SL6 ....40 B
Moor Furlong SL1 ....41 C
Moor La
 Harmondsworth UB7 ....70 A
 Maidenhead SL6 ....19 C
 Newbury RG14 ....104 C
 Staines TW18, TW19 ....96 B
Moor Park Ho RG12 ......117 C
Moor Pl GU20 ....146 A
Moorbridge Rd SL6 ....40 A
Moordale Ave RG42 ....90 C
Moore Cl SL1 ....42 A
Moore Grove Cres TW20 ..95 C
Moores Gn RG40 ....116 C
Moores La SL4 ....41 C
Moores Pl RG17 ....100 B
Moorfield Terr SL6 ....40 A
Moorfields Cl TW18 ......123 C
Moorhayes Dr TW18 .....124 B
Moorhen Dr RG6 ....87 A
Moorings The SL4 ....95 B
Moorland Rd UB7 ....70 B
Moorlands Dr SL6 ....38 C
Moorlands Pl GU15 ......151 A
Moorlands Prim Sch
 RG30 ....84 C
Moorlands Rd GU15 .....151 A
Moormede Cres TW18 .....96 C
Moors The Pangbourne RG8 .56 B
 Thatcham RG19 ....106 B
Moorside HP10 ....3 C
Moorside Cl
 Farnborough (Hants) GU14 .151 A
 Maidenhead SL6 ....19 C
Moorstown Ct 7 SL1 ......42 C
Moray Ave GU15 ....150 B
Moray Dr SL2 ....43 A
Mordaunt Dr RG45 ......143 A
Morden Cl RG12 ....118 C
Moreau Wlk SL3 ....43 C
Morecambe Ave RG4 ......58 C
Moreland Ave SL3 ....69 B
Moreland Cl SL3 ....69 B
Moreleigh Cl RG2 ....113 A
Morella Cl GU25 ....122 B
Morello Dr SL3 ....43 C
Moreton Ct RG1 ....86 B
Moreton Way SL1 ....41 B
Morgan Ct TW15 ....98 A
Morgan Rd RG1 ....86 B
Moriston Cl RG30 ....85 A
Morlais RG4 ....59 A

orlands Ave RG30 . . . . . . .85 A3
orley Cl Slough SL3 . . . . . . .43 C2
ateley GU46 . . . . .149 A3
orley Ct SL5 . . . . .120 C2
orley Pl RG17 . . . . .100 B3
ornington Ave RG40 . . . .141 C4
ornington Cl RG26 . . . . .134 C1
ornington Rd TW15 . . . . . .98 B2
orpeth Cl RG2 . . . . .86 B2
orrell Ct TW18 . . . . .97 A2
orrice Cl SL3 . . . . .44 A1
orris Ct SL4 . . . . .66 C3
orris Pl 5 SL7 . . . . .1 B1
orriss Ct 14 RG1 . . . . .86 B4
ortaine Rd TW15 . . . . .97 B3
ortimer Cl RG2 . . . . .113 B4
ortimer La RG7 . . . . .137 B4
ortimer Rd SL3 . . . . .43 B2
ortimer Sta RG7 . . . . . . .137 C3
OX10 . . . . .14 A3
oulsham Copse La
GU46 . . . . .149 A4
oulsham La GU46 . . . . .149 A4
oundsfield Way SL1 . . . . .41 C2
ount Cl
Farnham Common SL2 . . . .22 B4
Newbury RG14 . . . . .105 A1
ount Cl The GU25 . . . . . .122 B2
ount Felix KT12 . . . . .54 C3
ount La Bracknell RG12 . .118 B4
Chaddleworth RG20 . . . . . .49 A4
ount Lee TW20 . . . . .95 C2
ount Pleasant
Bracknell RG12 . . . . .118 B3
Reading RG1 . . . . .86 A3
Sandhurst GU47 . . . . .143 A1
Tadley RG26 . . . . .135 A1
Wokingham RG41 . . . . . . .115 C4
ount Pleasant Cl GU18 .146 A1
ount Pleasant Cotts
12 Bourne End SL8 . . . . . . .3 A2
Englefield Green TW20 . . . .95 B1
ount Pleasant Gr RG1 . . .86 A3
ount Rd RG18 . . . . .106 C2
ount St RG2 . . . . .86 A3
ount The Caversham RG4 . .58 C2
Reading RG1 . . . . .86 B3
Wentworth GU25 . . . . . . .122 B2
ount View RG9 . . . . .15 B1
ount View Ct RG9 . . . . . . .15 B1
ountain Ash SL7 . . . . .1 B3
ountbatten Cl
Newbury RG14 . . . . .105 B3
6 Slough SL1 . . . . .43 A2
ountbatten Rise GU47 . .142 C1
ountbatten Sq 8 SL4 . . . .67 B3
ountfield RG8 . . . . .34 B4
ounts Hill SL4, SL5 . . . . . .93 B2
ountsfield Cl TW19 . . . . . .70 A1
owbray Cres TW20 . . . . . .96 A1
owbray Dr RG30 . . . . .85 A4
ower Rd RG40 . . . . .116 C4
oyleen Rise SL7 . . . . .1 B1
uckhatch La TW20 . . . . .123 A4
ud La
Finchampstead RG27 . . . .140 C1
Peasemore RG20 . . . . .50 B3
uirfield Cl RG11 . . . . .86 B4
uirfield Ho RG12 . . . . . .117 C2
ulberry Ave TW19 . . . . . .97 C4
ulberry Bsns Pk RG41 . .116 A2
ulberry Cl
Crowthorne RG45 . . . . . . .143 B2
1 Sandhurst GU47 . . . . . .150 A4
Woodley RG5 . . . . .87 C4
ulberry Ct
1 Bracknell RG12 . . . . . .118 C2
Newbury RG14 . . . . .104 C2
Wokingham RG40 . . . . . . .116 B3
ulberry Dr SL3 . . . . .43 C1
ulberry Ho RG42 . . . . . . .91 A1
ulberry Trees TW17 . . . .125 B1
ulberry Way RG7 . . . . . . .83 C2
ulberry Wlk SL6 . . . . .39 B4
ulfords Hill RG26 . . . . . .135 A1
ulgrave Rd GU16 . . . . . . .151 C1
ullens Rd TW19 . . . . .96 B2
ullion Ct 22 RG1 . . . . .85 C4
ulroy Dr SL3 . . . . .152 A3
umbery Hill RG10 . . . . . . .36 C1
uncaster Cl TW15 . . . . . . .98 A2
uncaster Rd TW15 . . . . . .98 A2
unces Rd SL7 . . . . .1 B3
unday Ct RG42 . . . . .90 C1
undaydean La SL7 . . . . . . .1 A2
undesley St RG1 . . . . .86 A3
unkle Marsh RG19 . . . . .107 A2
unnings Dr GU47 . . . . . .150 C3
unro Ave RG5 . . . . .87 C2
urdoch Cl TW18 . . . . .97 A2
urdoch Rd RG40 . . . . . . .116 A3
urray Ct SL5 . . . . .120 B2
urray Ho RG41 . . . . .116 A3
urray Rd RG41 . . . . .116 A3
urrellhill La RG42 . . . . . .117 B4
urrells La GU15 . . . . .151 A4
urrin Rd SL6 . . . . .39 B4
us of Berkshire
Aviation The SL6 . . . . .88 A3
us of English Rural Life
RG2 . . . . .86 C2
us of Reading RG1 . . . . . .86 A4

Mushroom Castle La
RG42 . . . . .92 A1
Mustard La RG4 . . . . .60 C1
Mustard Mill Rd TW18 . . . .96 C2
Muswell Cl RG7 . . . . .83 C2
Mutton Oaks RG12 . . . . . .117 B4
Myers Way GU16 . . . . .152 B1
Mylne Sq RG40 . . . . .116 B3
Mylum Cl RG2 . . . . .113 B3
Myrke The SL3 . . . . .42 C1
Myrtle Ave TW14 . . . . .71 C1
Myrtle Cl
Burghfield Common RG7 . .111 A2
Lightwater GU18 . . . . .153 A4
Poyle SL3 . . . . .69 C3
Purley on T RG31 . . . . .57 B2
Myrtle Cres SL2 . . . . .42 C3
Myrtle Dr GU17 . . . . .150 B3
Myton Wlk RG7 . . . . .83 C2

N

Nabbs Hill Cl RG31 . . . . . .84 B3
Nairn Cl GU16 . . . . .151 C1
Nalderhill Rd RG20 . . . . .103 A3
Napier Cl RG45 . . . . .143 B3
Napier Dr GU15 . . . . .152 A4
Napier Lodge TW15 . . . . . .98 B1
Napier Rd Ashford TW15 . .98 B1
Crowthorne RG45 . . . . . . .143 B2
Harmondsworth TW6 . . . . .70 B3
Maidenhead SL6 . . . . .39 A4
Reading RG1 . . . . .86 B4
Napier Wlk TW15 . . . . .98 B1
Napper Cl SL5 . . . . .119 B4
Narromine Dr RG31 . . . . . .84 C2
Naseby RG12 . . . . .118 A1
Naseby Rise RG14 . . . . . .105 B3
Nash Cl RG6 . . . . .87 A2
Nash Gdns SL5 . . . . .119 C4
Nash Grove La RG40 . . . .115 C1
Nash Pk RG42 . . . . .90 A1
Nash Rd SL3 . . . . .44 A1
Nashdom La SL1 . . . . .21 A3
Natalie Cl TW14 . . . . .98 B4
Nathan Ct 20 RG1 . . . . . . .85 C4
Naylors The RG7 . . . . . . .139 B3
Neath Gdns RG30 . . . . . . .84 C4
Needham Cl SL4 . . . . .66 C3
Neil Cl TW15 . . . . .98 B2
Nell Gwynn Ave TW17 . . .125 B2
Nell Gwynne Ave SL5 . . .120 B3
Nell Gwynne Cl SL5 . . . .120 B3
Nelson Cl Bracknell RG12 .118 C4
East Bedfont TW14 . . . . . .98 C4
Slough SL3 . . . . .43 B1
Nelson Ct KT16 . . . . .124 A1
Nelson Rd Ashford TW15 . .97 C2
Caversham RG4 . . . . .59 B1
Harmondsworth TW6 . . . . .70 C3
Windsor SL4 . . . . .66 C2
Nelson Terr 22 RG1 . . . . . .86 A3
Nelson Way GU15 . . . . . .150 C2
Nelson's La RG10 . . . . .89 A3
Nene Rd TW6, UB7 . . . . . . .71 A3
Neptune Cl RG41 . . . . . . .115 C3
Neptune Rd TW6 . . . . .71 B3
Neptune Way SL1 . . . . . . .41 C2
Netherton RG12 . . . . .118 A3
Netley Cl RG4 . . . . .59 C3
Nettlecombe RG12 . . . . . .118 B2
Nettleton Rd TW6 . . . . . . .71 A3
Neve Ho SL6 . . . . .39 C4
Nevelle Cl RG42 . . . . .117 B4
Neville Cl Stoke Poges SL2 .22 C3
Waltham St Lawrence RG10 .62 C3
Neville Ct SL1 . . . . .21 B1
Neville Dr RG19 . . . . .106 C2
Nevis Rd RG31 . . . . .57 B2
New Bath Rd RG10 . . . . . . .61 B3
New Bldgs RG7 . . . . .81 B2
New Bright St 6 RG1 . . . . .86 A3
New Christ Church
CE Prim Sch RG1 . . . . .86 A3
New Cl RG9 . . . . .16 A4
New Ct SL7 . . . . .1 B1
New Forest Ride RG12 . . .118 C2
New Greenham Pk RG19 .131 C3
New Hill RG8 . . . . .57 B3
New Lane Hill RG30 . . . . . .84 C3
New Mdw SL5 . . . . .119 B4
New Mile Rd SL5 . . . . . . .120 B4
New Mill La RG27 . . . . . . .140 C1
New Mill Rd RG27 . . . . . . .140 C1
New Par TW15 . . . . .97 C2
New Park Rd TW15 . . . . . .98 B2
New Rd Bagshot GU19 . . .145 C2
Blackwater GU17 . . . . . . .150 C2
Bourne End SL8 . . . . .3 A2
Bracknell RG12 . . . . .118 B4
Burghfield Common RG7 . .111 C1
Cookham SL6 . . . . .19 C4
Crowthorne RG45 . . . . . . .143 B4
Datchet SL3 . . . . .68 B3
East Bedfont TW14 . . . . . .71 B1
Egham TW18 . . . . .96 B1
Harlington UB3 . . . . .71 B4
Holyport SL6 . . . . .65 A4
Hurley SL6 . . . . .17 C2
Littleton TW17 . . . . .125 C1
Marlow Bottom SL7 . . . . . .1 C3
Newbury RG14 . . . . .105 B1
North Ascot SL5 . . . . .92 C1
Reading RG1 . . . . .86 B3
Sandhurst GU47 . . . . .150 A4
Shiplake RG9 . . . . .36 A2
Slough SL3 . . . . .44 A1

New Rd continued
Twyford RG10 . . . . .61 B4
Twyford, Ruscombe RG10 . .61 C3
Windlesham GU19,GU20 . .146 A2
Wokingham RG41 . . . . . . .115 A4
New Road Hill RG7 . . . . . .108 A2
New Scotland Hill
Prim Sch GU47 . . . . .143 A1
New Sq East Bedfont TW14 .98 B4
Slough SL1 . . . . .42 C2
New St Beech Hill RG7 . . .138 A1
Henley-on-T RG9 . . . . .15 C1
Staines TW18 . . . . .97 A2
New Town Prim Sch RG1 . .86 B4
New Way RG7 . . . . .82 A1
New Wickham La TW20 . . .96 A1
New Wokingham Rd
RG45 . . . . .143 A3
New Zealand Ave KT12 . . .125 C1
Newall Rd TW6 . . . . .71 B3
Newalls Rise RG10 . . . . . . .36 C1
Newark Rd RG20 . . . . .146 A3
Newark St RG1 . . . . .86 A3
Newberry Cres SL4 . . . . . . .66 B3
Newbery Cl RG31 . . . . .57 B1
Newbery Way SL1 . . . . . . .42 B2
Newbold Coll RG42 . . . . . . .90 B1
Newbold Rd RG14 . . . . . .104 B3
Newbold Sch RG42 . . . . . .90 B1
Newbolt Cl RG18 . . . . . . .106 B3
Newbury Cl RG18 . . . . .61 A2
Newbury Coll RG14 . . . . .104 C2
Newbury District Hospl
RG14 . . . . .104 C1
Newbury District Mus
RG14 . . . . .105 A2
Newbury Dr SL6 . . . . .40 A3
Newbury Hill RG18 . . . . . . .52 C3
Newbury La RG20 . . . . .31 B2
Newbury Rd
Great Shefford RG17 . . . . . .48 A1
Harmondsworth TW6 . . . . .70 C3
Hermitage RG18 . . . . .79 A3
Lambourn RG17 . . . . .25 B1
Newbury Ret Pk RG14 . . .131 A4
Newbury St
Kintbury RG17 . . . . .102 A1
Lambourn RG17 . . . . .25 A1
Newbury Sta RG14 . . . . . .105 A1
Newcastle Rd RG2 . . . . . . .86 B2
Newchurch Rd Slough SL2 .41 C4
Tadley RG26 . . . . .135 A1
Newell Gn RG42 . . . . .91 B3
Newfield Gdns SL7 . . . . . . .1 C1
Newfield Rd SL7 . . . . .1 C1
Newfield Way SL7 . . . . .1 C1
Newhaven Cres TW15 . . . .98 B2
Newhaven Spur SL2 . . . . . .22 A1
Newhurst Gdns RG42 . . . . .91 B2
Newlands Ave RG4 . . . . . . .59 A2
Newlands Cl RG40 . . . . . .149 B3
Newlands Cty Prim Sch
GU46 . . . . .149 B3
Newlands Dr
Maidenhead SL6 . . . . .39 A4
Poyle SL3 . . . . .69 C2
Newlands Rd GU15 . . . . . .151 A1
Newlands Sch SL6 . . . . . . .39 A4
Newlyn Gdns RG2 . . . . . . .86 A1
Newmarket Cl 10 RG6 . . . .87 B1
Newnham Cl SL2 . . . . .22 A1
Newport Cl 11 RG14 . . . . .105 A2
Newport Dr RG42 . . . . .91 A1
Newport Rd
Harmondsworth TW6 . . . . .71 A3
Newbury RG14 . . . . .105 A2
Reading RG1 . . . . .59 A1
Slough SL2 . . . . .21 C1
Newquay Dr RG6 . . . . .87 A1
Newstead Rise RG2 . . . . . .86 C1
Newton Ave RG4 . . . . .59 B3
Newton Cl SL3 . . . . .43 C2
Newton Ct SL4 . . . . .68 A1
Newton La SL4 . . . . .68 A1
Newton Side Orch SL4 . . . .68 A1
Newtonside SL4 . . . . .68 A1
Newtown RG26 . . . . .135 A1
Newtown Gdns RG9 . . . . . .35 C4
Newtown Rd
Henley-on-T RG9 . . . . .35 C4
Marlow SL7 . . . . .1 C1
Newbury RG14 & RG20 . . .131 A3
Sandhurst GU47 . . . . .150 A4
Niagara Rd RG9 . . . . .35 C4
Nicholas Ct 28 RG1 . . . . . .85 C4
Nicholas Gdns SL1 . . . . . . .41 C3
Nicholas Rd RG9 . . . . .35 A4
Nicholls SL4 . . . . .66 B2
Nicholls Wlk SL4 . . . . .66 B2
Nicholson Wlk 3 TW20 . . .96 A2
Nicholsons Ctr 5 SL6 . . . .39 C4
Nicholsons La SL6 . . . . . . .39 C4
Nideggen Cl RG19 . . . . . .106 C2
Nightingale Cres RG12 . . .118 B2
Nightingale Gdns GU47 . .150 A4
Nightingale Ho 3 RG1 . . . .85 C4
Nightingale La
Maidenhead SL6 . . . . .19 B2
Mortimer RG7 . . . . .137 B3
Nightingale Pk SL2 . . . . . .21 C3
Nightingale Pl SL6 . . . . . . .19 C4
Nightingale Rd RG5 . . . . . .87 B2
Nightingale Wlk SL4 . . . . . .67 B2
Nightingales The
Newbury RG14 . . . . .131 A3
Stanwell TW19 . . . . .97 C4
Nimrod Cl RG5 . . . . .88 C4
Nimrod Way RG2 . . . . .86 A3
Nine Acres SL1 . . . . .41 C3

Nine Elms Cl TW14 . . . . . . .98 C4
Nine Mile Ride
Bracknell RG12, RG40 . . . .117 C1
Crowthorne RG40 . . . . . . .142 B4
Nine Mile Ride Prim Sch
RG40 . . . . .141 C3
Nire Rd RG4 . . . . .59 C1
Nixey Cl SL1 . . . . .43 A2
No 4 RG30 . . . . .85 B3
Noakes Hill RG8 . . . . .54 A4
Nobel Dr UB3 . . . . .71 C4
Noble Rd RG5 . . . . .35 C4
Nobles Way TW20 . . . . . . .95 C1
Nodmore RG20 . . . . .49 A4
Norcot Rd RG30 . . . . .84 C4
Norden Cl SL6 . . . . .39 B2
Norden Mdws SL6 . . . . . . .39 B3
Norden Rd SL6 . . . . .39 B3
Nores Rd RG2 . . . . .113 B4
Norfolk Ave SL1 . . . . .42 B4
Norfolk Chase RG42 . . . . . .91 C1
Norfolk Cl RG41 . . . . .115 C3
Norfolk Park Cotts SL6 . . . .39 C4
Norfolk Rd Maidenhead SL6 .39 B4
Reading RG30 . . . . .85 B4
Norland Dr HP10 . . . . .3 C1
Norland Nursery
Training Coll RG17 . . . . . .101 B4
Norlands RG18 . . . . .106 B3
Norlands La TW18, TW20 .123 C4
Norman Ave RG9 . . . . .15 C1
Norman Ct TW18 . . . . .97 A2
Norman Ho RG17 . . . . . . .125 A1
Norman Keep RG42 . . . . .118 C4
Norman Pl RG1 . . . . .59 A1
Norman Rd Ashford TW15 . .98 B1
Caversham RG4 . . . . .59 B2
Normandy Wlk TW20 . . . . .96 B2
Normanhurst TW15 . . . . . .98 A1
Normans The SL2 . . . . .43 A4
Normanstead Rd RG31 . . . .84 B4
Normay Rise RG14 . . . . . .130 B3
Normoor Rd RG7 . . . . .110 C1
Norreys Ave RG40 . . . . . .116 B4
Norreys Dr SL6 . . . . .39 B2
Norris Field RG20 . . . . .49 A4
Norris Ho SL6 . . . . .39 C4
Norris La RG20 . . . . .49 A4
Norris Rd Reading RG6 . . . .87 A3
Staines TW18 . . . . .96 C2
North Burnham Cl SL1 . . . .21 A2
North Cl East Bedfont TW14 .71 B1
Medmenham SL7 . . . . .17 B4
Windsor SL4 . . . . .66 C3
North Cotts SL2 . . . . .22 B1
North Croft HP10 . . . . .3 C3
North Dr Sulhamstead RG7 .110 B4
Wentworth GU25 . . . . . . .121 C2
North End La SL5 . . . . . . .121 A1
North Farm Cl RG17 . . . . . .25 B2
North Fryerne GU46 . . . . .149 B4
North Gn Bracknell RG12 . .118 B4
3 Maidenhead SL6 . . . . . .19 C1
Slough SL1 . . . . .42 C2
North Gr KT16 . . . . .123 C2
North Hatton Rd TW6 . . . . .71 B3
North Links Rd HP10 . . . . . .3 A4
North Lodge Dr SL5 . . . . .119 B4
North Lodge Mews RG30 . .85 B2
North Pk SL0 . . . . .44 B2
North Rd
East Bedfont TW14 . . . . . .71 B1
Maidenhead SL6 . . . . .39 C4
Moulsford OX10 . . . . .13 C2
Winkfield SL5 . . . . .119 A4
North Row SL3 . . . . .23 C4
North St Caversham RG4 . .59 A1
Egham TW20 . . . . .95 C1
Reading RG1 . . . . .85 C4
Winkfield SL4 . . . . .94 A1
North Standen Rd RG17 . .100 A2
North Star La SL6 . . . . .39 B3
North Town Cl 1 SL6 . . . . .19 C1
North Town Mead 4 SL6 . .19 C1
North Town Moor SL6 . . . . .19 C1
North Town Rd SL6 . . . . . .19 C1
North View Gdns 8
RG14 . . . . .105 A2
North Wlk RG18 . . . . .83 C2
Northam Cl RG6 . . . . .87 C2
Northampton Ave SL1 . . . .42 B4
Northampton Cl RG12 . . . .118 C2
Northborough Rd SL2 . . . . .22 A1
Northbourne Cl RG6 . . . . . .87 A1
Northbrook Copse RG12 . .118 C2
Northbrook Pl RG14 . . . . .105 A2
Northbrook Rd RG4 . . . . . .59 B3
Northbrook St RG14 . . . . .105 A2
Northbury Ave RG10 . . . . . .61 C3
Northbury La RG10 . . . . . . .61 C3
Northcott RG12 . . . . .118 A1
Northcourt Ave RG2 . . . . . .86 B2
Northcroft SL1 . . . . .22 A1
Northcroft Cl TW20 . . . . . . .95 A2
Northcroft Gdns TW20 . . . .95 A2
Northcroft La RG14 . . . . . .104 C2
Northcroft Rd TW20 . . . . . .95 A2
Northcroft Terr TW20 . . . .104 C2
Northcroft Villas TW20 . . . .95 A2
Northdean 6 SL6 . . . . .19 C1
Northend Cl HP10 . . . . .3 B4
Northern Ave RG14 . . . . . .105 A3
Northern Hts SL8 . . . . .3 A3
Northern Perimeter Rd
TW6 . . . . .71 B3
Northern Perimeter Road
(W) TW6 . . . . .70 B3
Northern Rd SL2 . . . . .22 B1

Mor–Oak 173

Northern Way RG2 . . . . . . .85 C1
Northern Woods HP10 . . . . .3 B4
Northfield RG42 . . . . .153 A4
Northfield Ave RG9 . . . . . . .36 A2
Northfield Ct
Henley-on-T RG9 . . . . .15 B2
Staines TW18 . . . . .124 A4
Northfield End RG9 . . . . . . .15 B2
Northfield Rd Eton SL4 . . . .41 C1
Maidenhead SL6 . . . . .19 C1
Reading RG1 . . . . .59 A1
Shiplake RG9 . . . . .36 A2
Staines TW18 . . . . .124 A4
Thatcham RG18 . . . . .106 A2
Northfields Chieveley RG20 .51 A2
Lambourn RG17 . . . . .25 A2
Northfields Terr RG17 . . . . .25 C2
Northgate Dr GU15 . . . . . .152 A4
Northington Cl RG12 . . . . .118 C2
Northlands Dr SL1 . . . . . . .21 B2
Northmead Rd SL2 . . . . . . .41 C4
Northolt Rd TW6 . . . . .70 C3
Northrop Rd TW6 . . . . .71 C3
Northumberland Ave RG2 . .86 B2
Northumberland Cl
Bracknell RG42 . . . . .91 C1
Stanwell TW19 . . . . .70 C1
Northumberland Cres
TW14 . . . . .71 C1
Northumbria Rd SL6 . . . . . .39 A2
Northview RG17 . . . . .100 B3
Northview Hts RG17 . . . . .100 B3
Northway Newbury RG14 . .105 A1
Thatcham RG18 . . . . .106 A2
Wokingham RG41 . . . . . . .115 C4
Northwood Dr RG14 . . . . .105 A3
Northwood Rd TW6 . . . . . .70 B3
Norton Cl RG14 . . . . .130 B3
Norton Pk SL5 . . . . .120 B2
Norton Rd Frimley GU15 . .152 B2
Reading RG1 . . . . .86 C4
Swallowfield RG7 . . . . . . .139 B2
Wokingham RG40 . . . . . . .116 B3
Woodley RG5 . . . . .87 C3
Norway Dr SL2 . . . . .43 A4
Norwich Ave GU15 . . . . . .151 C2
Norwich Dr RG5 . . . . .87 B4
Norwich Ho SL6 . . . . .39 C4
Norwood Cres TW6 . . . . . .71 B3
Norwood Rd RG1 . . . . .86 C4
Notley End TW20 . . . . .95 B1
Notton Way RG6 . . . . .113 C4
Nuffield Dr GU47 . . . . .143 C3
Nuffield Rd Barkham,
Arborfield Garrison RG2 . . .140 C4
Barkham, Langley
Common RG2 . . . . .141 A4
Nugee Ct RG45 . . . . .143 A3
Nugent Cl SL7 . . . . .1 C2
Nuneaton RG12 . . . . .118 C2
Nunhide La RG8,RG31 . . . .83 C3
Nuns Acre RG8 . . . . .34 A4
Nuns Wlk GU25 . . . . .122 B2
Nuptown La RG42 . . . . .91 C4
Nursery Cl Hurst RG10 . . . .88 C4
Shiplake RG9 . . . . .36 A2
Nursery Gdns
Purley on T RG8 . . . . .57 A3
Staines TW18 . . . . .97 A1
Sunbury TW16 . . . . .125 C4
Nursery La
North Ascot SL5 . . . . .119 C4
Slough SL3 . . . . .43 B3
Nursery Rd Burnham SL6 . .41 A4
Sunbury TW16 . . . . .125 C4
Nursery Way TW19 . . . . . . .68 B1
Nursery Wlk SL7 . . . . .1 A1
Nut La RG10 . . . . .62 C3
Nutbean La RG7 . . . . .139 C3
Nutbourne Ct TW18 . . . . . .96 C1
Nutfield Ct GU15 . . . . .151 B4
Nuthatch Dr RG6 . . . . .87 A2
Nuthurst RG12 . . . . .118 C2
Nutley Cl GU46 . . . . .149 B3
Nutley Cl GU46 . . . . .149 B3
Nutmeg Cl RG6 . . . . .86 C1
Nutter's La RG2 . . . . .140 A4
Nuttingtons RG20 . . . . .49 C3
Nutty La TW17 . . . . .125 B3

O

O' Bee Gdns RG26 . . . . . .134 C1
Oak Ave Egham TW20 . . . . .96 B1
Sandhurst GU47 . . . . .143 B1
Oak Dr
Burghfield Common RG7 . .110 C1
Newbury RG14 . . . . .104 C1
Woodley RG5 . . . . .88 A3
Oak End Way RG7 . . . . . . .109 B2
Oak Farm CI GU17 . . . . . .150 B3
Oak Gn RG2 . . . . .113 B4
Oak Hill SN8 . . . . .99 B2
Oak La
Englefield Green TW20 . . . .95 A3
Windsor SL4 . . . . .67 A3
Oak Leaf Ct SL5 . . . . .119 B4
Oak Lo 8 TW16 . . . . .98 C1
Oak Lodge RG45 . . . . .143 B4
Oak Stubbs La SL4 . . . . . . .40 C2
Oak Tree Ave SL7 . . . . .1 B2
Oak Tree Cl Marlow SL7 . . .1 A1
Tadley RG26 . . . . .135 A1

Oak Tree Cl *continued*
Wentworth GU25 .....122 B2
Oak Tree Copse RG31 .....57 C2
Oak Tree Dr TW20 .....95 B2
Oak Tree Rd Marlow SL7 .....1 B2
Reading RG31 .....57 C1
Thatcham RG19 .....106 C1
Oak Tree Wlk RG8 .....57 B3
Oak View RG31 .....84 B4
Oak Way
East Bedfont TW14 .....98 C4
Woodley RG5 .....87 B2
Oakdale RG12 .....118 B2
Oakdale Cl RG31 .....84 B4
Oakdale Wlk RG5 .....88 A4
Oakdene
Burghfield Common RG7 .....111 A1
Sunningdale SL5 .....120 C2
Oaken Copse GU15 .....152 B4
Oaken Gr Maidenhead SL6 .....19 B1
Newbury RG14 .....130 B4
Oakengates RG12 .....118 A1
Oakes Ct RG17 .....100 B3
Oakfield RG1 .....86 B3
Oakfield Ave SL1 .....42 A3
Oakfield Ct RG41 .....116 A3
Oakfield Cty Fst Sch SL4 .....67 A3
Oakfield Rd Ashford TW15 .....98 A2
Blackwater GU17 .....150 C2
Bourne End SL8 .....3 A2
Silchester RG26 .....135 C1
Oakfields GU15 .....151 A3
Oakhall Ct TW16 .....98 C2
Oakhall Dr TW16 .....98 C2
Oakham Cl RG31 .....57 B1
Oakhurst SL6 .....20 A2
Oaklands Reading RG1 .....86 B3
Yateley GU46 .....149 B3
Oaklands Cl SL5 .....92 C1
Oaklands Cty Jun Sch
RG45 .....143 A3
Oaklands Dr
North Ascot SL5 .....92 C1
Wokingham RG41 .....116 A3
Wokingham RG41 .....116 A3
Oaklands Inf Sch RG45 .....143 A3
Oaklands La RG45 .....143 A4
Oaklands Pk RG41 .....116 A2
Oaklea Dr RG27 .....140 C1
Oakleigh GU18 .....153 B4
Oakley HP10 .....3 C4
Oakley Cres SL1 .....42 C3
Oakley Green Rd SL4 .....66 A3
Oakley Rd
Camberley GU15 .....151 A2
Caversham RG4 .....58 C2
Newbury RG14 .....105 B2
Oakmede Pl RG42 .....90 B1
Oakridge GU24 .....153 C3
Oaks Rd Shiplake RG9 .....36 A2
Stanwell TW19 .....70 B1
Oaks The Bracknell RG12 .....118 B4
Staines TW18 .....96 C2
Yateley GU46 .....149 B3
Oakside Way RG2 .....113 C4
Oaktree Way GU47 .....143 A1
Oakview RG40 .....116 A2
Oakway Dr GU16 .....151 C1
Oakwood Rd
Bracknell RG12 .....118 C4
Virginia Water GU25 .....122 B2
Windlesham GU20 .....146 C2
Oareborough RG12 .....118 C2
Oast Ct TW18 .....96 C2
Oast House Cl TW19 .....95 C4
Oatlands Dr Slough SL1 .....42 B4
Walton-on-T KT13 .....125 C1
Oatlands Rd RG2 .....113 C3
Oban Ct SL1 .....42 B2
Oban Gdns RG5 .....87 C2
Obelisk Way GU15 .....151 B3
Oberon Way TW17 .....124 C3
Ockwells Rd SL6 .....39 B1
Octavia RG12 .....118 A1
Octavia Way TW18 .....97 A1
Oddfellows Rd RG14 .....104 C1
Odell Cl RG6 .....114 A4
Odencroft Rd SL2 .....22 A1
Odiham Ave RG4 .....59 C3
Odiham Rd RG7 .....139 B1
Odney La SL6 .....20 A4
Ogmore Cl RG30 .....84 C4
Okingham Cl GU47 .....143 B1
Old Acre La RG10 .....61 A3
Old Barn Cl RG4 .....59 A3
Old Bath Rd Charvil RG10 .....61 A3
Newbury RG14 .....104 C2
Sonning RG4 .....60 B1
Old Bisley Rd GU16 .....152 B2
Old Bothampstead Rd
RG20 .....51 B3
Old Bracknell Cl RG12 .....118 A3
Old Bracknell La E RG12 .....118 A3
Old Bracknell La W
RG12 .....118 A3
Old Charlton Rd TW17 .....125 B2
Old Court Cl SL6 .....39 A2
Old Crown 11 SL1 .....42 C2
Old Dean Rd GU15 .....151 B4
Old Elm Dr RG30 .....84 B4
Old Farm Cres RG31 .....57 B1
Old Farm Dr RG12 .....91 B1
Old Ferry Dr TW19 .....68 B1
Old Fives Ct SL1 .....21 A1
Old Forest Rd RG41 .....88 C1
Old Forge Cl SL6 .....40 A2
Old Forge Cres TW17 .....125 A2
Old Forge End GU47 .....150 A4
Old Green La GU15 .....151 B4
Old Hayward La RG17 .....73 B1
Old House Ct SL3 .....43 B4
Old Kennels Ct RG30 .....85 A3
Old Kiln Rd HP10 .....3 A4
Old La
Hamstead Marshall RG20 .....102 C1
Headley RG19 .....133 C1
Old La The RG1 .....85 C3
Old Lands Hill RG12 .....118 B4
Old Marsh La SL6 .....40 C2
Old Mill Ct RG10 .....61 B3
Old Mill La SL6 .....40 B2
Old Moor La HP10 .....3 C4
Old Newtown Rd RG14 .....104 C1
Old Nursery Pl TW15 .....98 A2
Old Orchard The RG31 .....84 C2
Old Palace Ct SL3 .....69 B3
Old Pasture Rd
GU16, GU15 .....151 C2
Old Pharmacy Ct RG45 .....143 B2
Old Pond Cl GU15 .....151 B1
Old Portsmouth Rd
GU15 .....152 A3
Old Post Office La 10 SL6 .....39 C4
Old Priory La RG42 .....91 B1
Old Sawmill La RG45 .....143 B3
Old Sawmills The RG17 .....127 C3
Old School Ct TW19 .....95 C4
Old School La GU46 .....149 B3
Old School The
Hampstead Norreys RG18 .....52 C3
Wooburn Green HP10 .....3 B2
Old School Yd The RG17 .....25 A1
Old Slade La SL0 .....44 C1
Old St Chieveley RG18 .....51 C1
Chieveley, Beedon
Common RG20 .....51 B3
Hermitage RG18 .....78 C4
Old Station Bsns Pk RG20 .....31 C2
Old Station Way HP10 .....3 C3
Old Station Yd The RG17 .....25 A1
Old Vicarage Way HP10 .....3 B2
Old Watery La HP10 .....3 C4
Old Well Ct RG4 .....60 B2
Old Welmore GU46 .....149 C3
Old Whitley Wood La
RG2 .....113 B3
Old Wokingham Rd
RG40,RG45 .....143 B4
Old Woosehill La RG41 .....115 C4
Oldacre GU24 .....153 C4
Oldacres SL6 .....40 A4
Oldbury RG12 .....117 C3
Oldbury Rd KT16 .....123 C1
Oldcorne Hollow GU46 .....149 A3
Olde Farm Dr GU17 .....150 A3
Oldean Cl RG31 .....57 B1
Oldershaw Mews SL6 .....39 A4
Oldfield Cl RG6 .....87 A4
Oldfield Prim Sch SL6 .....40 A3
Oldfield Rd SL6 .....40 A4
Oldfield Rd Ind Est SL6 .....40 A4
Oldhouse La GU18 .....146 B1
Oldstead RG12 .....118 B2
Oldway La SL1 .....41 B3
Oleander Cl RG45 .....143 A4
Oliver Dr RG31 .....84 B3
Oliver Rd SL5 .....120 A3
Oliver's Paddock SL7 .....1 B3
Ollerton RG12 .....118 A1
Omega Way TW20 .....123 B4
Omer's Rise RG7 .....110 C2
One Pin La SL2 .....22 B4
Onslow Dr SL5 .....93 A1
Onslow Gdns RG4 .....59 B2
Onslow Lodge TW18 .....96 C1
Onslow Mews KT16 .....124 A2
Onslow Rd SL5 .....121 A1
Opal Ct SL3 .....23 B1
Opal Way RG41 .....115 C4
Opendale Rd SL1 .....41 A4
Opladen Way RG12 .....118 C2
Oracle Ctr RG12 .....118 B4
Oracle Ctr The RG1 .....86 A4
Oracle Parkway
Reading RG6 .....86 C4
Sonning RG6 .....60 A1
Orbit Cl RG40 .....141 C3
Orchard Ave Ashford TW15 .....98 B1
Hatton TW14 .....71 B1
Slough SL1 .....41 B4
Windsor SL4 .....67 A3
Orchard Chase RG10 .....88 C4
Orchard Cl Ashford TW15 .....98 B1
Farnborough (Hants) GU17 .....150 C1
Henley-on-T RG9 .....15 C1
Hermitage RG18 .....79 B4
Maidenhead SL6 .....40 A2
Newbury RG14 .....105 B3
Purley on T RG31 .....57 B2
Shinfield RG7 .....113 A1
Shiplake RG9 .....35 C1
West End GU24 .....153 B3
Wokingham RG40 .....116 B3
Woolhampton RG7 .....108 B1
Orchard Ct
Bracknell RG12 .....118 B4
Harmondsworth UB7 .....70 B4
Reading RG2 .....113 B4
Thatcham RG19 .....106 C2
Walton-on-T KT12 .....125 C1
Orchard Dr Sunbury TW17 .....125 C3
Wooburn Green HP10 .....3 B2
Orchard Est RG10 .....61 C3
Orchard Gate
Farnham Common SL2 .....22 B4
Sandhurst GU47 .....150 A4
Orchard Gr Caversham RG4 .....59 C2
Flackwell Heath HP10 .....3 A4
Maidenhead SL6 .....39 B4
Orchard Hill Bourne End SL8 .....3 A1
Windlesham GU20 .....146 B2
Orchard Ho 6 SL8 .....3 A2
Orchard Park Cl RG17 .....100 B2
Orchard Pl RG40 .....116 B3
Orchard Rd Hurst RG10 .....88 C4
Mortimer RG7 .....137 A3
Old Windsor SL4 .....68 A1
Orchard St RG1 .....86 A3
Orchard The
Flackwell Heath HP10 .....3 A4
Lightwater GU18 .....153 A4
Marlow SL7 .....1 C2
Theale RG7 .....83 C2
Virginia Water GU25 .....122 C2
Orchard Way
Ashford TW15 .....97 C3
Camberley GU15 .....151 A1
Slough SL3 .....43 C3
Orchardene RG14 .....105 A2
Orchards The TW15 .....98 B2
Orchardville SL1 .....21 A1
Orchids The OX11 .....10 B4
Oregon Ave RG31 .....57 B2
Oregon Wlk RG40 .....141 C4
Oriel Hill GU15 .....151 B2
Oriental Rd SL5 .....120 B3
Orion RG12 .....118 A1
Orkney Cl RG31 .....84 C2
Orkney Ct SL6 .....20 C3
Ormathwaites Cnr RG42 .....91 C1
Ormonde Rd RG41 .....116 A3
Ormsby St RG1 .....85 C4
Orrin Cl RG30 .....85 A4
Orts Rd Newbury RG14 .....105 A1
Reading RG1 .....86 B4
Orville Cl RG5 .....88 A4
Orwell Cl Caversham RG4 .....58 C2
Windsor SL4 .....67 B2
Osborne Ave TW19 .....97 C4
Osborne Dr GU18 .....153 A4
Osborne La RG42 .....91 B2
Osborne Mews SL4 .....67 B3
Osborne Rd Egham TW20 .....95 C1
Reading RG30 .....85 A4
Windsor SL4 .....67 B2
Wokingham RG40 .....116 B3
Osborne St SL1 .....42 C2
Osbourne Ct SL4 .....67 B3
Osier Pl TW20 .....96 B1
Osman's Cl RG42 .....92 A1
Osnaburgh Hill GU15 .....151 A3
Osney Rd SL6 .....19 C1
Osprey Ct 4 RG1 .....86 B4
Osterley Cl RG40 .....116 C3
Osterley Dr RG4 .....59 C3
Ostler Gate SL6 .....19 B1
Oswald Cl RG42 .....91 B1
Othello Gr RG42 .....118 C4
Otter Cl RG45 .....143 A4
Our Lady of Peace
RC Inf Sch SL1 .....41 B4
Our Lady of Peace
RC Mid Sch SL1 .....41 B4
Our Lady of the Rosary
RC Sch TW18 .....97 A1
Our Lady's Prep Sch
RG45 .....143 A3
Ouseley Lodge TW19 .....95 B4
Ouseley Rd TW19 .....95 B4
Overbridge Sq RG14 .....105 C2
Overbury Ave RG41 .....88 C1
Overdale Rise GU16 .....151 C2
Overdown Rd RG31 .....57 B2
Overlanders End RG31 .....57 C2
Overlord Cl GU15 .....151 B4
Owen Rd Newbury RG14 .....105 A3
Windlesham GU20 .....146 B3
Owl Cl RG41 .....115 C3
Owlsmoor Cty Prim Sch
GU47 .....143 C1
Owlsmoor Rd GU47 .....143 B1
Owston RG6 .....87 B1
Oxenhope RG12 .....118 A3
Oxford Ave Burnham SL1 .....21 A2
Harlington UB3 .....71 C4
Slough SL1 .....41 C4
Oxford Cl TW15 .....98 B1
Oxford Rd Marlow SL7 .....1 B1
Newbury RG14 .....104 C3
Reading RG30 .....58 A1
Sandhurst GU47 .....143 C1
Windsor SL4 .....67 B3
Wokingham RG41 .....116 A3
Oxford Rd E SL4 .....67 B3
Oxford Road Prim Sch
RG1 .....85 C4
Oxford St Caversham RG4 .....59 A1
Hungerford RG17 .....100 C4
Lambourn RG17 .....25 A2
Newbury RG14 .....104 C2

P

Pacific Cl TW14 .....98 C4
Pack & Prime La RG9 .....15 B1
Packman Dr RG10 .....61 B3
Padbury Cl TW14 .....98 B4
Padbury Oaks UB7 .....70 A3
Paddick Cl RG4 .....60 C2
Paddick Dr RG6 .....87 B1
Paddock Cl
Camberley GU15 .....152 A3
Maidenhead SL6 .....39 A1
Paddock Cotts SL6 .....39 A1
Paddock Hts RG10 .....61 C2
Paddock Rd
Caversham RG4 .....59 B1
Newbury RG14 .....130 C4
Paddock The
Bracknell RG12 .....118 B3
Crowthorne RG45 .....143 A3
Datchet SL3 .....68 A3
Maidenhead SL6 .....19 B1
Newbury RG14 .....105 B1
Paddocks The HP10 .....3 A4
Paddocks Way KT16 .....124 A1
Padley Ct 7 RG1 .....86 B4
Padstow Cl SL3 .....43 C2
Padstow Gdns RG2 .....86 A1
Padstow Wlk TW14 .....98 C4
Padworth La RG7 .....109 C2
Padworth Prep Sch RG7 .....109 C1
Padworth Rd RG7 .....136 B4
Page Rd TW14 .....71 B1
Page's Croft RG40 .....116 B3
Paget Cl Camberley GU15 .....152 A4
Marlow SL7 .....1 C2
Paget Dr SL6 .....39 A2
Paget Rd SL3 .....43 C1
Pagoda The SL6 .....20 A1
Paice Gn RG40 .....116 B4
Paices Hill RG7 .....135 A3
Pakenham Rd RG12 .....118 B1
Palace Cl SL1 .....41 C3
Paley St SL6 .....64 A3
Palmer CE Jun Sch The
RG40 .....116 B4
Palmer Cl
Crowthorne RG40 .....143 A4
Peasemore RG20 .....50 B4
Palmer Park Ave RG6 .....87 A3
Palmer School Rd RG40 .....116 B3
Palmera Ave RG31 .....84 B2
Palmers Cl SL6 .....39 A2
Palmers Hill RG8 .....54 B3
Palmers La
Burghfield Common RG7 .....111 A1
Burghfield Common,
Poundgreen RG7 .....112 A2
Palmerston Ave SL3 .....43 A2
Palmerstone Rd RG6 .....87 A3
Pamber Heath Rd RG26 .....135 C1
Pamber Rd RG7 .....136 A1
Pamela Row SL6 .....65 A4
Pan's Gdns GU15 .....151 C2
Panbourne Hill RG8 .....56 B3
Pangbourne Coll RG8 .....56 A2
Pangbourne Prim Sch
RG8 .....56 C3
Pangbourne Rd RG8 .....55 B2
Pangbourne St 2 RG30 .....85 A4
Pangbourne Sta RG8 .....56 B3
Pankhurst Dr RG12 .....118 B2
Pannells Cl KT16 .....123 C1
Pantile Row SL3 .....44 A1
Papist Way OX10 .....13 C4
Papplewick Sch SL5 .....120 A1
Paprika Cl RG6 .....86 C1
Par The SL2 .....22 B3
Parade The Ashford TW16 .....98 C1
Bourne End SL8 .....3 A2
Earley RG6 .....87 A2
Egham TW18 .....96 B2
Reading RG30 .....85 B3
Tadley RG26 .....135 A1
Wentworth GU25 .....122 B2
Windsor SL4 .....66 B3
Woodley RG5 .....87 C4
Paradise Mews RG9 .....15 B1
Paradise Rd RG9 .....15 B1
Paradise Way RG7 .....108 B4
Park Ave Camberley GU15 .....151 B2
Egham TW20 .....96 B1
Staines TW18 .....97 A1
Thatcham RG18 .....106 B2
Upper Halliford TW17 .....125 C3
Wokingham RG40 .....116 A3
Wraysbury TW19 .....68 B2
Park Cl SL4 .....67 B3
Park Close Cotts TW20 .....94 C2
Park Cnr SL4 .....66 C2
Park Cres Reading RG30 .....85 A3
Sunningdale SL5 .....120 C2
Park Dr SL5 .....120 C2
Park End RG14 .....105 A2
Park Farm Ind Est GU15 .....151 B1
Park Gr RG30 .....85 A3
Park Ho SL6 .....39 C3
Park House Sch RG14 .....130 C3
Park La Barkham RG40 .....141 A3
Beech Hill RG7 .....137 B1
Binfield RG42 .....90 C1
Burnham SL1 .....21 C4
Camberley GU15 .....151 B3
Charvil RG10 .....61 A2
Horton SL3 .....69 A2
Newbury RG14 .....105 A2
Reading RG31 .....84 B4
Slough SL3 .....43 A2
Stockcross RG20 .....103 A1
Thatcham RG18 .....106 B2
Winkfield SL4 .....93 A4
Park Lane Prim Sch RG31 .....84 B4
Park Lane Prim Sch
Annexe RG31 .....84 B4
Park Lawn SL2 .....22 B1
Park Mews TW19 .....97 C4
Park Rd Ashford TW15 .....98 A2
Park Rd *continued*
Bracknell RG12 118
Camberley GU15 151
Egham TW20 .....96 A
Henley-on-T RG9 .....15 C
Lower Halliford TW17 .....125 A
Sandhurst GU47 .....150 B
Stanwell TW19 .....70 B
Stoke Poges SL2 .....22 C
Wokingham RG40 .....116 A
Park St Bagshot GU19 .....145 C
Camberley GU15 .....151 B
Hungerford RG17 .....100 B
Maidenhead SL6 .....39 C
Newbury RG14 .....105 A
Poyle SL3 .....69 B
Slough SL1 .....42 C
Windsor SL4 .....67 B
Park Terr RG14 .....105 A
Park The RG17 .....25 A
Park View Bagshot GU19 .....145 B
Beech Hill RG7 .....138 B
Park View Dr N RG10 .....61 A
Park View Dr S RG10 .....61 A
Park Wall La RG8 .....34 B
Park Way
Hungerford RG17 .....100 C
Newbury RG14 .....105 A
Park Wlk RG8 .....57 B
Parkcorner La RG41 .....114 C
Parker's La RG42 .....92 A
Parkers Ct GU19 .....145 C
Parkgate SL1 .....21 B
Parkhill Cl GU17 .....150 B
Parkhill Dr RG31 .....57 B
Parkhill Rd GU17 .....150 B
Parkhouse La RG30 .....85 B
Parkhouse Mews 9 RG30 .....85 B
Parkhurst 20 RG30 .....85 B
Parkland Ave SL3 .....43 B
Parkland Dr RG12 .....118 C
Parkland Gr TW15 .....98 A
Parkland Rd TW15 .....98 A
Parkside Henley-on-T RG9 .....15 B
Maidenhead SL6 .....19 B
Parkside Rd Reading RG30 .....85 B
Sunningdale SL5 .....121 A
Thatcham RG18 .....106 B
Parkside Wlk SL1 .....43 A
Parkstone Dr GU15 .....151 B
Parkview
Flackwell Heath HP10 .....3 A
Maidenhead SL6 .....39 C
Parkview Chase SL1 .....41 C
Parkway Camberley GU15 .....151 B
Crowthorne RG45 .....143 A
Marlow SL7 .....2 A
Parkway Dr RG4 .....60 C
Parlaunt Park Comb Sch
SL3 .....44 A
Parlaunt Rd SL3 .....44 A
Parliament La SL6 .....20 C
Parnham Ave GU18 .....153 B
Parry Gn N SL3 .....43 C
Parry Gn S SL3 .....44 A
Parsley Cl RG6 .....86 C
Parson's Wood La SL2 .....22 B
Parsonage Gdns SL7 .....1 C
Parsonage La
Farnham Common SL2 .....22 B
Hungerford RG17 .....100 B
Lambourn RG17 .....25 A
Windsor SL4 .....67 A
Parsonage Pl RG17 .....25 A
Parsonage Rd TW20 .....95 B
Parsonage Way GU16 .....151 C
Parsons Cl Barkham RG2 .....141 A
Newbury RG14 .....104 C
Parsons Down
Jun & Inf Schs RG19 .....106 A
Parsons Field GU47 .....150 A
Part La RG7 .....139 C
Parthia Cl RG1 .....86 A
Partridge Ave GU46 .....149 A
Partridge Cl GU16 .....151 C
Partridge Dr RG31 .....84 B
Partridge Mead SL6 .....19 C
Paschal Rd GU15 .....151 C
Pasture Cl RG6 .....114 A
Patches Field SL7 .....1 C
Paterson Cl GU16 .....152 B
Pates Manor Dr TW14 .....98 B
Patricia Cl SL1 .....41 C
Patrick Gdns RG42 .....91 C
Patrick Rd RG4 .....59 A
Patriot Pl RG1 .....86 B
Patten Ash Dr RG40 .....116 C
Patten Ave GU46 .....149 B
Pavenham Cl RG6 .....114 A
Pavilion Gdns TW18 .....97 A
Pavilions End The GU15 .....151 B
Pavy Cl RG19 .....106 C
Paxton Ave SL1 .....42 B
Payley Dr RG40 .....116 C
Paynesdown Rd RG19 .....106 A
Peace La SL6 .....19 C
Peach St RG40 .....116 B
Peachy Dr RG19 .....106 C
Peacock Ave TW14 .....98 B
Peacock Cotts RG12 .....117 B
Peacock La RG12 .....117 B
Peacock Rd SL7 .....2 A
Pear Ave TW17 .....125 C
Pear Tree Ct GU15 .....152 A
Pear Tree La RG14 .....105 B
Pear Tree Rd TW15 .....98 B
Pearce Cl SL6 .....19 C
Pearce Dr SL6 .....19 C

earce Rd SL6 19 C1
earces Orch RG9 15 B2
earl Gdns SL1 42 A3
earmain Cl TW17 125 A2
earmans Glade RG2 113 C4
earson Rd RG4 60 B2
earson Way RG5 87 C3
eartree Cl SL1 41 C3
eascod Pl 21 SL4 67 B3
eascod St SL4 67 B3
ease Hill RG7 107 C4
easemore Hill RG20 50 A4
ebble Hill RG17 128 A3
eckmoor Dr RG19 131 B4
eddlars Gr GU46 149 C3
eel Cl Caversham RG4 59 B1
Windsor SL4 67 A2
Woodley RG5 88 A4
eel Ct SL1 42 A4
eel Ctr The RG12 118 A4
eel Ho TW20 95 C1
egasus Cl RG19 106 A2
egasus Ct RG31 84 B4
eggotty Pl GU47 143 C1
egs Green Cl RG30 85 A3
eket Cl TW18 123 C4
elham Ct Maidenhead SL6 39 C4
12 Reading RG30 85 B3
Staines TW18 97 A2
elican La RG14 105 A2
elican Rd RG26 135 C1
ell St RG1 86 A3
elling Hill SL4 95 A4
emberton Gdns RG31 84 B2
emberton Rd SL2 21 C1
embroke RG12 118 A1
embroke Broadway
GU15 151 B3
embroke Cl Ascot SL5 120 B2
Burghfield Common RG7 111 B2
embroke Ho 3 RG4 59 B1
embroke Mews SL5 120 B2
embroke Pl RG4 59 B2
embroke Rd 22 RG14 105 A2
Pembury Ct UB3 71 B4
Pendals Cl RG18 52 C3
Pendeen Ct SL1 42 A3
Pendell Ave UB3 71 C4
Pendennis Ave RG4 59 C3
Pendine Pl RG12 118 A2
Pendlebury RG12 118 A1
Pendragon Ct RG30 85 B3
Pendragon Way GU15 152 B2
Pendred Rd RG2 113 B3
Peninsular Cl GU15 152 A4
Peninsular Cl TW14 71 C1
Penling Cl SL6 19 C3
Penn Cl RG4 59 A3
Penn Ct 8 SL7 1 C1
Penn Mdw SL2 22 C2
Penn Rd Newbury RG14 104 B3
Slough SL2 22 B1
Pennfields RG10 61 C3
Pennine Cl RG31 84 A3
Pennine Rd SL2 42 A4
Pennine Way Charvil RG10 61 A2
Harlington UB3 71 B4
Penny La TW17 125 C1
Pennylets Gn SL2 23 A3
Pennypiece RG8 34 B4
Pennyroyal Ct RG1 86 A3
Penroath Ave RG30 85 B3
Penrose Ave RG5 87 C3
Penrose Cl RG14 104 C3
Penrose Ct TW20 95 B1
Pensford Cl RG45 143 A4
Penshurst Rd SL6 39 B3
Pentangle The 13 RG14 105 A2
Pentland Ave TW17 125 A2
Pentland Cl RG30 84 C3
Pentland Pl RG19 106 B1
Pentland Rd SL2 42 A4
Pentlands The RG17 102 B1
Penton Ave TW18 123 C4
Penton Ct TW18 96 C1
Penton Hall TW18 124 A4
Penton Hall Dr TW18 124 A4
Penton Hook Marina
Chertsey KT16 124 A3
Egham TW18 123 C4
Penton Hook Rd TW18 124 A4
Penton Rd TW18 96 C1
Penwood Ct SL6 39 A4
Penwood Gdns RG12 117 B2
Penwood La SL7 1 B1
Penwood Rd RG20 130 B2
Penyston Rd SL6 39 B4
Penzance Spur SL2 22 A1
Peppard La RG9 35 C4
Peppard Rd RG4 59 B4
Pepper La RG2 86 C2
Pepys Cl SL3 69 A4
Perch Cl SL7 18 B4
Percival Rd TW13 98 C3
Percy Ave TW15 98 A2
Percy Bryant Rd TW16 98 C1
Percy Pl SL3 68 A3
Peregrine Cl
Bracknell RG12 118 A2
Wokingham RG41 115 C3
Peregrine Rd TW16 125 C4
Periam Cl RG9 35 B4
Perkins Ct TW15 97 C2
Perkins Way RG41 116 A3
Perrin Cl TW15 97 C2
Perry Ho SL1 21 A1
Perry Oaks RG12 118 C4
Perry Oaks Dr TW6, UB7 70 B3
Perry Way Bracknell RG12 118 C4
Lightwater GU18 152 C4
Perrycroft SL4 66 C2
Perryfields Way SL1 21 A1
Perryhill Dr GU47 142 C1
Perryman Way SL2 21 C1
Perserverance Hill RG9 35 A3
Perth Ave SL1 42 A4
Perth Cl RG5 61 A1
Perth Trad Est SL1 42 A4
Peterhead Mews SL3 44 A1
Peterhouse Cl GU47 143 C1
Petersfield Ave Slough SL2 43 A3
Staines TW18 97 B1
Petersfield Rd TW18 97 B2
Petrel Cl RG41 115 C3
Petts La TW17 125 A3
Petty Pl SL6 39 B2
Petworth Ave RG30 84 C2
Petworth Ct Reading RG1 85 C3
Windsor SL4 67 A3
Pevensey Ave RG4 59 C3
Pevensey Ct RG2 86 C1
Pevensey Rd SL2 42 A4
Pewsey Vale RG12 118 C2
Pheasant Cl RG41 88 B1
Pheasant La RG20 131 C2
Pheasants Croft SL6 39 A2
Pheasants Ridge SL7 1 B4
Philbye Mews SL1 41 C2
Philip Dr HP10 3 B4
Philip Rd TW18 97 B1
Phillimore Rd RG4 59 B4
Phillips Cl RG5 61 A1
Phipps Cl SL6 39 A1
Phipps Rd SL1 41 C4
Phoebe Ct RG1 86 A3
Phoenix Bsns Pk RG12 117 B4
Phoenix Cl RG41 115 C3
Phoenix Ct SL6 39 B2
Phoenix Pl TW18 97 A2
Phoenix Wlk RG14 130 B3
Phyllis Court Dr RG9 15 C2
Pickering RG12 118 A3
Picket Post Cl RG12 118 C3
Picketts La RG8 55 C2
Pickford Dr SL3 43 C3
Pickins Piece SL3 69 A3
Pickwell Cl RG6 87 B1
Pickwick Gdns GU15 152 A2
Picton Cl GU15 152 A4
Picton Way RG4 59 A2
Piercefield RG31 84 B2
Pierces Hill RG31 57 B1
Pierson Rd SL4 66 B3
Pigeonhouse La SL4, SL5 92 C2
Pigeons Farm Rd RG19 131 B4
Piggott Sch The RG10 61 B4
Piggotts Rd 4 RG4 59 B1
Pightle The RG7 111 C2
Pigott Ct RG40 116 B3
Pigott Rd RG40 116 C4
Pike Cl SL7 18 B4
Pike St RG14 105 A2
Pikeshaw Way RG31 57 B1
Pimento Dr RG6 86 C1
Pimpernel Pl RG18 106 C2
Pincents Kiln Ind Est
RG31 84 A2
Pincents La RG31 84 A3
Pinchcut RG7 111 A2
Pinchington La
RG14 & RG19 131 A4
Pindar Pl RG14 105 C3
Pine Ave GU15 151 B2
Pine Cl Maidenhead SL6 39 A4
Sandhurst GU15 150 C4
Pine Croft Rd RG41 116 A1
Pine Ct RG12 118 C3
Pine Dr Blackwater GU17 150 C2
Mortimer RG7 136 C3
Wokingham RG40 142 A4
Pine Gr Twyford RG10 61 B3
Windlesham GU20 146 B2
Pine Mount Rd GU15 151 B2
Pine Ridge RG14 105 B3
Pine Ridge Golf Ctr
GU16 152 B1
Pine Ridge Rd RG7 111 A2
Pine Trees Bsns Pk TW18 96 C2
Pine Way TW20 95 A1
Pinecote Dr SL5 120 C1
Pinecroft SL7 1 B2
Pinefields Cl RG45 143 A2
Pinehill Rd RG45 143 B2
Pinehill Rise GU47 150 B4
Pinehurst SL5 120 B2
Pinel Cl GU25 122 C3
Piner Cotts SL4 66 C2
Pineridge Cty Inf Sch
GU15 145 A1
Pineridge Gdns 10 RG30 85 B3
Pines Cty Inf Sch RG12 118 A1
Pines Cty Jun Sch RG12 118 A1
Pines The
Camberley GU15 151 C4
Twyford RG10 61 C4
Pinetree Ct RG4 59 A3
Pinewood Ave RG45 143 B3
Pinewood Cl RG26 134 B1
Pinewood Dr
Caversham RG4 58 C3
Newtown RG20 131 A1
Staines TW18 97 A2
Pinewood Gdns GU19 145 B2
Pinewood Mews TW19 70 B1
Pinewood Rd GU25 122 A3
Pingewood Cl RG30 85 A1
Pingewood Rd RG30 85 A1
Pingewood Rd S
RG7,RG30 112 B4
Pinglestone Cl TW6, UB7 70 C4
Pink La SL1 21 A2
Pinkneys Dr SL6 38 C4
Pinkneys Rd SL6 39 A4
Pinks La RG26 134 C1
Piper's End GU25 122 B3
Pipers Cl SL1 21 B1
Pipers Ct Burnham SL1 21 B1
Thatcham RG19 107 A1
Pipers Way RG19 107 A1
Pipit Cl RG19 106 A2
Pippins Ct TW15 98 A1
Pippins The SL3 43 C3
Pipsons Cl GU46 149 B3
Pitch Pl RG42 90 B2
Pitcroft Ave RG6 87 A3
Pitfield La RG7 137 B2
Pitford Rd RG5 88 A4
Pitts Cl RG42 90 B1
Pitts La RG6 87 A4
Pitts Rd SL1 42 B3
Plackett Way SL1 41 B3
Plaines Cl SL1 41 C3
Plaitinson Rd RG2 113 B3
Planes The KT16 124 B1
Plantagenet Pk RG42 118 C4
Plantation Cl RG18 78 C3
Plantation Rd Chilton OX12 9 C4
Tadley RG26 134 C1
Plantation Row GU15 151 A3
Platt Ct RG17 100 C2
Platt La RG17 45 B3
Play Platt RG7 83 B2
Players Gn RG5 87 C3
Playhatch Rd RG4 60 A3
Plough La Shiplake RG9 35 C1
Stoke Poges SL2 23 A2
Wokingham RG40 116 C3
Plough Rd GU46 149 C4
Ploughlands RG42 117 C4
Ploughlees La SL1 42 C3
Plover Cl Staines TW18 96 C3
Wokingham RG41 115 C3
Plover La RG27 140 C1
Plowden Way RG9 35 C1
Plummery The 1 RG1 86 B4
Plumpton Rd RG14 105 B1
Plumtrees RG6 87 A1
Pluto Cl SL1 41 C2
Pluto Rd OX11 9 C4
Plymouth Ave RG5 87 B3
Plymouth Rd SL1 41 C4
Plympton Cl RG6 87 C2
Pocket Cl RG12 117 B4
Pococks La SL4 42 C1
Poffley Pl RG19 107 A2
Point (L Ctr) The RG12 118 A4
Point Royal RG12 118 A2
Pointers Cl RG20 51 A1
Points The SL6 39 A2
Polehampton CE Inf Sch
RG10 61 B3
Polehampton Cl RG10 61 B2
Polehampton Jun Sch
RG10 61 C3
Pollard Cl SL4 68 A1
Pollard Gr GU15 152 B2
Pollardrow Ave RG42 117 C4
Pollards Way RG31 84 B2
Polsted Rd RG31 57 B1
Polyanthus Way RG45 143 A4
Polygon Bsns Ctr SL3 69 C3
Pond Cl RG14 130 B4
Pond Croft GU46 149 C3
Pond Head La RG6 87 B2
Pond La Hermitage RG18 79 B4
Mapledurham RG4 58 A3
Pond Moor Rd RG12 118 A2
Pond Rd TW20 96 B1
Pondside Cl UB3 71 B4
Pool End Cl TW17 125 A2
Pool La Slough SL1 42 C3
Waltham St Lawrence RG10 63 A3
Poole Cl RG30 85 A4
Pooley Ave TW20 96 A2
Pooley Green Cl TW20 96 B2
Pooley Green Rd TW20 96 B2
Poolmans Rd SL4 66 B2
Pope Cl TW14 98 C4
Popes Cl SL3 69 B4
Popes La SL6 19 B4
Popeswood Rd RG42 117 B4
Popham Cl RG12 118 C2
Poplar Ave Reading RG30 84 C3
Windlesham GU20 146 A3
Poplar Cl SL3 69 C3
Poplar Gdns RG2 86 C1
Poplar Ho SL3 43 C1
Poplar La Hurst RG10 62 A1
Winnersh RG41 88 B2
Poplar Pl RG14 105 A3
Poplar Rd TW15 98 B2
Poplars Gr SL6 20 A1
Poplars The SL5 120 A2
Poppy Dr RG18 106 C2
Poppy Pl RG40 116 A3
Poppy Way RG31 84 B3
Poppyhills Rd GU15 151 C4
Porchester SL5 120 A3
Porchester Rd RG14 105 A1
Porchfield Cl RG6 87 A1
Porlock Cl RG19 106 B1
Porlock Pl RG31 84 B2
Port Down RG17 100 C3
Porter Cl RG6 114 B4
Porter End RG14 131 A4
Portesbery Hill Dr GU15 151 C3
Portesbery Rd GU15 151 C3
Portesbery Sch GU15 151 B3
Portia Gr RG42 118 C4
Portland Bsns Ctr SL3 68 A3
Portland Cl SL2 21 B1
Portland Cres TW13 98 B2
Portland Gdns RG30 84 B4
Portland Rd TW15 97 C3
Portlands SL7 1 B1
Portlands Mews 8 SL7 1 B1
Portlock Rd SL6 39 B4
Portman Cl 5 RG42 118 A4
Portman Rd RG30 58 B1
Portmeirion Gdns RG30 57 C1
Portnall Dr GU25 121 C2
Portnall Rd GU25 121 C2
Portnall Rise GU25 121 C2
Portrush Rd RG5 87 B3
Portsmouth Ct SL1 42 C3
Portsmouth Rd GU15 152 A4
Portway Swallowfield RG7 139 B1
Tadley RG26 134 C1
Portway Cl RG1 85 C3
Post Horn Pl RG31 84 C2
Post Office Cotts SL2 23 A3
Post Office La
Burghfield Common RG30 111 B3
Slough SL3 43 B4
Post Office Rd RG17 127 C3
Posting House Mews
RG14 104 C2
Potley Hill Cty Prim Sch
GU46 150 A3
Potley Hill Rd GU46 149 C3
Pottery La RG17 127 C3
Pottery Rd RG30 57 C1
Poulcott TW19 68 C1
Pound Cres SL7 1 B1
Pound La Hurst RG10 89 A3
Little Marlow SL7 2 B2
Marlow SL7 1 B1
Newbury RG20 104 B2
Sonning RG4 60 C1
Thatcham RG19 106 A2
Windlesham GU20 146 B2
Pound Piece RG17 100 B3
Pound Rd KT16 124 A1
Pound St RG14 104 C1
Pound The Cookham SL6 19 C4
Slough SL1 21 B1
Poundfield La SL6 19 C4
Poundfield Way RG10 61 C2
Powis Cl SL6 39 A2
Powney Rd SL6 39 B4
Poyle 14 Trad Est SL3 69 C2
Poyle Cty Fst Sch SL3 69 C3
Poyle Gdns RG12 118 B4
Poyle La SL1 21 A2
Poyle New Cotts SL3 69 C3
Poyle Rd SL3 69 C3
Poyle Tech Ctr The SL3 69 C3
Poynings SL0 44 C1
Prancing Horse Cl RG19 106 C2
Precinct The TW20 96 A2
Precincts The SL1 21 B1
Prescott RG12 117 C1
Prescott Rd SL3 69 C3
Presentation Coll RG30 85 B3
Preston Pl RG14 105 B3
Preston Rd Littleton TW17 125 A2
Reading RG2 86 A3
Slough SL2 43 B3
Prestwick Ct 36 RG1 86 B4
Prestwood SL2 43 A4
Pretoria Rd KT16 123 C1
Price Gdns RG42 91 A1
Prides Crossing SL5 93 A1
Priest Ave RG40 116 C3
Priest Hill Caversham RG4 59 A2
Englefield Green TW19, SL4 95 B3
Priest La GU24 153 B3
Priestwood Ave RG42 117 C4
Priestwood Court Rd
RG42 118 A4
Priestwood Sq 1 RG42 118 A4
Primrose Cl RG8 57 B3
Primrose La RG41 88 B2
Primrose Walk GU46 149 A3
Primrose Way GU47 143 A1
Primrose Wlk RG12 118 B2
Prince Albert Dr SL5 119 B2
Prince Andrew Cl SL6 20 A1
Prince Andrew Rd SL6 20 A1
Prince Andrew Way SL5 119 B4
Prince Consort Cotts SL4 67 B3
Prince Consort Dr SL5 119 B3
Prince Consort's Dr
Old Windsor SL4 94 A3
Winkfield SL4 93 C2
Prince Dr GU47 143 A1
Prince Hold Rd RG19 106 A2
Prince of Wales Ave RG30 85 B4
Prince of Wales Wlk 1
GU15 151 B3
Prince William Ct TW15 97 C2
Prince William Dr RG31 57 B1
Princes Cl Bagshot GU19 145 C1
Eton SL4 41 C1
Princes Ct SL8 3 B2
Princes La RG20 50 B3
Princes Rd Ashford TW15 97 C2
Bourne End SL8 3 B2
Egham TW20 95 C1
Feltham TW13 98 C3
Princes St Reading RG1 86 B4
Slough SL1 43 A2
Princess Ave SL4 67 A2
Princess Christians Hospl
SL4 67 B3
Princess Margaret Hospl
The SL4 67 B3
Princess Margaret Royal
Free Sch The SL4 67 B2
Princess Marina Dr
Barkham, Arborfield
Garrison RG2 140 C4
Barkham, Langley
Common RG2 115 A1
Princess Sq RG12 118 A4
Princess St SL6 39 C3
Princess Way GU15 151 B3
Prior Croft Cl GU15 152 A2
Prior End GU15 152 A3
Prior Heath Cty Inf Sch
GU15 152 A3
Prior Rd GU15 152 A3
Prior's La GU17 150 A3
Priors Cl Maidenhead SL6 40 A1
5 Slough SL1 43 A2
Priors Court Rd RG18 78 C4
Priors Court Specl Sch
RG18 78 B4
Priors Ct 21 RG1 86 A3
Priors Rd Tadley RG26 135 A1
Windsor SL4 66 B2
Priors Way SL6 40 A1
Priors Way Ind Est SL6 40 A1
Priors Wood RG45 142 B2
Priory Ave Caversham RG4 59 A1
Hungerford RG17 100 B2
Priory Cl Hungerford RG17 100 B2
Sunningdale SL5 121 A1
Priory Ct Camberley GU15 150 C3
Caversham RG4 59 A1
Egham TW20 96 B1
Winnersh RG41 88 B2
Priory Cty Jun & Inf Sch
SL1 41 B4
Priory Gn TW18 97 A2
Priory La RG42 91 B1
Priory Mews TW18 97 A2
Priory Pl Greenham RG19 131 A3
Hungerford RG17 100 B2
Priory Rd Burnham SL1 41 B4
Hungerford RG17 100 B2
Newbury RG14 105 A1
Sunningdale SL5 121 A1
Winkfield SL5 119 A4
Priory The RG41 88 B2
Priory Way Datchet SL3 68 A4
Harmondsworth UB7 70 C4
Priory Wlk RG12 118 C3
Priscilla Ho 13 TW16 98 C1
Pritchard Cl RG19 131 B4
Privet Cl RG6 87 A1
Proctors Rd RG40 116 C3
Progress Bsns Ctr SL1 41 B4
Promenade SL4 67 B4
Promenade Rd RG4 59 A1
Prospect Cotts RG42 117 B4
Prospect Ct RG30 85 A3
Prospect La TW20 95 A2
Prospect Pl Hurley SL6 17 C2
Newbury RG14 105 A1
Staines TW18 96 C2
3 Windsor SL4 67 B2
Prospect Rd
Hungerford RG17 100 B3
Marlow SL7 1 B1
Prospect Sch RG30 85 A3
Prospect St
Caversham RG4 59 A1
Reading RG1 85 C4
Providence Ho GU19 145 C2
Providence La UB3 71 B4
Providence Pl SL6 39 C4
Prudential Bldgs 8 SL1 42 C2
Prune Hill TW20 95 C1
Prunus Cl GU24 153 C3
Pudding Hill RG10 37 B3
Pudding La RG20 28 C1
Puffers Way RG14 104 C1
Pullmans Pl TW18 97 A2
Pump La Ascot SL5 120 C4
Shinfield RG7 112 B1
Pump La N SL7 1 C3
Pump La S SL7 2 A2
Pumpkin Hill SL1 21 C3
Pundles La SL6 63 B3
Purbrook Ct RG12 118 C2
Purcell Rd RG45 143 A4
Purfield Dr RG10 36 C1
Purley CE Inf Sch RG8 57 B3
Purley La RG8 57 B3
Purley Rise RG8 56 C3
Purley Village RG8 57 B3
Purley Way RG8 56 C3
Pursers Farm RG7 113 A2
Purslane RG40 116 B3
Purssell Cl SL6 39 A2
Purton Ct SL2 22 B3
Purton La SL2 22 B3
Putman Pl RG9 15 C1
Pycroft Ct KT16 123 C1
Pyegrove Chase RG12 118 C1
Pyke Cl RG40 116 B3
Pykes Hill RG8 54 B2
Pyle Hill RG14 105 A1
Pyrcroft Grange
Prim Sch KT16 123 C2
Pyrcroft Rd KT16 123 C1

Q

Quadrant Ct RG12 . . . . .118 C3
Quadrant The SL6 . . . . .40 A3
Qualitas RG12 . . . . .117 C1
Quantock Ave RG4 . . . . .59 B3
Quantock Cl Charvil RG10 . . .61 A2
  Harlington UB3 . . . . .71 B4
  Slough SL3 . . . . .44 A1
Quantocks The RG19 . . . . . . .106 B1
Quarrington Cl RG19 . . . . . . .106 C1
Quarry Bank GU18 . . . . .153 A4
Quarry La Shiplake RG9 . . . . .36 A2
  Yateley GU46 . . . . .149 C3
Quarry Wood Rd SL6,SL7 . .19 A4
Quarrydale Dr SL7 . . . . .1 C1
Quartz Cl RG41 . . . . .115 B4
Quaves Rd SL3 . . . . .43 B2
Quebec Gdns GU17 . . . . .150 B2
Quebec Rd RG9 . . . . .35 C4
Queen Anne Fst Sch The
  SL4 .67 B2
Queen Anne's Cl SL4 . . . . . . .94 A3
Queen Anne's Ct 🔟 SL4 . . . .67 B3
Queen Anne's Ct SL4 . . . . . . .67 B2
Queen Anne's Rd SL4 . . . . . . .59 A2
Queen Annes Gate RG4 . . . . .59 B2
Queen Charlotte St 🔟 SL4 67 B3
Queen Cl RG9 . . . . .15 C1
Queen Elizabeth Rd
  GU15 . . . . .144 B1
Queen Mary Ave GU15 . . . . .151 B4
Queen Mary Rd TW17 . . . . . .125 B4
Queen St Caversham RG4 . . .59 A2
  Chertsey KT16 . . . . .124 A1
  Henley-on-T RG9 . . . . .15 C1
  Maidenhead SL6 . . . . .39 C4
Queen Victoria
  Cross Roads GU15 . . . . . . .151 A3
Queen Victoria Ho RG40 .116 B3
Queen Victoria St RG1 . . . .86 A4
Queen's Acre SL4 . . . . .67 B2
Queen's Cl
  North Ascot SL5 . . . . .119 C4
  Old Windsor SL4 . . . . .68 A1
Queen's Ct Slough SL1 . . . . .42 C3
  Staines TW18 . . . . .97 B1
Queen's Gate SL4 . . . . .67 B2
Queen's Pl SL5 . . . . .120 A3
Queen's La 🖪 SL6 . . . . .39 C4
Queen's Rd Ascot SL5 . . . . . .120 B2
  Datchet SL3 . . . . .68 A4
  Egham TW20 . . . . .95 C1
  Marlow SL7 . . . . .1 B1
  Newbury RG14 . . . . .105 A1
  Slough SL1 . . . . .42 C3
  Windsor SL4 . . . . .67 B3
Queen's Terr 🖪 SL4 . . . . . . .67 B2
Queens Acre Ho 🖪 SL4 . . . .67 B2
Queens Cotts RG1 . . . . .86 A4
Queens Ct 🔟 RG14 . . . . . . .105 A1
Queens Dr The RG2 & RG6 .86 C2
Queens Hill Rise SL5 . . . . . .120 B3
Queens Keep GU15 . . . . .151 B3
Queens Lawns RG1 . . . . .86 B3
Queens Park Gdns TW13 . .98 C3
Queens Pine RG12 . . . . .118 C2
Queens Rd Bisley GU24 . . . .153 C1
  Camberley GU15 . . . . .151 A4
  Caversham RG4 . . . . .59 B1
  Eton SL4 . . . . .41 C1
  Reading RG1 . . . . .86 B4
Queens Ride RG45 . . . . .143 A4
Queens Way RG17 . . . . .102 B1
Queens Wlk TW15 . . . . .97 B2
Queens Wlk Mall 🖪 SL6 . .39 C4
Queensborough Dr RG4 . . .58 C3
Queensbury Pl GU17 . . . . . .150 B2
Queenshill Lodge SL5 . . . . .120 A3
Queensmead
  Ashford TW15 . . . . .97 C2
  Camberley GU15 . . . . .152 A4
  Datchet SL3 . . . . .68 A3
Queensmere Rd SL1 . . . . . . .43 A2
Queensway Caversham RG4 .59 B3
  Maidenhead SL6 . . . . .19 C1
Quentin Rd RG5 . . . . .87 B3
Quentin Way GU25 . . . . .122 A3
Quinbrookes SL2 . . . . .43 B4
Quince Cl SL5 . . . . .120 B3
Quincy Rd TW20 . . . . .96 A2
Quinn Ct RG30 . . . . .85 B4
Quintilis RG12 . . . . .117 C1
Quoiting Sq SL7 . . . . .1 B1
Quoitings Dr SL7 . . . . .1 B1

R

R.E.M.E Mus RG2 . . . . .141 A4
Race Course Rd RG14 . . . . .105 A1
Race Course Sta RG14 . . . .105 A1
Raceview Bsns Ctr RG14 .105 A1
Rachaels Lake View RG42 .91 C1
Rackstraw Rd GU47 . . . . . . .143 B1
Radbourne Rd RG31 . . . . . . .84 B2
Radcliffe Way RG42 . . . . . . .117 C4
Radcot Ave SL3 . . . . .44 A2
Radcot Cl Maidenhead SL6 . .19 C2
  Woodley RG5 . . . . .60 C1
Radical Ride RG40 . . . . .141 C4
Radius Pk TW6 . . . . .71 C2
Radley Bottom
  Hungerford RG17 . . . . .101 B4

Radley Bottom continued
  Hungerford Newtown RG17 .74 A2
Radley Cl TW14 . . . . .98 C4
Radnor Cl RG9 . . . . .15 C1
Radnor Ho 🔢 RG1 . . . . .85 C3
Radnor Rd Bracknell RG12 .118 C3
  Earley RG6 . . . . .87 B2
Radnor Way SL3 . . . . .43 C1
Radstock La RG6 . . . . .87 A1
Radstock Prim Sch RG6 . .87 A1
Radstock Rd RG1 . . . . .86 C4
Raeburn Way GU47 . . . . . . .150 B3
Ragdale RG7 . . . . .111 A2
Ragglesswood 🔟 RG6 . . . . .87 B2
Raghill RG7 . . . . .135 B3
Raglan Ct RG2 . . . . .86 B1
Raglan Gdns RG4 . . . . .59 B2
Ragley Mews RG4 . . . . .59 B3
Ragmans Cl SL7 . . . . .1 B4
Ragstone Rd SL1 . . . . .42 C2
Railside RG7 . . . . .108 C1
Railton Cl RG2 . . . . .113 B4
Railway App KT16 . . . . .123 C1
Railway Rd RG14 . . . . .105 A1
Railway Terr Egham TW18 . .96 B2
  Slough SL2 . . . . .42 C3
Railways Cotts RG8 . . . . . . .34 B3
Rainbow Pk RG41 . . . . .88 A1
Rainsborough Chase SL6 .39 A2
Rainworth Cl RG6 . . . . .114 A4
Raleigh Cl Slough SL1 . . . . . .42 A3
  Woodley RG5 . . . . .87 C3
Raleigh Ct TW18 . . . . .97 A2
Raleigh Rd TW13,TW14 . . . .98 C3
Raleigh Way GU16 . . . . .151 C2
Ralphs Ride RG12 . . . . .118 C3
Rambler Cl SL6 . . . . .41 A4
Rambler La SL3 . . . . .43 B2
Ramptons La SL3 . . . . .43 B2
Ramsay Rd GU20 . . . . .146 C3
Ramsbury Cl RG12 . . . . .117 C2
Ramsbury Dr Earley RG6 . . .87 A2
  Hungerford RG17 . . . . .100 C3
Ramsey Cl
  Camberley GU15 . . . . .152 A4
  Earley RG6 . . . . .87 C1
Ramsey Ct SL2 . . . . .21 B1
Ramslade Rd RG12 . . . . .118 B3
Rances La RG40 . . . . .116 C3
Randall Cl SL3 . . . . .43 C1
Randall Ct SL4 . . . . .68 A1
Randall Mead RG42 . . . . .90 A1
Randell Cl GU17 . . . . .150 C1
Randolph Rd Reading RG1 . .59 C1
  Slough SL3 . . . . .43 C2
Ranelagh Cres SL5 . . . . . . .119 B4
Ranelagh Dr RG12 . . . . .118 B3
Ranelagh Sch RG12 . . . . . .118 B3
Range Rd RG40 . . . . .142 A4
Range Ride RG12 . . . . .150 C4
Range View GU47 . . . . .150 C4
Range Villas TW17 . . . . .124 C1
Range Way TW17 . . . . .125 A1
Rangewood Ave RG30 . . . . .84 C2
Ranikhet Prim Sch RG30 . .85 A4
Rapley Cl GU15 . . . . .151 C4
Rapley Gn RG12 . . . . .118 B2
Ratby Cl RG6 . . . . .87 B1
Raven Cl GU46 . . . . .149 A3
Ravendale Rd TW16 . . . . . . .125 C4
Ravenglass Cl RG6 . . . . .87 B2
Ravens Field SL3 . . . . .43 B2
Ravensbourne Ave TW19 .97 C4
Ravensbourne Dr RG5 . . . .87 C4
Ravenscote Cty Jun Sch
  GU16 . . . . .152 A2
Ravenscourt Marlow SL6 . . . .2 A2
  Sunbury TW16 . . . . .125 C4
Ravenscroft Rd RG9 . . . . . . .15 B1
Ravensdale Mews TW18 . .97 A1
Ravensdale Rd SL5 . . . . . . .120 A2
Ravensfield TW20 . . . . .95 B1
Ravenshoe Cl SL8 . . . . .3 A2
Ravenstone Rd GU15 . . . . . .152 B3
Ravenswing Mobile
  Home Pk RG7 . . . . .135 B1
Ravenswood Ave RG45 . . . .142 C3
Ravenswood Dr GU15 . . . . .152 A3
Ravenswood Village
  Settlement RG45 . . . . .142 C3
Ravensworth Rd
  Mortimer RG7 . . . . .136 C3
  Slough SL2 . . . . .22 A1
Rawcliffe Ho SL6 . . . . .40 A3
Rawdon Rise GU15 . . . . .152 A3
Rawlinson Rd GU15 . . . . . . .150 C3
Ray Dr SL6 . . . . .40 A4
Ray Ho 🖪 SL8 . . . . .3 A2
Ray Lea Cl SL6 . . . . .40 A4
Ray Lea Rd SL6 . . . . .40 A4
Ray Lodge SL6 . . . . .40 A4
Ray Lodge Mews SL6 . . . . . .40 A4
Ray Mdw SL6 . . . . .20 A1
Ray Mead Ct SL6 . . . . .20 B1
Ray Mead Rd SL6 . . . . .40 A4
Ray Mill Rd E SL6 . . . . .20 A1
Ray Mill Rd W SL6 . . . . .40 A4
Ray Park Ave SL6 . . . . .40 A4
Ray Park La SL6 . . . . .40 A4
Ray Park Rd SL6 . . . . .40 A4
Ray St SL6 . . . . .40 A4
Rayfield SL6 . . . . .40 A4
Raymond Cl SL3 . . . . .69 C3
Raymond Rd
  Maidenhead SL6 . . . . .39 B4
  Slough SL3 . . . . .44 A2
Rayners Cl SL3 . . . . .69 B4

Rays Ave SL4 . . . . .66 C4
Raywood Cl UB3 . . . . .71 B4
Reade Ct SL2 . . . . .22 B3
Reading Alternative Sch
  RG1 .86 B3
Reading Blue Coat Sch
  RG4 .60 B2
Reading Bridge RG1 . . . . . .86 A4
Reading Coll
  of Arts & Tech RG1 . . . . . . .86 C3
Reading Coll of Tech RG1 .86 B4
Reading Gate Ret Pk RG2 .85 C1
Reading Girls Sch RG2 . . .86 B2
Reading Gram Sch RG1 . . .86 B2
Reading Link Ret Pk RG2 .86 A3
Reading Rd Aldworth RG8 . .33 A1
  Arborfield RG2 . . . . .114 B2
  Blackwater GU17 . . . . .150 A2
  Burghfield Common RG7 . .111 A1
  Finchampstead RG27 . . . . .140 C2
  Goring RG8 . . . . .34 C3
  Henley-on-T RG9 . . . . .15 C1
  Moulsford OX10 . . . . .14 A4
  Pangbourne RG8 . . . . .56 B3
  Streatley RG8 . . . . .34 A3
  Wokingham RG41 . . . . .115 C4
  Woodley RG5 . . . . .87 B4
  Yateley GU46 . . . . .149 B3
Reading St Michael
  Cty Prim Sch RG30 . . . . . .85 A4
Reading Sta RG1 . . . . .86 A4
Reading West Sta RG30 . .85 C4
Recreation Cl GU14 . . . . . . .150 C1
Recreation La RG7 . . . . .113 A1
Recreation Rd
  Bourne End SL8 . . . . .3 A2
  Burghfield Common RG7 . .111 A1
  Reading RG30 . . . . .84 C4
  Wargrave RG10 . . . . .36 C1
Rectory Cl Bracknell RG12 .118 B3
  Farnham Common SL2 . . . . .22 A1
  Littleton TW17 . . . . .125 A3
  Newbury RG14 . . . . .104 C1
  Sandhurst GU47 . . . . .149 C4
  Windsor SL4 . . . . .67 A3
  Wokingham RG40 . . . . .116 B3
Rectory La
  Aston Tirrold OX11 . . . . .12 C4
  Bracknell RG12 . . . . .118 A3
  Letcombe Bassett OX12 . . . .6 C4
  Windlesham GU20 . . . . .146 A2
Rectory Rd Caversham RG4 .59 A1
  Padworth RG7 . . . . .135 C4
  Streatley RG8 . . . . .33 B4
  Taplow SL6 . . . . .20 C1
  Wokingham RG40 . . . . .116 B3
Rectory Row RG12 . . . . .118 A3
Rectory Terr SL2 . . . . .22 B2
Red Cottage Dr RG31 . . . . .84 B2
Red Cottage Mews SL3 . . . .43 B2
Red Cross Rd RG8 . . . . .34 B3
Red Ct SL1 . . . . .42 C3
Red Hill RG9 . . . . .35 A3
Red House Ct RG6 . . . . .114 A4
Red La RG7 . . . . .135 B3
Red Leaf Cl SL3 . . . . .43 C3
Red Lion Cotts SL2 . . . . .23 A1
Red Lion Way HP10 . . . . .3 C3
Red Rd GU18, GU24, GU15 .153 A4
Red Rose RG42 . . . . .90 B2
Red Shute Hill RG18 . . . . . . .79 A2
Red Shute Ind Est RG18 . .79 A2
Redberry Rd RG4 . . . . .59 B3
Redcrest Gdns GU15 . . . . . .151 C3
Reddington Dr SL3 . . . . .43 C1
Redditch RG12 . . . . .118 B1
Redfield Ct RG14 . . . . .105 B2
Redford Cl TW13 . . . . .98 C3
Redford Rd SL4 . . . . .66 B3
Redgauntlet RG40 . . . . .141 B3
Redgrave Pl SL7 . . . . .1 C2
Redhatch Dr RG6 . . . . .87 A1
Redlake La RG40 . . . . .116 C1
Redlands Pl RG40 . . . . .115 C1
Redlands Prim Sch RG1 . .86 C3
Redlane Ct RG1 . . . . .86 B3
Redlane Hill RG7 . . . . .135 B3
Redleaves Ave TW15 . . . . . .98 A1
Redmayne RG12 . . . . .152 B2
Rediriff Cl SL6 . . . . .39 B3
Redruth Gdns RG2 . . . . .86 A1
Redshots Cl SL7 . . . . .1 C2
Redvers Rd RG12 . . . . .118 A2
Redwood Burnham SL1 . . . . .21 A2
  Egham TW20 . . . . .123 C4
Redwood Ave RG5 . . . . .88 A3
Redwood Dr
  Frimley GU15 . . . . .152 B2
  Sunningdale SL5 . . . . .121 A2
Redwood Gdns SL3 . . . . .42 B3
Redwood Mews TW15 . . . . .98 B1
Redwood Way RG31 . . . . . . .57 B2
Redwoods The SL4 . . . . .67 B2
Reed Cl SL0 . . . . .44 C4
Reed Place Bsns Pk
  TW17 . . . . .124 C1
Reed Wlk TW15 . . . . .105 B2
Reed's Hill RG12 . . . . .118 A2
Reeds Ave RG6 . . . . .86 C2
Reedsfield Cl TW15 . . . . . . .98 A3
Reedsfield Rd TW15 . . . . . . .98 A2
Reeve Rd SL6 . . . . .65 A4
Reeves Way RG41 . . . . .116 A2
Reform Rd SL6 . . . . .40 A4
Regal Ct SL6 . . . . .40 A1
Regatta Ho TW18 . . . . .96 C2
Regency Hts RG4 . . . . .58 C2

Regent Cl Earley RG6 . . . . . .87 B1
  Hungerford RG17 . . . . .100 B3
Regent Ct Bagshot GU19 . .145 C1
  🗑 Maidenhead SL6 . . . . . . .39 C4
  Reading RG1 . . . . .86 A4
  Slough SL1 . . . . .42 C4
  Windsor SL4 . . . . .67 B3
Regent St RG1 . . . . .86 C4
Regent Way GU16 . . . . .152 A1
Regents Cl RG41 . . . . .104 C2
Regents Pl GU47 . . . . .150 B4
Regents Wlk SL5 . . . . .120 B1
Regis Cl RG2 . . . . .113 B4
Regis Ct TW14 . . . . .71 B1
Regnum Dr RG14 . . . . .105 A3
Reid Ave SL6 . . . . .39 C4
Rembrandt Cl RG41 . . . . . . .115 B3
Rembrandt Way RG1 . . . . . .85 C3
Remembrance Rd RG4 . . . .104 C1
Remenham Church La
  RG9 .16 A2
Remenham La RG9 . . . . .15 C2
Remenham Terr RG9 . . . . . . .16 B1
Renault Rd RG5 . . . . .88 A3
Renfree Way TW17 . . . . .125 A1
Rennie Cl TW15 . . . . .97 B3
Repton Cl SL6 . . . . .39 B2
Repton Rd RG6 . . . . .87 B2
Restwold Cl RG30 . . . . .85 B2
Retford Cl RG5 . . . . .60 C1
Retreat The
  Englefield Green TW20 . . . .95 C2
  Holyport SL6 . . . . .65 B4
Revel Rd HP10 . . . . .3 B4
Revesby Cl Maidenhead SL6 .39 B2
  West End GU24 . . . . .153 B3
Rex Ave TW15 . . . . .98 A2
Reynards Cl RG41 . . . . .88 B1
Reynolds Ct RG18 . . . . .106 B2
Reynolds Gn GU47 . . . . . . .150 B3
Rhigos RG4 . . . . .58 C3
Rhine Cl RG4 . . . . .59 B1
Rhodes Cl Earley RG6 . . . . . .87 C2
  Egham TW20 . . . . .96 A2
Rhodes Ct TW20 . . . . .96 B2
Rhododendron Cl SL5 . . . . .92 C1
Rhododendron Rd GU16 .152 A1
Rhododendron Ride
  SL4,TW20 . . . . .94 C2
Rhododendron Wlk SL5 . . .92 C1
Ribbleton Cl RG6 . . . . .87 C2
Ribstone Rd SL6 . . . . .39 A2
Ricardo Rd SL4 . . . . .68 A1
Richard Ct TW15 . . . . .97 C2
Richard Nevill Ct 🖪 RG4 .59 B1
Richards Cl UB3 . . . . .71 B4
Richards Way SL1 . . . . .42 A3
Richardson's Lawn Cotts
  SL4 .94 A3
Richborough Cl RG6 . . . . . . .87 A1
Richfield Ave RG1 . . . . .58 C1
Richings Way SL0 . . . . .44 C2
Richmond Ave
  Feltham TW14 . . . . .71 C1
  Thatcham RG19 . . . . .106 A2
Richmond Cl GU16 . . . . . . .151 C1
Richmond Cres Slough SL1 .43 A3
  Staines TW18 . . . . .96 C2
Richmond Dr TW17 . . . . . . .125 B2
Richmond Ho GU47 . . . . . . .150 C4
Richmond Rd
  Caversham RG4 . . . . .58 C2
  Reading RG30 . . . . .85 B4
  Sandhurst GU47 . . . . .150 C4
  Staines TW18 . . . . .96 C2
Richmond Rise RG41 . . . . .115 C4
Richmondwood SL5 . . . . . .121 A1
Rickman Cl
  Arborfield RG2 . . . . .114 C1
  Bracknell RG12 . . . . .118 B2
  Woodley RG5 . . . . .87 B3
Rickman's La SL2 . . . . .22 C3
Riddings La RG19 . . . . .133 B1
Riders La RG7 . . . . .112 A2
Rideway Cl GU15 . . . . .151 A2
Ridge Hall Cl RG4 . . . . .58 C2
Ridge Mount Rd SL5 . . . . . .121 A1
Ridge The Cold Ash RG18 . .106 B4
  Lower Basildon RG8 . . . . . . .34 C1
  Upper Basildon RG8 . . . . . . .55 C4
Ridge Way Iver SL0 . . . . .44 C3
  Virginia Water GU25 . . . . . .122 C2
Ridgebank SL1 . . . . .41 C3
Ridgemead Rd TW20 . . . . . .95 A3
Ridgemount Cl RG31 . . . . . .57 A1
Ridgeway
  Walton-on-T KT12 . . . . .125 C1
  Wargrave RG10 . . . . .36 C1
Ridgeway Cl
  Hermitage RG18 . . . . .79 A4
  Lightwater GU18 . . . . .153 A4
  Marlow SL7 . . . . .1 C2
Ridgeway Prim Sch RG2 . .86 B1
Ridgeway Sch RG8 . . . . . . .38 C3
Ridgeway The
  Bracknell RG12 . . . . .118 B3
  Caversham RG4 . . . . .59 A2
  Letcombe Bassett OX12 . . . .7 B3
  Lightwater GU18 . . . . .146 A1
  Marlow SL7 . . . . .1 C2
  Woodley RG5 . . . . .87 C3
Ridgeway Trad Est The
  SL0 .44 C3
Ridgewood Ctr (Hospl)
  GU16 . . . . .152 B2
Ridgewood Dr GU16 . . . . . .152 B2
Riding Court Rd SL3 . . . . . . .68 B4
Riding Ct SL3 . . . . .68 B4

Riding Way RG41 . . . . .115 C
Ridings The
  Caversham RG4 . . . . .59 B
  Frimley GU16 . . . . .152 A
  Iver SL0 . . . . .44 C
  Maidenhead SL6 . . . . .39 A
Ridleigh Ct TW15 . . . . .98 A
Ridlington Cl RG6 . . . . .87 C
Rigby Lodge SL1 . . . . .42 C
Righton Cl RG41 . . . . .61 A
Riley Rd Marlow SL7 . . . . .1 B
  Reading RG30 . . . . .84 C
Ring The RG12 . . . . .118 B
Ringmead Bracknell,
  Great Hollands RG12 . . . . .117 C
  Bracknell, Hanworth RG12 .118 A
Ringwood RG12 . . . . .117 C
Ringwood Cl SL5 . . . . .120 A
Ringwood Rd
  Blackwater GU17 . . . . .150 A
  Reading RG30 . . . . .58 A
Ripley Ave TW20 . . . . .95 C
Ripley Cl SL3 . . . . .43 C
Ripley Rd RG30 . . . . .58 A
Ripon Cl GU15 . . . . .152 B
Ripplemere RG12 . . . . .118 B
Ripplesmere Cl GU47 . . . . .150 A
Ripston Rd TW15 . . . . .98 B
Risborough Rd SL6 . . . . .39 C
Rise Rd SL5 . . . . .120 C
Rise The Caversham RG4 . . .59 A
  Cold Ash RG18 . . . . .106 B
  Crowthorne RG45 . . . . .142 C
  Finchampstead RG40 . . . . .141 A
  Wokingham RG41 . . . . .116 A
Riseley Rd SL6 . . . . .39 B
Rissington Cl RG31 . . . . . . .57 C
River Ct SL6 . . . . .40 A
River Gdns Maidenhead SL6 .40 B
  Purley on T RG8 . . . . .57 B
River Mount KT12 . . . . .125 C
River Park Ave TW18 . . . . . .96 B
River Pk RG14 . . . . .105 B
River Rd Caversham RG4 . . .58 B
  Reading RG1 . . . . .86 A
  Staines TW18 . . . . .123 C
  Taplow SL6 . . . . .40 B
  Yateley GU46 . . . . .149 A
River & Rowing Mus RG9 .15 C
River Side Cotts HP10 . . . . . .3 C
River St SL4 . . . . .67 B
River View HP10 . . . . .3 A
River Wlk RG14 . . . . .105 A
Riverbank TW18 . . . . .96 C
Riverdene Dr RG41 . . . . . . .88 A
Riverhead Ct SL7 . . . . .18 B
Rivermead Ind Est RG19 .106 C
Rivermead Prim Sch RG5 .87 C
Rivermead Rd
  Camberley GU15 . . . . .151 A
  Woodley RG5 . . . . .87 C
Riverpark Dr SL7 . . . . .1 C
Riversdale SL8 . . . . .3 A
Riversdale Ct RG1 . . . . .86 C
Riversdell Cl KT16 . . . . .123 C
Riverside Bradfield RG7 . . . .82 B
  Egham TW20 . . . . .96 A
  Lower Halliford TW17 . . . . .125 C
  Wraysbury TW19 . . . . .95 B
Riverside Ave RG18 . . . . . . .153 B
Riverside Cl TW18 . . . . .123 C
Riverside Ct 🔲 RG4 . . . . . . .59 A
Riverside Dr Egham TW18 . .96 C
  Staines TW18 . . . . .123 C
Riverside Pl TW19 . . . . .70 B
Riverside Rd Staines TW18 .96 C
  Stanwell TW19 . . . . .70 C
Riverside Way GU15 . . . . . .151 A
Riverside Wlk SL4 . . . . .67 B
Riverview TW17 . . . . .125 B
Riverview Rd RG8 . . . . .56 B
Riverway
  Great Shefford RG17 . . . . . .48 A
  Staines TW18 . . . . .124 A
Riverwood Ct SL7 . . . . .18 C
Riverwoods Ave SL7 . . . . . . .2 A
Riverwoods Dr SL7 . . . . .2 A
Rixman Cl SL6 . . . . .39 B
Rixon Cl SL3 . . . . .43 C
Robert Piggott CE Inf Sch
  RG10 . . . . .36 C
Robert Piggott CE Jun Sch
  RG10 . . . . .36 B
Robert Sandilands
  Prim Sch RG14 . . . . .104 C
Roberts Cl TW19 . . . . .70 B
Roberts Gr RG41 . . . . .115 C
Roberts Rd GU15 . . . . .151 A
Roberts Way TW20 . . . . .95 B
Robertsfield RG19 . . . . .105 C
Robertson Cl RG14 . . . . . . .131 A
Robin Cl RG7 . . . . .111 A
Robin Hill Dr GU15 . . . . . . .152 A
Robin Hood Cl SL1 . . . . .41 C
Robin Hood Way RG41 . . . .88 B
Robin La Newtown RG20 . . .131 C
  Sandhurst GU47 . . . . .143 B
Robin Par 🖪 SL2 . . . . .22 B
Robin Way Reading RG31 . . .84 A
  Staines TW18 . . . . .96 C
Robin Willis Way SL4 . . . . . .68 A
Robin's Bow GU15 . . . . .151 A
Robindale Ave RG6 . . . . .87 B
Robinhood La RG41 . . . . . . .88 B
Robins Cl RG14 . . . . .130 C
Robins Grove Cres GU46 .149 A
Robins Hill RG17 . . . . .127 C

Robinson Cl OX11 . . . . .12 A4
Robinson Ct RG6 . . . . .87 A1
Roby Dr RG12 . . . . .118 B1
Rochester Ave
Feltham TW13 . . . . .98 C3
Woodley RG5 . . . . .60 C1
Rochester Rd TW20 . . . . . . .96 B1
Rochford Way SL6 . . . . .41 A4
Rochfords Gdns SL2 . . . . . . .43 B3
Rockall Ct SL3 . . . . .44 A2
Rockbourne Gdns RG30 . . . .58 A1
Rockfel Rd RG17 . . . . .25 A1
Rockfield Way 7 GU47 . . . . .150 B4
Rockingham Rd RG14 . . . . .104 C1
Rockmoor La SP11 . . . . . . .147 A1
Rodd Est TW17 . . . . .125 B2
Rodney Ct 11 RG1 . . . . .86 A3
Rodney Way SL3 . . . . .69 C3
Rodway Rd RG30 . . . . .57 C1
Roebuck Est RG42 . . . . .90 B1
Roebuck Gn SL1 . . . . .41 C4
Roebuck Rise RG31 . . . . . . .57 B2
Roebuts Cl RG14 . . . . .130 C4
Rogers La SL2 . . . . .22 C2
Rogers's La RG17 . . . . .47 B3
Rogosa Rd GU24 . . . . .153 C3
Rokeby Cl Bracknell RG12 .118 A4
Newbury RG14 . . . . .131 A4
Rokeby Dr RG4 . . . . .58 B4
Rokes Pl GU46 . . . . .149 A3
Rokesby Rd SL2 . . . . .21 C1
Rolls La SL6 . . . . .64 C4
Roman Field RG7 . . . . .136 A1
Roman Lea SL6 . . . . .19 C4
Roman Ride RG45 . . . . .142 B3
Roman Way Bourne End SL8 . .3 A2
Earley RG6 . . . . .87 B2
Thatcham RG18 . . . . .106 A2
Winkfield RG42 . . . . .118 C4
Romana Ct TW18 . . . . .97 A2
Romano Ct 9 RG14 . . . . . .105 A1
Romans Gate RG26 . . . . . . .135 C1
Romany Cl RG30 . . . . .58 A1
Romany La RG30 . . . . .58 A1
Romeo Hill RG42 . . . . .118 C4
Romney Ct 11 SL7 . . . . .1 C2
Romney Ho RG12 . . . . .118 C3
Romney Lock Rd SL4 . . . . . .67 B4
Romsey Cl
Blackwater GU17 . . . . .150 B3
Slough SL3 . . . . .43 C2
Romsey Rd RG30 . . . . .58 A1
Rona Ct RG30 . . . . .85 A4
Ronaldsay Spur SL1 . . . . . . .42 C4
Ronita Ct RG1 . . . . .86 C3
Rood Hill RG20 . . . . .76 B2
Rook Cl RG41 . . . . .115 C3
Rook Rd HP10 . . . . .3 B2
Rookery Cl SL7 . . . . .1 B1
Rookery Rd TW18 . . . . .97 A2
Rookery The RG20 . . . . .50 B4
Rooksfield RG20 . . . . .132 A1
Rooksmead Rd TW16 . . . . . .125 C4
Rooksnest La RG17 . . . . . . .128 A3
Rookswood Bracknell RG42 . .91 A1
Stockcross RG20 . . . . .103 C3
Rookwood Ave GU47 . . . . . .143 C1
Rope Wlk RG19 . . . . .106 B2
Rosa Ave TW15 . . . . .98 A4
Rosary Gdns Ashford TW15 . .98 A2
Yateley GU46 . . . . .149 B3
Rose Cl RG5 . . . . .88 A4
Rose Cotts SL6 . . . . .39 B2
Rose Ct RG40 . . . . .116 B3
Rose Gdns TW19 . . . . .97 B4
Rose Hill Binfield RG42 . . . . .90 B2
Burnham SL1 . . . . .21 A3
Rose Ind Est
Bourne End SL8 . . . . .3 A2
Marlow Bottom SL7 . . . . .1 B3
Rose Kiln La RG1 & RG2 . . . .86 A2
Rose La Hurley RG9 . . . . . . .17 A1
Knowl Hill RG10 . . . . .37 A4
Rose St RG40 . . . . .116 B3
Rose Wlk Reading RG1 . . . . .86 A4
Slough SL3 . . . . .42 A4
Roseacre Cl TW17 . . . . .125 A4
Rosebank Cl SL6 . . . . .19 C4
Rosebay RG40 . . . . .116 C4
Rosebery Rd RG4 . . . . .58 B4
Rosecroft Way RG2 . . . . . . .113 C3
Rosedale RG42 . . . . .90 B2
Rosedale Cres RG6 . . . . .87 A4
Rosedale Gdns
Bracknell RG12 . . . . .118 A4
Thatcham RG19 . . . . .106 B1
Rosedene La GU47 . . . . . . .150 B4
Rosefield Rd TW18 . . . . .97 A2
Rosehill Cl SL1 . . . . .43 A2
Rosehill Ho RG4 . . . . .59 B4
Rosehill Pk RG4 . . . . .59 B4
Roseleigh Cl SL6 . . . . .39 A4
Rosemary Ave RG6 . . . . .86 C1
Rosemary Gdns GU17 . . . . .150 B3
Rosemary La
Blackwater GU17 . . . . .150 B3
Thorpe TW20 . . . . .123 A3
Rosemary Terr RG14 . . . . . .104 C1
Rosemead KT16 . . . . .124 A1
Rosemead Ave
Feltham TW13 . . . . .98 C3
Purley on T RG31 . . . . .57 A2
Rosen Ct RG19 . . . . .106 C2
Rosery The SL8 . . . . .3 A2
Roses La SL4 . . . . .66 A4
Rosewood RG5 . . . . .87 B2
Rosewood Dr TW17 . . . . . . .124 C2

Rosewood Way
Farnham Common SL2 . . . . .22 B4
West End GU24 . . . . .153 C3
Rosier Cl RG19 . . . . .106 C1
Rosken Gr SL2 . . . . .22 A2
Roslyn Rd RG5 . . . . .87 B3
Ross Ho 2 RG30 . . . . .85 B3
Ross Rd Maidenhead SL6 . . . .39 C2
Reading RG1 . . . . .59 A1
Rossendale Rd RG4 . . . . . . .59 B2
Rossett Cl RG12 . . . . .118 A3
Rossey Pl SL4 . . . . .42 B1
Rossington Pl RG2 . . . . . . .113 B4
Rossiter Cl SL3 . . . . .43 C1
Rosslea GU20 . . . . .146 A3
Rosslyn Cl TW16 . . . . .98 C1
Rothbury Wlk GU15 . . . . . . .152 B2
Rother Cl GU47 . . . . .150 B4
Rotherfield Ave RG41 . . . . .116 A4
Rotherfield Cl RG7 . . . . .83 C2
Rotherfield Rd RG9 . . . . . . .35 C4
Rotherfield Way RG4 . . . . . .59 A2
Rothwell Gdns RG5 . . . . . . .61 A1
Rothwell Rd RG45 . . . . .143 B2
Rothwell Wlk RG4 . . . . .59 B1
Rotten Row Hill RG7 . . . . . .81 C2
Roughgrove Copse RG42 . . .90 A1
Rounce La GU24 . . . . .153 B3
Round Cl GU46 . . . . .149 C3
Round End RG14 . . . . .130 B3
Roundabout La RG41 . . . . .115 B4
Roundfield RG7 . . . . .107 A3
Roundhead Rd RG7 . . . . . . .83 B2
Roundshead Dr RG12 . . . . .118 B4
Roundway Egham TW20 . . . .96 B2
Frimley GU15 . . . . .152 B3
Roundway Cl GU15 . . . . . . .152 B3
Routh Ct TW14 . . . . .98 B4
Routh La RG30 . . . . .84 C3
Row La RG4 . . . . .59 C4
Rowallan Cl RG4 . . . . .59 B3
Rowan 2 RG12 . . . . .118 C2
Rowan Ave TW20 . . . . .96 B2
Rowan Cl Camberley GU15 .151 C4
Wokingham RG41 . . . . .115 C3
Rowan Ct RG6 . . . . .87 A1
Rowan Dr
Crowthorne RG45 . . . . .143 B3
Newbury RG14 . . . . .105 A3
Woodley RG5 . . . . .87 C4
Rowan Ho 1 SL8 . . . . .3 A2
Rowan Way
Burghfield Common RG30 .111 A3
Slough SL2 . . . . .42 A4
Rowanhurst Dr SL2 . . . . . . .22 B4
Rowans Cl GU14 . . . . .150 C1
Rowans The TW16 . . . . .98 C2
Rowcroft Rd RG2 . . . . .140 C4
Rowdell Dr RG2 . . . . .86 B1
Rowdown RG17 . . . . .24 C1
Rowe Ct RG30 . . . . .85 A4
Rowland Cl SL4 . . . . .66 B2
Rowland Hill
Almshouses TW15 . . . . . . .98 A2
Rowland Way Earley RG6 . . .86 C1
Littleton TW15 . . . . .98 B1
Rowland's Cl RG7 . . . . .136 B3
Rowles Paddock RG20 . . . . .10 A1
Rowley Cl RG12 . . . . .118 C3
Rowley La SL3 . . . . .23 B2
Rowley Rd RG2 . . . . .86 A2
Roxborough Way SL6 . . . . . .38 C2
Roxburgh Cl GU15 . . . . . . .152 B2
Roxeth Ct TW15 . . . . .98 A1
Roxford Cl TW17 . . . . .125 C2
Roxwell Cl SL1 . . . . .41 C3
Roy Cl RG18 . . . . .78 C3
Royal Ascot Golf Club
SL5 . . . . .120 A4
Royal Ave RG14 . . . . .105 A2
Royal Cotts SL6 . . . . .19 B4
Royal Ct 10 RG1 . . . . .86 B4
Royal Free Ct 22 SL4 . . . . . .67 B3
Royal Holloway Univ
of London TW20 . . . . .95 B1
Royal Hunt Ho SL5 . . . . . . .119 B4
Royal Mans RG9 . . . . .15 C1
Royal Military Acad
GU15 . . . . .150 C3
Royal Military Acad
Hospl RG45 . . . . .151 A4
Royal Oak Cl GU46 . . . . . . .149 C3
Royal Oak Dr RG45 . . . . . . .143 A4
Royal Prim Sch The SL4 . . . .94 B2
Royal Victoria Gdns SL5 . . .120 A4
Royal Way RG2 . . . . .112 C4
Royal Windsor Race Course
SL4 . . . . .66 C4
Roycroft La RG40 . . . . .141 C4
Royston Cl RG30 . . . . .84 C4
Royston Way SL1 . . . . .41 B4
Rubus Cl GU24 . . . . .153 C3
Ruby Cl Slough SL1 . . . . . . .42 A2
Wokingham RG41 . . . . .115 C4
Rudd Hall Rise GU15 . . . . . .151 C2
Ruddlesway SL4 . . . . .66 B3
Rudland Cl RG19 . . . . .106 B1
Rudsworth Cl SL3 . . . . .69 B4
Rufus Isaacs Rd RG4 . . . . . .59 A1
Rugby Cl GU47 . . . . .143 C1
Ruggles-Brise Rd TW15 . . . .97 B2
Rumseys La OX11 . . . . .12 A4
Runnemede Rd TW20 . . . . . .96 A2
Runnymede Cotts TW19 . . . .96 B4
Runnymede Ct TW20 . . . . . .96 A2
Runnymede Rdbt TW20 . . . . .96 A2

Rupert Cl RG9 . . . . .15 C2
Rupert House Sch RG9 . . . .15 C1
Rupert Rd RG14 . . . . .130 C4
Rupert Sq 16 RG1 . . . . .86 B4
Rupert St RG1 . . . . .86 B4
Rupert Wlk 17 RG1 . . . . .86 B4
Rupert's La RG9 . . . . .15 C2
Ruscombe La RG10 . . . . . . .61 C3
Ruscombe Pk RG10 . . . . . . .61 C3
Ruscombe Rd RG10 . . . . . . .61 C3
Ruscombe Way TW14 . . . . . .98 C4
Rushall Cl RG6 . . . . .113 C4
Rusham Park Ave TW20 . . . .96 A1
Rusham Rd TW20 . . . . .95 C1
Rushbrook Rd RG5 . . . . .87 B4
Rushburn HP10 . . . . .3 C3
Rushden Dr RG2 . . . . .86 C1
Rushes The
Maidenhead SL6 . . . . .40 B3
Marlow SL7 . . . . .18 B4
Rushey Way RG6 . . . . .87 B1
Rushington Ave SL6 . . . . . . .39 C3
Rushmere Pl TW20 . . . . .95 C2
Rushmoor Gdns RG31 . . . . .84 A2
Rushy Ho 7 RG12 . . . . .118 C3
Ruskin Ave TW14 . . . . .71 C1
Ruskin Ct RG45 . . . . .142 C1
Ruskin Rd TW18 . . . . .96 C1
Ruskin Way RG41 . . . . .115 B3
Russel Cl RG12 . . . . .118 B1
Russell Ct
Blackwater GU17 . . . . .150 B3
Maidenhead SL6 . . . . .39 C4
Russell Dr TW19 . . . . .70 B1
Russell Ho 3 SL8 . . . . .3 A2
Russell Rd
Lower Halliford TW17 . . . . .125 B1
Mapledurham RG4 . . . . .58 B4
Newbury RG14 . . . . .104 C1
Russell St Reading RG1 . . . .85 C4
Windsor SL4 . . . . .67 B3
Russell Way RG41 . . . . .88 A1
Russet Ave TW16, TW17 . . . .125 C3
Russet Cl TW19 . . . . .69 C1
Russet Gdns GU15 . . . . . . .151 B2
Russet Glade
Burghfield Common RG7 . .111 A1
Caversham RG4 . . . . .59 B4
Russet Rd SL6 . . . . .39 B2
Russington Rd TW17 . . . . . .125 B1
Russley Gn RG40 . . . . .116 A1
Rustington Cl 5 RG6 . . . . . .87 B1
Ruston Way SL5 . . . . .119 C4
Rutherford Cl SL4 . . . . .66 C3
Rutherford Wlk RG31 . . . . . .84 A4
Rutherwyk Rd KT16 . . . . . . .123 C1
Rutland Ave SL1 . . . . .42 B4
Rutland Gate SL6 . . . . .39 B3
Rutland Pl SL6 . . . . .39 B3
Rutland Rd Maidenhead SL6 .39 B3
Reading RG30 . . . . .85 B4
Ruxbury Ct TW15 . . . . .97 C3
Ruxbury Rd KT16 . . . . .123 B2
Ryan Mount GU47 . . . . .150 A4
Ryans Mount SL7 . . . . .1 B1
Rycroft SL4 . . . . .66 C2
Rydal Ave RG30 . . . . .57 C1
Rydal Cl GU15 . . . . .152 B3
Rydal Dr RG19 . . . . .106 A2
Rydal Pl GU18 . . . . .153 A4
Rydal Way TW20 . . . . .96 A1
Ryde Gdns GU46 . . . . .149 A3
Ryde The TW18 . . . . .124 A4
Rydings SL4 . . . . .66 C2
Rye Cl 1 SL1 . . . . .43 A2
Rye Gr GU18,GU20 . . . . . . .146 C1
Ryecroft Cl Wargrave RG10 .36 C1
Ryecroft Gdns GU17 . . . . . .150 C2
Ryehurst La RG42 . . . . .90 C3
Ryeish Green Comp Sch
RG7 . . . . .113 B2
Ryeish La RG7 . . . . .113 B2
Ryemead La RG42, SL4 . . . . .92 B3
Ryhill Way RG6 . . . . .113 C4
Ryland Cl TW13 . . . . .98 C2
Rylstone Cl SL6 . . . . .39 B2
Rylstone Rd RG30 . . . . .85 B4
Ryvers Ave GU46 . . . . .149 A3
Ryvers End SL3 . . . . .43 C2
Ryvers Rd SL3 . . . . .43 C2
Ryvers Sch SL3 . . . . .43 B2

S

Sabah Ct TW15 . . . . .98 A2
Sackville St RG1 . . . . .86 A4
Sacred Heart Coll SL5 . . . .121 B2
Sacred Heart
RC Prim Sch The RG9 . . . .15 B1
Saddleback Rd GU15 . . . . . .151 C4
Saddlebrook Pk TW16 . . . . . .98 C1
Saddler Cnr GU47 . . . . .150 A4
Saddlewood GU15 . . . . .151 B2
Sadlers Cl RG41 . . . . .88 B1
Sadlers End RG41 . . . . .115 B3
Sadlers La RG41 . . . . .115 B4
Sadlers Mews SL6 . . . . .40 A4
Sadlers Rd RG17 . . . . .127 A3
Saffron Cl Datchet SL3 . . . . .68 A3
Earley RG6 . . . . .87 B2
Newbury RG14 . . . . .104 C2
Saffron Ct TW14 . . . . .98 B4

Saffron Rd RG12 . . . . .118 A3
Sage Cl RG6 . . . . .87 A1
Sage Rd SL1 . . . . .57 B2
Sage Wlk RG42 . . . . .91 B1
Sagecroft Rd RG18 . . . . . . .106 B3
Sailing Club Rd SL8 . . . . .3 A2
Sainsbury Ctr The TK16 . . . .124 A1
St Adrian's Cl SL6 . . . . .39 A2
St Agnes Mews RG2 . . . . . . .86 B1
St Agnes Terr RG17 . . . . . . .25 A1
St Alban's St SL4 . . . . .67 B3
St Albans Ct 18 SL4 . . . . . . .67 B3
St Andrew's Ave SL4 . . . . . .66 C3
St Andrew's Cl
Old Windsor SL4 . . . . .68 A1
Upper Halliford TW17 . . . . .125 B3
Wraysbury TW19 . . . . .68 C1
St Andrew's Cres SL4 . . . . . .66 C3
St Andrew's Way SL1 . . . . . .41 B3
St Andrews RG12 . . . . .117 C2
St Andrews Cl
Bradfield RG7 . . . . .82 B3
Crowthorne RG45 . . . . .142 C3
St Andrews Cotts 1 SL4 . . .67 A3
St Andrews Ct Ascot SL5 . . .120 B2
Colnbrook SL3 . . . . .69 B4
35 Reading RG1 . . . . .86 B4
28 Slough SL1 . . . . .42 C2
St Andrews Rd
Caversham RG4 . . . . .58 C2
Henley-on-T RG9 . . . . .35 C4
St Ann's Cl KT16 . . . . .123 C4
St Ann's Heath
Cty Mid Sch GU25 . . . . . . .122 C2
St Ann's Hill Rd KT16 . . . . .123 B2
St Ann's Rd KT16 . . . . .123 C4
St Anne's Ave TW19 . . . . . . .97 B4
St Anne's Cl RG9 . . . . .15 B1
St Anne's Prim Sch TW19 .97 C4
St Anne's RC Prim Sch
Caversham RG4 . . . . .59 A1
Chertsey KT16 . . . . .124 A1
St Annes Glade GU19 . . . . .145 B2
St Annes Rd RG4 . . . . .59 A1
St Anthony's RC Prim Sch
SL2 . . . . .22 B1
St Anthony's Way TW14 . . . .71 C2
St Anthonys Cl RG42 . . . . .118 A4
St Augustine's
RC Prim Sch GU16 . . . . . .151 C1
St Barnabas Rd
Caversham RG4 . . . . .59 A3
Earley RG2 . . . . .86 C1
St Bartholomew's Sch
RG14 . . . . .104 C1
St Bartholomews Rd RG1 .86 C4
St Bernard's Convent Sch
SL3 . . . . .43 B2
St Bernard's Prep Sch
SL1 . . . . .43 A2
St Bernards Rd SL3 . . . . . . .43 B2
St Birinus Rd RG31 . . . . . . .84 B3
St Catherines Cl RG41 . . . . .88 A1
St Catherines Ct
Staines TW18 . . . . .97 A2
3 Windsor SL4 . . . . .67 A3
St Catherines Hill RG7 . . . .136 C3
St Catherines Rd GU16 . . . .152 A1
St Cecelia Ct RG2 . . . . .86 B2
St Chad's Rd SL6 . . . . .39 C4
St Christophers Gdns
SL5 . . . . .119 B4
St Clements Cl RG6 . . . . . . .87 B1
St Columba's Cl SL6 . . . . . . .39 A2
St Crispin's Comp Sch
RG40 . . . . .116 C3
St Cuthbert's Cl TW20 . . . .95 B1
St Cuthbert's RC Prim Sch
TW20 . . . . .95 B1
St David's Cl SL6 . . . . .39 A2
St David's Jun Sch TW15 . .97 C3
St David's Rd RG14 . . . . . .104 C1
St Davids Cl RG4 . . . . .58 C3
St Davids Dr TW20 . . . . .95 B1
St Dominic Savio
RC Prim Sch RG5 . . . . . . .87 B4
St Donats Pl RG14 . . . . . . .105 A1
St Dunstan's Rd TW13 . . . . .98 C3
St Edmund Campion
RC Prim Sch SL6 . . . . .39 C4
St Edward's RC Sch
Reading RG30 . . . . .85 B4
Windsor SL4 . . . . .67 A3
St Edward's Royal Free
Ecumenical Mid Sch
Reading RG30 . . . . .85 B4
Windsor SL4 . . . . .67 A3
St Edwards Rd RG6 . . . . . . .87 A3
St Elizabeth Cl RG2 . . . . . .113 A4
St Elmo Cl SL2 . . . . .22 B1
St Elmo Cres SL2 . . . . .22 B1
St Ethelbert's RC Sch SL2 .43 A4
St Finian's RC Prim Sch
RG18 . . . . .106 B4
St Francis RC Sch SL5 . . . .120 C4
St Gabrial's Sch RG20 . . . .131 A3
St George's Ave RG14 . . . .104 C1
St George's Cl SL4 . . . . .66 C3
St George's Cres SL1 . . . . . .41 B3
St George's La SL5 . . . . . . .120 A3
St George's Rd GU15 . . . . .151 B3
St George's Sch
Ascot SL5 . . . . .120 A4
Windsor SL4 . . . . .67 B4
St Georges Ct GU47 . . . . . .143 C1
St Georges Ind Est GU15 .151 A2

St Georges Rd RG30 . . . . . .85 B4
St Georges Terr RG30 . . . . .85 A4
St Giles Cl RG1 . . . . .86 A3
St Giles Ct 14 RG1 . . . . .86 A3
St Helens Cres GU47 . . . . . .150 A4
St Helier Cl RG41 . . . . .116 A2
St Hilda's Ave TW15 . . . . . . .97 C2
St Ives Cl RG7 . . . . .83 B1
St Ives Rd SL6 . . . . .40 C4
St James Cl
Pangbourne RG8 . . . . .56 B3
Twyford RG10 . . . . .61 C3
St James Ctyd 4 SL7 . . . . . . .1 C1
St James Pl SL1 . . . . .41 B4
St James Rd RG40 . . . . . . .141 C4
St James Wlk SL0 . . . . .44 C2
St John the Evangelist
CE Sch RG14 . . . . .104 C1
St John's Beaumont
Prep Sch SL4 . . . . .95 A3
St John's CE Prim Sch
RG1 . . . . .86 B4
St John's Gdns RG14 . . . . .104 C1
St John's Rd
North Ascot SL5 . . . . .92 C1
Sandhurst GU47 . . . . .150 B4
St Johns Ct RG5 . . . . .87 C4
St Johns Ct TW20 . . . . .96 A2
St Johns Dr SL4 . . . . .67 A3
St Johns Hill RG1 . . . . .86 B4
St Johns Inf Sch RG7 . . . . .137 A3
St Johns Rd
Caversham RG4 . . . . .59 B1
Mortimer RG7 . . . . .137 A3
Newbury RG14 . . . . .105 A1
Reading RG1 . . . . .86 B4
Slough SL2 . . . . .43 A3
Thatcham RG19 . . . . .106 B2
Windsor SL4 . . . . .67 A3
St Johns St
Crowthorne RG45 . . . . .143 A2
Reading RG1 . . . . .86 B4
St Johns Way KT16 . . . . . . .124 A1
St Joseph's Convent Sch
RG1 . . . . .86 C3
St Joseph's Convent
Prep Sch RG1 . . . . .86 C3
St Joseph's Ct 7 RG14 . . . .105 A2
St Joseph's RC Prim Sch
Bracknell RG12 . . . . .118 B4
Newbury RG14 . . . . .105 A2
St Joseph's RC Sec Sch
SL2 . . . . .43 A4
St Jude's CE Sch TW20 . . . .95 B1
St Jude's Cl TW20 . . . . .95 B2
St Jude's Cotts TW20 . . . . . .95 B2
St Jude's Rd TW20 . . . . .95 B2
St Katherines Rd RG9 . . . . .35 B4
St Laurence Way SL1 . . . . . .43 B4
St Lawrence Sq RG17 . . . . .100 B3
St Leger Ct RG14 . . . . .104 C2
St Leonard's Ave 23 SL4 . . .67 B3
St Leonard's Rd
Windsor SL4 . . . . .67 B2
Windsor, Clewer Green SL4 . .66 B2
St Leonards Hill SL4 . . . . . .66 C2
St Leonards Wlk SL0 . . . . . .44 C2
St Luke's CE Prim Sch
SL6 . . . . .39 C4
St Luke's Rd
Maidenhead SL6 . . . . .39 C4
Old Windsor SL4 . . . . .68 A1
St Lukes Ct RG4 . . . . .59 C4
St Lukes Way RG4 . . . . .59 C4
St Margaret Clitherow
RC Prim Sch RG12 . . . . . .117 C1
St Margaret's Rd SL6 . . . . . .39 A4
St Margarets Ave TW15 . . . .98 A4
St Mark's Cl RG7 . . . . .83 A3
St Mark's Cres SL6 . . . . .39 A4
St Mark's Hospl SL6 . . . . . . .39 B4
St Mark's Pl SL4 . . . . .67 B4
St Mark's Rd
Binfield RG42 . . . . .117 B4
Henley-on-T RG9 . . . . .15 C1
Maidenhead SL6 . . . . .39 B4
Windsor SL4 . . . . .67 B3
St Marks Cl RG3 . . . . .106 B2
St Marks Rd Binfield RG42 . .90 B1
Henley-on-T RG9 . . . . .35 B4
St Martin's Ct TW15 . . . . . . .97 B2
St Martins Cl 3 RG6 . . . . . .87 B1
St Martins RC Prim Sch
RG4 . . . . .59 C3
St Mary's All Saints
CE Prim Sch RG1 . . . . .85 C3
St Mary's Ave TW19 . . . . . . .97 B4
St Mary's CE Comb Sch
SL3 . . . . .68 A3
St Mary's CE Jun Sch
RG18 . . . . .106 B2
St Mary's CE Prim Sch
Kintbury RG17 . . . . .102 A1
Slough SL1 . . . . .43 A2
Winkfield RG42 . . . . .92 B3
St Mary's CE Sch TW19 . . . .97 C4
St Mary's Cl
Maidenhead SL6 . . . . .40 A4
Stanwell TW19 . . . . .97 B4
St Mary's Cres TW19 . . . . . .97 B4
St Mary's Ct 6 RG14 . . . . . .105 A2
St Mary's Dr TW14 . . . . .98 B4
St Mary's Gdns GU19 . . . . .145 C2
St Mary's Hill SL5 . . . . .120 B2
St Mary's Jun Sch RG7 . . .137 B3

St Mary's Pl **14** RG14 ....105 A2
St Mary's RC Prim Sch
 SL6 ....19 C1
St Mary's Rd Ascot SL5 ..120 A2
 Camberley GU15 ....151 B3
 Slough SL3 ....43 C2
St Mary's Sch SL5 ....120 A1
St Mary's Wlk SL6 ....39 C4
St Marys Ave RG8 ....57 B3
St Marys Butts RG1 ......86 A4
St Marys Cl
 Henley-on-T RG9 ....35 A4
 Sandhurst GU47 ....150 B4
St Marys La SL4 ....92 B3
St Marys Rd
 Mortimer RG7 ....137 A3
 Newbury RG14 ....105 A2
 Wokingham RG41 ....88 A1
St Marys Way RG7 ....111 A2
St Matthew's Ct TW15 ....98 A2
St Michael's CE Prim Sch
 RG12 ....118 A3
St Michael's Ct SL2 ......21 B1
St Michael's RC Prim Sch
 TW15 ....98 A2
St Michael's Rd
 Newbury RG14 ....104 C1
 Reading RG30 ....84 B4
St Michaels CE Prim Sch
 GU47 ....149 C4
St Michaels Cl RG17 ......25 A1
St Michaels Cotts RG40 .143 B4
St Michaels Ct RG10 ......61 C3
St Michaels Rd
 Ashford TW15 ....98 A2
 Camberley GU15 ....151 A3
 Sandhurst GU47 ....149 C4
St Micheal's CE Sch SL2 .120 B2
St Nazaire Cl TW20 ....96 B2
St Nicholas CE Comb Sch
 SL6 ....20 C1
St Nicholas CE Prim Sch
 Hurst RG10 ....88 C4
 Shepperton TW17 ....125 A2
St Nicholas Dr TW17 .....125 A1
St Nicholas' Rd RG14 ....104 C1
St Nicolas CE Jun Sch
 RG14 ....105 A1
St Olave's Cl TW18 ....96 C1
St Patrick's Ave RG10 .....61 C3
St Patrick's Cl SL6 ....39 A2
St Paul's CE Comb Sch
 HP10 ....3 B2
St Paul's CE Jun Sch
 RG41 ....116 A3
St Paul's Cl TW15 ....98 B2
St Paul's Ct SL6 ....39 C3
St Paul's Gate RG41 ......116 A3
St Paul's RC Prim Sch
 RG31 ....84 B4
St Paul's Rd TW18 ....96 B1
St Pauls Ave SL2 ....43 A3
St Pauls Ct RG1 ....86 A3
St Peter St SL7 ....1 C1
St Peter's CE Comb Sch
 SL1 ....21 A1
St Peter's CE Mid Sch
 SL4 ....67 C1
St Peter's CE Prim Sch
 RG6 ....87 A3
St Peter's Cl Burnham SL1 ..21 A1
 Old Windsor SL4 ....68 A1
 Staines TW18 ....96 C1
St Peter's RC Comb Sch
 SL7 ....1 B2
St Peter's Rd SL6 ....19 B1
St Peters Ave RG4 ....58 C2
St Peters Gdns GU46 ....149 B3
St Peters Hill SL6 ....58 C2
St Peters Rd RG6 ....87 A3
St Pinnock Ave TW18 ....124 A4
St Pirans Ind Day Sch
 SL6 ....19 C1
St Richards Rd RG14 .....105 A2
St Ronans RG30 ....85 A4
St Saviour's Terr **9** RG1 ..86 A3
St Saviours Rd RG1 ....85 C3
St Sebastian Cl RG40 ....142 C4
St Stephens Cl RG4 ....59 A1
St Swithins Cl RG20 ....75 B2
St Swithuns Ct RG10 ......61 B2
St Theresa's RC Prim Sch
 RG40 ....116 B3
St Theresa's Rd TW14 .....71 C2
St Thomas Ct RG18 ......106 C2
St Thomas Wlk SL6 ....69 B4
St-Cloud Way SL6 ....40 A4
Salamanca RG45 ....142 C3
Salcombe Dr RG6 ....87 A2
Salcombe Rd
 Ashford TW15 ....97 C3
 Newbury RG14 ....104 C1
 Reading RG2 ....86 B2
Sale Garden Cotts RG40 .116 B3
Saleby Cl RG6 ....87 C1
Salesian Gdns KT16 .....124 A1
Salesian Sch KT16 ......124 A1
Salford RG2 ....113 B4
Salisbury Ave SL2 ....42 B4
Salisbury Cl RG41 ....116 A1
Salisbury Ct SL6 ....39 C3
Salisbury Mews SL2 ......19 C1
Salisbury Rd
 Blackwater GU17 ....150 B3
 Harlington TW6 ....71 B1

Salisbury Rd *continued*
 Hungerford RG17 ....100 B2
 Reading RG30 ....85 C4
Salmon Cl RG7 ....113 A1
Salmond Rd RG2 ....113 B3
Salt Hill Ave SL1 ....42 B3
Salt Hill Dr SL1 ....42 B3
Salt Hill Mans SL1 ....42 B3
Salt Hill Way SL1 ....42 B3
Salters Cl SL6 ....40 A4
Salters Rd SL6 ....40 A4
Saltersgate Cl RG6 ....87 B1
Saltire Gdns **2** RG42 ....118 A4
Salva Ct SL12 ....86 B3
Salwey Cl RG12 ....118 A2
Salwey Ct RG6 ....87 B1
Samarkand Cl GU15 .....152 A2
Samian Pl RG42 ....90 C1
Sampage Cl RG2 ....113 B3
Sampson Bsns Pk GU15 .151 A2
Sampson Ct TW17 ....125 B2
Sampson Pk RG42 ....117 B4
Sampsons Gn SL2 ....21 C1
Sanctuary Cl RG30 ....84 C4
Sanctuary Rd TW19, TW6 ..71 A1
Sandcroft Rd RG4 ....58 C3
Sanden Cl RG17 ....100 B3
Sandford Down RG12 ....118 C2
Sandford Rd SL6 ....60 C1
Sandford La RG5, RG10 ..88 B3
Sandgate Ave RG30 ....57 C1
Sandhills Cl RG25 ....122 C2
Sandhills La GU25, TW20 .122 C2
Sandhills Mdw TW17 .....125 B2
Sandhills Way RG31 ....84 C2
Sandhurst La GU17 ....150 A3
Sandhurst Rd
 Crowthorne RG45 ....143 A2
 Wokingham RG40 ....142 A4
 Yateley GU46 ....149 C4
Sandhurst Sch GU47 .....150 B4
Sandhurst Sta GU47 .....150 A4
Sandisplatt Rd SL6 ....39 A3
Sandleford Cl RG2 ....113 B3
Sandleford Hospl RG14 ..131 A4
Sandleford Rise RG14 ....131 A4
Sandlers End SL2 ....22 A1
Sandown Ave RG31 ....84 A2
Sandown Cl GU47 ....150 B3
Sandown Dr GU16 ....151 C1
Sandown Rd SL2 ....41 C4
Sandown Way RG14 .....105 B3
Sandpit Hill RG14, RG20 .130 B2
Sandpit La RG7 ....140 A3
Sandringham Ct SL1 ......41 B4
Sandringham Dr TW15 ....97 B2
Sandringham Rd
 Maidenhead SL6 ....19 C1
 Stanwell TW19, TW6 ......70 C1
Sandringham Way RG31 ..84 A2
Sands Farm Dr SL1 ....21 B1
Sandstone Cl RG41 ....88 B1
Sandy Cl RG18 ....79 A2
Sandy La Bracknell RG12 .118 B4
 Camberley GU15 ....151 C3
 Hermitage RG18 ....78 C2
 North Ascot SL5 ....119 B4
 Sandhurst GU47 ....143 A1
 Sunningdale SL5 ....121 A2
 Virginia Water GU25 .....122 C3
 Wokingham RG41 ....116 B3
Sandy Lane Inf Sch RG42 ..91 B1
Sandy Lane Jun Sch RG42 .91 B1
Sandy Mead SL6 ....40 B1
Sandy Ride SL5 ....120 C3
Sandy Way KT12 ....125 C1
Sandygate Cl SL7 ....1 C3
Sandygate Rd SL7 ....1 B2
Sapgood Ct RG19 ....106 C1
Sapphire Cl RG41 ....115 C4
Sarsby Dr TW19 ....96 A3
Sarum RG12 ....117 C1
Sarum Cres RG40 ....116 B4
Sarum Ct **1** RG30 ....85 B3
Sarum Rd RG26 ....135 A4
Sarum Way RG17 ....100 B2
Satis Ho SL3 ....68 B4
Saturn Cl RG41 ....115 C3
Saturn Croft RG42 ....92 A1
Saunders Cl RG10 ....61 C2
Saunders Ct RG8 ....57 A3
Saunton Ave UB3 ....71 C4
Savernake Cl RG30 ....84 C4
Savernake Way RG12 ....118 C2
Savill Gardens The TW20 .94 C1
Savill Way SL7 ....1 C1
Saville Cres TW15 ....98 B1
Saville Gdns GU15 ....152 A3
Savory Wlk RG42 ....90 B1
Sawmill Rd RG18 ....79 A2
Sawpit Rd RG10 ....88 C4
Sawtry Cl RG6 ....87 C1
Sawyer's Cl SL4 ....66 C4
Sawyers Cl SL6 ....39 A1
Sawyers Cres SL6 ....39 A1
Saxby Cl RG7 ....111 A2
Saxon Cl SL3 ....43 C2
Saxon Ct **22** Reading RG1 ..86 A3
 Stanwell TW15 ....70 A1
 Thatcham RG19 ....106 A2
Saxon Cty Jun Sch
 TW17 ....125 A2
Saxon Dr RG42 ....118 C4
Saxon Gdns SL6 ....20 B1
Saxon Rd TW15 ....98 B1
Saxon Way
 Harmondsworth UB7 .....70 B4

Saxon Way *continued*
 Old Windsor SL4 ....68 A1
Saxons Acre RG20 ....28 B2
Sayers Cl RG14 ....131 A4
Scafell Cl RG31 ....57 A1
Scafell Rd SL2 ....41 C4
Scampton Rd TW6 ....70 C1
Scania Wlk RG42 ....92 A1
Scarborough Rd TW6 .....71 B1
Scarborough Way SL1 ....42 A2
Scarlet Oaks GU15 ......151 C2
Scarletts La RG10 ....37 B1
Sch of Electronic
 Engineering RG2 ....114 C1
Scholars Cl Caversham RG4 .58 C2
 Great Shefford RG17 .....48 C1
School Cl GU24 ....153 C2
School Hill
 Crowthorne RG45 ....143 A1
 Sandhurst GU47 ....143 A1
 Wargrave RG10 ....36 B1
 Woolhampton RG7 ....107 C2
School Ho TW19 ....70 B1
School La Bagshot GU19 .145 C1
 Boxford RG20 ....76 C2
 Burghfield Common RG7 ..111 A1
 Caversham RG4 ....59 A1
 Caversham, Emmer
 Green RG4 ....59 A3
 Cookham SL6 ....20 A4
 Cookham, Cookham
 Dean SL6 ....19 A4
 East Garston RG17 ....47 B3
 Egham TW20 ....96 A2
 Froxfield SN8 ....99 A1
 Little Marlow SL7 ....2 B3
 Littlewick Green SL6 ......38 A2
 Lower Halliford TW17 ....125 A1
 Maidenhead SL6 ....19 C1
 Medmenham SL7 ....17 A3
 Silchester RG7 ....136 A1
 Stoke Poges SL2 ....23 A2
 Swallowfield RG7 ....139 C2
 Wargrave RG10 ....36 B1
 Windlesham GU20 ......146 B2
 Yateley GU46 ....149 A3
School of Military Survey
 RG18 ....78 C4
School Rd Arborfield RG2 .114 C1
 Ascot SL5 ....120 B2
 Ashford TW15 ....98 A1
 Burghfield Common RG30 .111 B3
 Chieveley RG20 ....78 A4
 Compton RG20 ....31 C2
 Harmondsworth UB7 .....70 B4
 Hurst RG10 ....88 C4
 Padworth RG7 ....109 C1
 Reading RG31 ....84 B4
 Swallowfield RG7 ....139 C2
 Waltham St Lawrence RG10 .62 C2
 Windlesham GU20 ......146 A3
 Wokingham RG40 ....116 B3
 Wooburn Green HP10 ....3 C1
School Terr RG1 ....86 C4
Schroder Ct TW20 ....95 A2
Scotland Hill GU47 ....150 A4
Scotlands Dr SL2 ....22 A3
Scots Cl TW19 ....97 B4
Scots Dr RG41 ....115 C4
Scott Cl Caversham RG4 ..59 A3
 Farnham Common SL2 ...22 B4
 Woodley RG5 ....88 A4
Scott Terr RG12 ....118 C4
Scott's Ave TW16 ....98 C1
Scott's Way TW16 ....98 C1
Scottalls La SL8 ....22 C3
Scours La RG30 ....58 A1
Scratchface La RG7 ....81 C3
Scrivens Mead RG19 ....106 C2
Scylla Cres TW6&TW14 ..98 A4
Scylla Rd TW14, TW6 .....71 A1
Seacourt Rd SL3 ....44 A1
Seafield Ct **28** RG1 ....85 C4
Seaford Gdns RG5 ....87 C3
Seaford Rd
 Stanwell TW19, TW6 ......70 B1
 Wokingham RG40 ....116 B3
Sealand Rd SL6 ....71 A1
Searing Way RG26 ....135 A1
Searles Farm La RG30 ....85 A1
Seaton Dr TW15 ....97 C3
Seaton Gdns RG2 ....86 B1
Seaton Rd GU15 ....151 A3
Second Ave RG7 ....135 B1
Second Cres SL1 ....42 B4
Second St E RG19 ....132 A3
Second St W RG19 ......131 C2
Seddon Hill RG42 ....91 A1
Sedge Gr RG18 ....106 C2
Sedgefield Rd RG14 .....131 B4
Sedgmoor Cl HP10 ....3 A4
Sedgmoor Gdns HP10 ....3 A4
Sedgmoor La HP10 ....3 A4
Sedgmoor Rd HP10 ....3 A4
Seebys Oak GU47 ....150 C3
Sefton Cl Stoke Poges SL2 .22 C2
 West End GU24 ....153 C3
Sefton Paddock SL2 ......23 A3
Sefton Park Cotts SL2 ....23 A2
Segsbury Gr RG12 ....118 C3
Selborne Cl GU17 ....150 B3
Selborne Ct **2** RG1 ....86 B4
Selborne Gdns RG30 .....58 A1
Selby Rd TW15 ....98 B1
Selcourt Cl RG5 ....87 B4
Sellafield Way RG6 ....87 B1
Selsdon Ave RG5 ....87 C4
Selsey Way RG6 ....114 A4

Selwood Cl TW19 ....70 B1
Selwood Gdns TW19 .....70 B1
Selwyn Cl SL4 ....66 C3
Selwyn Dr GU46 ....149 A3
Selwyn Pl **2** SL1 ....41 C3
Sen Cl RG42 ....91 B1
Send Rd RG4 ....59 B1
Servite Ho SL6 ....40 A4
Setley Way RG12 ....118 C3
Seton Dr RG31 ....84 C3
Sett The GU46 ....149 A3
Sevenoaks Dr RG7 ......113 A2
Sevenoaks Rd RG6 ....87 A2
Seventh St RG19 ....131 C3
Severalls The SN8 ....126 B2
Severn Cl Sandhurst GU47 .150 B4
 Thatcham RG18 ....106 A3
Severn Cres SL3 ....69 A4
Severn Way RG30 ....84 C3
Sewell Ave RG41 ....116 A4
Sewell Ct RG18 ....79 A1
Seymour Ave RG2 ....113 C3
Seymour Cl SL6 ....39 C2
Seymour Court La SL7 ....1 A3
Seymour Court Rd SL7 ....1 B2
Seymour Dr GU15 ....152 A2
Seymour Ho SL3 ....43 C2
Seymour Park Rd SL7 ....1 B2
Seymour Plain SL7 ....1 B3
Seymour Rd SL1 ....42 B2
Seymour Way TW16 .....98 C2
Shackleton Ct **6** TW19 ..70 C1
Shackleton La SL1 ....42 C3
Shackleton Way RG5 .....88 A4
Shafer Ct RG14 ....105 A1
Shaftesbury Cl RG12 ....118 B2
Shaftesbury Cres TW18 ..97 B1
Shaftesbury Ct
 Maidenhead SL6 ....39 C3
 6 Slough SL1 ....42 C2
 Wokingham RG40 ....116 B4
Shaftesbury Mount
 GU17 ....150 B2
Shaftesbury Rd
 Bisley GU24 ....153 C2
 Reading RG30 ....85 A4
Shaggy Calf La SL2 ....43 A3
Shakespeare Cl RG4 .....59 B3
Shakespeare Rd RG18 ..106 B2
Shakespeare Way RG42 .118 C4
Shalbourne Cl RG17 ....100 A3
Shalbourne Rise GU15 ..151 B3
Sharney Ave SL3 ....44 A2
Sharnwood Dr RG31 .....84 C3
Sharonelle Ct RG40 .....116 A3
Sharpethorpe Cl **2** RG6 ..87 A1
Shaw Ct SL4 ....68 A1
Shaw Farm Rd RG14 ....105 A1
Shaw Hill RG14 ....105 A3
Shaw Mill RG14 ....105 A3
Shaw Pk RG45 ....143 A2
Shaw Rd Newbury RG14 .105 A2
 Reading RG1 ....85 C3
Shaw The SL6 ....19 C3
Shaw-Cum-Donnington
 Parochial Prim Sch
 RG14 ....105 A3
Shears Ct TW16 ....98 C1
Sheehy Way SL2 ....43 A3
Sheep Fair Way RG17 ....25 A1
Sheep Leaze La RG20 ....29 B1
Sheep Wlk RG4 ....59 A2
Sheepcote La
 Bourne End SL1 ....3 C1
 Holyport SL6 ....64 B2
Sheepcote Rd Eton SL4 ..42 A1
 Windsor SL4 ....66 C3
Sheepdrove Rd RG17 .....25 B2
Sheephouse Rd SL6 ......20 A1
Sheephouse Way RG20 ..49 A3
Sheepridge La SL7,HP10 ..2 C3
Sheeps Ditch Cl TW18 ...97 A1
Sheepwalk Littleton TW17 .125 A2
 Shepperton TW17 ....124 C2
Sheepwash RG20 ....131 A1
Sheepways La RG4 ....58 A4
Sheerlands Rd RG2 ......140 C4
Sheet St SL4 ....67 B3
Sheet Street Rd SL4 ......94 A4
Sheffield Rd
 Harlington TW14, TW6 ....71 B1
 Slough SL1 ....42 B4
Sheffield Way TW14, TW6 .71 B1
Shefford CE Sch RG17 ....48 A2
Shefford Cres RG40 .....116 A4
Shefford Lodge **5** RG14 .105 A1
Sheldon Gdns RG2 ....86 B1
Shelgate Wlk RG5 ....87 B4
Shelley Ave RG12 ....118 B4
Shelley Cl Medmenham SL7 .17 B4
 Slough SL3 ....43 C1
 Wooburn Green HP10 ....3 C4
 Woodley RG5 ....87 C2
Shelley Ct
 Camberley GU15 ....151 B3
 28 Reading RG1 ....86 B4
Shelley Rd **12** Marlow SL7 ..1 C2
 Thatcham RG18 ....106 B2
Shelley Walk GU46 ......149 A3
Shelson Ave TW13 ....98 C2
Shelton Ct SL3 ....43 B2
Shenstone Cl RG40 ......142 A4
Shenstone Dr SL1 ....21 B1
Shenstone Pk SL5 ....120 C3
Shenstone Rd RG2 ....86 A2
Shephards La RG42 ....91 A1
Shepherd's Hill RG20 .....76 C2
Shepherds Ave RG6 ......87 A4

Shepherds Chase GU19 .145 C1
Shepherds Cl Hurley SL6 ..17 C1
 Shepperton TW17 ....125 A1
Shepherds Ct SL6 ....66 C1
Shepherds Hill
 Bracknell RG12 ....118 B3
 Compton RG20 ....31 C1
 Earley RG6 ....87 B1
 Woodley RG5 ....60 B1
Shepherds House La RG6 .87 A4
Shepherds La
 Caversham RG4 ....58 B1
 Hurley SL6 ....17 C1
Shepherds Mount RG20 ..31 C1
Shepherds Rise RG20 ....31 C1
Shepherds Way RG45 ...142 C4
Shepherds Wlk RG6 ......87 B1
Shepley Dr Reading RG30 .85 B4
 Wentworth SL5 ....121 B3
Shepley End SL5 ....121 B3
Shepperton Bsns Pk
 TW17 ....125 B2
Shepperton Court Dr
 TW17 ....125 A2
Shepperton Ct TW17 ....125 A2
Shepperton Rd
 TW17, TW18 ....124 B2
Shepperton Sta TW17 ..125 B2
Shepperton Studios
 TW17 ....124 C2
Sheraton Cl GU17 ....150 C2
Sheraton Dr RG31 ....57 A1
Sherborne Cl SL3 ....69 C2
Sherborne Ct SL6 ....39 C3
Sherborne Rd TW14 ......98 B3
Sherbourne Dr
 Maidenhead SL6 ....39 B3
 Wentworth SL5 ....121 B3
 Windsor SL4 ....66 C1
 Woodley RG5 ....87 C1
Sherbourne Gdns TW17 .125 C1
Sherbourne Wlk SL2 ......22 B4
Sherfield Cl RG2 ....86 B2
Sherfield Dr RG2 ....86 B2
Shergold Way SL6 ....19 C1
Sheridan Ave RG4 ....59 A2
Sheridan Cres RG26 ....134 C1
Sheridan Ct
 Maidenhead SL6 ....40 A4
 Newbury RG14 ....105 B2
 1 Slough SL1 ....41 C3
Sheridan Way RG41 .....115 C2
Sheringham Ct **9** RG1 ...86 B3
Sherman Rd Reading RG1 .86 A3
 Slough SL1 ....42 C4
Sherrardmead RG14 ....105 A3
Sherring Cl RG42 ....91 B1
Sherwood Cl
 Bracknell RG12 ....119 A4
 Slough SL3 ....43 C2
Sherwood Ct
 Colnbrook SL3 ....69 B4
 Slough SL3 ....43 C1
Sherwood Dr SL6 ....39 A3
Sherwood Gdns RG9 .....35 A4
Sherwood Ho **11** RG1 ....85 C3
Sherwood Pl RG8 ....57 A2
Sherwood Rd RG41 ....88 B1
Sherwood Rise SL5 ....57 A3
Sherwood St RG30 ....85 B4
Shield Rd TW15 ....98 B2
Shifford Cres SL6 ....19 C2
Shildon Cl GU15 ....152 B2
Shilling Ct RG30 ....85 A3
Shinfield CE Jun Sch
 RG2 ....113 C2
Shinfield Cty Inf Sch
 RG2 ....113 C2
Shinfield Rd RG2 ....86 C2
Shinfield Rise RG2 ....86 C1
Shiplake Coll RG9 ....35 C1
Shiplake Ho Bourne End SL8 .3 A2
 Bracknell RG12 ....118 C3
Shiplake Sta RG9 ....36 A2
Shipley Cl RG5 ....61 A1
Shipton Cl RG31 ....57 B1
Shire Cl GU19 ....145 C1
Shire's Head Cl RG30 ....85 B3
Shires The RG41 ....115 B2
Shires Way GU46 ....149 B4
Shirley Ave Reading RG2 .113 B4
 Windsor SL4 ....66 C3
Shirley Rd SL6 ....39 B3
Shoesmiths Ct **4** RG1 ...86 A4
Sholto Rd TW6 ....71 A1
Shooters Hill RG8 ....56 B3
Shooters Way RG2 ......112 C4
Shop La
 Leckhampstead RG20 ....49 C3
 Newbury RG14 ....104 C3
Shoppenhanger's Rd SL6 .39 C2
Shoreham Rd (E) TW6 ....70 C1
Shoreham Rd (W) TW6 ...70 C1
Shoreham Rise SL2 ....21 B1
Shorland Oaks RG42 .....91 B1
Short La TW15, TW19 .....97 C4
Short Rd TW19 ....70 C1
Short St Caversham RG4 ..59 A1
 Pangbourne RG8 ....56 B3
 Reading RG1 ....86 A3
Short The RG8 ....57 B3
Shortfern SL2 ....43 B4
Shortheath La RG7 ......110 C2
Shortlands UB3 ....71 B4
Shortlands Hill OX10 .....13 B2
Shortwood Ave TW18 ....97 A3
Shortwood Cty Inf Sch
 TW18 ....97 A3

Shrewbury Terr RG14 . . . .104 C1
Shrewsbury Rd
TW14, TW6 . . . . .71 B1
Shrivenham Cl **3** GU47 . .150 B4
Shropshire Gdns RG42 . . . .91 C1
Shrubs Hill La SL5 . . . . . .121 B2
Shrubland Dr RG30 . . . . . .85 A2
Shrublands Dr SL8 . . . . . .153 A4
Shute End RG40, 41 . . . . .116 A3
Shyshack La RG7 . . . . . . .134 C1
Sibley Park Rd RG6 . . . . . .87 A1
Sibson RG6 . . . . .87 B1
Sidbury Cl SL5 . . . . .121 A2
Sidestrand Rd RG14 . . . . .130 C4
Sidings The TW18 . . . . . . .97 A2
Sidmouth Ct **5** RG1 . . . . .86 B4
Sidmouth Grange RG6 . . . .87 A4
Sidmouth Grange Rd RG6 . .87 A4
Sidmouth St RG1 . . . . .86 B4
Sidney Rd Staines TW18 . . .97 A2
Windsor SL4 . . . . .66 B2
Silbury Cl RG31 . . . . .84 C2
Silchester CE Prim Sch
RG7 . . . . .136 A1
Silchester Ct TW15 . . . . . . .97 C3
Silchester Ho SL6 . . . . . . .40 A4
Silchester House Sch SL6 .40 B4
Silchester Rd
Reading RG30 . . . . .85 B2
Tadley RG26 . . . . .135 B1
Silco Dr SL6 . . . . .39 C3
Silk La RG10 . . . . .61 B2
Silver Birches RG41 . . . . .115 B2
Silver Cl SL6 . . . . .39 A3
Silver Dr GU16 . . . . .152 B2
Silver Fox Cres RG5 . . . . . .87 B3
Silver Hill GU47 . . . . .150 C4
Silver La RG10 . . . . .136 A4
Silver St RG1 . . . . .86 A3
Silver Street Flats **28** RG1 .86 A3
Silverdale Rd Earley RG6 . .87 B2
Tadley RG26 . . . . .135 A1
Wargrave RG10 . . . . .36 C1
Silverglades GU46 . . . . . .149 B2
Silverthorne Dr RG4 . . . . .58 C3
Silvertrees Dr SL6 . . . . . . .39 A3
Silverwood Dr GU15 . . . . .152 A4
Silwood RG12 . . . . .117 C3
Silwood Cl SL5 . . . . .120 B4
Silwood Pk
(Imperial Coll) SL5 . . . . .120 C3
Silwood Rd SL5 . . . . .120 C3
Simkins Cl RG42 . . . . .92 A1
Simmonds Cl RG42 . . . . . .117 C4
Simmonds St RG1 . . . . . . .86 A4
Simmons Cl SL3 . . . . .44 A1
Simmons Field RG18 . . . . .106 C2
Simmons Fields RG10 . . . .61 A2
Simmons Pl TW18 . . . . . . .96 C2
Simmons Rd RG9 . . . . .15 B2
Simms Farm La RG7 . . . . .136 C2
Simod Ct RG30 . . . . .85 B4
Simons Cl RG31 . . . . .57 B2
Simons La RG41 . . . . .115 B4
Simons Wlk TW20 . . . . . . .95 B1
Simpson Cl SL6 . . . . .40 A4
Sindle Cl RG41 . . . . .88 A1
Sindlesham Rd RG2 . . . . .114 C2
Sindlesham Specl Sch
RG41 . . . . .114 C4
Singer La RG9 . . . . .15 C1
Singers Cl RG9 . . . . .35 C4
Singers La RG9 . . . . .35 C4
Sinhurst Rd GU15 . . . . . . .151 A2
Sipson Cl UB7 . . . . .71 A4
Sipson La UB3, UB7 . . . . . .71 A4
Sipson Rd UB7 . . . . .71 A4
Sipson Way UB7 . . . . .71 A4
Sir Sydney Camm Ho SL4 .67 A3
Sir William Borlase's
Gram Sch SL7 . . . . .1 B1
Sir William Perkin's Ind
Sch for Girls KT16 . . . . .123 C1
Sirius Cl RG41 . . . . .115 C3
Sirl Cotts SL5 . . . . .120 B3
Six Acre La RG17 . . . . . . .126 A3
Sixth St RG19 . . . . .131 C3
Skarries View RG4 . . . . . . .58 B4
Skeffling Cl RG6 . . . . .87 C1
Skelmerdale Way RG6 . . . .87 B4
Skelton Fields RG42 . . . . . .91 B1
Skerries Ct SL3 . . . . .44 A1
Skerrit Way RG8 . . . . .57 B2
Skillman Dr RG7 . . . . .106 C2
Skilton Rd RG31 . . . . .57 B2
Skimpedhill La RG12 . . . . .118 A4
Skippons Cl RG14 . . . . . . .130 B3
Sky Bsns Pk TW20 . . . . . .123 B4
Skydmore Path SL2 . . . . . .21 C1
Skye Cl RG31 . . . . .84 C2
Skyes Dr TW18 . . . . .97 A2
Skylings RG14 . . . . .105 B2
Skyport Dr UB7 . . . . .70 B2
Skyway 14 Trad Est SL3 . . .69 C2
Slade Hill Gdns RG20 . . . .129 C1
Slaidburn Gn RG12 . . . . . .118 C2
Slanting Hill RG18 . . . . . . .79 A2
Sledmere Ct TW14 . . . . . . .98 C4
Slim Rd GU15 . . . . .151 B4
Sloan Cl RG8 . . . . .34 B3
Slopes The RG4 . . . . .59 B1
Slough & Eton CE Sec Sch
SL1 . . . . .42 B2
Slough Gram Sch SL3 . . . .43 A2
Slough Mus SL1 . . . . .43 A2
Slough Rd Datchet SL3 . . . .68 A4
Eton SL4 . . . . .42 C1

Slough Sta SL1 . . . . .42 C3
Slough Trad Est SL1 . . . . . .42 A4
Smallmead Rd
Burghfield Common RG2 . . .85 B1
Reading RG2 . . . . .86 A1
Smallridge RG14 . . . . .130 B2
Smith Hospl RG9 . . . . .15 A3
Smith Sq RG12 . . . . .118 B4
Smith's La SL4 . . . . .66 C3
Smitham Bridge Rd
RG17 . . . . .100 B3
Smithfield Cl SL6 . . . . .38 C2
Smithfield Rd SL6 . . . . .39 A2
Smiths Hill OX12 . . . . .6 C3
Smithy's Gn GU20 . . . . . . .146 B2
Snake La RG20 . . . . .104 A4
Snape Spur SL1 . . . . .42 C4
Snelsmore Common
Ctry Pk RG18 . . . . .77 C1
Snipe La RG20 . . . . .131 C1
Snowball Hill
Maidenhead SL6 . . . . .39 A1
White Waltham SL6 . . . . . . .64 A4
Snowberry Cl RG41 . . . . . .115 C3
Snowden Cl SL4 . . . . .66 B2
Snowden Dr RG31 . . . . . . .84 A3
Snowdon Cl RG19 . . . . . . .106 B1
Snowdon Rd TW6 . . . . .71 B1
Snowdrop Copse RG18 . . .106 C2
Snowdrop Gr RG41 . . . . . . .88 B2
Snows Paddock GU20 . . . .146 A4
Snows Ride GU20 . . . . . . .146 A3
Soane End RG4 . . . . .59 A4
Soham Cl RG6 . . . . .114 B4
Soho Cres HP10 . . . . .3 A4
Soho Mills Ind Est HP10 . . .3 B2
Soke Rd RG7 . . . . .135 C2
Soldiers Rise RG40 . . . . . .142 B4
Solent Ct **16** RG1 . . . . . . .86 A3
Solent Rd TW6 . . . . .70 C1
Somerford Cl SL6 . . . . .40 A4
Somersby Cres SL6 . . . . . .39 C2
Somerset Cl
Hungerford RG17 . . . . . . .100 B3
Wokingham RG41 . . . . . . .115 B3
Somerset Gr RG42 . . . . . . .91 C1
Somerset Hospital RG9 . . .15 A3
Somerset Lodge **3** SL6 . .39 C3
Somerset Way SL10 . . . . . .44 C2
Somerset Wlk RG31 . . . . . .84 A3
Somerton Gdns RG6 . . . . . .87 A1
Somerton Gr RG19 . . . . . .106 B1
Somerville Cres GU46 . . . .149 C3
Somerville Gr RG41 . . . . . .115 B2
Somerville Rd SL4 . . . . . . .42 B1
Sonning CE Prim Sch
RG4 . . . . .60 B2
Sonning La RG4 . . . . .60 B1
Sonning Mdws RG4 . . . . . .60 B1
Sonninge Cl GU47 . . . . . . .150 B4
Sopwith Cl RG5 . . . . .88 A4
Sorrel Cl
Burghfield Common RG7 . .111 A2
Newbury RG14 . . . . .105 B3
Wokingham RG40 . . . . . . .116 C4
Sorrel Dr GU18 . . . . .152 C4
Sospel Ct SL2 . . . . .22 B2
South Ave Egham TW20 . . .96 B1
Henley-on-T RG9 . . . . .35 C4
South Bank RG8 . . . . .14 B2
South Cl Burnham SL1 . . . .41 B3
Medmenham SL7 . . . . .17 B4
Wokingham RG40 . . . . . . .116 B2
South Dr Reading RG2 . . . .86 C1
Sonning RG4 . . . . .60 B1
Sulhamstead RG7 . . . . . . .110 B4
Wentworth GU25 . . . . . . .122 A1
Wokingham RG40 . . . . . . .116 B3
South End Rd RG7 . . . . . . .82 A1
South Farm La GU19 . . . . .146 A1
South Field Cl SL4 . . . . . . .41 B2
South Gate Ave TW13 . . . .98 B2
South Gn SL1 . . . . .42 C3
South Gr KT16 . . . . .123 C2
South Groves RG17 . . . . . .73 A3
South Hill Pk RG12 . . . . . .118 B1
South Hill Rd RG12 . . . . . .118 A2
South Lake Cres RG5 . . . . .87 C3
South Lake Inf Sch RG5 . . .87 C3
South Lake Jun Sch RG5 . .87 B3
South Lynn Cres RG12 . . .118 A2
South Mdw RG45 . . . . .143 B2
South Meadow La SL4 . . . .67 B4
South Oak Way RG2,RG7 .112 C4
South Path SL4 . . . . .67 B3
South Pl Marlow SL7 . . . . . .1 C1
Wokingham RG40 . . . . . . .116 B3
South Rd Bisley GU24 . . . .153 C2
Bracknell RG40, RG12 . . . .117 C1
Crowthorne RG45 . . . . . . .143 C2
Englefield Green TW20 . . . .95 C2
Maidenhead SL6 . . . . .39 C3
South Row Chilton OX11 . .10 B4
Fulmer SL3 . . . . .23 C4
South St Blewbury OX11 . .12 A4
Caversham RG4 . . . . .59 A2
Reading RG1 . . . . .86 B4
Staines TW18 . . . . .96 C2
South Stoke Cty Prim Sch
RG8 . . . . .14 A2
South View Cookham SL6 . .19 C4
Hungerford RG17 . . . . . . .100 B3
Wooburn Green HP10 . . . . . .3 C4
South View Ave RG4 . . . . . .59 B1
South View Pk RG4 . . . . . .59 B1
South View Gdns **9**
RG14 . . . . .105 A2
Southampton Cl GU17 . . . .150 B3

Southampton Rd
TW19, TW6 . . . . .70 C1
Southampton St RG1 . . . . .86 A3
Southbank Gdns RG17 . . . .25 A3
Southbourne Dr SL8 . . . . . .3 A2
Southbury La RG10 . . . . . . .61 C3
Southcote Dr GU15 . . . . . .152 A3
Southcote Farm La RG30 . .85 B2
Southcote La RG30 . . . . . . .85 B2
Southcote Lodge RG30 . . . .85 A2
Southcote Prim Sch RG30 .85 B2
Southcote Rd RG30 . . . . . .85 B3
Southcroft
Englefield Green TW20 . . . .95 A2
Slough SL2 . . . . .22 A1
Southdown Rd
Caversham RG4 . . . . .59 A3
Tadley RG26 . . . . .135 A4
Thatcham RG19 . . . . .105 C2
Southend RG18 . . . . .106 B3
Southern Cotts TW19 . . . . .70 A1
Southern Cl RG1 . . . . .86 A4
Southern Hill RG1 . . . . .86 B3
Southern Ind Area RG2 . .117 C3
Southern Perimeter Rd
East Bedfont TW6 . . . . .71 A1
Hatton TW14, TW6 . . . . . . .71 B1
Stanwell TW19, TW6 . . . . . .70 B1
Southern Rd GU15 . . . . . . .151 B4
Southerndene Cl RG31 . . . .57 B1
Southfield GU46 . . . . .149 A1
Southfields Boxford RG20 . .76 B2
Chieveley RG20 . . . . .78 A4
Southfields Ave TW15 . . . .98 A1
Southfields Sch RG40 . . . .116 B3
Southgate Ho SL6 . . . . . . .39 C4
Southglade RG2 . . . . .113 C4
Southlake Ct RG5 . . . . .87 B3
Southlands Cl RG40 . . . . . .116 B3
Southlands Rd RG40 . . . . .116 B2
Southlea Rd SL3 . . . . .68 A3
Southview Cl RG10 . . . . . . .61 C3
Southview Rd SL7 . . . . .1 C1
Southville Cl TW14 . . . . . . .98 C4
Southville Cres TW14 . . . . .98 C4
Southville Jun & Inf Schs
TW14 . . . . .98 C4
Southville Rd TW14 . . . . . .98 C4
Southwark Cl GU46 . . . . . .149 B3
Southway GU15 . . . . .151 A2
Southwell Park Rd GU15 . .151 B3
Southwick Cl RG19 . . . . . .145 C1
Southwick Ct RG12 . . . . . .118 C2
Southwold RG12 . . . . .117 C1
Southwold Cl RG6 . . . . .87 B1
Southwold Spur SL3 . . . . . .44 B2
Southwood RG40 . . . . .116 B2
Southwood Gdns
Burghfield Common RG7 . .111 A2
Cookham SL6 . . . . .19 C3
Southwood Rd SL6 . . . . . . .19 C3
Sovereign Dr GU15 . . . . . .152 A4
Sovereign Ho TW15 . . . . . .97 C2
Sovereign Way RG31 . . . . .84 C2
Sowbury Bank RG20 . . . . . .78 A4
Spackman Cl RG19 . . . . . .106 B1
Spade Oak Mdw SL8 . . . . . .2 C2
Span Hill RG4 . . . . .60 A4
Sparrow Cl RG41 . . . . .115 C3
Sparrowbill RG20 . . . . .28 C1
Sparvell Way GU15 . . . . . .151 B3
Speedbird Way UB7 . . . . . .70 B4
Speedwell Way RG18 . . . .106 C2
Speen Hill Cl RG14 . . . . . .104 C2
Speen La RG14 . . . . .104 C2
Speen Lodge Ct RG14 . . . .104 C2
Speen Pl RG14 . . . . .104 C2
Speenhamland Ct **5**
RG14 . . . . .105 A2
Speenhamland Prim Sch
RG14 . . . . .104 C2
Spelthorne Coll TW15 . . . . .97 C2
Spelthorne Cty Inf Sch
TW15 . . . . .98 C1
Spelthorne Gr TW16 . . . . . .98 C1
Spelthorne La
TW15, TW17 . . . . .125 B4
Spelthorne Mus TW16 . . . .96 C2
Spelthorne Sports Club
TW15 . . . . .98 B1
Spencer Cl
Silchester RG26 . . . . .135 C1
Wokingham RG41 . . . . . . .115 B3
Spencer Gdns TW20 . . . . . .95 B2
Spencer Rd
Bracknell RG42 . . . . .117 C4
Newbury RG14 . . . . .130 B3
Reading RG2 . . . . .113 A4
Slough SL3 . . . . .43 C2
Spencers Cl SL6 . . . . .39 B4
Spencers La SL6 . . . . .19 C3
Spencers Rd SL6 . . . . .39 B4
Spenwood Cl RG7 . . . . . . .113 A4
Sperling Rd SL6 . . . . .19 C1
Spey Rd RG30 . . . . .85 A4
Spinfield Cty Comb Sch
SL7 .1 A1
Spinfield La W SL7 . . . . . . .1 B1
Spinfield Mount SL7 . . . . . .1 B1
Spinfield Pk SL7 . . . . .1 B1
Spinis RG12 . . . . .117 C1
Spinner Gn RG12 . . . . .118 A4
Spinners Wlk Marlow SL7 . .1 B1
Windsor SL4 . . . . .67 B3
Spinney SL1 . . . . .42 A3
Spinney Cl RG4 . . . . .59 A4
Spinney Dr TW14 . . . . .98 A4

Spinney La SL4 . . . . .93 A4
Spinney The Ascot SL5 . . .120 C2
Frimley GU15 . . . . .152 B3
Reading RG31 . . . . .84 C2
Wokingham RG40 . . . . . . .141 C4
Yateley GU46 . . . . .149 B4
Spinningwheel La RG42 . . .90 B4
Spitfire Way RG5 . . . . .88 A4
Spittal St SL7 . . . . .1 B1
Splash The RG42 . . . . .91 A1
Spode Cl RG30 . . . . .84 C4
Spout La TW19 . . . . .70 A2
Spout La N TW19 . . . . .70 A2
Spray La RG20 . . . . .28 B1
Spray Rd Ham SN8 . . . . . .126 C2
Inkpen RG17 . . . . .127 A2
Spriggs Cl RG19 . . . . .106 B1
Spring Ave TW20 . . . . .95 C1
Spring Cl Maidenhead SL6 .19 C1
Pangbourne RG8 . . . . .55 B3
Spring Cnr TW13 . . . . .98 C3
Spring Gdns Ascot SL5 . . .120 C2
Bourne End SL8 . . . . .3 A2
Frimley GU15 . . . . .152 A3
Marlow SL7 . . . . .1 C2
Shinfield RG7 . . . . .113 A1
Wooburn Green HP10 . . . . .3 C4
Spring Gr RG1 . . . . .86 A3
Spring Hill RG9 . . . . .39 C2
Spring Ho SL7 . . . . .1 C2
Spring La
Aldermaston RG7 . . . . . . .135 B4
Aston Tirrold OX11 . . . . . . .12 C4
Caversham RG4 . . . . .60 A3
Cold Ash RG18 . . . . .106 B4
Cookham SL6 . . . . .19 B3
Farnham Common SL2 . . . .22 B3
Mortimer RG7 . . . . .137 A3
Slough SL1 . . . . .41 C3
Swallowfield RG7 . . . . .139 A2
Spring Mdw RG12 . . . . . . .118 B4
Spring Mdws RG17 . . . . . . .48 A2
Spring Rd TW13 . . . . .98 C3
Spring Rise TW20 . . . . .95 C1
Spring Terr **22** RG1 . . . . . .86 A3
Spring Wlk RG10 . . . . .36 B1
Spring Wood La RG7 . . . . .111 A1
Spring Woods
Sandhurst GU47 . . . . .143 B1
Virginia Water GU25 . . . . .122 A3
Springate Field SL3 . . . . . .43 C2
Springcross Ave GU17 . . . .150 B2
Springdale Earley RG6 . . . .87 A1
Wokingham RG40 . . . . . . .141 C4
Springfield
Lightwater GU18 . . . . .153 B4
Slough SL1 . . . . .43 A2
Springfield Cl SL4 . . . . .67 A3
Springfield Ct SL6 . . . . .40 A4
Springfield Cty Prim Schs
TW16 . . . . .125 C4
Springfield End RG8 . . . . . .34 B4
Springfield La Marlow SL7 . .1 A1
Newbury RG14 . . . . .131 A4
Springfield Mews RG4 . . . .59 A2
Springfield Pk
Maidenhead SL6 . . . . .40 B1
Twyford RG10 . . . . .61 C2
Springfield Prim Sch
RG31 . . . . .84 A4
Springfield Rd
Ashford TW15 . . . . .97 C2
Bracknell RG12 . . . . .117 B4
Brands Hill SL3 . . . . .69 A4
Frimley GU15 . . . . .152 A3
Silchester RG26 . . . . .135 C1
Windsor SL4 . . . . .67 A3
Springfields Cl KT16 . . . . .124 A1
Springhill Ct RG12 . . . . . . .118 A3
Springhill Rd RG8 . . . . .34 B4
Springmead Ct GU47 . . . . .143 C1
Spruce Cl **3** SL1 . . . . .42 C2
Spruce Dr GU18 . . . . .153 A4
Spruce Rd RG5 . . . . .88 A3
Spur The Slough SL1 . . . . . .41 B4
Wargrave RG10 . . . . .36 C2
Spurcroft Prim Sch
RG19 . . . . .106 B1
Spurcroft Rd RG19 . . . . . .106 B1
Square The Bagshot GU19 .145 C2
Earley RG6 . . . . .114 A4
Harmondsworth TW6 . . . . .70 A3
Lightwater GU18 . . . . .146 B1
Pangbourne RG8 . . . . .56 B3
Shinfield RG7 . . . . .113 A1
Squire's Bridge Rd
TW17 . . . . .125 A3
Squire's Rd TW17 . . . . . . .125 A3
Squires Bridge Rd KT17 . .124 C3
Squires Ct
Camberley GU15 . . . . .151 B2
Chertsey KT16 . . . . .124 A1
Squires Wlk TW15 . . . . . . .98 B1
Squirrel Cl GU47 . . . . .150 A4
Squirrel Dr SL4 . . . . .93 A4
Squirrel Rise SL7 . . . . .1 A2
Squirrels Drey RG45 . . . . .142 C4
Squirrels Way RG6 . . . . . . .87 A1
Stable Cl RG7 . . . . .111 A2
Stable Cotts SL7 . . . . .18 B2
Stable Croft GU19 . . . . . . .145 B1
Stable Ct RG14 . . . . .105 A3
Stable View GU46 . . . . . . .149 B4
Stables Ct SL7 . . . . .1 A1
Stacey's Ind Est RG26 . . .135 B1
Staddlestone Cl RG31 . . . . .57 B1
Stadium Way RG30 . . . . . . .58 A2

Staff Coll GU15 . . . . .151 B4
Staff College Rd GU15 . . . .151 A3
Stafferton Way SL6 . . . . . . .40 A3
Stafford Ave SL2 . . . . .22 B1
Stafford Cl Burnham SL6 . . .41 A4
Woodley RG5 . . . . .87 C4
Stafford Lake GU21,GU24 .153 C1
Staffordshire Cl RG30 . . . . .84 C4
Staffordshire Croft RG42 . . .91 C1
Stag Hill RG17 . . . . .73 A1
Stainash Cres TW18 . . . . . .97 A2
Stainash Par TW18 . . . . . . .97 A2
Staines By-Pass
TW15, TW18 . . . . .97 B2
Staines Central Trad Est
W18 . . . . .96 C2
Staines La KT16 . . . . .124 A2
Staines Lane Cl KT16 . . . .123 C2
Staines Prep Sch The
TW18 . . . . .97 A2
Staines Rd Chertsey KT16 .124 A3
East Bedfont TW14 . . . . . . .98 B4
Laleham TW18 . . . . .124 A4
Wraysbury TW19 . . . . .95 C4
Staines Rd W TW15,TW16 .98 B1
Staines Sta TW18 . . . . .97 A2
Stainford Cl TW15 . . . . .98 B2
Stamford Ave GU16 . . . . . .151 C1
Stamford Rd SL6 . . . . .39 B3
Stanbrook Cl RG7 . . . . .82 A1
Stanbury Gate RG7 . . . . . .113 A2
Stanfield RG26 . . . . .135 A1
Stanford Dingley
Circular Wlks RG18 . . . . . .80 C4
Stanham Rd RG30 . . . . .84 C4
Stanhope Heath TW19 . . . . .70 B1
Stanhope Rd
Camberley GU15 . . . . .150 C2
Reading RG2 . . . . .86 B2
Slough SL1 . . . . .41 B4
Stanhope Way TW19 . . . . . .70 B1
Stanlake La RG10 . . . . .61 C2
Stanley Cl SL7 . . . . .1 C2
Stanley Cotts SL2 . . . . .42 C3
Stanley Gn E SL3 . . . . .43 C1
Stanley Gn W SL3 . . . . .43 C1
Stanley Gr **5** RG1 . . . . . . .85 C4
Stanley Ho SL4 . . . . .67 A3
Stanley Rd Ashford TW15 . .97 C2
Newbury RG14 . . . . .105 A1
Wokingham RG40 . . . . . . .116 C3
Stanley St RG1 . . . . .85 C4
Stanmore Cl SL5 . . . . .120 A3
Stanmore Gdns RG7 . . . . .136 C3
Stanmore Rd Beedon RG20 .30 B1
East Isley RG20 . . . . .30 C4
Stanshawe Rd RG1 . . . . . . .86 A4
Stansted Rd TW6 . . . . .70 C1
Stanton Cl RG6 . . . . .87 B2
Stanton Way SL3 . . . . .43 C1
Stanway Cotts
7 Chertsey KT16 . . . . . .124 A1
Reading RG1 . . . . .86 C3
Stanwell Cl TW19 . . . . .70 B1
Stanwell Gdns TW19 . . . . . .70 B1
Stanwell Moor Rd
TW19, TW6, UB7 . . . . .70 A2
Stanwell New Rd
TW18, TW19 . . . . .97 A3
Stanwell Rd Ashford TW15 .97 C2
East Bedfont TW14,
TW19, TW6 . . . . .98 A4
Horton SL3, TW19 . . . . .69 B2
Stapleford Rd RG30 . . . . . . .85 B2
Staplehurst RG12 . . . . .117 C1
Stapleton Cl Marlow SL7 . . . .1 C2
Newbury RG14 . . . . .130 B3
Star La Knowl Hill RG10 . . .37 C2
Reading RG1 . . . . .86 A4
Star Post Rd GU15 . . . . . .151 C4
Star Rd RG4 . . . . .59 B1
Starling Cl RG41 . . . . .115 C3
Starlings Dr RG31 . . . . .84 A3
Starmead Dr RG40 . . . . . .116 C3
Starting Gates RG14 . . . . .105 A3
Startins La SL6 . . . . .19 B4
Starwood Ct SL3 . . . . .43 B2
Statham Ct RG42 . . . . .91 C1
Station App Ashford TW15 . .97 C2
Maidenhead SL6 . . . . .39 C3
Marlow SL7 . . . . .1 C1
Reading RG1 . . . . .86 A4
Shepperton TW17 . . . . . . .125 B2
Staines TW18 . . . . .97 A2
Virginia Water GU25 . . . . .122 B3
Station Cres TW15 . . . . . . .97 C2
Station Flats SL5 . . . . .121 A1
Station Hill Ascot SL5 . . . .120 A3
Cookham SL6 . . . . .19 C4
Hampstead Norreys RG18 . .52 C3
Reading RG1 . . . . .86 A4
Station Ind Est RG40 . . . . .116 A3
Station Par Ashford TW15 . .97 C2
Cookham SL6 . . . . .19 C3
Sunningdale SL5 . . . . .121 A1
Virginia Water GU25 . . . . .122 C2
Station Path TW18 . . . . . . .96 C2
Station Rd Ashford TW15 . .97 C2
Bagshot GU19 . . . . .145 C2
Ball Hill RG20 . . . . .130 A2
Bourne End SL8 . . . . .3 A2
Bracknell RG12 . . . . .118 A4
Chertsey KT16 . . . . .124 A1
Cookham SL6 . . . . .19 C4
Earley RG6 . . . . .87 B2

Station Rd continued
East Garston RG17 . . . . .47 B3
Egham TW20 . . . . .96 A2
Frimley GU16 . . . . .151 B1
Goring RG8 . . . . .34 B3
Great Shefford RG17 . . . . .48 A2
Henley-on-T RG9 . . . . .15 C1
Hungerford RG17 . . . . . . .100 B3
Kintbury RG17 . . . . .102 A1
Marlow SL7 . . . . .1 C1
Newbury, City RG14 . . . . .105 A1
Newbury, Speen RG14 . . . .104 B3
Pangbourne RG8 . . . . .56 B3
Reading RG1 . . . . .86 A4
Shepperton TW17 . . . . . . .125 B2
Shiplake RG9 . . . . .36 A2
Slough SL1 . . . . .41 C4
Slough, Langley SL3 . . . . . .44 A2
Sunningdale SL5 . . . . .121 A2
Taplow SL6 . . . . .40 C4
Thatcham RG19 . . . . .106 C1
Theale RG7 . . . . .83 C2
Twyford RG10 . . . . .61 B2
Wargrave RG10 . . . . .36 B1
Wokingham RG40 . . . . . . .116 A3
Woolhampton RG7 . . . . . .108 B1
Wraysbury TW19 . . . . .69 A1
Station Rd N 5 TW20 . . . .96 A2
Station Rise SL7 . . . . .1 C1
Station Road Ind Est
RG19 . . . . .106 C1
Station Yard Ind Est
RG17 . . . . .100 C3
Staunton Rd SL2 . . . . .42 B4
Staveley Rd TW15 . . . . . . .98 B1
Staverton Cl
Bracknell RG42 . . . . .91 A1
Wokingham RG40 . . . . . . .116 C3
Staverton Rd RG2 . . . . .86 B2
Stayne End GU25 . . . . . . .122 A3
Steam Farm La TW14 . . . .71 C2
Steeple Wlk RG6 . . . . .113 C4
Steerforth Copse GU47 . .143 C1
Steggles Cl RG5 . . . . .87 B4
Stepgates KT16 . . . . .124 B1
Stepgates Cl KT16 . . . . . . .124 A1
Stepgates Prim Sch
KT16 . . . . .124 A1
Stephanie Chase Ct
RG40 . . . . .116 B4
Stephen Cl Egham TW20 . . .96 B1
Twyford RG10 . . . . .61 C2
Stephen's Rd RG7 . . . . . . .136 C3
Stephens Cl RG7 . . . . .136 C3
Stephens Firs RG7 . . . . . . .136 C3
Stephenson Cl RG18 . . . . .106 B2
Stephenson Ct 21 SL1 . . . .42 C2
Stephenson Dr SL4 . . . . . . .67 A4
Stephenson Rd RG2 . . . . . .141 A4
Sterling Ave
Littleton TW17 . . . . .125 A3
Slough SL1 . . . . .42 C4
Sterling Cl SL6 . . . . .65 B3
Stewarts Dr SL2 . . . . .22 A4
Stewarts Way SL7 . . . . .1 B4
Stile Rd SL3 . . . . .43 B2
Stilton Cl RG6 . . . . .87 C1
Stilwell Cl GU46 . . . . .149 C1
Stirling Cl Caversham RG4 . .59 B3
Windsor SL4 . . . . .66 B3
Stirling Rd Slough SL1 . . . .42 A4
Stanwell TW19, TW6 . . . . . .70 C1
Stirling Way RG18 . . . . . .106 B2
Stirrup RG14 . . . . .131 A4
Stockbridge Way GU46 . . .149 B2
Stockbury Cl RG6 . . . . .87 A1
Stockcross CE Prim Sch
RG20 . . . . .103 C3
Stockdales Rd SL4 . . . . . . .41 C1
Stockton Rd RG2 . . . . .86 B1
Stockwells SL6 . . . . .20 B1
Stockwood Rise GU15 . . . .151 C3
Stoke Common Rd SL3 . . . .23 A4
Stoke Court Dr SL2 . . . . . . .22 C2
Stoke Gdns SL1 . . . . .42 C3
Stoke Gn SL2 . . . . .23 A1
Stoke Park Ave SL2 . . . . . .22 B1
Stoke Poges La SL1, SL2 . . .42 C4
Stoke Poges Sch SL2 . . . . . .23 A3
Stoke Poges Sch The SL2 . .22 C3
Stoke Rd SL2 . . . . .22 C4
Stoke View SL1 . . . . .42 C3
Stoke Wood SL2 . . . . .22 C4
Stokeford Cl 6 RG12 . . . .118 C2
Stokes La RG26 . . . . .134 B1
Stokes View RG8 . . . . .56 B3
Stokesay SL2 . . . . .42 C3
Stokesley Rise HP10 . . . . . . .3 C4
Stomp Rd SL1 . . . . .41 B4
Stompits Rd Holyport SL6 . .65 B4
Maidenhead SL6 . . . . .40 B1
Stone Copse RG14 . . . . . .105 C4
Stone Cres TW14 . . . . .98 C4
Stone House La SL6 . . . . . . .2 B1
Stone St RG30 . . . . .58 A1
Stonea Cl RG6 . . . . .114 B4
Stonebridge Field SL4 . . . .42 A1

Stonecroft Ave SL0 . . . . . .44 C4
Stonefield Pk SL6 . . . . .39 B4
Stonegate GU15 . . . . .152 B3
Stoneham Cl RG30 . . . . . . .85 A3
Stonehaven Dr RG5 . . . . . . .88 A3
Stonehill Rd GU18 . . . . . . .146 A1
Stonehouse Rise GU16 . . .151 C1
Stoneleigh Ct GU16 . . . . .151 C1
Stoney Cl GU46 . . . . .149 B2
Stoney La Burnham SL2 . . . .22 A2
Newbury RG14, RG18 . . . .105 A3
Thatcham RG19 . . . . .106 C2
Stoney Meade SL1 . . . . . . .42 A3
Stoney Rd RG42 . . . . .118 A4
Stoney Ware SL7 . . . . .18 C4
Stoney Ware Cl SL7 . . . . . .18 B4
Stoneyfield RG7 . . . . .109 A3
Stoneyland Ct 5 TW20 . . . .95 C2
Stoneylands Rd TW20 . . . .95 C2
Stookes Way GU46 . . . . . .149 A2
Stornaway Rd SL3 . . . . . . .44 B1
Stour Cl Reading RG30 . . . .85 A4
Slough SL1 . . . . .42 A2
Stovell Rd SL4 . . . . .67 A4
Stow Rd RG9 . . . . .35 C4
Stowe Rd SL1 . . . . .41 C3
Strachey Cl RG8 . . . . .56 B1
Straight Bit HP10 . . . . .3 A4
Straight La RG17 . . . . .46 C2
Straight Mile The
Hurst RG10 & RG40 . . . . . . .89 B3
Waltham St Lawrence RG10 . .62 C1
Straight Rd SL4 . . . . .68 A1
Strand La SL6 . . . . .19 C3
Strand View Wlk SL6 . . . . .19 C3
Strand Way RG6 . . . . .87 B1
Stranraer Gdns SL1 . . . . . .42 C3
Stranraer Way 1 TW6 . . . .70 C1
Stratfield RG12 . . . . .117 C1
Stratfield Cl SL6 . . . . .40 A4
Stratfield Rd SL1 . . . . .43 A2
Stratford Cl SL2 . . . . .21 B1
Stratford Dr HP10 . . . . .3 B2
Stratford Gdns SL6 . . . . . . .39 B2
Stratford Rd TW6 . . . . .71 B1
Stratford Way RG31 . . . . . .84 A3
Strathcona Cl HP10 . . . . .3 B4
Strathcona Way HP10 . . . . . .3 A3
Strathearn Ave UB3 . . . . . .71 C4
Stratheden Pl 9 RG1 . . . . .85 C4
Strathmore Ct GU15 . . . . .151 B3
Strathmore Dr RG10 . . . . . .61 A2
Strathy Cl RG30 . . . . .85 A4
Stratton Gdns RG2 . . . . . . .86 B1
Stratton Rd TW16 . . . . . . .125 C4
Strawberry Hill
Newbury RG14 . . . . .104 C2
Newell Green RG42 . . . . . . .91 C1
Streamside SL1 . . . . .41 C3
Streatley CE Sch RG8 . . . .33 C3
Streatley & Goring Bridge
RG8 .34 A3
Streatley Hill RG8 . . . . .33 C3
Street The
Aldermaston RG7 . . . . .135 A4
Bradfield RG7 . . . . .83 A4
Mortimer RG7 . . . . .137 B3
Moulsford OX10 . . . . .14 A3
South Stoke RG8 . . . . .14 A2
Swallowfield RG7 . . . . .139 B4
Tidmarsh RG8 . . . . .56 B1
Waltham St Lawrence RG10 . .63 A3
Streets Heath GU24 . . . . . .153 C4
Stretton Cl RG7 . . . . .82 A1
Strode St TW20 . . . . .96 A2
Strode's Coll TW20 . . . . . . .95 C2
Strode's Cres TW18 . . . . . .97 B2
Strodes College La TW20 . .95 C2
Stroller Ct RG19 . . . . .105 C2
Stroma Ct SL1 . . . . .41 B3
Strongrove Hill RG17 . . . . .100 B3
Strood La SL5 . . . . .93 B1
Strood Cl SL4 . . . . .66 B2
Strood Farm Rd SL6 . . . . . .65 A4
Stroud Way TW15 . . . . .98 A1
Stroude Rd Egham TW20 . . .96 A1
Virginia Water
GU25, TW20 . . . . .122 C3
Strouds Mdw RG18 . . . . . .106 B4
Strouds The RG7 . . . . .108 C3
Stuart Cl Caversham RG4 . . .59 A3
Windsor SL4 . . . . .66 C3
Stuart Ho RG42 . . . . .117 C4
Stuart Rd RG14 . . . . .130 B3
Stuart Way Staines TW18 . . .97 A1
Virginia Water GU25 . . . . .122 A3
Windsor SL4 . . . . .66 C3
Stubbington House Sch
SL5 . . . . .120 A1
Stubbles La SL6 . . . . .19 A3
Stubbs Folly GU47 . . . . . .150 B4
Studios Rd TW17 . . . . .124 C3
Studland Cl RG2 . . . . .113 B4
Studland Ind Est RG20 . . .129 A2
Sturbridge Cl RG6 . . . . .87 B1
Sturdee Cl GU16 . . . . .151 C1
Sturges Rd RG40 . . . . .116 B3
Sturt Gn SL6 . . . . .64 C4
Styventon Pl KT16 . . . . . . .123 C1
Sucks La SL6 . . . . .54 B2
Suffolk Cl Bagshot GU19 . .145 C1
Slough SL1 . . . . .41 C4
Wokingham RG41 . . . . .115 B3
Suffolk Combe RG42 . . . . .91 C1
Suffolk Ct SL6 . . . . .39 C4
Suffolk Rd Maidenhead SL6 . .39 B2
Reading RG30 . . . . .85 B4
Sulham La RG8 . . . . .56 C2

Sulham Wlk RG30 . . . . .85 A2
Sulhamstead Hill RG7 . . . .110 B3
Sulhamstead La RG7 . . . . .110 B2
Sulhamstead Rd
RG7,RG30 . . . . .111 A3
Sulhamstead & Ufton
Nervet Prim Sch RG7 . . . .110 B2
Sullivan Rd GU15 . . . . . . .151 A3
Sumburgh Way SL1 . . . . . .42 C4
Summer Gdns GU15 . . . . .152 B3
Summerfield Cl RG41 . . . . .88 C3
Summerfield Rise RG8 . . . .34 B4
Summerhouse La UB7 . . . . .70 B4
Summerlea SL1 . . . . .42 A3
Summerleaze Rd SL6 . . . . .20 A1
Summers Rd SL1 . . . . .21 B1
Summit Cl RG40 . . . . .141 C4
Summit Ctr UB7 . . . . .70 B4
Sun Cl SL4 . . . . .67 B4
Sun Gdns RG7 . . . . .111 A1
Sun La Maidenhead SL6 . . . .39 C4
Swallowfield RG7 . . . . .139 A1
Sun Pas SL4 . . . . .67 B3
Sun Ray Est GU47 . . . . . . .150 A4
Sun St RG1 . . . . .86 B4
Sunbury Cres TW13 . . . . . .98 C2
Sunbury Cross Ctr 14
TW16 . . . . .98 C1
Sunbury Ct SL4 . . . . .67 B4
Sunbury Int Bsns Ctr
TW16 . . . . .125 C4
Sunbury Manor Sch
TW16 . . . . .125 C4
Sunbury Rd Eton SL4 . . . . .67 B4
Feltham TW13 . . . . .98 C2
Sunderland Cl RG5 . . . . . . .88 A4
Sunderland Ct 11 TW19 . . .70 C1
Sunderland Pl RG18 . . . . .106 B2
Sunderland Rd SL6 . . . . . . .39 A4
Sundew Cl
Lightwater GU18 . . . . .153 B4
Wokingham RG40 . . . . . . .116 C4
Sundial Cl RG30 . . . . .85 A3
Sundon Cres GU25 . . . . . .122 B2
Sundown Rd TW15 . . . . . . .98 B2
Sunley Cl RG14 . . . . .130 B3
Sunning Ave SL5 . . . . .120 C1
Sunning Ho Ascot SL5 . . . .120 B3
Windlesham SL5 . . . . .146 C4
Sunningdale Pk (Civil
Service Coll) SL5 . . . . . . .120 C2
Sunningdale Sch SL5 . . . .120 C2
Sunningdale Sta SL5 . . . .121 A1
Sunninghill Cl SL5 . . . . . . .120 B3
Sunninghill Ct SL5 . . . . . . .120 B3
Sunninghill Lodge SL5 . . .120 B4
Sunninghill Rd Ascot SL5 . .120 B3
Windlesham GU20 . . . . . . .146 A4
Winkfield SL4, SL5 . . . . .93 C1
Sunnybank Ascot SL5 . . . .120 A3
Marlow SL7 . . . . .1 B2
Sunnymeads Sta TW19 . . . .68 C2
Sunnymede Cotts SL6 . . . .20 A1
Sunnyside RG14 . . . . .104 C3
Surbiton Rd GU15 . . . . . . .145 A1
Surley Row RG4 . . . . .59 A3
Surly Hall Wlk SL4 . . . . . . .66 C3
Surrey Ave
Camberley GU15 . . . . .151 A2
Slough SL2 . . . . .22 B1
Surrey Ct RG42 . . . . .91 C1
Surrey Heath Mus GU15 . .151 B3
Surrey Rd RG2 . . . . .86 A2
Surridge Ct GU19 . . . . . . .145 C1
Sussex Cl SL1 . . . . .43 A2
Sussex Gdns RG5 . . . . .87 C4
Sussex Ho SL2 . . . . .22 B3
Sussex Keep SL1 . . . . .43 A2
Sussex La RG7 . . . . .113 B1
Sussex Lodge 7 SL6 . . . . . .39 C3
Sussex Pl SL1, SL3 . . . . . . .43 A2
Sutcliffe Ave RG6 . . . . .87 B2
Sutherland Ave TW16 . . . .125 C4
Sutherland Chase SL5 . . . .119 C4
Sutherland Gdns TW16 . . .125 C4
Sutherland Gr RG31 . . . . . .84 C2
Sutherland Grange SL4 . . . .66 B4
Sutherlands RG14 . . . . . . .130 C4
Sutherlands Ave RG1 . . . . .86 B3
Sutton Ave SL3 . . . . .43 B2
Sutton Cl Cookham SL6 . . . .20 A4
Maidenhead SL6 . . . . .39 B3
Sutton La Brands Hill SL3 . . .69 A4
Slough SL3 . . . . .44 B1
Sutton Pl SL3 . . . . .69 A4
Sutton Rd
Camberley GU15 . . . . .145 A1
Cookham SL6 . . . . .20 A3
Newbury RG14 . . . . .104 B3
Sutton Wlk RG1 . . . . .86 B3
Suttons Park Ave RG6 . . . . .86 C4
Swabey Rd SL3 . . . . .44 A1
Swainstone Rd RG2 . . . . . .86 A3
Swaledale RG12 . . . . .118 A2
Swallow Cl Reading RG31 . . .84 B3
Staines TW18 . . . . .96 C1
Yateley GU46 . . . . .149 A3
Swallow Ho SL7 . . . . .2 A1
Swallow St SL0 . . . . .44 B4
Swallow Way RG41 . . . . . .115 C3
Swallowfield TW20 . . . . . . .95 A1
Swallowfield Dr RG2 . . . . .113 B3
Swallowfield Gdns RG7 . . .83 C2
Swallowfield Pk RG7 . . . .139 B3
Swallowfield Rd RG2 . . . . .114 B1
Swan Cl RG30 . . . . .104 C2
Swan Dr RG7 . . . . .109 A2
Swan Ho GU47 . . . . .150 A4

Swan La GU47 . . . . .150 A4
Swan Pl 10 RG1 . . . . .86 A4
Swan Rd SL0 . . . . .44 C4
Swan Wlk TW17 . . . . .125 C1
Swancote Gn RG12 . . . . . .118 A2
Swandrift TW18 . . . . .96 C1
Swangate RG17 . . . . .100 B4
Swanholm Gdns RG31 . . . .84 C2
Swanmore Cl RG6 . . . . .87 C1
Swanscourt RG10 . . . . .61 C2
Swansdown Wlk RG19 . . . .106 A2
Swansea Rd
Harlington TW14, TW6 . . . .71 B1
Reading RG1 . . . . .59 A1
Swansea Terr RG31 . . . . . . .57 B1
Swanston La RG8 . . . . .56 B4
Sweeps Ditch Cl TW18 . . . .97 A1
Sweeps La TW20 . . . . .95 C2
Sweet Briar Dr RG31 . . . . . .84 B2
Sweetbriar RG45 . . . . .143 A4
Sweetzer's Piece RG7 . . . .136 C3
Swepstone Cl RG6 . . . . .87 C1
Swift Cl RG41 . . . . .115 C3
Swift Ho SL7 . . . . .2 A1
Swift La GU19 . . . . .145 C2
Swinbrook Cl RG31 . . . . . . .57 B2
Swindon Rd TW6 . . . . .71 B1
Swinley County Prim Sch
SL5 . . . . .120 A2
Swinley Forest Golf Club
SL5 . . . . .119 C1
Swinley Rd SL5 . . . . .119 B2
Swiss Cottage GU31 . . . . . .84 B4
Switchback Cl SL6 . . . . . . .19 B1
Switchback Rd N SL6 . . . . .19 C2
Switchback Rd S SL6 . . . . .19 B1
Switchback The SL6 . . . . . .19 B1
Swithin Chase RG42 . . . . . .91 C1
Sycamore Cl 18
Bourne End SL8 . . . . .3 A2
Burghfield Common RG30 . .111 A2
Frimley GU16 . . . . .151 C1
Maidenhead SL6 . . . . .39 B2
Sandhurst GU47 . . . . .150 A4
Woodley RG5 . . . . .87 B3
Sycamore Ct SL4 . . . . .67 B2
Sycamore Dr
Frimley GU16 . . . . .151 C1
Marlow Bottom SL7 . . . . .1 B3
Twyford RG10 . . . . .61 B3
Sycamore Lo 11 TW16 . . . .98 C1
Sycamore Rd RG2 . . . . .86 C2
Sycamore Rise
Bracknell RG12 . . . . .118 B3
Newbury RG14 . . . . .105 B3
Sycamore Wlk
Englefield Green TW20 . . . .95 A1
Slough SL3 . . . . .43 C4
Sycamores The GU17 . . . .150 A3
Sydings The RG14 . . . . . . .104 B3
Sydney Cl
Crowthorne RG45 . . . . . . .143 B4
Thatcham RG19 . . . . .106 C2
Sydney Cres TW15 . . . . . . .98 A1
Sydney Gr SL1 . . . . .42 B4
Sydney Lodge RG19 . . . . .106 C2
Syke Cluan SL0 . . . . .44 C2
Syke Ings SL0 . . . . .44 C2
Sykes Cotts RG12 . . . . . . .118 C1
Sykes Rd SL1 . . . . .42 A4
Sylvan Ridge GU47 . . . . . .143 A4
Sylvan Wlk RG30 . . . . .85 B2
Sylvanus RG12 . . . . .117 C1
Sylverns Ct RG42 . . . . .91 B1
Sylvester Cl
Newbury RG14 . . . . .104 C3
Winnersh RG41 . . . . .88 B2
Sylvester Rd SL6 . . . . .19 C1
Symondson Mews RG42 . . .90 C2
Sympson Rd RG26 . . . . . . .135 B1

T

Tachbrook Rd TW14 . . . . . .98 C4
Tadcroft Wlk RG31 . . . . . . .84 C2
Tadham Pl RG19 . . . . .106 B1
Tadley Common Rd
RG26 . . . . .135 B1
Tadmor Cl TW16 . . . . .125 C3
Taff Way RG30 . . . . .85 A4
Tag La RG10 . . . . .37 A1
Talbot Ave SL3 . . . . .43 B4
Talbot Cl Caversham RG4 . . .59 B1
Newbury RG14 . . . . .104 C3
Talbot Ct 7 Reading RG1 . .86 A4
Windsor SL4 . . . . .67 A2
Talbot Pl Bagshot GU19 . . .145 C2
Datchet SL3 . . . . .68 B3
Talbot Rd TW15 . . . . .97 C2
Talbot Way RG31 . . . . .57 B2
Talbots Dr SL6 . . . . .39 A3
Talfourd Ave RG6 . . . . .87 A3
Talisman Cl RG45 . . . . .142 B3
Tall Trees SL3 . . . . .69 C3
Tallis La RG30 . . . . .85 B3
Tamar Ct RG30 . . . . .85 B3
Tamar Gdns RG2 . . . . .86 B2
Tamar Way Slough SL3 . . . .44 A1
Wokingham RG41 . . . . .115 C4
Tamarind Ct 3 TW20 . . . . .95 C2
Tamarind Way RG6 . . . . . . .86 C1
Tamarisk Ave RG2 . . . . .86 C1
Tamarisk Rise RG40 . . . . . .116 B4
Tamarisk Way SL1 . . . . .42 A4
Tamerisk Ct RG18 . . . . . . .106 C2
Tamesa Ho TW17 . . . . .125 A1
Tamesis Pl RG4 . . . . .59 A1

Tamworth RG12 . . . . .118 B1
Tamworth Cl 2 RG6 . . . . . .87 B1
Tangier Ct SL4 . . . . .67 B4
Tangier La SL4 . . . . .67 B4
Tanglewood RG40 . . . . . . .142 A4
Tanglewood Ride GU24 . . .153 C2
Tangley Dr RG41 . . . . .116 A2
Tanglyn Ave TW17 . . . . . . .125 A3
Tanhouse La RG41 . . . . . . .116 A3
Tank Rd GU15 . . . . .150 C3
Tanner Ct RG14 . . . . .105 A2
Tanners Cl RG4 . . . . .110 C1
Tanners La RG4 . . . . .58 C4
Tanners Yd GU19 . . . . .145 C2
Tape La RG10 . . . . .88 C2
Tapestries The SL4 . . . . . . .68 A1
Taplow Common Rd SL1 . .21 A2
Taplow Rd SL6 . . . . .41 A4
Taplow Sta SL6 . . . . .40 C4
Tarbat Ct 6 GU47 . . . . . . .150 B4
Tarbay La SL4 . . . . .66 A3
Target Cl TW14 . . . . .71 C1
Target Hill RG42 . . . . .91 B1
Targett Ct RG41 . . . . .88 C1
Tarlton Ct RG30 . . . . .84 C3
Tarn Howes Cl RG19 . . . . .106 A2
Tarn La RG14 . . . . .130 C4
Tarnbrook Way RG12 . . . . .118 C1
Tarragon Cl Earley RG6 . . . .86 C1
Newell Green RG42 . . . . . . .91 B1
Tarragon Way RG7 . . . . . . .111 A2
Tarrant Gn RG42 . . . . .91 B1
Tarrants Hill RG17 . . . . . . .100 B3
Tasker Cl UB3 . . . . .71 B4
Tasman Ct 1 TW16 . . . . . . .98 C1
Tatchbook Cl SL6 . . . . .40 A4
Tattersall Cl RG40 . . . . . . .116 C3
Tavistock Cl
Maidenhead SL6 . . . . .39 A4
Staines TW18 . . . . .97 B1
Tavistock Rd RG42 . . . . . . .86 A2
Tawfield RG12 . . . . .117 C1
Tay Rd RG30 . . . . .85 A4
Taylor Ct 18 RG1 . . . . .85 C4
Taylor's Cl SL7 . . . . .1 C1
Taylors Cl SL6 . . . . .39 A4
Taynton Wlk 32 RG1 . . . . . .86 A3
Tazewell Ct RG1 . . . . .85 C3
Tebbit Cl RG12 . . . . .118 B4
Teesdale Rd SL2 . . . . .41 C4
Teikyo Sch (UK) SL3 . . . . . .23 B4
Tekels Ave GU15 . . . . .151 B2
Tekels Ct GU15 . . . . .151 C2
Tekels Way GU15 . . . . .151 C2
Telford Ave RG45 . . . . .143 B4
Telford Cres RG5 . . . . .60 C1
Telford Dr SL1 . . . . .42 A2
Telston Cl SL8 . . . . .3 B3
Tempest Rd TW20 . . . . .96 B1
Templar Ct GU47 . . . . .150 A4
Temple Cl Crowthorne RG45 .143 B4
Thatcham RG18 . . . . .106 C2
Temple La SL7 . . . . .18 B3
Temple Mews RG5 . . . . . . .87 C4
Temple Mill Cotts SL7 . . . .18 B3
Temple Mill Island SL7 . . .18 B3
Temple Pk SL6 . . . . .17 C2
Temple Pl RG1 . . . . .86 A3
Temple Rd SL4 . . . . .67 B3
Temple Way Binfield RG42 . .90 C2
Farnham Common SL2 . . . . .22 B4
Templecroft TW15 . . . . . . .98 B1
Templedene Ave TW18 . . . .97 B1
Templeton Gdns RG2 . . . . .86 B1
Templewood La SL2 . . . . . .22 B4
Ten Acre La TW20 . . . . . . .123 B4
Tenaplas Dr RG8 . . . . .54 C3
Tenby Ave RG4 . . . . .59 B3
Tenby Dr SL5 . . . . .120 B2
Tennyson Rd
Ashford TW15 . . . . .97 C2
Thatcham RG18 . . . . .106 B2
Woodley RG5 . . . . .87 C2
Tennyson Way SL2 . . . . . . .21 C1
Tensing Ct TW19 . . . . .97 C4
Teresa Vale RG42 . . . . .91 C1
Tern Cl RG30 . . . . .85 A3
Terrace Rd N RG42 . . . . . . .90 B2
Terrace Rd S RG42 . . . . . . .90 B1
Terrace The Ascot SL5 . . . .120 B2
Camberley GU15 . . . . .151 A3
Crowthorne RG45 . . . . . . .143 B3
Maidenhead SL6 . . . . .40 B2
Wokingham RG40 . . . . . . .116 A3
Terrent Ct SL4 . . . . .67 A3
Terrington Hill SL7 . . . . .1 A1
Terry's La SL6 . . . . .19 C4
Tesimond Dr GU46 . . . . . .149 A3
Tessa Rd RG1 . . . . .58 C1
Test Cl RG30 . . . . .85 A4
Testwood Rd SL4 . . . . .66 B3
Tetbury Ct 14 RG1 . . . . . . .85 C4
Teviot Rd RG30 . . . . .84 C4
Thackery Lodge TW14 . . . .71 B1
Thakerays The RG19 . . . . .106 B1
Thames Ave
Chertsey KT16 . . . . .124 A3
Pangbourne RG8 . . . . .56 B3
Reading RG1 . . . . .59 A1
Windsor SL4 . . . . .67 B4
Thames Cl Bourne End SL8 . .3 A2
Chertsey KT16 . . . . .124 B1
Thames Cres SL6 . . . . .20 A1
Thames Dr RG10 . . . . .60 C4
Thames Ind Est SL7 . . . . . . .1 C1
Thames Mdw
KT12, TW17 . . . . .125 C1

Tha–Ver 181

Thames Mead SL4 66 C3
Thames Rd Goring RG8 34 A3
Slough SL3 44 A2
Thatcham RG18 106 A3
Thames Reach
Medmenham SL7 17 B3
Purley on T RG8 57 B3
Thames Side
Henley-on-T RG9 15 C1
Laleham KT16, TW18 124 B2
Reading RG1 59 A1
Staines TW18 96 C1
Windsor SL4 67 B4
Thames Side Prom RG1 59 A1
Thames St Sonning RG4 60 B2
Staines TW18 96 C2
Walton-on-T KT12 125 C1
Windsor SL4 67 B4
Thames Valley Bsns Pk RG6 60 A1
Thames Valley Univ SL1 42 C3
Thamesbourne Mews SL8 3 A2
Thamesfield Ct TW17 125 B1
Thamesfield Gdns SL7 1 C1
Thamesgate TW18 124 A4
Thameside Prim Sch RG4 59 A1
Thamesmead Sch TW17 125 B2
Thanington Way RG6 87 A1
Thatcham Nature Discovery Ctr RG19 106 A1
Thatcham Sta RG19 106 C1
Thatchers Dr SL6 39 A3
Theal Cl GU47 150 B4
Theale CE Prim Sch RG7 83 B2
Theale Green Com Sch RG7 83 B2
Theale Rd RG30 111 B3
Theale Sta RG7 83 C1
Theobald Dr RG31 57 B2
Theobalds Way GU16 152 B2
Thetford Ho 10 RG1 85 C3
Thetford Mews RG4 59 B3
Thetford Rd TW15 97 C3
Thibet Rd GU47 150 B4
Thicket Gr SL6 38 C4
Thicket Rd RG30 84 C4
Thickthorne La TW18 97 B1
Third Ave Marlow SL7 1 C1
Tadley RG7 135 B1
Third Cres SL1 42 B4
Third St Greenham RG19 131 C3
Newtown RG19 132 A3
Thirkleby Cl SL1 42 B3
Thirlmere Ave
Burnham SL1 41 B4
Reading RG30 57 C1
Thirlmere Cl TW20 96 A1
Thirlmere Wlk GU15 152 B2
Thirtover RG18 79 A1
Thistledown RG31 57 B1
Thistleton Way RG6 87 C1
Thomas Dr RG42 91 C1
Thomas La RG40 141 C4
Thomas Rd HP10 3 C4
Thompkins La SL2 22 A3
Thompson Cl
Hermitage RG18 78 C3
Slough SL3 44 A1
Thompson Dr RG19 106 C1
Thomson Wlk RG31 84 C2
Thorburn Chase GU47 150 C3
Thorn Cl RG41 115 B2
Thorn Dr SL3 43 C4
Thorn La 12 RG1 86 A4
Thorn St RG1 86 A4
Thornaby Pl HP10 3 C4
Thornbank Cl TW19 70 A1
Thornbers Way RG10 61 A3
Thornbridge Rd RG2 113 A4
Thornbury Cl RG45 143 A3
Thornbury Gn RG10 61 B3
Thorncroft TW20 95 B1
Thorndike SL2 42 A4
Thorndown La GU20 146 B2
Thorne Cl
Crowthorne RG45 143 A4
Littleton TW15 98 B1
Thorney Cl RG6 87 C1
Thorney La N SL0 44 C3
Thorney La S SL0 44 C3
Thornfield RG19 132 B2
Thornfield Gn GU17 150 C2
Thornford Rd RG19 132 C2
Thornhill RG12 118 C3
Thornhill Way TW17 125 A2
Thorningdown OX11 10 B4
Thornton Mews RG30 85 B4
Thornton Rd RG30 85 B4
Thorp Cl RG42 90 B2
Thorpe By-Pass TW20 123 A3
Thorpe CE Fst Sch TW20 123 A3
Thorpe Cl RG41 116 A2
Thorpe Ho 7 RG30 85 A4
Thorpe Ind Est TW20 123 B4
Thorpe Ind Pk TW20 123 B4
Thorpe Lea Prim Sch TW20 96 B1
Thorpe Lea Rd TW20 96 B1
Thorpe Pk TW20 123 C3
Thorpe Rd Chertsey KT16 123 B2
Egham TW18, TW20 96 B2
Thorpeside Cl TW18 123 C4
Thrale Mews RG30 85 A4
Three Acre Rd RG14 130 C4
Three Firs Way RG7 110 C1
Three Gables La RG8 34 A4
Three Post La RG17 25 A1
Threshfield RG12 118 A2
Thrift La Holyport SL6 64 B4
Maidenhead SL6 39 B1
Throat Handpost Cnr The RG40 116 A1
Throgmorton Rd GU46 149 A3
Thrush Cl RG7 111 A2
Thurlby Way SL6 39 B2
Thurlestone Cl TW17 125 B2
Thurlestone Gdns RG2 86 B1
Thurlestone Par TW17 125 B2
Thurleys Cotts SL3 23 A2
Thurnscoe Cl RG6 113 C4
Thurso Cl RG30 85 A4
Thurston Rd SL1 42 C4
Thyme Cl RG6 87 A1
Tichborne Cl GU17 150 B3
Tichbourne Cl GU16 151 C2
Tickenor Dr RG40 141 C4
Tickhill Cl RG6 113 C4
Tickleback Row RG42 91 A4
Tidmarsh La RG8 56 A1
Tidmarsh Rd RG8 56 B2
Tidmarsh St 1 RG30 85 A4
Tidwells Lea RG12 118 C4
Tierney Ct 10 SL7 1 C1
Tiffany Cl RG41 115 B3
Tiger Cl RG5 88 A4
Tigerseye Cl RG41 115 B4
Tilbury Cl RG4 59 B2
Tilbury Wlk SL3 44 A2
Tile Barn Row RG20 129 C1
Tilebarn Cl RG9 15 B1
Tilecotes Cl SL7 1 B1
Tilehurst La RG42 90 B2
Tilehurst Rd RG1 & RG30 85 B4
Tilehurst Sta RG31 57 C2
Tilling Cl RG31 57 A1
Tilly's La TW18 96 C2
Tilney Way RG6 113 C4
Tilstone Ave SL4 41 C1
Tilstone Cl SL4 41 C1
Timbers Wlk SL6 39 A3
Timline Gn RG12 118 C4
Timsway TW18 96 C2
Tindal Cl GU46 149 B3
Tinkers La SL4 66 B3
Tinsey Cl TW20 96 A2
Tinsley Cl RG6 113 C4
Tintagel Dr GU16 151 C1
Tintagel Ho SL1 42 B3
Tintagel Rd RG40 142 A4
Tintern Cl SL1 42 B2
Tintern Cres RG1 85 C3
Tinwell Cl RG6 87 C1
Tippett Rise RG2 86 A3
Tippings La RG5 88 A4
Tippits Mead RG42 117 B4
Tiptree Cl RG6 113 C4
Tiree Ho SL2 42 A4
Titcombe Way RG17 102 A1
Tite Hill TW20 95 B2
Tithe Barn Dr SL6 40 C1
Tithe Cl Maidenhead SL6 40 B1
Wentworth GU25 122 B2
Tithe Ct Slough SL3 44 A1
Wokingham RG40 116 B4
Tithe La TW19 69 A1
Tithe Mdws GU25 122 B2
Tithebarn Gr RG31 84 C2
Titlarks Hill Rd SL5 121 A1
Tiverton Cl RG5 60 C1
Tiverton Way GU16 151 C1
Toad La GU17 150 C2
Tocker Gdns RG42 91 A1
Tockley Way SL1 21 A1
Tofrek Terr RG30 85 B4
Tokers Green Rd RG4 58 C4
Tokersgreen La RG4 58 B3
Toll Gdns RG12 118 C3
Tollgate SL6 39 A3
Tolpuddle Way GU46 149 C3
Tomlin Cl RG19 106 C1
Tomlin Rd SL2 21 C1
Tomlins Ave GU16 151 C1
Tomlinscote Sch GU16 152 A1
Tomlinscote Way GU16 152 A1
Tomlinson Dr RG40 142 A4
Toogood Pl RG42 91 B2
Top Common RG42 91 B1
Topaz Cl Slough SL1 42 A3
Wokingham RG41 115 C4
Tope Cres RG2 140 C4
Tope Rd RG2 140 C4
Torcross Gr RG31 84 A2
Torin Ct TW20 95 B2
Torquay Spur SL2 22 A1
Torridge Rd SL3 69 A4
Torrington Rd RG2 86 B1
Toseland Way RG6 87 C2
Totale Rise RG42 91 A1
Totnes Rd RG2 86 B1
Tottenham Wlk GU47 143 B1
Totterdown RG7 110 C1
Toulouse Cl GU15 152 A4
Toutley Cl RG41 88 C1
Toutley Rd RG41 89 A1
Toutly Works RG41 89 A1
Tower Cl Caversham RG4 59 B4
Flackwell Heath HP10 3 B4
Tower Hill RG20 49 A4
Tower Ho Iver SL0 44 C4
4 Slough SL1 42 C2
Towers Dr RG45 143 A2
Town Farm Cty Prim Sch TW19 97 B4
Town Farm Way TW19 97 B4
Town La Stanwell TW19 97 B4
Town La *continued*
Wooburn Green HP10 3 B2
Town Mills 23 RG14 105 A2
Town Quay TW18 124 B3
Town Sq Bracknell RG12 118 B4
Camberley GU15 151 B3
17 Slough SL1 42 C2
Town Tree Rd TW15 98 A2
Townlands Hospl RG9 15 B1
Townsend Cl RG12 118 C2
Townsend Rd
Aldworth RG8 32 C2
Ashford TW15 97 C2
Streatley RG8 34 A4
Townside Pl GU15 151 B3
Towpath TW17 124 C1
Tozer Wlk SL4 66 B2
Trafalgar Cl RG41 115 C3
Trafalgar Ct RG1 85 C3
Trafalgar Way GU15 150 C2
Trafford Rd RG1 58 C1
Transport & Road Research Laboratory RG45 143 B4
Travic Rd SL2 21 C1
Travis Ct SL2 22 A1
Travis La GU47 150 B4
Treble Ho Terr OX11 12 A4
Tredegar Rd RG4 59 A3
Tree Cl RG30 84 B4
Tree Tops Ave GU15 152 A4
Trees Rd SL8 3 A2
Treesmill Dr SL6 39 B2
Treeton Cl RG6 113 C4
Trefoil Cl RG40 116 C4
Trefoil Dro RG18 106 C2
Treforgan RG4 58 C3
Trelawney Ave SL3 43 C2
Trelawney Dr RG31 57 A1
Trelleck Rd RG1 85 C3
Tremayne Wlk GU15 152 B2
Trenchard Rd SL6 65 A4
Trenches La SL0, SL3 44 A3
Trent Cl RG41 115 C4
Trent Cres RG18 106 A3
Trent Rd SL3 69 A4
Trent Villas Est SL3 68 A3
Trenthams Cl RG8 57 A3
Trenton Cl GU16 152 A1
Tresham Cres GU46 149 A3
Tressel The SL6 39 B3
Trevelyan RG12 117 C1
Trevelyan Mid Sch SL4 67 A3
Trevithick Cl TW14 98 C4
Trevor Ct TW19 70 A1
Trevor Ho 5 RG30 85 A4
Trevose Ho SL2 22 A1
Treyarnon Ct RG1 86 B3
Triangle The
Greenham RG14 131 A4
Reading RG30 84 B4
Trident Ind Est SL3 69 C2
Trilakes Ctry Pk GU46,GU47 149 C4
Trindledown RG42 91 A1
Tring Rd RG31 57 B1
Trinity GU47 143 C1
Trinity Ave SL7 1 B2
Trinity Cl TW19 70 B1
Trinity Cres SL5 121 A2
Trinity Ct RG7 83 B2
Trinity Ho SL6 19 C3
Trinity Pl Reading RG1 85 C4
Windsor SL4 67 B3
Trinity Rd SL7 1 B1
Trinity Sch RG14 105 A3
Trinity St Stephens CE Fst Sch SL4 67 A3
Triumph Cl Harlington UB7 71 B3
Woodley RG5 87 C3
Troon Ct Ascot SL5 120 B2
33 Reading RG1 86 B4
Troston Ct TW18 96 C2
Trotsworth Ave GU25 122 C3
Trotsworth Ct GU25 122 B3
Trotwood Cl GU47 143 C1
Trout Cl Earley RG6 87 A4
Marlow SL7 18 B4
Trout Wlk RG14 105 B2
Troutbeck Cl Slough SL2 43 A3
Twyford RG10 61 B3
Troutbeck Wlk GU15 152 B2
Trowes La Beech Hill RG7 138 B2
Swallowfield RG7 139 B3
Trumbull Rd RG42 91 A1
Trumper Way SL1 41 C3
Trumps Green Cl GU25 122 C2
Trumps Green Cty Fst Sch GU25 122 B2
Trumps Mill La GU25 122 C2
Trumpsgreen Ave GU25 122 B2
Trumpsgreen Rd GU25 122 B2
Truro Cl SL6 39 A4
Truss Hill Rd SL5 120 B2
Trust Cnr RG9 35 C4
Trusthorpe Cl RG6 87 C1
Tubbs Farm Cl RG17 25 A1
Tubwell Rd SL2 23 A2
Tudor Ave RG20 51 B2
Tudor Cl Ashford TW15 97 C2
Wokingham RG40 116 C3
Tudor Ct Maidenhead SL6 20 B1
3 Stanwell TW19 70 C1
Tudor Dr
Wooburn Green HP10 3 B4
Yateley GU46 149 B2
Tudor Gdns SL1 41 B4
Tudor Ho RG12 118 A2
Tudor La SL4 95 B4
Tudor Mill HP10 3 C3
Tudor Rd Ashford TW15 98 B1
Newbury RG14 105 A1
Reading RG1 86 A4
Tudor Way SL4 66 C3
Tull Way RG14 105 C3
Tunnel Link Rd TW6 71 A1
Tunnel Rd E TW6 71 A3
Tunnel Rd W TW6 71 A3
Tuns Hill Cotts RG6 87 A3
Tuns La Henley-on-T RG9 15 C1
Slough SL1 42 B2
Tupsley Rd RG1 85 C3
Turbary Gdns RG26 135 A1
Turf Hill Rd GU15 151 C4
Turks Head Ct SL4 67 B4
Turks La RG7 137 A2
Turmeric Cl RG6 86 C1
Turnberry RG12 117 C1
Turnberry Ct 30 RG1 86 B4
Turnbridge Cl RG6 114 A4
Turner Pl GU47 150 B3
Turner Rd SL3 43 B2
Turners Cl TW18 97 A2
Turners Dr RG19 106 C1
Turnery The RG19 106 B2
Turnfields RG19 106 B2
Turnoak Pk SL4 66 C2
Turnpike Comp Sch RG14 105 B2
Turnpike Ind Est RG14 105 B3
Turnpike Rd
Bracknell RG42 117 B4
Newbury RG14, RG19 105 C2
Turnstone Cl RG41 88 A2
Turnstone End GU46 149 A3
Turnville Cl GU18 146 A1
Turpin Rd TW14 71 C1
Turpins Gn SL6 39 A3
Turpins Rise GU20 146 A3
Turton Way SL1 42 B2
Tuscam Way GU15 150 C2
Tuscan Cl RG30 57 C1
Tuxford Mews RG30 85 A4
Tweed Ct RG30 85 A4
Tweed Rd SL3 69 A4
Twin Oaks RG4 59 A3
Twinches La SL1 42 A3
Twinwoods RG20 49 A2
Two Mile Dr SL1 41 C2
Two Rivers Sh Ctr TW18 96 C2
Two Rivers Way RG14 105 B2
Two Tree Hill RG9 35 A4
Twycross Rd RG40 116 C4
Twyford Rd
Binfield RG10 & RG42 90 B4
Waltham St Lawrence RG10 62 C3
Wokingham RG40 89 A1
Twyford Sta RG10 61 C2
Twynersh Ave KT16 123 C2
Twynham Rd SL6 39 A4
Tyberton Pl RG1 85 C3
Tydehams RG14 130 C4
Tyle Pl SL4 68 A1
Tyle Rd RG30 84 B4
Tyler Cl RG4 58 C3
Tyler Dr RG2 140 C4
Tylers La RG7 80 A1
Tylers Pl RG30 84 C4
Tylorstown RG4 58 C3
Tyne Way RG18 106 A3
Tyrell Gdns SL4 66 C2
Tyrrel Ct 8 RG1 86 B4
Tytherton RG12 118 B4

U

Uffington Cl RG31 84 B4
Uffington Dr RG12 118 C3
Uffoott Cl RG6 113 C4
Ufton Court Yd SL8 3 A2
Ufton Ct SL8 3 A2
Ullswater RG12 117 C1
Ullswater Cl Burnham SL1 41 B4
Lightwater GU18 146 A1
Thatcham RG19 106 A2
Ullswater Dr RG31 57 B2
Ullswater Rd GU18 146 A1
Ulster Cl RG4 59 B3
Umberville Way SL2 21 C1
Underhill OX10 14 A2
Underhill Cl SL6 39 C3
Underwood RG12 117 C2
Underwood Ct RG42 90 B1
Underwood Rd RG30 85 A2
Union Cl GU47 143 C1
Union Rd RG7 82 B2
Union St RG1 86 A4
Unity Cl RG4 59 A3
Unity Ct RG4 59 A3
Univ of Reading
Earley RG6 87 A3
Reading RG1 86 B3
Reading, Whiteknights RG6 86 C2
Unwin Ave TW14 71 B1
Upavon Dr RG1 85 C3
Upavon Gdns RG12 118 C2
Upcroft SL4 67 A2
Upcroft Prim Sch RG30 84 C4
Updown Hill GU20 146 B2
Upland Rd GU15 151 B4
Uplands Hungerford RG17 100 B3
Marlow Bottom SL7 1 B3
Uplands Cl GU47 150 A4
Uplands Cty Prim Sch GU47 150 A4
Uplands Rd RG4 58 C3
Upper Bray Rd SL6 40 B2
Upper Broadmoor Rd RG45 143 B3
Upper Charles St GU15 151 B3
Upper Chobham Rd GU15 152 A2
Upper College Ride GU15 151 C4
Upper Crown St RG1 86 A3
Upper Eddington RG17 100 C4
Upper End RG20 49 A4
Upper Gordon Rd GU15 151 B3
Upper Halliford Rd TW17 125 C3
Upper Halliford Sta TW16 125 C4
Upper Lambourn Rd RG17 25 A2
Upper Lees Rd SL2 22 A1
Upper Meadow Rd RG2 86 B1
Upper Nursery SL5 121 A2
Upper Park Rd GU15 151 C3
Upper Red Cross Rd RG8 34 B4
Upper Redlands Rd RG1 86 C3
Upper Ventnor Cotts SL6 19 B4
Upper Verran Rd GU15 151 B2
Upper Village Rd SL5 120 B2
Upper Warren Ave RG4 58 B2
Upper Wlk GU25 122 C3
Upper Woodcote Rd RG4 58 B3
Uppingham Dr RG5 60 C1
Uppingham Gdns RG4 59 B3
Upshire Gdns RG12 118 C3
Upton Cl Henley-on-T RG9 15 C1
Slough SL1 42 C2
Upton Court Rd SL3 43 A1
Upton Hospl SL1 42 C2
Upton House Sch SL4 67 B3
Upton Lea Par SL2 43 A3
Upton Pk SL1 42 C2
Upton Rd Reading RG30 85 A4
Slough SL1 43 A2
Urquhart Rd RG19 106 C1
Usk Rd RG30 84 C3
Uxbridge Rd SL1, SL2, SL3 43 B3

V

Vachel Rd RG1 86 A4
Vale Cres RG30 57 C1
Vale Gr SL1 42 C2
Vale Rd Camberley GU15 151 A2
Windsor SL4 66 C3
Vale View RG10 61 A2
Valentia Cl RG30 85 B4
Valentia Rd RG30 85 B4
Valentine Cl RG6 86 C1
Valentine Cres RG4 59 B2
Valentine Wood Ind Est RG7 135 C2
Valeview Dr RG7 138 B3
Valley Cl Caversham RG4 59 A2
Goring RG8 34 B3
Valley Cres RG41 116 A4
Valley End SL3 23 B1
Valley Gdns TW20,GU25 121 C4
Valley Rd
Burghfield Common RG7 111 A2
Frimley GU16 152 B1
Henley-on-T RG9 35 A4
Newbury RG14 130 C4
Valley Road Prim Sch RG9 35 B4
Valley View GU47 150 A4
Valley Way RG26 135 C1
Valon Rd RG2 140 C4
Valpy St RG1 86 A4
Valroy Cl GU15 151 B3
Vanbrugh Ct RG1 86 B4
Vandyke RG12 117 C2
Vanguard Ho 5 TW19 70 C1
Vanlore Way RG31 84 B3
Vanners La RG20 129 B3
Vansittart Est SL4 67 B3
Vansittart Rd Bisham SL7 18 C4
Windsor SL4 67 A3
Vantage Rd SL1 42 A3
Vanwall Bsns Pk SL6 39 B3
Vanwall Rd SL6 39 B2
Vastern Rd RG1 59 A1
Vaughan Almshouses TW15 98 A2
Vaughan Copse SL4 42 B1
Vaughan Gdns SL4 41 C1
Vaughan Way SL2 21 C1
Vauxhall Dr RG5 88 A3
Vegal Cres TW20 95 B2
Venetia Cl RG4 59 B4
Venning Rd RG2 140 C4
Ventnor Rd RG31 57 B1
Venus Cl RG41 115 C3
Verbena Cl RG41 88 A2
Verdon Ct SL2 22 A1
Verey Cl RG10 61 C2
Vermont Rd SL2 21 C1
Vermont Woods RG40 141 C4
Verney Cl SL7 1 B1
Verney Mews RG30 85 B4
Verney Rd SL3 44 A1
Vernon Cres RG2 113 A4
Vernon Dr SL5 119 C4
Vernon Rd TW13 98 C3
Verran Rd GU15 151 B2

Viburnum Ct GU24 . . . . . .153 C3
Vicarage Ave TW20 . . . . . .96 A2
Vicarage Cl Cookham SL6 . .20 A4
  Wokingham RG40 . . . . . .141 C3
Vicarage Cres TW20 . . . . .96 A2
Vicarage Ct
  East Bedfont TW14 . . . . . .98 A4
  Egham TW20 . . . . .96 A1
Vicarage Dr SL6 . . . . .40 B2
Vicarage Flats SL4 . . . . . .67 B4
Vicarage Gdns Ascot SL5 . .120 A2
  White Waltham SL6 . . . . . .63 C4
Vicarage La
  Cold Ash RG18 . . . . .106 B4
  Laleham TW18 . . . . .124 B3
  Wraysbury TW19 . . . . . . .95 C4
  Yateley GU46 . . . . .149 B4
Vicarage Rd Ashford TW16 .98 C1
  Bagshot GU19 . . . . .145 B2
  Blackwater GU17 . . . . . . .150 C2
  Egham TW20 . . . . .96 A1
  Henley-on-T RG9 . . . . . . .35 C4
  Maidenhead SL6 . . . . .39 C4
  Reading RG2 . . . . .86 B3
  Staines TW18 . . . . .96 C3
  Yateley GU46 . . . . .149 B4
Vicarage Way SL3 . . . . . .69 B4
Vicarage Wlk SL6 . . . . . . .40 B2
Vicarage Wood Way
  RG31 . . . . .57 A1
Vickers Cl Shinfield RG2 . .113 C2
  Woodley RG5 . . . . .88 A4
Vickers Ct 9 TW19 . . . . . .70 C1
Victor Cl SL6 . . . . .39 A4
Victor Rd Thatcham RG19 . .106 C2
  Windsor SL4 . . . . .67 B2
Victor Way RG5 . . . . .88 A4
Victoria Ave GU15 . . . . . .151 A3
Victoria Ct Bagshot GU19 .145 C1
  Henley-on-T RG9 . . . . . . .15 C1
  2 Marlow SL7 . . . . .1 C1
  Slough SL1 . . . . .42 C3
Victoria Dr GU17 . . . . . . .150 B2
Victoria Gdns RG14 . . . . . .105 A2
Victoria Ho SL4 . . . . .68 A1
Victoria La UB3 . . . . .71 B4
Victoria Mews RG30 . . . . .85 B4
Victoria Rd Ascot SL5 . . . .120 A2
  Caversham RG4 . . . . .59 A2
  Eton SL4 . . . . .41 C1
  Farnham Common SL2 . . . .22 B3
  Marlow SL7 . . . . .1 C1
  Mortimer RG7 . . . . .136 C3
  Reading RG31 . . . . .84 B4
  Sandhurst GU47 . . . . . . .143 C1
  Slough SL2 . . . . .43 A3
  Staines TW18 . . . . .96 C3
  Wargrave RG10 . . . . .36 C1
Victoria St
  Englefield Green TW20 . . . .95 B1
  Reading RG1 . . . . .86 B4
  18 Slough SL1 . . . . .42 C2
  Windsor SL4 . . . . .67 B3
Victoria Way 18 RG1 . . . . .86 B4
Victory Rd KT16 . . . . .124 A1
Vigo La GU46 . . . . .149 B2
Viking RG12 . . . . .117 C2
Villa Mews RG1 . . . . .86 C4
Village Cl RG2 . . . . .113 A3
Village Ct SL5 . . . . .120 B2
Village Gate TW17 . . . . . .125 A2
Village Rd Dorney SL4 . . . .41 A2
  Thorpe TW20 . . . . .123 B3
Village Sh Ctr The 13 SL1 .42 C2
Village The
  Finchampstead RG40 . . . . .141 C2
  Old Windsor SL4 . . . . .94 A3
Village Way Ashford TW15 .98 A2
  Yateley GU46 . . . . .149 B4
Villiers Ct SL4 . . . . .67 A4
Villiers Mead RG41 . . . . . .116 A3
Villiers Rd SL2 . . . . .42 B4
Villiers Way RG14 . . . . . . .130 B3
Villiers Wlk RG14 . . . . . . .130 B3
Vincent Cl Chertsey KT16 . .123 C1
  Harmondsworth UB7 . . . . .71 A4
  Woodley RG5 . . . . .87 C3
Vincent Dr TW17 . . . . . . .125 C3
Vincent Ho 10 RG1 . . . . . .85 C4
Vincent Rd Chertsey KT16 .123 C1
  Thatcham RG18 . . . . .106 C2
Vincent Rise RG12 . . . . . .118 C3
Vine Cl TW19 . . . . .70 A1
Vine Cres RG30 . . . . .85 A2
Vine Ct Newbury RG14 . . . .105 A1
  Stoke Poges SL2 . . . . .23 A3
Vine Rd SL2 . . . . .22 C3
Vineries Cl UB7 . . . . .71 A4
Vinery The RG10 . . . . .36 B1
Vines The RG41 . . . . .115 B2
Vineyard Dr SL8 . . . . .3 A3
Vinter Ct TW17 . . . . .125 A2
Viola Ave TW19 . . . . .97 C4
Viola Croft RG42 . . . . .118 C4
Violet Gr RG18 . . . . .106 C3
Virginia Ave GU25 . . . . . .122 B3
Virginia Beeches GU25 . . .122 B3
Virginia Cl TW18 . . . . . . .124 B3
Virginia Ct Ashford TW15 . .97 C2
  Virginia Water GU25 . . . . .122 B3
Virginia Dr GU25 . . . . . . .122 B3
Virginia Water SL5 . . . . . .121 C3
Virginia Water Prep Sch
  GU25 . . . . .122 B3
Virginia Water Sta GU25 . .122 C2

Virginia Way RG30 . . . . . .85 A3
Viscount 27 SL4 . . . . .67 B3
Viscount Ind Est SL3 . . . . .69 C2
Viscount Rd TW19 . . . . . . .97 C4
Viscount Way Hatton TW6 . .71 C2
  Woodley RG5 . . . . .88 A4
Vivien Cl SL6 . . . . .19 C3
Vivienne Ho TW18 . . . . . . .97 A2
Vo-Tec RG14 . . . . .105 C1
Voller Dr RG31 . . . . .84 B3
Volunteer Rd RG7 . . . . . . .83 B1
Vulcan Cl Sandhurst GU47 .150 A4
  Woodley RG5 . . . . .61 A1
Vulcan Way GU47 . . . . . . .150 A4

W

Waborne Rd SL8 . . . . .3 A2
Wade Dr SL1 . . . . .42 A3
Wadham GU47 . . . . .143 C1
Wadham Cl TW17 . . . . . . .125 B1
Wagbullock Rise RG12 . . . .118 B2
Waggoners Hollow
  GU19 . . . . .145 C1
Wagner Cl SL6 . . . . .38 C2
Wagtail Cl RG10 . . . . .61 C2
Waingel's Copse Sch
  RG10 . . . . .61 A1
Waingells Rd RG5, RG10 . . .61 A1
Wainscot SL5 . . . . .120 C1
Wakefield Cres SL2 . . . . . .22 C3
Wakeford Cl RG26 . . . . . . .135 C1
Wakeford Ct RG26 . . . . . . .135 C1
Wakelins End SL6 . . . . . . .19 C4
Wakeman Rd SL8 . . . . .3 A2
Wakemans RG8 . . . . .55 B2
Walbury RG12 . . . . .118 C3
Waldeck Rd SL6 . . . . .40 A4
Waldeck St RG1 . . . . .86 A3
Waldegrave Pl RG14 . . . . . .105 A2
Walden Ave RG2 . . . . .114 B2
Waldens Cl SL8 . . . . .3 A2
Waldorf Hts GU17 . . . . . . .150 B2
Waldron Hill RG12 . . . . . . .118 C4
Waldrons The RG17 . . . . . .47 B3
Waleys Pl 7 RG1 . . . . .59 B1
Walgrove Gdns SL6 . . . . . .63 C4
Walk The Ashford TW16 . . . .98 C1
  Eton SL4 . . . . .42 A1
Walker Cl TW14 . . . . .98 C4
Walker Rd SL6 . . . . .40 A2
Walker's Ridge GU15 . . . . .151 C3
Walkers La RG17 . . . . .25 A2
Walkers Pl RG30 . . . . .85 B4
Wall La RG7 . . . . .136 B1
Wallace Cl Marlow SL7 . . . . .1 C2
  Upper Halliford TW17 . . . . .125 B3
  Woodley RG5 . . . . .87 B3
Wallace Wlk SL4 . . . . .42 C1
Wallcroft Cl RG42 . . . . . . .90 C1
Walled Gdn The RG10 . . . . .36 B1
Waller Ct RG4 . . . . .59 A1
Waller Dr RG14 . . . . .105 C2
Wallingford Cl RG12 . . . . . .118 C3
Wallingford Rd
  Compton RG20 . . . . .31 C3
  Goring RG8 . . . . .34 B4
  South Stoke RG8 & OX10 . .14 B3
Wallington Rd GU15 . . . . . .145 A1
Wallington's Rd RG17 . . . . .101 C1
Wallis Ct SL1 . . . . .43 A2
Wallner Way RG40 . . . . . . .116 C3
Walmer Cl
  Crowthorne RG45 . . . . . . .143 B3
  Reading RG30 . . . . .85 A3
Walmer Rd RG5 . . . . .60 C1
Walnut Cl
  Wokingham RG41 . . . . . . .115 C3
  Yateley GU46 . . . . .149 B2
Walnut Tree Cl
  Bourne End SL8 . . . . .3 A1
  Twyford RG10 . . . . .61 C3
Walnut Tree Ct RG8 . . . . . .34 B3
Walnut Tree Ho TW20 . . . . .95 C2
Walnut Tree Rd TW17 . . . . .125 B4
Walnut Way Bourne End SL8 . .3 A1
  Reading RG30 . . . . .84 B4
Walpole Rd
  Old Windsor SL4 . . . . .95 A4
  Slough SL1 . . . . .41 B4
Walrus Cl RG5 . . . . .88 A4
Walsh Ave RG42 . . . . .91 C1
Walter Inf Sch RG41 . . . . . .116 A3
Walter Rd RG41 . . . . .115 C4
Walters Cl RG18 . . . . .106 B4
Waltham Cl
  Maidenhead SL6 . . . . .38 C1
  Sandhurst GU47 . . . . . . .143 B1
Waltham Rd
  Twyford RG10 . . . . .62 A3
  White Waltham SL6 . . . . . .38 C1
Waltham St Lawrence
  Cty Prim Sch RG10 . . . . . .62 C2
Walton Ave RG9 . . . . .35 C4
Walton Bridge Rd
  KT12, TW17 . . . . .125 C1
Walton Cl RG5 . . . . .87 B4
Walton Dr SL5 . . . . .119 C4
Walton Gdns TW13 . . . . . . .98 C1
Walton La Burnham SL2 . . . .21 C2
  Lower Halliford KT13,TW17 .125 B1
  Walton-on-T TW17 . . . . . .125 C1
Walton Way RG14 . . . . . . .105 B2
Wandhope Way RG31 . . . . .57 B1
Wansey Gdns RG14 . . . . . .105 B3
Wanstraw Gr RG12 . . . . . .118 C1
Wantage Cl RG12 . . . . . . .118 C1

Wantage Rd
  Great Shefford RG17 . . . . .48 B3
  Lambourn RG17 . . . . .25 B3
  Reading RG30 . . . . .85 B4
  Sandhurst GU47 . . . . . . .150 B4
  Streatley RG8 . . . . .33 C4
Wapshott Rd TW18 . . . . . .96 C2
War Memorial Pl RG9 . . . . .35 C4
Waram Cl RG17 . . . . .100 C4
Warbler Cl RG31 . . . . .84 A3
Warbler Dr RG6 . . . . .87 A1
Warborough Ave RG31 . . . .84 A4
Warborough Rd OX12 . . . . . .7 A4
Warbreck Dr RG31 . . . . . . .57 A2
Ward Cl Iver SL0 . . . . .44 C4
  Wokingham RG40 . . . . . . .116 B4
Ward Gdns SL1 . . . . .41 C3
Ward Royal SL4 . . . . .67 B3
Ward Royal Par 3 SL4 . . . .67 B3
Wardle Ave RG31 . . . . . . .57 B1
Wardle Ct GU19 . . . . .145 C2
Wards Pl TW20 . . . . .96 B1
Wards Stone Pk RG12 . . . .118 C1
Wareham Rd RG12 . . . . . .118 C2
Warehouse Rd RG19 . . . . .131 C3
Warfield CE Prim Sch
  RG42 . . . . .91 C1
Warfield Rd
  Bracknell RG12 & RG42 . . .91 B1
  East Bedfont TW14 . . . . . .98 C4
Warfield St RG42 . . . . .91 B2
Wargrave RG10 . . . . .36 B1
Wargrave Rd
  Remenham Hill RG9 . . . . . .15 C1
  Twyford RG10 . . . . .61 B3
Wargrave Sta RG10 . . . . . .36 B1
Wargrove Dr GU47 . . . . . . .150 B4
Waring Cl RG6 . . . . .114 B4
Warings The RG7 . . . . . . .109 A4
Warley Rise RG31 . . . . . . .57 B2
Warner Cl Harlington UB3 . .71 B4
  Slough SL1 . . . . .41 C3
Warners Hill SL6 . . . . .19 B4
Warnford Rd RG30 . . . . . . .84 C4
Warnsham Cl 1 RG6 . . . . . .87 A1
Warren Cl
  Burghfield Common RG7 . . .111 A4
  Sandhurst GU47 . . . . . . .150 A4
  Slough SL3 . . . . .43 C2
Warren Ct 7 SL2 . . . . .22 B4
Warren Down RG42 . . . . . .117 C4
Warren House Rd RG40 . . . .116 B4
Warren La RG40 . . . . .141 C3
Warren Rd Ashford TW15 . .98 C1
  Newbury RG14 . . . . .130 B3
  Woodley RG4,RG5 . . . . . . .60 B1
Warren Rise GU16 . . . . . . .151 C2
Warren Row SL5 . . . . .119 B4
Warren Row Rd RG10 . . . . .37 B3
Warren The RG4 . . . . .58 B2
Warrington Ave SL1 . . . . . .42 B4
Warrington Spur SL4 . . . . .95 A4
Warwick RG12 . . . . .118 C2
Warwick Ave Slough SL2 . . .22 B1
  Staines TW18 . . . . .97 B1
  Thorpe Lea TW20 . . . . . .123 B4
Warwick Cl Frimley GU15 . .152 A2
  Maidenhead SL6 . . . . .39 A2
Warwick Ct 34 SL4 . . . . . . .67 B3
Warwick Dr RG14 . . . . .105 A1
Warwick Ho RG2 . . . . .86 B2
Warwick Rd Ashford TW15 . .97 C2
  Reading RG2 . . . . .86 B2
Warwick Villas TW20 . . . . .123 B4
Wasdale Cl GU47 . . . . .143 C1
Wash Hill HP10 . . . . .3 C2
Wash Hill Lea HP10 . . . . . . .3 C2
Wash Water RG20 . . . . . . .130 A2
Washburn Ho RG14 . . . . . .130 C4
Washington St SL7 . . . . .2 A2
Washington Dr Slough SL1 . .41 B3
  Windsor SL4 . . . . .66 C2
Washington Gdns RG40 . . .142 A4
Washington Rd RG4 . . . . . .59 A1
Wasing La RG7 . . . . .134 B3
Watchetts Cty Jun Sch
  The GU15 . . . . .151 A1
Watchetts Dr GU15 . . . . . .151 B1
Watchetts Lake Cl GU15 . .151 B1
Watchetts Rd GU15 . . . . . .151 A2
Watchmoor Pk GU15 . . . . .151 A2
Watchmoor Rd GU15 . . . . .151 A2
Watchmoor Trade Ctr
  GU15 . . . . .151 A2
Water La RG19 . . . . .131 B4
Water Rd RG30 . . . . .85 A4
Water Splash La SL5 . . . . .120 C4
Water St RG18 . . . . .52 C3
Waterbeach Cl SL1 . . . . . . .42 B4
Waterbeach Rd SL1 . . . . . .42 B4
Waterfall Cl GU25 . . . . . . .122 A3
Waterford Way RG40 . . . . .116 B3
Waterham Rd RG12 . . . . . .118 C2
Waterhouse Mead
  GU47 . . . . .150 B4
Waterloo Cl
  Camberley GU15 . . . . . . .152 A4
  East Bedfont TW14 . . . . . .98 C4
  Moulsford OX10 . . . . .14 A4
Waterloo Cres RG40 . . . . . .116 C2
Waterloo Rd
  Crowthorne RG45 . . . . . . .143 A2
  Reading RG2 . . . . .86 A3
  Wokingham RG40 . . . . . . .116 C2
Waterloo Rise RG2 . . . . . . .86 A2
Waterman Ct 5 SL1 . . . . . .41 C3
Waterman Pl RG1 . . . . .59 A1

Watermans Bsns Pk The
  TW18 . . . . .96 C2
Watermans Rd RG9 . . . . . .35 C4
Watermans Way RG10 . . . .36 B1
Watermead TW14 . . . . .98 C4
Watermeadows The
  RG14 . . . . .105 A2
Watermill Ct RG7 . . . . . . .108 B3
Waters Dr TW18 . . . . .96 C2
Watersfield Cl 4 RG6 . . . . .87 A1
Waterside HP10 . . . . .3 C4
Waterside Ct RG14 . . . . . . .105 B2
Waterside Dr
  Purley on T RG8 . . . . .57 B3
  Slough SL3 . . . . .44 A2
  Theale RG7 . . . . .83 C2
Waterside Gdns 9 RG1 . . . .86 A4
Watersplash La RG42 . . . . .91 A1
Watersplash Rd TW17 . . . .125 A3
Watery La Kintbury RG20 . .128 C3
  Wooburn Green HP10 . . . . . .3 C4
Watkins Cl RG40 . . . . .141 C4
Watlington St RG1 . . . . . . .86 B4
Watmore La RG41 . . . . . . .88 B1
Watson Cl RG40 . . . . .115 C1
Watts La OX11 . . . . .12 A4
Wavell Cl RG2 . . . . .86 C1
Wavell Gdns SL2 . . . . .21 C1
Wavell Rd SL6 . . . . .39 A3
Wavendene Ave TW20 . . . .96 B1
Waverley RG12 . . . . .117 C2
Waverley Cl GU15 . . . . . . .151 C2
Waverley Ct 18 RG3 . . . . . .85 B3
Waverley Dr
  Camberley GU15 . . . . . . .151 C2
  Virginia Water GU25 . . . . .122 A3
Waverley Rd
  Bagshot GU19 . . . . .145 C2
  Reading RG30 . . . . .85 B4
  Slough SL1 . . . . .42 B4
Waverley Sch RG40 . . . . . .115 C1
Waverley Way RG40 . . . . . .115 C1
Waverleys The RG18 . . . . .106 B2
Waybrook Cres RG1 . . . . . .86 C3
Wayland Cl RG12 . . . . .118 C3
Waylands TW19 . . . . .68 C1
Waylands Cl RG7 . . . . .82 B2
Waylen St RG1 . . . . .85 C4
Ways End GU15 . . . . .151 C2
Wayside Mews SL6 . . . . . . .39 C4
WC Lee's Resthouses
  GU20 . . . . .146 B2
Weald Rise RG30 . . . . .57 C1
Wealden Way RG30 . . . . . .84 C4
Weardale Cl RG2 . . . . .86 B2
Weaver Moss GU47 . . . . . .150 A4
Weavers Ct 37 RG1 . . . . . . .86 B4
Weavers La RG17 . . . . . . .127 B3
Weavers Way RG10 . . . . . .61 B2
Weavers Wlk 20 RG14 . . . .105 A2
Webb Cl Bagshot GU19 . . . .145 C1
  Binfield RG42 . . . . .90 C1
  Slough SL3 . . . . .43 B1
Webb Ct RG40 . . . . .116 C4
Webb's Cl RG1 . . . . .85 C3
Webbs Acre RG19 . . . . . . .106 C1
Webbs La RG7 . . . . .109 A4
Webster Cl SL6 . . . . .19 A1
Wedderburn Cl RG41 . . . . .88 B1
Wedgewood Way RG30 . . . .57 C1
Weekes Dr SL1 . . . . .42 A2
Weighbridge Row SL8 . . . . . .1 C1
Weir Cl RG31 . . . . .84 C2
Weir Pl TW18 . . . . .123 C4
Weir Rd KT16 . . . . .124 A1
Weirside Ct 18 RG1 . . . . . .86 B4
Welbeck RG12 . . . . .117 C2
Welbeck Rd SL6 . . . . .39 B3
Welby Cl SL6 . . . . .39 A2
Welby Cres RG41 . . . . .88 A1
Weldale St RG1 . . . . .85 C4
Welden SL2 . . . . .43 B4
Welford Pk RG20 . . . . .75 C4
Welford Rd RG5 . . . . .88 A4
Welford & Wickham
  CE Prim Sch RG20 . . . . . . .75 B2
Well Cl GU15 . . . . .151 C2
Well House La RG27 . . . . . .140 A2
Well Mdw RG1 . . . . .105 A3
  Reading RG31 . . . . .57 B1
Wellbank SL6 . . . . .20 C1
Wellburn Cl GU47 . . . . . . .150 A4
Wellcroft Rd SL1 . . . . .42 A3
Weller Dr Barkham RG40 . . .141 A3
  Camberley GU15 . . . . . . .151 B2
Wellers La RG42 . . . . .91 B4
Wellesley Ave SL0 . . . . . . .44 C2
Wellesley Cl GU19 . . . . . . .145 B2
Wellesley Ct SL0 . . . . .44 C2
Wellesley Dr RG45 . . . . . . .142 C3
Wellesley Path SL1 . . . . . .43 A2
Wellesley Rd SL1 . . . . .43 A2
Welley Ave TW19 . . . . .68 C2
Welley Rd TW19 . . . . .68 C1
Wellfield Cl RG31 . . . . .84 B4
Wellhill Rd OX12 . . . . .27 B3
Wellhouse La RG18 . . . . . . .79 C3
Wellhouse Rd SL6 . . . . .19 C1
Wellington Ave
  Reading RG2 . . . . .86 B2
  Virginia Water GU25 . . . . .122 A4
Wellington Bsns Pk
  RG45 . . . . .142 C2
Wellington Cl
  Newbury RG14 . . . . .105 A1
  Sandhurst GU47 . . . . . . .150 B4
  Walton-on-T KT12 . . . . . .125 C1

Wellington Coll RG45 . . . . .143 A2
Wellington Cotts
  Ball Hill RG20 . . . . .129 A3
  Knowl Hill RG10 . . . . .37 B4
Wellington Cres RG26 . . . .134 B4
Wellington Ct
  Ashford TW15 . . . . .97 C2
  Shinfield RG7 . . . . .113 A4
  Stanwell TW19 . . . . .97 C4
Wellington Ctry Pk RG7 . . .139 C1
Wellington Dr RG12 . . . . . .118 C2
Wellington Gdns RG7 . . . . .82 A3
Wellington Rd
  Ashford TW15 . . . . .97 C2
  Crowthorne RG45 . . . . . . .143 A2
  Hatton TW6 . . . . .71 C1
  Maidenhead SL6 . . . . .39 B4
  Sandhurst GU47 . . . . . . .150 B4
  Wokingham RG40 . . . . . . .116 A3
Wellington St SL1 . . . . .43 A2
Wellington Terr GU47 . . . . .150 B4
Wellingtonia Ave
  RG45,RG40 . . . . .142 B2
Wells Cl SL4 . . . . .67 A4
Wells La SL5 . . . . .120 A3
Welsh La RG7, RG7 . . . . . .139 A1
Welshmans Rd RG7 . . . . . .136 A3
Welwick Cl RG6 . . . . .87 C1
Welwyn Ave TW14 . . . . . . .71 C1
Wendan Rd RG14 . . . . .130 C4
Wendover Ct TW18 . . . . . . .96 B2
Wendover Dr GU16 . . . . . .152 B2
Wendover Pl TW18 . . . . . . .96 B2
Wendover Rd
  Bourne End SL8 . . . . .3 A3
  Burnham SL1 . . . . .41 A4
  Egham TW18, TW20 . . . . .96 B2
Wendover Way RG30 . . . . .84 B4
Wenlock Edge RG10 . . . . . .61 C2
Wenlock Way RG19 . . . . . .106 B1
Wensley Cl RG10 . . . . .61 B3
Wensley Rd RG1 . . . . .85 C3
Wensleydale Dr GU15 . . . . .152 B3
Wentworth Ave
  North Ascot SL5 . . . . .119 A4
  Reading RG2 . . . . .113 A4
  Slough SL2 . . . . .22 A1
Wentworth Cl
  Ashford TW15 . . . . .98 A2
  Crowthorne RG45 . . . . . . .142 C3
  Yateley GU46 . . . . .149 B3
Wentworth Club GU25 . . . .122 A4
Wentworth Cres SL6 . . . . . .39 C3
Wentworth Ct RG14 . . . . . .105 A1
Wentworth Dr GU25 . . . . . .121 C3
Wentworth Way SL5 . . . . . .119 B4
Wescott Inf Sch RG40 . . . .116 B3
Wescott Rd RG40 . . . . .116 B3
Wesley Dr TW20 . . . . .96 A1
Wesley Pl SL4 . . . . .93 A3
Wessex Cl RG17 . . . . .100 B3
Wessex Ct 4 TW19 . . . . . . .70 C1
Wessex Gdns RG1 . . . . . . .61 C2
Wessex Inf Sch SL6 . . . . . .39 A2
Wessex Jun Sch SL6 . . . . . .39 A2
Wessex Rd Bourne End SL8 . .3 A2
  Harmondsworth TW19, TW6 .70 C2
Wessex Road Ind Est
  SL8 . . . . .3 A2
Wessex Way SL6 . . . . .39 A2
Wessons Hill SL6 . . . . .19 B4
West Cl Ashford TW15 . . . . .97 C2
  Medmenham SL7 . . . . .17 B4
West Cres SL4 . . . . .66 C3
West Ct RG4 . . . . .60 C1
West Dean SL6 . . . . .39 C4
West Dr Reading RG31 . . . .84 C3
  Sonning RG4 . . . . .60 B1
  Wentworth GU25 . . . . . . .121 C1
West End Ct SL2 . . . . .22 C2
West End La
  Harlington UB3 . . . . .71 B4
  Newell Green RG42 . . . . . .91 A3
  Stoke Poges SL2 . . . . .22 C2
West End Rd RG7 . . . . . . .136 C3
West Fryerne GU46 . . . . . .149 B4
West Gn GU46 . . . . .149 A4
West Green Ct RG1 . . . . . . .85 C3
West Hill RG1 . . . . .86 A3
West Ilsley Ho RG20 . . . . . .10 A1
West La RG9 . . . . .15 B1
West Mead SL6 . . . . .19 C1
West Mead Sch RG40 . . . . .116 C3
West Mills RG14 . . . . .104 C2
West Mills Yd RG14 . . . . . .104 C2
West Point SL1 . . . . .41 B3
West Ramp TW6 . . . . .71 A3
West Rd Bracknell RG40 . . .117 B1
  Camberley GU15 . . . . . . .151 B3
  East Bedfont TW14 . . . . . .98 B4
  Maidenhead SL6 . . . . .39 C4
West Ridge SL8 . . . . .3 A2
West Sq SL0 . . . . .44 C4
West St Henley-on-T RG9 . . .15 B1
  Maidenhead SL6 . . . . .39 C4
  Marlow SL7 . . . . .1 B1
  Newbury RG14 . . . . .104 C2
  Reading RG1 . . . . .86 A4
West Surrey Est TW15 . . . .125 B4
West View
  East Bedfont TW14 . . . . . .98 B4
  Peasemore RG20 . . . . .50 B4
West View Cotts RG18 . . . .52 C3
West Way TW17 . . . . .97 C4
Westacott Bsns Ctr SL6 . . .38 C2
Westacott Way SL6 . . . . . .38 B2
Westborough Ct SL6 . . . . . .39 B3
Westborough Rd SL6 . . . . . .39 B3

Westbourne Rd
Feltham TW13 ....98 C3
Sandhurst GU47 ....150 C4
Staines TW18 ....97 A1
Westbourne Terr
3 Reading RG14 ....105 A2
Westbrook
Reading RG30 ....85 B4
Westbrook Cl RG17 ....40 C1
Westbrook Cl RG17 ....100 B3
Westbrook Gdns RG22 ....118 B4
Westbrook Gn OX11 ....11 C4
Westbrook Rd
Reading RG30 ....58 B1
Staines TW18 ....96 C2
Westbrook St OX11 ....11 C4
Westbury Cl
Crowthorne RG45 ....143 A3
Shepperton TW17 ....125 A3
Westbury La RG8 ....57 A3
Westcombe Ct RG12 ....118 C1
Westcote Rd RG30 ....85 B3
Westcotts Gn RG42 ....91 B1
Westcroft SL2 ....22 A1
Westdene Cres RG4 ....58 C2
Westende RG40 ....116 B3
Westende Jun Sch RG40 ....116 C4
Westdale RG19 ....106 B2
Westerdale Dr GU16 ....152 A2
Westerham Wlk **33** RG1 ....86 A3
Western Ave
Chertsey KT16 ....124 A3
Henley-on-T RG9 ....35 C4
Newbury RG14 ....104 C2
Thorpe TW20 ....123 A3
Woodley RG5 ....60 C1
Western Cl KT16 ....124 A3
Western Ctr The RG12 ....117 C4
Western Dr
Shepperton TW17 ....125 B2
Wooburn Green HP10 ....3 C3
Western Elms Ave RG30 ....85 C4
Western End RG14 ....104 C1
Western House Inf Sch
SL1 ....41 C3
Western Ind Area RG12 ....117 C4
Western Oaks RG31 ....57 C1
Western Perimeter Rd
TW19, TW6, UB7 ....70 A3
Western Perimeter Rd
Rdbt TW19 ....70 A3
Western Rd
Bracknell RG12 ....117 C4
Henley-on-T RG9 ....35 C4
Reading RG1 ....85 C3
Westfield Bglws SL7 ....16 C3
Westfield Cotts SL7 ....16 C3
Westfield Cres
Shiplake RG9 ....36 A2
Thatcham RG18 ....106 A3
Westfield Inf Sch SL8 ....3 A2
Westfield Rd
Camberley GU15 ....151 A1
Caversham RG4 ....59 A1
Cholsey OX10 ....13 B3
Maidenhead SL6 ....39 A4
Slough SL2 ....22 A1
Thatcham RG18 ....106 A3
Winnersh RG41 ....88 A1
Westfield Way RG14 ....104 C1
Westfields RG20 ....31 B2
Westfields Inf Sch GU46 ....149 A3
Westgate Cres SL1 ....41 C3
Westgate Ct RG14 ....104 C1
Westgate Cty Sec Sch
SL1 ....42 A3
Westgate Rd RG14 ....104 C1
Westhatch Cnr RG42 ....91 B3
Westhatch La RG42 ....91 B3
Westhead Dr RG14 ....131 A4
Westhorpe Rd SL7 ....1 C2
Westland RG18 ....106 A3
Westland Cl TW19 ....70 C1
Westlands Ave Earley RG2 ....86 C1
Slough SL1 ....41 B4
Westlands Cl SL1 ....41 B4
Westlands Rd RG14 ....131 A4
Westley Mill Binfield RG42 ....90 C4
Westlyn Rd RG26 ....135 C1
Westmacott Dr TW14 ....98 C4
Westmead SL4 ....67 A2
Westmead Dr RG14 ....130 C4
Westminster Way RG6 ....87 B1
Westmorland Rd RG41 ....115 B3
Westmorland Dr
Bracknell RG42 ....91 C1
Frimley GU15 ....152 A2
Westmorland Rd SL6 ....39 B3
Weston Gr GU19 ....145 C1
Weston Rd SL1 ....41 C4
Westonbirt Dr RG4 ....58 C2
Westons RG20 ....51 B4
Westridge Ave RG8 ....57 B3
Westview Dr RG10 ....61 C3
Westward Rd RG41 ....115 C4
Westwates Cl RG12 ....118 B4
Westway RG8 ....34 B4
Westwood Farm Jun
& Inf Schs RG31 ....57 B2
Westwood Glen RG31 ....57 B1
Westwood Gn SL6 ....19 C3
Westwood Rd Marlow SL7 ....1 B1
Newbury RG14 ....105 B1
Windlesham GU20 ....146 B2
Westwood Row RG31 ....57 B1
Wetherby Cl RG4 ....59 B3
Wetherby Ho GU15 ....151 B4

Wethered Dr SL1 ....41 A4
Wethered Pk SL7 ....1 B1
Wethered Rd SL7 ....1 B1
Wetton Pl TW20 ....95 C2
Wexford Ct SL6 ....40 A4
Wexham Court Comb Sch
SL2 ....43 B4
Wexham Cty Sec Sch SL2 ....43 B4
Wexham Park Hospl SL3 ....23 B1
Wexham Park La SL3 ....23 B1
Wexham Pl SL3 ....23 B3
Wexham Rd SL1, SL2 ....43 A3
Wexham St SL3 ....23 A2
Wexham Woods SL3 ....43 B3
Wey Ave KT16 ....124 A3
Wey Cl GU15 ....151 A3
Weybridge Mead GU46 ....149 C4
Weycrofts RG42 ....90 C1
Weymead Cl KT16 ....124 B1
Whaley Rd RG40 ....116 B4
Wharf La Bourne End SL8 ....3 A2
Henley-on-T RG9 ....15 C1
Wharf Rd Newbury RG14 ....105 A2
Wraysbury TW19 ....95 B4
Wharf St RG14 ....105 A2
Wharf The Newbury RG14 ....105 A2
Taplow SL6 ....40 B4
Wharfedale Rd RG41 ....88 A2
Wharfside RG7 ....109 B2
Whatley Gn RG12 ....118 A3
Whatmore Cl TW19 ....70 A1
Wheatash Rd KT15 ....124 A3
Wheatbutts The SL4 ....41 C1
Wheatfields Cl SL6 ....39 A2
Wheatfields Rd RG2 ....113 C3
Wheatlands SL1 ....84 C2
Wheatlands La RG14 ....130 A3
Wheatlands Rd SL3 ....43 B2
Wheatley RG12 ....117 C2
Wheatley Cl RG2 ....86 C1
Wheatsheaf La
Newbury RG14 ....105 A2
Staines TW18 ....96 C1
Wheatsheaf Par SL4 ....68 A1
Wheble Dr RG5 ....87 B4
Wheeler Cl
Burghfield Common RG7 ....111 A2
Wokingham RG41 ....115 C3
Wheeler Ct RG31 ....57 C1
Wheelers Green Way
RG19 ....106 C3
Wheelton Cl RG6 ....87 C2
Wheelwrights Pl SL3 ....69 B4
Whins Cl GU15 ....151 A2
Whins Dr GU15 ....151 A2
Whinshill Ct SL5 ....121 A1
Whistler Gr GU47 ....150 B3
Whistlers La RG7 ....136 A1
Whistley Cl RG12 ....118 C3
Whitakers Cl RG18 ....106 A2
Whitamore Row RG9 ....35 C4
Whitby Ct RG4 ....59 B3
Whitby Dr **7** RG1 ....86 B3
Whitby Gn RG4 ....59 B3
Whitby Rd SL1 ....42 B3
Whitchurch Cl SL6 ....19 C2
Whitchurch Prim Sch
RG8 ....56 C4
Whitchurch Rd RG8 ....56 B3
White Bridge Cl TW14 ....71 C4
White City RG45 ....143 B3
White Cl Hermitage RG18 ....78 C3
Slough SL1 ....42 B3
White Gates RG20 ....75 B3
White Hart Ind Est GU17 ....150 C2
White Hart Rd
2 Maidenhead SL6 ....39 C4
Slough SL1 ....42 B2
White Hart Row **3** KT16 ....124 A1
White Hill
Remenham Hill RG9 ....16 A1
Shiplake RG9 ....35 A3
Windlesham GU20 ....146 A3
Wooburn Moor HP9 ....3 C4
White Horse La RG40 ....141 B3
White Horse Rd SL4 ....66 B3
White House Gdns GU46 ....149 B4
White House Prep Sch
RG41 ....116 A2
White House Rd OX10 ....14 C4
White Lilies Island SL4 ....67 A4
White Lion Way GU46 ....149 B4
White Lodge Cl
Marlow Bottom SL7 ....1 B3
Purley on T RG31 ....57 A2
White Paddock SL6 ....39 A1
White Rd Chilton OX11 ....10 B1
Sandhurst GU15 ....150 C3
White Rock SL6 ....20 A1
White Shoot OX11 ....12 A3
White Waltham
CE Prim Sch SL6 ....63 B4
Whiteacres Dr SL6 ....40 A1
Whitebeam Cl RG41 ....115 B2
Whiteford Rd SL2 ....42 C4
Whitegates La RG6 ....87 C4
Whitegrove Prim Sch
RG42 ....91 C1
Whitehall SL6 ....20 A1
Whitehall Rd SL6 ....42 C4
Whitehall Farm La GU25 ....122 C3
Whitehall La Egham TW20 ....95 C1
Horton TW19 ....69 A1
Whitehaven SL1 ....42 C4
Whitehill Cl GU15 ....151 B4
Whitehill Pl GU25 ....122 C4
Whitehills Cl SL7 ....1 B1
Whitehills Gn RG8 ....34 B3

Whitehouse Way SL3 ....43 B2
Whiteknights Prim Sch
RG2 ....86 C1
Whiteknights Rd RG6 ....86 C3
Whitelands Dr SL5 ....119 B4
Whitelands Park Prim Sch
RG18 ....106 B3
Whitelands Rd RG18 ....106 B2
Whiteley SL4 ....66 C4
Whitelocke Inf Sch
RG40 ....116 B4
Whitelocks Piece RG17 ....73 A1
Whitemoor La
Lower Basildon RG8 ....34 B1
Upper Basildon RG8 ....54 C3
Whitepit La HP10 ....3 B4
Whites Hill RG7 ....110 B3
Whites La Beenham RG7 ....109 A4
Datchet SL3 ....68 A4
Whitestone Cl RG6 ....87 C4
Whiteways Ct TW18 ....97 A1
Whitewell Cl RG2 ....114 C1
Whitley Cl TW19 ....70 C1
Whitley Park Inf Sch RG2 ....86 A1
Whitley Park Jun Sch
RG2 ....86 A1
Whitley Park La RG2 ....86 B2
Whitley Rd GU46 ....149 B2
Whitley St RG2 ....86 A3
Whitley Wood La RG2 ....113 B4
Whitley Wood Rd RG2 ....113 B4
Whitmoor Rd GU19 ....145 C1
Whitmore Cl GU47 ....143 B1
Whitmore La SL5 ....121 A3
Whitstone Gdns RG2 ....86 B1
Whittaker Rd SL2 ....21 C1
Whittenham Cl SL2 ....43 A3
Whittle Cl
Sandhurst GU47 ....143 A1
Wokingham RG40 ....141 C4
Whittle Parkway SL1 ....41 B4
Whitton Cl **6** RG12 ....87 B1
Whitton Rd RG12 ....118 C3
Whitworth Rd RG2 ....141 A4
Whurley Way SL6 ....19 C1
Whynstones Rd SL5 ....120 A2
Whyteladyes La SL6 ....19 C3
Wick Hill La RG40 ....142 A3
Wick La TW20 ....94 C2
Wick Rd TW20 ....95 A1
Wickets The
Ashford TW15 ....97 C2
Maidenhead SL6 ....39 B4
Wickford Way RG6 ....113 C4
Wickham La TW20 ....96 A1
Wickham Rd
Camberley GU15 ....151 C4
Earley RG6 ....87 C1
Wickham Vale RG12 ....117 C2
Wickhurst Cotts SL6 ....38 A3
Wicks Gn RG42 ....90 A2
Widbrook Rd SL6 ....20 A2
Widecroft Rd SL0 ....44 C4
Widmere La SL7 ....1 A3
Wield Ct RG2 ....86 C1
Wiggett Gr RG42 ....90 B1
Wigmore La Reading RG30 ....58 A1
Reading RG30 ....58 B1
Theale RG7 ....83 B1
Wigmore Rd RG26 ....134 C1
Wilberforce Mews SL6 ....39 C4
Wilberforce Way RG12 ....118 B2
Wilcox Gdns SW17 ....124 C3
Wild Briar RG40 ....141 C4
Wild Cl RG6 ....114 B4
Wildcroft Dr RG40 ....116 A1
Wilde Theatre RG12 ....118 B1
Wilder Ave RG8 ....56 C3
Wilderness Ct RG6 ....87 A2
Wilderness Rd Earley RG6 ....87 A2
Frimley GU16 ....151 C1
Wilders Cl Bracknell RG42 ....91 A1
Frimley GU16 ....151 C2
Wildgreen N SL3 ....44 A1
Wildgreen S SL3 ....44 A1
Wildridings Cty Prim Sch
RG12 ....118 A3
Wildridings Rd RG12 ....118 A3
Wildridings Sq RG12 ....118 A3
Wildwood Dr RG26 ....134 B1
Wildwood Gdns GU46 ....149 B2
Wilford Rd SL3 ....43 C1
Wilfred Way SL3 ....43 C1
Wilfrids Wood Cl HP10 ....3 A3
Willats Cl KT16 ....124 A2
William Byrd Sch UB3 ....71 B4
William Cl RG2 ....106 B1
William Ellis Cl SL4 ....68 A1
William Gray Cty Inf Sch
The RG5 ....87 B4
William Gray Cty Jun Sch
The RG5 ....87 B3
William Penn Comb Sch
SL2 ....22 B1
William Sim Wood RG42 ....92 A1
William St Reading RG1 ....85 C4
Slough SL1 ....42 C3
Windsor SL4 ....67 B3
Williant Cl SL6 ....38 C1
Willington Cl GU15 ....151 A1
Willink Sch The RG7 ....110 C1
Willis Rd RG18 ....79 A2
Willoners SL2 ....42 A4
Willoughby Rd
Bracknell RG12 ....117 C3
Slough SL3 ....44 A2
Willow Bank SL7 ....1 B3

Willow Bank Jun & Inf Schs
RG5 ....60 C1
Willow Cl
Burghfield Common RG30 ....111 A3
Colnbrook SL3 ....69 B4
Flackwell Heath RG10 ....3 B1
Newbury RG14 ....104 C1
Willow Cotts SL6 ....13 C3
Willow Court La OX10 ....13 C3
Willow Ct **2** Charlton TW16 ....98 C1
Frimley GU16 ....151 B1
Wokingham RG41 ....115 C3
Willow Dr Bracknell RG12 ....118 B4
Maidenhead SL6 ....40 A1
Twyford RG10 ....61 B3
Willow Gdns
Purley on T RG31 ....57 A1
Reading RG2 ....86 C1
Willow Gn GU24 ....153 C3
Willow Gr SL4 ....67 A2
Willow La
Blackwater GU17 ....150 B2
Wargrave RG10 ....36 C3
Willow Lo **10** TW16 ....98 C1
Willow Par SL3 ....44 A2
Willow Pk SL2 ....23 A3
Willow Pl SL4 ....67 B4
Willow Rd Newtown RG20 ....131 C1
Poyle SL3 ....69 C3
Willow St **3** RG1 ....86 A3
Willow Tree Glade RG31 ....84 B2
Willow Way GU47 ....142 C1
Willow Wlk
Chertsey KT16 ....124 A1
Englefield Green TW20 ....95 B2
Willow Wood Cl SL1 ....21 A2
Willowbrook SL4 ....42 B1
Willowbrook Rd TW19 ....97 C3
Willowdale RG40 ....141 C4
Willowford GU46 ....149 B3
Willowherb Cl RG40 ....116 C4
Willowmead TW18 ....124 A4
Willowmead Cl **10**
Marlow SL7 ....1 C2
Newbury RG14 ....130 B3
Willowmead Gdns SL7 ....1 C2
Willowmead Rd **8** SL7 ....1 C1
Willowmead Sq **9** SL7 ....1 C2
Willows Ct RG8 ....56 B3
Willows End GU47 ....150 A4
Willows Rd SL8 ....3 A2
Willows The
14 Bourne End SL8 ....3 A2
9 Bracknell RG12 ....118 C3
Caversham RG4 ....59 A1
Lightwater GU18 ....146 B1
Windsor SL4 ....66 B4
Willowside RG5 ....60 C1
Willson Rd TW20 ....95 A2
Wilmington Cl RG5 ....87 C4
Wilmot Cl RG42 ....90 C1
Wilmot Rd SL1 ....21 C1
Wilmot Way GU15 ....151 C2
Wilmot Wlk RG14 ....130 B3
Wilsford Cl RG6 ....113 C4
Wilson Ave RG9 ....35 C4
Wilson Cl RG20 ....31 C2
Wilson Ct RG41 ....88 B1
Wilson Prim Sch RG30 ....85 B4
Wilson Rd RG30 ....85 B4
Wilson Valkenburg Ct
RG14 ....104 C2
Wilstrode Ave RG42 ....90 C1
Wilton Cl UB7 ....70 A4
Wilton Cres SL4 ....66 B2
Wilton Rd
Camberley GU15 ....151 A2
Reading RG30 ....85 B4
Wiltshire Ave
Crowthorne RG45 ....143 A3
Slough SL2 ....22 B1
Wiltshire Cl RG17 ....100 B3
Wiltshire Dr RG40 ....116 B1
Wiltshire Gr RG42 ....91 C1
Wiltshire Lodge **2** SL6 ....39 C3
Wiltshire Rd Marlow SL7 ....2 B1
Wokingham RG40 ....116 B4
Wiltshire Wlk RG31 ....84 B3
Wilwood Rd RG42 ....117 C4
Wilwyne Cl RG4 ....59 B2
Wimbledon Cl GU15 ....144 C1
Wimbledon Rd GU15 ....144 C1
Wimblington Dr RG6 ....114 B4
Wimbourne Gdns RG30 ....58 A1
Wimbushes RG40 ....141 B4
Winbury Ct SL6 ....39 C4
Winbury Sch SL6 ....40 A2
Wincanton Rd RG2 ....113 B4
Winch Cl RG42 ....90 B2
Winchbottom La SL7, HP10 ....2 A4
Winchcombe Cty
Jun & Inf Schs RG14 ....105 A2
Winchcombe Rd
Newbury RG14 ....105 A1
Twyford RG10 ....61 C2
Winchester Cl SL3 ....69 C3
Winchester Dr SL6 ....39 C4
Winchester Ho **12** RG14 ....105 A1
Winchester Rd
Harlington UB3 ....71 C4
Reading RG2 ....86 C4
Winchester Way GU17 ....150 B3
Winchgrove Rd RG42 ....91 A1
Winchstone Cl TW17 ....124 C3
Wincroft Rd RG4 ....58 C2
Windermere Cl
East Bedfont TW14 ....98 C4
Stanwell TW19 ....97 B3

Windermere Cl *continued*
Thorpe Lea TW20 ....96 A1
Winnersh RG41 ....88 B2
Windermere Rd
Lightwater GU18 ....146 A1
Reading RG2 ....86 B2
Windermere Way
Slough SL1 ....41 B4
Thatcham RG19 ....106 A2
Windermere Wlk GU15 ....152 B3
Winding Wood Dr GU15 ....152 A2
Windle Cl GU20 ....146 B2
Windlebrook Gn **3** RG42 ....118 A4
Windlemere Golf Ctr
GU24 ....153 C4
Windlesham Ct GU20 ....146 B3
Windlesham Rd
Bracknell RG42 ....117 C4
West End GU24 ....153 C4
Windlesham Village
Cty Inf Sch GU20 ....146 A3
Windmill Ave RG41 ....115 C4
Windmill Bsns Village
TW16 ....125 C4
Windmill Cl Charlton TW16 ....98 C1
Windsor SL4 ....67 A3
Wokingham RG41 ....115 C4
Windmill Cnr RG7 ....137 A3
Windmill Ct RG7 ....137 A3
Windmill Field GU20 ....146 B2
Windmill La RG7 ....108 A3
Windmill Lodge TW16 ....125 C4
Windmill Rd
Bracknell RG42 ....118 A4
Charlton TW16 ....125 C4
Cookham SL6 ....19 C3
Fulmer SL3 ....23 B4
Mortimer RG7 ....137 A3
Slough SL1 ....42 B3
Windmill Rd W TW16 ....125 C4
Windmill Terr TW17 ....125 C1
Windmill Trad Est TW16 ....125 C4
Windrush Ave SL3 ....44 A2
Windrush Ct RG30 ....85 A4
Windrush Ho SL8 ....3 A2
Windrush Hts GU47 ....150 A4
Windrush Way
Maidenhead SL6 ....39 C4
Reading RG30 ....85 A4
Windsor Boys Sch SL4 ....67 A3
Windsor Bsns Ctr The
SL4 ....67 B4
Windsor Castle SL4 ....67 C4
Windsor Cl SL1 ....21 B1
Windsor Ct **16** RG1 ....85 C4
Windsor Dr TW15 ....97 B2
Windsor & Eton
Central Sta SL4 ....67 B3
Windsor & Eton
Riverside Sta SL4 ....67 B4
Windsor Forest Ct SL5 ....119 B4
Windsor Girls Sch SL4 ....67 A4
Windsor Great Pk SL4 ....94 B2
Windsor Hill HP10 ....3 C3
Windsor Ho RG9 ....35 C4
Windsor L Ctr SL4 ....67 A4
Windsor La SL1 ....21 B1
Windsor Park Rd UB3 ....71 C4
Windsor Pl KT16 ....124 A1
Windsor Rd Datchet SL3 ....68 A4
Englefield Green
TW19, TW20 ....95 C3
Fulmer SL3 ....23 A4
Holyport SL6 ....40 B1
North Ascot SL5 ....120 A4
Slough SL1 ....42 C2
Wraysbury TW19 ....68 C2
Windsor Ride
Bracknell SL5 ....119 B2
Sandhurst GU15 ....151 A4
Wokingham RG40 ....142 A4
Windsor Rise RG14 ....131 B4
Windsor Sq **24** RG1 ....86 A3
Windsor St KT16 ....124 A2
Windsor Way RG31 ....84 B2
Windsor Youth Hostel
SL4 ....67 A4
Wing Cl SL7 ....1 B1
Wingate Rd RG5 ....87 C3
Wingfield Gdns GU16 ....152 B3
Wingrove Rd RG30 ....85 B3
Winkfield Cl RG41 ....116 A2
Winkfield La
Oakley Green SL4 ....66 A1
Winkfield SL4 ....92 B4
Winkfield Rd Ascot SL5 ....120 A4
Windsor SL4 ....66 C1
Winkfield Row RG42 ....92 A2
Winkfield St SL4 ....92 B3
Winkworth Rd RG41 ....135 B1
Winnersh Gate RG41 ....88 B1
Winnersh RG41 ....88 B1
Winnersh Prim Sch RG41 ....88 B2
Winnersh Sta RG41 ....88 B1
Winnersh Triangle Ind Est
RG41 ....88 B2
Winnersh Triangle Sta
RG41 ....88 B1
Winscombe RG12 ....117 C2
Winser Dr RG30 ....85 B3
Winston Cl RG7 ....113 B1
Winston Way
Purley on T RG8 ....57 A3
Thatcham RG19 ....105 C2
Winter Hill SL6 ....2 B1

Winter Hill Rd SL6 . . . . . . .19 A2
Winterberry Way RG4 . . . .58 C3
Winterbourne Ct RG12 . . .118 B4
Winterbourne Rd RG20 . .76 C2
Winterton Dr RG14 . . . . .104 B3
Winton Cres GU46 . . . . . .149 B3
Winton Rd RG2 . . . . .113 B4
Wintoun Path SL2 . . . . .21 C1
Wintringham Way RG8 . . .57 B3
Winvale SL1 . . . . .42 C2
Winwood Slough SL2 . . . . .43 B4
  Windsor SL4 . . . . .66 C3
Wisdom Ct 14 RG30 . . . . . .85 B3
Wises Firs RG7 . . . . .110 B2
Wishmoor Cl GU15 . . . . . .151 C4
Wishmoor Rd GU15 . . . . . .151 C4
Wispington Cl RG6 . . . . . . .87 B1
Wistaria La GU46 . . . . . . .149 B3
Wisteria Cl RG41 . . . . . . .115 C3
Wiston Terr RG1 . . . . .86 A4
Witcham Cl RG6 . . . . .114 B4
Withey Cl SL4 . . . . .66 C3
Witheygate Ave TW18 . . . .97 A1
Withy Cl Lightwater GU18 . .146 B1
  Reading RG31 . . . . .84 B3
Withybed La RG17 . . . . . . .101 C2
Withybed Way RG18 . . . . .106 C3
Withycroft SL3 . . . . .43 C4
Withys The RG18 . . . . .53 C1
Wittenham Ave RG31 . . . .84 A4
Wittenham Rd RG12 . . . . .118 C4
Wittington Cotts SL2 . . . . .17 B3
Woburn Cl Caversham RG4 .58 C2
  Frimley GU16 . . . . .152 A1
Wokefield Row RG7 . . . . .137 B4
Wokingham Hospl
  RG41 . . . . .116 A3
Wokingham Rd
  Bracknell RG42 . . . . . . .117 C4
  Earley RG6 . . . . .87 B2
  Hurst RG10 . . . . .88 C4
  Sandhurst RG45,GU47 . . . .142 C1
Wokingham Sta RG40 . . . .116 A3
Wokingham Theatre
  RG40 . . . . .116 A4
Wolf La SL4 . . . . .66 C2
Wolseley St RG1 . . . . .86 A3
Wolsey Rd Ashford TW15 . . .97 C2
  Ashford, Felthamhill TW16 . .98 C1
  Caversham RG4 . . . . .59 A1
Wolsingham Way RG19 . .106 B1
Wondesford Dale RG42 . . .90 B2
Wooburn Grange HP10 . . . .3 B2
Wooburn Manor Pk HP10 . . .3 C3
Wooburn Mews HP10 . . . . .3 C3
Wood Cl SL4 . . . . .67 B2
Wood End RG45 . . . . .142 C2
Wood Gn RG2 . . . . .113 B4
Wood Green Cl RG30 . . . . .85 C4
Wood La Arborfield RG41 . .114 C2
  Beech Hill RG7 . . . . .138 C3
  Binfield RG42 . . . . .90 B1
  Iver SL0 . . . . .44 B4
  Slough SL1 . . . . .42 A2
Wood Moor RG40 . . . . . . .141 C1
Wood Rd Camberley GU15 .151 A1
  Littleton TW17 . . . . .125 A3
Wood Ridge RG14 . . . . . .130 C4
Woodberry Cl RG4 . . . . . . .59 A3
Woodbine Cl Earley RG6 . . .87 B1
  Sandhurst GU47 . . . . . . .150 B4
Woodbine Cotts TW20 . . . .95 C1
Woodbine La RG20 . . . . . .130 C4
Woodbourne Cl GU46 . . . .149 B3

Woodbridge Dr GU15 . . . .151 B4
Woodbridge Rd
  Blackwater GU17 . . . . . .150 A3
  Reading RG31 . . . . .84 A3
Woodbury RG17 . . . . .25 B1
Woodbury Cl SL8 . . . . .3 B2
Woodby Dr SL5 . . . . .120 C1
Woodcock Ct RG7 . . . . . .113 A2
Woodcote SL6 . . . . .39 B3
Woodcote House Sch
  GU20 . . . . .146 A3
Woodcote Pl SL5 . . . . . . .119 C4
Woodcote Rd
  Caversham RG4 . . . . .58 C2
  South Stoke RG8 . . . . .14 C2
Woodcote Way RG4 . . . . . .58 B3
Woodend Cl SL5 . . . . .119 C4
Woodend Dr SL5 . . . . . . .120 A2
Woodenhill RG12 Ascot SL5 .117 C1
Woodenhill Cty Prim Sch
  RG12 . . . . .117 C1
Woodfield Dr SL6 . . . . .39 A3
Woodfield Way RG7 . . . . . .83 C2
Woodford Cl RG4 . . . . .58 C2
Woodford Gn RG12 . . . . . .118 C3
Woodford Way SL2 . . . . . . .22 A1
Woodhall La SL5 . . . . .146 C4
Woodhaw TW20 . . . . .96 A2
Woodhouse La RG19 . . . . .133 C1
Woodhouse St RG42 . . . . .90 C1
Woodhurst La RG41 . . . . .115 C4
Woodhurst Rd SL6 . . . . . . .20 A1
Woodhurst South SL6 . . . . .20 B1
Woodies Cl RG42 . . . . .90 B1
Woodland Ave Slough SL1 . .42 B3
  Windsor SL4 . . . . .66 C2
Woodland Cl SL7 . . . . .1 C2
Woodland Cres RG42 . . . . .91 B1
Woodland Dr RG30 . . . . . . .84 B4
Woodland Way SL7 . . . . . . .1 C2
Woodlands GU46 . . . . . . .149 B2
Woodlands Ave
  Burghfield Common RG7 . .111 A2
  Wokingham RG41 . . . . . .115 C4
  Woodley RG5 . . . . .87 B4
Woodlands Bsns Pk SL6 . .39 A1
Woodlands Cl Ascot SL5 . .119 C2
  Farnborough (Hants) GU17 .150 C1
  Hermitage RG18 . . . . .78 C2
Woodlands Cotts 4 SL2 . .22 B4
Woodlands Ct GU47 . . . . .143 C1
Woodlands Gr RG4 . . . . . . .59 C2
Woodlands La
  GU20,GU24 . . . . .146 C2
Woodlands Par TW15 . . . . .98 B1
Woodlands Park Ave
  SL6 . . . . .39 A1
Woodlands Park Prim Sch
  SL6 . . . . .39 A1
Woodlands Park Rd SL6 . . .39 A1
Woodlands Rd
  Camberley GU15 . . . . . . .151 A3
  Shiplake RG9 . . . . .35 C2
  Tadley RG26 . . . . .134 B1
  Virginia Water GU25 . . . . .122 B3
Woodlands Rd E GU25 . . .122 B3
Woodlands Rd W GU25 . . .122 B3
Woodlands Ride SL5 . . . . .120 A2
Woodlands The RG41 . . . .115 B2
Woodlands Wlk GU17 . . . .150 C1
Woodlee Cl GU25 . . . . . . .122 B4
Woodley CE Prim Sch
  RG5 . . . . .88 A4
Woodley Gn RG5 . . . . .87 C4
Woodley Park Est RG5 . . . .87 B4
Woodman Cl RG2 . . . . . . .113 B3
Woodmancott Cl RG12 . . .118 C2

Woodmans La RG7 . . . . . .110 C2
Woodmere RG12 . . . . .118 C3
Woodmere Cl RG6 . . . . . . .87 A1
Woodmoor End SL6 . . . . . .20 A4
Woodpecker Cl RG10 . . . . .61 C2
Woodpeckers RG12 . . . . . .118 A3
Woodridge Cl RG12 . . . . . .118 B3
Woodrow Dr RG40 . . . . . .116 C3
Woods Rd RG4 . . . . .59 C2
Woodsend Cl RG6 . . . . . . .113 C4
Woodshore Cl GU25 . . . . .122 A2
Woodside
  Blackwater GU17 . . . . . .150 B2
  Cold Ash RG18 . . . . .79 B1
  Flackwell Heath HP10 . . . . .3 B3
  Newbury RG14 . . . . .130 B4
  andhurst GU15 . . . . .150 C4
Woodside Ave HP10 . . . . . .3 B4
Woodside Bsns Pk RG2 . .113 A4
Woodside Cl
  Bucklebury RG7 . . . . . . .107 B3
  Mortimer RG7 . . . . .137 A3
  Wokingham RG40 . . . . . .141 C3
Woodside Dr RG18 . . . . . . .79 A3
Woodside La SL4, SL5 . . . .93 B2
Woodside Rd SL5 . . . . .93 A1
Woodside Way
  Reading RG2 . . . . .113 B4
  Virginia Water GU25 . . . .122 A3
Woodstock RG40 . . . . . . .116 B3
Woodstock Ave SL3 . . . . . .43 B1
Woodstock Cl SL6 . . . . . . .19 C1
Woodstock St RG1 . . . . . . .86 C4
Woodthorpe Rd TW15 . . . .97 B2
Woodview Rd RG8 . . . . . . .56 B3
Woodville Cl GU17 . . . . . .150 A3
Woodward Cl RG41 . . . . . . .88 B1
Woodway GU15 . . . . .151 A3
Woodway Rd OX11 . . . . . . .12 A4
Woodwaye RG5 . . . . .87 B4
Woodyer Cl RG5 . . . . .87 C3
Woolacombe Dr RG6 . . . . .86 C1
Woolf Dr RG40 . . . . .116 A4
Woolford Cl RG42 . . . . . . .92 B1
Woolhampton
  CE Prim Sch RG7 . . . . . .108 B2
Woolhampton Hill RG7 . . .108 B2
Woolhampton Way
  RG12 . . . . .118 B2
Woolton Lodge Gdns
  RG20 . . . . .129 C1
Woosehill RG41 . . . . .115 C3
Woosehill Ct RG41 . . . . . .115 C4
Woosehill La RG41 . . . . . .115 C3
Wootton Cl RG31 . . . . .84 B4
Wootton Dr HP10 . . . . .3 C4
Wootton Rd RG9 . . . . .35 B4
Wootton Way SL6 . . . . .39 B3
Worcester Cl
  Maidenhead SL6 . . . . .39 B2
  Reading RG30 . . . . .85 A3
Worcester Ct
  Ashford TW15 . . . . .98 A2
  Staines TW18 . . . . .97 A2
Worcester Dr TW15 . . . . . .98 A2
Worcester Gdns SL1 . . . . .42 B2
Worcestershire Lea RG42 .91 C1
Wordsworth RG12 . . . . . .117 C2
Wordsworth Ave GU46 . . .149 A2
Wordsworth Ct RG4 . . . . . .59 B4
Wordsworth Rd
  Slough SL2 . . . . .21 B1
  Thatcham RG18 . . . . . . .106 B2
Worlds End Hill RG12 . . . .118 C2
Wormersley Rd RG19 . . . .131 B4
Worple Ave TW18 . . . . .97 A1
Worple Rd TW18 . . . . .97 A1

Worple The TW19 . . . . .68 C1
Worrall Way RG6 . . . . . . .113 C4
Worsley Pl RG7 . . . . .83 C2
Worster Rd SL6 . . . . .19 C3
Worton Dr RG2 . . . . .113 A4
Worton Grange Ind Est
  RG2 . . . . .113 A4
Wrabness Way TW18 . . . .124 A4
Wraysbury Cty Comb Sch
  TW19 . . . . .68 C1
Wraysbury Rd TW18, TW19 .96 B3
Wraysbury Sta TW19 . . . . .69 A1
Wren Cl
  Burghfield Common RG7 . .111 A2
  Wokingham RG41 . . . . . .115 C3
Yateley GU46 . . . . .149 A3
Wren Ct Egham TW20 . . . . .96 A2
  Slough SL3 . . . . .44 A2
Wrenfield Dr RG4 . . . . .58 C3
Wrens Ave TW15 . . . . .98 B2
Wrensfield SL7 . . . . .1 B1
Wrenswood Cl RG2 . . . . . .113 A4
Wright SL4 . . . . .66 B2
Wright Cl RG5 . . . . .88 A4
Wright Gdns TW17 . . . . . .125 A2
Wright Sq SL4 . . . . .66 B2
Wright Way SL4 . . . . .66 B2
Wroxham RG12 . . . . .117 C2
Wroxham Rd RG5 . . . . .87 B4
Wyatt Rd Staines TW18 . . . .97 A2
  Windsor SL4 . . . . .66 B2
Wychcotes RG4 . . . . .58 C2
Wychelm Rd
  Lightwater GU18 . . . . . . .153 B4
  Shinfield RG2 . . . . .113 C3
Wychwood Ave RG12 . . . .118 C3
Wychwood Cl RG6 . . . . . . .86 C1
Wychwood Cres RG6 . . . . .86 C2
Wycombe La RG12 . . . . .3 C4
Wycombe Rd SL7 . . . . .1 C2
Wye Cl Ashford TW15 . . . . .98 A2
  Reading RG30 . . . . .84 C3
Wye Rd HP10 . . . . .3 B4
Wye Valley Sch SL8 . . . . . .3 A2
Wykeham Cl UB7 . . . . .71 A4
Wykeham Rd RG6 . . . . .87 A3
Wylam RG12 . . . . .117 C2
Wylands Rd SL3 . . . . .44 A1
Wyld Court Hill RG18 . . . . .53 A3
Wyld Court Rainforest
  RG18 . . . . .53 B3
Wymers Cl SL1 . . . . .21 A2
Wymers Wood Rd SL1 . . . .21 A2
Wyncote Cl RG2 . . . . .86 C1
Wyndale Cl RG9 . . . . .15 C1
Wyndham Cl GU46 . . . . . .149 B4
Wyndham Cres
  Burnham SL1 . . . . .21 A2
  Woodley RG5 . . . . .60 B1
Wyndham Rd RG14 . . . . . .105 B3
Wynford Cl RG30 . . . . .85 B2
Wynnstay Gdns SL7 . . . . . .1 C3
Wynsham Way GU20 . . . .146 A3
Wyre Ct RG31 . . . . .57 B2
Wyresdale RG12 . . . . .118 C1
Wythe Mead RG42 . . . . . . .90 A1
Wythegate TW18 . . . . .96 C1
Wyvern Cl RG12 . . . . .118 A3
Wyvern Ct TW15 . . . . .97 C3

Y

Yale Cl GU47 . . . . .143 C1
Yard Mead TW20 . . . . .96 A3
Yardley RG12 . . . . .117 C2
Yarmouth Rd SL1 . . . . .42 B3

Yarnold Cl RG40 . . . . .116 C4
Yarnton Cl RG4 . . . . .59 B1
Yateley Common Ctry Pk
  GU17,GU46 . . . . .149 C
Yateley Inf Sch GU46 . . . .149 B
Yateley Manor Prep Sch
  GU46 . . . . .149 B
Yateley Rd GU47 . . . . .149 C
Yateley Sch GU46 . . . . . . .149 B
Yates Copse RG14 . . . . . .105 C4
Yattendon CE Prim Sch
  RG18 . . . . .53 C
Yattendon Ct RG18 . . . . . . .53 C
Yattendon La RG8,RG18 . . .54 B
Yattendon Rd RG18 . . . . . .79 B
Yaverland Dr GU19 . . . . . .145 B
Ye Meads SL6 . . . . .40 C
Yelverton Rd RG2 . . . . .86 B
Yeomans La RG20 . . . . . . .131 A
Yeomans Way GU15 . . . . .151 C
Yeosfield RG7 . . . . .139 B
Yeoveney Cl TW19 . . . . . . .96 B
Yeovil Ent Ctr SL1 . . . . . . .41 C
Yeovil Rd Sandhurst GU47 .143 C4
  Slough SL1 . . . . .41 C
Yew Cl RG41 . . . . .115 C
Yew Gate RG14 . . . . .104 C
Yew La RG1 . . . . .85 C
Yew Tree Cl SL6 . . . . .39 C
Yew Tree Ct RG8 . . . . .34 B
Yew Tree Rd SL1 . . . . .43 A
Yew Tree Rise RG31 . . . . . .84 B
Yew Tree Stables RG20 . . .31 C
Yew Tree Wlk GU16 . . . . .151 C
Yew Trees TW17 . . . . .124 C
Yewhurst Cl RG10 . . . . . . .61 B
Yews The TW15 . . . . .98 A
Yewtrees TW20 . . . . .123 B
Yield Hall La 11 RG1 . . . . .86 A
Yield Hall Pl RG1 . . . . .86 A
Yockley Cl GU15 . . . . .152 A
Yoreham Cl RG6 . . . . .87 C
York Ave Slough SL1 . . . . . .42 B
  Windsor SL4 . . . . .67 A
York Cl RG14 . . . . .105 A
York Ho RG42 . . . . .117 C
York Rd Binfield RG42 . . . . .90 B
  Camberley GU15 . . . . . . .151 B
  Henley-on-T RG9 . . . . .15 B
  Hungerford RG17 . . . . . . .100 B
  Maidenhead SL6 . . . . .40 A
  Marlow SL7 . . . . .1 B
  Newbury RG14 . . . . .105 A
  Reading RG1 . . . . .59 A
  Windsor SL4 . . . . .67 A
York Town Ind Est GU15 . .151 A
York Way GU47 . . . . .150 A
Yorkshire Pl RG42 . . . . . . .91 C
Yorktown Rd
  Sandhurst GU47 . . . . . . .150 A
  Sandhurst GU47 . . . . . . .150 C
Youlden Cl GU15 . . . . .152 A
Youlden Dr GU15 . . . . .152 A
Young Cres RG19 . . . . . . .131 B
Young's Ind Est RG7 . . . . .134 C

Z

Zealand Ave UB7 . . . . .70 C
Zenith Ct GU47 . . . . .143 B
Zetland Ct SL6 . . . . .40 A
Zinnia Cl RG41 . . . . .115 B
Zinzan St RG1 . . . . .85 C4